# Politics and Governance in the UK

www.palgrave.com
Companion Website

www.palgrave.com/politics/moran

# Politics and Governance in the UK

MICHAEL MORAN

First published 2005 by
PALGRAVE MACMILLAN
Houndmills, Basingstoke, Hampshire RG21 6XS and
175 Fifth Avenue, New York, N.Y. 10010
Companies and representatives throughout the world

PALGRAVE MACMILLAN is the global academic imprint of the Palgrave
Macmillan division of St. Martin's Press, LLC and of Palgrave Macmillan Ltd.
Macmillan® is a registered trademark in the United States, United Kingdom
and other countries. Palgrave is a registered trademark in the European
Union and other countries.

ISBN-13: 978–0–333–94511–7    hardback
ISBN-10: 0–333–94511–5        hardback
ISBN-13: 978–0–333–94512–4    paperback
ISBN-10: 0–333–94512–3        paperback


This book is printed on paper suitable for recycling and made from fully
managed and sustained forest sources.

A catalogue record for this book is available from the British Library.

Library of Congress Cataloging-in-Publication Data

Moran, Michael, 1946–
    Politics and governance in the UK / Michael Moran.
       p. cm.
    Includes bibliographical references and index.
    ISBN 1–333–94511–5 — ISBN 0–333–94512–3 (pbk.)
       1. Great Britain—Politics and government—1945– I. Title.

JN231.M66 2005
320.441—dc22                                    2005049753


10  9  8  7  6  5  4  3  2  1
14  13  12  11  10  09  08  07  06  05

Printed and bound in Great Britain by Arrowsmiths, Bristol

# Summary of contents

# Contents

# List of illustrative material

## IMAGES

## BRIEFINGS

## PEOPLE IN POLITICS

## TIMELINES

## DOCUMENTING POLITICS

# Preface

Writing a textbook is much more difficult than writing a scholarly monograph, and for the same reason that teaching an introductory course is harder than teaching advanced students. Introducing a subject involves ruthless but judicious selection and total clarity in exposition. Make a mess of things at advanced level and you can expect some help from the student and the reader, but the beginner cannot be expected to rescue the incompetent author.

I have attempted to meet these high standards, and any success I have achieved I owe to generous friends, colleagues and even family who read earlier drafts. I owe a special debt to the four anonymous referees commissioned by the publisher to review earlier drafts; their eye for detail and the larger shape of arguments helped me immensely. It is a pleasure to thank by name others who read all or part of the book in draft: Rodney Brazier, Martin Burch, David Denver, David Farrell, Joe Moran, Neill Nugent and Gerry Stoker. The legendary Steven Kennedy was an ideal editor: constantly encouraging, but insistent that I did not cut corners. Beverley Tarquini improved the finished product enormously with her publisher's eye for detail and style. I thank Ian Wileman for a wonderful design from a chaotic typescript, and Keith Povey and his collaborators Gail Sheffield and Marilyn Hamshere for eagle-eyed copy-editing and proof-reading.

I owe a very special debt of gratitude to Shaun Steele, who drew the witty and provocative cartoons used to illustrate the 'People in Politics' features. Special thanks are also due to Jo Wainhouse for smoothing the way so that I could take the photograph for Image 7.1; it is somehow characteristic of the Wainhouse family that only they could crack fortress Downing Street. I must also acknowledge the contribution of several thousand unnamed helpers – the students whom I have taught over more than 30 years at Manchester Polytechnic and Manchester University. In particular, I taught an introduction to British Politics for many years on the main first-year course at Manchester University: confronting over 700 students, hardly any of whom had come to university to study politics, concentrated the mind wonderfully.

I reserve special thanks for Tim May. He read the whole manuscript, corrected countless points of detail and offered numerous suggestions that improved the larger structure. I first began teaching British politics with him when I joined the politics staff at the (then) Manchester Polytechnic in 1970. He taught me much about British politics, and a lot more besides.

Michael Moran
*University of Manchester*
*September 2004*

# Acknowledgements

The author and publishers would like to thank the following who have kindly given permission for the use of copyright material: *Government and Opposition* for Table 5.1; Palgrave Macmillan for Image 6.1 and Briefing 7.1; The British Retail Consortium for Documenting Politics 9.1; *Political Studies* for Table 13.2 and Figure 18.1; The Labour Party for Image 15.1 (the 'Labour Rose' logo is a registered emblem of the Labour Party); Patrick Dunleavy for Figure 19.2; Oxford University Press for Figure 19.3; PA/Empics for Images 1.1, 5.1, 7.3, 10.2, 13.2, 17.1, 18.1, 20.1, 20.2 and 24.2; EPA/Empics for Image 4.3.

Crown copyright material in Tables 12.2 and 18.1; Figures 3.7, 3.8, 3.9, 12.1, 12.2, 21.1, 21.3, 22.1, 22.3 and 23.1; Images 4.1 and 4.2; Briefings 7.2, 8.2 and 23.3; Documenting Politics 4.1, 6.2, 7.2, 8.1, 8.3, 8.5, 10.1, 10.3, 10.4, 10.5, 10.6, 11.1, 18.1, 19.3, 20.1, 20.3, 22.1, 23.1, 23.2 and 23.3 is reproduced with the permission of the controller of Her Majesty's Stationery Office under click licence CO1W0000276. Image 1.2 and Documenting Politics 7.3 and 14.1 are reproduced under Crown copyright waiver. Documenting Politics 6.1 and 6.3 are European Union copyright.

Particular thanks to Clive Lacey at FCO for his help in obtaining Images 4.1 and 4.2.

# List of abbreviations

| | |
|---|---|
| BBC | British Broadcasting Corporation |
| BSE | bovine spongiform encephalopathy |
| CCTV | closed circuit television |
| CFSP | common foreign and security policy |
| CND | Campaign for Nuclear Disarmament |
| DEFRA | Department of the Environment, Food and Rural Affairs |
| DTI | Department of Trade and Industry |
| DUP | Democratic Unionist Party |
| ECJ | European Court of Justice |
| ECSC | European Coal and Steel Community |
| EEC | European Economic Community |
| EMU | European Monetary Union |
| EP | European Parliament |
| EU | European Union |
| FCO | Foreign and Commonwealth Office |
| FSA | Financial Services Authority |
| GDP | gross domestic product |
| GP | general practitioner |
| HFEA | Human Fertilization and Embryology Authority |
| HSE | Health and Safety Executive |
| IRA | Irish Republican Army |
| IT | information technology |
| JHA | justice and home affairs |
| LGA | Local Government Association |
| MEPs | Members of the European Parliament |
| MPs | Members of Parliament |
| NATO | North Atlantic Treaty Organization |
| NFU | National Farmers' Union |
| NHS | National Health Service |
| PAYE | Pay As You Earn |
| PC | personal computer |
| PFI | Private Finance Initiative |
| RSPB | Royal Society for the Protection of Birds |
| RSPCA | Royal Society for the Prevention of Cruelty to Animals |
| SDLP | Social Democratic and Labour Party |
| SDP | Social Democratic Party |
| SEA | Single European Act |
| SNP | Scottish Nationalist Party |
| SOCPO | Society of Personnel Officers in Local Government |
| SOPO | Society of Procurement Officers in Local Government |
| UK | United Kingdom |
| UN | United Nations |
| US | United States |
| UUP | Ulster Unionist Party |
| VAT | Value Added Tax |
| WHO | World Health Organization |
| WTO | World Trade Organization |

# Introduction

## What this book is about

This book is an introduction to the study of British politics for the beginning student. I assume little or no prior knowledge of British society, or British history or, obviously, of political life in the UK. I have tried to make the language of the text as accessible as possible, and to provide as comprehensive a survey as possible.

The book is therefore aimed at a wide audience. It is primarily intended for readers studying the subject at undergraduate level, though I have tried to write in the plainest English, with the intention of making it accessible also for students at AS and A2. I have two main aims: to give the reader as comprehensive a picture as is possible, within the available space, of political life in Britain; and to open up for the reader some of the important questions and debates in the study of British politics. Of course, any student of politics soon realizes that these two aims cannot be divorced. Any picture of British politics is not drawn innocently from life; it is the result of a whole set of assumptions brought, consciously and unconsciously, to the act of composing that picture. Description cannot be separated from theory. Indeed, one of my intentions is to make explicit throughout the assumptions about the character of British politics which underpin my descriptions.

Put more formally, the aims of the book are:

- to provide a comprehensive introduction to the context, ideas, institutions, practices and policies that are most important in British political life.
- to provide an introduction to the main analytical

issues and theoretical debates in the study of British politics.

The learning objectives of the book need to be more fully stated. By the end of the book student readers should have grasped the following:

- They should know fundamental institutional information about the workings of British politics.
- They should be able to think of British politics as a system of *multi-level governance*, stretching from the level of the European Union (EU) to the most local of political systems, and should appreciate what this means for the strategies and tactics employed by the most important actors in British political life. Below I explain what 'governance' means here.
- They should understand that British politics amounts to much more than the political institutions located in London, but now encompasses distinct systems of government in the different nations of the United Kingdom.
- They should realize that British politics is now also European politics: that Britain is – regardless of whether people like it or not – a part of the political system of the European Union.

## The intellectual structure of the book

The structure of a book is never the result of simple choices. Even mundane features – such as the order of chapters – often arise from important presuppositions and conceal key implications. Since a main aim of the book is to communicate how the study of British politics is affected by the theoretical 'lenses' used, it is only right that some of the assumptions governing this book's structure should themselves be laid bare.

Four important preoccupations lie at the heart of the book, and have shaped its organization:

- Territorial decentralization
- Europe
- Institutions
- Democracy.

## Taking territorial decentralization seriously

The events of recent years require that we undergo a change of mindset in approaching the British political system. For much of the twentieth century Britain's was a highly centralized system of government. This centralization partly reflected the domination – both in numbers and wealth – of one nation, England, and the dominance in turn of one city, London. London's predominance was particularly remarkable, whether we measure it by concentration of economic resources, concentration of the great institutions of culture such as the mass media, or concentration of important political institutions. That history of centralization naturally coloured the way the British political system was pictured: the institutions that were put at the centre were mostly the institutions of the capital. In the study of British politics most roads led to London. There were good justifications for shaping the study of politics in this way. The reality of power and decision indeed meant that it was mostly what happened in London that mattered. It still matters a great deal, and that explains why what, for shorthand, in this book is called 'The Westminster system' occupies several long chapters.

In recent years, however, things have changed; it is not enough to take this historically centralized state of affairs for granted. It must be recognized as the product of a particular set of hierarchies and those hierarchies must be exposed and examined. That exposure and examination is made easier because in political life itself those very hierarchies have been seriously challenged: in Ireland for decades; in Scotland and Wales more recently; and more recently still in the revival and reinvention of many English provincial cities and in the stirrings of

a movement for regional government. The devolution reforms put in place by the Labour Government after 1997 attempt to respond to these challenges. The predominant power still lies with London institutions, but these reforms have accelerated the establishment of distinctive national political systems in the British Isles.

## Taking Europe seriously

The devolution reforms referred to above are often thought of as weakening the centre 'from below'. But there is also a big challenge to the London-focused picture coming from a very different direction: the European Union. Of course, even the least knowledgeable student of British politics knows that membership of the European Union – which stretches back to the original accession to the European Economic Community, or the Common Market, in 1973 – is of outstanding importance, but understanding the significance of membership demands more than acknowledging this fact. It, too, demands a change in mindset. It is not enough to think of the Union as an important influence from 'outside' or 'above'. It is necessary to think of Britain as a European political system: that is, as a system of politics so woven into the government of the European Union that the two cannot easily be disentangled. That explains two big features of the book: the space given to European institutions and issues; and, something that is not obvious from simple inspection of the contents, the extent to which the European dimension is built into the substance of the discussion in individual chapters.

## Taking institutions seriously

A generation ago in political science, institutions were assigned only subordinate importance. It was widely believed that social, economic and cultural forces mattered above all in shaping politics, and that institutional life mostly reflected these wider and deeper forces. But since the mid-1980s political science has rediscovered institutions and formal organization (March and Olsen 1984 is the key text). The rediscovery is particularly important for British politics. 'Europeanization' has opened Britain to systems where formal organization and written rules – for example, in written constitutions – are very important. There are numerous examples in this text showing how the influence of Europe has made the practice of government in Britain more elaborately codified. There are also numerous examples showing that there is much more formal organization than in the past regulating the relations between the state and its citizens, and these are particularly important themes in, for instance, Chapters 5 and 22–4. Moreover, there are numerous examples showing that interest representation is increasingly populated by formal organizations. Finally, we will see that some of the greatest reforms of recent years – such as the devolution reforms discussed in Chapter 11 – have precisely been about changing the institutional shape of government.

## Taking democracy seriously

By this phrase I mean the following. All official accounts of the British system of government take pride in picturing it as democratic. Even critics of this official view usually only dissent because, while wanting democracy, they deny that it has been realized. Only a few authoritarians publicly argue that we should not have democratic government. This almost universal consensus about the desirability of democracy provides a powerful set of tools with which to evaluate British government. 'Democracy' is a hotly contested idea, but plainly it implies beliefs about the distribution of power, about participation in politics and about controls over government. An important purpose of the chapters that follow is to tackle the difficult matter of the reality or otherwise of British democracy. I try to show that we should take democratic claims seriously, and to show how we can evaluate the worth of these claims.

A word should also be said about something more mundane: how the chapters open and close. Under 'Aims' I start each chapter in the same way: with a short, bald summary of what is coming. Under 'Review' I end each chapter not with a summary, but with my 'take' on what have been the main themes of the chapter. The reader might not agree with the themes I have highlighted; indeed, for the student reader a useful exercise, and a prompt to active reading, is to compare my view of the important themes with the reader's own view.

## The title of the book

Why 'governance' in the title? The choice acknowledges the increasing use of the word in recent years to describe what is going on in the governing process in Britain. 'Governance' brings a new stress on the importance of coordination and bargaining, in place of issuing commands. It also reflects something not apparent from the title alone: that the governing process is increasingly 'multi-level' and 'multi-agency'. In other words, the business of governing involves drawing together a wide range of different institutions at many levels of a governing system. The development of devolution and the growing importance of Europe have both been important in reinforcing this multi-level system. The succeeding chapters show time and again that the complexity of modern society means that numerous agencies typically have to be involved in the governing process. Governing can never be a solitary vice, or virtue; it necessarily involves coordination between many different bodies.

I try in the pages that follow to use 'governance' as a summary description of the whole process, and to reserve 'government' for the institutions of, for instance, the Westminster or the devolved governing systems. The significance of this usage should not be exaggerated: 'governance' here is a shift of nuance rather than a wholesale shift of meaning. By contrast, in some other accounts it is indeed a shift in meaning: some radical versions of the 'governance' approach picture the state as a transformed 'network' state. I examine the pros and cons of this radical view in the concluding chapter.

## A note on presentation

This book will be in the main used as part of a course and, obviously, how it is used will be determined by the needs of the individual course. But a note is needed about two features, to explain why I have developed them: the 'visuals' – boxes, photos, charts, tables, graphs – and the website that accompanies the book.

The 'visuals' build on the innovations of a generation of textbooks that appeared in the 1990s. These departed from the traditional presentation of the book as a block of text. The innovations were a real breakthrough, exploiting technological developments in setting and printing in order better to convey material to readers. They also exploited something that everyone experiences in their daily lives: an idea or a fact is best understood and remembered if it is presented in more than one form. The choice of visuals nevertheless needs to be highly self-conscious if it is not simply to become a gimmick or just a way of breaking up blocks of text. I intend the book to be, within the limits of an introductory text, comprehensive and self-contained. Although most students will, naturally, wish to read widely beyond these chapters, my intention is that the beginning reader should not have to go beyond the book to understand its contents. The visuals, therefore, are intended to ensure that all the central concepts used, historical and social features invoked, and technical terms employed, are explained, without breaking up the flow of the text. The contents of the boxes, charts and other visual material represent my judgement of what the beginning reader needs by way of extra explanation and illustration. No doubt I have not made all the right choices, and I appeal to readers to tell me where I have made mistakes so that later editions can be improved.

For the most part the meaning of the various features is self-evident, but it is worth highlighting six.

- *Briefing boxes* are the commonest form of boxed material. This is where I try economically to summarize facts and ideas that, if inserted into the body of the text, would break up the flow, but which are nevertheless particularly important for the student.
- *Documenting politics* boxes try to give the student the raw flavour of political life: I use extracts from Parliamentary debates, official documents, and private (leaked) memos to show what language the political class uses to talk to itself, to talk to the rest of us, and also to talk *about* the rest of us.
- *People in politics* boxes recognize that politics is a people business, and that personalities matter. I usually group three figures together, normally to give some perspective, historical or otherwise, to their significance. The cartoons by Shaun Steele put faces to the text. Cartoons are used in homage to the great British tradition of political caricature.
- *Images* are used because political life is lived as vividly through images as through ideas. Most of these images are photographs, in the main taken by me. When people are asked to conjure up British politics they are likely to turn to images, perhaps of people (the Prime Minister) or of buildings (the Houses of Parliament). I grew up in traditional rural Ireland in the 1950s and my sense of the authority of the Irish state is still conveyed by memories of the old coins that pictured icons of rural Ireland: the hen on the penny, the salmon on the two shilling (ten pence) coin. The 'images' in this book are intended to illustrate how politics is represented to us. The images selected are usually deliberately mundane and everyday, precisely because they surround us and – like the icons of the state on coins – seep more or less unacknowledged into everyday consciousness.
- *Political issues* boxes recognize that politics is about much more than institutions, structures or people: it is about issues that form the stuff of everyday political argument. For virtually every chapter I have taken an issue linked to a main theme of the chapter, to convey some of the life of real politics in action. These boxes are intended to be self-contained narratives, and do not therefore come with any extra annotation.
- *Debating politics* boxes come at the end of each chapter, because the study of British politics is a contested subject, and debating these contested issues, as much as learning institutional detail, is central to its study. The debates are numerous

and endless; each single debate box at the end of the chapter can do no more than select one area of contestation. Like the *Political issues* boxes these are self-contained and have no external annotation.

Beyond the special cases of the last two categories of boxes, all the other visual features are annotated, and these annotations are an integral part of the features, since they try to explain both the placing of the feature and the point of the particular material chosen.

The website for the book at http://www.palgrave.com/politics/moran also tries to exploit technology to communicate more effectively. Virtually all students now have access to the web, and the site for the book has two purposes. First, on it is placed material (for example, extended guides to more reading, self-assessment tests to measure comprehension of the text) which it would simply be too bulky to put into hard copy. A good example of the distinction between the text and the website is provided by the guide to further reading. The 'further reading' sections at the end of the book chapters are deliberately pared down to the bare essentials: the four or five works that students should read first if they want to explore further. In the website these are supplemented by much longer lists. Second, the site is used to solve one of the main problems of textbooks that try to cover social and political life in an up-to-date way. The traditional text is, just because of the mechanics of book production, inevitably several months out of date even when it first appears. The website will contain regular up-dates of all important developments that affect the text.

Though I have provided a website linked to the text, I have not provided guides to websites in my 'Further reading' sections at the end of chapters. The omission is deliberate. As a glance at the sources for the boxed material will show, I have used the web widely in writing the book. In the age of Google it is all too easy to search the web. But this is an extremely inefficient way for the beginner to study a subject, and it runs the risk of detaching the beginner from what is essential: embedding knowledge in the developed scholarly understandings. The web is an important tool in the study of Britain. It is vital for the student (for example, in electronically accessing academic journals or in gathering original material for projects or dissertations), but it is a distraction for the beginner.

**CHAPTER 1**

# Why politics matters and why British politics matters

## CONTENTS

Why study politics?
Why study the state?
Why study democracy?
Why study British Politics?
Three big questions about British politics
Review
Further reading

## AIMS

This opening chapter has the following aims:

❖ To explain why we study politics

❖ To explain why we study the politics of a special sort of institution, the state

❖ To explain why we study British politics

❖ To sketch some of the main themes that we encounter when we study British politics.

## Why study politics?

Why study politics? Indeed, why be concerned with political life at all? For most citizens – including citizens of the United Kingdom – the answers to these questions are pretty obvious: there are no good reasons either to study politics or to take an active part in political life. Politics is a popular subject in most universities and in further education, but beyond these places the study of politics really is a minority interest – more accessible, say, than the study of theoretical physics, but not able to attract more interest among the wider population. The reader of this book is engaged in a minority activity, and the reader of this book who is engaged actively in politics is engaged in a more unusual activity still. There are perhaps no more than 100,000 really committed political activists in Britain – by which I mean people for whom, beyond work and the immediate demands of family life, politics is a really time-consuming activity. By contrast, surveys tell us that apparently marginal activities such as dressmaking and knitting are actually engaged in by 3 per cent of all British *men* over the age of 16 – about 700,000 in all. About double that number of people regularly play skittles or go ten-pin bowling. So one way to put politics into perspective is to realize that it is a lot less popular than either knitting or skittles (*Social Trends 2002*: 210, 216).

If politics is a minority interest, however, even in a democracy it is nevertheless a matter of the utmost importance – in a quite literal sense, a matter of life and death. We soon start to see this if we consider some of the commonest definitions of politics and political life, such as those illustrated in Documenting Politics 1.1. There are important differences in emphasis in the different definitions collected in that box, but we can nevertheless find in here a common theme. *Politics is a social activity involving the attempt to choose between competing views and interests in institutions.* It immediately becomes obvious that politics can happen in any of a variety of institutions: politics exist in families, in colleges and in business firms. It also immediately becomes obvious why politics is so important: the failure to make these choices by peaceful means, and to carry them out effectively and peacefully, has catastrophic results. Consider, for instance, the life of people unfortunate enough to live in poverty stricken countries of Africa, such as Zaire. What single thing would transform those lives: a great medical advance, or a great advance in biotechnology which would make farming more productive? Neither of these things: their lives would be transformed for the better by peace and the creation of a stable system of government, because since the then Belgian Congo achieved independence as Zaire over 40 years ago it has been racked by civil wars. Understanding politics, if we want to make the world a better place for our fellow human beings, is more urgent even than understanding medicine, biology or physics.

Since Britons usually live in peace and security they naturally take the contribution of politics to our well being for granted. But not all Britons, for when these conditions disappear we see immediately how important they are. That is the lesson of the last 30 years in the history of Northern Ireland. What single thing would transform the lives of the people of Northern Ireland? The answer is obvious: a peaceful political settlement. Indeed, when the first longstanding ceasefire in that province began in 1994 the transformation took place: not only did the threat of violence diminish, but everything from the biggest things – such as the state of the economy – to the smallest – the ability of people in Belfast to enjoy the life of their city on a Saturday night – was transformed.

Of course, these are very dramatic examples of the way politics matters in all our lives. But it is not just a matter of the way politics determines the biggest issues, including the very conditions of peaceful existence: politics shapes every detail of our lives, from the most dramatic to the most mundane. And it does for this for a particular historical reason: the importance of the institution called the state in a country such as the United Kingdom.

## Why study the state?

Politics has already been defined in very general terms – essentially as a social activity, which could

## DOCUMENTING POLITICS 1.1

## DEFINING POLITICS

- 'Politics are now nothing more than a means of rising in the world' (Samuel Johnson, English writer, 1709–84).
- 'Politics is perhaps the only profession for which no preparation is thought necessary' (Robert Louis Stevenson, Scottish writer, 1850–94).
- 'Whoever could make two ears of corn or two blades of grass to grow upon a spot of ground where only one grew before, would deserve better of mankind, and do more essential service to his country than the whole race of politicians put together' (Jonathan Swift, Irish writer, 1667–1745).

Definitions from students and practitioners are, predictably, more restrained:

- 'A human being is naturally a political animal' (Aristotle, Greek philosopher, c. 384–322BC, *Ethics*).
- 'Politics is the art of the possible' (Prince Otto von Bismarck, German statesman, 1815–98).
- 'Politics: who gets what, when, how' (Harold Laswell, American political scientist, title of introduction to political science, 1950).
- 'A political system [is] any persistent pattern of human relationships that involves, to a significant extent, control, influence, power, or authority' (Robert Dahl, American political scientist, 1984: 10).

➲ There is a popular cynicism about politics and politicians illustrated by our first three quotations. But our second four, though very different in their emphasis, all fasten on one key feature: that some form of political action is a necessary condition of all social life.

be carried out in a whole variety of institutional settings. That is why we can and do speak of the internal politics of a college or a tennis club. But in Europe from the seventeenth century – most observers, if pressed for a single date, would choose the Treaty of Westphalia in 1648 – a very particular institution began to take on responsibility for managing the political process in societies. That institution we normally call the state. A wide range of the social sciences studies politics as a general social process, but the study of the politics connected with the state is usually done within the field of political studies or political science. That is just a matter of the convenient division of labour in academic work. Courses conventionally called 'politics' or 'government' are mostly concerned with this state-focused system of politics, and books such as this one share the same preoccupation. The state is not the whole of politics; but since the seventeenth

century it has been a very important part of politics.

Why is this, and why is so much of modern political studies preoccupied with the state? What emerged out of the Treaty of Westphalia was a particular political form. The essence of that political form is contained in the most famous definition of the state, one offered by a founding father of the social sciences, the German sociologist Max Weber: 'the state is a human community that (successfully) claims *the monopoly of the legitimate use of physical force* within a given territory' (see Briefing 1.1).

There are three elements of this definition to note. First, the state is a territorial entity, as indeed a glance at a weather map of the United Kingdom in your morning paper will show. Second, the state claims to monopolize the means of coercion in this territory. This does not mean that physical coercion by other means does not take place; but it does mean that the state claims that coercion can only legitimately take place with its consent. The word 'legitimacy' refers to the third feature of the state: the claim to monopoly is tied to a claim to being the *legitimate* supreme power in a given territory.

What does legitimacy mean? It involves the state making a special kind of claim to the loyalties of the population. The idea is once again well conveyed by Max Weber, who linked the idea of legitimacy to the idea of *authority*. If I have power over you that means that I have the capacity, whether you like it or not, to get you to do something you would not otherwise do. But if I exercise authority I command you, not simply through fear or money, but because you recognize my moral right to demand your obedience: I have a legitimate right to get you to obey. This idea of *legitimate* authority conveys a key claim of the modern state.

The notion of legitimate authority opens up another key feature of the state: why and how states are in practice obeyed. States have great powers of coercion: they can take away our property, our liberty and even our lives, by war or execution. But if we only obeyed the state through fear of coercion the power of the state would actually be quite limited. We would disobey whenever we thought the state would not discover our disobedience, and that in turn would entail the state investing huge resources in spying and control of its population. Some famous modern dictatorships of the twentieth century have indeed done exactly that, and as a result they have turned out to be quite inefficient. The states most effective in commanding obedience have ruled by legitimate authority rather than fear.

That legitimate authority can rest on various grounds. Weber again made a famous distinction between three sorts of authority. *Traditional authority* rests on custom, often based on right of succession: for instance, the kind of authority claimed by a hereditary monarchy. Leaders with some extraordinary personal quality that commands obedience claim charismatic authority. Rational-legal authority is claimed on the grounds that the person or institution wielding it does so because of certain agreed rules and procedures.

One reason Weber's classification is so important is that it throws light on the changing nature of legitimate authority in the state. Traditional

# Briefing                                 1.1

## MAX WEBER'S DEFINITION OF STATE AND OF AUTHORITY

Weber on the state: 'The relation between the state and violence is an especially intimate one . . . the state is a human community that (successfully) claims the *monopoly of the legitimate use of physical force* within a given territory.'

Weber on the three grounds that can confer the legitimacy for domination:

- Traditional: 'the authority of the eternal yesterday . . . traditional domination exercised by the patriarch and the patrimonial prince of yore'.
- Charismatic: 'the authority of extraordinary and personal gift of grace (charisma)' exercised by 'the great demagogue, or the political party leader'.
- Rational-legal: authority 'by virtue of the belief in the validity of legal statute and functional competence based on rationally created *rules*'.

*Source*: Weber (1918/1948: 78–9).

➲ Max Weber (1864–1920) was a key figure in the development of modern social science but, as with all great social observers, his apparently universal statements grew out of particular historical experiences. His most often quoted statements on the state and authority, summarized above, come from a lecture, 'Politics as a vocation' delivered in Munich (the capital of what was then Bavaria) in 1918. The Great War (1914–1918) had led to the collapse of three empires: in Germany, in the Austro–Hungarian Empire and in Tsarist Russia. Weber had been a supporter of the monarchy in Germany; now he lived through upheaval, civil war, dictatorship and the threat of Communist revolution. His view of the state as an institution that secured authority in a territory was inseparable from this experience of collapse and turmoil.

authority was typically in the past claimed by monarchs. We can see faint traces in the case of the present British monarchy: the Queen is monarch through right of succession, even though the line of succession was often falsified. The original charismatic leader was the Pope, who claims to wield authority as the anointed successor of Christ. Charisma is a word of Greek origins, and its

### Image 1.1
### The tank and the piper

➲ Max Weber (see Briefing1.1) defined the state by its monopoly of coercion. But we also know that physical force is not enough: states need symbols that arouse loyalty. The photo, taken in 2004 during the military campaign in Iraq, encapsulates the two elements: the tank has for nearly a century been a hugely effective instrument of military conquest; the regimental piper has an even longer lineage, symbolizing the attachment of soldiers to their regiment and, through the regiment, to the Crown and the state. Both, though, can prove very fragile: tanks often prove ineffective against guerrilla campaigns such as that faced in Iraq after the original military conquest in 2003; the piper is from the Black Watch regiment, and in 2004 there occurred a bitter dispute because of British government plans to reorganize, and effectively abolish, the regiment.

original literal meaning conveys the idea of being an anointed one, marked with divine qualities. As a sign of this, at the coronation of a Pope the new Pontiff is anointed with an oil called chrism; and an even fainter sign can be seen in the fact that the coronation of a monarch in Britain also involves being anointed with oil of chrism. (Readers of this book who have been confirmed will know of a fainter echo yet: at the Christian ceremony of confirmation anointing with chrism takes place as a sign of joining the elect of the church.)

The genius of Weber's notion of charisma lay not in the way it interpreted the past, but the way it anticipated a terrible future. Elaborated at the start of the twentieth century, it anticipated the kind of authority claimed by the most notorious dictatorships of the twentieth century: both Hitler in Nazi Germany (1933–45) and Stalin in Soviet Russia (died 1953) were pictured as having superhuman, god-like qualities of leadership.

The other great form of authority in our age is rational-legal authority, which is now closely associated with the modern democratic state such as exists in Britain. From the core notion of rational-legality – that the exercise of authority is rule-bound – come several key ideas in modern politics, especially democratic politics. As our example of the British monarchy shows, there are faint traces of both traditional and charismatic authority in modern British government (see Image 1.2). But the most important source of authority claimed by the state in Britain is rational-legality: it is to be obeyed because what is does is governed by explicit rules covering both the substance of what it can do, and the ways it can do it. This idea that state authority is rule bound is also, we will now see, central to an equally important claim made by the state in Britain: that it is democratic.

## Why study democracy?

Until the twentieth century democracy was usually spoken of in hostile terms. That hostile tradition began at the very dawn of political theory. The Greek political philosopher, Aristotle, classified democracy as a form of tyranny, because it was a form of class rule: rule in the interests of the poor, propertyless masses in a society. That is why, until the twentieth century, it was viewed with hostility or suspicion, at least by anyone with property. But it is now most commonly thought of in procedural terms: democratic governments are democratic because they have been chosen by particular rules, usually involving winning some sort of majority in elections where all or most adults have the right to take part. In Britain, although formally we still speak of Her Majesty's Government, implying that authority is traditional, in reality the government's authority rests on the fact that it won a general election and has a majority in the House of Commons. *Democracy*, in this meaning, has shrunk to something quite narrow: it refers to a procedure (periodic elections involving most of the adult population) by which the government is selected.

Commanding a majority in the House of Commons is also critical to another aspect of rational-legal authority. A majority gives the capacity, in most cases, to pass laws, and government's ability to command obedience only stretches to those areas where it is backed by properly enacted laws. Not only do we not feel obliged to obey government if it makes demands beyond the law; we are entitled to, and often do, challenge it in the courts. In short, in Britain, the rational-legal authority of government is not only bound up with the fact that it has won a majority under defined rules of political competition, but that its claims to obedience rest on properly passed laws. This notion of the *rule of law* is thus central to claims to authority. That is why in our visual illustration of three kinds of authority, rational-legal authority is illustrated by a tax demand received by me (Image 1.3). If I do not pay the tax the authorities will seek a court judgment against me seizing my property to the value of the demand (plus an additional fine). But I can successfully appeal against the demand if I can show that the authorities have not acted in accordance with the law: for instance, if they have not applied the legally stated tax rate in calculating my bill. (This is the theory; later in the book, especially in Chapters 22 and 23, we will examine how far this optimistic view of British government as constrained by law fits the reality.)

In some political systems, but not yet in Britain, this notion of government under law is given a special force by a written *constitution*. A constitution lays down the most important rules of political procedure: for instance, how elections are to be organized, the powers of different branches of government, and the rights of citizens against government. One of the peculiarities of Britain is that, while it undoubtedly has a constitution, it does not have one in the form of a single written document.

The theory of modern democracy is thus that it is a form of rule involving the selection of government by some majority, and the exercise of restraint on government by compelling it to act only in accordance with the law. This theory in turn entails another key idea: *accountability*. Periodic elections are of course one important way in which governments are obliged to be held accountable: literally, to give an account of their stewardship over the preceding period. One of the marks of democratic government is the existence of a wide range of formal and informal practices and institutions designed to ensure that government is held accountable for its actions. The different meanings of accountability, and the tests of accountability, are central to debates about whether we do indeed have effective democracy in Britain.

Weber's famous definition of the state opened up for us the important notion of *authority*, but two other linked elements in his definition open up another key political concept: his notion that the state claims a monopoly of authority, and claims it in a bounded territory. These are encapsulated in the idea of *sovereignty*, a notion that was central to the emergence of the state as a key political unit after the Treaty of Westphalia in 1648. In legal theory sovereignty – the idea that a state commanded supreme authority in its own territory – was at the core of statehood. This has turned out to be one of the most difficult and contested ideas in modern British politics.

States in the seventeenth century could make these Weber-like claims, but in practice they often had very little impact on the daily lives of the populations over whom they ruled. The state in the twenty-first century is a very different matter, as the example of Britain below will show.

## Why study British politics?

Why should anyone be interested in the study of British politics? There are two linked answers, partly to do with the importance of Britain, and partly to do with the lives of those who live in Britain. Imagine first posing the question to someone who did not live in Britain; the British political system would nevertheless be highly relevant. Britain is an exceptionally important member of the international state system, because it is one of a small number of rich and powerful states that

**Image 1.2**
**Images of authority in Britain: banknote and coin**

⮕ The two illustrations convey in different ways Weber's famous classification of three kinds of authority. The first image is one we see every day: the monarch's head on a coin, and on a note. It is the most commonly available symbol of royal authority. The Queen's right to have her image on the currency derives in part from tradition: she is queen because she inherited the title of monarch from her father. But there are also traces of charisma in monarchical authority. Charisma is a claim to divinely sanctioned authority. The abbreviations on the coin identify the Queen (from the Latin) as monarch by the grace of God, and as defender of the (Protestant) faith. But as these examples suggest, both tradition and charisma are now mostly just curiosities: the bed rock of authority in British government is rational-legal. And as symptomatic of that, the more valuable currency – the note – is also backed by the entirely uncharismatic authority of the central bank, the Bank of England. The tax demand (received by the author) illustrates the most important kind of authority identified by Weber, now at the heart of the modern state: rational-legal authority. The power of the Inland Revenue to issue the demand derives solely from the law. The substance of the demand – the size of the bill – is the product of calculations according to explicit rules, referred to in the demand. And the ability to enforce the demand depends on the calculation having been made according to the rules: hence the invitation to the recipient to examine and if appropriate disagree with the calculation. (In Chapter 23 we discuss what remedies the citizen has against the misuse of this kind of authority.)

**Image 1.3**
**Images of authority in Britain: tax demand**

belong to what is sometimes called the 'first world' (see Table 1.1). It is also a member, through the European Union, of an organization which, as we shall see, is one of the most important economic and political players in world politics.

Britain also has a special historical significance in the development of the wider global system. The Industrial Revolution, which Britain pioneered in the eighteenth century, created the first industrial society, clearing a path in economics and politics which many other leading nations have followed. In short, you do not have to be particularly interested in Britain for its own sake to find the study of British politics important; you just have to be interested in our modern world, and how we got here.

For those who live in Britain the importance and relevance of politics is greater still. A century ago most people who lived in Britain could go through their daily lives without being significantly touched by the state: if you had wandered round a British town a century ago the only big public employer you would have seen evidence of, for example, would have been the Post Office (then, as now, it was publicly owned). But during the twentieth century the British state, like the states of other democracies, emerged as a major influence on the lives of all citizens. The typical Briton will profess herself entirely uninterested in government and politics, yet all our lives are profoundly shaped by what goes on in the political arena, and by what government does. Just consider some of the ways. British readers of this book will almost certainly have been born in a hospital run by the National Health Service, a state-funded and state controlled body. Bar a small minority they will have been educated in state schools, schools which are entirely funded by government and, over the last couple of decades, which have been subjected to close control by central government as to what they teach and how they teach. And now, if in further or higher education, the story will be repeated. Although students in higher education in England pay an annual fee, that fee falls far short of covering the cost of education, most of which comes from taxation raised by central government. And as in schools, what is taught, and how it is taught, is

increasingly prescribed by agencies of central government.

This sketch is just a miniature of the way government now looms large in the life of all of us. Figure 1.1 presents a summary measure of the long-term growth in the scale of government spending over this last century.

British politics is an important subject of study because of its size and historical importance, so we

**Table 1.1**  Britain as a rich and privileged country: the British and the poorest on earth

|  | Britain | Poorest countries on Earth* |
|---|---|---|
| Life expectancy (years) | 77.3 | 58.9 |
| Infant mortality rates (per live 1,000 births) | 5.6 | 76.1 |
| Electricity use per capita (kwh) | 5,240.7 | 345.8 |
| Gross national income, per head (US$) | 24,430 | 410.0 |
| Telephones (fixed line and mobile) per 1,000 people | 1,315.5 | 28.7 |
| Paved roads (% of total) | 100 | 16.7 |
| Personal computers (per 1,000 people) | 337 | 5.1 |

* The figures are for the poorest countries identified by the World Bank for its 'low income data profile', a collective portrait of the poorest countries on earth. Most figures date to 2000.

*Source*: Calculated from World Bank Data File 2003: www.worldbank.org

➲ The table summarizes the single most important feature of social and economic life in Britain: she is one of a small number of fabulously rich countries by the standards of most of the world's population (and by the standards of most Britons of earlier generations). The figures compare Britain with the poorest countries as identified by the World Bank. Some of the figures directly measure the huge disparities in income, such as that for gross national income per head. Some measure fundamental difference in life chances, such as those for mortality (both adult and infant). Some measure access to modern technology which most Britons now take for granted, such as telephones. And some measure the quality of the physical infrastructure, such as the percentage of roads that are paved.

**Figure 1.1** The growth in the scale of government over a century (% Gross Domestic Product accounted for by general government spending)

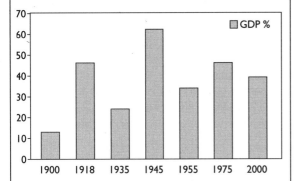

*Source*: Calculated from Clark and Dilnot 2002:3.

➲ The chart highlights the changing scale of spending by governments at various points over the course of the twentieth century. It measures 'general government spending' – a broad measure – as a proportion of Gross Domestic Product (GDP), the commonest measure of the size of the wider economy. It thus measures both the growing absolute scale of government and also its changing relative importance in the wider economy. It is a summary of why studying British government is so important: government is easily the biggest institution in British society. Notice three particularly important features: the way there are two huge peaks accompanying the two world wars in the century (these will be discussed more fully in Chapter 2); the way the century-long trend is ever-increasing; and the way there is little appreciable scaling back in the last quarter of the century, despite the fact that Britain was then run by governments who wanted to cut spending. These trends are discussed in more detail in Chapter 21.

try to make sense of it for academic reasons. But there are also reasons why as citizens we should study it, and those reasons are summarized below.

## Understanding

Anyone who follows the daily arguments that go on in British politics – in the House of Commons or in the media – will know that they are highly charged. They resemble more the argument of a courtroom, where competing prosecutors and defenders do battle, than the atmosphere of a scientific laboratory or a seminar room. But politics also needs to be *understood* just as dispassionately as we try to understand the workings of the natural world. In the broadest sense of the term the study of politics thus needs to be *scientific*. This does not mean that the key elements we study in politics – who are after all human beings – are like the key elements that a chemist or an astronomer studies, and neither does it mean that we expect to be able to develop the sort of highly formal, mathematically expressed theories common in the physical sciences. (Nevertheless in some areas, such as the most sophisticated studies of elections, mathematical formality is quite well advanced.) 'Science' is a word with a root in Latin and by origin it denotes only knowledge and its systematic study. To speak of the need to study British politics *scientifically* is thus only to speak of the need to study it as systematically and dispassionately as possible; to develop accounts of how the various parts of the system operate; and to debate the accuracy of those accounts, not by reference to our subjective views, but by reference to agreed bodies of evidence.

## Effective citizenship

Britain is run, we will discover, by an activist minority numbered in tens, rather than hundreds, of thousands. Some readers of this book will eventually form a part of that activist minority. There are many ways of obtaining knowledge about how the system of government operates in order to have an effective say in government, and practical participation in politics is one. But that sort of knowledge only comes with long experience. Not everyone wants to wait 20 years to pick up the hard truths about the realities of political power; systematic study is a way of short-circuiting that extended learning through experience.

## Making government effective

Governments make decisions and put those decisions into effect. Nothing guarantees that they are wise decisions or, if they are, that wise decisions actually take effect. One of the main lessons of the study of British government in recent years, as we shall see in these pages, is that good government is more than a matter of good intentions or good people (see Briefing 1.2). It also depends on how government is *run*. Getting things wrong can be catastrophic. Northern Ireland, for instance, was very badly run between the 1920s and the 1960s, and part of what was bad about how it was run can be found in the way government in the province was organized. Since the end of the 1960s several thousand people have paid with their lives for that bad history. Lesser (but still significant) catastrophes occur every day. Government manages the economy, sometimes for better, sometimes for worse. Look around your neighbourhood. Is the way it is laid out – the amount of green space, the safety of the roads, the quality of the buildings – satisfactory? If not, at least some of the blame can be laid at the door of government in its role as the planner of our local environment. Understanding how government is organized, and how it fails or succeeds in particular policies, does not guarantee more effective government; but without this knowledge we have no chance at all of improving the quality of governing institutions.

## Three big questions about British politics

It is time to turn to more particular questions: those that focus on British politics itself. These questions anticipate the most important themes that recur throughout the pages of the rest of this book, and we return to them in the final chapter. Three are sketched below because they recur so commonly in later pages.

### Who has power in Britain and under what conditions do they exercise that power?

This is the most fundamental of all questions about British government, and for very obvious reasons. The struggle for power lies at the heart of all political life, and it bears in particular on the most important moral claim made about British government: that it is democratic. As Briefing 1.3 illustrates, there are many meanings that can be attributed to democracy, and many ways of conceiving power. But at the very minimum the theory that Britain is democratic

---

# Briefing                                    1.2

## WHY WE CANNOT TAKE SUCCESS IN GOVERNMENT FOR GRANTED

- Northern Ireland was ruled from the 1920s to the 1960s by sectarian devolved government which systematically discriminated against Catholics and Irish Nationalists (whom it mostly treated as equivalents). Governments of both parties in Westminster turned a blind eye. At the end of the 1960s civil strife resulted. Since then governments of both parties have struggled with the consequences, the most disastrous of which has been the loss of over 3,000 lives.
- The poll tax was introduced in the 1980s by Mrs Thatcher's government, and almost as quickly abandoned. It was intended to be a new way of levying taxes by local government. It led to large scale civil disobedience, did huge damage to local government finance and wasted about £1.5 billion in public money.
- Rail privatization was carried out in the mid- to late 1990s. It replaced an inefficient and poorly funded publicly owned system (British Rail) with a network of badly coordinated private companies. Since then the rail system has been notorious for delays, unreliability, overcrowding and missed targets.

⮕ Government successfully carries out many complex tasks. But the very scale of the modern state in Britain means that when things go wrong, they often go wrong in a spectacular fashion. Success has to be worked for and, as the three cases show, when it is not achieved the result is a fiasco (often, as in the case of Northern Ireland, on the scale of a grand tragedy). For more on fiascos in government see Chapters 19 and 24.

---

demands two things: that power be widely distributed, and that those who exercise power should do so in an open way according to clear rules, and be held accountable for its exercise. In terms of the theories outlined in Briefing 1.3 power in Britain should at least match the requirements of the 'pluralist' model of power distribution.

An equally important claim about British government concerns not the direct question of the distribution of power, but the conditions under which it is exercised: that the system of government is *consti-*

# Briefing

## THEORIES OF DEMOCRATIC GOVERNMENT

|  | *Class rule* | *Direct democracy* | *Elitist democracy* | *Pluralist democracy* |
|---|---|---|---|---|
| How are decisions made? | By direct participation of the poor and propertyless | By direct participation of all people, either in assemblies or through devices such as referenda | By political and administrative elites; the former elected through competition by parties for the popular vote | By political and administrative elites, and by numerous competing organized interests and opinion groups |
| In whose interests? | Those without property | Decisions reflect the general will of the community, as expressed by choices made after collective deliberation. | Decisions reflect the balance of power between competing elites, modified by the need to compete for the popular vote every four or five years. | Decisions reflect the balance of power between different groups at different times, no one interest dominates and no interest has a monopoly of the different means of exercizing power over decision. |
| Influence in Britain | Almost nil | Historically nil; some growth in the use of referenda, public opinion polling and a few experiments with mass electronic voting allowing direct popular say in particular decisions | Was the dominant form of democratic rule in Britain throughout the twentieth century following the creation of near universal adult voting rights after 1918 | Is the commonest 'official' approved account of how Britain has been, and continues to be, governed |

➲ 'Democracy' comes in many shapes and sizes. Before the twentieth century most people – both practical politicians and political theorists – thought of democracy as 'class rule', and were fearful of it. 'Direct democracy' was long associated with small communities since it was believed that only when numbers were small was real direct participation in decisions possible. The device of the referendum – a vote on a particular issue put to the mass of the population – has spread as an alternative, and the rise of opinion polling in the last 50 years has added more elements of the 'direct'. Electronic voting using the latest technology promises to expand the range further. 'Elitist democracy' was the dominant academic theory of how democracy functions for most of the second half of the twentieth century. Its intellectual father is the great Austrian social scientist Joseph Schumpeter (1883–1950): his masterpiece, *Capitalism, Socialism and Democracy* (1943/1976) offered a vision of democracy as the competitive struggle for the popular vote by elites. It is not surprising that a book written in the shadow of two tyrannies that had used the forms of popular rule – German Nazism and Soviet Stalinism – should have been sceptical of direct popular influence over government. 'Pluralist democracy' is a close cousin of elitism, but it stresses the importance of popular participation through the web of organized (and unorganized) interests and opinions in society, and sees group organization and participation and voting in elections as complementary.

*tutional*. What this amounts to is the claim that government is constrained by law, and that the liberties of citizens are protected by the independent power of law. It is easy to see that we could all live under such a system of limited, constrained government even if the system were not democratic in the sense of allowing us a positive say in the making of policy. The claim that the British system is constitutional in this sense is intensely debated. The preference for imposing constitutional limitations on government goes alongside a powerful apparatus – through, for instance, Official Secrets legislation – ensuring secrecy in the operation of a large part of the state machine. In institutions such as the security services the state has institutions that can seriously infringe the liberties of citizens. In at least one part of the kingdom – Northern Ireland – many of the established mechanisms for ensuring liberty, such as jury trial for some categories of offence, have been suspended for a generation on the grounds that this suspension is needed to combat the bigger threat to liberty posed by terrorism. Britain is also quite special in not having a written constitution that incorporates a bill of rights for citizens, which is one of the main legal mechanisms used in other democratic countries to try to ensure that citizen liberties are protected. But Britain has undergone a constitutional revolution in recent years. Later chapters (especially from 22 onwards) try to discover how far this has strengthened the forces making the exercise of power open and accountable.

## Is British government 'hollowed out' government?

Arguments about power and accountability assume that there is some worthwhile power to be struggled over, yet in recent years doubts have grown over the degree to which power actually is any longer exercised at the traditional centre of British government, in London. The argument is that the centre is being 'hollowed out', that power is forcibly being distributed across many levels of society – and that as a result, government in Britain is necessarily 'multi-level' government: policy is made and executed at many different levels, and is the result of bargaining and manoeuvring by a wide range of

forces at these different levels. The biggest problem for the 'centre' is trying to coordinate this multilevel system in order to produce some consistency and effectiveness in what government does.

Three big forces lie behind these claims. First, the spectacular policy failures illustrated in Briefing 1.2 show that modern government is a highly complex business. (There is further discussion of policy fiascos in Chapters 19 and 24.) British government was traditionally very centralized in London, but this centralization makes government highly vulnerable to policy disasters. Only by recognizing that the power to shape successful policy is nowadays distributed widely through many social networks can governments have any hope of governing effectively. The age of successful policy made by command from the centre in London is at an end, although governments in London do not necessarily recognize this fact. Second, British government is being 'hollowed out' from the top, as a result of our membership of the European Union. A large number of important decisions, especially about the critical matter of economic policy, can no longer be made independently in London; at best they have to be negotiated through the institutions of the European Union, mostly in Brussels. This second force obviously connects to one of the major themes of this book: the thoroughgoing interpenetration between the institutions of government in Britain and the institutions of government in the European Union. These changes now date back a long time: they can be traced to Britain's original entry into what was then the European Economic Community (EEC) in 1973, something we look at in more detail in Chapters 2 and 6. But the third force is more recent: it is produced by the large scale constitutional changes introduced by the new Labour Government after 1998, especially the establishment of devolved executives for Wales and Scotland. This last change, according to the hollowing-out theory, amounts to hollowing out 'from below'.

## What is the Thatcher legacy in British government?

The election of a new Conservative Government under Margaret Thatcher in 1979 was a momen-

**POLITICAL ISSUES**

## 1.1   LIBERAL FREEDOMS UNDER PRESSURE: THE CASE OF BELMARSH INTERNEES

We saw in Briefing 1.1 that a defining feature of the modern state is the ability to exercise physical compulsion. In the last resort that means imprisoning us, or worse. In most cases in a liberal democracy that cannot be done without a public trial, which is in turn surrounded by a variety of safeguards. But in extreme cases in the twentieth century the British state imprisoned those suspected of threatening state security without trial: during the Second World War, 1939-45, and in Northern Ireland in the 1970s. Following the terrorist attacks in New York and Washington on 11 September 2001 the state in Britain took power to intern terrorist suspects without trial, in the Anti-Terrorism Crime and Security Act, 2001. Following the passage of the Act 13 men were held without trial in Belmarsh High Security Prison by order of the Home Secretary. They had no right to examine the evidence on which they were held, or the charges against them. Their only appeal was through a Special Immigration Appeals Commission. In July 2002 the Commission found that there was a public emergency justification for their detention. But all are foreign nationals, and the Commission found that the detention was unlawful because discriminatory: the powers in the Act concern only foreign nationals; British subjects retain the right to be charged and tried, or released. In October 2002 the Court of Appeal overturned this ruling, finding that there was no discrimination. In 2005 the Courts ruled that the detentions were unlawful.

The case illuminates four key issues about state power:

- It shows the critical connection between national citizenship and the exercise of power: the state makes a clear distinction here between the rights of British nationals and foreigners.
- It illuminates in a particularly clear way the heart of coercive state power.
- It illuminates one of the central dilemmas of a liberal democracy, such as Britain claims to be: how far the safeguards conventional in a liberal democracy, including those against imprisonment without trial, can defensibly be violated.
- As with earlier episodes of internment without trial, this case occurred at a time of heightened fears for public security: in this case, fears of terrorist attacks in Britain and abroad. And as with earlier episodes, it raises the question of how robustly the institutions of the liberal democratic state can be preserved in the face of terrorism.

tous event in British politics – perhaps the single most momentous peacetime event in British politics during the twentieth century. Mrs Thatcher remained Prime Minister for over 11 years, the longest tenure of any Prime Minister of modern times. The 1980s were the decade of 'Thatcherism': unusually, a whole political programme was identified with a leading politician. Thatcherism produced revolutionary changes in Britain. It transformed economic life: it greatly reduced the power of trade unions; it sold off many large publicly owned industries, including gas and telecommunications, and disposed of over a million council house dwellings to sitting tenants; it forced numerous industries to abandon restrictions on competition. It also transformed government: as we will see (for instance, in Chapter 8) it fundamentally reorganized the structure of the civil service. Thatcherism also led to a wider transformation of political life. The Labour Party spent the 1980s

## DEBATING POLITICS

### 1.1    THE STUDY OF POLITICS: PRACTICALLY USEFUL OR PRACTICALLY USELESS?

| The study of politics is of practical importance: | The study of politics is practically useless: |
|---|---|

**The study of politics is of practical importance:**

■ Most of the big sources of human misery are political in origin: wars, revolution, poverty. Curing or alleviating these would immeasurably benefit humanity.

■ Governments frequently perpetrate policy disasters and it is important to understand the causes of those disasters.

■ British democracy demands informed citizens – and being informed about how government operates is a vital kind of information.

■ The study of politics in a university or college provides a valuable training for a political career.

**The study of politics is practically useless:**

■ After more than 2,000 years of studying politics we are still no nearer remedying the political causes of human misery.

■ Understanding disasters after they have occurred is like locking the stable door when the horse has bolted.

■ Most citizens get by, and get active in politics, without opening a single academic text or attending a single politics lecture.

■ Not one British Prime Minister for the last 25 years has studied politics at university. We have been ruled by lawyers, chemists and some who did not attend university at all.

---

trying to work out how to cope with Mrs Thatcher, suffering three successive election defeats at her hands (in 1979, 1983 and 1987). It ended up by accepting most of the elements of the Thatcher revolution. All these changes not only happened under Mrs Thatcher's leadership; they could also be traced to her influence. By energy, determination and luck she dominated her governments in a way never achieved before by a Prime Minister in peacetime.

Yet the Thatcher legacy is hotly contested. She is the most revered and admired political figure in Britain of recent decades – and also the most detested. For some, she was the saviour of the British economy, turning an economy that was descending into chaos and impoverishment into a model that most of our European neighbours would now seek to emulate. In saving the economy, and cutting back a large and incompetent state, she also preserved the liberties of the British people (see Political issues 1.1). For others, her legacy is poisonous: she helped destroy many traditional British manufacturing industries, and produced an economy where a tiny minority

### REVIEW

Four themes dominate this chapter:

1 The importance of politics as an activity in securing for any community the basics of a peaceful and prosperous life;

2 The importance of the state as an arena where the most vital political issues are contested;

3 The importance of the British system of government, both for anyone interested in government across the universe of rich industrial nations on earth, and for anyone who actually lives in Britain;

4 The importance of studying British government in the light of hotly contested questions about the nature of power and democracy, the nature of decision-making in Britain, and the impact of the era of Thatcherism in Britain.

enrich themselves fabulously while millions work under the threat of dismissal. For many Conservatives her legacy is uncertain. The Conservative Party that she led utterly dominated British politics in the 1980s. Her successor as Leader, John Major (1990–7) was Prime Minister of a divided and declining government. The once dominant Conservatives suffered three catastrophic election defeats (in 1997, 2001 and 2005) and are now reduced to the position of by-standers as Labour dominates government. (See also Image 1.1 and Debating politics 1.1).

## Further reading

The classic introduction to the nature of politics is Crick (2000). A standard American work that is particularly strong on the study of power and authority is Dahl (1984). Professor Crick chaired a committee on the teaching of citizenship: its report (Crick 1998) is a very good introduction to the study of the subject in a British setting. Harrison (1996) provides a clear, compressed thematic introduction to British politics covering more than a century. A very good introduction to the historically controversial meaning of democracy is Macpherson (1971).

**CHAPTER 2**

# British politics: the historical context

## CONTENTS

## AIMS

The most important aim of this chapter is to sketch the main routes by which we have arrived at the present condition of modern British politics. Five are summarily described:

❖ The historical development of democratic politics

❖ The historical development of the British economy

❖ The historical development of the British welfare state

❖ The historical development of Britain's place in the world

❖ The arrival of Britain at a historical crossroads involving a choice between a more 'European' and a more 'Americanized' future.

## The development of democratic politics

Britain belongs to an exclusive club of countries: those that can make a fairly convincing claim to be democracies. Chapter 1 demonstrated that the meaning of 'democracy' is uncertain, and we will discover time and again in later chapters that the British claim can in many details be disputed. But nevertheless the claim in the British case is credible. Although it is a monarchy, the monarch in Britain has long been stripped of any serious publicly exercised power (though it is almost certain that considerable private influence is still wielded). Elections are contested under almost universal suffrage – the large majority of adults (defined as over 18) is entitled to the vote. (But the exclusion of a significant minority is examined in Chapter 17.) Political parties compete openly for votes, and the result of this competition at national level decides (though sometimes in an arithmetically odd way) who occupies the offices of government. Finally, there exist freedoms that are usually thought to be essential to the operations of liberal and democratic politics: freedom of speech, of assembly, of the press. Later in the book we will see that many of these working features of democracy are often limited and breached, but they are nevertheless of real significance. Where did they come from?

The histories of the monarchy and of the suffrage are both critical (see People in Politics 2.1). Britain limited the power of its monarch before it empowered its people – became, in other words, a limited monarchy before it became any sort of democracy. In the seventeenth century a number of kings claimed unrestricted power, and that the absolute character of this power came from God: in the language we used in Chapter 1, they claimed a mixture of traditional and charismatic (divine) authority. Those claims were rejected in two events. In 1649 the head of one king (Charles I) was chopped off, and in 1688 another (James II) was forced to flee London, and was then defeated in battle. The events of 1688 are sometimes called the 'Glorious Revolution'. After it, kings in England always had to share power with others, and always had their power limited in important ways by law.

The limiting of royal power also produced measures which led to limits on the power of government arbitrarily to detain subjects, and after a long struggle in the eighteenth century led to freedoms of conscience and expression. It was nevertheless a long time before monarchs shared their power with elected representatives of the people, and a longer time still before the monarchy was reduced to a point of marginal importance in the system of government. Queen Victoria (1837–1901) was still powerful in blocking many reforms, and her successors Edward VII (1901–10) and George V (1910–36) were able to exercise significant influence when there were constitutional crises. We do not yet definitively know whether the long reign of Elizabeth II (1953–) has led to similar behind-the-scenes influence, but we do know that the Queen and other royals (notably the Prince of Wales and the Duke of Edinburgh) have easy access to political leaders of all the main parties.

The transformation of the monarchy from an absolute to a limited one had, however, been achieved before the issue of suffrage became central to political struggle. Who should be entitled to the vote was the great political issue of the nineteenth century. The struggle was conducted in the shadow of two revolutions, one foreign and one domestic. The French Revolution (which began in 1789) overthrew traditional powers, executed royals and aristocrats, developed political philosophies which used the language of equality, and soon turned into an aggressive military power which conquered large parts of Europe. It faced ruling elites in Britain with a stark choice: to accommodate demands for political change from below; or to repress those demands by using coercion.

Making that choice was both complicated and helped by the second (domestic) revolution, the Industrial Revolution. The Industrial Revolution had by the middle of the nineteenth century created two powerful classes in Britain: the owners of the new industries and the workers employed in those industries. Constitutional change in the first half of the nineteenth century was mainly concerned with accommodating the former of these: for example, the first great piece of electoral reform in the century, the 1832 Reform Act, mostly extended

## People in politics

### 2.1  THREE WHO MADE THE MODERN BRITISH STATE

Cartoons: Shaun Steele

**Elizabeth I** (reigned 1558–1603). The Tudor monarchs ruled from 1485 to 1603 and Elizabeth was the last, and the greatest. She consolidated the Protestantism that had started with the Reformation begun by her father Henry, finally wiping out the Catholic Church as a rival power to the state. Under her the Church of England was settled as the official keeper of the state religion. She also consolidated central executive power, a process begun by her grandfather, Henry VI (reigned 1485–1509). The defeat of an invading Spanish Armada in 1588 was soon mythologized as a great feat of national defence. National mythologies were also developed by the great burst of creative theatre that coincided with her reign, notably in the historical dramas of Shakespeare. Long after her death, the concept of a glorious 'Elizabethan Age' became central to notions of British, and especially English, national identity.

**Oliver Cromwell**, born of minor gentry in Huntingdon in 1599, emerged as, first, the leading general of the Parliamentary forces in the English Civil War (1642–49). He played a key part not only in the military defeat of the Crown but in the political debates that arose out of the conflict. Following the defeat of the Royalists and the execution of King Charles I in 1649 he then emerged as the most powerful figure in the state. He imposed a brutal military settlement on Ireland, and in the execution of the King decisively banished the royalist claim to rule by absolute monarchy. Though he contemptuously dismissed Parliament, and though the monarchy was restored following Cromwell's death, his impact was decisive: after it, the monarchy was always limited and a long process of decline in its powers began. Ironically, a figure who ruled in an authoritarian way had thus begun the long road to a system of rule by a constitutional and parliamentary government.

**David Lloyd George** (1863–1945) was the most creative political figure of the early decades of the twentieth century. He first emerged as a leader of Liberal radical politics from a political base in north Wales. From 1905 to 1922 he served continuously in the Cabinet, and from 1908 to 1915 as Chancellor. His period as Chancellor was marked by radical social policy innovations – such as the introduction of old age pensions – that helped found the modern welfare state. This radicalism also provoked fierce opposition and resulted in a decisive curtailment of the power of the House of Lords. As Prime Minister 1916–22 he first presided over the great wartime expansion of state controls. Despite postwar retreat by the state this also marked the first appearance of the twentieth-century interventionist state. He negotiated the independence of the Irish Free State in 1921. And in 1918 he split from, and broke, the Liberal Party, thus allowing Labour to supplant it as the Conservatives' main opponents for the whole of the twentieth century.

➲ Many historical figures have shaped the British state, but these three were decisive in different ways at different times: Elizabeth in consolidating state power and defeating foreign (Spanish) threats; Cromwell in preparing the way for a limited, constitutional monarchy; Lloyd George in shaping the large scale interventionist state that still rules Britain. In all three cases there is a distinctive combination: a mix of great military demands coupled with a powerfully commanding personality. The examples show how British political history has been governed by a mix of great historical forces and human agency. All three of these personalities were remarkable enough to shape history, and not just to be shaped by it. The most remarkable was Elizabeth, a commanding woman in an era when the subjection of women was almost total.

Parliamentary representation to the new owners of property created by economic change. In the 1867 Reform Act there was some limited extension of the vote to the most prosperous of *male* manual workers, but even the progressive extensions of the suffrage later in the nineteenth century maintained two key principles: that the right to vote should be restricted to those who owned some specified amount of property and should be restricted to men. (The two were connected since property laws made it difficult for women, especially married women, to own property independently.) It was not until the Representation of the People Act of 1918 that something akin to a modern democratic system of suffrage emerged: entitlement to a vote was in the case of men disconnected from property, being extended to all adult men (aged 21 and over). But property was still used to restrain the political power of women: those 30 and over were given the vote if they were ratepayers or married to ratepayers. The qualifying age for women to vote was reduced to that for men in 1928 and the qualifying age for everyone was reduced to 18 in 1969 (see Timeline 2.1).

The years after the First World War were also marked by a series of other developments that are now recognized as central to the modern political system. In the 1918 general election, fought on the new franchise and in the immediate aftermath of the First World War, the party system that has since dominated Britain first appeared: Conservatives and Labour emerged as the two dominant parties and the Liberals, who had been the Conservatives' main opponents for over half a century, began to be pushed to the margins of politics. The emergence of this two-party system also coincided with the rise of class-based political conflict in Britain, since (in very broad terms) the Conservatives established themselves as the party of property holders and the Labour Party presented itself as the party of the newly enfranchised working class. Something like the organization of the system of government that characterized Britain for most of the twentieth century also matured at around this time. In 1910, the end of a long struggle for power between the House of Lords (which was dominated by traditional aristocratic interests) and the House of

Commons was settled in favour of the latter through a law that greatly reduced the ability of the Lords to obstruct legislation passed in the Commons.

By 1918, a series of reforms in the civil service (which originated in proposals dating from as far back as the mid-1850s) finally produced a unified civil service, one which recruited by competitive selection rather than connections. In 1921 the establishment of the Irish Free State redefined for the remainder of the century the boundaries of the United Kingdom, creating an independent Irish state in 26 of the 32 counties of Ireland. In the 1920s itself the foundation of the BBC, and the development of radio as a means of mass communication, heralded two very important developments: the creation of a national system of mass communication focused from, and controlled from, the capital; and the rise of a system of political communication (including mass campaigning by the parties) which relied heavily on mass communication rather than the sort of face-to-face contacts which had been the norm in the nineteenth century. From the 1920s most important events and political messages were communicated to people via mass communication, first through radio and, from the early 1950s, through television.

Thus the historical development of the modern political system in Britain can be thought of as involving three processes.

- First, there developed before the nineteenth century restraints on the exercise of arbitrary power by government. The most important aspect of this was the growing limitation of the power of monarchs.
- Second, in the century up to the end of the First World War (1918) a democratic franchise was developed, after much struggle. That involved both extending the right to vote to most adults and largely disconnecting voting entitlements from property ownership.
- Third, after 1918 the shape of modern British politics was established: the two dominant parties, Labour and the Conservatives, emerged; politics was dominated by the struggle for control of the governing machine in London;

| | Measure | Main provisions |
|---|---|---|
| **1832** | Reform Act | Abolishes 'rotten boroughs', constituencies with no or few electors owned by rich patrons; creates new constituencies in the growing urban/industrial districts; extends voting rights to middle-class property owners. |
| **1867** | Representation of the People Act | Relaxes property qualifications so as to enfranchise many skilled male manual workers; creates more additional new constituencies in urban/industrial districts. |
| **1884** | Representation of the People Act | Adds 2.5 million new votes by enfranchising virtually all male householders and many tenants. |
| **1918** | Representation of the People Act | Votes for all men over 21 and women over the age of 30 who were ratepayers or married to ratepayers. |
| **1928** | Representation of the People Act | Reduces the qualifying age for voting for women to 21. |
| **1948** | Representation of the People Act | Abolishes plural voting for business and professional classes: (the practice of giving an extra vote to owners of businesses and graduates of some prestigious universities). |
| **1969** | Representation of the People Act | Reduces the qualifying age for voting from 21 to 18. |

**TIMELINE 2.1   THE RISE OF UNIVERSAL SUFFRAGE IN BRITAIN**

➲ There are three important themes to bear in mind in reading this chronicle of the single most important development of democratic politics in Britain. First, the spread of the franchise was not simply a matter of the mere quantitative extension in the numbers of voter: it consisted in the principle of gradually severing the connection between property ownership and the vote. The connection was vital to most nineteenth-century thinkers about these matters, since they feared that a democracy of the 'propertyless' would confiscate property. Second, the old principles of advantaging property lingered remarkably late: notice that only in 1948 was a separate 'business vote' (based on location of business property) abolished. Third, the struggle to extend the franchise overlapped with, but was in key respects distinct from, the struggle to enfranchise women.

*Source*: Adapted from Butler and Butler (2000); Cook and Stevenson (2000)

and the modern mass media became central instruments of the political struggle.

As we saw, two great revolutions helped shape nineteenth-century politics: the French Revolution and the Industrial Revolution. Since the second was uniquely British and still reverberates through our society and politics, it requires separate discussion.

## The development of the British economy

Britain pioneered a new kind of economy for the whole world and this pioneering role and its after-math have left indelible marks not just on the economy, but on the whole of government and society. Around the middle decades of the eighteenth century – economic historians dispute the exact sequence – the economy began to grow at what was then an unprecedented pace, and this expansion marked out Britain from other national economies for a century.

This change in pace, though important, was merely a sign of much more fundamental developments. The Industrial Revolution created a society with distinct ways of making a living and generating wealth. For most of human history land had been the most important form of wealth and the farm the most important place of work. Now, industry became the most important form of wealth and the factory the most important place of work. That in turn had incalculable consequences for the class structure. One of the most important classes in the societies of most European nations until recently was that of peasants, a social group that lived by cultivating small plots of land. Britain wiped out this peasantry early by enclosing the land it worked on and handing it over to landlords, thus forcing peasants and their descendants into labouring in the new factories. As a consequence people were also driven from the countryside to the town, so that Britain not only became a pioneering industrial economy; she also became a highly urbanized society where, by the middle of the nineteenth century, the majority of her population lived in towns and cities.

The Industrial Revolution also transformed the class structure. Among the rich it created a new group of industrial property owners, an industrial bourgeoisie, that emerged in the nineteenth century as one of the most important influences on political reform, and as a rival to the traditionally powerful aristocracy whose wealth and power depended on land. Among the mass of the population the Revolution also transformed class structure. It created the first large, well-organized and self-conscious industrial working class in history. By the end of the nineteenth century this class had its own trade unions, its own cultural institutions, its own distinct religious preferences and its own leisure patterns. At the start of the twentieth century it also founded its own political party, Labour.

Almost everything that is presently significant about British politics is about working out the social consequences of this pioneering role in industrialism. But the Industrial Revolution's consequences were not limited to their impact at home: it also had dramatic consequences for Britain's place in the world (see Figure 2.1). When it began Britain was a small, comparatively poor and not particularly powerful nation on the edge of Europe. Within a century she was the 'workshop of the world': by the last quarter of the nineteenth century she produced over one-fifth of all world manufacturing output. Since political power tends to follow economic power, she also dominated international politics. By the end of the nineteenth century she had acquired

the largest Empire on earth, probably the largest Empire in history, and was the world's greatest military power. The nineteenth century was 'the English century'. A symbolically important moment of domination occurred, fittingly, in the middle of the century, at the high point of British economic dominance. It took the form of the Great Exhibition of 1851, a huge international exhibition of the arts, crafts and products of the new industries that served to showcase British success. Britain by then was well on the way to completing the assembly of her vast Empire and she was a dominant naval and diplomatic power. She also ruled the international financial system. The pound sterling was the dominant international currency and the City of London was the world's greatest financial centre.

The Industrial Revolution gave Britain a flying start ahead of all other nations into the world of industrial society, and provided the foundations for British world domination for most of the nineteenth century. It continues to mark British society deeply and irrevocably. As far as contemporary politics are concerned – and indeed as far as the politics of the second half of the twentieth century were concerned – it also provided some of the most important problems on the agenda of government. Of these, perhaps the most significant was the perception that precisely because of its pioneering role Britain suffered uniquely a problem of economic decline. The Great Exhibition of 1851 turns out in retrospect to have marked the apogee of British economic power. Never again would the British economy be quite so dominant. In the last 30 years of the nineteenth century, when the world economy entered a prolonged depression, it became obvious that other nations were imitating British economic success: Germany, the United States and Japan all emerged as formidable industrial rivals. As the gap with rivals closed it also became increasingly clear that that this was not just a matter of other nations naturally catching up; rather, whatever had been the secret of the astounding economic revolution in Britain seemed to have been lost.

Britain's relative economic decline accelerated in the twentieth century, especially in the second half of the century. In 1945, at the close of the Second World War, Britain seemed to have a unique

**Figure 2.1** How Britain dominated the world economy at the height of the Industrial Revolution (shares of world exports in 1870)

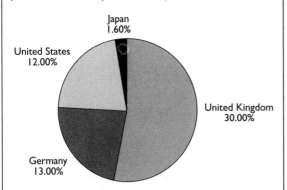

*Source*: Calculated from Alford (1996: 7).

➲ These figures date from 1870, just about the high point of British industrial and imperial power. They show how far ahead of her main competitors Britain was at the height of the Industrial Revolution, and they show to what extent this lead rested on her domination of global markets. They also alert us to how much ground was made up by some of those competitors: look at the share enjoyed by Japan, which by the second half of the twentieth century had far outstripped Britain.

opportunity to recover some of the lost economic ground. The world economy stood on the edge of a sustained 30-year long boom. The world was hungry for production, and some of the most successful rivals to the British economy – notably Germany and Japan – were defeated, under military occupation and large parts of their industry had simply been flattened out of existence by the destruction of war. Yet when the great world economic boom came to an end in the middle of the 1970s, as far as Britain was concerned it only highlighted what had been partly concealed by the wider international buoyancy: that the British economy was one of the weakest of those in the advanced industrial world. In industry after industry it was possible to find instances where, as recently as a quarter of a century before Britain had been a world leader and now had no industry at all, or only a weak, reduced version, often foreign owned: the examples stretched from shipbuilding to car and motorcycle manufacture. The 1970s were the lowest point of despair about the fate of the British economy: it was a moment when the possibility of Britain simply dropping out of the small club of First World, prosperous nations seemed a distinct possibility.

This apocalyptic scenario never came to pass, but the closing decades of the twentieth century saw the continuation of long-term historical trends in the development of the British economy. The old industries that had been the bedrock of the economy created in the Industrial Revolution continued to decline virtually to the point of extinction. An example is deep mining for coal, which almost completely disappeared in the closing decades of the twentieth century. More modern manufacturing sectors, such as automobiles, were also transformed. Britain became important once again in car building, but now as a site for assembly by large foreign-owned multinational automobile companies. Domestically-owned British car production disappeared except among a few small specialist producers.

The next chapter shows that these trends – notably the declining importance of the industrial economy that once made Britain so powerful and so distinctive – have had big social consequences.

## The development of the British welfare state

The great age of the British economy, when she pioneered the Industrial Revolution, was also marked by the domination of a particular kind of social philosophy. It was first expressed systematically by the great Scottish political economist Adam Smith in his *The Wealth of Nations* (1776). Smith argued that an economy based on market principles was the most just and efficient social arrangement that could be conceived. This meant that the state was assigned a marginal role, principally providing the goods and services that could not be guaranteed through the workings of supply and demand. The first century of the Industrial Revolution was the age of *laissez-faire* – a preference for a minimal state, and in particular for the minimum of public support for poverty relief. Even the modest public measures of poor relief that dated from the reign of Elizabeth I (1558–1603) were dismantled. Now, when poverty could not be dealt with by the operations of the market it was to be the responsibility of private charity. Most of the measures regulating working conditions, providing social services and providing income for those unable to earn a living in the marketplace that we now take for granted were entirely absent. If we look at Britain in 1850, for instance, at the very height of her industrial power, we find: no compulsory or state provided free schooling at any level; no national system of unemployment benefit; no public provision for pensions in old age; no public provision for free or subsidized health care; and only the barest regulation of the health and safety of workers.

Even in the golden age of *laissez-faire*, however, the state still retained an important place. Indeed, enforcing the free market itself demanded a highly active, often centralized, system of government. Perhaps the greatest attempt to oblige people to rely on the labour market for their own welfare was the Poor Law Amendment Act of 1834. This was an attempt organized nationally to create a uniform, and harsh, system of poor relief. It obliged those who claimed relief to subject themselves to a punitive regime in specially constructed workhouses. This involved building new workhouses around the country, and setting up a system of central control to ensure that conditions were sufficiently unpleasant to drive the poor into making every effort to avoid seeking public welfare. Thus *laissez-faire* actually demanded a strong, centralized state with high physical visibility. Many of these substantial buildings can still be seen. In the twentieth century they were very often converted into hospitals.

State power in nineteenth-century Britain was thus used to enforce a punitive welfare system that provided the barest of human necessities. By contrast, the European state that by the end of the nineteenth century was Britain's most formidable rival, Germany, already had a comprehensive system of welfare provision. It was far in advance of Britain in the provision of free education, income support in poverty and old age, access to free health

care and regulation of health and safety at work. The patchwork of limited measures that existed in Britain at the turn of the century could by no stretch of the imagination be described as a welfare state. What we now understand by that term is the product of two linked processes: a long-drawn-out process of piecemeal reforms which were addressed to very particular social problems; and three self-conscious bursts of innovation designed to build ambitious programmes of reform. The three were: by the Liberal Government between 1906 and 1911; by a variety of governments in the period stretching from the end of the First World War to the start of the Great Depression in the 1930s; and by the Labour Government headed by Attlee between 1945 and 1951. As this list shows, it is difficult for any single party to claim special responsibility for the establishment of the welfare state. The Liberal reforms, which were principally driven through by Lloyd George after he became Chancellor of the Exchequer in 1908, did three main things: introduced pensions for some of the old; established a system of compulsory national insurance which created an entitlement to some benefits for those paying if they became unemployed; and introduced a system of compulsory health insurance, partly modelled on that already existing in Germany. (The threat of a better-educated and more efficient Germany was one of the most important reasons for the introduction of these measures.)

The second burst – after the First World War (see Image 2.1) – was focused on two areas: financing a programme of housing construction by local governments for the poor; and reforming, and eventually all but abolishing, the Poor Law system originally created in 1834. The reforms of the Labour Government after 1945 built upon a consensus between all the parties that had been reached during the Second World War. They were inspired in particular by a famous official report produced by William Beveridge in 1942. Although the details of policy in the welfare state would have been different had the Conservatives won the 1945 election there can be little doubt that what we now recognize as the welfare state was the result of a consensus between all the parties about implementing the

**Image 2.1**
**The mark of war in twentieth-century Britain**

Photo: Michael Moran

➲ Virtually every town and large village in Britain has one of these war memorials. Most were constructed right at the beginning of the 1920s. They testify to the shaping experience of war in the history of Britain in the twentieth century. They record the astonishing loss of (mostly young male) lives, especially in the First World War, 1914–18. As we have seen in this chapter, war was critical in reshaping the role of the state in Britain, but it also had a huge human cost. This picture is taken sideways on because the slaughter was so great that the names of the dead run over more than one face of the memorial. The photo is taken in Drymen, a Scottish village just outside Glasgow. A picture of a Scottish memorial is fitting testimony, since Scotland contributed disproportionately: over one-quarter of all UK troops who landed in June 1944 in the Normandy invasion which led to the conquest of Hitler were Scots, though Scotland's proportion of the total UK population at the time barely exceeded 10 per cent.

main features of the Beveridge Report. For instance, one of the key measures that we associate with the welfare state, the 1944 Education Act, was prepared and passed by a Conservative Minister of Education in the wartime coalition.

The measures passed by Labour after 1945 are unusual, however, in two ways. The first is their range and ambition, typified by the most ambitious of all, the establishment of the National Health Service in 1948. This replaced an incomplete patchwork of provision with a nationally organized service. It extended to everyone an entitlement to the services, free of charge, of a medical practitioner, and free hospital care if the medical practitioner thought it appropriate. While an insurance levy was still imposed on those in work, in practice the welfare state after the Labour reforms was paid for out of general taxation, and its services were available to all. This linked to the second feature of the reforms introduced by Labour. After the post-1945 reforms the provision of welfare was linked to the idea of *citizenship*. In other words, access to the social goods and services produced as a result of the taxes levied by the state was an entitlement that was open equally to all in the community. The National Health Service, again, was the ideal of this. Everyone was entitled to the services of a general practitioner (GP), and to any further care that their GP might think appropriate, regardless of how rich or poor they were, regardless of what demands they had previously made on the service, and regardless of whether they had previously made contributions to the cost of the service. Conversely, every tax payer was obliged to contribute, through their taxes, to the cost of the welfare state, regardless of whether they were likely to need its services. Welfare services were an entitlement of citizenship and paying for welfare services was an obligation of citizenship.

The foundations of the welfare state laid down in the first half of the twentieth century (see Timeline 2.2) have proved remarkably resilient, but throughout the second half of the century there was continuous argument about its viability. Four issues have proved particularly contentious. First, is provision of welfare services by the state, at central or local level, an efficient mode of delivery? In the last 20

| TIMELINE 2.2 | BUILDING THE WELFARE STATE, 1900–50 | | |
|---|---|---|---|
| | Title of legislation | Main provisions | Party in government |
| 1901 | Trade Boards Act | Fixed minimum wages in some low wage industries. | Conservative |
| 1902 | Education Act | Established local authorities with power to provide secondary education. | Conservative |
| 1909 | Old Age Pensions Act | Established means-tested pensions for all over 70. | Liberal |
| 1911 | National Insurance Act | Levied insurance contributions in selected industries to provide income support in sickness and unemployment. | Liberal |
| 1915 | Rent Restrictions Act | Introduced rent control. | Liberal |
| 1918 | Education Act | Raised minimum school-leaving age to 12; abolished fees for elementary education. | Conservative–Liberal coalition |
| 1919 | Housing Act | Provided subsidies for building council housing. | Conservative–Liberal coalition |
| 1924 | Housing Act | Increased subsidies for council house building leading to construction of 500,000 houses in next eight years. | Labour |
| 1929 | Local Government Act | Poor Law Guardians abolished and replaced by elected local councils. | Conservative |
| 1930 | Poor Law Act | Poor Law replaced by Public Assistance, and provision that relief could only be provided to inmates of a workhouse abolished. | Labour |

⇨

years one of the biggest areas of social provision – housing owned and managed by local authorities – has been greatly scaled down, both by selling off houses to tenants and by shifting management responsibilities to voluntary housing associations. These changes were partly due to the belief that the system of local state delivery was inefficient. Second, the citizenship principle has imposed great pressures because it demands high levels of solidarity: that is, a willingness to contribute to the upkeep of others by tax payers who may themselves get nothing out of a particular service. For example, very high levels of spending on the upkeep of university students have benefited the middle and upper classes, which disproportionately supply the body of university students. The pressures on soli-

darity explain why over the last 50 years there has been a steady shift to more targeted and selective welfare services and a growing reliance on charges.

Third, the long struggle to cope with the problems of the ailing British economy have led to arguments that levels of welfare spending, while not high by international standards, are still too high for the British economy to fund. A counter-argument in this debate has been that many of the services of the welfare state – such as education and health care – are actually vital to the functioning of an efficient economy. Finally, the culture of the welfare state has been challenged by long-term social change. The citizenship principle at the heart of the welfare state meant that access to services was governed by legal entitlements, and that meant in turn that

## TIMELINE 2.2  (CONTINUED)

| | Title of legislation | Main provisions | Party in government |
|---|---|---|---|
| **1942** | Beveridge Report published | An official report which proposed a comprehensive system of national insurance for protection against unemployment, poverty and illness. | Author was a civil servant and supporter of the Liberal Party. |
| **1944** | Education Act | Provided free secondary education for all children, subsidized school meals, free medical inspection; raised school-leaving age to 15. | Conservative–Labour coalition |
| **1946** | National Insurance Act | Implemented 1942 Beveridge Report: compulsory insurance for all in work to fund pensions, income support in sickness, unemployment benefit and free health care for all. | Labour |
| **1948** | National Health Service founded | Implemented effects of 1946 National Insurance Act for health care. | Labour |
| **1948** | National Assistance Act | Abolished last traces of Poor Law and provide cash payments for poverty relief. | Labour |

⮕ The timeline covers the key era in the building of the welfare state in Britain. Notice two things: that no single party can lay claim to be the builder; and that the measures are a mix of scattered reforms over time and bursts of innovation, the latter often coinciding with the great national crisis of war. The simple device of identifying in the third column the party colour of the government in office at the time of the measure also overstates single-party influence: for instance, both the Beveridge Report and the reforms that it produced were the result of arguments advanced by people of all parties, and by many with no party affiliation at all.

*Source*: Adapted from Cook and Stevenson (1983) and Butler and Butler (2000).

services were rationed administratively, by those who delivered the service in the light of their judgement of need. In health care, for instance, rationing was mostly done in this way by doctors. In the 1940s that did not feel strange, because most of the necessities of life – food, clothes, petrol, coal – were administratively rationed because of shortages. By the end of the twentieth century, in contrast, most goods and services in Britain were bought on the open market. Welfare rationing, which had once seemed perfectly normal, now seemed unusual. If we could use our money to buy the food we wanted why could we not do the same with health care or higher education? As we will see in Chapters 19 and 21, these questions have turned into difficult policy problems for government.

## Britain in the wider world

Three hundred years or so ago Britain was a power of minor significance in the international system. Its population was small, its economy backward and its military capacity slight. Geographical isolation, while protecting it from the turmoil of wars on the European continent, also consigned it to the margins of European power politics. Two hundred years later, in 1900, after a dizzyingly rapid ascent to world domination, Britain was already observably on a steep downward path as a world power.

This astonishing trajectory is the essential historical background to Britain in the wider world. Indeed, the history of rise and fall is more compressed even than this suggests, for the story of Britain as a dominant world power spans barely more than a century.

The fundamental cause of Britain's transformation into a world power was the economic domination produced by the Industrial Revolution, but to appreciate the full significance of that it is necessary to understand the particular form taken by that Revolution. It was not just that the economy and society were transformed domestically; that domestic transformation was connected to a wider transformation in the international economic system. Britain was both a beneficiary of, and a driving force behind, this wider transformation. The Industrial Revolution was intimately bound up with creation of a truly global economy. Britain created world markets for her manufactured products, and created a worldwide financial system for trade and foreign investment. The latter financial system was especially important. Not only was Britain for much of the nineteenth century the world's greatest industrial power; she was for all the century its greatest financial power. The financial capital of the country – the City of London – was also the financial capital of the world. It funnelled investment funds around the world: by the end of the nineteenth century the country was a major investor in large scale projects abroad, such as the development of railways in both North and South America. In this period there also emerged a particular kind of international monetary system, normally summarized as the Gold Standard, in which national currencies had their values assessed against gold. Britain, and especially its central bank, the Bank of England, was the most important manager of this system. The pound sterling was 'as good as gold' because the Bank guaranteed to exchange it for gold.

Britain partly ruled the world financially because of imperialism. In the last quarter of the eighteenth century she looked to be past her peak as an imperial power, in the 1780s losing the American colonies, her most impressive imperial possessions. But almost at exactly the same moment an extraordinary expansion of imperial reach elsewhere was beginning: as she was losing America Britain was acquiring, and then consolidating, a vast stretch of Empire in India. Within a

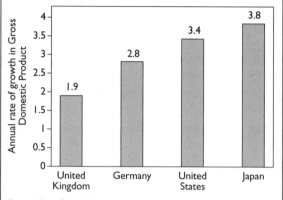

**Figure 2.2**  How Britain fell behind in the world economy, 1870–1989 (average annual rates of economic growth)

*Source:* Data from Alford (1996: 335).

➲  The chart is a summary of the comparative performance of the British economy for over a century. At its start Britain led the world as a result of her pioneering Industrial Revolution; by the end, it seemed that she was in danger of being relegated from the 'premier league' of industrial countries. The differences in annual rates of growth do not look dramatic, but it must be remembered that these are averaged over more than a century; the cumulative difference in economic performance was tremendous. In the final chapter of this text we bring the story up to date, showing how from the 1990s Britain's relative economic record greatly improved.

century of the loss of the American colonies, not only India but large parts of Africa were incorporated into the Empire. Huge areas of the new world, including Australia, were settled and organized into a subordinate relationship with British power. Her power also extended to a kind of informal empire: for instance, parts of the Middle East, while not formally under imperial rule, were effectively controlled by the British.

This impressive imperial reach was bound up with two other aspects of British power: her military capacity and the place she enjoyed in the international political system. The defeat of Napoleon at the battle of Waterloo in 1815 brought to an end a generation of war in Europe, and was succeeded by a century of virtual peace. Between 1815 and the outbreak of what we now call the First World War in 1914 Britain was involved in only one major 'European' campaign, and that – the Crimean War – was itself on the periphery of Europe. This long period of freedom from great wars was also a period of what is sometimes called the 'pax Britannica'. Britain, as a great economic and imperial power, was able to convert that power into a role as a kind of policeman for the world system. British naval power in particular was a key factor in international diplomacy and in the international military system.

British power in what is sometimes called the 'English century' therefore rested on three pillars: on the country's dominant position in a rapidly globalizing international economic system; on the reach of British power through Empire, and through less formal means of foreign rule; and on Britain's capacity to regulate, partly through her naval domination, an international diplomatic system which delivered a century of peace. The breakdown of this system of peace was signalled by the outbreak of the First World War in 1914. Although Britain emerged in 1918 as one of the victors, the War and its aftermath marked the moment when British world domination decisively ended.

The nineteenth century was the century of British world domination; the twentieth century was the century of British world decline (see Figure 2.2). This decline took four main forms.

## Economic decline

As we saw earlier, British economic decline was already well set before the First World War; indeed, one cause of the War was the challenge of a great industrial power that was supplanting Britain, Germany. But the First World War hastened British economic decline. It exhausted much of the country's overseas investments, and resulted in the loss to competitors of many important overseas markets. It destroyed the wider international financial system – based on open frontiers – which Britain had played a dominant part in regulating. It also helped destroy one of the critical features of the international economic system in which Britain had prospered for most of the nineteenth century, free trade between nations.

## Military decline

World wars also helped destroy British military supremacy. The First World War, and even more the Second World War (1938–45), saw the emergence of an international power system where Britain was relegated to a position of, at best, second rank. Her successor was the United States.

## Imperial decline

Before the First World War, British imperial power had already become fragile. A disastrous war in South Africa had exposed the limits of Britain's ability to control her scattered overseas possessions. Already by the turn of the century the great settlements of the eighteenth and nineteenth centuries – such as Canada and Australia – were beginning to move to full independence. After the First World War Britain found herself supplanted as the leading power in many parts of the globe (the Middle East and Latin America) where she had previously been dominant. A significant independence movement developed in India, and the beginnings of independence movements started in other parts of the empire, notably in Africa (see Timeline 2.3).

## English decline

It has often been remarked that 'England' and 'Britain' are frequently used interchangeably, and that this was especially true in the great days of British world domination. Nor is this surprising. England was the dominant partner in what is formally called the United Kingdom: she had most of the population, most of the wealth and, in London, most of the powerful institutions. The rise of Britain to world dominance was preceded by the rise of England to domination of the British Isles. An important symbolic moment was the Act of Union with Scotland in 1707, the takeover by England of an independent political system. During the nineteenth century English influence, and the English language, dominated the British Isles. But out of the First World War came a powerful challenge to English dominance in the form of an Irish War of Independence. That led to the foundation in 1921 of the Irish Free State: to all intents and purposes, the setting-up of a fully independent state in what had been hitherto a United Kingdom that covered the whole of the British Isles.

The decline of British world power in the twentieth century was not gradual. There were two great blows, in the form of the costs and consequences of the First and Second World Wars. By the end of the second of those wars in 1945, her Empire was on the point of vanishing, her military might was overshadowed by the United States and her economy was in deep trouble.

---

## TIMELINE 2.3    BUILDING AND DISMANTLING AN EMPIRE

**1713**
Treaty of Utrecht: Britain gains Gibraltar, Nova Scotia and Newfoundland.

**1750**
Settlement begins on West Africa's 'Gold Coast'.

**1757**
Military victories in Bengal lay foundations for conquest of India.

**1763**
Treaty of Paris: all French possessions in North America east of the Mississippi ceded to Britain.

**1768**
First separate Secretary of State for colonies established.

**1773**
Act establishes that British rule in India will be carried on by the Crown.

**1776**
American colonies declare Independence.

**1783**
Treat of Versailles: recognizes American independence.

**1791**
Canada Act divides Canada into provinces with limited self-government under a Governor General.

**1814**
Britain gains possessions in the West Indies and Malta after defeat of Napoleon.

**1823**
New South Wales (Australia) becomes Crown Colony.

**1833**
First Governor General of India installed.

**1840**
Canada Act unites Canada under single administration; New Zealand annexed.

**1842**
Hong Kong acquired.

**1857**
First Secretary of State for India installed.

**1867**
British North America Act creates Dominion status (home rule) for Canada.

**1876**
Queen Victoria created Empress of India.

**1886**
Control of Nigeria strengthened; Britain and Germany partition East Africa and possessions in the Pacific.

**1888**
Zululand in South Africa annexed.

**1900**
First Pan-African Congress (in opposition to Empire) meets in London.

**1901**
Commonwealth of Australia established.

**1902**
Peace of Vereeniging ends second Boer War with annexation of Transvaal and Orange Free State by Britain.

**1907**
Australia and New Zealand gain Dominion (home rule) status.

**1910**
Union of South Africa formed.

## Britain at a historical crossroads

This moment of imperial exhaustion brings us close to the present day; as Timeline 2.3 shows, Britain is still divesting herself of various fragments of Empire. But it also introduces the very latest historical strand in the British story. If Britain could not be a 'Great Power', if her economy was in decline, and if her Empire was dismantled, what historical role was open to her? Arguments about how to make that choice have been the great historical divide in British politics for the last generation (see Political Issues 2.1). Two broad alternatives have divided political leaders and the country at large: to

---

### TIMELINE 2.3    (CONTINUED)

**1920**
Mahatma Gandhi begins campaign for Indian independence.

**1921**
Irish Free State given formal home rule and effective full independence.

**1930**
Nehru proclaims Indian independence and Gandhi begins mass campaign of civil disobedience to win British recognition of the proclamation.

**1942**
Japanese capture of Singapore delivers major blow to British imperial prestige.

**1947**
India and Pakistan granted independence.

**1948**
Ceylon and Burma become independent.

**1956**
Fiasco of British attempt to launch a military expedition to conquer the Suez Canal in Egypt delivers blow to British imperial power and self-confidence.

**1957**
Ghana and Malay states become independent.

**1960**
Cyprus, Nigeria and British Somaliland become independent.

**1961**
Tanganyika, Sierra Leone and British Cameroons become independent.

**1963**
Zanzibar and Kenya become independent.

**1967**
Aden becomes independent.

**1973**
Bahamas gain independence.

**1982**
Argentine troops invade Falkland Islands in South Atlantic, shortly after a secret proposal by the British to hand the islands over to Argentina; British expeditionary force recaptures the islands.

**1990**
Namibia becomes fiftieth independent member of British Commonwealth.

**1997**
Hong Kong returned to China.

**1998**
Remaining scattered pieces of Empire renamed United Kingdom Overseas Territories.

➲ The summary of a long story here both conceals and reveals key features. The most important revelation is the picture we get here of the twentieth century as the century of British imperial retreat. And this retreat was closely connected to the way the two great World Wars damaged British power: the First World War was succeeded not only by the secession of Ireland, but by the rise of independence movements across the Empire. After the Second World War there was a huge cascade of decolonization. What the table cannot convey is the extent to which the building of this Empire involved military conquest and brutal force; and the extent to which, even as the Empire was decaying in the twentieth century, at home Imperial language and symbols remained central to domestic political life.

---

*Sources*: Adapted from Cook and Stevenson (1983 and 2000) and Butler and Butler (2000).

**POLITICAL ISSUES**

### 2.1   BRITAIN'S HISTORICAL MISSION?

The historian Linda Colley (1996) argued that Britain's rise to world eminence in the eighteenth and nineteenth centuries was accompanied by a sense of special mission: a belief that providence had granted her a unique historical role in spreading Protestant civilisation. The end of Empire, and Britain's decline as a world economic power, had by the 1960s virtually destroyed that belief in special destiny; and in a society where the Christian religion had declined to insignificance few believed in the mission of a Protestant nation. But in the last 20 years a providential mission has been rediscovered in new ways. Two kinds are especially important. First, each of the last three British Prime Ministers (Thatcher, Major, Blair) has believed that Britain has a historic role in teaching other European nations about the merits of free, deregulated markets, and each has seen Britain as the leader of free market reform in the European Union. Second, each has seen Britain as enjoying a special world role as the main partner of the United States when it acts as a 'super-power', notably in great military missions in two Gulf Wars (1991 and 2003) and in Afghanistan (2002).

This renewed sense of destiny has raised issues which now cause deep divisions in British politics. Three are particularly important.

- The stress on Britain as a teacher of free market economics to much of the rest of the European Union has strengthened 'Euroscepticism' in Britain. Broadly, Euroscepticism correlates with the belief that the British economy is a superior model to the more regulated European one.
- Deep divisions have been caused by the renewal of British commitment to foreign wars. The deepest occurred in the Iraq War of 2003, much of which was justified in the language of providence: that the war was part of Britain's wider international responsibilities in international pacification, ridding the world of dictators such as Saddam Hussein.
- Since the most controversial foreign military commitments have been as junior partners of the United States – notably in the Gulf War of 1991, the Afghanistan War of 2002 and the Iraq War of 2003 – a third controversy has arisen over attitudes to America as a world power: should it be opposed, or supported as fundamentally a force for good?

The divisions created by this new sense of providence are far from simple: for example, many of those who are enthusiastic Europeans, such as the Liberal Democrats, were also opponents of involvement in the Iraq War. (For more on British providence, see Chapter 24.)

incorporate Britain ever more closely into the European Union; or to incorporate Britain into a wider global order dominated by the United States. Few British political leaders want to make a stark choice between these options, but there is serious division over which of the alternatives to favour most.

The attractions of European integration grew from the early 1960s. As Chapter 6 will show, the politics and economics of Western Europe were transformed in the 15 years after the Second World War: a continent that had been on the brink of mass starvation became a region with a record of economic growth and prosperity that the British could not match. Much of the credit for the transformation, rightly or wrongly, went to the 'Common

# DEBATING POLITICS

## 2.1   BRITISH DECLINE: INEVITABLE OR SELF-INFLICTED?

| British decline was normal and inevitable because: | British decline reflects fatal flaws in British society because: |
|---|---|
| ■ Other nations were bound to catch up on the economic lead established by the Industrial Revolution.<br>■ British Imperial power was always a transient phenomenon – like all Empires in the past.<br>■ Britain is naturally a 'middle ranking' country rather than a great power because of her size, location and limited natural resources.<br>■ The really striking feature of the last 100 years is the success with which Britain has retained her place in the front rank of rich nations. | ■ Her pioneering early lead in the Industrial Revolution meant that she entered the twentieth century with already outdated industries.<br>■ Her education system and wider society valued inherited position over ability and achievement.<br>■ The power of the City of London inhibited the growth of efficient modern manufacturing industries.<br>■ Attempts to defend the Empire led Britain into a series of ruinous world wars out of which she emerged the weak, junior partner of the United States. |

Market' created by six countries of Western Europe in the Treaty of Rome in 1957. After a history of argument at home, and rejection abroad by France, Britain became a member of this Common Market in 1973. As this text shows at numerous points, membership of what is now the European Union has deeply shaped British government and politics. The progress of economic integration was such that, within 30 years of joining, political leaders were divided over a momentous decision: whether to replace the pound sterling, the traditional historic symbol of British power and sovereignty, with a new Europe-wide currency, the Euro.

Divisions over how far to integrate with Europe in part reflected a lingering inability fully to appreciate the extent of Britain's historic decline from imperial and military might (see Debating Politics 2.1). But they also reflected the existence of an alternative to a European future which was credible in the minds of many political leaders: as a partner of the United States, albeit a junior partner, in an American-dominated world order. The United States succeeded Britain as the dominant world power after the end of the Second World War in 1945. She was joined as a 'super-power' by the

## REVIEW

Five themes dominate this chapter:

1 The key British century was the nineteenth, when Britain dominated the world economically, militarily and politically;
2 The twentieth century was dominated by decline from this domination and by the attempt to cope with the decline;
3 Though world decline marked the twentieth century domestically, it was also a period of great innovation and growth: a system of democratic politics, and a fully-fledged welfare state, developed in Britain;
4 English domination of the British Isles, whose roots can be traced back to the start of the eighteenth century, continued throughout the twentieth but was increasingly challenged by the Celtic nations;
5 The choice between a 'European' or an 'American' historical path is the latest great historical choice to divide the British.

Soviet Union, and for over 40 years the two super-powers conducted a 'Cold War' of mostly non-violent struggle. Britain cultivated a 'special relationship' with the United States during the era of the Cold War, though it is not certain that the United States thought her at all special. The collapse of the Soviet Union and of its 'empire' in Eastern Europe after 1989 left the United States utterly dominant as the only world super-power. All British governments in the 1990s, even those that contained enthusiastic supporters of European integration, were more enthusiastic supporters of the United States than were other members of the European Union. And opponents of economic integration, especially opponents of abolition of the pound in favour of the Euro, looked to this American-dominated world as the alternative to a more European future.

## Further reading

Colley (1996) is a famous interpretation of the emergence of British identity. Although not on Britain alone, a wonderful introduction to the historical background is Hobsbawm (1962/1997), which introduces the idea of the significance of the 'two revolutions' (French and Industrial) referred to in this chapter. More ruminative, and more focused on domestic politics, is Harrison (1996). Gamble (1981/1994) is definitive on 'decline'. Timmins (1995) vividly tells the story of the welfare state.

**CHAPTER 3**

# Economy and society

## CONTENTS

## AIMS

This chapter:

❖ Explains why and how the economic and social contexts matter to politics

❖ Describes the traditional model of class society in Britain

❖ Shows how this model is being reshaped by different social identities

❖ Shows how the ownership of property is organized, and how its distribution affects our general view of the connection between democracy and capitalism in Britain.

## Why the social context matters

In an introduction to British politics why should we spend time considering matters that are not immediately obviously political at all; in other words, why consider the economic and social contexts of British politics? Even to raise the question is to see some immediate and compelling links. Three are particularly convincing.

### Democratic politics and capitalism

Just as the government of a country is inseparable from its history – something we have already seen –

so it is inseparable from its wider social structure. Take one of the most important features of any system of government: whether it is stable, and whether it is, if only in some rough and ready way, democratic. Most of us, if asked to rank the desirable features of government, would probably say that we want to live in a stable democracy. Such systems do exist, and Britain is, exceptions such as Northern Ireland apart, a good example. But these systems are not randomly distributed across the globe; they coincide with certain wider social and economic arrangements. For example, stable democracies are mostly clustered on either side of the North Atlantic and in a few states – such as New Zealand and

**Images 3.1, 3.2 and 3.3**
**Diverse Britain: how diversity shapes even the most mundane aspects of everyday life**

Image 3.1    Street sign

Image 3.2    Library sign

Image 3.3    Temple

Photos: Michael Moran

➲ The three images illustrate how diversity is reflected in the everyday appearance of Britain: Image 3.1 is a street sign in Liverpool's Chinatown, one of the oldest established in the UK, in English and Cantonese; 3.2 is the entrance sign for a public library in the West Midlands, in a town with a long history of immigration (the sign is in the several languages of the incoming communities); 3.3 is the handsome temple, which also functions as an important social centre, built by the Sikh community in the same town.

Australia – in the Southern Hemisphere. Why is this? Part of the explanation has to do with the historical development of institutions and the influence of the wider international system, but a lot has to do with the social and economic structures within which these systems of government are set. They are all, to varying degrees, rich societies and they are all, to varying degrees, capitalist societies – their economies are organized on market principles. This does not mean that a country inevitably has to be to be rich to be a democracy: India has been a noticeable exception for over half a century. Neither does it mean that being capitalist is a guarantee of either stability or democracy: the history of numerous countries in Latin America and, in the last decade or so, of the former Soviet Union, shows otherwise. But a market economy and a rich economy are a good start in building a stable democracy, and Britain has both.

## Political interests and the social setting

British government is organized partly to ensure the representation of interests in Britain. Where do these interests come from? The answer lies in the wider economic and social contexts. And how do they change over time? The answer also lies in the wider society. The last chapter provided an example: the Industrial Revolution profoundly changed the nature of interest representation to the benefit of industrial workers and industrial capitalists, at the expense of agricultural interests. After the Industrial Revolution new interests had to be accommodated in the system of government: they included the new capitalists who controlled industrial firms and the new industrial workers who organized in trade unions.

## Politics shapes society

As the example just examined shows, social change can shape the way government functions. But the reverse is also true: the decisions taken by government can shape social change. Government is the biggest organization in Britain. It is charged with the overall task of managing society: with managing the economy, with managing social institutions such as schools, and with preventing social evils, including crime. In other words it consciously tries to shape and reshape society. A striking example is provided by the 'Thatcher Revolution', which is examined at various points in later chapters. In the last two decades of the twentieth century the social structure was fundamentally altered by government policies. Whole social groups that had been a key part of the social landscape – such as coalminers – virtually disappeared as a result of public policy. At the other end of the social scale, changes in tax policies made the rich markedly richer. Thus government was able consciously to engineer an increase in economic inequality in Britain. A more long-term, and less consciously chosen reshaping concerns the ethnic mixture of Britain. At the end of the Second World War Britain was, Irish immigrants excepted, a white Anglo-Saxon country. Now, it is one with high levels of diversity in colour, creed and ethnic culture (see Images 3.1–3). That diversity is partly the result of public policies which in the early post-war years encouraged immigration into Britain from many of the countries of the former Empire.

Thus there is a two-way relationship between the social context and the political system: they can mutually affect each other.

## Class, gender and ethnicity

Since it was the first society to experience large scale industrialization Britain was also a pioneer of a new kind of social structure, one where class and class relations were exceptionally important. *Class* is one of the most contested and shifting ideas in the social sciences, but the commonest usage in Britain refers to *occupational class*: to the identification of the class of an individual – and even of a complete family – by the occupation of the 'breadwinner' in the family. Our everyday colloquial use of class tries to catch this, but does so inadequately. Thus 'working class' usually identifies manual workers and their families; 'middle class' usually refers to professional and other 'white-collar' workers. But we can see immediately that this language is anomalous because while 'working' refers to kinds of job, 'middle' suggests a location in a range. The language of a range dates from the nineteenth century when there existed above the middle class an aristocracy: holders of huge wealth and power, clearly separated from the other classes in society by wealth, culture and attitude.

The Industrial Revolution made class the key to social division in Britain in a way unusual among advanced industrial societies. In the United States and Western Europe other lines of social division – such as religion, race or regional loyalty – were as significant. We shall see later in this chapter that these other lines of division have either been created or have reappeared in modern Britain. Two – gender and ethnicity – are examined in particular detail.

## Traditional class society

The Industrial Revolution turned Britain into a class society and this dominated British politics for much of the twentieth century. What were the most important elements of this society?

*Occupational class* was central to defining identity. The vast mass of the population had its social location fixed by the occupation of the male breadwinner in a family. This was particularly true of working-class families (that is, those where the breadwinner was a manual worker). Belonging to this kind of family meant a particular, and predictable, social fate. Most of this class owned hardly any property. The modern consumer goods economy – of cars and suchlike – had not developed, and home ownership was rare. The members of this working class left school early; they worked with their hands; they had high risks of unemployment and poverty, especially in old age; and they had high risks of suffering poor health and early death.

*Manual workers* were by far the numerically dominant class: we can see this by looking at the first bar in Figure 3.1, which charts change over much of the twentieth century.

*Wealth inequality* was striking. The most numerous class owned least, earned least and had the worst 'life chances': that is, chances of actually living a

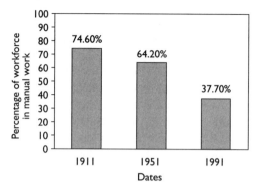

**Figure 3.1**   The declining numerical importance of the working class in Britain

*Source*: Calculated from Gallie (2000: 288).

➲ The figures summarized in this bar chart draw on the most comprehensive studies of the labour force structure over the course of the twentieth century. We do not yet have definitive, comparable figures for the present, but we can be certain that the proportion of manual workers has declined further. In a democracy such as Britain where much turns on competition for the vote, and where election winners are largely determined by the size of popular vote, the implications for the political strategies of parties are immense.

long life, living a healthy life, or living a life with access to either material goods or to cultural goods such as education.

The history of class in the twentieth century is a history partly of the decline of this class society, and partly of its strengthening. Here we highlight only those changes that will, in later chapters, turn out to have a particular importance for political life.

*Occupational class* has declined in importance as a sign of social location. In part this is a function of cultural changes that are hard to measure objectively over a long period of time. Class accents have become less distinct, partly because of the influence of the mass broadcasting media. Mass production and consumption in clothes, and cultural products such as pop music, have helped create more uniformity. A century ago we could have more or less immediately identified working-class people in a street: they would have been smaller, would have dressed distinctively, talked with distinctive accents, perhaps even smelt differently because so few had access to bathrooms. All these outward signs of class location have now become much less important. But the changes are also due to more measurable developments, and the most important we examine next.

*Manual workers* have declined in numerical importance, as Figure 3.1 clearly shows. Traditional class society was one where workers were in a clear majority. This had immense political consequences: it provided the basis for the original organization of a separate Labour Party at the start of the twentieth century. Once all workers had the vote it deeply shaped the strategies of the Conservative Party, which realized that it would never win elections with the votes of white-collar workers and the business class alone. But we can see that, from being a majority, manual workers declined to a minority of the workforce, and therefore of the population. This change was due to two connected forces. The class of manual workers was created by the original Industrial Revolution, and as we know from the last chapter the twentieth century was a century of decline for the old industries of that revolution. Coal, steel, shipbuilding: the emblems of industrialism faded away.

However, to this history of decline we need to add a history of remarkable growth and expansion, something brought out clearly in Figure 3.2. Behind this change lie developments which are observable in all advanced industrial economies: as they develop manufacturing declines as a source of jobs, and the service sector – everything from cleaning to teaching to insurance broking – expands. This has happened in all industrial economies because they are all subject to similar forces. Advances in manufacturing productivity mean that vastly more goods can be produced with fewer people: cars that were assembled by hand in the 1920s are now put together with the help of computer-controlled robots. That cuts the demand for jobs in manufacturing. Conversely, huge rises in prosperity in the twentieth century produced expanded demands for services, and for the provision of new services: the range covers everything from tourism to health care. (The National Health Service, which has existed for barely 50 years, now employs over a

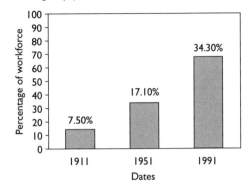

**Figure 3.2**  The rise of the professionals, managers and administrators (percentage of workforce composed of these groups)

*Source*: Calculated from Gallie (2000: 288).

➲ Just as the category 'manual worker' covered a huge range of very different occupations, so this category, created by me from the most authoritative study of long-term change, includes a very diverse range of occupations. It measures the proportion of the workforce who are 'upper' and 'lower' professionals, managers and administrators. It spans, for example, managers in the private sector receiving millionaire salaries and primary school teachers earning less than £20,000 per annum, but when viewed alongside Figure 3.1 it reinforces our picture of the long-term transformation of class society in Britain. We do not yet have authoritative comparable, up-to-date figures, but we can be sure that this group now outstrips manual workers in numbers. 'The workers', as traditionally understood, are now in a minority.

million people.) The expansion of job numbers in the service sector has also had a third set of consequences to which we now turn.

*Class mobility* has increased. Where have all the workers (and their descendants, once employed in traditional manufacturing industries) gone? The immediate effect of the decline of industries such as shipbuilding and coalmining was to pitch workers into unemployment, but this has not always been the long-term effect. In part, jobs displaced in manufacturing have been replaced by service jobs that are themselves badly paid, regimented and allow little discretion to workers. Thus there are now more people answering telephones in highly regimented call centres in Britain than work in the steel industry.

This history of unemployment, and the creation of poorly paid jobs in services such as catering or call centres, is only part of the story, however. Another important part is the huge long-term expansion in professional occupations. The scale of expansion meant that these could only be filled by recruiting from the families of manual workers. The expansion of education was another factor in the change. At the start of the twentieth century compulsory schooling ended at the age of 12 and fees were the norm in secondary education. By the end of the century compulsory schooling ended at 16 and was free. As we can see from Figure 3.3, the century was also a century of upward social mobility, some of it out of the ranks of the families of manual workers.

The changes summarized here have been experienced by all advanced market economies, but they are particularly important in the British case, especially in their political significance. This is because traditional 'class society' of the kind summarized above was especially important in Britain: the Industrial Revolution left Britain with a society where class divisions and identities overrode, to an unusual degree, other identities, including ethnicity. Conversely, when change to industrial structures came in Britain it was particularly dramatic: the economic history of the country was dominated by the decline of the industries of the old Industrial Revolution.

The changes summarized here, although important, were moderated in three key ways, and all these three ways are politically relevant.

*Regionally*, the transformation of 'class society' was highly variable, and one effect of this was also to increase the significance of regional inequalities in Britain. The greatest divide opened up between the economy of the south east, dominated by London, and the rest. In the nineteenth century producing *things* was still important in London; by the end of the twentieth century its economy was dominated by services, especially by the gigantic financial services industries spilling over from the City of London. As we can see from Figure 3.4, this has given the economy and society of the south east a most distinctive aspect by comparison with the rest of the United Kingdom.

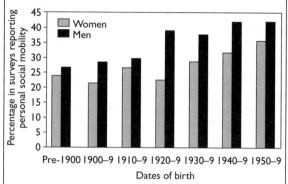

**Figure 3.3**   Patterns of class mobility in twentieth-century Britain

*Source*: Calculated from Heath and Payne (2000: 265, 267).

➔ Plotting changes in social mobility over a long period of time – the only period that is of any importance – demands something rare: data sets that allow us to reach back into the distant past. Heath and Payne achieve this by exploiting data from surveys of the whole population that go back now over 40 years. One obvious limit of these surveys is that they rely on the accuracy of what people tell interviewers. The figures on the horizontal axis refer to the birth dates of those interviewed; those on the vertical axis are the proportion who reported upward mobility by comparing their occupation with those of their fathers. The figures show two striking features: the expansion of professional and managerial jobs over the century created room for upward mobility; but men were distinctly, if modestly, greater beneficiaries.

*Social mobility*, though it took many out of the old working class, was also very unequally distributed. A striking example is provided by one of the most important means of modern access to professional careers: higher education. There was a vast expansion of the proportion of young people in higher education in the last four decades of the twentieth century. In the early 1960s about 5 per cent of 18 year olds were in universities; 40 years later it is 40 per cent and rising. One of the most rapid expansions took place in the 1990s; but as we can see, by glancing ahead to Figure 21.8 (p. 466), most of this expansion advantaged students from middle-class homes. The expansion now virtually guarantees higher education to the middle class, while providing access for only a small minority of the children of the poorest.

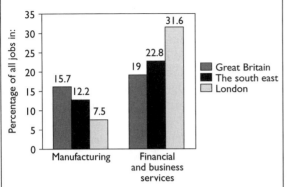

**Figure 3.4**  Regions apart: the class uniqueness of London and the south east

*Source*: Calculated from *Regional Trends* (2001: 68–9).

➲ These figures date from 1999, and illustrate an important feature of the link between economic change and class society in Britain: they have made London, and to a lesser extent, the south east, very different from the rest of the country. The single most important reason for this – vividly reflected in the figures for London – is the overwhelming presence of the City of London, one of the world's leading financial centres, and an overwhelming influence on both jobs and wealth. In later chapters we will see this uniqueness, and the wealth of London, reflected also in numerous parts of political life.

**Figure 3.5**  Unequal Britain: how she compares with other leading economies

*Source*: Adapted from Atkinson (2000: 367).

➲ This reproduces an attempt to compare income inequality in Britain and other leading economies by the leading British student of wealth and income distribution. The technical measure used is the 'Gini coefficient' and the simplest intuitive interpretation is that the higher the coefficient – and thus here the longer the bar – the more unequal is income distribution. Britain belongs to a class of high inequality countries. The causes of these variations are complex. It is sometimes argued that economies such as Britain and the United States 'trade off' income equality for job creation. But notice that Germany, which has a poor record on job creation, is only slightly less unequal. Conversely, the Netherlands has an outstanding record on job creation and is low on inequality.

*Class inequality* is, by some important measures, on the increase. The decline of manufacturing industries disproportionately destroyed secure and (by manual working standards) well-paid jobs in the old industries of the Industrial Revolution. Those who did not benefit from the social mobility opened up by education found that the opportunities for unskilled work were highly restricted. By contrast, a mixture of reductions in tax rates for the highest paid, and rapid increases in rewards for the managers, greatly increased income inequality in Britain as the twentieth century closed. This is illustrated and explained in Figure 3.5.

## Gender

We could once speak of Britain as a 'class society' because occupational class differences were the overwhelmingly important divide, but one reason class seemed so dominant was that it actually hid other lines of division and inequality. The case of gender strikingly illustrates this. Class society was based heavily on a 'male breadwinner' model: hence the common practice of measuring the class of everyone in a household by the occupational class of the male head of the household. But this unthinking practice reflected deeper assumptions: for instance, that the preferences and interests of women could simply be 'read off' from those of male members of 'their' class or household. Thus we saw in the last chapter that a major theme of political conflict in the early decades of the twentieth century was the struggle for votes for women. A common argument against this extension of the franchise was that women did not need the vote since they could be represented by men: by their husbands, fathers, sons or brothers. A similar attitude decreed that at marriage control of a woman's property fell to her husband: this practice only finally ended with the Married Women's Property Act of 1925.

The rising consciousness of gender as a divide in British society is thus in part a rediscovery of an older social divide that the dominance of class concealed; but, in addition, important changes have come over the condition of women in Britain in recent decades and have also made important contributions to the rising importance of gender division. Some of these changes are cultural and are hard to measure objectively. For instance, the development from the 1960s of effective means of female contraception have allowed women to control a vital and delicate aspect of their lives, and have contributed to a sense of empowerment in numerous areas, ranging from the most intimate of all personal relations to choices in the labour market.

However, some of the sources of change are straightforward and not at all elusive. The lives of women were transformed by changes in the linked domains of the labour market and the education system. In work, there was a long-term rise of women in employment over the course of the twentieth century, from under 30 per cent to well over half the workforce over the century's course. By international standards the participation of British women in work is unusually high: for example, over two-thirds of adult women in Britain are in the workforce, while the comparable figure for Italy is under a half (*Social Trends 2001*: 73). Participation by women in the workforce in Britain is consistently above the average for the whole European Union.

The changes in participation in higher education – the commonest road to high status and high pay occupations – have been even more dramatic, because they have occurred in a shorter space of time. In the 30 years after 1970 the number of male undergraduates in Britain doubled; but the increase was fivefold for women, who now account for a majority (55 per cent) of undergraduates.

These sketches of changes in the conditions of women can be, and have been, read in a variety of ways. Two contrasting ones are summarized here.

*Convergence.*   One obvious way to read change is to argue that gender, far from rising in objective importance, is declining. Women were once marked out both legally and in terms of how they were in practice treated socially. Until a generation ago, it was both legal and common to pay women less and to offer them worse employment conditions. Many big employers obliged women to resign on marriage and motherhood. Colleges of prestigious universities openly barred women, and many others practised informal discrimination. Now the law enforces formal equality, and discrimination by employers is illegal. Women's participation in key social arenas, such as the workforce and higher education, approaches or even exceeds that of men. While there remains gender inequality, we can expect this to reduce with the passage of time, just as the grosser inequalities from the past have now disappeared.

*Persistent inequality.*   An alternative interpretation points to the apparently stubborn persistence of gender inequality inside and outside the workplace. One sign of this is the continuing income gap between men and women. A second, related to this, is the pattern of women's participation in the workforce. Women have found it difficult to gain access to the best-paid and high status jobs; their increasing participation is disproportionately concentrated on lower status occupations, such as retail selling and clerking. The pattern is illustrated in Figure 3.6. Most discouraging of all for those who believe in the convergence theory is evidence about the wider division of gender roles in social life. Although it is hard to study these with the precision of, say, figures concerning enrolment in education, they nevertheless are vital: they tell us about the practical relations between men and women in such everyday activities as sharing the work of running a home and raising a family. Evidence from 'time budgets' about who does what

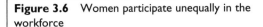

**Figure 3.6**  Women participate unequally in the workforce

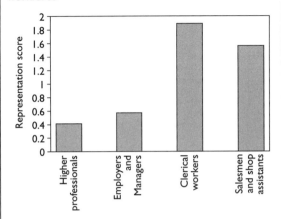

*Source*: Calculated from Gallie (2000: 295).

➲  These figures are taken from Gallie's survey of changes in the workforce over the course of the twentieth century. They date from 1991 but are useful in showing the orders of distribution. Women in Britain do participate to a high degree in paid employment but they are concentrated in lower status and lower paid jobs, and are underrepresented in the most lucrative jobs. The easiest intuitive way to appreciate the figure is to see any figure above 1 as marking higher representation given the numbers of women, and below 1 as indicating a lower than expected representation. While they may of course only reflect the delayed effect of other changes, such as participation in higher education, they do also reflect powerful forces in the labour market. Women in Britain gravitate towards, or are pushed towards, particular kinds of jobs. A glance in the offices of any college or university will illustrate the social reality behind the figures in the third column: secretarial offices will mostly contain women, and professorial offices will mostly contain men.

suggests that in families and partnerships women still disproportionately carry the burden of what is traditionally considered domestic work: for instance, cleaning and childcare. This evidence is particularly discouraging for advocates of gender equality; it suggests that there are large areas of social life that are hard to change by alterations in law. Furthermore, it suggests that gender inequality may actually have increased over time: women have added the burdens of paid employment to more traditional domestic burdens.

## Ethnic Britain

*Ethnicity* refers to a broad range of social identities, encompassing national, religious and racial consciousness. The growing importance of gender as a line of social division was due, we saw, to two factors: to the way the weakening of the old class model allowed suppressed ideas and interests to resurface; and to real changes in the place of women in society. The same two factors are at work in the case of ethnic identity.

A century ago Britain seemed a very homogeneous society: even the Irish were just incomers from another part of the United Kingdom. This picture of homogeneity, though, was itself partly a mixture of invention and repression. The Irish were widely despised as alien, Catholic and feckless. In all three Celtic nations of the United Kingdom there was a long history of attempts to suppress diversity: the language in Wales; the language and Catholicism in Ireland; and the traditional clan society in the Scottish Highlands. There was also already a long history of migration into Britain, for instance, from groups fleeing persecution abroad, such as the Huguenots fleeing France in the seventeenth century or the Jews fleeing Russia at the end of the nineteenth.

Nevertheless, important truths lay behind the image of homogeneity. The high point of the class society described above – which lasted for about 50 years from the end of the First World War, 1918 – was also the high point of homogeneity: class issues, and class identities, overrode religious, national or racial identities. Three important changes have come over British society in the last generation, and have greatly increased the importance of ethnicity in the wider society and in politics.

● *Revival of old identities*. There has been a revival of once suppressed national and religious identities, principally in the Celtic nations of the British Isles. As we shall discover in Chapter 11, these have now produced important changes in the way the United Kingdom is governed, and in the case of Northern Ireland they produced the single most serious domestic problem faced by Westminster governments over the last 40 years.

● *Immigration from the old Empire.* Until the middle of the twentieth century Britain was an overwhelmingly white society. For about the next 30 years immigration into Britain was largely dominated by immigration from the countries of the old Empire, especially from parts of the Indian sub-continent and from the Caribbean. The total scale of this immigration was modest: even by 2000 only 8 per cent of the population of England, and 2 per cent of Scotland and of Wales, originated from these ethnic groups (*Regional Trends 2001*: 42). But since immigrants naturally concentrate in certain areas – principally where there is work – they are not evenly distributed: the comparable figure for London, for instance, is 28 per cent.

● *Immigration from a globalizing world.* Since the nineteenth century there have been great waves of immigration across the globe by peoples fleeing hunger, war and persecution. Immigration into Britain in recent decades has increasingly come from this source (see Figures 3.7 and 3.8). Thus the national, linguistic and religious diversity of immigrants has widened greatly.

The sources of this new migration have also become more complex. From the Irish in the nineteenth century to Bangladeshis a century later the motivation for immigration was essentially the same: poverty. But immigration now involves a mix of flight from war, persecution, collapsing economies and the simple, traditional desire to find work. The wave of immigration from the old Empire was something that was mostly special to the old imperial powers; but this new world of immigration in a globalizing world is a phenomenon which Britain shares with most other rich, stable countries as populations flee war, persecution and economic collapse.

The impact of a half a century of immigration on a society which traditionally pictured itself as homogeneous, and which was indeed homogeneous racially, has been profound. Even the Irish – who in skin colour and language were barely distinguishable from the inhabitants of mainland Britain – aroused extraordinary feelings: as recently as 50

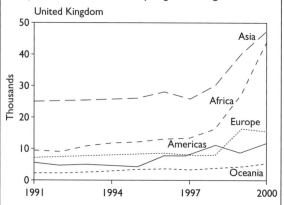

**Figure 3.7**   The changing pattern of immigration: acceptances for settlement by region of origin

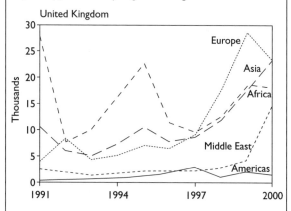

**Figure 3.8**   The changing pattern of immigration: asylum applications by region of origin

*Source: Social Trends 2002 (36)*

➲ Figures 3.7 and 3.8 sum up the new world of immigration which has succeeded the world dominated by immigration from the old Empire. Three features should be noticed. First, the figures emphasize the diversity of modern immigration flows, and the continuing contribution immigration is now making to the diversity of the United Kingdom. Second, the 'European' figures for asylum applications show how far movements of population are affected by war and its aftermath: these figures are heavily influenced by the chaos in the Balkans following a series of particularly brutal wars after the break-up of Yugoslavia. Third, notice what is missing from these figures: immigration into Britain from the other member states of the European Union. The rules guaranteeing free movement of citizens across the Union now make these movements officially not 'immigration' at all. The number of Greeks who have migrated to London is for these purposes as irrelevant as the numbers of Mancunians who have migrated to London.

years ago it was common in British cities for hotels and boarding houses to display notices barring Irish clients. The arrival of Jewish immigrants fleeing persecution in Eastern Europe at the end of the nineteenth century aroused powerful anti-Semitic emotions. And the arrival of black and brown immigrants from the old Empire was bound to arouse some racial hostility in a society where the old ideas of Empire were associated with native British, white supremacy over colonized peoples. But the impact of immigration cannot be reduced to any simple generalizations; it has been extraordinary and subtle in its transforming consequences. From the point of view of the system of government we highlight three consequences.

*Public policy.* The growth of ethnic diversity (see Figure 3.9), especially as a result of large scale immigration, has compelled what was hitherto unknown in Britain: a series of laws and policy innovations designed to combat ethnic discrimination. Open discrimination on grounds of race or religion, commonplace in work and elsewhere a generation ago, is now illegal.

*The new politics of immigration.* After a brief period in the 1950s when all the main British parties welcomed immigrants from the old Empire, all have since moved to compete to limit, and in some cases to try to halt, immigration. From the 1990s this political competition was immensely complicated by a number of features. The transformation of what had been immigration from the Empire into immigration produced by global strife and poverty made the task of managing immigration more difficult. At the same time Britain, with an ageing population and low birth rates, was desperately in need of immigrant labour. And while a half-century of immigration had transformed Britain into a highly cosmopolitan society – London being probably the most ethnically diverse city in the European Union – the diversity of the new immigration still presented immense challenges for a society with a history of homogeneity. Finally, managing the new wave of immigration has illustrated a major theme of this whole book: the interpenetration of British and European Union politics, for the new immigration control is impossible without common agreement with other partner states.

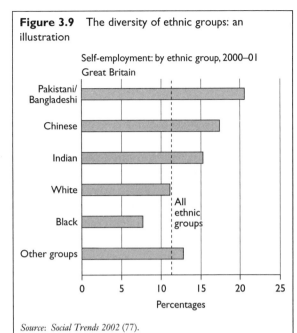

**Figure 3.9**   The diversity of ethnic groups: an illustration

Self-employment: by ethnic group, 2000–01
Great Britain

*Source: Social Trends 2002 (77).*

➲ 'Ethnic Britain' is diverse Britain. This figure provides one narrow, but telling, illustration: the proportion of different ethnic groups who are self-employed. Encouraging self-employment has been one of the main aims of all governments in Britain for a quarter of a century. Notice that the figure also assimilates 'whites' to the diversity of ethnic Britain. It shows striking variations in the proportions of different groups who are self-employed.

*Diversity.* It is natural for a society with a history of homogeneity, and an image of itself as homogeneous, to view immigrants as a single 'other' group, whether the observers are sympathetic to, or hostile to, immigration. But the most important consequence of immigration is also the most obvious: it is making British society more ethnically diverse. Immigrants conform to no template: they are diverse in their languages, religions, cultures, aptitudes and ambitions.

## Ownership, control and capitalism

Britain's is a capitalist economy, which is to say that it has two defining features: goods and services are allocated by being traded for prices that, broadly,

**POLITICAL ISSUES**

### 3.1  'FAT CATS'

'Fat cats' is journalistic coinage for a phenomenon that has existed in the British economy now for nearly two decades. It refers to groups of senior company executives and directors who draw huge, and widely publicised, rewards, in the form both of high salaries and lucrative fringe benefits, such as options to buy shares in the companies that employ them at preferential prices, allowing capital gains often running into tens of millions of pounds. The original arguments about fat cats appeared in the late 1980s and 1990s in newly privatized companies, which on privatization often awarded large pay increases to bring executives up to comparable private sector levels. (For privatization, see Timeline 21.1, p. 455) At a shareholders' Annual General Meeting of the privatized British Gas, a fat pig (not a cat) was let loose to symbolize protests about the pay package of the Chief Executive. But in recent years the fat cats issue has fixed increasingly on rewards at the top of the private sector. Typical cases have included: executives making huge capital gains when companies are 'floated' (offered for sale) on the Stock Exchange; performance bonuses which greatly increase executive pay against very undemanding performance targets; and 'rewards for failure', where executives are dismissed when companies perform poorly, but depart with large compensation packages.

The 'fat cats' problem was usually focused on particular individuals, but it raised issues central to economic management in a market economy such as Britain's. These included:

- How much economic inequality is desirable in a market economy, where it is common to argue that the most enterprizing should be highly rewarded?
- How far should the state intervene, either by persuasion or the law, to regulate top salaries?
- How far, if unequal rewards are the price of economic efficiency and enterprize, should failure be compensated by lucrative dismissal packages?
- How far should the existence of an international market in top executives mean that rates in Britain have to be bid up to attract the best in the world: in short, to what extent are top executives subject to the same kinds of market forces as star footballers?

are determined by market demand; and property is largely in private hands. The nature of property ownership is therefore crucial to understanding the economy. It also highlights a powerful tension in the relationship between the economy and the system of government. Democratic politics presumes equality of citizenship entitlements: the symbol of that is the long struggle, summarized in the last chapter, to ensure 'one person one vote' and to disconnect voting entitlements from property ownership. But the economy makes no such presumption: on the contrary, it functions by the unequal distribution of economic resources. Thus, while it is common to find across the world that

most working democracies are also working capitalist economies, there are powerful tensions between the principles of democratic citizenship and the principles of market capitalist organization. This tension is the single most important reason why we have to preface a study of the governing institutions of Britain with a sketch of the nature of ownership in the British economy.

The most important form of ownership in an advanced capitalist economy such as exists in Britain is corporate ownership: of the firms that are at the heart of any market economy. Three features of corporate ownership stand out.

## Size

Giant firms dominate the British economy. Everyday life in Britain provides numerous examples of this, as illustrated by a daily experience that most readers of this book will have: food shopping. Nearly three-quarters of all groceries bought in Britain are purchased in one of four supermarket giants (Tesco, Sainsbury, Asda and Morrisons). Britain is not alone in this respect. The giant firm is a characteristically dominant form in the economies of most advanced capitalist societies. It is not difficult to realize some of the important political implications of this. As we shall see in Chapter 9, examining interest representation, giant firms have giant resources and these resources can make them important political lobbyists. Giant firms also make decisions that are vital to the interests of government because they affect so many: to take only an obvious instance, a decision by a giant firm to make an investment, or to close a investment, can create or destroy thousands of jobs.

## Multinational reach

These giant firms have another important characteristic: they are more often than not multinational in nature. A multinational firm is one that organizes its functions (notably research, production and marketing) across many different countries. The biggest firms – such as automobile firms or oil companies – in effect treat the whole globe as their sphere of operations. In the most complete versions of multinationalism the internal division of labour inside the firm is such that production operations are organized with little reference to national boundaries: a multinational automobile firm will often produce (or buy) engine and body parts in different countries and then assemble the final automobile in yet another different country entirely. Multinational firms are common across the globe, but they have a special significance in Britain, and this significance is tied to membership of the European Union: since Britain entered originally in 1973 she has been the most important location for investment by non-European multinationals in the European Union. In addition, the City of London is by far the most important location in the Union for the activities of multinational financial services firms trading in world financial markets.

## Institutional ownership

The big firm in Britain shares a feature common across the advanced capitalist world, a feature sometimes called 'the managerial revolution'. Even as recently as a century ago big firms within Britain were 'owner controlled' – which meant, as the phrase implies, that more often than not they were run by their owners. In the intervening century business management has emerged as a distinctive series of professions and big firms are run by professional managers: accountants, production engineers, personnel managers, and so on. It is common for leading managers to become fabulously wealthy by being given options to buy company stock at preferred prices, but most big firms are now institutionally controlled (see Political Issues 3.1). That is, share ownership is vested in institutions such as life insurance companies and pension funds which are funded by the individually small contributions of individual members. Institutions such as these now own close to 60 per cent of the share market in the UK; 40 years ago the figure was under 30 per cent.

These features have important political implications, which we now describe.

## Ownership, control and inequality

The rise of institutional share ownership has important implications for how to understand the wider social and economic context of British politics. One important set of implications concerns the location of power in the modern economy. When the original theories of the separation of ownership from control (which date from the 1930s) were applied, it was common to argue that managerialism was transforming capitalism by making it more bureaucratic, less driven by the search for profit, and – because firms were so large – more able to limit competitive

**Figure 3.10** A glass half full or half empty? Recent trends in the distribution of wealth in Britain

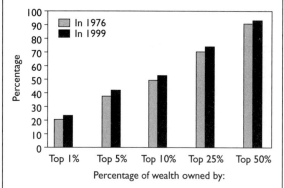

*Source*: Calculated from *Social Trends 2001* (102).

⮕ This standard measure of the distribution of the 'stock' of wealth, derived from Inland Revenue estimates, can be read in a variety of ways. The figures cover a period when defenders of government policies argued that a determined attempt was being made to distribute wealth more equally in order to create a people's capitalism. Critics of policy, by contrast, argued that Britain had entered a new age of inequality when the rich were growing fabulously wealthier. But the most striking feature of the figures is the lack of change they show over the period. And the glass can be seen as 'half full' or 'half empty' because it can be understood in one of two very different ways: wealth is widely spread over half the population; or, alternatively, the poorest 50 per cent owns only 6 per cent of the nation's stock of wealth.

conditions in markets. Capitalism, at least in its more intensely competitive form, was being superseded.

In the last quarter of a century we have heard a great deal less about the taming of the capitalist spirit, and much more about the *Anglo-Saxon model of capitalism*, of which Britain is usually (alongside the United States) held up as a prime example. This model links the managerial revolution to the nature of corporate ownership. In advanced capitalist economies the 'joint stock' company is the usual ownership form: literally, individuals or institutions own stock/shares jointly in an enterprise, which is run in its daily operations by managers. In the theory of Anglo-Saxon capitalism this produces anything but a restrained, bureaucratic capitalism. The shares in firms are very actively traded on the stock market, and there is intense pressure to maxi-

mize the return on the investment of shareholders: to maximize 'shareholder value'. Dissatisfaction with management performance often leads owners to sell shares; the most radical form of this is the takeover, often hostile (against the wishes of managers). The buying and selling of companies in this way is common in the British system. In the original 'managerial revolution' version of the separation of ownership and control, managers were pictured as escaping the controls of the market and owners; but in this latter view of Britain as a species of Anglo-Saxon capitalism the picture is very different. Managers are under constant pressure from owners to maximize short-term returns and the interests of other participants in companies – such as those employed over the long term – are subordinated to the search for maximum shareholder value.

The issues raised here concern power and motivation, but another set of issues goes to the heart of a great tension in a capitalist democracy like Britain: a tension between the equality assumptions that underpin democratic citizenship, and the inequalities that are a necessary part of a capitalist economy. In part we have already encountered these in discussing earlier income inequality in Britain. However, income refers only to what can be called the 'flow' of economic resources; there is also the issue of the distribution of the 'stock' of resources, the fixed wealth of a community at any particular moment; and the fixed wealth in a rich country such as Britain is immense. The connection with issues of institutional share ownership is highlighted by the figures summarized in Figure 3.10, the commonest effort in recent decades to measure the distribution of wealth in Britain. We can read the figures in a variety of different ways, as the annotation makes clear. The figures are, however, derived from Inland Revenue statistics and these statistics exclude wealth embodied in pension schemes (a perfectly reasonable exclusion since most pensions are obviously not 'marketable' in the way a house or shares can be sold). However, wealth embodied in pensions is important: over 60 per cent of men in work, and over 50 per cent of women, are in pension schemes of some kind. In calculating my own personal wealth, for instance, is it sensible to include the

# DEBATING POLITICS

## 3.1   POLITICS: REFLECTOR OR SHAPER OF SOCIAL FORCES?

| Politics is shaped by social forces: | Politics can reshape social forces: |
|---|---|
| ■ In capitalist Britain government must work within the constraints set by a market economy: defending private property and fostering profit. | ■ The growth of inequality in recent decades shows the power of politics: it is the result of conscious decisions by government. |
| ■ Political influence rests on command of economic resources. Power follows money. | ■ Since the development of formal democracy welfare policy has consistently tried to protect the poorest. |
| ■ Despite formal democracy Britain has become a more class-unequal society in the last 30 years. | ■ Wealth is only one kind of political resource: others include sheer numbers and organizing skill. |
| ■ The poorest rarely participate in politics; the rich very often do. Wealth inequalities translate into differences in the ability of the rich and poor to enter the political arena. | ■ In a free society people do not have to participate directly in politics to exert influence: others, such as politicians seeking votes, will be advocates on their behalf. |

value of my house but not my share of the University Teachers' Pension Fund (value of investments at latest estimate in excess of £19 billion)?

## Politics, economics and society in Britain

Even this simple sketch of the social and economic context of British politics shows the importance of that context to the country's political life. We can see immediately that the effects we identified at the start of the chapter are all at work. Changes in the economy and society are reshaping the kind of interests that enter the political arena; and inequalities in the distribution of resources affect the ability of different groups to enter that arena. The interaction between domestic society – what happens in Britain – and wider international social trends is also a powerful shaping influence, as we can see in cases as different as flows of migration and the multinational organization of large corporations.

This all-encompassing and all-permeating influence of the social and economic context explains why the link between the political and the social (see Debating Politics 3.1) is one of the most contentious areas not only in the study of British politics, but in social science as a whole. For some, politics is largely a mirror of the wider society: a passive reflector of these social forces, in particular a reflector of social inequalities. For others, politics – and especially government – has a degree of autonomy from society: political institutions can themselves independently shape social outcomes, and can thus either produce new inequalities, or modify old ones.

## REVIEW

The four themes that dominate this chapter are:

1  The reshaping of the class relationships inherited from Britain's role as a pioneer of industrialism;
2  The rise, or rediscovery, of new lines of social division, such as gender and ethnicity;
3  The persistence of inequalities in the distribution of the stock of wealth;
4  The importance of the interaction between the domestic British society and the wider international social setting.

## Further reading

The single most illuminating collection of studies of British society is edited by Halsey and Webb (2000); it is comprehensive in range, and has an especial value because it traces changes across the twentieth century. Two annual official publications from the UK Office of National Statistics – the government's publishing arm – are invaluable, their value increasing yearly since they commonly contain time series going back over more than 30 years: they are *Social Trends* and *Regional Trends*. A most useful account of models of capitalism that 'sets' Britain internationally is Coates (2000a).

CHAPTER 4

# Britain and the world

## CONTENTS

## AIMS

The chapter starts from a self-evident assumption: Britain may be literally a set of islands, but it can only be understood within the setting of the wider world. The chapter has four aims:

❖ To describe two overlapping sets of foreign relations that are critical to British government: Britain in the global economy, and Britain in the international political system created by a world of separate sovereign states

❖ To describe how Britain traditionally managed these relations

❖ To show how this traditional model is changing

❖ To describe the main influences causing change.

## Britain and the global economy

Look at a simple map of the world, or even the traditional schoolroom globe. It makes clear the underlying point of this chapter: that Britain is a collection of islands, but one set in a wider world. This is most obviously true when considering the British economy. All economies develop what economists call a 'division of labour': a system where people specialize in different trades and services. That division of labour can be seen in something as comparatively simple as the local economy of a town or district. Just consult the Yellow Pages of your local telephone directory to see how refined and elaborate a division of labour can exist even in quite small communities; it will show the development of specialized trades of which you were not even aware.

What is true of the modest and limited economy of a local community is even truer of the global economy. Since the sixteenth century there has been developing a global economy where different parts of the world occupy different positions in the division of labour. Countries or regions specialize in different economic sectors, depending on climate, natural resources or the skills of the population. Understanding Britain's place in this global economy depends on understanding the different places she has occupied in this evolving system. We already know something of this from Chapter 2. We saw there that Britain pioneered the world's first industrial revolution. In terms of the global division of labour, in the nineteenth century she specialized with great success in two fields: in the production of manufactured goods for export; and, through the world importance of the City of London, in channelling financial resources into economic development right across the globe. In the twentieth century, as we also saw in Chapter 2, she lost her specialized roles, notably in manufacturing exports. But despite all these changes she still stands out in four key respects in the global economy: she is rich; market capitalist; a world financial centre; and a major trader.

### Britain is rich

For over a century public debate about the economy in Britain has been dominated by an assumption that in this country we have serious economic problems. But looked at against a wider global setting a rather different picture emerges: Britons live in incredibly fortunate economic circumstances. They belong to a small group of outstandingly rich economies. The most obvious contrast is with a group of economies, mostly clustered in Africa below the Sahara, which are extremely poor. The total wealth of each of these nations is, measured in standard ways, often less than the turnover of a single business corporation in a rich nation. Most of the populations of these countries live in the direst poverty. They do not get to eat enough of even the simplest food to ensure health; they do not have basic public facilities, such as reliable sources of clean water, to protect them against infectious disease; they are always at risk of sudden death in famine; and even when they do not die of famine they die young by British standards, worn out by lack of decent food and exposure to a myriad of diseases. Most of the people of these countries live lives of hardship virtually inconceivable, let alone experienced by, any imaginable reader of this book. Viewing Britain in the world requires us to maintain a variety of perspectives: in part viewing where Britain stands within the club of the rich, but in part viewing her as one of a small club of the rich distinguished from the mass of humanity across the globe (see Figure 4.1).

In Chapter 1 we isolated Britain and compared her with the poorest nations on earth (see Table 1.1). But this isolation conceals an important truth: Britain is not only rich; she is part of a select group of very rich nations, mostly clustered around Western Europe and North America. It is a group that commands a disproportionate share of the globe's resources. This is a premier league of wealth, and Britain has been in the premier league for at least a couple of centuries. What is more, this premier league is getting richer all the time. (This is indisputable. There is a complex debate about whether the poor at the same time are getting more impoverished, or are sharing modestly in wealth growth.) Beyond the two national groups identified here – the long-term very rich and the very poor – there are nations which have changed their status over a century or so. For example, Japan 'joined' the

**Figure 4.1**   Britain and the premier world league of the wealthy (per capita income, $)

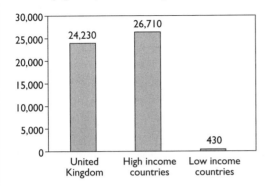

*Source*: Calculated from World Bank Data File 2003: www.worldbank.org

➲ These figures, derived from World Bank sources, measure a standard indicator of wealth for the year 2001 (there are rarely dramatic changes from year to year). 'Per capita' income is a form of average: we simply divide total wealth by total population. The World Bank divides countries into wealth categories: Britain belongs to the very richest, the high income group. Suppose the wealth of someone were indicated by their height: as the figure suggests the British, alongside other fortunate high-income nations such as the Americans and the Swiss, would be giants; those unfortunate enough to live in the poorest countries would be tiny.

premier league of wealth over the course of the twentieth century. By contrast, Argentina was one of the richest countries on earth at the start of the twentieth century; it now has difficulty in feeding, let alone employing, large parts of its population. Within the group of the very wealthy there have also been changes in the league of wealth rankings over time.

Most of the debates about the failings of the British economy are about the fact that, while becoming ever more fabulously wealthy, Britain in the course of the twentieth century slipped down the rankings of the super-wealthy. That is a serious matter, because this process of decline has inflicted great suffering, mostly through unemployment caused by the decline and disappearance of particular industries. But the single most important fact about Britain in the world economy remains: she is a securely rich society.

## Britain is market capitalist

We have already encountered a definition of what it means to be market capitalist: it involves an economy where most wealth takes the form of privately owned property and where resources are allocated chiefly by the workings of supply and demand in markets. Britain has been a market capitalist economy since at least the beginning of the Industrial Revolution in the middle of the eighteenth century. If we look across the globe now we find that most nations aspire to market capitalism, but in the fairly recent past taking market capitalism seriously made Britain fairly unusual. Even a quarter of a century ago a large part of the globe – stretching more or less continuously from the borders of West Germany to China – was governed by Marxist dictatorships which claimed to run their economies according to socialist, anti-capitalist principles: that is, property was mostly owned by the state and resources were allocated by government rather than by market demand. If we had gone further back in the twentieth century, to the 1930s, we would have found large parts of the globe governed by another rival to market capitalism: some of the most important countries of Western Europe, including Germany, as well as Japan and some parts of Latin America, were governed by Fascist regimes: Fascism allowed private property but tried to suppress the market as a mechanism for allocating resources.

The domination of the market capitalist model now gives Britain a special significance in the world economy. It makes her one of the pioneers of the system of economic organization that seems to be the pattern for the foreseeable future across the globe.

## Britain is a world financial centre

We saw in Chapter 2 that Britain was the dominant financial power in the world during the nineteenth century. She no longer occupies that dominant position, but she remains one of the world's leading centres where financial trading takes place. The most important reason for this is the City of London, which is one of the three dominant financial capitals on earth. (The other two are New York and Tokyo.) Chapter 3 described some of the domestic consequences of this importance: most notably the way the economy of London singled it out from the rest of the British economy. The country's financial importance amounts to a further development in the specialized global division of labour: the British lead in manufacturing has disappeared, but she specializes heavily in the provision of financial services for large parts of the globe. This specialization has produced, in London and the south east, an economy of high prosperity and employment; it is therefore a key feature of the domestic British economy and society. But it also gives the country a special international importance. Financial services encompass activities such as trading in currencies, debt raising for governments and firms, and dealings in the shares of firms. These are activities that in recent decades have been organized on a unified, global scale. London's dominance means that she is part of a global system of round the clock, round the year trading. If manufacturing can be thought of as the muscle of an economy, financial services are its nerves; and Britain, through London, is thus part of the nerve centre of the global economy (see Figure 4.2).

## Britain is a trading economy

All national economies live partly by trading with the world around them. But some trade more than others, because some are more self-sufficient than others. The United States for example, which is of course a continent-wide economy, is able to produce most of its goods and services within its own borders. But Britain has comparatively few natural resources, and its climate means that the range of food that it can grow is limited. Self-sufficiency is impossible, at least at present high standards of living: a glance at the product origins of the goods in any supermarket greengrocery or wine section will show the daily reality of this fact. The global division of labour is therefore especially important to Britain, because it is only by importing a huge variety of goods that she can maintain the standard of life of a rich country (see Figure 4.3). And, conversely, it is only by exporting either goods, or services such as those carried out in the City of

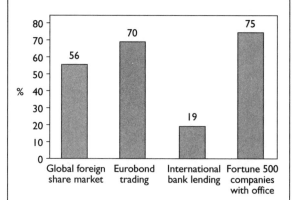

**Figure 4.2**   London as a global financial capital

*Source*: Calculated from Corporation of London at www.cityoflondon.gov.uk

⮕  The most 'global' part of the British economy is the City of London, the leading financial centre in the European Union. The figure provides some illustrative examples of London's global financial prominence. They measure, respectively: the proportion of the global trading in 'equities' (company shares) done from London; London's share of Eurobond trading, trading in the most important kinds of bonds issued on international capital markets; the percentage of international bank lending issued from London; and the percentage of the biggest corporations (measured by *Fortune* magazine) with offices in London. The City is also a bed-rock for London's economy, the single most important reason why the London economy leads the rest of the United Kingdom. The figures reflect the state of affairs at the start of the millennium.

London, that can she pay for the products that make a high standard of living possible. If we think back for a moment to Chapter 2 we can see that this state of affairs is a continuation of a feature that was central to Britain from the very start of her Industrial Revolution: her economy is bound in with the fate of the world economy to an unusual degree. This in turn affects many important domestic policy problems. Whether the British economy prospers or not depends critically on relations with the rest of the world, and the condition of the rest of the world. It depends, for instance, on the following:

● On whether other countries allow British goods and services freely to circulate in their home markets

- On how competitive British goods and services are, whether measured by price or quality
- On how buoyant generally is the wider world economy.

In short, issues of global economic policy are uniquely important to Britain.

Britain is a trading economy but not all parts of the world are equally important to her as trading partners. Britain actually shares an important characteristic with the rest of the club of rich capitalist countries: they trade increasingly, but increasingly they trade with each other, not with the poorer parts of the world. Thus trading patterns 'lock in' Britain even more tightly to the most economically privileged and powerful part of the globe. This fact in turn has consequences for the patterns examined in the next section.

## Britain in the international political system: the traditional model of management

Britain is part of a world of nations. If we look at a map of the globe we will find that every square kilometre is either claimed by some sovereign state or – as in the case of parts of Antarctica – is under some system of shared dominion. It is usual to date the beginning of this world 'state system' from the Treaty of Westphalia, whose conclusion in 1648 brought to an end the Thirty Years War in Europe. This international system of states that claim sovereign control over their own territory is thus long established. Moreover, dismantling empires such as those of Britain in the last 50 years has multiplied the number of states. In 1945, when the United Nations (UN) was founded, it consisted of 51 member states; now there are 191.

British government has to manage the country's relations with this world of states. But this management has not always been done in the same way, and it is helpful to distinguish a 'traditional' model that was built up out of the Westphalian system from more recent patterns. (This traditional model was not unique to Britain; on the contrary, Britain prac-

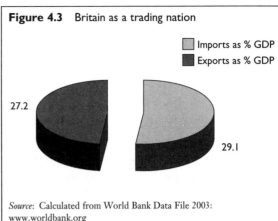

**Figure 4.3**  Britain as a trading nation

☐ Imports as % GDP
■ Exports as % GDP

27.2

29.1

*Source*: Calculated from World Bank Data File 2003: www.worldbank.org

➲ The simple divided pie chart shows how immensely 'open' the British economy is. It also reveals an important structural feature of that economy: Britain is a net importer. A private household that consistently spent more than it brought in would soon go bankrupt. How does the British economy avoid this? In part because it has other sources of overseas income, notably the income from investments abroad on which the profits can be 'repatriated'. So, for all her economic power, the United Kingdom is a bit like an old-fashioned 'rentier': a rich figure living partly on the proceeds of investment income that is derived from the enterprize of others, to wit foreigners.

tised it precisely because it was the norm for other powers.)

Traditionally, managing Britain's interests in the world of states was done by three means.

### Specialized domestic institutions

The most important and enduring of these actually still exists. It is the Foreign Office whose political head (the Foreign Secretary) is always a leading member of any British government. The Foreign Office's comprehensive management of Britain's foreign relations covers a huge range: it encompasses the organization of public, highly ceremonial occasions, such as the visit of a foreign head of state to Britain; and the most secret – the management of a large network of spies by which Britain (like most other nations) tries to spy on the rest of the world. In the past other domestic institutions have also been important: for instance, at the height of the

Empire described in the last chapter a separate Colonial Office was an important domestic institution in managing relations with imperial possessions.

## Specialized institutions abroad

Of these, the most important are embassies. Britain still maintains separate embassies for virtually all nations, and always for all important nations. Before global communication and travel became comparatively easy, embassies often enjoyed a high level of autonomy in how they managed relations with 'their' state. The Diplomatic Service, which was the career of the most important embassy staff, was a distinct service within British government. The heads of embassies – ambassadors – were often major figures in their own right. Embassy buildings were often imposing, acting as major statements of national power and prestige (see Images 4.1 and 4.2).

## Alliances

One of the main functions of both 'domestic' institutions such as the Foreign Office and of embassies was to maintain, or create, alliances with other national states in the 'world of nations'. These alliances could range from informal, friendly relations to elaborately specified treaties detailing the obligations of Britain and the other signatories, in the event of such occurrences as attack by a third party, such as another state. These alliances could often shift in a historically drastic manner. Britain's relations with Germany and with the United States in the twentieth century provide the most historically striking illustration. In the first half of the century Britain fought two world wars against Germany and created a powerful alliance with the United States. Yet at the start of that century foreign policy makers in Britain were still debating the uncertain question of whether it would be better for Britain to go to war with Germany or with the United States. The dilemma, and the way it was resolved in favour of a long-term alliance with the United States, shows that, in the traditional model of foreign relations, calculations of the national interest were the most important influence on the

alliances made by Britain. As we shall see, in the conduct of foreign affairs the United Kingdom, along with other sovereign governments, continues to be very hard-headed.

The traditional model of managing Britain's place in the world, therefore, can be summarized in three ways:

● Foreign policy was a specialized area dominated by a few institutions, notably the Foreign Office and the Diplomatic Service.
● There was heavy reliance on management of foreign relations country by country, through relatively autonomous embassies.
● Alliances and treaties were struck between Britain and other sovereign nations in an ad hoc fashion depending on which foreign alliance was held to serve Britain's short-term interests.

There are still important elements of this traditional 'model' in place: for example, the Foreign Office and individual embassies still retain great influence, and still stand as important physical symbols of national prestige (see Images 4.1–2). But it has gradually been modified; the process has lasted more than 50 years, and still continues.

## Modifying the traditional model of management

The traditional model of managing Britain's place in the international political system has been changed in three important ways.

### Foreign policy has ceased to be a uniquely specialized policy field

The divide between 'domestic' and 'foreign' policy is no longer automatically recognized. This is partly because most important areas of domestic policy are now seen as having a 'foreign policy' aspect. Areas as traditionally domestic as crime management, control of immigration, customs control, health

**Images 4.1 and 4.2**
**Icons of government: the physical face of the British state abroad: embassies**

Image 4.1 Prague embassy

Image 4.2 Brasilia embassy

Photos: Foreign and Commonwealth Office Services; Crown Copyright

➲ When Britain was a world 'super-power' the British embassy in any foreign capital was a building of great importance. Embassies, and their ambassadors, played a large independent part in conducting foreign policy, in part because slow and difficult communication often gave them considerable freedom from London. That independence has now declined, and British power has also declined, but embassies can still be used to try to make an important statement about national 'image'. Contrast the two examples here: the traditional 'grandeur' of the British embassy in Prague, Czech Republic, a mansion dating from the seventeenth century; and the self-consciously modern image presented by the purpose built embassy in Brasilia, the capital of Brazil, opened in 1961 – a modern building to match a purpose built modern capital.

care and education are all seen as impossible without coordination with powers abroad. Conversely, traditional areas of foreign policy are now seen as impinging in important ways on the management of government at home. The management of the world economy, which is periodically discussed at 'summits' of the leading industrial nations, or bargained over in the World Trade Organization (WTO), has obvious effects on the domestic management of the British economy. At a more particular level, Britain's large arms exporting industry depends heavily on the kind of alliances and deals made in foreign negotiations; and the prosperity of that industry in turn affects the jobs of tens of thousands at home. Foreign Secretaries can no longer treat foreign affairs as their unique domain. Decision-making has to be shared, and not only with the most important figures in the government, such as the Prime Minister and the Chancellor of the Exchequer. Virtually every

Cabinet Minister, and every government department, will have a continuing interest in foreign affairs (see Briefing 4.1).

## Specialized institutions have lost much of their autonomy

The most important effect here is observable in the case of embassies and ambassadors, which were a product of a historical epoch when international communication was slow. In the early nineteenth century it could take weeks to communicate between London and embassies abroad; now it can be done instantaneously via e-mail and secure telephone links. As these examples show, part of the reason for the change is technological: embassies can now be incorporated into communications almost as easily as if they were located in London. But the decline of autonomy is also due to changes in policy priorities. As Britain declined in the twentieth century from the status of a major world power, the point of foreign relations changed. Britain was no longer a main manager of the international political system. The job of embassies became increasingly mundane, and centred on trying to improve British commercial relations and

# Briefing                                    4.1

• • • • • • • • • • • • • • • • • • • • • • • • • • • • •

## EXAMPLES OF HOW FOREIGN AND DOMESTIC POLICY ARE ENTWINED

*Education*
British universities balance their books by selling their services abroad, often with the help of local British embassies.

*Employment*
Tens of thousands of jobs at home depend on foreign defence contracts.

*Health*
Many diseases (from AIDS to malaria) imported by travellers from abroad, or 'exported' by British tourists. Shortages of medical staff alleviated by overseas recruitment.

*Drugs*
Many prohibited drugs cultivated abroad and imported illegally into Britain.

*Animal welfare*
Welfare of animals depends on regulation of import and export of animals for trade or for pleasure.

*Child protection*
Worldwide web creates new opportunities for child abuse.

*Broadcasting*
Broadcasts from foreign radio and television stations force reform of home regime for regulating broadcasters.

• • • • • • • • • • • • • • • • • • • • • • • • • • • • •

➲ The chief lesson of these examples is the inextricable intertwining of the conventionally 'domestic' and 'foreign'. Notice how foreign influences produce a complex mixture: some straightforward 'problems', some benefits and some more neutral opportunities.

to promote British exports (see Documenting Politics 4.1).

## The nature of alliances and treaties has changed

When Britain was a great power she made alliances with states as and when it seemed to suit her individual interests. But as her power and prestige declined, she increasingly relied on participation in alliances and institutions as one of a number of states, albeit often an important one. Three examples illustrate the point. For over 50 years the most important military alliance of which Britain has been a member has been the North Atlantic Treaty Organization (NATO). This is an organization dominated by the United States, with its own command hierarchy and command headquarters. A second example is the United Nations, which was founded in 1945 to try to promote collective international security. As a legacy of her former Great Power status Britain is one of small number of states with a permanent place on the UN Security Council, the most important decision-making body of that organization. A third example anticipates a major theme of this whole book, and is discussed in more detail in Chapter 6: the majority of Britain's foreign relations is now conducted through the institutions of the European Union. Two important examples are negotiations on trade relations in the World Trade Organization, where the Union negotiates on behalf of its member states; and bargaining over treaties to control climate change, where Britain again negotiates as part of the European Union because the Union plays such a large part in environmental regulation.

In the 'new model' of managing Britain's international political relations, therefore, we can see three important developments:

- At home, foreign policy is much more closely integrated into the wider domestic system of policy making.
- The integration has greatly reduced the autonomy of traditional foreign policy-making institutions.

● Britain's foreign relations are increasingly managed collectively in institutions with other states.

## Why the traditional model has changed

Some of the reasons for the changes summarized here have already been referred to: for instance, the rise of rapid means of global communication, and easier travel, now make it much simpler to manage foreign relations from London rather than relying on far-flung embassies. But at the root of the changes lie long-term developments in the nature of

the international economic and political system, and of Britain's place in that system (see People in Politics 4.1).

### Increasing global interdependence

The growth of an increasingly interdependent economic and political global system is one of the most important reasons why foreign policy is no longer viewed as a distinct domain separate from domestic policy. The 'global dimension' exists in economic production, in crime control, in regulation of broadcasting and telecommunications, and in a host of other fields: this helps explain why virtually every department of government now feels it

---

## DOCUMENTING POLITICS 4.1

### HOW THE FOREIGN AND THE DOMESTIC ARE ENTWINED: THE CASE OF STEEL TARIFFS

'In a joint effort between the FCO [Foreign and Commonwealth Office], DTI [Department of Trade and Industry] and other Departments, trade teams in London and our Posts in Washington, Brussels and Geneva pulled together to win major concessions for UK industry at the outset of the steel trade dispute with the US.

In March 2002 the Bush Administration announced a programme of tariffs on steel imports to the US ... Whitehall and our Embassy in Washington worked with UK companies to mitigate the effects of steel tariffs for UK producers and workers. The Embassy reported, early on, the likelihood of tariffs, and was able to advise the FCO and DTI of key players for lobbying efforts and the best timing for deployment. The companies provided ample substantive justification for their request, and were pleased with the advice and high-level lobbying support from us. Trade policy teams in London, Washington, Brussels and Geneva worked together to provide a full picture of action in capitals and the implications for UK interests.

This team effort paid off. At the end of the first round of the exclusion process, some 70% of UK steel exports were free of the tariffs. A good example of joined-up government.'

➲ The boastful and partisan tone of this extract derives from its origin, in the annual report of the Foreign and Commonwealth Office, essentially a piece of propaganda both for the Foreign Office and for the government in power. But it illustrates very well the hard-headed nature of modern diplomacy, notably the extent to which it involves the active defence of private corporate interests by the state. It also shows how far modern foreign policy is now conducted in a world of multi-level institutions. Among those central to this story are: our Embassies abroad; the Foreign Office itself; the Department of Trade and Industry, the department that speaks for industrial interests at home; the European Commission, the key institution in the European Union, whose importance for the British economy is spelled out in Chapter 6; the WTO which tries to adjudicate on trade disputes of this kind; and the United States Government, the promoter of the biggest and richest economy in the world.

*Source*: Foreign and Commonwealth Office, *Annual Report 2003* (61).

## *People in politics*

### 4.1   THREE WHO MADE MODERN BRITISH FOREIGN POLICY

Cartoons: Shaun Steele

**Ernest Bevin** (1881–1951). Bevin was the greatest trade union leader in Britain in the years between the two world wars and only entered government as a result of the great crisis of war, in 1940. He became Foreign Secretary in the Labour Government elected in 1945 and throughout the next six years was one of its dominant personalities. He set the direction of British foreign policy for the next half century: scepticism about European unification, and a commitment to an alliance with the United States. He was one of the architects of the North Atlantic Treaty Organization, a military alliance dominated by the Americans, which opposed the Soviet Union when it was one of the two world super-powers.

**Edward Heath** (1916–) was only Prime Minister for just over three-and-a-half years (1970–4) but he changed the direction of British foreign policy in one vital respect: he led the government which negotiated the terms of British entry into the then European Economic Community in 1973. A decade earlier he had also unsuccessfully tried to negotiate entry into the original Common Market. He thus critically modified, though did not extinguish, the 'Eurosceptic' tone of British foreign policy set by Ernest Bevin. He spent the years following his deposition as leader of the Conservative Party (1975) advocating closer integration between Britain and the European Union, in an increasingly 'Eurosceptic' Conservative Party.

**Margaret Thatcher** (1925–), by common consent the most forceful peacetime Prime Minister in modern British history, in some respects reinforced the pro-European direction of Mr Heath: under her, Britain became increasingly integrated into the wider European economy. But in the later years of her Premiership she became increasingly hostile to European integration, and out of office became the focus of a powerful Euro-sceptic movement in the Conservative Party. She also throughout the 1980s reinforced the strength of the Anglo–American alliance, thus continuing work begun by Ernest Bevin a generation before. The fact that for two decades Britain has been America's closest military ally testifies to her influence.

➲ These three great figures are important because they left different, indelible prints on British foreign policy, but they are also important because their policies encapsulate the tensions about where Britain should locate itself in the international power system. Bevin was a convinced 'Atlanticist', who strengthened the alliance with the United States; Heath decisively pushed the country in a European direction; and in Mrs Thatcher's foreign policy career she was alternately Europeanist and Atlanticist.

must have a say over some aspect of foreign policy. We saw one of the most dramatic examples of this in the last chapter. The rise of immigration as a major issue for government inside Britain, and the changing sources of immigration in the 1990s, are due to wider changes in the nature of the international political system. The rise of immigration as a problem for governments at home is also due to the difficulty of policing national borders in a world of increasing global movement of goods and people. The fact that the British government has to manage the economy in a world of global economic organization is now a commonplace in discussions of economic policy but, as examples such as crime control and immigration show, there is now a global dimension to virtually everything that government attempts to do domestically.

## American domination

From the beginning of the twentieth century it became obvious, even in Britain, that she was no longer the supreme world power and was being challenged by the two rising powers of the United States and Germany. In the two great wars of the twentieth century (1914–18 and 1939–45) America eventually intervened on the side of Britain. After the Second World War the United States replaced Britain as a world super-power. Since then, all British governments have followed essentially the same foreign policy strategy: to position Britain as a close ally, and junior partner, of the United States. The calculation has been that since everyone is now living in an American-dominated world, Britain's best interests would be served by alliance with the dominant power. This helps explain, for instance, why Britain's most important military alliance for over 50 years has been the American-dominated North Atlantic Treaty Organization.

One important legacy of great power status, and of the conviction that Britain is an especially important partner of the United States, is British military power. Britain rapidly acquired nuclear weapons – then thought to be the badge of the super-power – after the Second World War. She remains one of a small number of countries that possess nuclear weapons, despite being virtually completely reliant

on American rockets to deliver these (the weapons are virtually useless without means of delivery). The country also retains a most unusual conventional military capability. This military capacity is bought partly by high levels of spending (see Figure 4.4). We have been emphasizing how the 'traditional' model of foreign relations has changed over time, but here we see two striking continuities: the importance of war, and the importance of the arms economy to Britain.

Britain still uses force as an important means of managing its foreign relations. In the last quarter of a century alone she has participated in five important military campaigns: to recover the Falkland Islands colony from Argentina after that country invaded in 1982; to expel the Iraqi invaders from Kuwait in 1991, as an important part of a multinational force led by the United States; to intervene in the civil war in the Balkans in 1999 as leading member of a NATO force; to help the Americans conquer

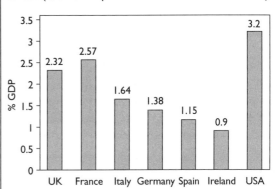

**Figure 4.4** The importance of the arms economy in Britain (% of GDP spent on arms in selected countries)

*Source*: Data from CIA, *World Fact Book 2002*.

➲ Britain is among the highest defence spenders in the democratic world, and this in turn makes the arms economy especially important to the wider UK economy. The figures are for a range of dates at the end of the 1990s and the beginning of the millennium, but are broadly comparable because spending does not vary dramatically from year to year. They compare the UK with other big EU states, and as a point of reference with her immediate neighbour, a tiny EU state, and the world's super-power, the USA. Among her main EU partners only France outspends the UK. The two share a common past as imperial powers.

**POLITICAL ISSUES**

### 4.1   THE IRAQ WAR OF 2003–05

The Iraq War of 2003 could be considered the 'second' Iraq war. The first was the Gulf War of 1991, which involved expelling the Iraqi regime from Kuwait, a small oil-rich kingdom in the Gulf which it had invaded. The 'second' Iraq war involved the invasion of Iraq, the toppling of the regime headed by Saddam Hussein, and the attempt to create a new political regime in the country. The invasion was led by the United States, with the United Kingdom as her main ally. The war had many claimed justifications, the most important of which was that the Saddam regime possessed 'weapons of mass destruction' which could be used against Iraq's neighbours, and even further afield. A successful military campaign which toppled Saddam rapidly in 2003 was followed by a succession of catastrophes: large scale loss of Iraqi lives as the occupying forces tried to maintain order; the emergence of rival groupings struggling for power, often violently, in Iraq; the revelation in 2004 of large scale abuse and torture of Iraqi prisoners by American forces; allegations of abuse and torture made against British forces, some of which, though not all, turned out to be fabricated; growing hostility in both the British and the American electorates to the military operation; and increasing pressure on the British government publicly to separate itself from support for American policies. The war led key groups of swing voters to desert Labour in the 2005 general election, either for the Liberal Democrats or for abstention.

The war raised many issues, most of which are still unresolved at the time of writing. For the conduct of British foreign policy the most important issues were:

- How closely should the UK ally itself in foreign policy with the United States, over an issue where there were deep divisions between member states of the European Union?
- 'Weapons of mass destruction' have not been discovered. How far should foreign policy decisions be made on the basis of secret intelligence, in this case about the existence of weapons of mass destruction, which cannot be tested in the public arena?
- How far should a government go in making foreign policy commitments which are intensely opposed by a large section – by some measures the majority – of its domestic electorate?

Afghanistan in 2001–2, following the terrorist attacks on the United States on 11 September 2001; and to invade Iraq as the main ally of the United States in 2003 (see Political Issues 4.1).

We saw in Chapter 2 that British manufacturing suffered a long historical decline. One exception to this is arms manufacturing and export, where Britain remains a world leader. There is a connection between the importance of war and the importance of arms production. At the start of the twentieth century British firms were important in helping build the Japanese Navy, thus laying the foundations of a military power that Britain then had to fight in the Second World War. At the end of the twentieth century British firms were important in equipping the Iraqi dictator, Saddam Hussein, who then had to be fought in the invasion of 2003.

### The rise and fall of the Soviet Union

One reason Britain – and other west European states – so quickly became junior allies of the American super-power after 1945 was fear of a new super-power that had arisen in Eastern Europe, the Soviet Union. The Marxist doctrines and dictatorial system of the Soviet Union were a threat to both capitalism and democracy. For over 40 years there was a Cold War across the globe. The war was 'cold' because it involved little open military conflict, in Europe at least. Both super-powers had nuclear weapons and were held back by the fear of mutual nuclear annihilation. The Soviet Union controlled a set of Marxist dictator-ships across Eastern Europe. It was believed that only American nuclear protection defended Western Europe against Soviet ambitions. This naturally helped to support alliances such as NATO, and to encourage Britain to cultivate her place as a junior ally of the United States (see Image 4.3).

The Soviet Empire in Eastern Europe collapsed dramatically at the end of the 1980s. This was followed in 1991 by the collapse of the Soviet Union itself. But these collapses, though they changed much, did not change Britain's role as a junior partner of the United States. In the 1990s, as we saw above, she fought a number of wars alongside the United States. The collapse of the Soviet Union, though it removed a threat to democracy and capitalism in Western Europe, also meant that in the 1990s America was now the unchallenged super-power. This made even stronger the logic of Britain's long-term strategy, which was to seek influence in foreign relations as an ally of this super-power. The collapse of Soviet power in Eastern Europe and over large parts of Asia has made these areas unstable, and has drawn in the United States and her ally in a policing role.

## The rise of the European Union as a regional power

The most important factors cited so far as influ-ences changing the traditional model of foreign relations – such as the rise of America to super-power position and the collapse of the Soviet Union – have all pointed Britain in a particular direction: strengthening her role as a junior partner of the United States in an American-dominated world. But as we anticipated at the end of Chapter 2, the rising importance of the European Union poten-

### Image 4.3
### Britain as the junior partner of the United States

Photo: EPA/EMPICS

➲ The photo of Prime Minister Blair and President Bush at a summit meeting in Istanbul is taken from a mischievous angle: by omitting Britain's name plate it suggests that Mr Blair is actually a member of the American delegation. But it highlighs an important issue surrounding Anglo–American relations in the twenty-first century, and one that forms a major theme of this chapter: just how closely should Britain ally herself as a junior partner with the world's super-power, the United States? The photo dates from June 2004.

tially pulls Britain in very different directions. In Chapter 6 we will see that the government of Britain and of the European Union are now so intertwined that it is hard in many instances to make any clear separation between the two. Not surpris-ingly, this is having important consequences for managing Britain's place in the international politi-cal system. It is the best example of one of the big changes identified earlier: the tendency for Britain now to be an international actor, not as a separate sovereign state, but as one member of a group. As we have noticed, in some important fields such as international trade negotiations in the WTO, Britain effectively has no separate presence at all. Since the European Union is a single trading unit, all important trade negotiations have to be carried on by the Union collectively. This does not mean

## DEBATING POLITICS

### 4.1   AMERICAN JUNIOR PARTNER OR EUROPEAN REGIONAL POWER?

**The case for an American partnership:**

■ The United States will be the dominant super-power for the foreseeable future, and the collapse of the Soviet Union has left her as the unchallenged sole world super-power: it makes sense to stay in close alliance with her.

■ Britain is the most important European centre of American investment in Europe.

■ The United States was Britain's key ally in the two great world wars of the twentieth century.

■ Britain and the United States share important cultural features, such as a common language.

■ The British and American economies share impor-tant structural features: notably, they are lightly regu-lated by comparison with the economies of the leading members of the European Union.

**The case for European regional power**

■ The EU is emerging as an important world economic power and it makes sense to maximize UK influence within its institutions.

■ The EU is the most important trading partner for the UK, and can be expected to become more so.

■ Britain's democratic institutions and cultures are shared with most important member states of the EU.

■ The EU will largely regulate the British economy unless we take the radical step of withdrawal, so it makes sense to maximize influence over how that regulation works.

■ Full membership of an enlarged European Union offers Britain a part of a largely self-sufficient European-wide economy with protection from both American power and global economic disturbances.

---

that Britain has no influence, but it does mean that influence has to start by shaping the collective posi-tion adopted by the Union as a whole. Britain can no longer take independent decisions on these key aspects of foreign economic policy. The Union is an economic super-power. Its economic interests are often sharply opposed to those of the United States. Here, then, is one important area where Britain is often constrained from acting as a junior ally of the United States.

## Tensions and choices in Britain's international relations

Discussion of the forces that have contributed to the changing model of managing Britain's international relations returns us to a key theme examined at the end of Chapter 2. The collapse of the Soviet Union has made more severe the tension between Britain's position as an EU member, and her historically established close alliance with the United States.

The collapse of Soviet power strengthened the tendency for Britain to position herself as a junior partner in an American-dominated world order. But the removal of much of the threat of Soviet power had a rather different effect across the rest of the European Union. Freed from the threat of Soviet domination, the Union has felt able to act increas-ingly independently of the United States. The passing away of the Soviet Empire has led, as we shall see in Chapter 6, to the entry of a large number of new members who were formerly under the control of the Soviet Union. In some key cases a divide has opened up between the United Kingdom and other leading members of the European Union in their attitude to the exercise of American power (see Debating Politics 4.1). After a series of terrorist attacks on the United States on 11 September 2001 the United States began to pursue a much more active policy of military intervention (for instance, in Afghanistan and Iraq). It tried to do this mainly with the support of the United Nations. In these efforts Britain has stood out from other

## REVIEW

Four main themes have been developed in this chapter:

1  British government lives in a world of other nation-states and has to manage British interests in that world;
2  Britain's economy makes her particularly sensitive to global developments;
3  The traditional division between the management of foreign policy and the management of the rest of government at home has been eroded over the last 50 years;
4  The dominant strategy of British governments for at least half-a-century has been to position the country as a junior ally of the United States, but this is now seriously complicated by the influences of European Union membership.

leading members of the Union in its willingness to support the United States, both in diplomatic negotiations to secure UN support and on the battlefield.

These examples are thus a concrete instance of the 'historical crossroads' that we identified for Britain at the close of Chapter 2. She finds herself pulled between American and European influences, often trying to conciliate between the two. One effect of these tensions has been to make the domestic management of foreign policy an especially important preoccupation at the top of British government. When we come to examine the core executive in Chapter 7 we will see that foreign policy management is one of its key concerns. This active management is needed because British government is not internally united. Some institutions, and some important personalities, will incline towards the American 'signpost' at the crossroads; some will incline towards the European. The core executive is constantly trying to sort out these tensions.

## Further reading

The most stimulating, authoritative, and partly sceptical, study of the economic globalization which has done so much to transform the traditional model of foreign relations is Hirst and Thompson (1999). A vast, stimulating and highly readable panorama of the history of the international system in which Britain plays a key part is Kennedy (1989). The most important scholarly study of the European movement is Milward (1992). Gamble (2003) is very illuminating on the tensions between American and European fates for the United Kingdom.

CHAPTER 5

# The constitution and the political culture

## AIMS

This chapter:

❖ Explains why we need to explore the constitution and the political culture together

❖ Locates the sources of the constitution

❖ Describes the sources of, and the content of, constitutional change

❖ Describes the traditional pattern of the political culture and how it is changing

❖ Shows that there is a close connection between constitutional change and cultural change.

## The constitution and the political culture

Constitutions are at the heart of democratic politics. Formally, a constitution prescribes the rules of the game in a system of government: it describes both the rules by which decisions in government can be made, and defines the broad boundaries of the content of those decisions – laying down the range of potential powers of government, in other words. A constitution does not have to be democratic: we can find numerous examples historically of 'the rules of the game' that are *not* democratic; but part of the essence of modern democratic government is that the state is subject to explicit constraints. It cannot act arbitrarily, but has to observe some 'rules of the game'. That is one reason why a common alternative summary of the system of government in Britain is 'constitutional democracy'.

The state has to be subject to constitutional restraints, but the form of these restraints varies enormously. One of the common kinds of variation concerns the extent to which a constitution is *codified*. The most highly developed kind of codification occurs when we can identify a single written document called a constitution. If we were, for instance, examining political life in the United States our natural starting point would be precisely this: a document originally written in 1787 and subsequently amended 26 times. The American constitution is a document, even with all its amendments, of only about 8,000 words – the length, in other words, of a typical student project.

By contrast, the British constitution is more elusive. It is sometimes said that Britain is distinguished by the fact that it has an unwritten constitution. This is not strictly correct because, as we shall see shortly, many key elements of the constitution are indeed written, some in the form of law; but it is true that the constitution is not systematically codified in a single document. We have an uncodified constitution which comes from a wide range of sources, and which takes many forms: it is what might be called an eclectic, 'pick and mix' constitution.

The fact that the constitution is uncodified and eclectic has a number of important implications. Three are especially important.

First, the uncodified and eclectic nature of the constitution means that the nature of the constitution depends heavily on constitutional understandings, but it is the nature of understandings that different groups can understand them differently. The result is that both the boundaries of the constitution, and even the meaning of its core content, are widely contested. The British constitution should not therefore be understood as a single definitive, settled set of rules. Conflict about the meaning of the constitution is one important way in which wider political conflict is expressed in Britain.

Second, the uncodified and eclectic nature of the constitution means that it cannot be conceived as a set of formal doctrines; it is an expression of, and is closely connected to, the wider *political culture* of the community. Political culture is the term we apply to what might be thought of as the wider pattern of popular understandings about the 'rules of the game' of government. Not many people think about the nature of the British constitution; but most of us have a view about the system of government in Britain. Do we trust the institutions of government to act fairly and truthfully? Do we believe that the United Kingdom should remain united under the single symbol of the Crown? Do we approve of the most important institutions and practices of British politics, such as universal suffrage? These attitudes form the core components of the political culture.

Third, the shifting and uncertain meaning of the British constitution makes it ideally suited to performing two very different functions. These were famously identified in the greatest of all books on the constitution as the *dignified* and the *efficient* (see Documenting Politics 5.1). In making this distinction the nineteenth-century political commentator Walter Bagehot argued that the 'dignified' elements of the constitution were important in creating loyalty and political attachment to the system of rule. His most important example was the monarchy, which performed no serious governing function but which inspired popular loyalty to the system of government. By contrast, Bagehot argued that the 'efficient' elements of a constitution concerned those parts where the rules of the governing game were actually specified and operated. The exact words used by Bagehot can mislead in our time. The Royal

**DOCUMENTING POLITICS 5.1**

## WALTER BAGEHOT ON THE MONARCHY AS A 'DIGNIFIED' INSTITUTION

'The best reason why Monarchy is a strong government is, that it is an intelligible government. The mass of mankind understand it, and they hardly anywhere in the world understand any other ... A *family* on the throne is an interesting idea also. It brings down the pride of sovereignty to the level of petty life. No feeling could seem more childish than the enthusiasm of the English at the marriage of the Prince of Wales. They treated as a great political event, what, looked at as a matter of pure business, was very small indeed. But no feeling could be more like common human nature as it is, and as it is likely to be. The women – one half of the human race at least – care fifty times more for a marriage than a ministry.'

⬤ The passages here can be found on pp. 82 and 85 of the 1963 edition of *The English Constitution* (see Bibliography), first published in 1867. Bagehot was a worldly journalist, a distinguished editor of *The Economist*. He thought of politics, even in this age before the rise of democracy, as the art of manipulating popular beliefs; hence the distinction between highly public, 'dignified' bodies such as the monarchy, that commanded public loyalty, and the real, informal and often hidden practical mechanisms of government. Notice also the reflection – common for the time – of the view that women were especially likely to care for the dignified over the efficient. Yet despite the lapse of time, the passages on the Prince of Wales' wedding (in the 1860s) have an uncanny application to the present Prince of Wales' first wedding (in 1981).

*Source*: Bagehot (1867/1963: 82, 85).

Family remains a 'dignified' part of the constitution, but a glance at any issue of a tabloid newspaper will show that its members often behave in a very undignified way. Often the 'efficient' parts of the constitution work in a blundering, ineffective way. But the heart of Bagehot's argument stands: that some elements of the constitution are there to induce loyalty to the system of rule, and some are there actually to guide the practice of government. The importance of the 'dignified' function of the constitution, however, makes the meaning of the constitution even more contested and uncertain, since different interests and groups will want to attach the magic of 'constitutional' to their own view of what the system of rule should be.

## Where will we find the constitution?

This simple question is the obvious first step in identifying the British constitution. Yet it is actually a more difficult question than appears at first sight, and for a highly revealing reason. Because the constitution is eclectic and uncodified its sources are many and varied; and for this reason, we can stress different sources depending on what we want to make of the constitution.

There are six important sources we can look to in identifying the constitution, as explained below.

### 'Normal' statutes

It is hardly surprising to find that the law of the land is an important source of the constitution. It stretches historically as far back at least as the constitutional turmoil of the seventeenth century. For instance, the law of *habeas corpus* passed in 1679 put explicit legislative restraints on the power of the state – which at that time largely meant the Crown – to detain subjects without trial: it codified on the statute book what had long before been a common law remedy. At the other end of the historical spectrum, two more recent pieces of legislation significantly qualify the protections of *habeas corpus*. The Prevention of Terrorism Act was originally passed in the 1974 as a 'temporary' measure following horrific bomb attacks on the British mainland, at the height of a bombing campaign by Irish Republicans. It has been renewed each year since. It proscribes certain organizations because they are concerned with terrorism, and gives police the power to detain and exclude persons from Great Britain on grounds that they are suspected of terrorism. In December 2001, following terrorist attacks on the World Trade Center in New York in September of that year, the Anti-Terrorism, Crime and Security Emergency Act was passed. It greatly strengthened the power of the state to restrict civil liberties (see Table 5.1.) These examples emphasize the point made earlier: the Constitution is not a single, consistent set of provisions but rather a set of domains where different views of the 'rules of the government game' are contested.

## 'Super' statutes

Until recently it was commonly argued that there were no distinct constitutional statutes in Britain: any statute, from the most momentous for civil liberty to the most mundane, was passed through Parliament in the same way, and could be repealed in the same way. Parliament was the supreme arbiter of the constitution. In the words of Albert Dicey, the most influential constitutional theorist of the nineteenth century; Parliament 'has, under the English constitution, the right to make or unmake any law whatsoever' (see Bradley 2000: 27). It is doubtful if this is any longer the case. There now exist a set of laws that restrict government in Britain in unique ways (see Timeline 5.1). The most obvious of these arise from our obligations as signatories of the various Treaties that govern our membership of the European Union. While these obligations are embodied in statute passed by Parliament it is hard to imagine that Parliament could repeal them – for instance, withdraw from the European Union – except in the most dramatic circumstances. The same is true of the laws that led

**Table 5.1** The challenge of terrorism and the challenge to liberal freedoms: restrictions to civil liberties after the 11 September 2001 terrorist attacks

|  | France | Germany | United Kingdom |
|---|---|---|---|
| Law expires | 31.12.03 | 1.01.07 | No expiry date |
| Privacy | X | X | X |
| Freedom of the person | X |  | X |
| Private property |  |  | X |
| Freedom of movement |  | X | X |
| Jurisdiction of secret services |  | X | X |
| Personal identification |  | X |  |
| Freedom of expression |  |  | X |
| Miscellaneous | X | X | X |

*Source*: Haubrich 2003: 19.

➲ Following terrorist attacks in the United States on 11 September 2001 (notably on the New York World Trade Center) most states in North America and Western Europe passed legislation restricting civil liberties in the attempt to combat terrorism. Table 5.1 draws on a study which compares the severity of the restrictions in the three biggest countries of the European Union. An 'X' in the box means that a measure was passed that enhanced the state's power to infringe liberties or the power of its security services to exercise surveillance over citizens. Britain 'scores' highest on the list. Why should this have been so?

to the establishment of a Scottish Parliament and a Welsh Assembly in 1999. Similarly, the principle of hereditary membership of the House of Lords was all but abolished by the Labour Government in the House of Lords Act of that year, and it is hard to imagine a return to the previous state of affairs; the statute has a special quality marking it out from 'normal' legislation. All of these statutes have the character of a constitutional Rubicon: that is, once

| TIMELINE 5.1 | THE SPREAD OF 'SUPER' STATUTES IN DEFINING THE CONSTITUTION |
|---|---|

| | Statute | Main effect |
|---|---|---|
| **1972** | UK government signs Treaty of Accession to European Economic Community | Confirms British membership of 'Common Market' from January 1973, and subjects British government to the law of the Community as interpreted by the European Court of Justice. |
| **1986** | Single European Act | Commits British governments to implementation of final measures to create free movement of goods, services and people across the EEC. |
| **1993** | Maastricht Act | Confirms UK as signatory of Maastricht Treaty: creates European Union; extends range of decisions taken by majority decision of members of the Union |
| **1998** | Scotland Act | Following referendum supporting devolved powers in 1997 creates an elected Scottish Parliament and Scottish executive in 1999 with control of most domestic policy and some tax-raising power. |
| | Government of Wales Act | Following referendum supporting some devolved power in 1997 creates an elected Welsh Assembly with a Cabinet and First Minister, but with no tax-raising power and more limited control of policy than in Scotland. |
| | Human Rights Act | Incorporates into law the provisions of the European Convention on Human Rights. |
| **1999** | House of Lords Act | Removes from Lords all but 92 specially selected hereditary peers. |

➲ Four features should be noticed about this timeline. First, it illustrates a long-term development which we highlight again at the end of the chapter: the shift from a constitution dominated by informal conventions to one increasingly laid down in law. Second, it shows how important has been membership of the (now) European Union in this process. Third, it shows how far election of New Labour brought constitutional innovation to the centre of policy making. Finally, notice a missing feature: Northern Ireland. Since 1972 – when direct rule from Westminster was first imposed – there have been numerous constitutional innovations, culminating in the 'Good Friday' Agreement of 1998 described later (in Chapter 11). Although all the innovations in this box are subject to change, a return to the condition that they replaced is inconceivable. They cross a 'constitutional Rubicon'; but no such certainty surrounds constitutional change for Northern Ireland, for at the time of writing the devolved institutions created out of the Good Friday Agreement are suspended and the province is under direct rule from Westminster.

*Sources*: Butler and Butler (2000); Cook and Stevenson (2000); www.wales.gov.uk

crossed they are irreversible, definitive changes in the constitutional order.

## Judge-shaped law

Notice the word 'shaped' rather than 'made' here. It recognizes that Parliament has in the last analysis been the source of law; but it also recognizes an important role for judicial decisions. Judges have until recently been reluctant to review and strike down law passed by Parliament, but they have been able to exercise a huge influence on the way law is put into effect. In part the influence comes through an accumulation of decisions in the courts. We usually summarize this as the 'common law': a law that comes out of customary understandings and the accumulation of cases decided by judges over centuries. But judges have also felt able to practise 'judicial review'. Since parliamentary statutes are typically general in character their application in any particular instance can be unclear and contested. And it is in the interpretation and clarifi-

# Briefing

## TWO GROUPS THAT CONTEST THE DOMAINS OF THE CONSTITUTION: CHARTER 88 AND LIBERTY

**Charter 88** is an independent pressure group for constitutional reform. As its name implies, its name dates from a 'charter' drafted in 1988 which argued for major constitutional reform in a number of areas. These included devolution, electoral reform and the framing of a written constitution including a bill of rights. Although some of these changes have been partly introduced Charter 88 continues to agitate, organizing networks of groups at local and national level. It claims over 80,000 supporters, by which it means that over 80,000 people have signed its charter of reform measures. The language of 'charter' is designed to recall another era of radical constitutional agitation: the 'Chartists' who in the 1840s unsuccessfully organized mass demonstrations demanding then unheard-of radical changes, such as universal male suffrage. Charter 88 also uses the modern technology of lobbying and mass participation which we discuss in later chapters: see www.charter88.org.uk

**Liberty** traces its organized history back to 1934, when the *National Council for Civil Liberties* was formed. It shares many of the same values as Charter 88, but is much more focused on campaigning on particular issues: it takes human rights cases through the UK courts and the European Court of Human Rights; it conducts research into current government policies that affect the rights of groups such as refugees; it provides practical advice and training to human rights lawyers, runs specialist advice lines and offers guidance to individual members of the public who have fallen foul of the authorities. These activities are intended to push the boundaries of individual rights as far as possible, and limit the powers of the state as far as possible. See www.liberty-human-rights-org.uk

⟳ The boundaries of what is constitutionally acceptable are especially unclear in a system where there is strong resistance to writing down constitutional rules, and a heavy reliance on unwritten conventions. As the meaning of the constitution has become more and more uncertain, radical constitutional groups, such as Liberty and Charter 88, have emerged to contest key constitutional domains.

cation of meaning that judicial review is important: judges can pronounce on the mind of Parliament even when (especially when) Parliament's mind is not obvious. In Chapter 22 we show that, notably in the form of judicial review, this kind of judicial intervention has assumed a growing importance in constitutional practice.

### Institutional rules

Many of the most important governing institutions in Britain have their own internal 'rule books' and these are so central to the way government life is conducted that they can be considered part of the constitution. The best example is *Erskine May*, the 'bible' covering matters of procedure in the House of Commons. It originated as a codification of the rules of Commons behaviour by a nineteenth-century clerk to the Commons, Sir Thomas

Erskine May (1815–86), and each successive edition has governed the conduct of business in the Commons.

### Conventions

The original title of Erskine May's handbook of parliamentary procedure was *A Treatise Upon the Law, Privileges, Proceedings, and Usages of Parliament* (1844). The variety of sources of parliamentary authority, and especially the reference to 'usages', catches the importance of constitutional conventions, and perfectly expresses the historically uncodified and eclectic character of the constitution in Britain. Conventions are understandings that guide behaviour; and as with understandings in any walk of life they can vary in the degree to which they are openly expressed, and can vary in the degree to which they actually do shape behaviour. A convention of social life with which most readers will be familiar is the convention that teachers do not swear at students. But we know that what is viewed as swearing varies from place to place and time to time; and we know that in extreme exasperation teachers have been driven to swear. A parallel example in British government is provided by the convention (sometimes called doctrine) of collective ministerial responsibility. This is a convention that decrees that members of the British Cabinet (see Chapter 7) are publicly bound to defend a collective policy decision made by Cabinet. The convention undoubtedly does constrain the public utterances of Cabinet members; even if they disagree privately with what has been decided they will (in many cases at least) keep their disagreement publicly silent. But the way the convention works shows how elastic is the idea of a convention and how much fiction it contains. The convention originated when the Cabinet normally debated in full session all important policy matters and tried to arrive at a common view. But as we will discover in Chapter 7, this kind of collective debate hardly ever happens now. Most business is done in bodies such as Cabinet committees. Ministers can thus often find themselves publicly committed to policies without ever being present at the debate where the decision was made.

Cabinet ministers cope with the convention of collective responsibility in this changed world in various ways. They stretch the meaning of 'public' disagreement. While remaining silent 'on the record' they can 'off the record' brief journalists about their dissent; the fact of a minister's disagreement is reported but with no sources named. They can informally let their allies outside government know of their dissent. This is then often reported as 'friends' of the minister briefing journalists about internal Cabinet disagreements. There have been a few occasions when Cabinets were so divided that they have agreed openly to license disagreement on an issue (the political equivalent of the exasperated teacher actually swearing). The most famous came in 1975, when members of the then Labour Cabinet campaigned on different sides in the referendum on the country's continuing membership of the European Economic Community. But this open breach with the convention is less important than the continuous informal leaking of disagreements by cabinet Ministers as they battle with each other over policy and career ambitions.

The shifting and uncertain meaning of conventions is one of the most important mechanisms in the British constitution. It allows the 'rules of the game' to be adapted to the demands of the most powerful, and it helps the process by which interests can struggle to appropriate the magic of 'constitutional dignity' to their own view of the rules of the governing game. But conventions have an added importance: for the most part they cover the daily conduct of business, as the example of the convention of collective ministerial responsibility shows. But they shade off into the larger understandings described below, and thus are the point where the constitution as conventionally understood shades off into the wider character of the political culture.

## Cultural understandings

Most constitutional conventions of the sort described above can and do change, and are often abandoned. It is not hard to imagine the doctrine of collective cabinet responsibility being openly abandoned (for instance, if we had a series of governments composed of coalitions from different parties). But suppose a government proposed reinstating the link between property ownership and the right to vote that was broken by the long struggle for universal adult suffrage as described in Chapter 2? It is not hard to imagine here that the attempt would provoke widespread popular resistance. The example shows that at the foundations of the constitution lie features engrained in the wider political culture: understandings that are thought to be the moral core of the system of government. Like conventions, these cultural understandings can themselves be elusive, will shift over time and will often not command universal support. The understanding that there should be universal suffrage unqualified by property qualifications is a good example of this. It is a comparatively recent understanding historically: as we saw in Chapter 2, only in 1948 were the last property qualifications finally abolished. It is uncertain as to exact meaning: until 1969 an 'adult' was anyone over 21; after that date, anyone over 18; and some reformers would like to reduce the age to 16 (see Political Issues 17.1, p. 385). And there are undoubtedly some traditionalists – though numerically few – who actually would like to see property or educational qualifications reinstated as a precondition of an entitlement to vote.

## The domains of the constitution: the core and the contested

We have stressed the diverse sources of the constitution, and the shifting and contested nature of many key constitutional understandings. Does this mean that the constitution has no settled identifiable existence? Is it simply a fiction that can be dreamt up by whichever group is most powerful?

The answer is that the meaning of the British constitution is not a fiction, but its meaning is uncertain. The reason takes us back to Bagehot's insight about the functions of a constitution: that it is invoked as a symbol to command loyalty and obedience; and is a practical means of specifying the game of government. The symbolic importance of the constitution means that it will be given different meanings by different powerful groups in different circumstances, but these groups cannot simply invent the constitution to suit themselves. The constitution is best thought of a series of domains or territories. The boundaries of all these domains are often contested, but some are more contested than others (see Briefing 5.1, p. 75). We can express this by a simple distinction between the *core domains* of the constitution, and the *contested domains* of the constitution: between its heartland and its more disputed outer regions. And we will see that one of the fascinating features of the constitution is that the core and contested domains shift over time.

### The core domains of the constitution

Four important core domains of the British constitution are described here.

*Rule of law.* Governments can change the law; they can manipulate it since the meaning of law is often unclear; and they do even on some occasions

covertly break it. But they cannot openly breach the law. One technical but important expression of this is the legal doctrine of *ultra vires.* A literal translation from the Latin is 'beyond powers'; and one important practical meaning is that government decisions can be overturned in the courts if they are held not to be based on a capacity conferred by a law. Government ministers and their civil service advisers therefore spend a great deal of time trying to gauge the state of law and gauging how far it limits or empowers them. As we will see later in this text (see notably Chapters 22 and 23) the rising importance of judicial review, and of the Human Rights Act, means that they have to spend increasing amounts of time in making these calculations. The central value attached to the rule of law also explains why the Westminster Parliament remains central to the governing process. To introduce a policy innovation of any significance at all will require a change in law. That is why, as shown in Chapter 10, any government's legislative timetable in any particular year is at the heart of its governing activity.

Three developments have strengthened the significance of the rule of law as a central feature of the constitution: the long-term expansion in the role of government in social life has meant that ever wider areas of life are covered by the statute book; our membership of the European Union means that governments now have to ask not only whether what they are doing agrees with UK law, but whether it is consistent with the law of the European Union; and the value attached to the rule of law means that citizens and pressure groups now increasingly use the courts to try to establish that some policies are in breach of (or are required by) the law. (Many important changes in policy relating to employment protection, we will see later, have come about in this way.) We return to the rising importance of law in the constitution in describing the changing constitution later in this chapter.

*Procedural democracy.* This second 'core' domain of the constitution refers to what might be called the bare bones of democratic life: the requirement to hold elections within specified periods; to allow those registered on the electoral roll to vote; and to organize the process of electoral registration so as to make it simple for all adults to register. Since the passage of the Parliament Act in 1911 the life of a parliament has been limited to five years, in effect obliging the governing party to submit to a general election at least every fifth year. It is easy to see that the bare bones of procedural democracy are a powerful influence on the conduct of political life. They are so engrained that it occurs to virtually nobody to even imagine changing them. Imagine the reaction if a government proposed a new Representation of the People Act restricting the right to vote to university graduates.

Yet even the bare bones of procedural democracy can change shape. Under the great crisis of the Second World War the general election that was due in 1940 was postponed until 1945. And while governments do not dare attack head-on the principle of universal adult suffrage, it is qualified at the boundaries in numerous ways. For instance, most inmates of prisons and mental hospitals are disqualified from voting. Rules governing registration to vote – a precondition of actually voting – are framed so as to exclude, or make difficult, registration by many voters: for example, until recently registration had to be at a fixed address, so large numbers of the very poorest (the homeless) were disqualified. That these restrictions are not fixed by some clear theory of the democratic franchise is shown by recent changes relaxing some of the restrictions summarized here: remand prisoners can now vote; those who voluntarily enter a mental hospital may do so; and the homeless can qualify if they can give an address where correspondence can be collected.

*Accountability.* Try this simple thought experiment. Imagine a cabinet minister who declined to answer questions in Parliament, and who told journalists to mind their own business when they asked questions about his or her department. Such a figure is actually very hard to conceive in Britain, and were one to appear he or she would not last long in government. That expectation reflects a central constitutional value: that governments are obliged to be accountable at least in the bare sense of giving an account in public of what they are doing and why they are doing it. That requirement can be set aside in some circumstances (for example, on the grounds that an account would be contrary

to national security). Ministers can often decline to give an account by claiming some such exceptional dispensation, but they do not have to make that claim. They can also evade questioning, and indeed an important part of the skill of being a minister is fending off questions from journalists and political opponents while giving away as little as possible. But they cannot just tell inquirers to push off and mind their own business. The presumption of accountability, though its meaning and application are varied and contested, is a central constitutional value. One of the most famous modern examples of this occurred in 1997, when in a gruelling television interview the then Home Secretary refused to answer 14 times the same question from an interviewer. But the exchange was repeated so often, and threatened to show the Home Secretary in such an unfavourable light, that he felt obliged to offer an extended defence of his behaviour in another bruising interview a few days later (see Documenting Politics 5.2, p. 79)

*Liberal freedoms.* Liberal freedoms in the core domain of the constitution refer to the freedoms such as those of the press, of speech and assembly. We can see how central they are to constitutional understandings by again performing a simple thought experiment. Imagine turning on the radio news tomorrow morning to find that all but government-controlled papers had been closed; that any criticism of the government was outlawed; that no public meetings could be held without the permission of the Home Secretary. We would be in no doubt that major (and damaging) changes in the constitution had taken place.

This example also shows just how uncertain and contested even the 'heartland' of the constitution is, however. The sudden abolition of one or all of these liberal freedoms would be a major and damaging change to the constitution. Yet all these liberal freedoms are constantly breached in some particulars, and there is constant debate about just how widely they can be set (see Image 5.1, p. 80). Freedom of the press is not absolute: for instance, it is restricted by libel laws that are stricter than in many other democracies. Likewise freedom of speech is not absolute: it is not allowed, for instance, where its exercise would threaten public order, and making

**DOCUMENTING POLITICS 5.2**

## THE MODERN ADVERSARIAL INTERVIEW: JOHN HUMPHRYS INTERVIEWS MICHAEL HOWARD

HUMPHRYS: But what's intrigued some people is that when Jeremy Paxman asked you that very question on Tuesday night you declined to answer it. He asked you the question fourteen times and the interview has been replayed on various other forms since then and you wouldn't answer it now ...

HOWARD: I wanted to be scrupulously accurate in answering that question. I'd been thinking of lots of other things that day. I wanted to check the documents, I did not want there to be any question at all of my giving an answer that wasn't entirely true and accurate. The next day I checked the records, I gave the answer, I did not threaten to overrule Derek Lewis.

HUMPHRYS: But surely the only reason you could have had for wanting to check the documents, the minutes or whatever they were, was that you yourself weren't sure whether you had threatened to overrule him or not.

HOWARD: This was a meeting that took place two-and-a-half years ago and before answering a question to which I knew importance would be attached, I wanted to make absolutely sure that I got the right, honest and accurate answer and that's what I did.

HUMPHRYS: But there must have been some doubt in your mind therefore.

HOWARD: No, I just wanted to check absolutely that there was no question of my giving an answer that wasn't entirely accurate...

HUMPHRYS: So you had to check the minutes to make sure that you hadn't said something about which you were sure ...

➡ In May 1997 Michael Howard, then Home Secretary, was confronted in a famous interview by the BBC *Newsnight* interviewer, Jeremy Paxman. Paxman was interested in discovering whether the Home Secretary had given orders to the director of the Prison Service in a critical episode in the recent history of the Service – orders which would have exceeded his powers. Mr Howard initially declined to answer, and Mr Paxman repeated the question 14 times, each time failing to extract a direct answer. The widespread assumption that he was declining to answer because he had indeed exceeded his powers was what Mr Howard now tried to counter in a radio interview a few days later with an interviewer with an almost equal reputation for ferocity, John Humphrys. The extract (and the wider episode) shows how far the broadcasting interview has emerged as the main method of grilling government ministers.

*Source*: BBC *On The Record* interview, 1997

racist attacks is prohibited. Freedom of assembly is not absolute: meetings and marches that might provoke racial violence or otherwise pose a threat to public order are often banned. In Northern Ireland the 'right to march' is governed by an elaborate set of rules administered by a specially appointed 'parades commission'.

The domain of liberal freedoms is one of the key domains of the constitution, not because it is settled and stable, but for the reverse reason. It is a key area where disputes about the meaning of the constitution are conducted. Rival invocations of the meaning of what liberal freedoms are guaranteed by the constitution are one important means by which conflicting understandings of the constitution are expressed. The process returns us once again to Bagehot's insight about the importance of the constitution as a source of political loyalty and obedience: invoking the constitutional status of liberal freedoms is an important way in which advocates of particular meanings of these freedoms try to capture the magic of the constitution for their particular understandings.

## The contested domains of the constitution

The contested territories of the constitution are important and revealing. Part of the appeal of the constitution in Britain is that it has a 'magic' to which contesting groups can appeal to give legitimacy to their view of what the rules of the political game should be. The areas of contestation therefore reveal something about the nature of conflict and competition over how Britain should be ruled. Four important contested domains are discussed here.

*Territorial unity*. Britain is the 'United Kingdom' and this represents an important historical ambition: to unite the different territories of the islands under a single Crown and a single Parliament. Chapter 2, however, showed that this was only achieved by military conquest. In the twentieth century it was sundered by one great civil war followed by secession: the 'Irish War of Independence' led to the establishment of the 'Irish Free State' in 1922 following a Treaty of 1921. Dismantling the Empire also amounted to a break-up of territorial unity. When George VI was ceremonially crowned crowned King in May 1937, having succeeded his brother in the preceding year, he was also Emperor of India; when his daughter was crowned Elizabeth II in 1953 the title had disappeared because India had disappeared from the Empire into an independent republic. For nearly 40 years the dominion of Parliament and Crown in Northern Ireland has been contested by a Republican movement prepared to use acts of terrorism to separate the province from the United Kingdom. For a generation there have also been nationalist parties in both Wales and Scotland that have by peaceful means advocated separation from the United Kingdom. Chapter 11 will show that this has now resulted in a separate Parliament for Scotland with distinct powers, and an Assembly in Wales with lesser, but still significant, powers. The most influential modern definition of a state – that

**Image 5.1**
**The new politics of the Constitution: contesting identity cards**

Photo: Stefan Rousseau/PA/EMPICS

⮕ A major theme of this chapter is the new politics of the Constitution, as groups contest what was previously accepted without much debate. Contestation has been intensified by innovation on the side of government. Under David Blunkett as Home Secretary (2001–4) the government used the occasion of new terrorist threats to propose the introduction of identity cards for all – a radical innovation in Britain, though quite common in other European states. The photo encapsulates the 'civil liberties' tone of resistance to the proposal. At the end of 2004 Mr Blunkett, the object of so much criticism here, was swept from office in a scandal involving the procurement of a visa for the nanny of his rich American mistress; but the government remains committed to the introduction of identity cards. However, the Bill had to be abandoned in 2005 when Parliament was dissolved for the general election. With a much reduced majority, its chances of enactment are uncertain, without great concessions to opponents.

given by Max Weber, as discussed in Chapter 1 – pictured it as a system of rule over a physically identifiable territory. The geographical boundaries of rule are thus central to any account of a country's constitution. In the case of the United Kingdom these boundaries are subject to sustained dispute.

*Parliamentary supremacy*. The territorial unity of the United Kingdom and doctrines of parliamentary supremacy are connected, because the parliament in question is the Westminster Parliament.

The Westminster Parliament remains central to any understanding of the constitution: the rule of law remains a core part of the constitution and the Westminster Parliament is still a main source of the law. But this supremacy is now contested in two main ways. First, there is the constraining importance of 'super statutes': legal commitments that arise out of legislation originally passed in Parliament but that now constrain its ability to exercise supremacy. The legal obligations of European Union membership, as Chapter 6 shows, are a prime example of this: it has been estimated that 80 per cent of the rules that govern trade in the single market of the Union now originate in EU institutions, rather than in national parliaments such as Westminster. Since 1998 the establishment of separate assemblies in Wales and Scotland has further diminished Westminster supremacy especially, as we shall see later, in the case of Scotland. The boundaries of Westminster supremacy are now an even more contested domain of the constitution than the territorial boundaries of the United Kingdom itself.

However, the most serious challenges to parliamentary supremacy have not come from the conscious transfer of power to other institutions; they have come from the rise of rival forms of representation. The Westminster Parliament owes its authority to territorial representation: the 'bare bones' of democracy that were sketched above involve elections in territorially defined constituencies. But territory is not the only possible basis on which interests and ideas can be represented. An important alternative is sometimes called 'functional' representation. Groups claim legitimacy because they speak for members who perform functions in the community – as teachers, doctors, firefighters or accountants. Governments have to deal all the time with these functional groups, and a number of constitutional crises have arisen because the demands of functional and territorial representation could not be reconciled. That was true of some of the bitterest industrial disputes of the twentieth century: for instance, a 'general strike' called by all trade unions in 1926; and a strike by coalminers in 1973–4, in defiance of the government which led to widespread social chaos and, eventually, the

fall of the government itself. The balance between the supremacy of a territorially elected Parliament and groups claiming authority through functional representation, is one of the most unstable and contested domains of the constitution.

*Crown legitimacy.* When Bagehot published his famous work in 1867 he put the Crown at the centre of the constitution. It was the most important way the 'dignified' constitutional function was performed, and was therefore vital to supporting the system of rule (see Images 5.2 and 5.3). It was strengthened in the twentieth century by the invention of a 'Royal Family' with a carefully managed public image which presented that Family as simultaneously glamorously remote but very ordinary in its family preoccupations. The dignified role of the Royal Family probably reached its highest point in the Second World War. The King and Queen insisted on staying at their palace in London for the express purpose of being bombed by the Germans, thus sharing the dangers of normal Londoners. But in the last generation this dignified effect has worn away. Royal ceremonial at great public occasions is still commonplace, but a key device identified by Bagehot – the cultivation of an aura of magic and mystery – has disappeared. The troubles and foibles of royalty (both sexual and financial) are now a commonplace of media reporting. While polling evidence shows little sustained support for a republic it shows also that the public routinely 'grades' different members of the Royal Family according to their performance, usually awarding high marks to the Queen herself, and much lower marks to most of the rest. This grading of performance profoundly undermines the cultivation of a remote, magical mystique.

The Crown as pictured by Bagehot is therefore being pushed to the margins of the constitution, and is becoming decreasingly important in performing 'dignified' roles. At times of great national distress it is now common for Prime Ministers – most of whom have a gift for public communication – to play a consoling, dignified role. How far this marginalization continues depends on many factors, not least the intelligence with which the monarchy manages its public roles. It is possible to imagine a reinvention of the monarch's role in which the

**Images 5.2 and 5.3**
**The 'dignified' Constitution made flesh**

Image 5.2   Queen Victoria (Belfast)

Image 5.3   Queen Victoria (Manchester)

◗ Documenting Politics 5.1 quoted Bagehot on the monarchy as the key 'dignified' part of the Constitution. Queen Victoria – monarch when Bagehot wrote – was the personal incarnation of this dignified role. Statues of the Queen such as those pictured here can be found in numerous towns and cities. The two here, however, show how differently 'dignity' is revealed: 5.2 shows the Queen's pristine statue outside Belfast City Hall. Note the Union Jack flying above. Here the statue represents Protestant Union dominion in Ireland: see Chapter 11 for this history. Image 5.3 shows a similar statue in the centre of Manchester: but here, ignored, occasionally vandalized and usually covered with pigeon droppings.

Crown once again assumes an important place in the emotional life of the nation (for instance, by the development of something like the 'people's monarchies' so successful in parts of Scandinavia). Alternatively, it may simply become part of the celebrity world of the international *demi-monde*, like the royal family of Monaco, providing the same sort of tabloid entertainment as movie stars, footballers and contestants in reality television shows.

*Citizens not subjects.* Traditionally the British were subjects, not citizens: that is, they had impor-

tant legal protections such as those detailed above in our sketch of the rule of law. But these were not rights that they could claim against the authority of the state; rather, they were protections that they could claim by virtue of being subjects of the Crown. Protection was granted by the state, rather than being enforceable against the state. But the language of citizenship is now increasingly used to speak of rights in Britain. This is partly reflected in the rise of campaigning groups who simply do not accept the constitutional language of the subject, and assert that individuals should have rights against the state as citizens. They include groups campaigning to reform the constitution, such as Charter 88; and groups dedicated to the defence of what they conceive as civil liberties, such as Liberty. (See Briefing 5.1, p. 75). The passage of the Human Rights Act 1998 incorporates into law the provisions of an international charter, the European Charter of Human Rights. It thus has some of the features of what we above called a 'super' statute: it entrenches the rights of citizens against the state, and its language of 'rights' departs from the traditional language of concessions granted to subjects by the Crown.

We should not overstate the extent to which the language of 'subjection' is now contested by the language of 'citizenship'. The British government – in the name of the Crown – retains the power to curb these rights in emergency conditions. It has done this in respect of the detention of some groups of suspects without trial in the search for terrorists after the bombing of the World Trade Center in New York on 11 September 2001. But the very acrimony this has created reveals the shift in assumptions that is taking place. The idea that we were 'subjects' of the Crown was once a settled part of the constitution; but this is now contested territory because of the rise of a vocabulary that pictures us as 'citizens' with rights that we can assert against state authority.

## The sources of constitutional change and conflict

The British constitution has never been a stable settlement. The constitution performs Bagehot's 'dignified' function: whatever can convincingly be described as part of the constitution has a special legitimacy conferred on it. This is why it resembles a series of territories or domains over which conflicting groups compete. No domain is ever entirely settled, but some are more securely at the heart of the constitution than others. Obviously changes in what is at the heart of the constitution, and what pushed to the margins or even excluded, depends on the operation of many forces. Three are identified here, because they help reinforce an

important point; that there is a powerful connection between the constitution as narrowly understood and the wider political culture in Britain.

## The decline of deference

The British constitution was traditionally a deferential constitution. Deference has many shades of meaning, but the core meaning is straightforward; it refers to a willingness to obey without undue questioning. That willingness can arise from a number of sources: from a belief, for instance, that others have an innate superiority in the art of government; or from a belief that some social groups are by birth or training uniquely suited to government. This latter 'deference' was once an important part of the constitution. It explains, for example, why Bagehot set such store by the magic of monarchy. That was shorthand for a political culture in which the mass of the population accepted that social superiors in the aristocracy had a special entitlement to rule. Even when the aristocracy declined as an important source of political leadership in Britain – and that did not happen until the second half of the twentieth century – deference carried over into modern times in a special willingness to obey the authority figures of the state, such as the police. It also showed itself in a special willingness to 'defer' to key ideas; for instance, the notion that one should scrupulously obey laws and the values that underlay those laws. As Figure 5.1 shows, there is now convincing evidence that this deference is in decline.

Changes in cultural patterns such as deference are hard to document, partly because cultural patterns are complex and partly because we often lack systematic evidence that will allow us to compare the past and the present. But there does seem to be compelling evidence that deference is declining. Social deference has almost disappeared: aristocrats who seek elected office now usually find it expedient, indeed, to modify the evidence of their aristocratic origins, such as their accents. Survey evidence shows a long-term decline in a special willingness to obey authority: for instance, a rising willingness, especially among the young, to claim that they would openly resist laws that they felt to be

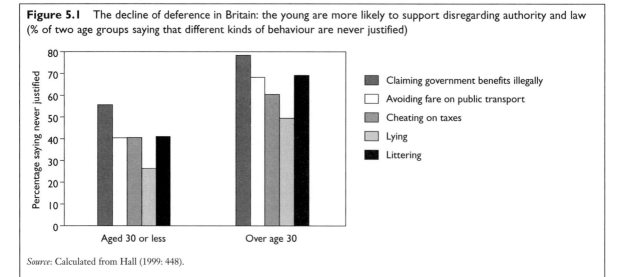

**Figure 5.1**    The decline of deference in Britain: the young are more likely to support disregarding authority and law (% of two age groups saying that different kinds of behaviour are never justified)

*Source*: Calculated from Hall (1999: 448).

➲ The political scientist, Peter Hall, combined responses to two large scale surveys to produce these figures, which relate to the 1980s and 1990s. They show a remarkably consistent pattern: older people are more consistently disapproving of both law-breaking and general anti-social behaviour than are young people. The inference is that this reflects a historical change: that the old are reflecting values from the past that are now, literally, dying out. But, bear two cautions in mind: there is the possibility that the young are simply more frank than the old, and that the differences do not always reflect real differences in behaviour; and the possibility that the difference is simply age-related, and that as people mature in years they adopt more socially responsible attitudes.

unjust. There is also some evidence from behaviour of a declining willingness to do something just because authority figures say so. In the 1980s a major reform of local government finance – the replacement of the rates on property by a tax levied on each individual – was destroyed by mass civil disobedience, especially in Scotland. The state has long prohibited consumption and sale of a wide range of narcotics, such as cannabis; but there is compelling evidence that this is disregarded by a large part of the population. Political demonstrations, from all ends of the political spectrum, now involve open use of civil disobedience: examples include opposition to construction projects, such as motorway or airport extensions; tax protests, such as protests against fuel taxes which virtually brought the country to a halt briefly in the autumn of 2000; and generalized campaigns such as those against the perceived threats of globalization.

The decline of deference is more, however, than a change in wider popular attitudes. There have been demonstrable long-term changes in the treatment of rulers in media reporting, and these too are signs of declining deference. This decline of deference is one important reason for the damage inflicted in recent years on a once key 'dignified' part of the constitution: the Royal Family. The Royal Family now routinely provides material for the scandal sheets of newspapers. Historical evidence suggests that present royalty are no odder in behaviour than previous generations of royals: no more given to marital infidelity, boorishness or drug use than the average royal in history. But in the past these were rarely reported. When King Edward VIII abdicated in 1936 to marry his mistress, the occasion was the first that country at large knew that he actually had a mistress. In the case of the present heir to the throne there has been intimate reporting of the Prince of Wales, his late wife and her lovers, and the Prince's own mistress.

## Declining trust

The decline of deference helps explain one of the most striking features of modern popular attitudes to politicians: the fact that politicians are among the least trusted of all groups in the community (see Figure 5.2). There is a connection between declining deference and low trust because willingness to defer partly arises from a high level of trust: if I have strong faith in your integrity and competence I will be more willing to do what you command without questioning. The evidence of low trust comes from surveys where representative samples of the population have been asked about their willingness to trust public authority figures such as educators, the police and politicians. This survey evidence of course only reveals what people tell opinion pollsters, but other evidence supports it. Although there is widespread participation in a range of political demonstrations and protests, there is declining enthusiasm to participate in more conventional politics: membership of political parties is in long term decline; we will examine these themes in detail in Chapters 13, 14 and 17.

Of course, taken by itself declining participation in official politics might easily be taken as a sign of satisfaction, arising from a feeling that government was run so well that one could let it run unhindered. But the evidence of surveys contradicts this complacent conclusion. In addition, the 1990s were an era of sleaze and scandal at the top of British politics. Two prominent public figures ended up in jail for perjury: one was a former cabinet minister and one a former Deputy Chairman of the Conservative Party (Jonathan Aitken and Jeffrey Archer). There were newspaper exposures of the willingness of backbench members of Parliament to 'plant' parliamentary questions to ministers in return for personal payments. A campaign by the Prime Minister, John Major, in the early 1990s to assert the importance of traditional Victorian values was destroyed by the revelation of numerous sexual indiscretions by leading members of his government and party. It later transpired that Mr Major had himself conducted a protracted illicit extra-marital affair with a fellow Conservative MP. In 1994 the same Prime Minister, John Major, was obliged by the volume of scandal to establish a special Committee on Standards in Public Life. This is still in existence over a decade later, and is still investigating standards across a wide range of public life; as we shall see next, it has made an

**Figure 5.2**  Don't trust me: I'm a politician (% expressing trust in different occupations)

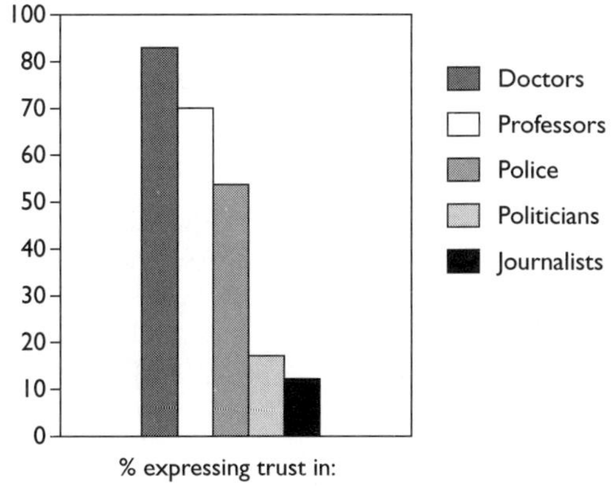

Legend: Doctors, Professors, Police, Politicians, Journalists

% expressing trust in:

*Source*: Calculated from *Politics Review* (2003: 2).

➲ The figure reports the proportion of a representative national sample who expressed trust in a variety of important groups in the community in 2002. Only journalists are less trusted than politicians – and, in the mind of the public, the two groups are often closely linked. Similar proportions are reported when people are asked about satisfaction with performance rather than trust: satisfaction with groups such as teachers, doctors and the police is high, but low with politicians.

important contribution to the rise of a more formally codified constitution.

## The rise of codification

What would you do if your trust in someone – an authority figure such as a priest or a lecturer – was badly damaged? If you were obliged to continue dealing with them a natural response would be to want to write down clearly what their obligations amounted to, and to check closely that they were meeting those obligations. In short, you would explicitly codify what had hitherto been only informally understood and probably never openly expressed. This describes an important change that is reshaping constitutional understandings in Britain. As we noted at the start of this chapter the British constitution was traditionally described as uncodified: more accurately, codification was piecemeal and fragmented, and many key parts of the constitution consisted of informal understandings.

# Briefing

## FROM CONVENTION TO CODIFICATION: THE RECOMMENDATIONS OF THE COMMITTEE ON STANDARDS IN PUBLIC LIFE

| Number and title of report | Summary of main recommendations |
|---|---|
| First Report: Standards in Public Life | All public bodies to draw up Codes of Conduct incorporating the Seven Principles of Public Life. |
| Second Report: Local Public Spending Bodies | • Set limits to terms of office of public appointments<br>• Develop independent complaints processes<br>• Establish codes for 'whistleblowers'. |
| Third Report: Standards of Conduct in Local Public Bodies | • Set new rules on declaration of interests by councillors<br>• Replace existing National Code with codes tailored to individual councils<br>• Create new framework for standards of discipline for councillors and officers. |
| Fourth Report: Standards of Conduct of non-departmental public bodies, NHS Trusts and Local Public Spending Bodies | More open and transparent appointment rules in accordance with the principles of the Committee's First Report and specific recommendations of its Second Report (above). |
| Fifth Report: Funding of Political Parties | • Clear rules for full disclosure of all donations<br>• Limit to total campaign spending in a general election<br>• Regulation of any organization or individual spending more than £25,000 in a general election campaign. |
| Sixth Report: Reinforcing Standards | The Report reviewed progress on implementing the recommendations of earlier reports, especially the First Report. |
| Seventh Report: Standards of Conduct in the House of Lords | • House to adopt a Code of Conduct<br>• Interests of peers to be declared and registered. |

*Source*: Information from where these reports can be accessed together with background briefing at www.public-standards.gov.uk

➲ As this summary of the existing seven reports shows, the Committee on Standards in Public Life has developed into a permanent feature of public life in Britain. Not all its recommendations have been accepted, but most have; and it is one of the most important sources of pressure to shift constitutional understandings from the realm of informal understandings to formal codification.

These 'conventions' are still important, but there is a growing tendency to codify understandings, mostly by the simple act of writing down what they mean. This may seem a trivial change, but it has momentous consequences. Once an understanding is written down it is much more difficult to keep it out of the public domain. And while words written down may often be ambiguous, they are less ambiguous than unwritten understandings; they therefore provide an openly available standard against which behaviour can be judged. The rising importance of codification reflects wider social and cultural changes: a growing tendency to codify all kinds of hitherto informal social relations.

**POLITICAL ISSUES**

### 5.1   CONSTITUTIONAL REFORM: NEW LABOUR'S BIG IDEA

Since the return of Labour in 1997 the pace of constitutional change has accelerated. Three radical innovations can be traced directly to New Labour: the virtual abolition of the hereditary element in the House of Lords, as part of an unfinished wider reconstruction of the composition of the Lords; the introduction of a new regime of human rights, notably in the Human Rights Act of 1998; and the creation of new devolved systems of government in Scotland, Wales and Northern Ireland. The years of the Blair Governments have also seen major changes in constitutional practice in fields as different as the regulation of political parties, the methods of making public appointments, and the regulation of the declaration of interests by public servants.

New Labour's constitutional reforms raise three big issues:

- Though irreversible, they are not necessarily stable. Devolution provides a key example. It was intended to stifle support for nationalism, notably in England and Wales, and it has indeed created tactical problems for nationalism in both countries (see Political Issues 14.1, p. 313). But Scottish Nationalism remains committed to a referendum on independence if it ever attains the position of governing party in the devolved system.
- Though radical, their democratic credentials are widely contested. This is particularly true in the case of the reformed House of Lords. The present unfinished business has largely removed the hereditary element (see Timeline 10.1, p. 209) and has left the House dominated by appointees of the leadership of the two Westminster parties, Labour and the Conservatives.
- The demand for constitutional reform, especially for more developed reform, is uncertain. In particular, the attempt to extend reforms to the English regions has aroused little popular enthusiasm (see Political Issues 12.1, p. 264).

In the case of the constitution, the rise of codification has some obvious, particular origins. One of the most important is the influence of the Committee on Standards in Public Life originally established in 1994. The Committee has not only developed a set of general standards of conduct in public life but has produced detailed recommendations covering some of the most important institutions of government: for more open rules governing appointment to public bodies; for rules regulating the relations between members of Parliament (MPs) and special interests; for rules governing the financing of political parties; and for rules governing standards of conduct in local government (see Briefing 5.2). Many of these recommendations are now embodied in written codes, and some are even embodied in laws. In later chapters – for example,

when we turn to political parties – we shall find widespread evidence of this growth in codification.

Law is the most developed form of codification. Laws are backed by the power of the state, and their breach attracts its coercive power. Governments that claim to be bound by the rule of law – as do governments in Britain – therefore have to frame laws carefully. Laws need to say as unambiguously as possible what obligations they impose, and on whom. Since they are backed by the state's coercive power – in the last analysis through police and courts – clear rules are needed: to show when coercion will be applied, how, and what safeguards citizens have against the improper use of that coercion. All these considerations make codification in law special: the rules are spelt out in an especially clear and elaborate way. Hence embodying constitutional

# DEBATING POLITICS

## 5.1    POLITICAL AUTHORITY IN BRITAIN: DEMOCRATIC CHANGE OR DECAY?

### Political authority is simply being subjected to more democratic scrutiny

- Unthinking deference to authority is in decline.
- The Committee on Standards in Public Life is obliging public bodies to obey clear rules and give clear accounts of their activities.
- Constitutional conventions are increasingly openly debated rather than being settled without public discussion.
- Constitutional 'lobby groups' such as Liberty are increasingly contesting the meaning of the constitution. Political authority in Britain is in decay

### Political authority in Britain is in decay

- Trust in politicians is lower than among almost any other group in the community.
- Readiness to act unlawfully and dishonestly is growing.
- The power of the ceremonial role of the monarchy is decaying.
- Media treatment of government figures is increasingly adversarial, treating the politician as a kind of permanent 'accused' in the dock.

understandings in law moves the constitution further away again from its traditional uncodified, informal understandings (see Briefing 5.2, p. 86). In recent years important laws have regulated key domains of the constitution, as the three following examples show.

- The Human Rights Act 1998, to which we have already referred, seeks to codify legally the relations between the state and the individual citizen.
- The Political Parties, Elections and Referendums Act of 2000 now legally codifies what was hitherto largely a matter of informal understanding: the roles of political parties, and especially the conditions under which they can raise finance. It has also established an agency to regulate these activities, in the form of the Electoral Commission.
- The legislation creating devolved government in Scotland and Wales, which we shall examine in Chapter 12, naturally codifies also the

relations between the different levels of government in the newly created multi-level system (see Political Issues 5.1).

### REVIEW

Four important themes have been stressed in this chapter.

1 The very diverse sources of the constitution in Britain;
2 The importance of the constitution's dual functions: the *dignified* and the *efficient*;
3 The continually contested nature of the constitution;
4 The gradual transformation of the constitution from a patchwork of informal understandings to something more explicitly and systematically codified.

## Further reading

This chapter is, in the widest sense, about the 'political culture' of the UK: about the understandings, popular and elite, which shape thinking and behaviour about the rule of the game. Any beginner to the study of Britain should read the great historic classic, Bagehot (1867/1963). Two modern 'classics' are Almond and Verba (1963 and 1980). The authoritative modern collection on constitutional theory and practice is Jowell and Oliver (2000); Brazier (1999) is the best single-author study on the constitutional foundations of political practice.

CHAPTER 6

# The European political system

## AIMS

The aims of this chapter are to introduce the wider political system of the European Union, a political system of which Britain is an important component part. The chapter:

❖ Summarizes the history of European integration, showing why it is so important in British politics

❖ Describes the main ways the European Union now permeates British politics

❖ Shows, conversely, how deeply embedded Britain is in European political institutions

❖ Describes the European Union as a legal creation, and explains why that is so important

❖ Summarizes how the 'Europeanization' of British politics has added key elements to the development of multi-level governance in Britain.

## Britain as a European political system

In a textbook on British politics why do we begin our account of the institutional structure of the system with a chapter on institutions outside Britain – the political institutions of the European Union? The answers not only justify the chapter: they tell us something very important about the system of government under which the British live.

The reasons for treating Europe in such an important way are threefold:

- *Impact of the Union on the British government.* A large amount of what government actually undertakes in Britain is done as a result of decisions taken by the institutions of the European Union. We would utterly fail to understand why and how government functions in Britain if we did not grasp this fact.
- *Resources.* A key issue in all government is: where do resources get allocated, and by whom? In British government resource allocation is increasingly a European matter: the British contribute large amounts annually to the budget of the Union; and they receive large amounts annually in subsidies and grants. The figure for 2002 can stand as typical of recent years: the United Kingdom contributed more than £6 billion gross, and over £2 billion net, to the Union's budget. (The gap exists because the gross figure simply measures all contributions; the net figure is the result of subtracting grants and subsidies.)
- *Impact on the wider political system.* Because the European Union is so important in decision making and in resource allocation, the British political system is increasingly organized along 'European' lines: government runs itself so as to try to act effectively in Europe; pressure groups organize themselves to exert pressure in Brussels; and parties increasingly argue about how best to organize Britain as a member of the European Union.

## European union since 1945

In 1945, most of Western Europe lay in ruins, and most of Eastern Europe – roughly, Europe east of the river Elbe – was under the control of a new communist military super-power, the Soviet Union. Two world wars (1914–18 and 1939–45) had been fought largely because of rivalry between three west European nations: Germany, Britain and France. The outcome not only produced the untold suffering of the conflict itself; such was the physical devastation and social dislocation that on several occasions after 1945 the people of Western Europe were on the verge of starvation.

These catastrophes eventually produced what we now call the European Union (EU). The origin of the movement for integration lay in the effort to solve the key problem in Europe that had led to the Great Wars: the inability of France and Germany to live in peace. The first important step was taken in 1951 with the signing of the Treaty of Paris, which founded the European Coal and Steel Community (ECSC), an organization designed to integrate the coal and steel industries of six countries into a single unified market: France, Germany, Italy and the three Benelux countries (Belgium, the Netherlands and Luxembourg). These industries were targeted for a first stage of integration because they were at that time the foundations of military and industrial power: integrated coal and steel industries would make it exceptionally difficult for any single nation to build a separate military capacity such as had led Germany to the aggressive military policies that had produced war in 1939.

In 1955 at Messina in Italy a meeting of the six countries that had joined the European Coal and Steel Community attempted, successfully, to repeat for their wider economies what had been achieved in coal and steel. This agreement led to the signing in 1957 of the Treaty of Rome, the founding Treaty of a new European Economic Community (colloquially called 'the Common Market'). The Treaty became effective at the start of 1958, and is the founding treaty of what we now know as the European Union.

The Messina meeting and the Treaty that it produced are momentous historical events in the history of Europe – easily the most momentous for Western Europe in the second half of the twentieth century. They were in part the product of a vision of a united Europe which was held by a number of public servants and politicians: the French civil servant, Jean Monnet, the French politician, Robert Schuman, and the German politician, Konrad Adenauer (see People in Politics 6.1).

If there was a grand vision of what a united Europe would become, however, the first version of

## People in politics

### 6.1   THREE WHO SHAPED EUROPEAN INTEGRATION

Cartoons: Shaun Steele

**Konrad Adenauer** (1876–1967) was a German statesman. He was deprived of all political office by the Nazis in 1933. He helped found the Christian Democratic Party after German defeat in 1945, and was Chancellor (Prime Minister) of the Federal Republic of Germany, 1949–63, and simultaneously Foreign Minister, 1951–55. Adenauer's determination to stabilize a new German democracy by binding Germany into a new united Europe was the key element in German support for European unification.

**Jean Monnet** (1888–1979) was a French public servant. He held numerous public offices in the years between the First and Second World Wars, and lived in exile when France was occupied by the Nazis, 1940–45. The Monnet Plan, 1946, created the foundations for French economic revival. He made the blueprint for the European Coal and Steel Community (and was its President 1952–55), the forerunner of what became the European Union. The 'Monnet method' – to use economic integration as a foundation for political integration – has been the key to the development of the European Union.

**Robert Schuman** (1886–1963) was a French statesman. His life and history graphically illustrate the tortured history of early twentieth-century Europe. He was educated mostly at German universities, but made his career in French public life. Briefly Prime Minister (1947–8) his greatest impact was as French foreign minister, 1948–52, when he gave his name to the plan that created the European Coal and Steel Community. He was President of the European Parliament 1958–60.

➲ Three key figures in the founding period of what became the European Union. They shared the experience of economic depression and war in Europe in the first half of the twentieth century and conceived European integration as a way of ensuring that the experience was not repeated. Notice that none was British.

the Treaty of Rome seems, nearly 50 years later, quite modest in its ambitions, at least by the standards of what has now been achieved. The modesty of these practical ambitions is shown in three ways.

- *Modest formal powers.* The formal powers of the institutions of the Community were very limited. The most important sign of this limitation was a voting rule designed to ensure that the sovereign independence of no member country could be overruled: all important decisions required unanimity among the national members.
- *Modest resources.* The resources of the Common Market were few. Virtually the only sizable pot of money which it controlled was a fund designed to provide subsidies for agriculture, itself the product of the most important single economic bargain at the heart of the Common Market: the creation of a Common Market promised to open up the markets of other member nations to the industrial goods of the biggest, most efficient industrial economy in Europe, that of Germany. In return Germany contributed a disproportionate amount to a common budget that was largely used to subsidize small farmers in the other countries, especially in France.
- *Modest economic aims.* The commonest colloquial title for the new creation has already been used: the 'Common Market'. In fact this is a misnomer, because it implies that the only ambition was to create a free trade area – an area where goods and services would be traded without the imposition of any national barriers. But from the beginning the aim was to create something more: a *customs union*, which means an area not only where there is internal free trade but also a common set of external tariffs imposed on all goods and services imported into the new union.

From the present vantage point of European Union these are modest aims, though in 1957 they were startlingly radical – far too radical, as we saw in Chapter 2, for British governments of the time. How was this limited attempt to create a modest amount of European integration between six countries transformed into the present European Union? Four important factors were at work.

## Economic success

From the very beginning the various efforts at economic integration (both the ECSC and the Common Market) were accompanied by staggering economic success. The economies ruined by two world wars and the great depression of the 1930s were transformed by years of high economic growth in the 1950s and 1960s. For instance, between 1950 and 1973 (the year when Britain joined the EEC) British economic growth was 3 per cent per annum; the corresponding German figure was exactly twice that, and the French figure was 5.1 per cent per annum. How far this economic transformation could be attributed to economic integration can be debated, but what mattered was what the association did to belief in the whole European enterprize. It gave confidence to those with a vision of building a *single Europe*, and created wide public support for their continuing efforts.

## Enlargement

As we saw in Chapter 2 one of the most important results of this economic success was its effect on Britain. She had stood aside from the original Messina negotiations, and most of her initial responses to the Common Market consisted of efforts to create alternatives – for example, a European Free Trade Area – that, if successful, would have turned the integration movement into something much more limited than that envisioned by the Common Market's founders. The success of the economies of the Common Market, coupled with the continuing relative failure of the British economy, destroyed this effort to create an alternative. It led to the decade of attempts – described above in Chapter 2 – which culminated, finally, in British accession in 1973. Britain joined at the same time as Ireland and Denmark, which until then had been closely tied to Britain because she was an important market for their agricultural products. In the 1980s three Mediterranean countries joined after they had reconstructed their political systems along democratic lines following periods of dictatorship: Greece in 1981 and Spain and Portugal in 1986. A fourth

**Image 6.1**
**The growth of the European Union**

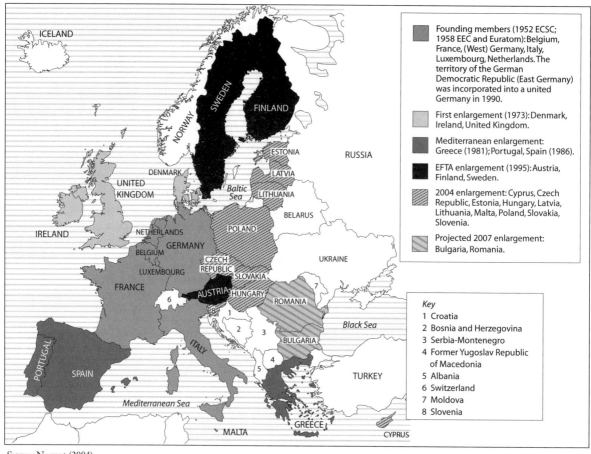

Founding members (1952 ECSC; 1958 EEC and Euratom): Belgium, France, (West) Germany, Italy, Luxembourg, Netherlands. The territory of the German Democratic Republic (East Germany) was incorporated into a united Germany in 1990.

First enlargement (1973): Denmark, Ireland, United Kingdom.

Mediterranean enlargement: Greece (1981); Portugal, Spain (1986).

EFTA enlargement (1995): Austria, Finland, Sweden.

2004 enlargement: Cyprus, Czech Republic, Estonia, Hungary, Latvia, Lithuania, Malta, Poland, Slovakia, Slovenia.

Projected 2007 enlargement: Bulgaria, Romania.

Key
1 Croatia
2 Bosnia and Herzegovina
3 Serbia-Montenegro
4 Former Yugoslav Republic of Macedonia
5 Albania
6 Switzerland
7 Moldova
8 Slovenia

*Source*: Nugent (2004).

➲ The map shows the growth of the EU over a period spanning more than 50 years: the very first integration involved the coal and steel industries of six west European states in 1952. This period of more than half-a-century has seen both geographical widening and institutional 'deepening': the expansion of the original limited coverage of a couple of industries to the wholesale government of the economies of the member states. The biggest single enlargement measured by increase in members was in 2004 – the fifth enlargement identified here – and is a direct consequence of the collapse of the Soviet Empire in Eastern Europe after 1989.

wave in 1995 brought three more members, Austria, Finland and Sweden, making the total 15 in all. The most dramatic enlargement occurred in May 2004 when ten new members joined: these were mostly states that had until the end of the 1980s been ruled by Communist dictatorships under the control of the Soviet Union. (For more explanation see the section on 'Crisis' below, and also Image 6.1).

## Policy innovation

For much of the 1970s and 1980s the European Union barely seemed to develop, and the economies of the member states struggled with a succession of economic problems. The most important policy innovation breaking away from this stagnation was the programme to complete the Single Market that was formally launched by a treaty implemented in legislation passed by all member states (the Single European Act, or SEA) in 1986. The Single European Act marked the moment when Europe decisively turned from the limited aims of the original Treaty of Rome – creating a customs union – to something much more active: building a single European economy where the movement of goods, services and labour would be as free as within the former national economies (see Timeline 6.1). Building this economy would not be possible without extensive political intervention by the institutions of the European Union to ensure that economic conditions across Europe were regulated to give equality of competitive conditions across the whole Union. In other words, the commitment to completing the Single Market also meant a commitment to a great expansion in the powers of the institutions of Europe: it meant creating not just a single European economy but a unified system of economic government. The Treaty of Maastricht, signed in 1992 (though ratified in Britain only the following year after bitter debate) was a further striking stage of policy innovation. It marked four key advances:

● It made provision for the creation of single European currency, an ambition realized, we shall see below, with the introduction of the Euro in 1999. The Euro is now the single currency for 12 members of the Union, and the new 2004 entrants are expected to adopt it. Only Britain, Denmark and Sweden have explicitly rejected membership of the Eurozone.
● It strengthened Europe's capacities in foreign, defence and social policy.
● It formally introduced the coinage of the European Union.
● It conferred on the people of the member states the common status of citizens of the new Union.

## Crisis

As we have seen, the original moves towards integration were the product of the great and ruinous historical crises of the first half of the twentieth century. The spread in the range and influence of the European Union was greatly helped after the 1980s by another great crisis, the collapse of the Communist systems of Eastern Europe, and the dissolution of their controlling power, the Soviet Union, after 1989. It created a gap in the international power system that the European Union has begun to fill by expanding its diplomatic and even its military capacities. It directly led to the accession of one new member, Finland, which had previously been greatly limited in its foreign commitments by the domination of its immediate neighbour, the Soviet Union. It led to applications for membership from a large number of former Soviet bloc countries. In May 2004, as we noted above, ten new states joined, mostly from the former Soviet bloc. The enlargement added 75 million new citizens to the EU and necessitated, as we shall see, important changes in both institutions and policies.

## Europe in Britain

### The scope of EU power and influence in Britain

The influence of Britain's membership of the European Union permeates numerous aspects of British government, and indeed of British life. The most important influences are fivefold:

● In the markets for goods and services
● In the market for labour
● In regional and environmental policy
● In foreign economic policy
● In foreign diplomacy and defence.

The *market for goods and services* is the first and most important area. Historically the Union above all has had an economic face. Membership involved both negative surrender of power by British government and positive acquisition of power by the institutions of the Union. The most obvious example is that, even on entry to the old EEC in 1973, British governments surrendered any right to impose import duties or other restrictions on the flow of goods from other members of the Union, just as Britain acquired corresponding rights in other member states. These areas of 'negative integration', as they are sometimes called, have been joined now by 'positive' integration – the positive use of

## TIMELINE 6.1    LANDMARKS IN EUROPEAN INTEGRATION

**1951**
The Six sign the Treaty establishing the European Coal and Steel Community (ECSC) in Paris.

**1955**
The foreign ministers of the Six, meeting in Messina, decide to create a customs union covering their economies.

**1957**
The Treaty establishing the European Economic Community is signed in Rome.

**1962**
A Common Agricultural Policy is introduced.

**1963**
General de Gaulle announces at a press conference that France will veto the United Kingdom's accession to the Community.

**1970**
Negotiations open with four prospective member states (Denmark, Ireland, Norway and the United Kingdom).

**1973**
First enlargement: Denmark, Ireland and the United Kingdom join the Community (Norway withdraws following a referendum).

**1979**
The first direct elections to the (then) 410-seat European Parliament are held.

**1981**
Second enlargement: Greece becomes member.

**1985**
Jacques Delors is appointed President of the Commission. At the Luxembourg European Council the Ten agree to amend the Treaty of Rome and to revitalize the process of European integration by drawing up a 'Single European Act'.

**1986**
Third enlargement: Portugal and Spain join. The Single European Act is signed in Luxembourg and The Hague.

**1991**
Collapse of Soviet Union clears way for eventual entry into the Union of many former Soviet controlled states (see 2004, below).

**1992**
The Treaty on European Union is signed in Maastricht.

**1993**
The Maastricht Treaty comes into force.

**1995**
Fourth enlargement: Austria, Finland and Sweden join the Union.

**1997**
'Consolidated' Treaty unifying all the preceding Treaties into a single document signed in Amsterdam.

**1998**
Negotiations begin for accession of range of former Soviet controlled states.

**1999**
Eleven countries of the European Union enter the third phase of European Monetary Union (EMU) and adopt the Euro as a currency in foreign exchange.

**2002**
Euro coins and notes come into circulation, and the Euro becomes the sole currency of the Eurozone.

**2004**
Accession of 10 new member states from central and Eastern Europe.

➲ There are two important lessons here. The first is obvious even from a casual glance: the movement to European integration is now deeply rooted, lasting more than half a century. It is thus already more enduring than the catastrophic period of world wars and economic depression that preceded it in Europe in the twentieth century. The second is that the progress of integration comes in irregular spurts, often produced by great external changes: for example, the developments since the early 1990s are inseparable from the collapse of the old Soviet-ruled bloc of countries after 1989.

*Sources*: Butler and Butler (2000); Cook and Stevenson (2000).

the power of the EU institutions to create equal competitive conditions right across the Union. This move to positive integration has grown stronger since the movement to complete a Single Market began in the 1980s. An important example of this is the power of the European Commission, the Union's most important institution, directly to regulate competition between firms across the Union: the Commission has direct power to prosecute and fine firms that break EU competition regulations.

The *market for labour* provides examples of both the positive and negative power of the Union. Negatively, no government (or any other institution) can prohibit any citizen from any member state of the Union entering Britain to work and, conversely, Britons have the same entitlement across the whole Union. (There are some transitional restrictions on free movement from the ten new members who joined in May 2004 but these will eventually disappear.) Positively, a wide range of working conditions are now the subject of the Union's jurisdiction: they include health and safety at work, aspects of collective bargaining, and even working hours.

The examples of *regional and environmental policies* are striking instances of how the Union is now deeply woven into the fabric of domestic policy making. Europe is a major distributor of funds for the development of economically depressed regions. In environmental policy it is the single most important source of regulation: everything from the purity of the water that we drink to the purity of the air that we breathe is subject to EU regulations.

The *foreign economic policy* of Britain is now substantially conducted through the European Union. For instance, because Europe is a single trading bloc with common rules governing trade and investment, agreements governing such areas with other trading nations have to be settled in common by the Union. This means that in international negotiations, such as those conducted within the framework of the WTO, the Union is the key negotiator rather than individual separate members.

*Foreign diplomacy and defence* cannot be sealed off from economic policy, so in foreign affairs generally the Union's importance is growing. Any great international crisis that affects the interests of a member state such as Britain is likely to draw in the Union in some role. From the 1990s (through the Treaties of Maastricht, 1992, and Amsterdam, 1997) this participation has been increasingly regularized: Maastricht provided for a common foreign and security policy (though carefully drawn to ensure that any state could have a veto); while Amsterdam provided for the appointment of the Union's own High Representative for foreign and security policy.

The Union thus penetrates deeply into the policy world in Britain. What are the main instruments of this penetration?

## The means of EU power and influence

The means of EU power and influence in Britain can be divided into the formal and the informal.

The most important formal instruments are threefold: treaties; legislation; and court rulings. In combination, they both specify areas where British decision makers are *obliged* to take action and other areas where they are *prohibited* from action.

*Treaties* (such as those of Rome and Maastricht discussed above) are the great legal compacts that bind the Union together (Documenting Politics 6.1). The legal obligations of the Treaties explain, for instance, why British governments now do not have the right to impose tariffs on goods coming into Britain from elsewhere in the Union. Conversely, the Treaties explain why any British goods can likewise be traded freely across the Union and why any British citizens can settle in any other member state. The chief institution 'policing' breaches of Treaty law by either national governments or institutions such as firms is the Commission: there have, for example, been several cases of British firms being fined for breaches of the Union's competition policy.

*Directives* are by far the most important instruments by which the Union 'legislates' on particular policies. For instance, the whole Single Market programme depended heavily on Directives that were designed to ensure parity of competitive conditions in the different industries and sectors across the nations of the Union. The formal

## DOCUMENTING POLITICS 6.1

### THE PREAMBLE TO THE TREATY OF ROME 1957

HIS MAJESTY THE KING OF THE BELGIANS, THE PRESIDENT OF THE FEDERAL REPUBLIC OF GERMANY, THE PRESIDENT OF THE FRENCH REPUBLIC, THE PRESIDENT OF THE ITALIAN REPUBLIC, HER ROYAL HIGHNESS THE GRAND DUCHESS OF LUXEMBOURG, HER MAJESTY THE QUEEN OF THE NETHERLANDS,

DETERMINED to lay the foundations of an ever closer union among the peoples of Europe,

RESOLVED to ensure the economic and social progress of their countries by common action to eliminate the barriers which divide Europe,

AFFIRMING as the essential objective of their efforts the constant improvements of the living and working conditions of their peoples,

RECOGNIZING that the removal of existing obstacles calls for concerted action in order to guarantee steady expansion, balanced trade and fair competition,

ANXIOUS to strengthen the unity of their economies and to ensure their harmonious development by reducing the differences existing between the various regions and the backwardness of the less favoured regions,

DESIRING to contribute, by means of a common commercial policy, to the progressive abolition of restrictions on international trade,

INTENDING to confirm the solidarity which binds Europe and the overseas countries and desiring to ensure the development of their prosperity, in accordance with the principles of the Charter of the United Nations,

RESOLVED by thus pooling their resources to preserve and strengthen peace and liberty, and calling upon the other peoples of Europe who share their ideal to join in their efforts,

HAVE DECIDED to create a EUROPEAN COMMUNITY.

⮕ There were actually two Rome Treaties. The lesser known created a joint authority for the management of nuclear power. This box reproduces the preamble – the aspirations – of the Treaty that created what is now the European Union.

position is that Directives are the result of joint decision by the Council of Ministers and the European Parliament (EP: for details of this see below). The reality is that they emerge from a complicated process of negotiation in which interest groups and the Commission bargain hard over drafts, and this is often followed by more bargaining in the Council of Ministers, in the European Parliament and between the EP and the Council. The best way to think of Directives is as a form of what is sometimes called 'framework legislation': a Directive will apply across the whole Union, but will typically only prescribe certain goals to be achieved, not the exact means or timing. Directives are 'translated' into law at national level, and this process of translation allows a large area of discretion to national states. This discretion even extends to the promptness with which Directives are translated and enforced, there being large variations between different members.

*Court rulings* are a vital source of law precisely because of the discretion just referred to. No legislation ever covers all eventualities. Courts in substance make law by interpreting the meaning of legislation in particular circumstances. Later in the chapter we examine in detail the workings in these respects of the most important EU legal institutions, notably the European Court of Justice (ECJ).

To these formal sources, we can add three important *informal* means of influence.

*The reputation of Commissioners.* Members of the Commission, undoubtedly one of the most important institutions in the European Union, have a high profile in many arguments about policy in Britain. It is increasingly common for Commissioners to give interviews to the British media, and directly to take part in discussions within British Government. (This is described in more detail below.) The President of the Commission, the leading Commissioner, has since the Presidency of Jacques Delors (1985–95) become a significant figure in arguments about Britain's place in the Union. The significance of this public reputation is reinforced by the fact that until 2004 there were always two British Commissioners, usually highly visible politicians who have not hesitated to intervene in 'European' debates within the United Kingdom.

*The allocation of Union resources.* The Union has become a significant distributor of resources within Britain, and these offer high-profile opportunities to both influence policy priorities and also raise the profile of European institutions. A wide range of programmes funnels resources into public investment infrastructure and into higher education. For instance, under the rules of regional development funding certain areas are designated as eligible for substantial funding, especially for building projects; in higher education, the Union both funds extensive student exchange schemes and even a range of academic posts, all designed to encourage the study of Europe in Britain and to make Britons more European minded. (Image 6.2 illustrates how assiduous is the Union in publicising its contribution to public investment projects within Britain.)

*Propaganda and public relations.* The Commission maintains its own office of representation in London, and three other outposts in Cardiff, Edinburgh and Belfast. The office is unashamedly a means of propaganda and public relations. It pumps out a ceaseless stream of advocacy of the European 'idea', highly partial accounts of recent developments, and constant attempts to demolish what it describes as the myths and mistakes of those in Britain who are sceptical of the EU or the European idea in general. It thus contributes to the symbolic presence of the Union in Britain. Just how common is that symbolic presence is illustrated again by Image 6.3. It is the very ordinariness of these images, the way they are encountered so often in everyday life, that so impressively testifies to the Union's success in propaganda and public relations.

## The European Union in the core executive

By far the most important presence of the European Union in British politics is felt in the *core executive*, the area of government covering the most senior ministers and civil servants gathered at the apex of the big departments of state in London and in the machinery organized around the Cabinet Office and the Prime Minister in Downing Street. (The concept of the core executive, and its organization, is described more fully in Chapter 7.) The presence of the EU stretches right across the institutions of

**Images 6.2 and 6.3**
**Europe in everyday life: the daily symbolic presence of the EU in Britain**

Image 6.2    EU project funding

Image 6.3    Car number plate

⮑ These two everyday images show how pervasive a symbolic presence the EU is now in Britain. The first image illustrates how the EU uses its financial resources to expand its symbolic presence. It is a noticeboard on a public spending project of a kind that can be seen all over Britain: it advertises the fact that the project is part funded from the Union budget, and uses the occasion once again to publicize the EU symbols, notably its flag. The project is part of a huge injection of EU funding to infrastructure projects in Liverpool, 2001–6. The Union is very attentive to these symbols: grants for European funding include detailed instructions on the design of these boards, including instructions on the relative size of EU symbols. The second image is of a car number plate carrying the EU flag, one of millions of similar plates on Britain's roads. Flags are a vital symbolic image for a state, and the spread of the EU flag has been extraordinarily rapid: it was adopted only in 1986.

government, though naturally the magnitude of that presence varies by institution, and has also changed over time. In summary, the most 'Europe-engaged' departments are: the Treasury; the Department of Trade and Industry (DTI); the Department of Environment, Food and Rural Affairs (DEFRA); the Foreign and Commonwealth Office; and, increasingly since the 1990s, the Home Office.

The Union's impact on the core executive is displayed in four particularly important ways.

*Organization of the core executive.* Within British government most issues are handled by a 'lead' department: for example, on anything to do with immigration policy the Home Office would be the natural 'lead'. But very few issues of any importance arising from EU membership are confined in their implications to a single department. Most, for instance, have some spending implications, so the Treasury is very commonly an interested party. Coordinating the cross-departmental management of issues is a particularly important function of the European Secretariat of the Cabinet Office.

*Conflict and bargaining in the core executive.* In the higher reaches of the core executive much of the bargaining and struggle that takes place over policy is about what stances to take up in bargaining within the European Union itself. The most dramatic example is provided by the case of membership of the European Monetary Union (EMU), the project to create a single currency already described above. Under Major (1990–7) and Blair (1997–) the question of whether, or when, Britain should join the Euro has been the biggest single subject of debate about economic policy inside the core executive.

*The daily business of political leaders.* The daily business of the most important political leaders is now as concerned with Europe as with domestic institutions; indeed, in the daily round of business the two are inextricably woven together. A large part of the job of being Prime Minister, Chancellor, Foreign Secretary or Secretary of State for Trade and Industry is engaging in the diplomacy of negotiation with European colleagues, either opposite numbers in other member states or officials in Brussels.

*Processing policy in the core executive.* Just managing the daily business of government is now closely shaped by the fact of EU membership. We saw above that a major concern of the core executive – especially in the European Secretariat of the Cabinet Office – is coordinating European policy across government. But in individual departments specialized groups are also charged with examining the European dimensions of policy. Documenting Politics 6.2 illustrates just how detailed and pervasive the guidance to 'think European' now is.

## The European Union in the wider political system

We should already have a sense by now of how the European Union permeates the political system, through such means as the media presence of prominent officials of the Union, and the use of money both to influence policy and to raise the public profile of the Union. But the Union's presence in the wider political system is more pervasive than even this would suggest. Three signs of that presence are particularly noticeable.

---

**DOCUMENTING POLITICS 6.2**

### HOW MEMBERSHIP OF THE EUROPEAN UNION SHAPES EVERY ASPECT OF POLICY MAKING IN THE CORE EXECUTIVE: THE GUIDANCE GIVEN TO POLICY MAKERS

'There are very few areas of policy making that no longer have a European dimension of any kind. From areas of exclusive Community competence such as international trade to those where the Community involvement is more one of promotion of common interests and information sharing such as culture or sport, we need to be aware of how our decisions fit in to this context. The questions the policy maker must address early on include:

- What, if anything, is happening elsewhere in the EU – in other Member States or at the EU level?
- Experience of others in addressing similar problems can be very useful. Plus, if there is already an initiative at EU level, the UK should seek to be an influential part of it.
- If there is nothing happening at the EU level, should we seek concerted action at that level? Action at EU level may be more effective and can help to ensure that the UK competes on a level playing field.
- Maintenance of the Single Market is a key UK objective.
- Is the suggested policy compatible with European law? Any proposed policy must be in line with European law. As it has supremacy over national law (i.e. overrules contradictory national law), failure to ensure this could lead to legal challenge, the policy being overturned.
- If the policy is within the context of an EU level initiative, then compatibility of that initiative should also be checked.
- Is the suggested policy compatible with the UK's European policy? The UK's aim is to be a positive and pro-active member of the EU. The UK is committed to transposing legislation promptly and implementing it fully.'

➲ This is guidance from the European Secretariat of the Cabinet Office to all senior officials involved in making policy across the full range of government. It shows how far membership of the Union now demands that everyone concerned with formulating and implementing policy must 'think European' from the very start.

*Source*: Extracted from original at www.cabinet-office.gov.uk.

- *In British political argument.* Since the 1950s the question of what Britain's attitude to the movement for an integrated Europe should be has provided a major point of division and debate. It has periodically divided the two main governing parties, Conservative and Labour, and it has always divided those parties internally, just as it has internally divided most important interests in Britain – industry, finance and the unions. Since the original decision in the early 1960s to apply for membership of what was then the Common Market, right through to the present divisions over Britain's participation in a single European currency, the question of how to respond to the challenges of European integration has provided a major line of division in British politics.

- *In government beyond Whitehall.* As we shall see in later chapters on the devolved institutions established in Scotland and Wales by the Blair government in 1999, Europe is potentially very important in the new devolved system. The administration of EU Structural Funds – which help finance large public works projects – are in the hands of the newly devolved institutions. For local government, too, the Union is important: it is a potential source of funds for local development projects, and this has encouraged both active individual lobbying in Brussels and cooperation with other local governments in other member states.

- *In the resolution of political problems.* The resources and (sometimes) the prestige of the European Union on occasion play an important part in attempts to resolve difficult domestic problems. In the case of the 'Good Friday' Agreement that attempted in 1998 to resolve the Northern Ireland problem, for instance, an important incentive to the parties to settle was the promise held out of significant sums of EU money to help rebuild the province's economy. (For the significance of the Good Friday Agreement, see Chapter 11.) The photograph of a building project in Image 6.2 is another illustration: behind the signboard of EU presence in Liverpool is a commitment by the Union to spend over £800 million of EU 'structural funds'

investing in the rundown infrastructure of Merseyside, an area with a long history of industrial decline.

In summary, we can say that the European Union is far from being just an important external influence on British politics; since the country's original accession at the start of 1973 it has become incorporated into the workings of the political system itself. At the same time, the traffic has not been all one way: a large amount of what goes on in British government and politics is now designed to influence what happens in the rest of the European Union. This is the theme of the next section.

## Britain in Europe: Britain in the Brussels political system and in the European Parliament

### Britain in the European Commission

Perhaps the single most important institution of the European Union is the European Commission. The Commission has three main functions:

- It is the most important institutional initiator of policy proposals for the Union: for instance, much of the important preparatory work on the original proposals that led to the widening of the Single European Market from the middle of the 1980s came from within the Commission.
- It is the most important means by which the terms of the Treaties governing the Union are adhered to: for instance, it scrutinizes all subsidies paid by national governments to ensure that they do not infringe the Union's competition rules.
- The Commission as a whole is the Union's 'civil service': it manages Union policies and negotiates international trade and cooperation agreements. For instance, the Commission leads negotiations on international trade rules with the WTO.

These functions explain why, if we went to Commission headquarters in Brussels, we would soon come across numerous instances of British political presence. But even these functions, impressive though they look, only hint at why national, (including British) presence is so important in the life of the Commission. Perhaps the single most important feature of the European Union is that it in effect operates an indirect system of government. In other words, having taken a decision it relies heavily on individual national institutions to implement that decision. In practice things are even more complex: the making of policy, and its implementation, cannot be separated into watertight compartments. The result is that, as far as British government is concerned, relations with the Commission consist of a virtually continuous dialogue and negotiation, at many different levels and at all stages of the policy process. The responsibilities extend across the whole range of government; there is no government department that does not spend a large amount of time consulting and negotiating with the Commission in Brussels (see Briefing 6.1).

The mode of appointing the Commission also increases the presence of national governments such as that of Britain in Brussels. About 10 per cent of all Commission staff are UK nationals, and until the last enlargement two Commissioners came from the UK. (From 2004 this was reduced to one.) Although the appointment of Commissioners as a group – and of the President of the Commission – has to command the support of the European Parliament, in effect the British Government can presently nominate the British Commissioner. Although there are powerful expectations that Commissioners will not act in their own national interests in managing their 'portfolio', nevertheless the effective power of nomination gives an important piece of patronage; there has been a tendency for this patronage to be shared between the two main political parties. A still more important lever of national influence over the Commission comes in the nomination of the President of the Commission, its leading figure and one who can therefore, with sufficient skill and force of personality, deeply influence the direction of the European Union. The French President, Jacques Delors (1985–95), is acknowledged to have played a big part in reviving the whole integration movement in the 1980s, for example. Formally, the President is nominated by

the European Council (see below); in practice, the name is the result of horse-trading between member states. It is impossible for Britain, or any other member, to impose a particular President. Until the Treaty of Nice it was possible to veto a candidate, and indeed Britain did so in one case where a likely President was thought to be too enthusiastic for further integration. New voting rules introduced in Nice in 2003 mean that selection of the President is now done through qualified majority voting (QMV); but the post is so sensitive that in practice strenuous efforts are made to ensure the emergence of a compromise candidate acceptable to all.

The British government is therefore an important player in all aspects of the life of the Commission, from the significant initial choices about selecting Commissioners to the most detailed negotiations about the making of policies. It is an even more direct participant in the Council of Ministers.

## Britain in the Council of Ministers

The 'Council', despite being a singular noun, is actually a set of institutions: whenever the ministers from member states with responsibility for a particular domain assemble (for instance, all finance ministers) they constitute a Council of Ministers. There are now nine specified Council domains, and thus nine separately constituted Councils. Naturally there are therefore numerous meetings of the Council, covering the different policy domains, in the course of a year. In addition, the formally distinct title of 'European Council' is reserved for the meetings of heads of government, the 'summits' that take place four times a year. Formally the Council makes decisions about policy based on proposals from the Commission; in practice, the issues considered by meetings of the Council of Ministers come from a wide range of sources and, in respect of policy proposals, will be the result of a large amount of toing and froing with the Commission.

Britain makes its voice heard in the Council usually in one of four ways.

# Briefing

## THE STRUCTURE OF THE COMMISSION OF THE EUROPEAN UNION

*Policies*
- Agriculture and Rural Development
- Competition
- Economic and Financial Affairs
- Education and Culture
- Employment, Social Affairs and Equal Opportunities
- Enterprize and Industry
- Environment
- Fisheries and Maritime Affairs
- Health and Consumer Protection
- Information Society
- Internal Market and Services
- Joint Research Centre
- Justice, Freedom and Security
- Regional Policy
- Research
- Taxation and Customs Union
- Transport and Energy

*External relations*
- Development
- Enlargement
- EuropeAid – Cooperation Office
- External Relations
- Humanitarian Aid Office – ECHO
- Trade

*General services*
- European Anti-Fraud Office
- Eurostat
- Press and Communication
- Publications Office
- Secretariat General

*Internal services*
- Budget
- Group of Policy Advisers
- Informatics
- Infrastructure and Logistics
- Internal Audit Service
- Interpretation
- Legal Service
- Personnel and Administration
- Translation

➲ This box conveys a picture of the Commission as a complex and comprehensive bureaucracy. The impression of complexity is accurate. Not only does the Commission cover a huge range of policy fields, but it has had up to now many of the marks of a 'spoils' system: that is, in appointing officials it has had to bear in mind the need to share out posts between different national members. As a result it also reflects the very different national administrative traditions of the Union's many members. This helps explain why it has become a by-word in Britain for bureaucratic impenetrability. But it is far from huge. Its total staff is 17,000, including all routine support staff; it has only 5,500 administrators. This imposes a particular style of doing business on the Commission: in formulating policy it relies heavily on specialized advisory committees, which are often dominated by experts and special interests; and in implementing policy it virtually relies totally on national-level institutions.

*The threat of veto.* A range of policy areas – principally to do with common foreign and security policy (CGSP) and cooperation on justice and home affairs (JHA) – are subject to a unanimity rule. Since a policy cannot be agreed without the assent of all members, the British Minister attending, like any other minister, can veto any policy not to her liking. In practice this veto is less useful than at first appears, for a number of reasons. The range of poli-cies settled by QMV has tended to widen over time. But even when a veto is formally available, it must be used, or threatened, with subtlety. The Union is a *community*, and a member state that vetoed constantly would be viewed as an obstructive member of that community – something sustainable in the short, but not the long, term. More importantly, Britain, like any other member state, has policies that she both wants to promote and kill. But where a unanimity rule applies, Britain must ensure that another member state does not kill the policies she favours. The natural way to do this is to horse-trade: to agree not to veto a policy desired by another member state in return for a similar promise concerning policies that are in British interests. In practice, therefore, the 'veto' converts into an opportunity to influence policy by bargaining and compromise with other members of the Council of Ministers.

*Bargaining in QMV.* Some of the policy areas most important to the historical development of the Union (for example agriculture, transport, energy, environment) are largely decided by QMV, with countries assigned different weights in the vote. As we have noted, majority voting of this kind is becoming increasingly important, and is a natural consequence of the expansion in the number of members. A unanimity rule when there only six founding members, or even the nine created by the accessions of 1973, could still allow policies to be made; but with 25 members, the threat that one single state could veto a decision obviously carries the danger of not being able to make policies at all. QMV is 'qualified' in an attempt to recognize the fact that member states vary greatly in size, power and wealth: members are allocated different voting weights, rather than being each given a single vote, as would happen under 'simple' majority voting. QMV is also 'qualified' in a second sense. In simple majority voting 50 per cent plus one of votes carries the day. But the threshold for a majority in the Council has, after the 2004 enlargement, been set in many cases at over 70 per cent. The present formula in the wake of the 2004 enlargement is summarized in Briefing 6.2. It is the result of hard bargaining, and is in turn intended to promote bargaining and compromise. The important consequence for the United Kingdom is that she must form coalitions consisting of more than 50 per cent of the votes to carry the day. Indeed the practical working of the Union creates even more pressure to compromise. Up to now only about 20 per cent of decisions in any one-year have been decided by a qualified majority vote. A commoner practice has been to try to bargain until a point is reached where there is unanimity, and for a very good reason: members

# Briefing 6.2

## THE UNITED KINGDOM AND THE TACTICS OF QUALIFIED MAJORITY VOTING IN THE COUNCIL OF MINISTERS AFTER ENLARGEMENT (FROM NOVEMBER 2004)

| | |
|---|---|
| Total votes in the Council | 321 |
| Votes required for a qualified majority | 232 (72.3%) |
| Number of votes allocated to United Kingdom | 29 (9%) |

➲ The simple arithmetic shows why the UK – like every other member of the Union – must build coalitions to influence decisions. Despite belonging to the group of members with the largest proportional allocation (alongside France, Germany, Italy, Poland and Spain), the UK needs lots of allies to be in a winning coalition. The procedures also create other hurdles to success: some proposals require the support of two-thirds of the individual national members of the Union, and some require referendum support from 62 per cent of the population of the Union. As we will see in Chapter 10, British governments are used to ruling by simple majorities in the Westminster Parliament; the European Union demands a very different, more consensual approach to decision making.

that persistently lost majority votes would soon become disillusioned with the Union.

*Summits in the European Council.* The 'summits' of heads of government held four times a year as the 'European Council' give member states particularly important opportunities to bargain with each other, both formally in meetings and, perhaps even more important, informally. But the summits are only the tip of an iceberg. The British Prime Minister is engaged in a constant round of negotiations – sometimes face to face, sometimes by telephone or e-mail – with other heads of government in the Union.

*The Presidency.* The Presidency (chair) of the European Council rotates between all members for six-monthly periods. Britain's periodic occupancy of the Presidency provides an opportunity, as it does for the other member states, both to play the lead in the Union's diplomacy with the rest of the world and to promote British policy priorities in a particularly visible way.

This summary of the opportunities for influence offered by the Council of Ministers contains a particularly important lesson. British influence rests less on the exercise of particular powers – such as the power of veto – and more on the ability of ministers and their advisers to build coalitions with other member states, and to bargain with member states that have different views and policy interests. This means that exercising influence in the Union is not something that just happens in the periodic meetings of the Council; it is a continuous process of negotiation that is meshed with the everyday business of government inside Britain. It also means that the growing importance of the Union in British government has now added a new talent to the requirements of a successful minister within the United Kingdom: the ability successfully to bargain within EU institutions.

## The British government in Brussels

One important means by which Britain monitors the whole EU political system, and continually channels its views through that system, is via the Office of Permanent Representation in Brussels which is Britain's 'embassy' to the EU, so to speak. The Office is rather like a 'mini-Whitehall' in Brussels, with desk officers overseeing all the major policy and departmental areas. Officials are formally seconded to the Foreign and Commonwealth Office (FCO) during their Brussels tour of duty, but are usually drawn from across the span of Whitehall departments. The role of the Office nicely illustrates how far the gap between governing in Brussels and governing in Whitehall is now quite unclear. The Office puts in a large amount of effort in Brussels functioning as might an Embassy abroad: making as wide a range of contacts as possible in order to put the UK government's point of view. But a large proportion of time is also spent in

Whitehall, serving on the interdepartmental committees that manage the processing of EU business in Whitehall, and liaising more informally with officials. Thus we see again how the processes in Brussels and in London are tightly stitched together.

## Britain in the European Parliament

The EP was first directly elected in 1979; now all its 732 members from the 25 member countries are subject to re-election every five years. (The United Kingdom is allocated 78 of these seats: see Table 6.1.) The shift to direct election, coupled with the periodic reconstruction of the Union's powers in successive Treaties, has gradually augmented the functions of the Parliament, notably in three areas: legislation; budgetary decision making; and supervision of the institutions of the Union. Legislation is formally the subject of co-decision with the Council of Ministers: that is, the Commission is the formal originator of legislative proposals, which to succeed must be adopted by both the Council of Ministers and the Parliament. In practice, the Commission and the Council are the two dominant actors; but this does not make the Parliament insignificant. As we shall see later in Chapters 10 and 11, the domestic elected assemblies in the United Kingdom, such as the Westminster House of Commons or the Scottish and Welsh Assemblies, have little real control over the shaping of legislation. Measured by their standards, the European Parliament is probably a more effective amending body. One reason for this is that the resources of European Members of Parliament (MEPs) – 'back office' support such as research assistants – are more impressive than those until very recently available to, for instance, members of the Westminster Parliament. Another reason is that, while there are party groupings of members of the European Parliament, they are more fluid and less internally disciplined than in domestic assemblies, giving individual MEPs more freedom to scrutinize and criticize.

The significance of the EP is generally undervalued within the United Kingdom, probably for two reasons. The public visibility of the European Parliament in Britain is reduced because it is rare

**Table 6.1**  National allocations of seats in the European Parliament after the 2004 enlargement: examples

|  | Number of seats | Percentage of seats |
|---|---|---|
| Germany | 99 | 13.52 |
| United Kingdom | 78 | 10.66 |
| Poland | 54 | 7.38 |
| Netherlands | 27 | 3.69 |
| Ireland | 13 | 1.78 |

➲ Allocation of seats is *roughly* proportional to population: Germany has the largest allocation; the smallest goes to Malta (0.68 per cent, five seats). The United Kingdom has the second largest allocation, equal to Italy and France, behind Germany, but national allocations are only part of the picture. It is natural to expect members from the same nations to share some common positions and interests. However, party groups crossing national frontiers, encompassing tendencies as various as conservatism, socialism and environmentalism, are well organized in the Parliament.

simultaneously to occupy seats in the Westminster and the European Parliaments. Thus the most ambitious British politicians continue to prefer the latter, which then guarantees it a higher domestic salience. In addition, the basis of election to the Parliament – as we shall see when we consider electoral systems in a later chapter – has created very large constituencies, and little incentive for MEPs to connect directly with voters. This is reflected, as we shall also see in Chapter 17, in the persistently lower British 'turnout' in EP elections.

These undoubtedly interesting features of the European Parliament should not, however, obscure its importance. Measured by the standards of influence we would apply to domestic elected assemblies, it emerges as a significant institution.

## Britain in the European Union lobbying system

Any system of government that takes vital decisions – whether these involve distributing resources, or exercising power and authority – affects interests in society, and prompts those interests to organize so

as to influence government. That is the simplest explanation for the existence of *lobbying groups* – groups that organize so as to influence the outcome of a decision. 'Lobbying' is an archaic image for an activity central to all modern government. The original 'lobby' was that of the House of Commons where people with special interests accosted members of parliament (MPs) to try to influence laws. Now it is shorthand for the pervasive presence of numerous special interests in the governing process.

Groups end up in the governing process in different ways. Some 'spontaneously' emerge in society – out of businesses, churches, leisure groups, and a myriad of other areas. Others are actually engineered into existence by governing institutions, which often find it immensely helpful to be able to work out, and even to implement, policy through such groups.

Both these effects can be seen in the case of the European Union, and both shape the presence of British 'lobbies' there. (In Chapter 9 we shall describe these patterns in more detail in 'setting' the Europeanization of interest representation into the wider system of interest group organization.)

*Adaptation by pre-existing groups.* When Britain became a member of the EEC in 1973 the country already had a large, and well-organized, lobbying system that was focused mainly on trying to shape the decisions of government in London. These groups included the familiar interests in society: those organized in professions, in trade unions, in numerous associations representing different sections of business, as well as a huge diversity of important groups representing every conceivable inclination and view. As the range and penetration of the European Union into Britain increased, something unsurprising happened: this pre-existing world of groups increasingly organized itself to supplement its activities within Britain itself with participation in the lobbying system that now surrounds decision making in the EU institutions. No significant British lobby group now lacks some representation in Brussels, principally aimed at influencing the Commission. The largest and best funded have their own permanent offices; others use the services of the increasingly large industry of professional lobbyists that operates in Brussels. Neither are they confined to Brussels: the EP is also a useful supplementary arena for lobbying and, as we shall see below, the European Court of Justice is also an important focus of argument and pressure. A good example is provided by agriculture. One of the best-organized domestic interest groups is the National Farmers' Union (NFU), with over 200 full-time staff in its London headquarters. In cooperation with separate farming organizations from Scotland and Ulster it also maintains a Brussels office (the Brussels Office for Agriculture). But the NFU is also a leading member of the Committee of Agricultural Organizations in the European Union (COPA), a Union-wide grouping of all the important national farming interest groups.

*Groups created within Britain to exploit EU opportunities.* The effect of the European Union just described, although important, is the most conventional and obvious: membership of the Union obliged the pre-existing groups to adapt their lobbying tactics to reflect the creation of this new level of government. A second effect is more profound: many groups in Britain (and, for that matter, in other member states) have formed solely because of the country's membership of the European Union. One of the most obvious examples is provided by the rise of the EU, since the 1980s, as a major player in regional development policy, through a succession of programmes designed to channel aid to poorer regions of the Union. But EU resources never come spontaneously; they have to be won competitively, usually by making an elaborate case and typically backed up with co-funding from other sources. Effective organization, both in putting together bids and in ensuring that those bids are presented to decision makers in the most favourable way, is one of the keys to success. Across Europe, regional and local governments, intent on managing economic development, have organized so as to secure this funding more effectively. Organizing is encouraged by the very structure of the EU grant-making process, because it is premised on the assumption that development projects will be partnerships, both between different public bodies and between public and private sector institutions. This process produces some novel attempts to organize a mix of public and private lobbying. Since 2000, for example, there has been a lobbying office in Brussels run jointly by the North West Development Agency (an official public body) and the North West Regional Assembly (an

---

## DOCUMENTING POLITICS 6.3

## THE LANGUAGE OF EUROPEAN POLICY MAKING: EXTRACT FROM A DIRECTIVE ON THE LEGAL PROTECTION OF DESIGNS

'Whereas it is unnecessary to undertake a full-scale approximation of the design laws of the Member States, and it will be sufficient if approximation is limited to those national provisions of law which most directly affect the functioning of the internal market; whereas provisions on sanctions, remedies and enforcement should be left to national law; whereas the objectives of this limited approximation cannot be achieved by the Member States acting alone.'

➲ Protection of copyright in designs is vital in any market and this Directive is concerned with ensuring this in the new Single Market. Notice how the Directive, the single most important instrument of policy making in the Union, tries to balance two different considerations: common action ('limited approximation cannot be achieved by the Member States acting alone') and delegation to member states ('provisions on sanctions, remedies and enforcement should be left to national law'). Notice, too, that while the language is that of the legal draftsman, it is perfectly straightforward, contradicting the common British picture of 'EU language' as impenetrable. The source for the full original can be found most easily in Nugent (2002: 250).

unofficial body) designed to lobby for EU funds for the North West of England.

The world of lobbying in Europe is one of the prime examples of the key theme of this chapter: that the European Union must not be considered simply as an important external influence on British politics. That image is inadequate because it misleadingly separates the Union from Britain; in practice, British and European politics are now entwined in a single system.

## The European Union as a legal creation: courts, laws and British politics

It is necessary to deal in separate detail with the legal dimension to the EU both because this is of profound and growing importance for Britain, and because it adds a new dimension to British politics. As we saw in Chapter 5, Britain famously has not had a codified constitution. One result has been that – by contrast with countries in possession of a single, written constitutional document – it has been impossible for citizens in Britain to appeal to courts against actions of government on the grounds that they violated some constitutionally entrenched rights (though of course actions of government could be overthrown on other grounds, such as that existing law did not sanction the exercise of authority).

The European Union represents a very different conception of the exercise of state authority. It is the product of successive Treaties, a series of self-conscious 'contracts' negotiated by members at various moments (such as the Treaty of Rome, and the Treaty of Accession that brought in Britain and others in 1973). These Treaties attempt to lay out in an explicit form how the important institutions of the union (such as the Commission and the Council) will be constituted, and they also attempt to lay out the principles governing the exercise of authority by these institutions. They thus amount to something close to a written constitution for the Union, attempting to specify, among other things, the extent of the Union's jurisdiction over its member states and over the citizens of those states.

(At the time of writing, indeed, an attempt is being made to consolidate everything into a single constitutional document.)

All written constitutions are subject to dispute in their interpretation, and the fundamental purpose of the ECJ is to adjudicate in any cases of uncertainty about the scope of Union jurisdiction. In this sense, it can be considered analogous to other constitutional courts, such as the Supreme Court of the United States. And, like the United States Supreme Court, the ECJ has emerged as a very important centre for the government of the European Union. The Court, though of vital importance because it is the final 'referee' in any disputed view of the EU's powers, is only the more public face of this judicial process. More quantitatively important still is the Court of First Instance. As the title implies it is the first resort of most cases that go to the level of the Union's judicial institutions; the Court of Justice itself will only usually be invoked when the continuing dispute concerns a point of law rather than the substance of a case.

### The Court: composition and significance

The European Court of Justice consists of 25 members, one from each member state, nominated by member governments for renewable terms of six years. A President of the Court is elected from among the 25 judges. The issues dealt with by the Court, though they can have a momentous bearing on the other institutions of the Union and on the lives of citizens in all member states, usually involve complex arguments on points of law, and are therefore mostly conducted through written submissions and responses to those submissions, rather than through the sort of oral argument which is usual in British courts.

The significance of the ECJ for Britain lies in three important effects of its judgments.

*Effects on the wider integration process.* Important decisions of the Court, even when not made with direct reference to Britain, have had a profound effect because they have shaped the whole nature of the process of European integration. Perhaps the greatest example is provided by the so-called *Cassis*

# Briefing

## THE INS AND OUTS OF EU MEMBERSHIP FOR BRITAIN

*Britain into the EU*

- Power: examples include the use of the British veto and British voting power in the Council of Ministers
- People: examples include the widespread presence of Britons in key official positions in the Union, such as British Commissioners
- Money: examples include the British annual contribution to the Union's budget
- Symbols: examples include the flying of the Union Jack across the Union as one of the flags of Union member states.

*The EU into Britain*

- Power: examples include judgments of the European Court of Justice that are binding on British governments
- People: examples include the intervention in British debates of prominent officials of the Union, such as Commissioners
- Money: examples include EU support for public investment projects from Development funds
- Symbols: examples include the widespread display in numerous settings of the Union's flag (see Image 6.3).

➲ This simple overview highlights only the most important components at work in EU/British relations, but it emphasizes two features that have recurred throughout the text of this chapter. First, there is no one simple factor at work in the relationship: the diversity of components show that simple images of 'the power of Brussels' or the 'sovereignty of the UK' miss the point, which is that many different resources are being employed. Second, it shows that there are very complicated exchanges in these relationships: for instance, the EU is often trading money, in the form of support for public investment, for visibility, of the kind illustrated in Image 6.2 of this chapter.

*de Dijon* judgment of 1979. It shows graphically how abstruse and technical Court judgments can have great historical effects. Cassis de Dijon is a liqueur produced in France and the Court ruled that efforts to prevent its sale in other member states were unlawful. The principle behind the Court's decision was one of mutual recognition: that a product which met national standards in its own home state was entitled to circulate throughout the Union. The principle applies widely beyond the comparatively trivial original case, since it establishes an important principle on which much economic integration now proceeds. Applied generally, it means that a good need conform only to the standards in its own country of origins (concerning, in this instance, liquor production and marketing); member states must then mutually recognize each other's regulatory standards, thus allowing goods licensed in one country free circulation throughout the Union. Integration can thus happen without establishing centrally decided, single standards for the whole

Union. The range of the Cassis de Dijon effect shows the subtlety of the connection between Court judgments and the integration process. The principle of mutual recognition is not applied universally and mechanically. For instance, where mutual recognition raises issues of the safety of goods, or the competence of services, it can apply only when minimum standards have been negotiated to apply in all member states of the Union. This explains why, for instance, the entitlement of doctors qualified in one member country to practise across the Union depends on the negotiation of minimum training standards. But this very process of negotiation – which is often largely determined by non-state bodies such as professional associations – is itself an important influence in stimulating the creation of Union-wide networks of groups and institutions.

*Critical judgements directly affecting Britain.* As the Cassis de Dijon judgment shows, the decisions of the Court do not have to directly concern the

**POLITICAL ISSUES**

## 6.1   BRITAIN AND THE EURO

The 'Eurozone' presently unites 12 members of the European Union under a single currency, the Euro. Since 2002 the Euro has totally replaced the separate national currencies of those countries. The United Kingdom has so far declined to join the zone. In office before 1997, a deeply divided Conservative government had adopted a 'wait and see' policy on the prospect of Euro membership. In Opposition the party moved virtually to a root and branch opposition to membership, though a large minority of leading figures from the 1990s, such as Michael Heseltine and Kenneth Clarke, remained in favour of joining. The Labour government agreed a set of 'tests' which would have to be met before joining; the tests are formally economic, but are so general that in practice their interpretation is a political judgement. They arose out of tensions between the Prime Minister, Tony Blair, and his Chancellor, Gordon Brown: the Treasury has responsibility for deciding whether the tests are met, thus giving the Chancellor control over the government's decision. Labour has also committed to a referendum on the question of joining before a final decision is made, but the prospect of this has gradually receded into the distance. The Prime Minister, who is instinctively favourable to deeper involvement in the European Union, has been boxed in by more than his Chancellor. He has also feared a tabloid press which is virtually unanimously hostile to replacement of sterling by the Euro; and has faced strong adverse public opinion which has consistently polled against adoption of the new currency.

The case of the Euro highlights a number of key issues:

■ A powerful tension, both personal and built into the nature of institutions, between the Prime Minister and Chancellor, for control over big decisions of foreign economic policy
■ Serious questions of economic strategy: notably, whether the unusually light regulation in the British economy could be maintained as a member of the Eurozone
■ The enduring scepticism about not only the Euro but the whole idea of the European Union among the electorate at large
■ The great power of the tabloid press in the minds of politicians, shaping their fear of adopting positions to which the tabloids are hostile.

United Kingdom to have a profound effect within Britain. But the Court has also in a number of important cases handed down judgments that have obliged governments in Britain to change both policy and legislation, since under the 1992 Treaty of Union governments are obliged to observe ECJ judgments. Judgments that have obliged changes in equal opportunities legislation (for instance, concerning equal treatment of men and women as far as pay and pensions are concerned) have so far been the most important for the United kingdom.

*Effects on the form of British political debates.* Perhaps the most important influence of the ECJ involves what can be called 'anticipated reaction'. Knowing that the Court has made judgments in the past, and can make judgments in the future, has influenced the whole nature of arguments about policy in Britain. The *threat* to take an issue to the ECJ is in itself a resource that advocates of a policy now have at their disposal, since this forces government to calculate whether or not it can win. If opponents of a group calculate that they might lose, this is in itself an incentive to compromise, since a loss

## DEBATING POLITICS

### 6.1    THE EU: WEAKENING OR STRENGTHENING BRITISH DEMOCRACY?

| Weakening British democracy: | Strengthening British democracy: |
|---|---|
| ■ Membership transfers power from elected politicians in Westminster to an unelected Commission in Brussels<br>■ Brussels policy making is dominated by powerful special interests<br>■ The elected European Parliament draws low turnouts in Britain, and has huge constituencies that make it difficult for MEPs to connect to voters<br>■ The process of making policy in the Union is unclear and complex: lack of clarity results in deals done behind closed doors; complexity means that the normal citizen, as distinct from the policy professional, usually cannot make sense of what is going on. | ■ Membership of a Union where power ultimately rests on Treaties gives powerful new legal safeguards to citizens against government<br>■ The Council of Ministers is the key institution where elected ministers from across Europe are obliged to bargain and compromise<br>■ The Commission's financial and personnel weaknesses oblige it to consult widely with affected interests before making policy proposals<br>■ 'Indirect' government means that the Commission delegates most responsibility for policy implementation to the national level, thereby strengthening, rather than weakening, many British institutions. |

at the ECJ is a definitive defeat – not to mention the cost and embarrassment of a reversal to the British government by a 'foreign' body. Thus, for the first time in history appeal to a 'Supreme Court' has itself become integral to the tactics used by the contending parties in policy making. This also stretches to the drafting of legislation. The fact that a whole range of British law is now subject to review by what is in effect a constitutional court to determine its conformity with Treaty obligations has influenced the whole law-writing process within Britain. Look back, for example, at Documenting Politics 6.2 (p. 101) to see how the guidance given to civil servants emphasizes how all decisions about policy now have to be made in the light of Britain's obligations as an EU member.

## The 'Europeanization' of British politics

The most important theme of this chapter is that British politics is, after several decades of member-

ship of the European Union, now thoroughly Europeanized. This chapter is placed at the head of our examination of specifically British institutions to emphasize this point; we have to look, in the succeeding chapters, at all the important institutions through European eyes. A summary account of what Europeanization means can be fairly brief: Europeanization is a *process* rather than a final product. In other words, it refers to sets of changes that are coming over Britain, changes that are still in progress. These changes can be considered under three headings.

### Economic Europeanization

This is the most easily measurable change. Since the 1970s the British economy has become inextricably intertwined with the economies of the other member states of the Union. One simple measure of that is trade: nearly 60 per cent of UK exports now go to another member economy of the European Union. A less tangible measure is that the rules (legal and otherwise) governing the conduct of economic life are becoming standardized across Europe: they include everything from 'big' issues (for instance, about the regulation of competition or recognition of trade unions) to the most detailed (the packaging of products).

## Europeanization of the process of government

This has been the main focus of this chapter, and will re-emerge in the chapters that follow. It refers to two linked processes: the growing extent to which the business of government *within* Britain is carried out by reference to the European Union; and the growing extent to which the activities of British government involve participating in the business of governing the European Union (see Debating Politics 6.1).

## Europeanization of the political system

This refers to the wider interpenetration of the political system with the European Union: the way political debate turns on the sort of tactics and strategies that should be adopted in Britain's position as a member of the Union; the way representing interests has acquired a European dimension; and the way the Union is itself present within Britain, allocating resources and intervening in the terms of the political argument.

### REVIEW

Three themes have dominated this chapter:

1  A limited attempt to create an area of free trade between six economies in the 1950s has been now been transformed into a hugely ambitious enterprize to create a common system of government across Europe;

2  Britain was a late and reluctant participant in this transformation;

3  Despite this late start, the 'Europeanization' of British government and politics is now profound: the EU, far from being only an important external influence, is now woven into the everyday fabric of British government.

## Further reading

The most important overview of the government of the European Union is Nugent (2002). The most important historical study of the development of the Union is Milward (1992). George (1998), though now dated, is the standard history of the relations between Britain and the Union. An exceptionally important chapter-length study of the Europeanization of the system of government is Bulmer and Burch (2000), while Bulmer *et al.* (2002) explore the impact of Europe on the devolved system.

# CHAPTER 7

# The core executive in the Westminster system

## CONTENTS

## AIMS

The aims of the chapter are:

❖ To outline the most important current general framework for understanding government at the centre: the 'core executive'

❖ To describe the institutions of the core executive

❖ To describe the main functions performed by these institutions, and the way these functions are carried out

❖ To describe the tensions within the core executive

❖ To return the discussion of the core executive to key debates about British government, notably about the location of power.

## Understanding British government: the traditional pyramid

The traditional theory of British government pictures it as a kind of pyramid. At the top of the pyramid are the elected members of the executive: ministers drawn from Parliament, mostly elected to the House of Commons. And at the very tip of this pyramid are the ministers who head the most prestigious departments, and the Prime Minister as the political head of the government. This group of elected politicians takes the most important decisions. It receives advice from lower down the pyramid, especially from permanent civil servants, who also put the decisions of ministers into effect (see Images 7.1 and 7.2).

This pyramid model has much to recommend it.

- *It highlights the importance of democratic control.* It is important for our theories of British democracy, since the theory of British democracy says that the most important decisions in government should be taken by those selected by the people in competitive elections.
- *It highlights struggles for power.* This is a feature which is undoubtedly central to the everyday workings of the top of central government: a constant struggle for power and status between different departments and the political heads of those different departments.
- *It highlights the debate about prime ministerial power.* It has been the starting point for one of the most frequently argued theories of power at the centre in Britain: the theory that we are shifting to a system of prime ministerial government, where the single figure of the Prime Minister is held increasingly to dominate British government.

However, this pyramid has come to be seen as inadequate, for a number of reasons.

- *Unrealistic division of labour in government.* The division of labour it suggests in policy making (between taking decisions, taking advice and putting decisions into effect) is unrealistic. At the top of government, where decisions are usually very complex and involve subtle judgement, no simple division exists between politics and administration.
- *Unrealistic concept of a hierarchy of departments.* The notion that departments are organized in a clear hierarchy is likewise unrealistic. The departmental structure of British government is much more like a series of tribes – the Treasury tribe, the Home Office tribe – who have their own recognized territory, their own distinctive cultures and their own distinctive policies. The tribes are, of course, not equal (the Treasury tribe is more powerful and prestigious than the tribe at the Department for Culture, Media and Sport) but much of what goes on in government involves bargaining between the tribes over their territory and their policies.
- *Unrealistic picture of prime ministerial power.* In focusing on the Prime Minister the pyramid model both overstates and understates the importance of the individual who holds that office. It overstates because prime ministerial government is impossible, in the sense that the government machine at the centre is too complex, and too much power is lodged with the departmental 'tribes', for any single individual tightly to control government. But it understates it because, in focusing on an *individual*, it risks missing what we will see to be a very important source of power: the growing machinery of decision making and policy coordination that surrounds the Prime Minister in Downing Street.

## The idea of the core executive

These points explain why the 'pyramid' notion of government, with a few powerful individuals at the top controlling the important decisions, has been increasingly replaced by the notion of a 'core executive'. Four key features mark out this notion.

### It breaks down the policy/administration division

It identifies institutions and individuals that are at the heart of decision making in government. As a

**Images 7.1 and 7.2**
**The dignified and efficient working faces of the core executive**

Image 7.1    10 Downing Street

Image 7.2    Entrance to the Cabinet Office

➲ In Chapter 5 we encountered Walter Bagehot's distinction between the dignified and the efficient – between the ceremonial and the working faces of government. Here they are embodied in two images. The front face of 10 Downing Street shows the importance of image and presentation in government. It presents a public face of government as venerable (the house was originally a gentleman's residence of the eighteenth century) and as serene and elegant (the main door has ten coats of varnish to give it a beautiful sheen). A posse of press photographers wait outside to snap the comings and goings of the famous. Round the corner is a very different entrance, to the Cabinet Office. On the day I took the photograph it was even covered in tarpaulin for building work. Here the movers and shakers of the core executive quietly slip in and out. There are no photographers to record their comings and goings.

result, it downplays the traditional distinction between ministers and civil servants, and offers a more realistic picture of the way decisions are made at the heart of government.

### It stresses interdependence and coordination

It focuses on a feature that is a fact of life in modern government: policy is not divided into separate 'boxes' labelled 'the economic', 'the educational' or 'the social'. At the centre of government policy is interdependent, both in the sense that decisions in one field often have consequences for the rest of government, and in the sense that at the centre government is attempting to manage a stream of decisions which it has to coordinate, and to present as in some sense consistent. A good example of interdependence is provided by the mundane fact of

money. The Treasury is permanently in the core executive because every time it agrees a substantial commitment of resources to one field – say, education – it is denying that resource to another set of claimants. A second example concerns the presentation of policy. In practice modern government is so complicated, and the decisions demanded of government so difficult, that governments often take wildly contradictory decisions. But they can never admit this, and a huge amount of energy goes into trying to convince the outside world – and, indeed to convince government itself – that what it does in one area is quite consistent with what it is doing elsewhere.

### It stresses roles more than structures

The concept of the core executive focuses on *roles* rather than on structures alone. We all play different roles, and some roles dominate our lives more than others: my role as a university teacher is a big part of my life; my role as a supporter of the Irish national rugby team is more marginal. Some people and institutions are permanently part of the core executive. A good example is the Prime Minister, whose whole life is given over to managing the centre of government; but many people shift in and out, as is the case with most departmental ministers. A very senior minister such as the Home Secretary, for example, will spend a large amount of his or her working life operating in the core executive: formally, serving on committees in the Cabinet system, for example; less formally, negotiating the most important Home Office policies with other leading members of the core executive, such as the Prime Minister. But the Home Secretary is chief of one of the departmental 'tribes', and will also spend a large amount of time on the business of that tribe. One of the biggest sources of tension inside the core executive as a whole, and in the lives of ministers, is between the demands of their 'own' departments and the demands of business in the core executive.

### It stresses decisions

The concept of the core executive alerts us to the fact that government is about *doing things*: about making decisions, or trying to avoid making decisions. It is not about the relations between static 'blocks' such as departments, or abstractions such as ministers and civil servants. At the centre life is a constant struggle to respond to one problem after another, and to present and defend the result to an outside world that is always intensely critical. There is no fixed agenda of business for the core executive; demands for decision just flow in remorselessly. Neither are the boundaries of the core executive fixed. At the centre government cannot pick and choose the subjects for decision. Often they will be self-evidently important: how to decide, say, Britain's policy on the Euro. Often they will be unexpected and detailed: a riot by drunken football fans abroad suddenly calls into question the government's law and order policy, and the machinery of the core executive suddenly has to be mobilized to respond. As a consequence, the *boundaries* of the

core executive are constantly shifting. An issue that was once routine (managing football fans who travel abroad) suddenly rises right to the top of the concerns of the core executive. Individuals who normally work in obscurity within the Home Office tribe suddenly find themselves at meetings with the senior ministers and officials trying to explain how best to manage the problem.

In summary, we increasingly think of government in terms of the core executive because it focuses on government as an activity; and it encourages us to examine how the most important parts of government cope (or fail in coping) with the constant need to make, present and defend decisions.

## The main components of the core executive

The boundaries of the core executive are flexible, but that does not mean that we cannot describe its most important components. Here we summarize three: the prime ministerial machine; the Cabinet machine; and the machinery of departmentalism (see Figure 7.1).

### The prime ministerial machine

At the heart of the core executive lies institutional machinery that is organized to serve the prime minister. We should beware of thinking of this in excessively personal terms since the complexity of government in Britain is too great for a single individual to control what is going on. But undoubtedly prime ministers have the potential to be immensely powerful within the core executive, and at least two recent prime ministers – Margaret Thatcher and Tony Blair – have at various periods of their time in office realised that potential very fully. The central place of the prime minister is reflected in the institutional machinery that has now grown up to support the office.

One of the features of the organization of the prime ministerial machine is that it is very sensitive

**Figure 7.1    The wiring of the core executive**

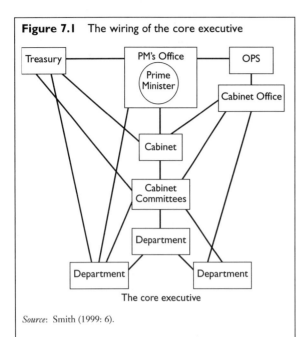

The core executive

*Source*: Smith (1999: 6).

➲ Smith's diagram of the core executive perfectly catches three of its key features. First, the office of Prime Minister is its heart. Second, it is not a simple hierarchy but an elaborate network of exchanges of communication and resources between a shifting population of institutions and individuals. Third, it pays little attention to one of the traditionally sacred divisions in British government: that between elected politicians (Ministers) and appointed officials. Indeed, for the latter it also mixes together civil servants and 'political' appointments made by the government of the day.

to the moods of each particular prime minister. The details constantly change, partly because prime ministers constantly fret about whether they are being adequately served, and partly because life at the centre has a frenetic, hothouse quality: little empires are constantly being built (and dismantled) as different people struggle for the ear of the prime minister and for their own personal advancement. The atmosphere is rather like that of the court of a monarch, where the skill consists in catching the ear and the eye of the powerful one. A small sign of this is that between the various drafts of this chapter the titles assigned to various components of the machine were changed, as were alterations in their formal organization. The practical consequence is that the best place to go for an up-to-date picture of

organization is the latest official web page (www.number-10.gov.uk). Figure 7.2 provides an adapted version of the latest available 'organogram' provided by Number 10. In describing the components below I recognize the constantly shifting formal structure by identifying the 'functional components' of the machine: the functions that always have to be performed whatever particular structure the prime minister at the moment chooses.

*The Private Office function.*    This is staffed by the civil service and is the single most important official form for managing the prime minister's business life: processing all advice and papers that come in both from elsewhere in government and from outside; managing the prime minister's day, and indeed the whole diary; managing all correspondence in and out of the office; and recording all prime ministerial meetings. There is a team of private secretaries who are generally civil servants marked out for a high-flying career, headed by a principal private secretary. The calibre of the last will be the highest the civil service can provide: most principal private secretaries end up later in their career at or near the very top of the civil service. Supporting the private secretaries in turn is a cohort of more routine administrators and secretaries, who ensure that the office is staffed 24 hours a day.

*The policy analysis function.*    This consists of a mixture of civil servants and special advisers appointed by the prime minister from outside. The latter will often, though not invariably, be close political allies of the ruling party. If the Private Office function is designed to ensure that business is processed effectively, the policy analysis function is designed to provide specialist policy advice to the prime minister, and to work with departmental ministers and civil servants to produce sound specialist advice and to chase policy implementation. The existence of this function is prompted by worries that bother all prime ministers: worries that they should not just be reacting to problems as they arise, but should be thinking ahead; worries that they lack the expert resources available to Cabinet ministers who head big departments; worries that the policies they want to happen will not actually be

**Figure 7.2**    The components of the Prime Ministerial machine

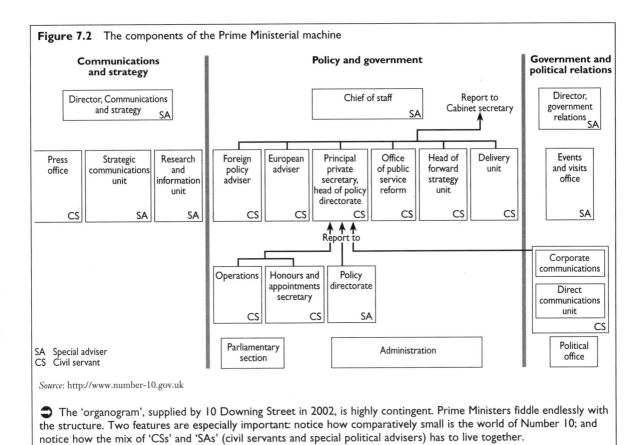

*Source:* http://www.number-10.gov.uk

➲ The 'organogram', supplied by 10 Downing Street in 2002, is highly contingent. Prime Ministers fiddle endlessly with the structure. Two features are especially important: notice how comparatively small is the world of Number 10; and notice how the mix of 'CSs' and 'SAs' (civil servants and special political advisers) has to live together.

implemented within departments. In practice, the actual roles played by the special advisers are heavily shaped by what prime ministers feel they need. They might spend time working on detailed policy problems; they might try to think about long-term strategy, something prime ministers are usually anxious to do but almost never get around to; or they might just as well suddenly be called on to draft a speech for the prime minister.

*The press relations function.*    This is a permanent 24 hours a day operation. It manages the presentation of news from Number 10. It also tries to coordinate news management across government and it manages all the prime minister's relations with the media. The official spokesman holds briefings virtually daily (indeed, commonly twice daily) for the journalists who specialize in covering the core executive. Even the mechanics of managing all this are onerous: a prime minister, for example, often

spends a large part of the working day giving press interviews. But this sort of news management is only part of the job. The core executive is at heart about policy coordination, and policy presentation is inseparable from coordination. So those who manage communications, and especially the official spokesman, are critical: they need to know the prime minister's mind, and to convey his mind to the media. This is a 24 hours a day operation because, in addition to presenting the prime minister's views, the centre has to stand ready to respond at an instant to press enquiries about any urgent matter. 'Urgent' here can be almost anything, from a great international crisis to an embarrassment resulting from the private behaviour of a member of the Cabinet or even a member of the prime minister's family.

*The party political function.*    Prime ministers head the government of the whole nation, but they only get there in the first place because they head a political party. A critical measure of their success is how far they put into effect the policies of their party and how far they succeed in winning partisan general elections. The bottom line for all prime ministers is success in winning partisan elections; otherwise, they cease to hold that position and, almost certainly, cease to be a prominent politician altogether. This function is a recognition of these facts: it is designed to manage all those areas where the prime minister's role overlaps with party leadership duties. It is therefore staffed by the party of government.

It is straightforward to describe in broad terms these different functions performed by parts of the Number 10 machine. But it will be obvious to anyone who spends even a short time looking at the actual life of the prime minister that no easy division of labour exists between them. If we glance at Image 7.1, for instance, we will see that the public face of Downing Street is elegant and impressive. Notoriously, however, crammed into this house are cramped, often tiny working offices. There is constant pressure on space. In Mr Blair's time, for instance, the prime minister's machine colonized the whole of the house next door, Number 12, which used to be occupied by the chief whip, and spread into part of Number 11, which is the house of the Chancellor of the Exchequer. Those inside are forced into close contact with each other all the time. A few matters are very obviously party political and the job of the political office (for example, the prime minister's relations with his own constituency party). But at root a prime minister's whole life is party political, since he functions in a political system dominated by adversarial competition between government and opposition. This sketch of the prime ministerial machine makes it look superficially impressive, but actually what is striking about this part of the core executive, relative to the responsibilities and public profile of the prime minster, is how little institutional support the office has, as Figure 7.2 illustrates. This is to some extent counter-balanced by the fact that the Cabinet machinery is also to a large degree at the disposal of the prime minister.

**Image 7.3**
**The public face of a troubled political partnership**

➲ The photo shows the Prime Minister, leading the applause after a speech by his Chancellor. Mr Brown is not praying; in a show of mock modesty, he is 'damping down' the applause. Mutual public admiration is needed for the most successful partnership in modern British politics. But the institutional tensions within the core executive between Prime Minister and Chancellor, coupled with the personal ambitions of the two men, have created a partnership that behind the public façade has been viciously antagonistic. The 2005 general election campaign and result both strengthened Mr Brown's hand.

## The Cabinet Machine

The Cabinet consists of the 20 or so leading ministers in government. In this bare sense it has hardly changed in over a century. An up-to-date membership list is on this book's website. But in that period, and especially since the 1950s, Cabinet roles (and the machinery that surrounds them) have been transformed. A century ago the Cabinet machinery meant only the Cabinet itself; there was not even a permanent arrangement for making a formal minute of what the Cabinet had discussed and decided. Now the machinery is elaborate, its most important components being as follows.

*The Cabinet itself.* The Cabinet still usually meets weekly, normally chaired by the prime minister. The Cabinet will never lose significance as long as it is constituted as it is now. It contains all the big power figures, the most senior ministers in a government, and so when big issues arise that divide the government it will always be important as an arena where those are argued out. But the Cabinet has increasingly taken on the character of a place where occasionally a really divisive issue is argued out, but otherwise it is a meeting which tends to do little more than hear reports of doings elsewhere, especially from the system of Cabinet committees.

*The system of Cabinet committees.*   A century ago the Cabinet had no permanent committees, and until the 1990s their existence was not even formally acknowledged. But we have known for a long time that the committee system of Cabinet is one of the most important means of processing business. At any one moment there will be in existence over 20 of these committees. An idea of the range and complexity of the business done in the committee structure is conveyed in Documenting Politics 7.1 (p. 122), which lists examples of the two characteristic Cabinet committees: a permanent committee dealing with broad areas of government business; and a temporary committee convened to deal with more short-term issues.

Why is the committee system so important? At the simplest level the answer is obvious: the volume of business in government is such that it would be impossible for Cabinet to cope were it to attempt to deal with all business in full session. But this resort to committees has reshaped the whole nature of power within the core executive, for three reasons. First, in almost all cases, to dominate an issue in government it is now necessary to dominate it in Cabinet committee, since the chance of appealing to the full Cabinet or the prime minister (still less of winning that appeal) is slight. Second, Cabinet committees are now the main focus of activity for senior ministers within the core executive. They spend far more time attending committees than attending Cabinet, and Cabinet committee documents dominate their paperwork. Even when a committee is not actually meeting it provides a framework for business: much consists of an exchange of ministerial correspondence between members, often in the form of an exchange of letters with the chair checking agreement to a proposal. Finally, assignment to Cabinet committees is an important indicator of place in the political pecking order, with the prize as chair of the most important committees going to the most powerful ministers in government. This explains a feature noticeable in Documenting Politics 7.1: that a really important Cabinet committee is often not much smaller than the full Cabinet as all the major figures demand the right of representation. This feature shows a powerful tension in the whole arrangement: the committee system exists with the avowed aim of doing business more efficiently; but the insistence of departments and ministers on being represented on committees means that the most important committees are often almost as unwieldy as the full Cabinet.

*The Cabinet Office.*   This elaborate machinery of committees could not exist without a machinery of support: to prepare and circulate papers, and to minute decisions and discussions. That is the fundamental job of the civil servants in the Cabinet Office. The Office originated in the first decision – taken in the First World War – to appoint an official to record the minutes of Cabinet discussions and conclusions. Out of that has grown one of the most powerful parts of the machinery of government. The head of the Office, the Cabinet secretary, is the most senior civil servant of all and will virtually work to the prime minister of the day as his most senior official adviser. The title of 'Cabinet Secretary' is potentially misleading since it suggests almost a passive, high-level clerical role. In fact it is intensely political, and in recent decades the Cabinet secretary has typically been one of the most powerful figures in government (see People in Politics 7.1, p. 124). Prime ministers in turn often rely on the Cabinet secretary to deal with delicate issues that they wish to keep at arm's length: for instance, when Jonathan Aitken, a senior member of the Conservative Cabinet in the 1990s, was accused of impropriety it was the Cabinet secretary, not the prime minister, who sought assurances from him as to the propriety of his conduct.

Just as the Cabinet secretary occupies a powerful and delicate political role, so the whole Cabinet Office is much more than an institution for preparing and circulating official papers, though this remains an important function. It is also a key institution in attempting to perform what is in many ways the central function of the core executive: managing policy that will not fit neatly into

## DOCUMENTING POLITICS 7.1

## TWO EXAMPLES OF CABINET COMMITTEES

### i) A major, permanent Cabinet Committee

**Ministerial Committee on Domestic Affairs (DA)**

*Composition*
Deputy Prime Minister and First Secretary of State (Chairman)
Chancellor of the Exchequer
Lord President and Leader of the House of Commons
Lord Chancellor
Secretary of State for the Home Department
Secretary of State for Environment, Food and Rural Affairs
Secretary of State for Transport
Secretary of State for Health
Secretary of State for Northern Ireland
Secretary of State for Wales
Secretary of State for Defence
Secretary of State for Work and Pensions
Secretary of State for Scotland
Lord Privy Seal and Leader of the House of Lords
Secretary of State for Trade and Industry
Secretary of State for Education and Skills
Secretary of State for Culture, Media and Sport
Parliamentary Secretary, Treasury and Chief Whip

Minister without Portfolio
Chief Secretary, Treasury
Attorney General
Minister for the Cabinet Office and Chancellor of the Duchy of Lancaster
Minister of State, Office of the Deputy Prime Minister.

*Terms of Reference*
'To consider issues relating to the Government's broader domestic policies, ensuring the work of its sub-committees contributes to achieving the Government's overall agenda.'

### ii) An ad hoc sub-committee with specialized terms of reference

**Ministerial Sub-Committee on Biotechnology (SCI(BIO))**

*Composition*
Lord President of the Council and Leader of the House of Commons (Chair)
Secretary of State for Environment, Food and Rural Affairs
Minister of State, Foreign and Commonwealth Office
Minister of State, Department for Environment, Food and Rural Affairs

$\Rightarrow$

existing departmental responsibilities. It tracks interdepartmental issues and advises when they need Cabinet committee consideration (in many ways, this is the key task of the core executive). It sets agendas, writes committee position papers and, crucially, briefs the ministers who chair committees. One of its rarely publicised but vitally important functions is also to coordinate the machinery for both domestic and external security intelligence. (For more details see Chapter 22.) And, as we saw in the last chapter, through its European Secretariat it is the critical bit of the machinery of government for trying to coordinate policy on the EU. Thus it makes sense to distinguish between the Cabinet Secretariat, which is largely concerned with 'servicing' the Cabinet system, and the wider Cabinet Office which has important responsibilities for managing the wider civil service system.

## The machinery of departments

No matter how much prime ministers try to control and coordinate from the centre, British government

**DOCUMENTING POLITICS 7.1**   (continued)

Economic Secretary, Treasury

Parliamentary Under Secretary of State, Home Office

Parliamentary Under Secretary of State, Department for International Development

Parliamentary Under Secretary of State, Department for Transport

Parliamentary Under Secretary of State, Department of Health

Parliamentary Under Secretary of State, Northern Ireland Office

Parliamentary Under Secretary of State, Wales Office

Parliamentary Under Secretary of State, Scotland Office

Parliamentary Under Secretary of State, Department for Trade and Industry

The Chief Scientific Adviser and the Chief Medical Officer are invited to attend.

The Chairman, Food Standards Agency will be invited to attend as appropriate.

*Terms of Reference*

'To consider issues relating to biotechnology – including those arising from genetic modification, biotechnology in healthcare and genetic issues – and their economic impact; and to report as necessary to the Committee on Science Policy.'

➲ The illustration, dating from 2003, is for the purpose of example only. Some of the offices referred to have actually now disappeared: for instance, Secretary of State for Scotland has been abolished. But notice two features illustrated by these examples of very different parts of the Cabinet Committee system:

- The first Committee is one of the most important of all, since it deals with the full range of domestic business that the government has to cope with. All the major Cabinet ministers therefore demand a place; the result is that it virtually matches the full Cabinet in size and complexity.
- The second example is an ad hoc sub-committee constituted to deal with a particular set of issues, to do with the impact of biotechnology on food, health care and other issues. It shows how far the 'Cabinet committee' system draws in people and institutions from right across government, well beyond the range of official membership of Cabinet: note that several members of this sub-Committee are not Cabinet ministers at all, and that those attending include figures not even within the conventionally defined civil service, such as the head of the Food Standards Agency. This emphasizes an observation made earlier in the chapter: the boundaries of the core executive are fluid, and actors who normally live in their own special worlds, such as the head the Food Standards Agency, will find themselves drawn in as occasion demands. In this way one of the aims of the Committee system – to economize on time and effort – is subverted.

is still at heart departmental. The departmental tribes command fierce loyalty from permanent civil servants, and even from their relatively short-lived ministerial heads.

As we noted in passing earlier, some tribes are more powerful than others. Two need to be highlighted.

*The Treasury.* This is virtually a permanent part of the core executive. It is a comparatively small department, and that reflects its importance in formulating advice and making policy decisions, rather than having executive responsibility for

putting policy into effect. Its political head, the chancellor of the Exchequer, occupies a central part in the machinery of the core executive, and almost invariably will have ready access to the prime minister. Its policy responsibilities encompass the whole of economic policy and it dominates decisions about the allocation of public spending. All governments believe, probably rightly, that their chances of re-election turn on the perceived success of economic policy; all departments need money to carry out their responsibilities. Both these considerations

## *People in politics*

### 7.1   GREY EMINENCES: THREE POWERFUL FIGURES BEHIND THE SCENES IN THE HISTORY OF THE CORE EXECUTIVE

Cartoons: Shaun Steele

**Maurice Hankey** (1877–1939). Secretary, Committee on Imperial Defence 1912–38; Secretary War Cabinet 1916–18, Cabinet 1918–38. Hankey created the Cabinet Secretariat, mostly by exploiting the pressures of war. He then dominated it for over 20 years. His relatively unusual background by comparison with later Cabinet Secretaries (his early career was as a soldier) typified his status as an institutional pioneer. Not only was his career route unusual – compare Brook and Armstrong – but his long tenure allowed him to dominate the system to a degree never later achieved.

**Norman Brook** (1902–67). Secretary to the Cabinet 1947–62; head of the Home Civil Service 1955–62. Brook entered the civil service in the Administrative class in 1925, after education at Wadham College Oxford. His career typified that of the civil service elite in the mid-twentieth century: progression from high early academic achievement, early appointment to the Administrative class as a recognition of future leadership of the service, and domination of the administrative apparatus in the great years of war time crisis and post war British decline. He finished his career as Chair of the BBC Board of Governors.

**Robert Armstrong** (1927–). Secretary to the Cabinet, 1979–87, head of the Home Civil Service 1983–87. Armstrong entered the Administrative class in the Treasury in 1950, after an education at Christ Church Oxford, the most socially exclusive college in a socially exclusive university. He typified in education and style the administrative elite that governed Britain in her years of post war decline, a style that put a premium on quick thinking, social skills and diplomatic subtlety. But he also served during his years at the very top the Prime Minister (Margaret Thatcher) who most fundamentally challenged that style and sought to reverse decline.

➲ Top civil servants are among the most powerful figures in British government. These three important figures from different eras in the modern history of British government were barely known to the general public at the time they exercised great power.

reinforce the position of the Treasury at the centre.

*The Foreign Office.* This is central for two reasons. First, it is a critical institution in dealing with the European Union, an increasingly vital part of British government (as we have already seen). Second, prime ministers define foreign affairs as a key part of their responsibility, so they naturally tend to draw the Foreign Office into their domain.

## Doing business in the core executive

Most of what has been described so far is intended to give an overview of the institutional structure of the core executive in Britain, but it is also necessary to know how this structure works. Government is important because it does things: it takes decisions, or decides to avoid decisions, and tries to implement decisions once taken. This next section is all about how business is done in the core executive (see Documenting Politics 7.2).

The very first condition for business to be processed by the core executive is that it must come to the attention of the executive machine. How does this happen? We can, broadly, observe three mechanisms.

### Business comes in from departments

The core executive is part of the huge organizational machine that is British central government. Most business is processed in the departments, and many issues start life quite far down a departmental hierarchy. The most important instrument of management is the file, still even in this electronic era usually a set of papers and memos written by civil servants about a particular issue. If we just did a count of decisions made within central government we would find that most are made by permanent officials inside departments, not by elected ministers or by others within the core executive. (This is not to mention something that will loom large in the next chapter: the importance of the executive agencies.) A complex mixture of things decides where the file lands for decision. A general

principle is that matters should be decided at the lowest level possible, but what that level should be in any particular case can be affected by many things: a judgement about the substantive importance of the issue; precedents; whether it involves a clear shift in policy direction; even the simple urgency of being seen to do something. Most important of all, however, is perceived political sensitivity. Ministers will always want to know about an issue that is politically sensitive: one that might damage or advance their careers, or the fortunes of their government. Quite often they will be alerted to it outside the department, perhaps by being formally lobbied or by hearing about the issue on the morning radio news. (Most politicians are obsessed by the reporting of politics but pressure of work means that senior ministers have a highly unusual experience of reporting. Early morning broadcasting, such as the *Today* programme on BBC Radio 4, can be particularly important because it is one of the few 'unfiltered' forms of news that senior ministers receive as they prepare for work or are driven to the office. Senior politicians hardly ever watch television since they are usually out in the evening, and ministers rely, again because of pressure of time, on digests and cuttings from the press prepared by their advisers and civil servants.)

Political sensitivity is the overriding influence determining whether the issue will be brought to the attention of the minister. The end of the line within the department is when the file is put onto the minister's desk or into the 'red box' (the box that is usually replenished daily with the papers and files that require ministerial attention). Since most ministers spend their working day in a whirlwind of meetings, the contents of the red box will usually be dealt with in the small hours of the morning. At this point a minister may decide that an issue is so sensitive that it needs to go into the core executive, and going further can take many different forms: being formally processed by the machinery of the Cabinet, usually starting in Cabinet committees; or being the subject of discussions of varying levels of formality with other senior figures. But while this route into the core executive is very important because it will

**DOCUMENTING POLITICS 7.2**

## THE WORKING DAYS OF PRIME MINISTERS IN DIFFERENT ERAS

### William Gladstone's routine as Prime Minister 1880–85

'He rarely slept beyond 9 am, and until the official day began at 11 am he read the newspapers and – if there was nothing especially urgent – literature. He would then have a meeting with the Chief Whip and deal with the day's letters and papers, which the Private Secretariat had sifted for him. In this period policy was often developed by correspondence. A lunch and then a walk would follow before he went to the House of Commons, where he remained, with breaks for tea and dinner, until the end of sitting. He would spend seven hours a day in the Commons chamber, sitting on the Treasury bench.' (Kavanagh and Seldon 1999: 37–8)

### A Day in the Life of Winston Churchill, Prime Minister in wartime, 1940–45

8.00am   Churchill woke, had breakfast and went into the bathroom.

8.30am   Churchill looked through all of the daily newspapers.

9.00am   One of Churchill's secretaries would sit on the end of his bed with a noiseless typewriter while he dictated. The Prime Minister would work on his black locking box which contained secret papers and documents. If there were no visits or meetings with the Cabinet or Chiefs of Staff scheduled, he would stay in bed until lunchtime.

1.00pm   Churchill would have a bath.

1.30pm   Lunch in Number 10.

After lunch Churchill would go to the House of Commons and/or work on speeches in the Cabinet Room in Number 10 with a secretary waiting in the room next door to take dictation when necessary.

6.00pm   Churchill would get undressed, put on his nightclothes and have an hour's sleep.

7.00pm   After waking and getting dressed he would eat, and then work in Number 10 or in the Annex until 2–3 am.

*Source:* www.org.uk/cabinet/winroom

identify the issues that are most sensitive, it is quantitatively not the most important – after all, there is an obvious physical limit to the volume of papers that a minister can process through the red box. Many issues will go out of the department into the core executive early in their lives. Some are just foreordained by the rules of government: legislative proposals prepared within a department, for instance, have to be dealt with by an important Cabinet committee that settles the legislative timetable of the government of the day. A huge number of issues in government are cross-departmental: a single department cannot settle them alone. These issues are naturally within the domain of the core executive.

### Business comes from inside the core executive

If most decisions in British government start and end their lives within a single department, a minority (usually particularly important ones) start and end their lives inside the core executive. Three kinds would, without question, be processed within the core executive. First, the Cabinet Office has

**DOCUMENTING POLITICS 7.2** (continued)

**A working day for Tony Blair, 7 July 2003**

- 'I had a breakfast with an information technology consultant.
- I had several meetings to deal with the issue of school funding.
- I then had quite a big speech on the criminal justice system in the QE2 Centre at 12.15.
- There was also a meeting with the head of the International Olympic Committee.
- Then I had interviews with European newspapers.
- And a meeting of Junior Ministers and a Government reception in the evening.
- It was a fairly busy time obviously. One of my preoccupations through this too was that I had the Liaison Committee on the Tuesday and Prime Minister's Questions on the Wednesday, both of which obviously were going to continue to be dominated by these allegations.'

*Source*: Transcript from www.the-hutton-inquiry.org.uk

These three descriptions show not only how the role of the prime minister has changed, but how much more stressful and busy life in the core executive has become. Gladstone, one of the greatest of nineteenth-century prime ministers, led a routine of what now looks like gentlemanly leisure. Mr Gladstone, we see, rose typically at 9; his greatest twentieth-century counterpart, Mrs Thatcher, was reputed normally to begin work at 5 a.m. Churchill, though prime minister in a time of great national crisis, followed his own eccentric work routines. Blair's description concerns one of the most important days of his premiership. The latter part of the transcript covers a key meeting he attended where there was discussion over what information to release to the public about the identity of Dr David Kelly, whose suicide following his exposure as a possible source for a BBC report on a dossier used to justify the war of 2003 in Iraq led to the setting-up of the Hutton Inquiry (see Hutton 2004). The striking feature is how this key meeting had to be squeezed into a day with numerous meetings on a wide variety of mostly unrelated subjects. The Prime Minister's remarks about the Liaison Committee and Prime Minister's Questions look forward to other stressful engagements. Mr Blair's description not only conveys the sense of a crammed timetable; it also shows how stressful and difficult decisions have to be made swiftly, allowing the Prime Minister to move on to other stressful issues.

managed over time to establish the convention that interdepartmental issues (its language) are naturally within its domain. An obvious example of this (discussed earlier) is the way the European Secretariat has established the right to process the range of European issues. Second, the core executive is the natural home for two areas of decision making that are central to the lives of all governments: managing the legislative programme and managing the economy. The first is largely done through the network of Cabinet committees, including a committee charged with managing the whole legislative timetable itself. The second is centred on the Treasury. Third, at any one moment there will be a small number of issues that are so central to the survival of a government that they will never leave the core executive. In the last few years

the most important of these has concerned the Euro: in particular, the question of whether, and when, Britain should join the single European currency.

### Business comes from 'firefighting'

So far, the picture we have drawn stresses routine and stability. And indeed it is the case that, because government is a machine, these are important features. Routines are established; precedents create conventions about who takes what decision, when, and where; papers are produced for meetings. Precedent and conventional understandings about how business is processed are important not because individuals are necessarily conservative but because observing routines is the only way a large complicated machine can process a huge volume of business. But there is another roller coaster aspect to the business in the core executive, and it is one that is missed completely by this stress on routine. A large part of the job of the core executive is fire-fighting: managing crises that appear suddenly, often apparently out of nowhere. Sometimes these are huge matters of life and death: every British prime minister in the last 25 years has been involved in a large scale war, and each of these was created by a short notice crisis: the Falklands, 1982; the Gulf War, 1990; the war against the Serbs in Kosovo in 1999; the wars in Afghanistan in 2002 and Iraq in 2003. Some issues of life and death just appear without notice: every British prime minister in the last 35 years has had to react in some way to violent deaths in Northern Ireland. The physical and emotional stress of these crises is immense.

Equally, however, a crisis can appear in the core executive arising from something apparently quite minor. The cause can be totally trivial but intensely embarrassing: the children of two leading figures in the Labour Government after 1997 were apprehended by the police, causing a flurry of activity to manage the embarrassment. In 2002 the Prime Minister's wife was involved in a series of revelations about the purchase of a flat for her son, involving an alleged confidence trickster who claimed to be her intermediary. At a moment when the country faced problems ranging from a strike of all fire-fighters to a possible war in Iraq the resources of the core executive were substantially devoted to 'fire-fighting' the embarrassing revelation.

Sometimes ministers themselves cause short-term crises because their sexual or financial lives get into the newspapers. The Home Office is a particularly important source of comparatively minor issues that suddenly require the attention of the core executive, chiefly through its responsibilities for policing: issues as various as dangerous dogs, British

---

## DOCUMENTING POLITICS 7.3

### EDITED EXTRACTS FROM THE REPORTS OF A DAILY PRESS BRIEFING BY THE PRIME MINISTER'S SPOKESMAN

'Lobby Briefing: 4 p.m. Monday 30 April 2001

**PM's glasses**
In answer to questions about the Prime Minister's glasses, the Prime Minister's Spokesman said he had no intention of going into details about the make ... following a speech he had made recently when he had confused the words 'teenagers' and 'teachers', he had recognized that he couldn't put off the inevitable forever and had taken the decision to wear them today for his speech.

**Europe**
Asked again about reports in today's papers about Chancellor Schroeder's ideas relating to the future of Europe debate, the Prime Minister's Spokesman said that ... a debate was ongoing about the future of Europe in the context of what institutional changes were necessary to deal with the enlarged EU which we were going to see in the coming years.'

➲ This edited extract of a lobby briefing by the Prime Minister's Spokesman, taken from the 10 Downing Street website, shows the jumble of the trivial and the momentous which government has to manage for presentation: the Prime Minister had just appeared for the first time in public with reading glasses and journalists were as interested in this as in bigger issues.

football hooligans, binge drinking, and escapes from jails, have in recent years arisen in this way. To get a sense of how the large scale and tragic is often mixed up with the trivial on the agenda of the core executive, glance at Documenting Politics 7.3.

## Managing the coordination of policy in the core executive

One of the most difficult things in modern government is trying to ensure that policy fits together in some consistent way. Modern governments are huge and complex organizations, making large numbers of important decisions daily. Without constant effort, there is no reason to suppose that these decisions will be coordinated in a consistent way. On the contrary, every day of the week provides examples of one government department pursuing a policy which directly contradicts that of another. Sometimes the contradiction is inside the same department: in recent years British government has been unable to make up its mind on whether it wants people to use their cars more, or less. A central task of the core executive is to try to ensure some coordination and consistency, even where it is absent.

The attempt is made by three means:

● Institutions
● Formal rules for coordinating policy
● Informal understandings and contacts.

### Institutions

The most important institution of coordination is the office of prime minister, the components of which we described earlier. We speak of the 'office' rather than the 'person' because this role attaches to the prime minister regardless of who the individual occupant of the office is. In any 'job description' of the office of prime minister coordinating government policy and ensuring its consistency would be right at the top of the list. Neither is any prime minister likely to neglect this part of the job, for on doing it well can depend the life of the government, and therefore the prime minister's own job. Prime

Ministers have a number of means of shaping institutions to achieve coordination. They not only chair Cabinet, but also chair some important Cabinet committees. They have extensive powers of appointment, including appointment to, and dismissal from, Cabinet; and while these cannot be used in an unrestrained way they do allow a prime minister to set the tone of the government, including influencing the likelihood that ministers will try to work cooperatively together in the first place. prime ministers can see all the important papers flowing through the core executive. Perhaps more important, both the civil servants in the Cabinet Secretariat and those who work in the 'prime ministerial' units (such as the Private Office and the Policy Unit) are primed to alert both each other and the prime minister as to what papers might be sensitive from the point of view of the government. On the skill and sensitivity with which this 'alerting' function is performed can depend the ultimate fate of the prime minister and his government.

### Formal rules of business

The whole formal organization of business in the core executive is designed to ensure coordination and consistency. That is the purpose of the existence of orderly rules for the preparation and circulation of papers and files through the Cabinet system. In recent years governments have often tried to strengthen coordination by appointing a senior Cabinet minister without departmental responsibilities at the centre as an 'enforcer': in other words, with the responsibility to chase policy initiatives through to see that they do not conflict with other parts of the government's programme, and to see that they are being implemented in a way consistent with that programme. The Cabinet machinery is also dominated by the task of trying to manage business in an orderly way. One of the most important examples of this is the management of the government's legislative programme. The yearly policy cycle in government is heavily dominated by the cycle of legislation. New laws are one of the main ways governments try to make policy and put their stamp on affairs. There is always less parliamentary legislative time available than there are potential proposals for legislation coming out of departments. The Cabinet Committee on the Legislative Programme therefore has the particularly important job of putting the proposals in some order of priority, and ensuring some balance and coherence in the government's legislative programme.

## Informal understandings and contacts

Beyond this formal world, coordination relies heavily on informal contacts and sources. Here again the prime minister is critical. Even more than departmental Cabinet ministers, prime ministers spend most of their time talking to people: in bi-lateral meetings with particular officials and Ministers; picking the brains of their staff who in turn are their eyes and ears in government; talking formally and informally to senior figures in their own party, including senior cabinet ministers, in the knowledge that if the party goes down at the next general election they all go down with it; spending a large part of each day talking on the telephone; even listening to early morning radio news to try to be alerted to any banana skins that might await them for the rest of the day. Prime ministers usually feel at a disadvantage when they contemplate the formidable civil service resources available to their departmental Cabinet colleagues, but there is also an advantage to their position: they are not chained to the backbreaking job of running a large specialist department, and have correspondingly more freedom to range widely over the whole range of government. A particularly energetic prime minister with ability to master detail quickly, such as Margaret Thatcher (1979–90), can in this fashion intervene widely in government.

## Managing the presentation of policy in the core executive

One reason policy coordination is so important in government is that it affects public presentation and perception. British politics is highly adversarial. A government always faces an official opposition in Parliament, and will have large numbers of critics of almost any policy it decides to pursue. Opponents are constantly trying to highlight inconsistencies in policy and splits within government. Few things are more damaging to the image of a government than the impression that it is disunited and not in control of all aspects of policy. Since governments are almost always disunited, and rarely in control, policy presentation is vital. Three forms of presentation are especially important and will be examined in turn.

## Briefing

The most important means of presenting policy is through the mass media – newspapers and broad-casting – since it is here that electors chiefly obtain information about what government is currently up to. Briefing of journalists goes on constantly, and always has. Politicians and political journalists in London inhabit the same world, mixing together both formally and socially. Politicians, whether in or out of government, are always briefing: putting their side of any argument to journalists. Since leading politicians are also almost always intensely ambitious and have large egos, this briefing about policy is usually mixed up with more personal briefings: defending their own positions, and criticizing those of their opponents and rivals in their own government. In the core executive in recent years, however, this briefing process has become more organized, a bit more open, and more like systematic news management. Press officers in departments, once simply career civil servants, are increasingly being displaced by specially recruited 'spin doctors' (a term originating in the expression 'to put a spin' on something, meaning to manipulate the way it is perceived). This exactly expresses the role of the spin-doctor, which is not just to present information, but also to take events and announcements and put on them the 'spin' most favourable to the minister and the government (see Documenting Politics 7.4). Cabinet ministers usually have their own dedicated spin-doctors to manage relations with the media. The shift to more organized briefing is most obvious right at the centre of the core executive, where the prime minister's personal spokesman has in recent decades emerged as a distinctive public figure in his own right.

The first to become a substantial media celebrity was Bernard Ingham, 1979–90, who acquired the title of Chief Press Secretary and who spanned exactly the years of Mrs Thatcher's prime ministership. In Sir Bernard's period the role of the Chief Press Secretary as the public 'voice' of the prime minister was permanently established. This has accompanied growing openness about the role of the prime minister's official spokesman. Originally, lobby briefings were totally unattributable; then they were acknowledged as coming from the prime minister's spokesman; then, since everyone knew his identity informally, that was acknowledged openly. At present, we are at a point where by click-ing on the Downing Street website it is possible to read an account of the daily briefing meetings (www.number-10.gov.uk, the source of the material in Documenting Politics 7.3). As the role has become more open it has also become more overtly political in a partisan sense. The best known spokesman of the Blair era was Alistair Campbell, a former journalist and long-term Labour Party supporter. He became so identified with the communication of the Prime Minister's view that following the 2001 election his role and title were redesigned in an attempt to give him a lower profile. The growing politicization of the communications function in the core executive has had the side effect

---

**DOCUMENTING POLITICS 7.4**

## THE IMPORTANCE OF NEWS PRESENTATION TO THE MODERN CORE EXECUTIVE: TWO LEAKED MEMOS SENT WITHIN GOVERNMENT

**Example 1:**   On 11 September 2001 a terrorist attack on the World Trade Center, resulting in the loss of several thousand lives, was relayed live around the globe by television. Watching in London, Jo Moore, special adviser to the Secretary of State for Transport, Local Government and the Regions, sent the following e-mail to her colleagues: 'It is now a very good day to get out anything we want to bury. Councillors' expenses?' The suggestion was that a potentially embarrassing news item about payment of expenses to councillors in local government might safely be released because the media in the coming days would be focused on the tragedy in New York.

**Example 2:**   In July 2000 the Prime Minister, faced with a run of bad publicity about a range of issues, sent the following memo to close colleagues in government. It was leaked and widely reproduced in the press. Headed 'Touchstone Issues', it ran in part as follows:

'There are a clutch of issues – seemingly disparate – that are in fact linked. They range from the family ... where we are perceived as weak; asylum and crime where we are perceived as soft ... We need a thoroughly worked out strategy, stretching over several months, to regain the initiative in this area ... Something tough, with immediate bite, which sends a message through the system. Maybe the driving licence penalty for young offenders ... On the family, we need two or three eye-catching initiatives that are entirely conventional in terms of their attitude to the family. Despite the rubbish about gay couples, the adoption issue worked well. We need more. I should be personally associated with as much of this as possible.'

---

⮕  The first e-mail became notorious as an example of a cynically manipulative approach to news but, as the second extract from a leaked memo of the then prime minister shows, it was only an extreme example of a key concern of the core executive: managing the presentation of news.

of making its formal organization more unstable, as prime ministers try to shape it to their immediate concerns.

Although the prime minister's official spokesman is very important, focusing only on that role can be misleading. Modern government is far too big for briefings to be controlled by one person. This partly explains the rise of an increasingly well-resourced news management capacity in the core executive. This news management capacity is also increasingly linked to news management inside the governing party. Modern technology, especially text retrieval via such devices as keywords, allows almost instant rebuttal of criticism. If a government is accused of a particular policy failure the retrieval system can usually locate quickly some contradictory, supporting bits of evidence. If the accusation comes from the parliamentary opposition, text searches can often locate some embarrassing contradiction between the opposition's present stance and one it occupied in the fairly recent past.

The problem of organizing the communications function at the heart of the core executive resurrects a difficulty we examined earlier: the difficulty of separating the party political from the governmental roles of a prime minister. In daily business the two are usually hopelessly entangled, but governments are very sensitive to the charge that they are manipulating the news for partisan purposes (though this is exactly what all governments have to do to survive). This explains the continuing instability in the organization of the media management functions in the prime ministerial machine. As we saw above, Alistair Campbell tried to adopt a less publicly visible role after 2001 in the belief that he had become too visible and too identified with partisan briefing. On Mr Campbell's departure in 2003 the Prime Minister commissioned a review whose recommendations have now been implemented. Essentially these try to organize the 'governmental' and the 'partisan' communication separately: there is now an 'official spokesman' who briefs for the Prime Minister at the regular meetings with lobby correspondents, and a 'Director of Communications' who leads for the more partisan aspects of media management.

How far this separation in practice can be managed is uncertain.

## Broadcasting

'Broadcasting' is used here in the general sense of positively putting out the government's case, not merely broadcasting on radio or television. It means the open presentation of policy. This is particularly important when new policies are made. Governments spend a lot of time preparing those policies, but they equally spend a huge amount of time working out how to launch them in the media. All ministers are skilled in this; otherwise, they would probably not reach top office and certainly would not survive there. The most skilled is usually the prime minister. All modern prime ministers are past masters at radio and television broadcasting: they can manage the 20-second sound bite for the evening news; the extended statement commending some new initiative; or the tough adversarial interview.

## Defending

Mention of the adversarial interview connects to the third key aspect of presentation, because in British government policy hardly ever has a neutral, dispassionate reception. Just imagine the following. Suppose we saw a student presenting a paper to a seminar, and then found that everyone in the seminar, including the tutor, denounced the paper as worthless in the strongest possible language, and impugned the motives of the paper giver. We would certainly conclude that they were all mad or malicious, and yet that is the atmosphere in which government policy is presented. Journalists define their role as the sceptical questioning of ministers, even if they privately agree with them; and the government's political opponents will always try to put the worst possible construction on what is being done. The core executive therefore is in a kind of permanent court where it is perpetually in the dock. This means that the ability to defend effectively against ferocious criticism is at a premium. This again puts the prime minister at the centre of the process, and a prime minister who seems to be losing this capacity to defend is usually thought to be failing. This also explains why, when Parliament is sitting, Prime Minister's Question Time looms so large. Just how far success and failure at Question Time, which increasingly involves a joust with the leader of the Opposition, actually influences the public is uncertain; but it is certain that prime ministers put enormous resources into preparing for the event, and feel shaken if they do badly. (See Documenting Politics 10.1, p. 188 for an example.)

## Tensions within the core executive

Summarized above were the most important separate components of the machinery of the core executive, but this gives little sense of the powerful tensions that constantly shape the way that machinery operates in practice. There are three great sources of tension, explored in turn below.

### The tension between the formal and the informal

Although the machinery described here is complex and generates a huge amount of business (not to mention paper), it actually involves a comparatively small number of regular participants. Most of these people work in close physical proximity to each other, and constantly meet both formally (in committees) and informally. The image of a village is often used to describe the atmosphere of the core executive and it is an accurate image. The result is that, outwith the formal machinery, all sorts of informal groupings and contacts – cabals, bi-lateral meetings, casual contacts in a corridor while waiting to go into a meeting, drinks, and dinners – are important in building alliances and making deals. The telephone (increasingly the mobile phone) and e-mail are important modes of doing business informally. Prime ministers are particularly important in fixing the balance between the formal and the informal at the top. All prime ministers like to fix things informally. That can range from having a 'kitchen cabinet' of trusted confidants with whom they discuss things constantly off the record; regular off-the-record

meetings with their most senior ministerial colleagues; periodic on-the-record meetings with senior colleagues, often to try to sort out some particular problem. ('On the record' here means that a civil servant will be present to make a note of the discussion.) The balance between the informal and formal is partly a function of prime ministerial temperament and partly a matter of prime ministerial ascendancy over colleagues, which tends to change with, for instance, the prime minister's perceived value in winning the next election. Broadly, the more in the ascendant a prime minister feels, the more he or she is likely to do business informally; the less in the ascendant, the more likely to feel obliged to go through the machinery of committees.

### The tension between the departmental and the central

British government is still a government of departments. Ministers, including most Cabinet ministers, spend most of their time on departmental business. They define their current political identity largely by reference to their departmental roles: they are the Home Secretary, for example, or the Secretary of State for Health. Most of the resources – technical expertise, staff – vital to government are lodged within departments, and most of the spending is done by departments, rather than by the core executive. This imparts another powerful source of tension: between the core executive and the distinct departments. In part that tension is personal and institutional. There are some important people (the prime minister, the Cabinet secretary) whose whole life is the core executive, and there are others (for example, ministers not in the Cabinet) whose life is spent in the departments. There are institutions (notably the Cabinet Office) whose whole territory is the core executive. Departments, by contrast, have a different territory to defend. The tension also exists inside the minds of all senior ministers: the Home Secretary, or the Secretary of State for Trade and Industry, is constantly being pulled between the departmental territory and the territory of the core executive.

## The tension between the personal and the political

The core executive is a small world, and an intensely stressful one. Part of the stress is built into the demands we have described in this chapter: the need to manage across the range of government everything from the most momentous (a war) to the trivial but potentially embarrassing (a minister's private life). But stress also arises from the personalities of this small group of people who work so closely with each other. All are intensely ambitious; most have large egos; all live to work, never switching off. Most are trying to rise up the career ladder. Virtually the only two people in the core executive who are content with their present jobs are the prime minister and the Cabinet secretary, who have reached the top of their respective hierarchies. Many of their immediate colleagues have their eye on the jobs of these two. Thus there is intense competition; ferocious jealousy; non-stop plotting; constant forming and re-forming of alliances behind powerful patrons; continual briefing against each other to the media; and never-ending manoeuvring to catch the ear of the most senior figures (see Political Issues 7.1).

## Power in the core executive: an overview

The concept of the core executive helps us avoid some pitfalls in the study of central government in Britain. In particular, it helps us avoid imposing an overly rigid division between the roles of politicians and permanent officials, and it stresses the importance of central coordinating institutions and offices, such as the Cabinet Office and the prime minister. But we should never forget a process central to the workings of the core executive: the struggle for power. The outcome of this struggle is vital for the workings of British democracy. There remains one key difference between elected politicians and the rest: the former can be held accountable to the people in free elections, even if the mechanisms of accountability are often imperfect. Traditional questions about the balance of power

between ministers and officials, and of the balance between different parts of the core executive, are therefore of central importance to the workings of British democracy. There are many complex issues here, but three are especially important.

## Struggles between the centre and departments

Central government in Britain is departmental, in the sense that the departments have a huge say in the delivery of policy and are important concentrations of staff, expertise and money. The department is still the funnel through which most important things run. More subtly, as we have emphasized, departments are tribes: they tend to be the institutions to which fierce loyalty is felt. The development of the concept of the 'core executive' reflects the growth of central coordinating capacities, but a constant struggle exists between the departments and the centre. On the side of the centre is the fact that it contains the most prestigious institutions in the system, notably the Treasury and the Cabinet Office. It also contains the most prestigious individuals, including the leading politicians (the prime minister and the chancellor).

Its weaknesses in the struggle with departments are twofold, however. First, the 'muscle' in government – the specialized expertise and other resources – lies in the departments. The centre has a huge span of issues to cover, and its resources are thinly spread. Second, the 'centre' is of course an abstraction: in reality, most of the time it just imports all the divisions and struggles that exist elsewhere in government. In every modern government, for example, there have been powerful tensions between the prime minister and the chancellor of the Exchequer – and, by extension, between the Treasury and the office of the prime minister.

## The power of the prime minister

The role of the prime minister was transformed during the twentieth century, but the significance of this transformation is difficult to agree upon. That there has occurred a long-term growth of prime ministerial authority and prominence is undeniable.

**POLITICAL ISSUES**

### 7.1   WHO SHOULD BE TOP? THE BLAIR/BROWN SOAP OPERA

'Issues' in politics are not only about clashes of ideas and interests; they can also be about clashes of personal ambition and personal style. For over ten years at the top of the Labour Party, and after 1997 at the top of government, one such clash consumed enormous energy: that between Prime Minister Blair and his Chancellor, Gordon Brown. They entered the Commons on the same day, shared an office, and were young leaders in the reform of the Labour Party in the 1980s (see Chapter 15). The sudden death in 1994 of John Smith, Leader of the Labour Party, opened the path to the Leadership for both. At a famous dinner at an Islington restaurant the two agreed a pact. Brown stood aside allowing Blair a clear run at the Leadership, and thus Prime Ministerial Office in 1997. But some of the terms of the pact have long been disputed, usually in competing leaks to journalists and in often unreliable memoirs. Brown, and the large 'Brownite' faction at the top of the Labour Party, believe that by now Blair should have relinquished office in favour of his Chancellor. The tension is aggravated by personality differences: though both are, like all leading politicians, obsessively ambitious, Blair is by temperament a conciliator, with a genius for managing personalities face to face; Brown often appears brusque and adversarial but is more forensic.

Beyond personal ambition the long running soap opera illuminates three key issues:

- The ideological tensions at the heart of New Labour. Though a champion of the core New Labour economic innovations, Brown has managed to position himself publicly as also being sympathetic to old Labour values.
- The engrained tensions between the two most powerful ministers in any Westminster government. Bad relations between prime ministers and chancellors are the norm. Mrs Thatcher's Chancellor, Nigel Lawson, resigned in 1989 in a row over a mixture of policy on Europe and the sources of economic advice. Mr Major sacked his chancellor in 1993, leading the ex-chancellor bitterly to denounce his government as 'in office but not in power'. The tensions partly reflect institutional tensions between the Treasury and Number 10. Even were the prime minister and chancellor two contemplative saints there would still be stand-up rows.
- The engrained tension over succession. Every prime minister has several colleagues who would like to succeed him. After the 2005 general election Brown was confirmed in the dangerous role of heir apparent.

The break-up of the Cabinet system into a large number of specialized committees, working groups and bi-lateral negotiations has made the prime minister, as the figure most able to operate across all these, especially important in the vital role of coordinating policy. The widened public roles of the prime minister, in the presentation and defence of policy, and in the diplomacy of the European Union, has made it much easier for prime ministers to intervene at will in any area of government policy. To that extent, the hold of departmentalism has been weakened. Electoral competition has put increasing emphasis on the role of party leaders, and when prime ministers are successful in this kind of personality competition – for instance, after a great election victory, or when riding high in the polls – their authority over the rest of government is greatly enhanced.

# DEBATING POLITICS

## 7.1    DO WE HAVE PRIME MINISTERIAL GOVERNMENT?

| Arguments in favour: | Arguments against: |
|---|---|
| ■ Prime ministers command enormous powers of patronage by virtue of the huge range of appointments in their gift. | ■ The patronage powers of modern prime ministers are so vast that they can only allocate jobs after advice from others. |
| ■ Prime ministers have a particularly important source of patronage: appointing ministers. | ■ Prime ministers usually find that in appointing and dismissing ministers they have to pay regard to their most powerful Cabinet colleagues, who are usually also rivals. |
| ■ Modern elections are dominated by the prime minister of the day, and their main rival, the leader of the chief opposition party. | ■ Prime ministers who are thought to be unlikely to win the next election will be weak in dealing with senior colleagues and will be subjected to constant conspiracies to remove them. |
| ■ Prime ministers do not have to run a large specialized department and can roam widely across the whole of government. | ■ Prime ministers have to cover the whole span of government with staff resources that are quite small by comparison with the resources of most ministers who head big departments. |
| ■ Prime ministers are the single most important figures in ensuring coordination and consistency in government policy. | ■ Prime ministers who become fascinated by their role on the European or world stage often find that some rival at home has taken over control of key parts of domestic policy. |
| ■ Prime ministers are the single most important voice and symbol of their government abroad, in Europe and elsewhere. | |

A popular way in the past to summarize the consequences of these developments was to argue that we were developing prime ministerial government to replace Cabinet government (see Debating Politics 7.1). But this theory, though it alerted us to the growing importance of the prime minister, suffered from a number of defects. 'prime ministerial government' implied a model of executive organization, and it was not clear what this model really was. Sometimes it seemed to suggest that what was developing was a 'presidential' system, but since there are numerous kinds of presidency, that characterization was not illuminating. The theory of prime ministerial dominance also glossed over the great limits, both in resources and authority, that still hem in prime ministers.

These limits take three particular forms. First, *the break-up of the Cabinet system* into so many small parts constantly strains the ability of even the most energetic Prime Minister to keep abreast of issues. Most people the prime minister deals with are specializing in one policy area; the prime minister is trying to keep abreast of them all. This is one reason why prime ministers are often tripped up by surprise developments and unforeseen crises, and why they fret so much about problems of coordination and presentation. Second, *the resources available* to the prime minister, either to analyse policy or to see it through to conclusion, are severely limited. Most of the time a prime minister relies on other parts of government to provide expert analysis and to execute a prime ministerial decision. Finally, the *authority* that comes from electoral success can as easily drain away with electoral failure, or the threat of electoral failure. Within a year of winning a third successive general election by a large majority in 1987, Mrs Thatcher was being conspired against; by late 1990 she had been deposed.

## The struggle between ministers and officials

Finally, an age-old tension still lies at the heart of British government. Departments are tribes, and the most loyal members of the tribe are the officials. They have often spent a working lifetime living with the tribe. By contrast, ministers are transients. Most politicians spend most of their working lives outside government: for instance, in the long years of Conservative rule between 1979 and 1997 – an ideal opportunity therefore to create stability – only two members of the House of Commons other than Margaret Thatcher served in government positions throughout the period (Kenneth Clarke and Malcolm Rifkind). A good example of the impact of transience is provided by the case of the office of Chief Secretary to the Treasury, a Cabinet-level appointment which, because it chiefly involves detailed negotiations with departments about public spending plans, demands great command of complex detail: there were ten chief secretaries between 1990 and 2005. The sources of the ingrained tensions are obvious. The lives of politicians are dominated by a short-term institutional objective (how to ensure that their party is re-elected) and by a short-term personal objective (how to move on up the hierarchy by switching out of their present department to a higher level). Just about the only politician who wants to stay for a prolonged period in the same job is the prime minister. A couple of senior ministers (such as the chancellor) will always be sizing up the prime minister's job; and below them will be the whole government of more junior ministers, extending to the most obscure junior minister in Culture, Media and Sport, all jockeying for advancement. Officials, of course, are moved by institutional and career ambitions, but these are rather different. They build their careers usually for the most part inside a single department. They have a long-term interest in the department, and they often develop a strong emotional identification with that department.

## Further reading

The most important work on the core executive is by Burch and Holliday (1996); they have updated many of their findings in Burch and Holliday (2004). Smith (2000) reports detailed research on relations in the core executive. Marsh, Richards and Smith (2001) report important work on the reshaping of the Whitehall system. The two volumes collected by Rhodes (2000) report the most ambitious modern studies of how the centre of British government is changing.

## REVIEW

Three themes have dominated this chapter:

1 The 'core executive' defines an unstable world of shifting actors, frenetic activity and unclear boundaries;
2 Inside the core executive are distilled most of the great tensions at the heart of government: between elected and appointed officials; between prime ministers and their ministers; between specialized departments and those concerned to coordinate the totality of government policy;
3 Inside the core executive coordination of policy is inseparable from the presentation of policy. 'Spin' is central to the core executive, because above all it has to manage appearances to give a picture of consistency and strategic coherence, even if there is none in reality.

CHAPTER 8

# Departments and agencies in the Westminster system

## CONTENTS

## AIMS

The aims of the chapter are to:

❖ Describe the new, more fragmented organization of government in the Westminster system

❖ Describe the continuing importance of civil service departments despite this fragmentation

❖ Outline the origins and development of the Next Steps (executive) agencies

❖ Explain why regulation of privatized industries has become so important, and to sketch its organization

❖ Describe the rapidly expanding world of government through regulatory agencies in Britain

❖ Examine how far all these developments suggest that Britain is turning into a regulatory state centred on Westminster.

# The new world of agencies in British government

The growing acceptance of the concept of the core executive, which dominated Chapter 7, was due to two developments. One concerned the study of government at the centre in Britain; the other the actual practice of government. The first, involved the realization that there was needed a more adequate method of describing minister/civil servant relationships than traditional models offered, in order to make sense of things right at the top of British government. The second concerned the rising demand for one of the key services fulfilled by a core executive: centrally coordinating the management and presentation of policy. Coordination and presentation have become increasingly important because of changes in the structure of British government in the last couple of decades, changes that dominate this chapter.

Since the 1980s, British government at the centre has become more fragmented. What was once the dominant form of government – the civil service department controlled by a minister in Whitehall – has been supplemented, and in some instances displaced, by new kinds of agencies (see Images 8.1 and 8.2). Departments do still remain important, but since the 1980s three developments have greatly altered the traditional structure, and 'dispersed' the executive through a wide range of institutions. This chapter is mostly about the structures created by these changes.

The first set of changes examined here dates back to reforms begun in the 1980s. They are sometimes called the *'Next Steps' reforms*, after the title of the report which heralded them. The report led to the creation of a wide range of specialized agencies, either newly created or 'hived off' from the traditional civil service departments. These new executive agencies took over responsibility for the delivery of a large number of government services. The next section of the chapter is about this new generation of 'Next Steps' executive agencies, as they are commonly called.

The second momentous change also dates back to the 1980s, when the Conservative Government began an ambitious programme of *privatization*:

## Images 8.1 and 8.2
## The declining giants

Image 8.1   The Foreign Office

Image 8.2   The Department of Trade and Industry

➲ The dominant institutions in British government for most of the twentieth century were the central departments located on or close to the street named Whitehall in London (hence 'Whitehall' as the common shorthand for executive government in Britain). These two images show that legacy, but also show how the giants have declined. The first is of the main Foreign Office building. It is traditionally dignified and was meant to impress at a time when the British Empire covered large parts of the globe. The much more workaday building in Image 8.2 houses the Department of Trade and Industry. It is a typical 1960s office block, and it echoes another era of Westminster government ambition: that period in the 1960s and 1970s when government sought to exercise detailed control over British industry. Notice the physical contrasts, reflecting the traditionally higher prestige of the Foreign Office. And while the Foreign Office is right at the heart of the cluster of governing buildings, a footstep away from Parliament, the Treasury and the Prime Minister's residence, the DTI building is located further away, at the periphery of the main collection of buildings. But both the Foreign Office and the DTI have an antiquated look in the twenty-first century as British government has shifted from reliance on the giant Whitehall department. After the 2005 general election it was renamed Productivity, Energy and Industry. Within a week the Prime Minister had revoked the name change, reverting to the Department of Trade and Industry.

selling to private owners a large range of industries which for many decades had been publicly owned. These industries included some of the most important in the British economy. They covered, among others, telecommunications services, water supply, electricity generation, gas and electricity supply, coalmining and rail transport. The importance of these industries meant that they could not be transferred to private ownership without any safeguards over how they would be operated in private hands. Consequently, each privatization was accompanied by the creation of a specialized agency, with legal powers, charged with regulating the privatized industry in the public interest. The creation of these new *regulatory agencies* is the second great institutional change which is examined in this chapter. It created a virtually new, and very important, area of economic government.

Alongside the creation of regulatory agencies for the privatized industries there also occurred a wider change: *agencies were created to regulate a wide range of markets and other social spheres.* The spheres, we shall discover, were strikingly diverse: they encompassed things as different as the regulation of financial markets, the regulation of food safety and the regulation of human fertility. This is the third momentous change examined in this chapter.

## The departmental world

If the core executive is the coping stone which holds together the whole structure of government in the Westminster system, departments have been the building blocks of that system. Departments vary hugely in size, function and political weight, but taken together they are outstandingly important. The five major reasons for this importance are summarized below.

### They are key to accountability

Departments remain one of the most important institutions through which attempts are made to practise the *accountability* which lies at the heart of the theory of British democracy. The team which forms the political head of the department – the Secretary of State and the more junior members of the ministerial team – are answerable to Parliament through the workings of the doctrine of individual ministerial responsibility. Historically, this doctrine developed when government was small and ministers could

realistically hope to control everything of importance that happened in their department. Palmerston, the greatest of the nineteenth-century Foreign Secretaries, wrote by hand most of the letters going out of the Foreign Office. Today ministers would not even expect to see most of what is written on their behalf. Ministerial responsibility, in the literal sense of believing that ministers can be held responsible for all that is done in their name, is therefore no longer a serious influence on British government. But it has turned into a living doctrine of ministerial accountability, if only in this restricted sense: both in Parliament and through the media ministers expect to have to give an account of (to explain and defend) what is done by their departments. The internal life of a department at the most senior levels is heavily concerned with equipping ministers with the information to give these accounts. A further sign of the accountability functions of departments is that the senior civil servant in a department – the Permanent Secretary – is that department's 'accounting officer', who is responsible for accounting for the resources committed by the department.

### They are key arenas of politician/civil service tension

Departments are run by a team made up of elected politicians – usually ministers with a seat in the House of Commons – and appointed civil servants. Like most teams, the departmental team tries to work together but is also often subject to great internal tensions. Because ministers expect to have to give an account of departmental policy and actions, they also expect both to be able to shape the most important decisions made within the department and to be kept informed of what is going on. The day-to-day to life of departments, especially at the most senior levels, is dominated by making sure that ministers are indeed informed and able to defend the department's position. But into this is built one of the great tensions in the Westminster system. Ministers are usually more transient than civil servants: just how transient they can be is illustrated in Table 8.1. Perhaps even more important, they have their own special priorities: above all, since they are ministers only because their party has a

**Table 8.1** Brief lives: tenure of political and civil service heads of departments 1945–2004

|  | Ministerial heads* | Civil service heads* |
|---|---|---|
| Cabinet Office | 12 (Prime Ministers) | 7 |
| Foreign Office | 21 | 15 |
| Treasury | 21 | 11 |
| Home Office | 21 | 10 |
| Education | 27 | 11 |
| Industry | 33 | 12 |

\* 'Heads' refers to the senior (usually Cabinet) minister and civil service Permanent Secretary. The figures count the numbers of office holders; some politicians held the same office more than once. The departments have often undergone name changes over time: 'Industry' begins as the Board of Trade in 1945 and ends as the Department of Trade and Industry.

*Source*: Calculated from standard directories and author's files.

➲ Time in office is a crucial influence over the ability to affect policy. Experience not only brings more time to master the details; many projects in government are long term, so the longer someone is around the greater the likelihood that they will shape policy. The turnover of senior ministers is roughly double that of their civil service counterparts, and in some cases is almost three times higher. The very high turnover in Education and in Industry reflects the lower prestige of these ministerial offices: they have tended to be staging posts for politicians on the way up, or on the way down. Only exceptionally does a really able minister want to stay long term in a middle-ranking department.

majority in the House of Commons, they are focused on electoral success. Individually, they have little loyalty to the department: their career depends on moving on, and up, as quickly as possible. Their horizons are short term. But the time scale of much that government does is long term: new ministers inherit projects that began long ago, and will be completed long after they have departed. Civil servants, by contrast, are typically deeply concerned with these long-term commitments. It has been usual until now – though as we shall see in the next section this may be changing – for civil servants to spend virtually their whole career in one department. This is what gives departments the 'tribal'

culture that we discussed in Chapter 7. The tension between the preoccupations of civil servants, who have to live with projects in the long term and who develop emotional commitments to a department, and more transient and electorally focused ministers, makes departmental life an important arena of tension in British government. And since elected, accountable ministers running departments form a key element in the theory of democratic government in Britain, the way these tensions are resolved is important well beyond the immediate preoccupations inside departments; it affects how real democracy is in Britain.

One of the most important signs of this tension in recent years has not involved ministers and civil servants directly, but permanent civil servants and the rising number of *special advisers* that ministers now bring with them into departments. These advisers are usually active supporters of the governing party. Their rising number and importance is due to the politicians' belief that, alone, they cannot exercise sufficient influence over policy and its presentation in the department. Their job therefore directly expresses the politician/bureaucrat tension, which has often in recent years spilled over into acrimonious public dispute. A striking case is illustrated in Briefing 8.1.

## They are key arenas for struggles over the allocation of resources

We saw in the last chapter that life in the core executive is dominated by a *struggle for resources* – especially for money and, in planning the government's legislation, parliamentary time to pass laws. Departments are key institutions in this struggle: they compete with each other for money, for jurisdiction over policy. A great deal of argument inside government concerns which department has the right to make decisions about policy. For example, which should be the lead department in managing policy over asylum seekers: the Home Office or the Foreign Office?

## They are a symbol of status and prestige

Not all departments are equal. The 'pecking order' is often unclear, and it often changes, but there are great and persistent inequalities. Nobody doubts that the Treasury, though a department with a comparatively small staff, is way ahead in both influence and status of the Department for Culture, Media and Sport. This has some obvious consequences. The most important players in government – the leading politicians and the leading civil servants – measure their success by the status and prestige of 'their' department. For civil servants this will often turn into a struggle to augment the department's resources and policy jurisdiction. For ambitious ministers it turns into a constant struggle to move up the departmental hierarchy. The ambitious Secretary of State for Education, say, wants to move on to the Home Office or the Treasury. The fact that these departments are a symbol of status and prestige also explains why they are so often being remade and renamed. Several departments have in effect been created to meet the ambitions of powerful political figures. This was true of the Deputy Prime Minister under the two last Prime Ministers: both Michael Heseltine (Deputy under John Major) and John Prescott (Deputy under Tony Blair) have had large administrative empires created to meet their ambitions.

The unstable boundaries of departments also point to one of the longest dilemmas in departmental organization: on what principles should they be organized? At the end of the First World War – after a period of huge expansion in the scale of the state – a committee of enquiry recommended that departments be organized along functional lines: that is, according to the responsibilities they carried out. This has never been implemented more than approximately. Departmental structures are more frequently the product of historical accident, and the departmental 'tribes' powerfully resist reform: what they have, they defend. And the ambitions of politicians, as we have just seen, constantly intervene to compromise general organizational principles.

## They are a means of policy formulation and implementation

The core executive, as we saw in Chapter 7, is very important to policy coordination and presentation, and to the making of some key areas of high strate-

# Briefing                                      8.1

**A CIVIL WAR IN A DEPARTMENT: HOW TENSIONS BETWEEN MINISTERS, THEIR ADVISERS AND CIVIL SERVANTS CREATED CHAOS**

In Documenting Politics 7.4 (p. 131) we saw the case of the infamous e-mail sent by Jo Moore, an adviser in the Department of Transport, advising colleagues to 'bury' bad news by issuing it the day after the cataclysmic terrorist attack on the World Trade Center in New York on September 2001. Moore was eventually forced to resign but the aftermath only revealed more clearly the chaotic and hate-filled working relationships in the Department. In February 2002 the Department's Chief of Communications (Martin Sixsmith) was forced out, in part because supporters of Byers and Moore believed that he had helped orchestrate the campaign against her and had briefed journalists against his minister (both charges denied by Sixsmith). A vicious farce ensued, in which Sixsmith insisted that he had not resigned, and the Department (and the Prime Minister's Office) insisted he had. Leaked accounts of meetings included the Department's Permanent Secretary (senior civil servant) using language that would have been shocking even on the Stretford End at Manchester United's football ground, revelations that that minister and the Permanent Secretary had bad personal relations, and a complicated set of negotiations designed to try to secure a severance package for Sixsmith in return for a 'gagging' clause – negotiations that failed. Finally, later in 2002 Byers himself resigned, in part because of the bad blood created by the whole affair.

⮑ 'Official' accounts of working relations between ministers and civil servants paint a picture of settled constitutional understandings, but there is also a human face to Department life. Members of the departmental 'tribe' live in an intensely stressful atmosphere where work almost entirely dominates their lives. Here, differences about policy and poisonous personal relations often combine. The civil war in the Department of Transport in 2001–2 is unusual only in the way it spilled over into the public arena and allowed us to see the messy human reality behind the constitutional theory.

gic policy – for instance, the big historical decisions such as whether Britain should replace the pound sterling by joining the 'Eurozone'. But most policy arguments and struggles in British government are departmental struggles, either within or between departments. Within departments, life is dominated by providing advice about policy decisions to ministers. These ministers in turn expect their lives to be dominated by making (and publicly defending) policy decisions. Some of the biggest will be embodied in legislative proposals – parliamentary bills – for which the minister will have to fight for time and space in the core executive: for instance, in the Cabinet committee on the legislative timetable which we encountered in Chapter 7. But even a senior Cabinet minister would not expect to deal normally with more than one big piece of legislation per session. Daily life will be dominated by an unpredictable mixture: making and defending some decisions, ranging from those involving huge resources to those concerning individuals. Ministers will expect to advocate and defend these decisions in both Parliament and the media, and they will expect their senior civil servants to provide them with the ammunition for defence. It is a foolish, or badly served, minister who appears on *The World at One* on Radio 4 or *Newsnight* on BBC2 without a briefing note from the civil service.

Policy ranges unpredictably from the minute to the grand, and the public importance attached to it can also be unpredictable. A Home Office minister can often spend large amounts of time defending decisions affecting single individuals – such as an individual prisoner or an individual asylum seeker. Not surprisingly, ministers and civil servants often feel overloaded by the volume of decisions needing to be taken and defended. As we shall see in a moment, this was one of the sources of the initiative to create executive agencies. But another source concerned not the making of policy but its implementation. Not all departments have been historically closely involved in policy implementation: the Treasury, for example, is largely concerned with strategic policy advice and formulation. But many departments have historically been huge policy delivery institutions: for example, the Home Office in its concern with prison administration, or social

security departments concerned with the administration of the whole benefit system for the unemployed. A feeling that the culture and skills of the London-based civil service elite was not well suited to administering large, complex delivery systems also lay behind the initiative which we examine next: the creation of the executive agencies.

## The world of the new executive agencies

The development of the new executive agencies, which date from the reforms of the Conservative governments at the end of the twentieth century, was the most ambitious reform of the structure of central government in modern times. The question of how those fundamental institutional reforms have actually changed the working of government in the Westminster system is now one of the great issues in studying British government.

### The Next Steps agencies: the context

The cryptic label 'Next Steps' agencies dates from the title of a report on the reform of the management of central government produced in 1988 by a team headed by Sir Robin Ibbs, then head of the Efficiency Unit established in the core executive by the prime minister in the 1980s (see Documenting Politics 8.1). As the title implies, the purpose of the report was to carry forward the 'Next Steps' of the Conservatives' revolutionary programme, which by the end of the 1980s was already well on the way to privatizing most of the big publicly owned industries. (The regulatory bodies created as a result of privatization are examined later in this chapter.)

As these historical origins suggest, the creation of the agencies cannot be considered in isolation, or as only an institutional change in the form of central government. They are part of a more long-drawn-out process of reform in the administrative centre of the state in Britain, a process which dates back to the 1960s. For the 50 years after the end of the First World War the administrative centre was dominated by a model which put the civil service department, headed by a minister advised by permanent

## DOCUMENTING POLITICS 8.1

### THE CREATION OF THE NEXT STEPS AGENCIES: THE PICTURE PAINTED BY THE CREATORS.

'The main strategic control must lie with the Minister and Permanent Secretary. But once the policy objectives and budgets within the framework are set, the management of the agency should then have as much independence as possible in deciding how these objectives are met. A crucial element in the relationship would be a formal understanding with Ministers about the handling of sensitive issues and lines of accountability in a crisis. The presumption must be that, provided management is operating within the strategic direction set by Ministers it must be left as free as possible to manage within that framework.'

➲ The passage here reproduces the central argument from perhaps the most important modern document about the organization of central government in Britain. It launched the 'Next Steps' agencies, whose multiplication fundamentally changed the traditional organization of the civil service. Notice a key assumption in the passage: that a consistent separation could be made between 'strategic control' which was to remain where it traditionally lay, with the minister and the most senior civil servant; and daily management which was to be done independently by the agencies. As we shall see, this distinction proved hard to preserve in practice.

*Source*: Jenkins, Caines and Jackson (1988: 9).

civil servants, right at the centre of the governing process. We saw in the last section that this model still remains enormously influential, but it has been increasingly challenged, on three chief grounds:

- *That is it uncoordinated.* The rise of the core executive, described in Chapter 7, represents an attempt to assert central control over the coordination, the presentation and even, in some cases, the making of policy. This can be seen as a reaction against the power of the departmental 'tribes' that have traditionally dominated the Westminster system.
- *That is it overloaded.* As we saw in the last section, departments are a frenetic focus of demands for decisions about matters large and small. Ministers and their most senior civil service advisers instinctively search for some ways of 'off-loading' responsibilities, thus allowing them to concentrate on a smaller range of strategic issues.
- *That it lacks the necessary skills.* Modern government demands high levels of managerial skills: in data analysis; in managing large-scale projects,

such as construction projects, from start to finish; in managing huge numbers of people in complex, multi-layered bureaucracies. Since the 1960s – when a report on the civil service chaired by Lord Fulton argued that the organization lacked these managerial skills – there have been periodic reforms designed to remedy these perceived defects. The result was that over a period of 30 years, the perception of the skills needed to administer modern government changed hugely: just how hugely is illustrated in Documenting Politics 8.2.

The Next Steps initiative can therefore be seen as the most determined attempt yet to respond to perceived problems in the civil service as traditionally organized, notably to the problems of overload and skill deficiency.

### The Next Steps agencies: the principles

Four principles lay behind the initiative that has led to the large-scale creation of executive agencies in British government.

**DOCUMENTING POLITICS 8.2**

## HOW THE PERCEIVED SKILLS NEEDED TO MANAGE MODERN GOVERNMENT HAVE CHANGED

'If you entered the civil service in, say, the 1960s (as I did) the literature would have told you that senior civil servants were policy makers. They were not expected to know the cost of the resources that they controlled or the staff who worked for them. They would not have had budgets. They would not have described themselves as managers. We now require people in public service to be good managers and good leaders of their organizations and to know how to achieve results through the people who are working for them and through the application of project management skills.' (Sir Richard Wilson, Cabinet Secretary, 1999)

➲ Sir Richard Wilson was the most successful civil servant of his generation, reaching the very top of the tree – Secretary to the Cabinet – in the 1990s. His recollection of how the job of managing government changed over more than 30 years is therefore authoritative. And his picture of greater demands for technical managerial skills, and more systematic managerial information, illustrates precisely the pressures for change that helped created the Next Steps agencies.

*Source*: Wilson (1999).

*Separating strategic policy advice and decision from delivery.* As the extract from the report in Box 8.1 shows, this was the key principle that lay behind the initiative. The attractions of this to senior civil servants and ministers are clear. The sense of being 'overloaded' arises partly from the sheer volume of demands for decision made on departments, and partly from the way those at the top of departments often feel uncomfortable in dealing with the details of policy implementation. Politicians in particular often struggle with detail, in part because they have so many competing demands on their time, and in part because temperamentally they often have a limited attention span. Senior, highly educated civil servants are used to playing the game of policy advice in the upper reaches of departments; their training has traditionally prepared them less well to get on top of the often tedious details of policy delivery. Making a supposedly clear separation between strategic priorities (a phrase which readily trips off the tongues of senior ministers and their advisers) and daily management is thus immensely attractive.

*Making the relationship between the agency and the department explicit and clear.* It is one thing to say in general terms that strategic decision is to be separated from daily management; another to operate this distinction in practice. The creation of the agencies has thus been accompanied by an important innovation: the laying down, usually in a written 'framework document', of the details of the division of responsibility between the agency and its department (see Documenting Politics 8.3 for an example). This marks a significant innovation in the organization of government, for hitherto the division between strategic decision and management had been 'bundled up' inside the department.

*Guiding Agency management by performance indicators.* The creation of the agencies coincided with another shift in the culture of British government: the rise of a concern with measuring the performance of government and judging the adequacy of government by the extent to which quantifiable performance targets had been met. From the start the framework of agency behaviour has been shaped by quantitative performance indicators, and the targets set to reach those indicators.

*Loosening the ties with traditional civil service organization.* Agencies come in all shapes and sizes,

**DOCUMENTING POLITICS 8.3**

## EXTRACT FROM A FRAMEWORK AGREEMENT: THE CASE OF THE PRISON SERVICE

'2.1 The Prison Service is a part of the criminal justice system which works to two overarching aims:

- to reduce crime and the fear of crime, and their social and economic costs;
- to dispense justice fairly and efficiently, and to promote confidence in the rule of law.

These aims and their associated targets are set out in the Public Service Agreement for the Criminal Justice System.

AIM

2.2 Deriving from these overarching aims, the Prison Service works within the Home Office to the following specific aim and associated targets set out in the Home Office Public Service Agreement:

- effective execution of the sentences of the courts so as to reduce re-offending and protect the public.

OBJECTIVES

2.3 In support of that aim the objectives set for the Prison Service are:

- to protect the public by holding in custody those committed by the Courts in a safe, decent, and healthy environment;

and there is no one single template guiding relationships with the civil service; but because the creation of agencies in part resulted from dissatisfaction with the civil service as a manager of policy delivery, the 'Next Steps' reforms also attempted to depart from traditional models of civil service organization. There are three particularly important signs of this. First, the heads of the new agencies have been appointed by *open competition*, not by internal promotion from within the civil service, although many heads are indeed drawn from the civil service. Second, there have been conscious attempts to introduce *private sector working practices and management styles* into the new agencies. These take a variety of forms. Market testing has become widespread. This involves measuring the efficiency of 'in-house' service provision against the terms offered in competitive tendering by private sector providers. The service can range from office cleaning to the provision of large-scale information technology (IT) support. Some of the changes are symbolic, but the symbols are designed to communicate a change in culture. Agencies now routinely speak of their 'customers', for instance, and try to measure customer satisfaction with their services. The overall effect of these changes has been to make relationships much more contractual in nature. The relationships between the agency and the department are rather like those of a supplier and customer, with the framework agreement and

**DOCUMENTING POLITICS 8.3**   (continued)

- to reduce crime by providing constructive regimes which address offending behaviour, improve educational and work skills and promote law abiding behaviour in custody and after release.

PRINCIPLES

2.4  In support of the specified aim and objectives is a statement of the ways in which the Prison Service works towards them and the conduct expected from staff:

In undertaking our work, all members of the Prison Service will:

- deal fairly, openly, and humanely with prisoners and all others who come into contact with us;
- encourage prisoners to address offending behaviour and respect others;
- value and support each other's contribution;
- promote equality of opportunity for all and combat discrimination wherever it occurs;
- work constructively with criminal justice agencies and other organizations;
- obtain best value from resources available.'

⮑ The work of each new executive agency is governed by a 'framework agreement'. This is intended to govern the principles by which it operates – both how it treats its clients and how it deals with its 'parent' department of state. The example here comes from one of the largest and most politically sensitive of the agencies, that concerned with running the Prison Service. In its early years, despite the attempt to establish working principles in the framework agreement, the prison service agency was beset with controversy, culminating in the sacking of its head by the Home Secretary. The issue of the division of responsibilities between the Home Office and the Prison Service is also documented in Chapter 5.

*Source*: www.hmprisonservice.gov.uk

performance targets embodying the terms of the contract. Working relationships inside agencies are also heavily contractual in nature, working life being governed by the need to achieve specified performance targets. The agency is itself increasingly involved in contractual relationships with private sector suppliers of services.

The third and final institutional change takes the logic of these developments to their fullest expression: to *privatize the agency itself*. The agency then becomes a private enterprize which has a contract with government to deliver services under specified conditions, for instance governing price and quality. A good example is provided by an agency which the readers of this book will probably use at some time

to buy an official publication: The Stationery Office (see Documenting Politics 8.4).

### Executive agencies: scale and range

Briefing 8.2 (p. 149) summarizes the scale and variety of the executive agencies. Their history of creation has three key features, only two of which are readily clear from the box itself.

*Scale*.   The scale of agency creation is immense: over 140 agencies now employ over 370,000 staff (see Briefing 8.2). Measured by this, not unimportant, indicator the rise of the executive agency is one of the most important changes in British government in modern times.

**DOCUMENTING POLITICS 8.4**

## THE STATIONERY OFFICE AS A PRIVATIZED AGENCY

ABOUT US

'TSO (The Stationery Office) was created in September 1996, when most of the assets and commercial activities of Her Majesty's Stationery Office (HMSO) were sold to The Stationery Office Group Ltd (TSOL). This company demerged its operations on 31 March 1999, creating The Stationery Office Holdings Ltd and three new independent companies.

  In July 1999 The Stationery Office Holdings Ltd was sold to funds managed by a leading venture capital company, Apax Partners, with additional finance provided by the Bank of Scotland. Apax Partners manages more than 5 billion euros for major institutional investors, both public and private. They own 74% of the shares of The Stationery Office Holdings Ltd, with the rest held by TSO management and staff.'

➲ The case of the Stationery Office is a striking example of how the changes in the structures of public administration have reshaped the line dividing the public and the private sector. Once the very epitome of a public service organization, the Office is now a privately owned company like any other, contracted with the public sector to produce official documents.

*Source*: www.tso.co.uk

*Diversity.* The diversity of agencies is an obvious implication of their very scale of creation. But this diversity goes beyond the obvious: as Briefing 8.2 makes clear, we are looking here at institutions that vary hugely in size and responsibilities. Close studies of the experience of agency working suggests a deeper diversity: in the extent to which the creation of an agency really does result in a change in institutional culture and working practices. For some, the effects of separation from the department have been comparatively modest. For others – obvious examples would be those that have been fully privatized – the changes have been quite fundamental.

*Political visibility.* One of the most important sources of diversity arises from the political visibility of the functions for which the agency is responsible. Some of these agencies are not only small, but they inhabit routine backwaters of British government. It takes a lot to reveal them to the public eye, and in particular for their activities

to cause problems for ministers. But others are highly visible, not only in the scale of the services they deliver, but in the potential for political problems that they create. Despite the formal separation of 'strategy' from 'daily management', political problems usually draw ministers into daily operations. In some cases this visibility and sensitivity is engrained in the agency. The best example is the Prison Service Agency: everyday details of prison policy – for instance, whether particular notorious prisoners might be eligible for parole – are the subject of intense party argument and media interest. No Home Secretary can keep his fingers out of that aspect of daily management. Some agencies are catapulted into political visibility by a failure of service delivery: for example, both the Passport Agency and the Child Support Agency have attracted the direct intervention of ministers because problems of daily service delivery were causing political embarrassment.

# Briefing

## THE VARIETY AND SCALE OF THE NEW EXECUTIVE AGENCIES

| Agency | Numbers employed | Main function |
|---|---|---|
| Civil Service | 220 | Provides in-service training for civil servants |
| Companies House | 839 | Receives, stores and disseminates company reports |
| Wilton Park | 37 | Runs an up-market conference centre, chiefly for foreign policy conferences |
| Employment Service | 28,612 | Runs all high street employment services |
| Serious Fraud Office | 149 | Investigates major financial frauds |
| Social Security Benefits Agency | 66,296 | Administers all social security benefits |
| Social Security Child Support Agency | 7,909 | Administers rules involving, chiefly, obligations of non-resident spouses to contribute to upkeep of dependents |
| HM Prison Service | 39,363 | Runs prisons in England and Wales |

*Source*: Extracted from *Next Steps Report 1998*, Annex A, at www.official-documents.co.uk

➲ These data derive from an official overview published in 1998. At the time, there were over 140 agencies employing over 370,000 staff. The examples are designed to show the diversity of the agencies. They range from tiny bodies carrying out utterly uncontroversial functions, to huge bureaucracies delivering large-scale public services that constantly arouse political controversy: notice the presence of the Prison Service, a crisis in the government of which was the occasion of the issue decribed in Chapter 5. But notice also that size is no measure of controversy: the medium-size Child Support Agency has been constantly at the centre of controversy, principally because of its pursuit of payments from divorced parents; and the tiny Serious Fraud Office has likewise been in continuing controversy, chiefly because of the collapse of high-profile trials involving financial fraud.

## Regulatory agencies and privatization

Although the creation of the executive agencies was a major change in the structure of British government it was not the biggest single change of recent years. That distinction belongs to the *privatization programme* which was carried out principally by the Conservative governments in power between 1979 and 1997. In those years, and especially in a few revolutionary years of the 1980s, whole industries were sold to the private sector, mostly through flotation on the Stock Exchange. (For a summary of the main privatizations, see Chapter 21). Privatization dismantled a whole range of public enterprize that had been organized in nationalized corporations (such as British Steel or British Rail) or in publicly owned authorities, (for instance, those

that controlled the water supply). It thus *contracted* the scale of British government, but it simultaneously *expanded public authority* because at the same time it created new kinds of public agencies to regulate these privatized enterprizes.

### The special features of regulatory agencies for privatized industries

The regulatory agencies for the privatized industries, though they bear some superficial resemblance to the executive agencies, differ from them in four important respects.

*They are new creations.* The executive agencies were carved out of civil service departments and have mostly retained close relationships with those departments. The regulatory agencies for the privatized industries are for the most part new creations (see Briefing 8.3). They are an important innovation in British government, for while some historical ancestors can be found in the nineteenth century they really amount to a new way of governing the economy.

*They regulate.* Public ownership created huge organizations that produced and delivered goods and services, ranging from coal to water to rail travel. That often gave departments in the Westminster system the opportunity for direct hands-on control of large parts of the economy. The new regulatory agencies are of outstanding importance because they span equally important domains of the economy. But unlike either the old nationalized corporations or the new executive agencies they deliver no goods or services. Their importance lies in the fact that they regulate how goods or services – ranging from water to electricity

# Briefing                                                                 8.3

## THE NEW WORLD OF REGULATORY AGENCIES, AT JUNE 2004

| Name | Date established | Responsibilities |
| --- | --- | --- |
| Office of Communications (OFCOM) | 2003 | From the end of 2003 has been responsible for all broadcasting regulation hitherto carried out by a range of separate bodies. |
| Office of the Rail Regulator | Established under the Railways Act 1993 | Regulates train and track operators in the privatized rail industry; replaced by Office of Rail Regulation in July 2004. |
| National Lottery Commission | 1999 (succeeded OFLOT, established 1993) | Regulates all aspects of the national lottery from sales to proceeds distribution. |
| Office of Gas and Electricity Markets (OFGEM) | 2000, fusing hitherto separate authorities regulating gas and electricity markets. | Regulates firms in energy markets. |
| Human Fertilization and Embryology Authority (HFEA) | 1991 | Regulates scientific research into, and use of embryos for, intervention in human fertility. |
| Financial Services Authority (FSA) | 1997 (fully operational 2000) | Regulates all financial institutions for honesty and stability. |
| Food Standards Agency | 2000 | Regulates all stages of food production in the interests of public health. |
| Office of Telecommunications (OFTEL) | 1984 | Regulates telecommunications markets. |

➲ The closing decades of the twentieth century saw a major institutional innovation in British government: the rise of the specialized regulatory agency charged with control of an industry or social domain. The dates of foundation chart the recent rise of the agencies. The agencies are commonly associated with the aftermath of the privatization programme of the Conservative governments in the 1980s and 1990s, and some of the examples above are indeed charged with regulating privatized enterprizes: in telecommunications, energy and rail. But some other examples show that the regulatory agency is now a standard way of exercising public control. In some cases the new agency replaces other public arrangements: for instance, the Food Standards Agency took over duties hitherto carried out by a central department, the old Ministry of Agriculture, Food and Fisheries; while the Financial Services Authority displaced the Bank of England from banking regulation.

to phone services – are produced or delivered: they literally control the rules under which markets operate. They thus have an important say in such vital matters as: what firms can enter a market; what prices they can charge, and by how much they can increase prices; when they can cut off services to customers, (for instance, for non-payment of bills); and what service standards (for instance, governing speed of response to customers) they must observe.

*They have unusual independence.* The executive agencies, we saw, have a complex relationship with civil service departments and with ministers. Although they often have a large amount of operational independence they are constantly subject to intervention, especially if their activities prove sensitive to the careers and priorities of ministers. The regulatory agencies are not immune to this sort of intervention, but they have established a much clearer tradition of independent operation. They are usually governed by a single Director-General whose powers and authority are specified by statute. They have from the beginning recruited from outside the civil service and have established their own management styles and career patterns, separate from the civil service. The individual Directors-General have, since they first emerged in the 1980s, established themselves as independent public figures in their own policy domains.

*They are a vital form of economic government.* The new regulatory agencies have existed in their present form for less than two decades: the first, OFTEL, which regulates Telecommunications, was established only when the old nationalized telephone service provider was privatized in 1984; but in the years since then they have emerged as major instruments for governing the economy in Britain. The privatized sector is a major part of the economy (see Documenting Politics 8.5). It includes industries, such as telecommunications, that are at the leading edge of modern technology, are organized on a global scale, and are dominated by large multinational firms. It includes those providing public services that are vital to the economy and everyday life, such as rail services. And it also includes services that we hardly think about but whose maintenance is vital to the very fabric of community life: every time we turn on a tap expecting an instanta-

neous flow of clean water we are drawing on the services of a regulated, privatized industry. (Not, however, in Scotland, where water privatization was never implemented.) The importance of the industries helps answer a vital question which we examine next: why were these major new public institutions created?

## Why the agencies were created

At first glance it is not at all clear why regulatory agencies should have been created for the newly privatized industries. We know from earlier chapters that Britain is primarily a market economy where private ownership dominates. Large parts of the economy have historically been run by private firms and, beyond general laws such as those concerned with preventing fraud, it has not usually been thought necessary to establish special regulatory bodies for individual industries: we do not have a special regulator for the chemical or the automobile production industries. The creation of important state regulatory agencies in the privatized sphere tells us a lot not just about the privatized sector. The range of their responsibilities also throws an important light on the new world of *multi-level government*: agencies to regulate the water industry do not have jurisdiction in Scotland for the simple reason that Scottish water has not been privatized. It throws an important light on a key question that has to be settled in any system which, like Britain, is simultaneously *democratic* and *capitalist*: how much control can the democratic state exercise over private enterprize?

There are three main reasons why it was felt necessary to create special regulatory agencies. All point to conditions where state intervention is needed in a market economy.

*Controlling monopoly.* Some of the privatized industries are near perfect examples of what is sometimes called *natural monopoly*: that is, the nature of the good supplied, and the network through which it is supplied, means that it is all but impossible for there to be competition between suppliers. The water industry is a good example. Although in principle it is possible to envisage a system of competitive supply of water, in practice

## DOCUMENTING POLITICS 8.5

## REGULATION ON THE GROUND: THE REACH OF A REGULATORY AGENCY

'*Debt and disconnection*

One and a half million consumers are repaying debts to their fuel supplier. A joint priority for Ofgem and energywatch is a reduction in this number. During 2002, we have examined the main causes of fuel debt, and the good practices which fuel suppliers can adopt to prevent debt problems occurring. Consumer representatives and energy companies have been consulted. Taking account of their views, Ofgem and energywatch have invited suppliers to develop strategies designed to help consumers avoid running up debts, by the adoption of best practice.

In developing strategies, suppliers have been asked to focus on six key areas:

1.   Minimizing billing errors
2.   Using incoming calls to identify consumers in difficulty
3.   Using consumer records to target energy efficiency improvements
4.   Demonstrating flexibility in debt recovery
5.   Offering sustainable solutions to consumers in extreme hardship
6.   Helping consumers who are unable to manage their own affairs.

Under each of these six headings, energywatch and Ofgem have identified guidelines reflecting good practice. Suppliers have been asked to incorporate these guidelines into their strategies.

All fuel suppliers already have codes of practice that set out the services they provide to domestic consumers. These cover payment of bills and dealing with customers in difficulty; energy efficiency advice; use of prepayment meters; services for customers who are elderly, disabled or chronically sick; and services for customers who are blind or deaf. In some areas, the debt prevention guidelines reflect best practice in respect to interpretation and operation of existing code of practice obligations. In other areas, the debt prevention guidelines go beyond existing obligations and encourage suppliers to consider new and innovative approaches to help consumers avoid getting into debt.'

➲ Although the privatized industries resemble conventional private sector firms in respect of ownership, their operations are very closely controlled by public regulatory bodies. This document shows just how close is the regulator's scrutiny. It was issued by OFGEM, the Office of Gas and Electricity Markets, the main energy regulator. It lays down guidelines on what is essentially a commercial matter: how the companies are to deal with bad debtors. Because of the social implications of disconnecting gas or electricity supplies from individual customers, it obliges the companies to develop strategies to manage those social consequences.

*Source*: www.ofgem.gov.uk

no such competition exists in Britain: citizens have no option but to take their water from the network supplied by the privatized company that delivers water in their town. It is common ground virtually right across the political spectrum that where monopoly exists, and market competition cannot therefore control the monopolist, a potential for abuse of power exists, and must be restrained by special regulation. Beyond natural monopoly there are other privatized industries where one firm is so dominant that, while competitors exist, its weight is so great that we cannot depend on competition to restrict its power. For most of the history of the privatized telecommunications industry, for example, that has been the situation with British Telecom (now BT).

*Regulating franchises.*   In many privatized industries there is in effect a special kind of monopoly: a 'franchise' or licence granted to a firm to provide a service, usually for a fixed time period under specified conditions. This is how the train operating companies following rail privatization provide services in different regions of Britain. A franchise obviously gives special privileges to the franchisee: Virgin Rail holds the franchise to provide the west coast inter-city rail link between Manchester and London, and thus has a monopoly on that line for the life of the franchise. Part of the job of regulators in the rail industry is to 'police' franchises: to award the franchise in the first place, to measure how well firms are meeting the conditions of their franchise, and to penalize them when they fail to meet service targets.

*Ensuring the supply of essential services.*   If I take out a loan to buy a new Mercedes, find that I cannot keep up the payments and have the car repossessed, everybody will conclude that I have been unlucky or foolish; nobody will think that I have an entitlement to a new Mercedes. However, many of the goods and services provided by the privatized industries are of a different order. They are widely perceived as essential for anyone to have a decent everyday existence in modern Britain. If I cannot pay my gas, electricity or water bills, disconnection of supply is not so obvious a solution as is repossession of my Mercedes. Apart from my own needs, how are others in my family to cook, keep warm, and wash? Special rules are needed for the disconnection of these essential supplies of the sort that are not needed in repossessing luxury cars. Formulating and enforcing those special rules is an important function of a regulator. That function connects with the regulation of price, for obviously the price at which a good or service is set will affect the chances of the poorest in the community being able to meet its charges.

Behind these reasons for creating special regulators for the privatized industries lies an important general principle: the principle of making economic power accountable. What all the particular reasons lead up to is the conclusion that in the privatized sector we have created important domains of economic power, and that democratic government has a duty to hold this power openly accountable. But of course it is not only in privatized industries that there exist important domains of economic power: parallel to the rise of the regulatory agencies in the privatized industries there has been a wider adoption of the public regulatory agency to control economic and social life. We examine these agencies next.

## General regulatory agencies in Britain

One of the most remarkable features of government in Britain since the 1980s has been the rise of regulatory agencies charged with control of important domains of economic and social life. There are four particularly important areas where we can observe the rise of the regulatory agency.

### Reorganization of traditional 'inspectorates'

There is nothing new in the principle of government inspecting and controlling particular fields of social and economic activity: for instance, regulation of safety at work and regulation of the environment to control air pollution have nineteenth-century origins (the former dates back to the establishment of the Factory Inspectorate in 1833; the latter to the Alkali Inspectorate in 1863). But this was a piecemeal, fragmented system of inspection built up by a long period of gradual historical change. Since the 1970s we have seen these piecemeal, fragmented state inspectorates organized into centrally coordinated agencies. Two examples are the Health and Safety Executive (HSE), which in 1974 reorganized all the nineteenth-century inspectorates concerned with health and safety at work into a single agency; and the Environment Agency, which in 1996 did the same thing for a variety of different specialized agencies concerned with the control of environmental pollution.

## Transformed self-regulation

There has long been regulation of social and economic life in Britain, but it has been dominated by self-regulation. Under *self-regulation* the state is usually a marginal influence and legal rules are rarely important. Institutions, such as firms in markets, agree voluntarily to controls and themselves police obedience to those controls. Some of the most important areas of British life were historically governed by self-regulation: the single most important sector of the British economy, the financial markets in the City of London, were governed in this way, and self-regulation was also the manner in which sport was governed. Recent changes have dramatically altered self-regulation. Some have involved a wholesale transformation of what were once independent domains of self-regulation into domains now regulated by public agencies with statutory powers: that is the situation in the financial services industry since the establishment of the Financial Services Authority (FSA), backed by statutory powers in the Financial Services and Markets Act of 2000. Some changes are less dramatic but are still significant: the founding of Sport England in 1997 meant the establishment of an important state agency, which distributes substantial public funds in a domain which traditionally was governed by pure self-regulation (see Briefing 8.4 for more details).

## Growing regulation inside government

Regulation 'inside the state' is one of the most rapidly growing areas of regulatory activity. This is partly due to a trend which we noticed in our description of the new Executive Agencies: the trend towards setting targets, monitoring performance and imposing sanctions when targets are not met. As Table 8.2 shows, there has been a proliferation of these new regulatory agencies inside government.

## Regulating new social domains

The regulatory agency is now established as a standard response by government in Britain to the problem of controlling economic and social life. This means that when new social problems appear,

or when innovation creates new social activities, it is almost instinctive to create a regulatory agency to exercise control. Three important recent examples illustrate this process:

● The Food Standards Agency was created in 2000 as a result of a series of scandals in food safety, especially the discovery that Bovine Spongiform Encephalopathy (BSE) had infected large parts of the national cattle herd in Britain. Although there had been hitherto some regulation of food standards, the establishment of the Agency represented a step change in the control of safety standards in agriculture, in food processing and in food retailing.
● The establishment of OFLOT (Office of the National Lottery) in 1993 showed another important development: new social and

**Table 8.2**   The rise of regulation inside government

Public-sector regulation, 1976 compared with 1995

| Regulators | No. of bodies, 1995 (and % change since 1976) | Estimated staffing increase 1976–95 | Estimated increase in real terms spending 1976–95 |
|---|---|---|---|
| Public audit bodies | 4 (same) | +60% | +130% |
| Inspectorates and equivalents | 27 (+17%) | +75% | +100% |
| Ombudsmen and equivalents | 17 (+78%) | +150% | +200% |
| Central agency regulators | 18 (+38%) | same | same |
| Funder-cum-regulators | 14 (+133%) | +10% | +100% |
| Departmental regulators of agencies | 26 (–10%) | n.a. | n.a. |
| Central regulators of local public bodies and the NHS | 29 (+11%) | n.a. | n.a. |
| All regulators in government | 135 (+22%) | +60% | +106% |

*Source*: Extracted and adapted from Hood *et al.* (1999: 30).

➲ This material is extracted from the standard study of 'regulation inside government', by Hood and his colleagues (1999). Their work paints a picture of long-term growth in the scale and intensity of regulation right across the public sector. The material here is a snapshot, and emphasizes the diversity of regulatory forms, the diversity of institutions covered, and the diverse ways regulation of public bodies is funded.

economic activities – in this case the establishment for the first time of a national lottery in Britain – can now expect to be subject to specialized regulatory control. The example of OFLOT also shows how operational problems can reshape agencies: after a history of ineffectiveness, OFLOT was replaced by the National Lottery Commission in 1999.

● The establishment of the Human Fertilization and Embryology Authority (HFEA) in 1991 marks the extension of the agency idea to another important social arena: the control of scientific research and the application of that research. The Authority is concerned with regulating the conditions under which women can benefit from the new technologies of artificial reproduction. But the importance of this body goes beyond this particular field, important though it is to those who seek IVF (*in vitro* fertilization): it establishes the principle that scientific technologies, and especially new technologies, can be applied only when they are subject to public controls through a regulatory institution.

## Explaining the rise of regulatory agencies

The rise of the new regulatory agencies marks an important long-term change in the way the state operates in Britain. The change has two particularly important features. In part it signifies a *retreat* by the state. For the first three-quarters of the twentieth century, the state relied on steadily growing public ownership to give it control over social and economic life. That was reversed in the privatization programmes of the 1980s and 1990s. But in part it signifies an *advance* by the state: some domains that governed themselves by self-regulation no longer enjoy that independence, and some entirely new domains of regulation have been created. Many particular factors explain these transformations, but three general forces can be identified.

### Crisis and scandal

Some of the most important creations in the world of agencies have been the result of large-scale breakdowns of traditional control, and these break-downs have led to public scandal and crisis. Two of most important agencies created in recent years, the Food Standards Agency and the Financial Services Authority, owe their existence in part to these forces. The Food Standards Agency was the direct result of a great crisis of public confidence in the safety of the food we eat arising from a run of fail-ures. These culminated in the great BSE crisis of the mid-1990s, when a public inquiry established that there had been a total breakdown of safety regulation in farming: BSE had spread throughout the national cattle herd, resulting in the entry into the human food chain of diseased meat and the possible infection of humans by a fatal, incurable disease. The Financial Services Authority was also partly the response to more than a decade of scan-dals, and collapses, of important financial institu-tions.

### The European Union

The traditional British system of self-regulation put the law at the margins of regulation. But with Britain's increasing integration in the European Union a very different regulatory culture was encountered: in both the Union itself, and in the most influential members of the Union such as Germany and France, law has been much more important in the regulation of social and economic life. As we saw in Chapter 6, the Union itself is a legal creation – through the Treaties that marked its foundation and extension – and it is natural that it should therefore work through law. As we also saw, the ECJ, and the interpretations it delivers, are important to the way public power works. An important consequence for Britain, therefore, is that traditionally non-legal systems of self-regula-tion have often had to be recast in legal language. This was a subsidiary reason for the reorganiza-tion of self-regulation in the financial markets, and it has been important in reshaping self-regulation in another important area, the regulation of professions such as medicine, the law and account-ing.

### Power and democracy

The theory of British democracy pictures the state as an institution concerned with the control of private power, such as great private economic power. The retreat of the state from many fields of economic intervention in recent decades – a retreat most obvious in the privatization of public enter-prize – raises an obvious question: how is public control now to be exercised? The regulatory agency has emerged as one answer to that question. How adequate an answer it amounts to, we now examine.

## The new regulatory state: achievements and problems

The developments described in this chapter summarize a great transformation of the Westminster model of British government since the 1980s. Two key components of that model have been fundamentally changed:

● The civil service department, while remaining important, is no longer the kingpin for policy delivery.
● Publicly owned industries are no longer impor-tant as a means of controlling economic life.

The changes amount to the rise of a new 'regulatory state', which is marked by three features:

● The new executive agencies are in essence contracted to deliver policy, and are regulated to measure how effectively they manage delivery.
● The new privatized sector is subject to a network of specialized regulatory agencies.
● Government has turned to the specialized regu-latory agency to control large areas of economic and social life.

The achievements of this new regulatory state are considerable. From the point of view of the func-tioning of democratic government in Britain two are particularly valuable.

## POLITICAL ISSUES

### 8.1   A NEW ERA OF PRIVATIZATION? THE PRIVATE FINANCE INITIATIVE

The Private Finance Initiative (PFI) was introduced by the Conservative predecessor to New Labour and, after denouncing it in Opposition, Labour in office fine-tuned the scheme and adopted it enthusiastically. The PFI is basically a mixture of franchising and hire purchase. Traditionally, large public investments such as hospitals and schools were paid for 'up front' from taxes. Under PFI, private consortia contract to design, build and manage projects over periods as long as 30 years. The cash for the project is raised on the financial markets, and is repaid with interest over the life of the project: hence the 'hire purchase' element. The consortium also collects fees for managing the project: hence the 'franchising' element. The initiative has been used by the government to create a new generation of public sector projects even in such traditionally 'non-commercial' areas as schools and hospitals. But the adoption of a scheme originally created by the Conservatives has bitterly divided the Labour movement, raising four key issues:

- The conditions of workers. Critics in the Labour Party and the trade unions assert that it is privatization by another name: that the private management of projects, in particular, means that profits are made by worsening the pay and conditions of those employed, by comparison with traditional pay and conditions in the public sector.
- The economics of the projects. Although there are standard tests designed to ensure that the only projects funded are those that could not be funded more cheaply with traditional public financing, these tests are inevitably uncertain. And the financial markets have to be paid the going rate for the money raised. This raises the common complaint that PFI is simply a more expensive way of funding public projects.
- The constraints on public funding. Defenders of the projects point out that funding out of current taxation sets huge limits to what can be done in an era when there is strong public resistance to tax increases: PFI is being used to repair a generation of neglect of the public sector infrastructure in areas such as schools and hospitals.
- The limits to public sector efficiency. One reason trade union opposition is so intense is precisely because PFI is being used to circumvent working practices in the public sector which stand in the way of the efficient use of labour and facilities.

## Transparency

The most obvious feature of the new regulatory arrangements is that they oblige increasing openness and explicitness in the way institutions are run, and in how they deal with each other. This is illustrated by the way the relationship between the new executive agencies and departments is formally described in the founding 'Framework Document'; by the way the powers of privatized regulators are laid down in law, and the obligations of regulated industries are made explicit; and by the way the new regulatory agencies such as the Food Standards Agency both have their powers explicitly stated and are obliged publicly to report their proceedings and decisions. All this marks a great advance, because it strengthens a value which is central to democratic decision making: the value of transparency. It is now much easier to find out how decisions are made in the new regulatory state than under the system that preceded it; and knowing who is making decisions, and how they are being made, is a first condition for the exercise of democratic control.

## A focus on performance

We have seen that the rise of the new world of regulation has been accompanied by a parallel movement: an increasing emphasis on target setting, and the measurement of how far targets have been achieved through measurable performance indicators. There is room for argument about the practical effect of many of these changes – it is obviously not certain, for instance, that just renaming an agency's clients its 'customers' will produce more responsive service delivery. There are many examples of performance targets being manipulated (and even fraudulently falsified) both by managers in agencies and by political leaders. But the rise of target setting marks an important set of cultural changes in governing institutions. It brings into the open important questions about the purpose of those institutions, and creates a continuing debate about whether those purposes are being realized in practice.

To set against this, the rise of the new regulatory state has created serious problems. We highlight two here.

## Accountability

Much of the advance in transparency outlined above is formal in nature: that is, much more is now spelt out in documents about the powers, duties and relationships of regulators and regulated. But that is not the same as the practical exercise of accountability and control. The creation of the executive agencies and regulatory agencies greatly increases the range and complexity of 'quasi-government' in Britain: that is, of institutions that have an ambiguous relationship with the state. This ambiguity can have serious consequences for public accountability. For example, it is recognized that traditional forms of Parliamentary accountability that could be exercised over civil service departments and nationalized industries were often ineffective. But nevertheless, doctrines of accountability and responsibility did usually oblige ministers, for example, to give an account of activities in which their departments were involved. It has been an avowed purpose of the creation of executive and regulatory agencies to 'hive off' these activities, and the result has been to make it much more difficult than hitherto to exercise Parliamentary control. This is made more difficult still by the ambiguous legal status of many of the new bodies. The Financial Services Authority supplies a good example. It exercises great public powers derived from the law, notably from the authority given it in the Financial Services and Markets Act of 2000. But it is not actually a public body: it is a company limited by guarantee, and it is funded by a levy on firms in the financial services industry. In other words, the impressive public powers of regulation in financial markets are wielded by an institution which is 'owned' by the private interests that it is designed to regulate.

## Effectiveness

A culture stressing the importance of effective performance is embedded in the agencies created by the new regulatory state. But how far that culture actually delivers more effective services is a separate matter (see Debating Politics 8.1). Whether we think the new regulatory state more effective than what preceded it will depend in part on our values. Those values will, for instance, help determine whether we think regulated privatized water companies deliver better services than the old publicly owned water authorities. In some cases the agencies have simply not been operating for sufficient time to permit a realistic judgement: we do not really know, for instance, whether the Food Standards Agency is an improvement on what went before, and probably will not know for a decade or so. But some parts of the new regulatory state have ruled over what everyone agrees is a shambolic state of affairs: most people would not contest such a judgement, for example, about regulation of the privatized rail service.

A more fundamental obstacle to effectiveness than problems in particular sectors, however, is the danger of 'regulatory capture'. The new regulatory state deliberately sets up relationships between regulators and regulated which are close, involving daily contact: in the case of the Financial Services Authority, for example, the regulated actually 'own'

# DEBATING POLITICS

## 8.1 TARGET SETTING IN THE NEW REGULATORY STATE: IMPROVING OR DAMAGING DEMOCRACY?

| Target setting aids democratic government | Target setting damages democratic government |
|---|---|
| ■ Targets set measurable standards by which government agencies can be judged.<br><br>■ Targets provide standards against which public servants can be held accountable.<br><br>■ Targets make open and transparent what would otherwise not be publicly debated.<br><br>■ Performance targets are widely and successfully used in business, so why not in government? | ■ Targets involve crude measurements which fail to capture the subtlety of social life.<br><br>■ Targets lead to 'top down' control by managers, making government excessively hierarchical.<br><br>■ Pressure to 'hit' targets encourages public servants to manipulate indicators.<br><br>■ Business can use profits – the bottom line – as an authoritative target, but profit levels are not relevant in government. |

the regulator. There is an obvious danger in this, a danger often observed in the case of the United States, from which much of the theory of the new regulatory state has been borrowed: that the regulator will grow so like the regulated that the two will simply share common interests and a common view of the world, and the independence so vital to the new regulatory agencies will be undermined.

## REVIEW

Four themes have dominated this chapter:

1 The decline of a model of state control in which the department located in Whitehall was the central institution;
2 The rise of a system of rule in which institutions 'contract' much more explicitly than in the past to deliver public services;
3 The passing away of public ownership as a means of public economic control and the rise of the regulatory agency as an alternative;
4 The spread of the regulatory agency model beyond the privatized sector, and its rise as the characteristic institution of the new regulatory state in Britain.

## Further reading

Moran (2003) is a study of the 'regulatory state' in Britain. Hood *et al.* (1999) study the reorganization of inspectorates and regulators. Rhodes (1997) studies the impact of the new governance theories on the structure of government. Skelcher (1998), though now a little dated, is an exceptionally important study of quasi-government and British democracy.

# CHAPTER 9

# Representing interests in the Westminster system

## CONTENTS

## AIMS

The aims of the chapter are:

❖ To describe why interest representation is of growing importance

❖ To distinguish the most important forms of interest groups

❖ To explain what determines interest group influence in government

❖ To sketch some of the most important ways the world of interest representation is changing.

# The rising importance of interest representation

No government makes policy in a vacuum. One of the most important set of influences over what governments do comes from the wider interests in society. That is true even of the most dictatorial of governments, and is truer still of governments which, like Britain's, have to function within the rules of democratic politics. These elementary points help explain the central part played by the representation of interests in British politics.

The importance of interest representation long pre-dates the rise of democracy. Even the most traditional political institutions reflect this fact: thus the historical division of Parliament into Lords and Commons, which we discuss in the next chapter, was intended to reflect a wider social and economic division between great aristocratic landed interests and other forms of property.

There is therefore nothing new about interest representation in politics. The development of interest representation in modern British politics has, however, been marked by four distinctive features:

- *Growing complexity of economic interests.* 'Interests' to an important extent mean economic interests. Historically, they referred overwhelmingly to particular forms of property, especially ownership of land. But the rise of a modern economy has greatly diversified the forms of material interests. Land ownership has been supplanted by more important forms of ownership, in industry and commerce, and by the great range of interests contained in the modern workforce – managers, the professions, industrial manual workers.
- *Growing range of campaigning groups.* 'Interests' always meant something more than material interests. Were we to describe interest representation in British politics in the nineteenth century, for example, our account would have to go well beyond material interests. The first half of the century was marked by a large number of campaigns – such as those against slavery – which united people who shared passionately held ideas.

Just as the complexity of a modern economy has multiplied the range of economic interests, so the complexity and diversity of modern society has widened the range of groups mobilizing to campaign for different, but intensely felt preferences about moral questions. This will be an important theme later in the chapter.
- *Growing formal organization.* Groups come in all shapes and sizes, from the biggest and more formally organized institutions (such as churches or big business corporations) to those that spontaneously spring up from public demonstrations. But over the long term there has been an increasing tendency for groups formally to organize, if only because the scale and diversity of modern society is marked by large scale, formal social organization (see Images 9.1–3).
- *Growing involvement with government.* One of the important reasons for the growth of formal organization is that groups have become more and more important to the process of government. Although the extent to which the state is willing to share control of policy with particular interests waxes and wanes, the complexity of modern government, and the need to rule by consent, means that governments rely to a huge extent on what groups tell them by way of specialized information and advice, and what groups tell their own supporters about the decisions made by government.

Interest representation in modern government, viewed in the historical long term, therefore means something more than the common-sense proposition that groups beyond the formal organization of the state are important in the governing process. It means that, in modern government, organized groups (sharing either economic interests or common moral preferences about issues) are deeply involved in the whole business of making policy and putting it into effect.

## The varieties of groups

Groups span churches, professions, unions, corporations, sports clubs (and more), so it is obvious that

**Images 9.1, 9.2 and 9.3**
**The interest groups around the corner**

Image 9.1    Church

Image 9.3    Charity shop

Image 9.2    Bank

➲ Chapter 1 stressed a key feature of modern political life: that overt participation in politics is a minority interest. In a modern society such as Britain's, government is also a specialized activity with its own institutions – including a bureaucracy – distinct from civil society. This gives the institutions that are the subject of this chapter a unique importance, because what we usually call interest groups are a key means of linking the state to civil society, and a key means by which millions of us, even if we do not realize it, make a contribution to the process of government. These three images are designed to emphasize this point. They are all the local 'branches' of important interests, and all were photographed within a few minutes walk of the author's home. You could easily perform a similar exercise. All, as it happens, are also branches of giant multi-national organizations. The Church is Roman Catholic, a universal organization with its headquarters in Rome. It is involved with the governing process at every conceivable level, from the most morally contentious to the most mundanely material. For instance, the Church constantly lobbies to influence policy on abortion and on research on human embryos; but at a much more mundane level, when this photo was taken the church pictured here was lobbying the National Lottery Commission (a public body) for a grant to replace the church roof. The bank is a branch of the Hong Kong and Shanghai Banking Corporation (HSBC), one of the largest and most powerful banks in the world. And as a sign of how the national and multinational can be linked in complex way, the HSBC itself originated in Hong Kong in the nineteenth century as a bank founded by Scottish colonizers. The Oxfam shop is a familiar sight on British high streets. But Oxfam, which originated in Oxford in the 1940s, is Britain's biggest charity delivering aid to the developing world, and a persistent lobbyist to influence the overseas economic policy of British governments. Its charity shops can now be seen on the streets of many cities in continental Europe.

they are huge in number and wide in diversity. It is also obvious that we could systematically classify these groups in a whole variety of different ways. Indeed, the simple language used above already classifies them just by the way they identify themselves; but it is plain that no one form of classification is definitive. We can see this by carrying out a thought experiment of our own. How might we classify ourselves? The answer is clear: it depends on the purpose of the classification. For sporting identification someone might be an Irish, not an English, football fan; for musical purposes an opera lover and a ballet hater; for the purposes of the tax inspector, an employee rather than self-employed.

The fact that purpose determines classification explains the single most important way of classifying interest groups. 'Interest' is a word with two different meanings: it commonly refers to a material interest (the interests of firefighters or students); or it can more widely mean a preference in the sense of a taste or belief (a shared interest in soccer or opera.) The commonest division of groups separates them in this way: into groups that band together people who believe they share a common economic interest because of the functions they perform in the economy; and groups that join people who believe they share common preferences, whether these are profound (religious belief) or more trivial (such as an interest in sport).

Many different terms have been employed to try to catch this divide: interest/promotional groups; interest/cause groups. In this chapter the distinction is made between *functional* and *preference* groups.

*Functional groups* arise out of a feature central to any modern economy, the division of labour. This is obvious in the range of groups that represent professionals and other workers, but it is also central to the wide range of important groups that cater for different parts of business whether they be the British Bankers' Association or the Chemical Industries Association. All these groups reflect the occupational and industrial specialization by which our economy operates. Membership of groups might consist of individuals: doctors make up the membership of the British Medical Association. It might consist of organizations: the membership of the Chemical Industries Association consists of

firms in the industry. All these groups are vital not just to the economy but to the governing process, precisely because they are the expression of the division of labour. They create and deliver goods and services. No government expects effectively to govern without at least some measure of their cooperation; but, as we will see shortly, for many groups this importance goes well beyond cooperation with government; their active participation is a necessary condition of effective policy making. The language of 'function' expresses this importance: these groups represent people and institutions that perform functions vital to social and economic life.

*Preference groups* are created when people or organizations believe they are united by some set of common preferences. Two features of these groups are immediately obvious: they cut across the functional groups created by the division of labour, but unlike functional groups their range is potentially infinite. They cut across functional groups because they unite people with different functional interests: churches, for instance, contain both employers and workers. And while the range and variety of functional groups is wide, limits are set by the division of labour in the economy. By contrast, the perceived preferences that we share with others are only bounded by our imagination and the way we want to combine. We might be linked with others because of sexual preferences, a common link in recent decades expressed, for example, by the foundation of gay rights groups such as Stonewall. We can be linked by religious preference (and the rise of immigration into Britain has widened the potential range beyond the Christian denominations that traditionally dominated religious preferences). We can also be linked by combinations of these preferences: gays and Christians have united, for example, in a variety of gay Christian groups.

This distinction between groups that spring from the division of labour and groups that spring from shared preferences is very helpful in ordering the complex multitudes of the group worlds, but we should not imagine that groups are sealed off into the two worlds of the functional and the preference. Functional groups often develop philosophies which unite their members: professions (such as medicine) have elaborate ethical codes; many trade

**Image 9.4**
**The giant firm as an organized interest**

Photo: Michael Moran

➲ There could hardly be anything more everyday than this image. Tesco is Britain's largest and most successful supermarket chain, and a store such as this can be found in virtually any town of any size in Britain, and increasingly in cities across the world. Yet every time we shop here, we encounter a formidable political organization. Tesco is entirely typical in having a huge range of interests to defend, and in organizing to defend them. Some of the most immediately obvious are:

- Interests in tax law, to protect both corporate profits and the incomes of senior executives
- Interests in company law: when the photo was taken Tesco, like other large firms, was resisting changes in company law intended to reform the rules governing the pay of senior executives which would have forced greater disclosure and more consultation with shareholders
- Interests in farm policy: together with other large supermarkets, Tesco is accused by farming interests of not passing on reductions in farm gate prices
- Interests in competition policy: Tesco and other big supermarkets have had constantly to defend themselves against official investigations of uncompetitive price fixing
- Interests in land use planning policy: supermarkets such as the one pictured here occupy a large amount of space, and any new supermarket usually involves an acrimonious planning argument. In the case of the example pictured here Tesco circumvented the problem by buying an existing store from a rival chain
- Interests in food safety policy: big supermarkets such as Tesco are the key organizations in 'delivering' food safety regulation under Britain's food safety laws
- Interests in employment policy: supermarkets are large employers of labour, especially part-time labour, and they have a keen interest in issues such as minimum wage legislation.

All this takes place within the framework of multi-level government: see Documenting Politics 9.1 (p. 166).

unions have been shaped by socialism, or by more general ideas about fraternity. Conversely, many preference groups also have a functional life. Churches are not just groups of people sharing the same religion. They are also often large property owners, sharing interests with other property owners; and they are often large employers, sharing interests with other employers. Some of the most important examples of groups that straddle the divide are provided by those that unite people who have the shared experience of being *clients* or *customers* of functional groups. For example, suffering a long-term chronic disease or disablement often powerfully unites groups: we have in recent decades seen the rise of groups representing categories of patients (for instance, those suffering chronic diseases such as multiple sclerosis) and groups representing those who are united by the experience of what is conventionally viewed as physical disablement.

## The main forms of functional representation

The division of labour in a modern economy is complex so the range of organized functional interests is also wide and complex, but the main lines of division in Britain are nevertheless not hard to identify: they are capital and labour.

Britain's is a market economy. This means that private ownership of property is central to economic life. In particular, economic life is concentrated in a comparatively small number of big enterprizes. Many of the household names that supply the goods and services that we consume are giant multinational firms. You will almost certainly do your food shopping at a branch of the giant multinational supermarket chain pictured in Image 9.4, or at one of its competitors. This book is being written with hardware (a personal computer, or PC) produced by a Japanese multinational (Toshiba) using software produced by an American giant (Microsoft Corporation). These institutions are central to economic life, and to political life. Their organized presence takes a variety of forms. *Capital* is organized in Britain in a number of so-called 'peak organizations', such as the Confederation of British Industry. In effect these are specialized lobbying organizations that exist to do little more than try to speak for business as a whole. But just as important are the 'peak' organizations that speak for particular industries and sectors. This is indeed the characteristic form of business organization, usually organized into a trade association for an industry or sector. Any industry of any importance has at least one trade association. As a single example: the Retail Consortium is vital in speaking for retailers, especially the big retailers that dominate our high streets (see Documenting Politics 9.1). The domination of industries by a few giant firms has also made the individual big firm itself a vital institution of interest representation. It is easy to see why. In many economic sectors, only a handful of firms really matter, something we saw in Chapter 3 in describing the domination of the economy by giant firms. The organization of a large firm (say Tesco or ICI) makes the task of organizing to present views to government much more straightforward than if coordination were necessary with other groups of firms. The biggest firms also have the resources – most obviously the money – to organize for this purpose. Any giant firm nowadays will therefore have a department that specializes in putting the firm's views to government.

*Labour*'s organized importance in interest representation comes in two, sometimes overlapping, forms. The most visible is the organization of labour into trade unions, most of which are in turn affiliated to labour's own specialist lobbying 'peak' organization, the Trades Union Congress. For over a century unions, while they have risen and fallen as regards the number of members and degree of influence over government, have been an exceptionally important medium of interest representation for labour.

Overlapping with unions, however, is a second critical set of institutions: that representing the interests of *professions* in British society. Professionals (such as doctors and lawyers) resemble any other group of workers in the sense that they make a living by selling their labour. But professions are different in the way they function in the labour market, in the way they are internally organized and

in their capacity to exercise influence. They are different in the labour market because the most successful professions exercise a large amount of influence over entry into the occupation: one of the marks of a profession is the control exercised through qualifying examinations, or by control of entry to the courses which prepare candidates for qualifying examinations. This is the key difference between, say, doctors and window cleaners: the latter labour market we can all freely enter if we have a ladder and a bucket of water. Professions are also distinctive in their internal organization, because they usually have their own governing institutions, setting standards of behaviour, and establishing the profession's identity, both internally and externally. And professions are different in the way they exercise influence in government precisely because so much of modern political and economic life is professionalized. If we look at big organizations in Britain, whether in the public or private sector, we will find that they are substantially run by groups of professionals: for instance, lawyers, accountants, engineers. Thus professions exercise influence not just by openly arguing about government policy; they are part of the very process by which policy is made and put into effect.

The divisions identified here are handy analytical distinctions but they should not be used too rigidly. In the real world people are not so neatly divided. The managers of big firms are more often than not also professionals, as we have noted. Nevertheless, one reason for creating the whole category of functional groups is that it identifies those with very distinctive resources: these resources often make them vital both to interest representation within government, and vital to the making and delivery of government policy.

### The resources of functional groups

Imagine you were a Cabinet minister or a senior civil servant. Why would you ever take notice of functional groups? The answer is simple: if you systematically ignored them you would never get far in making or putting into effect public policy. The most important reason for this state of affairs is that these groups have at their disposal vital resources.

## DOCUMENTING POLITICS 9.1

## A PEAK ASSOCIATION AS AN ORGANIZED INTEREST UNDER MULTI-LEVEL GOVERNANCE

```
                              BRC Members

                           BRC London,
                         SRC and BRC Brussels

   UK Government      Other relevant                                            European
   Departments,      interest groups,                    EuroCommerce:         Retail Round
   UKREP: UK          EMOTA, FEDSA,        CBI Brussels   the main voice for    Table (13 large
   government office      NFU                             retail and wholesale  retailers), other
   in Brussels                                                                  sectoral groups
                                                                                e.g. EuroCo-op
                         UNICE – the
                          European
                       employers' lobby

                           EUROPEAN UNION
   • European Commission: proposes legislation, oversees its implementation
   • European Parliament: amends Commission proposals and sometimes shares the final say with the Council
   • Council of Ministers:  represents the national governments and has the final say (sometimes together with the
     Parliament) on legislation after looking at the Parliament's amendments.
```

⮕ Peak associations developed a central role in interest representation because they offered great economies of scale, and because they could claim to speak for a wide range of interests. The British Retail Consortium (BRC) is a key peak association, because it speaks for one of the most dynamic parts of the British economy, and of course it represents firms that are part of the daily lives of us all. This figure, which appeared on the BRC website, perfectly sums up the complex institutional world in which an important peak association has to operate. It is obliged to organize at three different levels of government: 'BRC London' works with the Scottish Retail Consortium, its Scottish sister organization, whose importance derives from the devolution reforms discussed in Chapter 11; and with BRC Brussels, the Consortium's EU permanent lobbying operation. Note too how the web spins out from Brussels: back to Britain to the central departments in Westminster; to other interest groups, such as farmers (NFU); to other employer/business peak associations, such as the Confederation of British Industry (CBI Brussels); to a Europe-wide lobby for retailing (Eurocommerce); and to the European Retail Round Table, a separate organization for the biggest retailers in Europe. This last is especially important in the light of what we saw in Image 9.4: the retail sector across Western Europe is dominated by a small number of big chains, including Aldi (German), Casino (French) and Tesco (UK). A key tension that the Consortium, like other peak associations, has to manage is that between these giant member firms and the larger number of comparatively smaller firms.

*Source*: www.brc.org.uk

Four are especially important:

- Their place in the working of the economy
- Organization
- Expertize
- Money.

*Economic role*. We call these groups functional precisely because they are central to the division of labour, the most important feature in turn of a modern economy. Unless firms, workers and professionals do their job, the modern economy does not function. This gives functional groups a presumptive right to a say in making policy: that is why, for instance, no government would ever introduce a big reform of business taxation without consulting widely with firms. But economic role is the source of a deeper importance. The way firms and workers go about their daily business shapes the success or failure of government: in the end, the fate of economic policy depends on firms investing and utilising capital, and on workers producing goods and services. Suppose, for instance, that government wishes to change tax policy so as to increase the level of investment by firms in the economy. It cannot compel firms to invest more; it can only create the circumstances that induce them to do so. For this reason it would be foolish to frame changes in tax policy without close consultation with the industries where it is hoped to promote more investment.

*Organization*. Every major functional interest is organized, whether that organization be the Trades Union Congress for union members, the Retail Consortium for big retailers, or Tesco for a single giant firm. This kind of organization is one of the keys to success in shaping policy in modern government. Organization brings a continuous presence: a perpetual nagging away at issues; a build-up of expertize about issues; a permanent capacity to argue a public position; and a place in stable networks of contacts both with government and with other functional interests (see Briefing 9.1).

*Expertize*. Organization allows expertize to be assembled and used. One of the great strengths of functional groups is that they are natural repositories of expertize, by virtue of their position in the

## Briefing    9.1

### THE RESOURCES OF ONE POWERFUL FUNCTIONAL GROUP: THE CASE OF THE BRITISH MEDICAL ASSOCIATION

The British Medical Association (BMA) is one of the best documented of powerful functional groups. Its 'functional' importance derives from the fact that its members are vital to the delivery of a key public service: health care. We have probably all encountered a member of the BMA, when visiting our local GP, or if we have been unfortunate enough to be in hospital.

- The Association has 126,000 members, covering 80 per cent of all UK practising doctors.
- It is simultaneously a trade union for doctors, a major publisher (the *British Medical Journal* is both an important scientific weekly and a leading journal of medical opinion) and a scientific and educational body.
- Its annual income at the most recent count (2003) exceeded £80 million.
- It ran its own Parliamentary Affairs team in London (and separate teams in Scotland, Wales and Northern Ireland) providing briefing material for politicians, advising members on how to lobby public officials and coordinating BMA activities with Parliamentary Committees.

➲ The British Medical Association is one of a family of powerful functional groups. As the details above show, this is in part because it has considerable 'muscle' (resources of both money and people). But it is also because the modern state in Britain is a state that relies very heavily on professionals, such as doctors, to put policies into effect: imagine the National Health Service without their cooperation. To read more about the BMA as a powerful functional group, see www.bma.org.uk

division of labour. Governing Britain is, among other things, a highly complex business; doing it properly demands a command of great technical detail. Sometimes government itself is on top of this detail; more often than not it has to rely on functional groups. We can see this immediately if we think about some of the tasks of government. Imagine trying to do such things as devizing safety standards for the pharmaceutical drugs that can be sold to patients, the safety standards for the construction of offices, or the standards for the prudent conduct of banking business. All three involve dealing with immensely complex technical detail; and in all three cases the best informed groups are, respectively, pharmaceutical firms, architects and bankers themselves.

*Money.* Not all functional groups are rich, but many are; we only have to think of the resources of the biggest firms to realize that. Using lots of cash is no guarantee of success in lobbying, but it helps. Money brings some obvious advantages. Organization, which we have already identified as an important independent resource, is much easier if money is available. Rich organizations can hire the best experts, to consolidate their position as centres of expertize. Big firms operating in the City of London, for instance, are some of the most authoritative commentators on the British economy simply because they have the money to pay salaries commanding the full-time service of top economists. Later in this chapter we will see the rising importance of professional lobbyists in Britain: hired guns who will lobby for any interest prepared to pay them. Usually these hired guns do not come cheap. Money can also bring some ancillary advantages. Most of the really successful functional interests in Britain have their headquarters located in central London, for an obvious reason: it is where a great deal of the policy action is located. Office premises in central London are not cheap; neither are they cheap in Edinburgh or Cardiff, close to the new devolved administrations.

## Functional interests and the governing process

Enough has already been said in the last section to suggest that functional interests are absolutely central to the governing process in Britain. Indeed, this is the single most important point about this part of the world of interest representation. The great functional interests – the biggest firms, the key professions – are not just important interests trying to influence government from outside, though they may sometimes do that; they are integral to the whole process of making and putting policy into effect. This is perhaps the single most important change that came over British government in the twentieth century. If we had looked at British government in 1900 we would have found numerous important functional interests, but they were mostly organized lobbies trying to influence government from the outside. In the course of the century this changed: the greatest functional interests on the sides of capital and labour were integrated into the governing machine. They became de facto governing institutions: consulted at every turn; entitled to places on government advisory committees; and even entitled to places on public bodies concerned with the implementation of such policies as the regulation of health and safety at work, or the regulation of environmental pollution.

This connection to the governing process has, certainly, varied in strength at different moments. It was especially close at moments of great national crisis, notably in the two world wars of the twentieth century. It was also very close during the two decades after 1960, when governments of all parties usually accepted a doctrine of 'tri-partism': a doctrine that the economy should be managed in a partnership between government, business and labour. It was probably least close in the last two decades of the century, during the period of Conservative rule that began with Mrs Thatcher's election victory of 1979. The Conservatives were particularly determined to push the trade unions outside the governing machine, but they also showed less interest than their predecessors in sharing policy making with 'peak' business organizations, such as the Confederation of British Industry, or with the professions. But much of this rejection was at the 'headline' level; in the daily routines of government – the area where the functional groups have usually exercised most influence – groups remained, for all the short-term ups and downs, partners in the governing process.

The reasons for this enduring presence as governing institutions arise from the hard facts about the resources of groups that we sketched above. Functional groups need government; but government needs the groups even more. Above all, groups can perform three vital services for government (see Briefing 9.2).

# Briefing                              9.2

## WHAT'S ON OFFER? WHAT FUNCTIONAL GROUPS CAN GIVE AND WITHHOLD

| What's on offer? | Example |
| --- | --- |
| Legitimacy | Consultants attack proposals to change their working practices. |
| Expertize | Vets provide advice on practicality of combating foot and mouth disease by vaccination of cattle. |
| Policy implementation | Big supermarkets voluntarily run their own food safety systems. |
| Votes | Farmers have threatened to switch votes or run their own candidate. |
| Money | Unions have threatened to 'disaffiliate' from Labour, thus cutting off their affiliation fees. |

➲ What this schematic listing of resources does not convey is the way groups can simultaneously use, or threaten to use, different combinations of this battery of weapons.

*Provide advice and hard information.* Almost all policy made by government in Britain – or in any other advanced industrial country for that matter – involves judgements about highly specialized matters. In many cases, this specialization is highly technical: consider the kinds of issues involved in making policy concerning health and safety in the construction industry, or the standards governing emissions of pollutants from chemical plants. The most important functional interests – big firms, trade associations, trade unions, professional institutions – are the obvious sources of specialized advice and hard data. Governments sometimes make policy without consulting the affected groups, but they usually regret the omission. Hence, the business of policy formulation involves a continuous exchange with functional interests as government tries to winkle out this advice and information.

*Offer cooperation.* Passing laws is one thing; actually doing the surveillance and enforcement to ensure compliance is another. Government often has few resources to put policies into effect. The life of government is made much easier if important functional groups recommend cooperation with policies; but cooperation often goes further than just commending a policy. In the case of professions, for instance, the actual job of implementing is very often delegated to the professional organizations. In the case of health care professions – the most notable examples are doctors, dentists and nurses – there are national councils (such as the General Medical Council for doctors) which are responsible for such matters as prescribing and putting into effect standards of professional education and proper conduct, under authority delegated to them by the state. This is a world of government which rarely gets onto the front page or into the battle between the front benches in Parliament but it is part of the important everyday reality of government, and the functional interests are full partners in that reality.

*Provide legitimacy.* Legitimacy, you may recall from Chapter 1, is a vital condition of effective government. Legitimate authority means that those subject to laws and institutions obey because they believe government has a right to claim obedience. If policies are not seen as legitimate, the policies are likely to fail. The extent to which citizens can be made to obey policy by force, or the threat of force, is very limited. Governments claim legitimacy by many means. One of the most important general foundations for the claim invokes the rules of democratic politics: government has the right to govern because it won that right fair and square in a free election. But the legitimacy that comes from democratic elections is itself restricted: in Britain it is almost unheard of for a government to win a clear majority of the popular vote. In Chapter 17, for example, we shall see that Labour recorded huge majorities in the House of Commons in the general elections of 1997 and 2001 without ever getting close to a majority of the popular vote. The Conservative government that introduced the 'poll tax' (a new form of local taxation) in the late 1980s had a huge majority in the House of Commons; but the tax had to be abandoned because it produced large scale civil disobedience from those who refused to accept its legitimacy.

The rise of the great functional interests in the twentieth century was a recognition that there were limits to the legitimacy that could be gained by winning elections on votes of individual citizens organized in territorial constituencies. When policies are made in consultation with affected groups – still better if they are put into effect by those groups, as in the example of the professions given above – then the claim by government to legitimate authority is greatly strengthened. But the flow of legitimacy is not one way. There is an exchange of legitimacy between groups and government, and this helps explain why groups so often cooperate. Being consulted – or, better still, being designated by government as the authority with responsibility for a policy – changes what would just be a sectional interest into an institution with a responsibility for safeguarding the public interest: the group can see itself, and be seen, as a governing institution.

Of course, things do not always run smoothly. The price of advice, cooperation and legitimacy is giving groups a share in deciding the content of policy. Often governments decide that this price is too high and make policy in defiance of functional interests. When and why this sort of exclusion happens will be examined in the next section.

## The powerful and the excluded in the functional world

The world of functional representation is an unequal world (see Briefing 9.3). How far groups get into a position where they are accepted as natural partners in the policy making process is determined by their resources, and the skill with which they use those resources. In the case of the most important groups they more often than not do not even have to shout to be heard. When government makes policy about the taxation rules to be applied to the profits of oil exploration in the North Sea, for example, it will more or less automatically consult the big oil companies; and if by some oversight it fails to do so, the companies have battalions of tax lawyers, accountants and professional lobbyists to make their views clear. The chief executives of the oil companies will never have to march in the rain behind banners denouncing the government. The same point can be made about a second important set of functional groups, the most important professions. Indeed, in the case of professions the advantage is even more marked because the point of professional organizations is that much of the business of governing is actually delegated to the professional organizations themselves.

This is not to say that big business and the most important professions automatically get their way in policy making but, if the effort to influence policy by groups is like a race, then these functional groups always have a flying start; everyone else has to try extra hard to catch up.

The most powerful functional groups are identified by their wealth, expertize and efficient organization; the weakest are those that strikingly lack these attributes. Being badly organized, or not organized at all, not only contributes to weakness; it also usually tells us that such groups lack other attributes, such as economic resources. The obvious way employees can try to influence government is through organizing in trade unions; but only about 10.5 million workers belong to unions, and the numbers fell by nearly 2.5 million during the course of the 1990s. Many rich and powerful people decline to organize in unions, but the unorganized also include some of the poorest paid and most insecure people in the workforce: workers in low-paid jobs, in part-time jobs and in jobs where the risk of being sacked is very high. Within business, too, there are great variations in influence. Small businesses, for example, are usually much less well organized to influence government than are big firms. It is not difficult to see why. It is partly a matter of numbers: it is much easier to coordinate action by half-a-dozen big supermarket firms than by thousands of corner shops. It is partly a matter of resources: again it is easy to see why a group dominated by half a dozen giant firms would have fewer problems commanding the resources needed for effective lobbying than would one representing small shopkeepers.

# Briefing                    9.3

● ● ● ● ● ● ● ● ● ● ● ● ● ● ● ● ● ● ● ● ● ● ● ● ● ● ● ●

## THE LOW PAY UNIT AND THE HIGH PAY UNIT: CONTRASTING FORTUNES OF TWO INTEREST GROUPS IN BRITAIN

**The Low Pay Unit** was founded in 1974. For nearly 30 years it was the main group lobbying for the interests of the most poorly paid in Britain. It operated in three important ways:

● By gathering and publicizing research about low pay and the wider issue of poverty among those in work
● By lobbying government in Britain about the problem of low pay
● By joining and supporting European-wide networks to lobby the institutions of the European Union.

Low-paid workers did not generally give active support to the Unit: the low paid tend to have poor skills at lobbying, and have little money left over to contribute to political campaigns. The Unit therefore depended heavily on donations, and when in 2003 its main supporter decided to withdraw financial support, the Unit ceased to exist.

**The Institute of Directors** is, as the name suggests, Britain's leading organization for company directors. Membership is for individuals. At the time of writing a yearly subscription cost £240 (life membership £4,800). The Institute offers a wide range of special services to its members, such as free legal advice. It also lobbies government for those policies that its members favour; unsurprisingly, these often advocate lighter regulation of business. At the time of writing the Institute had 55,000 members and an annual income exceeding £28 million. Readers can enjoy an interactive tour of the Institute of Directors' beautiful headquarters in Pall Mall (in the centre of London's clubland) by visiting www.iod.co.uk

● ● ● ● ● ● ● ● ● ● ● ● ● ● ● ● ● ● ● ● ● ● ● ● ● ● ● ●

➲ It is not hard to form interest groups in Britain; there are literally tens of thousands. But running an effective group is hard work and demands both skill and financial resources. The two cases show just how different can be the resources, and the fates, of different groups.

However, if the big battalions – large firms, powerful unions, prestigious professions – have a flying start in influencing policy, there are lots of compensating mechanisms which ensure that they do not always win the race. Often the large, well resourced groups are competing against each other: even within a single industry such as supermarket retailing it is not automatically the case that the interests of Sainsbury's and Tesco will be identical. While governments depend on the biggest groups for all the things we identified earlier (approval, expertize, and so on), they also need things that the biggest groups cannot always deliver. Above all, governments need to win the support of millions of voters. Unless they win elections politicians are out of business. This does mean that a well organized functional interest that can influence votes is doubly powerful. Thus big media corporations that own the popular press in Britain have all the usual resources of giant firms, but are also believed by politicians to be able to sway voters. Thus they are deferred to particularly obsequiously. (See Chapter 16 for more discussion of this.) But even the most badly organized, if they are prepared to vote, and to switch their vote, can influence policy through the ballot box. As we will see when we turn in a moment to preference groups, this consideration may be growing as an influence over policy. There is also some evidence that the ability of the unorganized spontaneously to mobilize and force governments onto the defensive is growing. Consider the case in Briefing 9.6 (p. 179) which documents the astonishing speed with which an apparently unorganized coalition of small farmers, road hauliers and taxi drivers almost brought the economy to a halt in the autumn of 2000 in a protest over government tax policies on vehicle fuel.

## The main forms of preference groups

There is one striking difference in the way functional and preference groups are created. The variety of functional groups is wide, but the limits of the functional world are defined by the division of labour in a modern economy: there exist a finite, though very large, number of occupations and industries. In the case of preference groups, by contrast, the potential range is infinite, because here people form groups because they share some preference, and the combination of human preferences is infinite. Not all possible human preferences are realized, of course, but even so the variety in this part of the group world is staggering. In Britain today people are organized because they share common religious beliefs, sexual preferences, sporting interests, hobbies, tastes in beer – and virtually infinite combinations and recombinations of all these. You can experience this diversity by a simple personal experiment. Do a count for yourself, and for a couple of friends or a couple of members of your family, of the preference groups to which they belong. I guarantee that even for the most solitary the total will soon reach double figures.

Functional groups can be fairly readily classified by their place in the division of labour, but no obvious parallel way of categorizing preference groups exists. One illuminating way to think about the variety is by reference to the way groups fit into the wider fabric of society, because this difference often has important consequences for the importance of the group to the making of policy. Viewed thus, it is possible to see four important kinds of preference group:

- Established social institutions
- Charities
- New social movements
- Specialized lobbies.

*Established social institutions*: some groups are, so to speak, only incidentally part of the world of interest representation. They have historically well established alternative roles which make them central to the lives of communities. Some of the best examples are the long-established Christian denominations. They plainly do not exist primarily for the purpose of trying to exert influence on public policy, but equally plainly they in practice spend a great deal of effort trying to do precisely that. Churches have views about education, about policy affecting the family, about foreign aid, about how and when war can be waged; and naturally they intervene in

debates about these issues. There is thus virtually no area of government policy where we might not expect to find a Christian denomination trying to shape policy and to influence public opinion.

*Charities*: what we have called social institutions central to the fabric of social life overlap with the huge array of charities in the community. Indeed, institutions such as churches are usually registered as charities to gain the tax breaks that come with charitable status. But charities are worth separating because they often have a special importance in particular policy fields. Over 163,000 are presently registered with the Charity Commission (the main regulator), concerned to protect or promote some value or interest. Take as an example the Royal Society for the Prevention of Cruelty to Animals (RSPCA), a charity founded in 1824 in response to growing sensitivity about the treatment of animals. The RSPCA is probably the best known, and best resourced, animal charity in Britain (see Documenting Politics 9.2). It stands for a value now central to the life of the community – the humane treatment of animals – and devotes most of its energies to promoting that value and to the practical care of animals. But as a consequence of the commitment to these values, a large amount of energy is also devoted to trying to influence public policy: directly to persuading government, and indirectly trying to shape the wider climate of public opinion. Charities have indeed become increasingly important in recent decades in actually delivering public services, especially in the field of welfare.

*New social movements*: The huge array of charities in turn shade into something more diffuse which can be labelled social movements. The best way to understand these is through examples: think of the women's movement, the movement for gay rights or the environmental movement as instances. They all represent loosely connected constellations of many different kinds of groups: some are formally organized nationally, others are local, informal and often short lived. Like the great charities and churches they obviously serve a wide range of social purposes. Take what is loosely called the gay rights movement. It encompasses particular charities such as the Terence Higgins Trust, which is devoted to support for those diagnosed as HIV positive. More widely, it

## DOCUMENTING POLITICS 9.2

## MODERN CAMPAIGNING BY A POWERFUL PREFERENCE GROUP: THE CASE OF THE RSPCA

'Around 21 million hens are living in battery cages in the UK. These birds have almost no space to stretch their wings, move around properly or behave naturally. The cramped living conditions in battery cages can lead to dangerously fragile bones – up to a third of hens suffer broken bones after they are removed from cages at the end of their productive lives.

The UK government recently implemented the EU Laying Hen Directive to ban barren battery cages by 2012. However, so-called 'enriched' cages will still be allowed. These are very similar to barren battery cages allowing only a little more room and are totally inadequate to meet the welfare needs of hens.

Germany has voluntarily decided to ban barren battery cages five years earlier and is also banning enriched cages by 2012.

The RSPCA welcomes Germany's decision but is extremely disappointed the UK has implemented only the minimum requirements. The RSPCA believes the UK government should demonstrate that it is committed to improving hen welfare by banning all cages by 2007.

The government has completed its consultation on the use of enriched cages for laying hens. On the basis of this, the government will decide if all cages will be banned or if birds will continue to be kept in these cruel systems. The RSPCA is calling for a ban on all cage systems to prevent many millions of hens being condemned to a needlessly miserable life.

Sign the petition

Dear Secretary of State,

I am angry that the UK government will allow barren battery cages to be used until 2012. I urge the government to ban all cages for laying hens by 2007 and ensure birds have proper room in which to exercise and behave naturally.'

➲  The Royal Society for the Prevention of Cruelty to Animals (RSPCA) has its origins in the nineteenth-century discovery of a new sensibility about cruelty to animals, but its concerns and campaigning techniques are strikingly modern. This extract from the Society's web pages illustrates these. It continues the Society's campaign against cruelty in battery rearing of hens. Three features are especially striking:

• The invoking of international examples (the reference to superior German practices)
• The operation within multi-level governance: the aim of the campaign is to pressure the UK government in Whitehall to implement an EU Directive on battery rearing in a fuller way than the UK government has hitherto
• The range of pressure tactics used. The page here provides a facility to sign and e-mail a petition against UK practices. In addition (not shown here) the page details a range of other measures that the individual can take: for instance, refusing to buy eggs from battery-reared hens, buying only products that have the Society's own 'farm assurance' label, and donating financially to the Society.

The Society backs these campaigns with formidable resources: in its most recently reported financial year it spent more than £74 million.

*Source*: www.rspca.org

has been important in helping create social worlds where gay people can feel secure and free from some intimidation and discrimination. Many large English cities (such as Manchester) now have informally identified 'gay villages' where gay people can live and spend leisure time in a culture which they find non-threatening. Some religious denominations often also have these social movement-like characteristics: they provide social networks where people mix with the like-minded, and they elaborate philosophies which give moral meaning to the wider social movement. And, equally, they put a great deal of energy into trying to influence public policy: health, education and, of course, the environment are only the most obvious examples. As the example of religious denominations shows, there is in principle nothing novel about a social movement. Nevertheless, the other examples given here are of comparatively new social groupings. We shall see that they have a double importance: not only are they of growing importance in the world of interest representation; we shall find in Chapter 13 that they are important in pioneering new kinds of political participation.

We commonly speak of 'new' social movements because some of the most striking truly are new, such as the example from the gay community used here (and see Table 9.1). But in reality these movements hark back to an older tradition of political action in Britain, a tradition where lifestyle, intellectual commitment and political action united large numbers of people. Their ancestors include, for example, the great movements against alcohol, slavery and the subjection of women that were so important in the nineteenth century.

*Specialized lobbies*: one important feature of the preference groups identified so far is that interest representation in the sense of arguing with, or bargaining with, government is a by-product of their larger social purposes. But just as there are groups in the functional world who exist only to lobby, so there are specialized lobbies in the preference world. Take the case of the Society for the Protection of Unborn Children. This is not, as one might imagine from the name, an organization concerned with encouraging practices that foster the health of babies in the womb, or with developing more effective ante-natal care, it is an organiza-

| **Table 9.1** The rise of a movement: the case of environmentalism (membership of selected organizations, in thousands) | | |
|---|---|---|
| | 1971 | 1997 |
| National Trust | 278 | 2,489 |
| Royal Society for the Protection of Birds | 98 | 1,007 |
| Greenpeace | – | 215 |
| Friends of the Earth | 1 | 114 |
| Ramblers' Association | 22 | 123 |

*Source*: Data from *Social Trends*, 1999, Table 11.4.

➲ The figures show the extraordinary growth in membership of groups concerned with the environment in the closing decades of the twentieth century, which continues apace. Of course, membership of Greenpeace, an international campaigning group, does not have the same meaning as membership of the National Trust, an organization mostly dedicated to the preservation of ancient stately buildings and the protection of parts of the landscape. But this is precisely the character of a movement such as environmentalism: it is not a single organization, but a loose and shifting network linking a wide variety of groups whose members often have very different world views and aims.

tion that was created largely in response to the changes in the law in the 1960s that allowed legal abortion in some circumstances; and it is it devoted to resisting the extension of that original reform, to ensuring that such law as presently exists is enforced as strictly as possible and, as an ultimate objective, to returning the law to the state it was in before the original reforms of the 1960s.

Specialized lobbies, by their very nature, obviously devote their energies to intervening as effectively as possible in debates about public policy. It is natural to think of them as particularly important in the world of preference groups. However, as this sketch of the variety of preference groups shows, they actually only form a minority of the population of the preference world.

## The resources of preference groups

Since functional groups exist through their place in the division of labour it would be natural to assume that this automatically gives them access to resources superior to those of preference groups. The assumption would be wrong. There are many preference groups which can command impressive resources. Five kinds of resource are especially important.

*Some are quasi-state bodies.* We saw earlier that over the course of the twentieth century many functional groups became de facto governing institutions. Some preference groups have an even more impressive claim: they are so closely connected to parts of the state that they can be considered to be at least quasi-state institutions themselves. A perfect example is the Church of England. As the 'Established' Church it is actually headed by the monarch. Anglican bishops presently sit in the House of Lords, and any leading Anglican clergyman can offer opinions about almost any aspect of public policy with the certainty of commanding a hearing and, often, extensive publicity. As a very different example consider the National Trust. This is legally a charity formed at the end of the nineteenth century to protect the natural beauty of our landscape and buildings. It is now a rich and well connected institution: a membership of over two million brings it an annual income of more than £200 million. It owns and cares for some of the most important parts of the British landscape and hundreds of historic properties. On its governing council sit members of some of the most socially prestigious families in the land.

*Most have great cultural resources.* 'Culture' here does not refer narrowly to the arts, but to the wider culture of our society. Many preference groups have important cultural resources in this latter sense: that is, they can appeal to values which are deeply held and uncontestable across the community. It is possible, for example, for governments to decline particular demands from the RSPCA, or from the National Society for the Prevention of Cruelty to Children. But in any debates about policy these groups can naturally occupy the moral high ground, and no politician could safely question their general objectives. Their opposition can damage, or their support enhance, the legitimacy of a policy; and, as we know from our earlier discussions, legitimacy is a key condition of effective policy making.

*Many preference groups have wealth and numbers.* Some preference groups have precisely the resources that we saw conferring influence on functional groups. They are rich. Many religious denominations, and older environmental groups such as the National Trust and the Royal Society for the Protection of Birds (RSPB), have large memberships and huge incomes from subscriptions, donations and property holdings. They have the precious gift of permanent organization. For instance, while religious observance in Britain is low by international standards, nevertheless millions of Britons are available weekly in the church, the mosque or the synagogue to listen to the views of clergy. Minority religions often command particularly powerful allegiance. For instance, issues that affect Islam became central to British foreign policy after the terrorist attacks on the New York World Trade Center on 11 September 2001. Though only 2 per cent of Britons profess the Islamic faith, weekly attendance at the mosque is particularly high, and thus what is said at the mosque about British government policy is a highly sensitive matter for politicians.

*They deliver policy.* Many preference groups also resemble functional groups in playing a central role in the delivery of public policy, and are particularly important in the delivery of welfare policy. Primary and secondary education in Britain would be utterly different without the contribution of church schools. But this role in policy delivery has grown in recent years: charities are vital to the care of the young, the old, the sick, and the long term disabled. It is only natural that when a group delivers policy it claims, and is granted, a right to a say in how the policy is made.

*They are experts.* Many preference groups have expertize quite as valuable to policy makers as the expertize of big firms or professions. Governments concerned with the large issue of how to manage a sustainable environment, or with something as specific as the impact of particular farming practices on a bird species, will naturally look for expert advice to the RSPB; indeed, they will not even have to look, because the Society is already geared up to supply a constant stream of information and advocacy.

## Briefing                                    9.4

**THE POWERFUL AND THE EXCLUDED IN THE PREFERENCE WORLD: TWO EXAMPLES**

**The Campaign to Protect Rural England** (formerly the Council for the Preservation of Rural England) dates from 1926. It has more than 59,000 members organized in a network of over 200 local groups. The Campaign's aim is to protect and enhance the countryside. It now markets itself as one of Britain's leading environmental groups, and appeals both to modern ideologies of environmentalism and traditional visions of rural Britain. In the most recently available yearly accounts it spent £2.7 million. Its Patron is Her Majesty the Queen.

**The London Detainee Support Group** was founded in 1997. It aims to alleviate poverty, sickness and distress amongst refugees, asylum seekers and others who are, or have been, detained in London and elsewhere. It spent £74,000 in the most recently reported financial year. It has no Patron.

*Sources*: Information from Charity Commission Annual Reports: www.charity-commission.gov.uk-register

➲ We saw earlier that there are huge variations in the power, resources and acceptability of different 'functional' groups. The same is true for preference campaigning groups, and the two examples document the range. The wealth and support base of the Campaign to Protect Rural England are evident; the identity of its Patron exemplifies its acceptable 'insider' status. The Campaign appeals to a vision that nobody dares contradict: the beauty of nature. By contrast, the London Detainee Support Group was founded at a time when both leading parties, and most newspapers, pictured the arrival of asylum seekers to Britain as a serious problem and sought various ways of containing both their numbers and their movements. It is hard to imagine the Queen agreeing to be a patron of a group designed to protect detained asylum seekers.

In short, the most important preference groups have exactly the same potential to participate in the governing process as we identified earlier for the key functional groups: for government they are vital sources of advice, cooperation and legitimacy.

## The powerful and the excluded in the preference world

We have seen that it is wrong to think of preference groups as inevitably less powerful than their functional counterparts. But just as there is a power hierarchy in the functional world, so there is one among preference groups (see Briefing 9.4). This point nevertheless brings us to an important difference between the two worlds. Although short-term factors shape power in the functional world, in the long run importance depends on economic weight. For instance, 150 years ago agriculture was probably the dominant interest in government; now, with the decline in the economic importance of farming, agricultural interests, (although important) no longer have that commanding position.

The leverage preference groups can wield in government is partly a function also of these familiar factors. Groups such as the National Trust and RSPB are important because they are rich, and can use their wealth to buy expertize and organization. But a much more subtle process of inclusion and exclusion also affects preference groups, and it takes us back to the question of the *cultural* approval that they can command. Any Minister or senior civil servant can readily argue about particular policy options with the Royal National Lifeboat Institution or the National Society for the Prevention of Cruelty to Children, but only someone insane or malign would oppose the general aims of these groups. But by no means all groups command the same, or any, cultural approval. Even among 'approved' groups there can be striking variations in intensity of approval, and these differences are often culturally founded. For instance, it is much easier for charities speaking for the blind than for the deaf to organize in Britain, because while everyone perceives the seriousness of blindness, deafness is of much lower salience and, in some circumstance, is even treated as a subject of sick humour. Even more important, some groups are so subject to hostility that they are overtly excluded from influence over policy. Historically, some forms of religious discrimination functioned in this way. In the past, it was hard to speak for and represent Catholicism and Judaism, and indeed both religions faced legal bars to participation in political life and in the wider life of the community.

In modern Britain some of the same cultural (though not legal) obstacles exist in speaking for and representing Islam. Until the late 1960s it was also virtually impossible to speak for, and represent, gay people. Anyone who did so faced possible criminal prosecution (because same sex relations between men were illegal) and certain social hostility and career damage. In contemporary Britain, groups that attempt to speak for, and represent, asylum seekers also face official and popular hostility. At the most extreme points of hostility, to try to speak for some groups actually leads to the danger of prosecution and harassment by vigilantes, since they arouse deep popular animosity: imagine, for example, trying to organize a group that defended the views of paedophiles in Britain now.

## New worlds of interest representation

Interest representation in what we have been calling the Westminster system remains hugely important. It shapes the patterns of inclusion and exclusion which we outlined above. It is heavily centralized on a small geographical area covered by the main political institutions of the Westminster system, notably the government departments headquartered in central London. Functional groups that have the wealth and expertize to be useful in this governing world enjoy privileged access. This Westminster world helps shape the cultural preferences and prejudices which, as we have also just seen, are so important in determining which preference groups are 'in' or 'out'.

The world of interest representation is nevertheless changing. Some of these changes are reinforcing the dominance of the powerful and privileged, and some are challenging existing hierarchies. The changes are in part traceable to wider developments which are a major theme in this book: the reshaping,

and the decline, of the Westminster system of government.

Three sets of changes are particularly important: the rise of professional lobbying; the development of new forms of group mobilization, often linked to new social movements; and the 'Europeanization' of interest representation.

### The rise of professional lobbying

One of the most obvious features of the groups considered so far in this chapter is that, for most, interest representation is largely a by-product, albeit a vital by-product, of their main activities: firms need to make profits; professions need to organize their bit of the labour market; churches need to save souls. But in the last generation a different kind of figure has appeared on the interest representation stage: the professional lobbyist, a 'hired gun' available to speak on behalf of any group willing to pay. There have indeed always been well placed individuals – backbench MPs, former ministers, 'fixers' in leading law firms – who would lobby on behalf of clients; but the new world of professional lobbying, which is influenced by the much more highly developed lobbying system that exists in the United States, is distinctive in three ways.

● It is openly organized in firms that advertise their services, rather than being a discreet service offered by individual 'fixers'.
● It is developing into an industry in its own right, with trade associations that attempt, in turn, to promote codes of professional conduct.
● The firms in the industry claim a special expertize in the act of lobbying government itself.

The grounds for this last claim to special expertize and effectiveness are various: that lobbying firms are especially well placed to obtain access to government; that they have a unique expertize in assembling a case in terms that will appeal to policy makers; and that they command the technology (for instance, to produce well directed mail shots) that will maximize the effectiveness with which a case is presented. (See Briefing 9.5.)

# Briefing

## THE WORLD OF THE PROFESSIONAL LOBBYIST

Professional lobbying has been a boom industry in recent years. After a number of scandals in the 1990s, attempts have been made to organize self-regulatory bodies in the industry. The most important of these is via the Association of Professional Political Consultants. (Lobbyists prefer to call themselves consultants, or specialists in political communication.) Over 80 per cent (by turnover) of Britain's political consultancies are in membership. The Association maintains a highly informative register of consultants detailing, for instance, all the clients represented most recently by individual firms. It also promotes a code of conduct: for instance, it forbids the offer of financial inducements to promote business.

The style and scale of the work of the professional lobbyist is well illustrated by the account offered of its activities by Bell Pottinger Communications, one of the leading firms. (One of its partners was once an adviser to Margaret Thatcher.) The firm:

- advised Newport Borough Council on its campaign to achieve city status
- advised the Association of Friendly Societies on a campaign to secure changes in the regulations governing the operations of its members, thus strengthening their competitive position in financial services markets
- organized a mass campaign by the National Federation of Sub-Postmasters against threats to close small post offices
- advised the Guide Association in a successful campaign to scrap proposed charges to carry out security checks on volunteers working with young people, thus helping the Association save £450,000 annually.

*Sources*: Information from www.appc.org.uk and bell-pottinger.co.uk

➲ This material provides both a 'bird's eye' and a 'worm's eye' view of the modern lobbying industry from the point of view of the organization of the whole industry, and the daily business of lobbying, with examples from the website of Bell Pottinger. The material should be read with care, however. It is all from the public material provided by the industry. It says nothing of the scandals that compelled greater organization in the 1990s. The examples of work provided by Bell Pottinger also focus on the most socially acceptable groups and causes: while one might argue with particular features of the four campaigns documented, nobody would argue with the desirability of ensuring that these groups have their voices heard in policy making.

The rise of the special lobbying firm is due partly to a refinement of the division of labour in interest representation. The biggest and most powerful groups – giant firms, trade associations – already have specialized government relations divisions, even if they do not always call them by that name. It is quite a small step to recreating this specialization for the whole lobbying world. Likewise, there is an obvious cross-over between the work of the professional lobbyist and some longer established firms: for instance, those that specialize in public relations, advertising and offering legal advice. There is thus a growing supply of specialized lobbyists, as entrepreneurs spot a potentially lucrative business niche. There is also a growing demand for their services. Government is a huge and complex organization.

Exercising influence often depends on knowing exactly who to target. Personal contacts date very quickly since, as in every organization, people change jobs. Groups are experts in their policy field, but they are not naturally experts in government. Professional lobbyists claim precisely this latter sort of knowledge.

The rise of the professional lobbyist is important for understanding the nuts and bolts of British government, but it has also has raised issues about the workings of democratic politics. Three issues are especially sensitive.

*Privilege*. Professional lobbying is not cheap. It is a service therefore only available to rich groups, and in the main professional lobbyists are used by well organized functional groups, such as firms and trade associations. If we make the assumption that using professional lobbyists raises the chances of success in influencing government, then we must conclude that professional lobbying is a privileged service disproportionately available to the rich.

*Probity.* The rise of professional lobbying has been accompanied by a number of newspaper exposures of scandals involving privileged access by special interests. Both Mr Major's Conservative governments (1990–7) and Mr Blair's first administration (1997–2001) were damaged by such scandals (see Political Issues 9.1, p. 183). In Chapter 5, for example, we documented the importance of the Committee on Standards in Public Life in pressing for more openly codified standards of conduct in public life. The Committee owes its existence to scandals publicized in the early 1990s: newspapers revealed that backbench MPs in the House of Commons were covertly paid substantial sums of money by professional lobbyists for 'placing' questions to ministers. These particular instances reflect a more general problem of ethical standards. At heart, what the professional lobbyist offers is access. The lobbyist claims an expertize, not in the client's particular subject, but in government itself: how it works; who the people in government are who will really make a difference to a policy decision. Very often this knowledge itself comes from a period in public service or in political activity. Most lobbyists, if successful, are successful because their previous careers equipped them with a good contacts book and with the friendship of those who have power in government. This is why probity is an important issue: it concerns the moral rightness of using privileged connections with public figures to exercise influence over policy on behalf of special interests. In other walks of life using contacts in this way would be viewed as improper. Suppose, for instance, that I were to set up a business charging to advise sixth formers applying for places at the University of Manchester; and suppose I were to claim that my years of service in the University gave me lots of contacts with admissions tutors to help applicants make their case for admission. That would be highly improper and would lead, rightly, to my dismissal from the University; yet it is not clear how the exploitation of privileged connections by lobbyists differs from this.

## Briefing 9.6

### 'A REGULAR AND NORMAL PART OF BRITISH POLITICAL LIFE': THE CASE OF THE FUEL PROTESTS, 2000

In September 2000 a network of farmers and road hauliers launched a campaign of direct action protest against diesel fuel prices. Their main tactic was to blockade oil refineries. Within days a fuel shortage paralysed distribution networks, leading to food shortages and a dramatic collapse of public support for the government. But an attempt to widen the protests, and to organize the protesters more formally, entirely failed, and by October the protests had collapsed.

Doherty *et al.* (2003) explain the rise and success of the protests in terms already used in this chapter: learning lessons from other protesters, notably French farmers; the use of new technologies of communication, such as mobile phones; the vulnerability of modern economies to disruptive action; the existence of numerous 'outsiders' who think 'insiders' in government are indifferent to them. They explain the collapse of the protests as the product of tactical errors, and the difficulty of imposing permanent organization on spontaneously arising groups. But they emphasize that 'disruptive and confrontational protest is now a regular and normal part of British political life' (Doherty *et al.* 2003: 19).

➔ The fuel protests were spectacular; but they are only one of dozens of examples of confrontational protest organized through loosely coordinated networks. I guarantee that a week's reading of a good newspaper will produce at least one example, local or national.

*Power.* Issues of privilege and probity in turn imply issues to do with the exercise of power. Professional lobbying is not a charitable activity. The lobbyist serves those who can afford to pay, and those who can afford to pay are, naturally, already rich. In short, the activities of the professional reinforce existing power imbalances in the interest group system.

To these worries, the professional lobbyist can make a number of replies. Although there is a need

## People in politics

### 9.1    THREE LEADING POLITICAL ENTREPRENEURS IN THE WORLD OF PREFERENCE GROUPS

Cartoons: Shaun Steele

**Des Wilson** has claims to be founder of the modern political entrepreneur in preference groups. A campaigning journalist originally from New Zealand, his CV reads like a history of modern campaigning groups: he has been both director of Shelter (the campaign for the homeless) and chairman of Friends of the Earth, the leading environmental group. But his last job was as head of corporate affairs at a leading economic interest, the British Airports Authority.

**Eamonn Butler's** career shows that the modern political entrepreneur need not work on the left of politics. In 1977 he co-founded the *Adam Smith Institute*, a think tank which has campaigned for more free market forces. He now directs the Institute. Under him the Institute pours out a stream of advocacy for the market, commissioning research and publishing working papers, all of which is designed to reinforce the message that the market is best.

**Jonathan Porritt's** career is highly modern but he is also a familiar figure in the history of British politics: the toff with a conscience. Educated at Eton, he inherited the family baronetcy. He has been both director of Friends of the Earth and chair of the Ecology Party. He is probably the best known face of 'green politics' in Britain. His patrician connections latterly surfaced when he became the informal 'green guru' to the Prince of Wales.

➲ The three sketches show the diverse sources of political entrepreneurs who have done so much to revitalize issue campaigning in Britain, especially on behalf of groups who do not have the resources to defend their own interests: an immigrant, a university meritocrat, and an upper-class product of Eton.

for professional standards, and although there are periodic lapses from the highest standards, this is nothing unique to professional lobbying. It is true of all professions, and it is particularly true of professions that have traditionally been closely connected to professional lobbying, such as the law, public relations and politics itself. Lobbying has always gone on. The rise of professional lobbying makes open and organized, and therefore available for scrutiny and regulation, what was once hidden from public view. While undoubtedly professional lobbyists have to be paid, the best solution to problems of power and inequality is to encourage the growth and diversity of professional lobbying as an occupation, because with growth and diversity firms will emerge that specialize in different groups of clients and policy areas. Some lobbying firms have already been set up, for instance, with the aim of only serving clients of whose aims they approve. This is not hugely different from the way law firms, for example, specialize in different kinds of legal representation: some work in commercial law, some in human rights law. Professional lobbying is a service offered in the marketplace, and in any flourishing marketplace there will be a diversity of firms serving a diversity of clients.

## New forms of group mobilization

Consider Amnesty International, a group that campaigns on behalf of prisoners of conscience, which has a large individual membership both in Britain and worldwide; or a group such as Shelter, which for 40 years has campaigned on behalf of the homeless in Britain. Groups of this kind illustrate what is sometimes called the 'bumble bee' problem in studying interest groups. According to the laws of aerodynamics the bumble bee should not be able to fly, but it does. Likewise, these groups should not exist, or at least not flourish. Prisoners of conscience and the homeless do not have the obvious resources – like money and organization – that support flourishing and effective groups. Yet Amnesty and Shelter exist and flourish. The campaigning group, often with a large membership, and often campaigning on behalf of some dispossessed group or cause, is an increasingly important part of the political system. Three connected factors lie behind this important development.

*Creative leadership.* In the jargon of political science this is sometimes called *political entrepreneurship.* Many groups are brought into existence by energetic and idealistic figures, prepared to commit their energy and idealism wholesale to a cause. Sometimes these individuals become well known national figures: consider the examples given in People in Politics 9.1. Sometimes the groups emerge locally, and rapidly fade away: many environmental campaigns against projects such as new roads are sparked in this way. Of course, creative leadership and idealistic people have always existed. Some wider

conditions must now be helping creative leaders to have an impact. Two factors considered next may provide clues.

*Political skills and confidence.* Organizing and acting politically in an effective way comes naturally only to a gifted few. For most of us, the ability to run things, and to make a case, depends heavily on possessing skills and confidence: for instance, the skills and confidence needed to write, address public meetings and broadcast. There is no doubt at all that formal education helps foster these. The figures for formal education tell a straightforward story. More and more Britons are now able to raise their skill and confidence levels through extended secondary and tertiary education: 40 years ago about 5 per cent of 18–21 year olds entered universities; now about 40 per cent are in higher education.

*Technology.* Organizing and campaigning depend heavily on being able to communicate – with government, with supporters and with those among the public whom one wishes to persuade. We only have to contrast technologies of communication now with conditions 50 years ago to see how much easier, cheaper and quicker communication has become. Then, the telephone was a luxury available only to the minority of the population, and was limited to landline systems; now almost everyone has a phone, and about 80 per cent of households have access to a mobile. Then, telephoning abroad was cumbersome and expensive; now, virtually instantaneous global communication networks can be used via the Internet. These changes in hard technology have in turn reshaped what are sometimes called 'social' technologies – techniques of campaigning and communication. Creative political leaders have learnt how to exploit the new conditions: targeted mailshots using databases that identify potential groups of supporters provide an important way to raise funds quickly; confident and well educated members learn how to work the media so as to maximize reporting of their activities and views; use of mobile phones and e-mail networks allows rapid communication and the organization of widely spread groups without the need for traditional, formal, permanent organization in offices. (For a case study of what can be accomplished, see Briefing 9.6).

**DOCUMENTING POLITICS 9.3**

## PROFESSIONAL LOBBYING AT THE EU LEVEL: THE VIEW FROM THE PROFESSIONALS

'There are many interest groups and offices which are based in Brussels, playing an indispensable role in the European institutions' decision-making process ... But what kind of a future does a profession in constant evolution and of growing importance have if no training exists and there is no preparation for it ? What are the social consequences?

These thoughts led in 1994 to the creation of the European Institute for Public Affairs and Lobbying, EIPAL, the first of its kind in Brussels.

The EIPAL training programme allows managers, experienced professionals, company heads and even young university graduates to gain a thorough grasp of the decision-making process at the European level and of the different methods of defending public or private group interests. The programme allows participants not only to learn the basics of the lobbying profession, but also to follow the latest developments in this sector. It also helps them discover and understand the links between the European Union and all sectors, both public and private.

Since 1994, EIPAL has trained more than 250 professionals including diplomats, civil servants, consultants, graduates, corporate and multinational executives, officials from interest groups and european federations. Experience gained over the previous thirteen sessions is our trump-card for efficiency and professionalism.'

➲ This extract from a very successful professional training organization for lobbyists in the European Union shows how the rise of the Union is transforming the world of interest representation. The scale, diversity and complexity of policy making, especially in Brussels, means that many old British patterns simply no longer work. In particular, the informal cultivation of personal relationships by insiders is giving way to much more systematic organization of the activity of lobbying: skills which bodies such as this one offer to teach.

*Source*: www.eipal.be

Creative leadership, the spread of political skills, and technological innovation have all helped produce a more diverse and open world of interest representation. Thus these developments help counteract the historical inequalities in the system. They have also made the interest group world more unstable: groups often rise and die with extraordinary swiftness. Briefing 9.6 not only documents the rapid emergence of an alliance that depended heavily on the mobile phone for coordination; it also documents a movement that faded away almost as quickly as it had appeared.

### The Europeanization of interest representation

Interest group representation tends to follow the contours of political power. Since Britain's original entry into the (then) EEC in 1973 the European Union has emerged as a powerful political presence in Britain. Naturally, interest groups have responded to this. The consequence has been a profound *Europeanization* of interest representation. This has a number of different faces.

The most obvious is the tendency of existing groups to direct some of their activities to Union

### 9.1  SLEAZE AND LOBBYING

The common view that British politics is marked by high standards was damaged by a series of episodes under both the Conservative government of John Major, and under the governments of Tony Blair. The episodes produced allegations that economic interests could buy special access for cash. Under Major, Conservative MPs were revealed as willing to ask 'planted' parliamentary questions for money in a 'sting' organized by a newspaper. A government minister (Neil Hamilton) resigned over revelations of his connections with the owner of Harrods, and lost his seat in the 1997 general election to an 'anti-sleaze' independent, the television journalist, Martin Bell. The Conservative Cabinet Minister, Jonathan Aitken resigned from the government to sue *The Guardian* for libel over stories concerning his business connections; he lost, and ended in jail for committing perjury. The stream of cases led to the setting-up of the Committee on Standards in Public Life in 1994 (see Documenting Politics 23.3, p. 513). The Labour Leader Tony Blair announced that in office he would run a rigorously clean Administration. The promise was soon badly damaged. A 'sting' by a newspaper led to the revelation that a special adviser in the Blair Government was boasting of his ability to gain preferential access for clients. A string of decisions – ranging from the treatment of cigarette advertising in Formula One motor racing to the awarding of government contracts – was soon suspiciously linked to donations to the Labour Party. Members of the government were involved in bitter arguments about the investigations by the officer concerned with the maintenance of standards among members of the House of Commons.

'Sleaze' was a journalistic coinage to express the dark, discreditable world thus revealed. The immediate rows over individuals often obscured the wider issues. These included:

- What should be the connections between public servants and private interests?
- Should the connections be declared?
- Should they involve payments? In particular, how legitimate is it for Members of the House of Commons to benefit from payment as 'consultants' (for which read lobbyists) for commercial interests?
- Should they be regulated, and if so by whom? Is 'self-regulation' by bodies such as the House of Commons sufficient, or is some outside regulatory body needed?

institutions, especially to the Commission in Brussels (see Documenting Politics 9.3, p. 182). One of the simplest but most invariable rules of political life is that well organized interest groups go to where the power lies. If we came across a novel political system and wanted to find out quickly where power lay, just about the quickest way to find out would be to look at where the big functional groups – business, professions, large trade unions – were directing their lobbying. And a couple of days in Brussels (or even a couple of hours on the web navigating the sites of the big British functional groups) soon shows us that any group of weight has a big presence in Brussels. That presence can take a variety of forms: intensively lobbying at home – for instance, of ministers – to influence how national governments behave in Union-level bargaining; establishing a permanent office in Brussels; or perhaps periodically hiring professional lobbyists to navigate through the complicated EU decision-making system. 'Brussels' is shorthand here for all the major institutions of the Union, but it has become universal shorthand because the single most important object of pressure is the Commission, which has its headquarters in that city.

When we look at lobbying in the Commission, and in lesser institutions such as the European Parliament, we find not only British groups at work. All this British lobbying is replicated for the other member states. Another face of Europeanization has therefore been created by the unification of separate nationally organized interest groups into European-wide federations of groups. They range from the European Fishing Tackle Trade Association to the European Federation of Pharmaceutical Industries and Associations (EPPIA). Tremendous obstacles often lie in the way of creating these groups: for example, even within national associations representing firms in the chemical industry there can be huge differences of opinion and interest; these internal differences are obviously magnified when representation becomes pan-European. But Europeanizing interest representation in this way is helped greatly by the institutions of the Union itself. The Commission in particular is committed to a style of decision making which involves close consultation with affected interests before decisions are arrived at; and where there is no obvious organized European voice for an interest, the Commission often takes an active part in promoting the creation of such a voice. Thus many of these bodies are in practice *governing* institutions at the European level: more than 100 organizations influence, set and direct standards for products traded across the Union.

The tendency of the Union actually to promote Europeanization of representation is strengthened by the way the Union typically tries to implement policy. One feature of the Union we noted in Chapter 6 was that its financial and administrative resources were actually quite weak. It has neither the money nor the people to put policy into effect on the ground. It relies on nations to implement its Directives, and within nations it relies particularly heavily on well organized functional groups for implementation. For example, under the rules of economic integration there are now, in most profes-

sions, well developed systems of accreditation for ensuring that professional qualifications from the different member states are mutually recognized. These systems of mutual accreditation have more often than not been negotiated between the separate national professional associations, and responsibility for their implementation is delegated to those associations.

The Union has also widened the range of arenas and issues where groups can campaign. One of the most important instances of this concerns the courts. As Chapter 6 showed, the Union, because it is the creation of Treaties, has a well developed system of laws and entitlements whose exact interpretation is adjudicated by the European Court. In recent years the Court has been an important place where organized British groups have been able to go to test, or challenge, the validity of a policy.

## Interest representation in the Westminster system: change and continuity

The Westminster system is shorthand for a highly centralized arrangement that governed Britain until recently. It was geographically centralized, dominated by institutions located in central London, mostly clustered around the Westminster Parliament. The most important of these institutions were the core executive and the civil service departments discussed in the preceding two chapters. This system has been fragmenting. A world of interest representation grew up around this centralized system, with many of its centralized features. It too is changing, in part due to the fragmentation of the Westminster system. In part the changes consist of developments that are outside the range of this chapter but which will become clear later: for example, we will find that the creation of newly devolved administrations in Edinburgh and Cardiff has switched important interest group activity away from the London metropolis. The traditional Westminster system of interest representation, because it was highly centralized, was also very hierarchical and unequal. It divided the interest group world pretty clearly into 'insiders' and 'outsiders'.

# DEBATING POLITICS

## 9.1   INTEREST GROUPS: UNDERMINING OR PROMOTING DEMOCRACY IN BRITAIN?

| Interest groups undermine democracy | Interest groups promote democracy |
| --- | --- |
| ■ The most powerful and wealthy are always best organized, so strengthening inequality.<br>■ Groups promote sectional interests over the common interest.<br>■ Groups can challenge the authority of democratically elected governments.<br>■ There is no check on the extent to which groups are themselves democratic, and indeed most are run by small minorities of members or by professional officers. | ■ Group representation complements and extends the representation of territorially elected democratic governments.<br>■ Groups use their expertize and legitimacy to support and improve the policies of elected government.<br>■ Group organization is flexible and changing, allowing new and hitherto excluded interests a voice.<br>■ Groups are a counter-balancing power against that of the state. |

Some of the changes sketched in this chapter have made this centralized, unequal system less so: social and cultural change have stimulated the formation

## REVIEW

Five themes have been important in this chapter:

1   The diversity and complexity of worlds of interest representation that span both the functional and the world of preference groups;
2   The weight that accrues to functional groups from their place in the wider division of labour;
3   The importance of cultural preferences in determining the political weight of preference groups;
4   The way social and institutional change are reshaping what was a closed, hierarchical Westminster-focused system of interest representation;
5   The way change is both making the new system more open, but also more vulnerable to groups speaking for the already rich and powerful.

of groups and equipped many of them with the resources and skills to exercise much more open pressure. But some other changes have actually made wealth and the things that go with wealth even more important in interest group mobilization. These changes are partly reflected in the rise of professional lobbyists (the expensive 'hired guns' available to those who can afford to pay).

The ambiguous nature of change is perfectly illustrated by the consequences of Europeanization. On the one hand, the European Union has shifted much interest group lobbying away from the world of insiders in Westminster, and it has opened up new possibilities for exercising influence and created new arenas of influence (for instance, in the courts); but it has also made the activity of lobbying even more complex, and therefore more manipulable by those groups that can invest heavily in professional skills (see Documenting Politics 9.3, p. 182).

## Further reading

Three exceptionally important works which have stood the test of time to achieve the status of 'classics' are: Beer (1969/82); Middlemas, (1979); and Grant and Marsh (1977). Grant (2000) is an authoritative survey of the field.

CHAPTER 10

# Parliament in the Westminster system

## CONTENTS

## AIMS

The chapter:

❖ Stresses the physical presence of Parliament as an important symbol of the system of government

❖ Describes the practical organization of the House of Commons

❖ Describes how the functions of the House are in some degree determined by this organization

❖ Summarizes some important sources of change and stress in the place of the Commons in the Westminster system

❖ Describes the roles, organization and reform of the House of Lords.

## Parliament: dignity and efficiency

The very fact that we use the phrase 'Westminster system' to describe the most important institutions of British government conveys something of the significance of Parliament. In our everyday speech when we refer to 'Westminster' we more often than not mean the Houses of Parliament, the buildings that lie beside the Thames in the borough of Westminster. Even a first inspection of Parliament shows the importance of the famous distinction in the English Constitution made by Walter Bagehot, which we discussed in Chapter 5: between the dignified (the symbolic) and the efficient (the practical working). Parliament, we will discover, has some importance in the efficient working of the system; but it is absolutely central to the dignified, the symbolic. Indeed, it provides just about the most commonly reproduced image of British government (a version of which is also reproduced in Image 10.1 of this chapter). It has appeared on everything from a famous label on a sauce bottle which you can probably find in the kitchen cupboard at home (HP sauce) to cartoons, to official accounts of the British way of life. Parliament is, to state the obvious, a place, a set of buildings. The layout and form of these buildings is highly revealing about the roles of Parliament in the wider Westminster system. It will help us greatly, therefore, to begin with a quick tour of Parliament. It will have to be selective, for the 'Palace of Westminster', to use its more formal title, is a vast, rambling collection of buildings.

## A tour of Parliament

If you want to tour Parliament the first thing you will discover is that you cannot do this at will. Most of the Palace of Westminster is closed to the public. Virtually the only way to see beyond a few selected areas is to be given a tour by a member of the House. This is not difficult: backbench MPs in the House of Commons spend a fair part of their time escorting groups of their constituents around the Palace. Your MP guide will meet us in the central lobby. This was historically a place of unregulated contact where constituents could accost members –

**Image 10.1**
**The face of the Westminster Parliament**

Photo: Michael Moran

➲ The photograph shows in part the single best known image in British politics: the clock tower of the Palace of Westminster, Big Ben. The clock tower is an icon of British democracy and, via the chimes broadcast to announce numerous radio and television news bulletins, is also a powerful symbol of the London-focused system of government. But the angle of the photograph also shows the complexity of the physical and political reality of the Westminster Parliament. Big Ben seems a timeless symbol of traditional British government (though it only dates from the nineteenth century). The closer building is Portcullis House, the recently completed state-of-the-art offices provided for backbench MPs. One of the many ironies of this juxtaposition is that the completion of this enormously expensive addition to the facilities of the Westminster legislature coincided with its increasing loss of powers and functions, both downwards to devolved government, notably in Scotland, and outwards, to the institutions of the European Union.

**DOCUMENTING POLITICS 10.1**

## THE CULTURE OF THE HOUSE OF COMMONS: THE PARTISAN BATTLE AT FULL PITCH

### 'PRIME MINISTER
#### The Prime Minister was asked –

#### Engagements

**Mr. Eric Illsley (Barnsley, Central):** If he will list his official engagements for Wednesday 18 June.

**The Prime Minister (Mr. Tony Blair):** This morning I had meetings with ministerial colleagues and others. In addition to my duties in the House, I will have further such meetings later today.

**Mr. Illsley:** Will my right hon. Friend take this opportunity to reject the artificially generated hysteria about the Convention on the Future of Europe? Will he confirm that, when it comes to the ratification of any future European treaty, he will do exactly what previous Conservative Prime Ministers have done – reject a referendum and ratify through an Act of Parliament in this House?

**The Prime Minister:** That is the procedure that we will follow. There is no need to have a referendum on the Convention or the intergovernmental conference because they do not alter the fundamental constitutional arrangements. I certainly agree with my hon. Friend that it is very important to reject the position of those who, as we have seen from the Conservative spokesman on the Convention, would want to change the essential terms of Britain's membership of the European Union.

**Mr. Iain Duncan Smith (Chingford and Woodford Green):** Yesterday, the new Leader of the House – part-time Leader of the House – said that he had given up a third of his job in order to be an effective Welsh Secretary. Can the Prime Minister tell the House how much time the Secretary of State for Transport has given up to be an effective Scottish Secretary?

**The Prime Minister:** My right hon. Friend will spend as much time on Scottish affairs as is required, as he has already said, but let me point out to the right hon. Gentleman what the Conservative position is on the Secretary of State for Scotland. [Hon. Members: 'Order!'] The position on which he stood at the last election is this – [Hon. Members: 'Order!'] This is what the Conservative manifesto said: "We – [Hon. Members: 'Order!']

**Mr. Deputy Speaker:** Order. I appeal for calm and dignity in the House, and I would ask the Prime Minister to remember that his prime responsibility is to answer for the Government.

**The Prime Minister:** And in answering for the Government, I want to say why I agree with the proposition that I am about to read out from the Conservative party manifesto:

> 'We will keep the position of Secretary of State for Scotland with the holder of that position also having an additional UK role within the Cabinet.'

So we have implemented Conservative party manifesto policy.

**Mr. Duncan Smith:** Let me remind the Prime Minister that he was elected to implement his own manifesto, and ask him where in his manifesto did he make a pledge to have a part-time Welsh Secretary, a part-time Scottish Secretary, a part-time Leader of the House or, for that matter, a part-time Secretary of State for Transport?

The Prime Minister *rose* –

**Mr. Duncan Smith:** I have not finished yet. The Prime Minister will not get away as easily as that. Let me remind the Prime Minister what he actually did pledge. Eight months ago, at the Labour party conference, he said that transport under Labour was 'probably the worst area of public services'. Will he explain how full-time chaos on the roads can be dealt with by a part-time Secretary of State for Transport?

**DOCUMENTING POLITICS 10.1**    (continued)

**The Prime Minister**: I am sorry if the right hon. Gentleman is not prepared to acknowledge that I now agree with Conservative party policy, at least in relation to the Secretary of State for Scotland. As for transport, we are investing billions of pounds in our transport system. That is public investment, and also private sector investment.

The problem that the right hon. Gentleman must explain is this. That investment programme was put to the House a short time ago, and it was voted against by the Conservative party. How can the right hon. Gentleman say that he is going to improve the state of Britain's roads and railways when he has opposed the investment that will make that possible?

**Mr. Duncan Smith**: It is the usual story. The Prime Minister is rattling out the same old Labour lie machine, every single time. *[Interruption.]* Oh yes.

Let us remind the Prime Minister exactly what state all his transport policy is in. One in five trains is now late. Train services are being cut by his Government. Train fares are set to be increased by his Government. Congestion on the roads is growing every single day.

So the Prime Minister thinks that a record like that—a record of chaos like that—can be dealt with by appointing a part-time Secretary of State for Transport....

**Mr. Charles Kennedy (Ross, Skye and Inverness, West)**: When both the former Foreign Secretary and the former Secretary of State for International Development told the Foreign Affairs Committee yesterday that they had been told by MI6 that Iraq did not possess weapons of mass destruction capable of posing a direct threat to British security, were they correct?

**The Prime Minister**: The intelligence that we put out in the dossier last September described absolutely accurately the position of the Government. That position is that Saddam was indeed a threat to his region and to the wider world. I always made it clear that the issue was not whether he was about to launch an immediate strike on Britain: the issue was whether he posed a threat to his region and to the wider world. *[Interruption.]* I must say that I thought that Conservative Members, who are muttering, agreed with that on the basis of the same intelligence.

**Mr. Kennedy**: But given the seriousness of the charges made by those two former Cabinet Ministers yesterday, does the Prime Minister think that this can be adequately investigated by a Foreign Affairs Committee to which he refuses to give evidence and a Joint Intelligence Committee which he controls? Can we not have a proper independent judicial inquiry?

**The Prime Minister**: The right hon. Gentleman says that I control the Intelligence and Security Committee, but he has a member of his own party on that Committee; I do not believe that he would agree with the assessment that he is controlled by me.'

➲ The dominant theme of this chapter is that the House of Commons is an institution that exists mainly to fight battles between parties. Prime Minister's Questions (normally taken weekly on Wednesdays when the Commons is in session) epitomize this partisan culture. The extract catches the mixture of elaborately choreographed theatre and often chaotic intervention of the issues of the day. The Questions open with the same standard meaningless question every week: a request to the Prime Minister to list his engagements. The supplementary allows a friendly Labour backbencher to lob a substantive question to the Prime Minister on a topic where he has a prepared answer – in this case on the question of referenda on issues of important change in the European Union. This is followed by the heart of the session: the attempt by the Prime Minister and the Leader of the Opposition (Iain Duncan Smith) to score points off each other in an atmosphere where backbenchers shout at each other across the Chamber. (Note the Deputy Speaker's vain attempt to secure some order.) The topics on which abuse is exchanged, as on this occasion, simply, reflect the immediate issues of the week. The sarcastic references to the part-time Leader of the House, for example, attempt to exploit a muddled government reshuffle. The Leader of the third largest party, the Liberal Democrats (Charles Kennedy) is allowed a pot shot over the aftermath of a war fought in Iraq earlier in 2003. The Prime Minister will have arrived in the Commons after a detailed briefing that attempted to anticipate questions, and with a large annotated folder containing drafts of replies and supporting material. (That is why he could quote so easily from the Conservative Election Manifesto of 2001.)

*Source*: HC Debates, 18 June 2003, cols 347–51.

hence the origin of the modern verb, to lobby, which is commonly used to describe interest representation (see Chapter 9). But threats from terrorist attack in the last three decades have now turned the lobby into a meeting place where access is tightly regulated. You can only get into the lobby on evidence of a confirmed appointment with an MP guide.

Parliament is technically a bi-cameral legislature: it consists of the two 'chambers', the Commons and the Lords. Since the tour is swift and selective you should spend most of your available time on the Commons, the more important of these.

It is natural to want to begin a tour with the actual chamber of the House of Commons. Since Parliamentary debates were first televised in 1991 this is the arena where you are most likely to have viewed Parliament in action. What will immediately strike you if you have done a little homework is how little the Chamber, nominally the heart of Parliament, is occupied. Business is only formally conducted there for about 150 days in the Parliamentary year (even this is more than was typically the case a century ago). At any one time the visitor will see remarkably few of the 659 MPs actually present in the Chamber. Indeed, the Chamber is designed on the assumption that all members will rarely attend. On the few occasions when there is a full turnout there is standing room only: the long benches (rather than the special designated desks for each member usual in other parliaments) mean that nobody is guaranteed a reserved seat. These rare occasions include: Prime Minister's Question Time, when both sides join noisily in adversarial abuse between the Prime Minister and Leader of the Opposition (see Documenting Politics 10.1); the annual Budget statement by the Chancellor of the Exchequer; and a great national crisis, such as a war or a government scandal. Unless you have turned up one of these rare occasions you will see sparsely occupied benches. The benches, the panelling of the Chamber, fittings such as the lighting, the high ceiling: all these make the Chamber resemble an assembly hall in an ancient school, or even a church. At first glance the Chamber, like the view of the Palace of Westminster from the outside,

suggests that you are looking at an ancient building dating from medieval times. In fact the shape dates from the middle of the nineteenth century. After a great fire in 1834 the present Palace of Westminster was constructed after extensive debate and an elaborate architectural competition, the chamber only opening in 1850. The present chamber only dates from 1950. It was rebuilt as a modified version of the original following destruction in an air raid in 1941.

At this point the shape of the tour will depend on how friendly and influential is your guide. But if a compliant MP is showing you round you can now see important parts of the Palace to which members of the public are not normally admitted unaccompanied. These are the tea rooms, the bars and the restaurants. The House of Commons resembles a large and well equipped club which until recently kept unusual hours – at least by the standards of most conventional work places. Until very recently it normally began business in mid-afternoon, and often did not conclude until late at night. (Below are summarized some recent reforms.) It is the custom to keep these social facilities open at least as long as the Chamber of the House is in session. Because MPs represent territorial constituencies, only a minority of members have their main dwelling within commuting distance of the Commons. Most live in rented flats and houses, often shared with other members of the same party. In these circumstances the 'social' institutions (the bars and dining rooms) become very important for many members. The fact that for the most part access to these is highly restricted strengthens the atmosphere of a private club – a place where members can eat and drink (sometimes to excess) out of the public gaze. This intense and privileged social aspect to Commons life helps explain why, despite the fact that much of the actual business of parliamentary life is tedious and tiring, MPs often become intensely attached to the place and suffer serious traumas when they lose their seat. One prominent Conservative who lost his seat in the 1997 election could not bring himself to re-enter the precincts of the House as a guest until he was eventually returned as an MP in a subsequent by-election.

Until recently a tour of this part of the Palace would have also allowed you to examine MPs' offices. Office accommodation was cramped, office sharing being the norm – indeed, until a generation ago many MPs only acquired a locker on first being returned to Parliament, but now you can cross to the other side of Westminster Bridge and examine Portcullis House. This is a recently erected purpose-built edifice to provide office accommodation for members (see Image 10.1). Its existence reflects an important development, which, we shall see later, is a source of great tension about the role of the Commons: the development of a more conventional model of professional organization. The physical impression conveyed here is deliberately different from that of the traditional Palace. It has all the trappings of the modern. The visitor enters a large atrium, rather like the entrance to a large business corporation. Suites of offices for members provide room for secretaries and research assistants, and the offices have all the facilities of state-of-the-art IT.

Parliament consists of both the Houses of Commons and Lords, and since the former is by far the more important it is natural that on any tour it attracts the most attention. But you should now retrace your steps to the lobby of the Palace of Westminster where you originally entered. Now go down the corridor opposite to that taken to explore the Commons in order to explore 'the other place', as the House of Lords is quaintly called in formal House of Commons language. The tour replicates the main features you would have noticed in the Commons: a main chamber fitted out in mock medieval manner; committee rooms and bars; tea rooms and places to dine. The main difference is that the Lords is physically even grander than the Commons. Indeed the main ceremonial occasion in the Parliamentary year is held in the chamber of the Lords. This is the televised 'speech from the throne', when the monarch reads a speech written by the government of the day outlining its main legislative plans. The 'dignified' function of the Lords has been even more prominent than the dignified function of the Commons. What the future holds for the Lords is examined near the end of this chapter.

## The House of Commons: organization and powers

The House of Commons lies at the heart of the Westminster system – indeed, as we have noted, it is its best known public symbol. The organization and functions of the Commons, and the way these two elements are changing, are in turn important emblems of the way the once dominant wider Westminster system of governing Britain is changing.

If we imagined designing an institution from scratch, it would be rational first to decide its functions and then to design its organization. Real-world institutions are hardly ever like this, and the House of Commons is no exception. The way it is organized is a function of long-term historical evolution punctuated by dramatic changes, such as those associated with the great extensions of the franchise described in Chapter 2. Thus organization has often determined function, rather than vice versa. We can see this by describing three key influences that shape the organization of the House:

● The way members are selected
● The connected question of the importance of political parties
● The organization of the business of the House.

### Territorial representation

The Commons is made up of 646 individual members elected for separate territorial constituencies in the United Kingdom. Numbers have varied over time, though there has been a gradual tendency towards the expansion of the House. In Chapter 17 we describe the UK's electoral systems, but the distinctive feature operating for the House of Commons should be immediately noted: constituencies are represented by a single member, and the House is composed solely of these representatives of the individual constituencies. (We shall see very different principles at work when we turn to the new elected institutions for Scotland and Wales.) This basic principle of territorial representation, and its focus on the constituencies represented by a single member, has a number of important consequences for the way the Commons functions, but the most obvious can be simply stated: the working life of the Commons is deeply affected by the problem of how to occupy these territorial representatives.

## Party organization

As it happens, party organization provides the most important solution to the problem identified above. The dominance of party organization (see Figure 10.1) is the single most important influence on both the way the House runs its business and, we shall see later, on the functions it performs. The House of Commons is a party institution, and there are two key signs of this, as explained below.

*Affiliation of members.* It is almost unknown for a member of the Commons to be returned as an independent: that is, without the label of a political party. Indeed for most of the period of modern British politics – which we can date from 1918 – the overwhelming mass of MPs has been drawn from two parties, Conservative and Labour. The last two Parliaments have returned only one 'independent' member. While the representation of smaller parties has grown in recent decades, partisan domination of the House, and the domination of the two main parties, remain its most striking features.

*Party cohesion.* Members with party affiliations dominate many modern legislatures, but the influence of party goes deeper than mere affiliation in the Commons. Party organization shapes the behaviour of members, the styles of debate and the practicalities of working. When members of the Commons vote, they vote overwhelmingly on party lines. While this unity has declined in recent decades, partisan voting is still the overwhelming norm. This party cohesion is supported by a powerful system of internal party organization based on the 'whipping' system. The language of 'whipping' is itself an illustration of how the culture and organization of the House echo its historical evolution. The original 'whippers in' operated on the fox-hunting field, whipping the hounds into line. The adoption of the language as parliamentary reflects the Commons' historical domination by upper-class

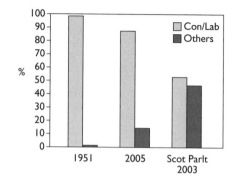

**Figure 10.1**   Party domination of the House of Commons, and the Scottish Parliament

*Source*: 1951 data from Butler and Butler (2000); other data from Electoral Commission.

➲   The bars measure percentages of the total Parliamentary representation. In the middle of the twentieth century the House of Commons had no British rival as a legislature, and was virtually monopolized by the two leading parties: only 1 per cent of seats were in other hands. By 2005 there had been an appreciable rise in rivals to Labour and the Conservatives, although, as we shall see in Chapter 17, the electoral system used for the Westminster Parliament meant that the rise did not reflect changes in the distribution of the popular vote. But one feature was virtually unchanged: the Commons was a party-dominated chamber. There were no non-party independents in 1951, and only 3 in 2005. Under a very different, more proportional electoral system in Scotland the two big UK parties had virtually lost their dominant position. And in the case of Scotland, summing Labour and Conservative numbers gives a misleading picture in one respect: most of these seats (50) are Labour-held; the Conservatives have been reduced to fourth place in Scotland, behind Labour, Scottish Nationalists and the Liberal Democrats.

representatives of rural constituencies, for whom fox hunting was part of a way of life and a natural source of everyday imagery. In modern parties, styles of whipping vary enormously, from the autocratic to the most diplomatic; but what unites them all is that the whipping system is vital to the maintenance of party unity, and helps organize the daily life of the member of the Commons. All the parties, both in government and out, have a Chief Whip who leads a team of Whips. The Whips' key functions are to – depending on style – discipline or cajole members into public support of the party, to

---

**DOCUMENTING POLITICS 10.2**

## HOW WHIPS MANIPULATE COMMONS' PROCEEDINGS: EXTRACT FROM AN MP's DIARY

'May 14

Late this morning DD of the SS [David Davis of the Government Whips Office] found me and handed me a slip of paper, a little strip, no more than two inches deep and four inches wide.
  'What's this?', I asked.
  'It's a question for the PM', he smirked. 'You're asking it. This afternoon.'
  'But I haven't got a question down for the PM', I protested.
  'Stand up and you'll be called.'
  'How do you know?'
  'I know. Trust me. Just learn the question. You've got to have it off by heart, no reading, no glancing at notes. Just wait for the Speaker to say your name then spit out the question. We've put a joke in for you.'

➲ The central place of Whips and whipping is a sign of a theme emphasized throughout this chapter: the way the Westminster Parliament, especially the House of Commons, is driven by the partisan battle. A good Whip tries to manipulate the apparently spontaneous battle in the Chamber. This extract from the diary of a Conservative back-bencher under the Government of Mr Major shows a good Whip at work.

*Source*: Brandreth (1999: 96).

---

monitor the state of opinion within the party in parliament, and to advise party leaders about the state of opinion (see Documenting Politics 10.2). More immediately, when Parliament is in session a key influence over individual MPs is the communication from the Whips indicating when an MP has to be present for a vote in the chamber of the Commons. So important is this last that its forms of expression have entered the wider language: for instance, a 'three-line whip'. (The urgency of attending to vote is indicated by underlining, three lines being a virtual command.)

The formalities of the whipping system, though important, are only the outward expression of even more profound ways in which party organization shapes the Commons. Although the physical layout of Parliament encourages a huge amount of informal contacts in those bars and tea rooms referred to earlier, and while there are occasional friendships across party lines, party organization is very impor-

tant in shaping even this informal life. Furthermore, it is also central to the conduct of parliamentary business.

### The organization of Commons business

When we look at the practical details of how the Commons organizes itself, three features stand out. First, *the organization of debate*, because the Chamber in particular is above all a debating forum; second, the *organization of time*, because the cycle of the parliamentary year is vital to the way the House runs itself; and third, the *practical organization of daily business*, because it is here that we see vivid illustrations of the House in action. Let us examine each of these three in turn.

*The organization of debate.* The first, revealing clues to the organization of Commons business we will already have gleaned from our quick tour of the Palace of Westminster. As we looked down on the

Chamber of the House we will have seen a layout that is actually quite unusual among legislatures in modern democracies. The important features of physical layout to notice are: the separation of the governing party from the rest of the Commons, and the physical line of division between the two halves, ensuring that they face each other across the Chamber; and the symbolic placing of the Speaker – the chair of the session – between the two. But another important physical feature only becomes clear when we look a bit more closely at the actual seating of members. If we can recognize our political personalities we will soon see that the leading members of the two main parties all occupy the front benches on either side: government ministers on one side, leaders of the main opposition party on the other. (Hence 'backbencher' as a term for rank-and-file MPs.) In other words, this is a House organized to conduct a public battle, albeit a non-violent one, between the supporters of the governing party and the rest. On the side of the opposition this is further organized by the now long-established practice in the opposition parties of forming a 'shadow' administration: a front-bench team which confronts its rivals on the opposition benches, stretching from the Leader of the Opposition (a paid position) to that of the most obscure shadow minister of sport. If we have chanced on the House on one of its big set piece occasions – such as Prime Minister's Question Time, which will be examined later – we will soon see that the organization of business is dominated by a public adversarial contest between the governing party and the opposition.

*The organization of the parliamentary timetable.* Our immediate first impression from the Chamber of the House that party is vital to organizing the conduct of business will be supported when we look more closely at how the Commons organizes its time. The most basic of all organizing facts – the organization of the Commons year – shows this. The governing party largely determines the organization of parliamentary time, and indeed what remains is largely shaped by the opposition's reactions to the governing party and by the desire to prosecute the adversarial party battle.

The shaping influence of parliamentary time comes in three particularly important forms. The first is that the legislative programme of the government of the day dominates the parliamentary year. The present conventions of passing legislation through the Commons (and then through the Lords, which we examine next) reinforce this domination. Legislation must pass through a series of stages (see Briefing 10.1), the most important of which are a debate on the principles of the legislation (Second Reading) and a virtual line-by-line examination of the proposals (Committee Stage). If all stages are not concluded in both Houses in the space of a year then the legislation lapses. (This is itself a marginal relaxation, being the result of a series of changes to working practices introduced in 2002. Before that, legislation not passed at the end of the parliamentary year was lost irrevocably.) For over a century, therefore, the single most important influence on the organization of parliamentary business has been a virtual imperative for the governing party: to use its majority to control parliamentary time in order to see through its legislative programme.

*The organization of daily business.* Imagine that we could examine the daily diary of a member of the Commons. What we would discover would depend greatly on the role of that MP. Members of the government are drawn predominantly from the House of Commons, and if our MP were a minister he or she would spend most of the time in the relevant department rather than in the House. (If we look back at Documenting Politics 7.2, p. 126 we will find that this marks an important historical change: the nineteenth-century Prime Minister, Gladstone, would expect to spend the largest part of his day actually in the Chamber when the House was in session.) If we examined the diary of a government backbencher – numerically the commonest form of parliamentary life – we would notice four striking features. First, the actual amount of time spent in the Chamber, still less speaking in the Chamber, is quite small. For most of the time when the Chamber is in session it is occupied by only a handful of members. Second, a significantly larger proportion of time spent on official Commons business is devoted to hearings of House of Commons committees. (For more details of these, see Briefing 10.2.) Third, the extensive network of tea rooms, bars and restaurants

# Briefing

## THE STAGES OF PARLIAMENTARY LEGISLATION

The pre-Parliamentary stages:

- Most legislation has a long gestation. It may be preceded by formal consultations with affected interests in the form of Green Papers or White Papers: the former indicate the government has a truly open mind, the latter that it is committed to proposals in outline.
- Even in the absence of formal public consultation, there will typically be extensive consultation and debate, between central departments, between departments and organized interests, and within the department that proposes to sponsor legislation.
- Most important legislation to be proposed by the governing party will be announced in outline in an annual Queen's Speech – an elaborate, 'dignified' occasion, but one that also announces the government's legislative programme for a session. To reach this stage a proposal will have had to win a slot in the government's allotment of Parliamentary time, an allotment made by a Cabinet Committee (see Chapter 7).
- The final proposal (a bill) is drafted by a team of lawyers in the Parliamentary Counsel Office of the Cabinet Office.
- The Labour government elected in 1997 has experimented with pre-legislative scrutiny of draft bills by Parliamentary Select Committees.

The Parliamentary stages:

Bills go through identical stages in both Houses, though most important bills begin life in the Commons:

- First Reading: a purely formal laying of the bill before the House – often done not by the minister with substantive responsibility, but by a government Whip.
- Second Reading: a wide-ranging debate on the broad principles of the Bill. Although focused on the proposals, the broad range of the Second Reading often means that debate is integrated into the partisan battle which is ever present, especially in the House of Commons.
- Committee Stage. Most bills are considered by one of a series of Standing Committees, typically consisting of about 18 members. Though committees are composed to reflect the partisan make-up of the wider House, their smaller size, more informal procedures and a focus on detail means the process is not as shaped by the party battle.
- Report Stage. This 'reports out' the amended bill to the wider House, at which stage committee amendments can be overturned and new amendments inserted.
- Third Reading. Formally a brief overview of the final product, but more commonly an opportunity to resume the full partisan battle using the bill as an instrument.

The post-Parliamentary stages

- Royal Assent: a purely formal stage of assent by the monarch (last withheld in 1707) followed by printing as an Act, the law of the land.
- Implementation: a far from formal stage. Even the most detailed pieces of legislation cannot prescribe the details of implementation. How a piece of legislation works, (indeed, if it works at all) depends on how it is carried out 'on the ground'; and that in turn depends on how those affected by the Act, as well as those responsible for carrying it out, approach the job of putting it into effect. The greatest failures of government policy (see Chapter 19) often happen at this implementation stage.

➲ This schematic outline of the stages of parliamentary legislation omits numerous important variations. One (private members' legislation) is summarized in Briefing 10.3, p. 198. Beyond 'standard' legislation there are often important variations in procedures: for instance, for bills of particularly important constitutional significance, such as the bill in 1998/9 reforming the Lords, the Committee is taken as a Committee of the Whole House: in effect the whole house operating under more informal debating rules. Each bill must complete all stages within a Parliamentary year and will lapse if this is not accomplished. Thus the management of Parliamentary time – which is heavily controlled but not monopolized by the governing party – is a vital part of the business of legislative management. A small number of experiments allowing bills to be 'carried over' from one session to the next have now begun.

that we saw on our tour would have alerted us to the large proportion of the working day spent in these. 'Socializing', dining, drinking and working are thus all mixed up together in the daily business of the Commons, and in the daily life of the member. Fourth (and finally), we would notice that the MP spends a large amount of time on constituency business: either actually in the constituency, where most MPs have their main residence, or in the office, dealing with issues raised by constituents.

Why the organization of daily business takes this form is something that now becomes clear in describing the functions of the Commons.

## The House of Commons: functions

The House of Commons is part of the legislature, and if we simply looked superficially at how it spends time daily we might decide that passing laws is indeed its main function: quantitatively, most debate and argument is about legislation, proposed or passed. But the House of Commons is misunderstood if viewed as a legislator. Virtually all legislative proposals originate from, and are shaped by, the executive, which means the government of the day advised by the civil service. Neither are the Commons' extensive debates on either the principles or details of legislative proposals of great significance in shaping the law: secure government majorities (the usual state of affairs) mean that legislative proposals are hardly ever overturned wholesale, and detailed amendments are usually the result of concessions by ministers.

The only significant departure from this pattern is Private Members' legislation (see Briefing 10.3, p. 198). A small amount of parliamentary time is allotted for the consideration each session of a number of bills sponsored by backbench MPs. Access to this privileged time – confined to a share of about ten Friday sessions and some Wednesday morning sessions per parliamentary year – is governed by an annual ballot. Drawing a 'winning number' in the ballot can do wonders for the reputation of the individual backbencher. Some highly contentious issues which divide parties internally (such as abortion law reform) have been dealt with in this way, since

'unwhipped' votes are normal on Private Member's Bills. Nevertheless, Private Members' legislation is of marginal importance.

The fact that the Commons is neither a serious originator nor a shaper of legislation does not mean that the time spent on debate about legislation is pointless; only that its point must be understood within the setting of the wider functions performed by the Commons, and within the context of the dominant feature of the Commons 'culture': the fact that it is a party-dominated institution. This partisan culture both enables, and hinders, the ability of the Commons to perform key political functions. Six of these are particularly important, and are now considered. They are:

- Supplying and supporting the government
- Fighting the partisan battle
- Scrutinizing legislation
- Scrutinizing the executive
- Representing interests
- Protecting individual constituents.

### Supplying and supporting the government

There is intense competition to enter the House of Commons, as we shall discover in Chapter 18. The single most important reason is that membership of the Commons is a virtual requirement for any politician who wishes to serve as a Westminster government minister. (When we turn to the Lords we shall discover an alternative route, mostly to office outside the Cabinet, which some find more congenial.) This fact defines perhaps the single most important function of the Commons in the wider Westminster system: it provides the main pool of talent from which members of the government – and the rivals who would like to replace them from the opposition front benches – are chosen. It helps explain why, despite the development of other legislatures such as the EP, most ambitious British politicians still aim for a seat in the Commons. What is more, those who become ministers retain their seat in the legislature (a practice not universal in the other democracies). While the demands of ministerial office inevitably reduce the time spent at Westminster, this membership is

# Briefing

## COMMITTEES IN THE HOUSE OF COMMONS: EXAMPLES

| | |
|---|---|
| **Broadcasting** | Advises the Speaker on issues to do with broadcasting the proceedings of the Commons – one of a class of committees to do with the domestic business of the House. |
| **Environment, Food and Rural Affairs** | Oversees the Department for Environment, Food and Rural Affairs and its associated public bodies. |
| **European Scrutiny** | Examines the legal and/or political importance of each EU document, and generally keeps the EU under review. |
| **Foreign Affairs** | Scrutinizes the expenditure, administration and policy of the Foreign and Commonwealth Office and its associated public bodies. |
| **International Development** | Scrutinizes the expenditure, administration and policy of the Department for International Development and its associated public bodies. |
| **Public Accounts** | A long-established Committee chiefly concerned to examine the reports produced by the Comptroller and Auditor General (C&AG) on his value for money (VFM) studies of the economy, efficiency and effectiveness with which government departments and other bodies have used their resources to further their objectives. |
| **Public Administration** | Examines reports of the Parliamentary Commissioner for Administration, of the Health Service Commissioners for England, Scotland and Wales and of the Parliamentary Ombudsman for Northern Ireland, which are laid before the House; more generally scrutinizes the system of government. |
| **Regulatory Reform** | Scrutinizes government proposals for regulatory reform orders under the Regulatory Reform Act 2001. |
| **Science and Technology** | Scrutinizes expenditure, administration and policy of the Office of Science and Technology and the Research Councils. |
| **Statutory Instruments** | Scrutinizes all statutory instruments laid only before the House of Commons. Its work is closely related to that of the Joint (with Lords) Committee on Statutory Instruments. |
| **Transport** | Scrutinizes the expenditure, administration and policy of the Department for Transport and its associated public bodies. |
| **Treasury** | Scrutinizes expenditure, administration and policy of HM Treasury, the Board of the Inland Revenue, the Board of HM Customs and Excise, and associated public bodies, including the Bank of England and the Financial Services Authority. |

➥ The exact titles, responsibilities and number of Select Committees varies. This selection is taken from the list as at July 2003, when there were 33 in existence. The selection is therefore only designed to indicate the range of work being done. It shows us that there are three kinds of Select Committee:

• Those concerned with the domestic management of the House itself: for instance, the Broadcasting Committee
• Those that are a legacy of a time when the Commons was a much more powerful controller of the Executive: notably, the Public Accounts Committee dates from the nineteenth century and reflects the historical role of the Commons in attempting to ensure *financial* accountability of the executive
• Committees that embody the larger architecture of the governing system, designed to ensure that the main functional divisions of the executive are covered (for instance, the Treasury Committee). This architecture was substantially redesigned in reforms introduced in 1979 by Mrs Thatcher's first Leader of the House of Commons, Norman St John Stevas.

# Briefing

## PRIVATE MEMBERS' LEGISLATION

Most bills that pass into law by receiving the Royal Assent originate as proposals from the executive. A small number, and a tiny proportion of the whole, originate as bills from backbench MPs. Although Private Members' legislation can originate in either House, most successful bills originate in the Commons. Formally, there are three sources of proposals for bills in the Commons, but only the third one described below is of significance as a source of legislation.

- Ten Minute Rule Bills: a Member may move a motion to seek House approval to introduce a bill. The proposer is allowed ten minutes to make a case. The motion is rarely allowed and this method is recognized not as a serious attempt to move legislation, but as an attempt to gain publicity for an issue that concerns the Member. Between 1983 and 2001 only 10 bills passed into law through this route.
- Ordinary Presentation Bills: these are laid before the House, but not debated. The proposer will have little prospect of turning the Bill into legislation, but will typically use it as part of continuing process of keeping 'alive' an issue on which the Member has legislative ambitions. Between 1983 and 2001, some 39 Bills passed into Law through this route.
- 'Ballot Bills': early in each session a ballot is held allocating an allotment of Parliamentary time – principally on Fridays – for Private Members' bills. Up to 400 MPs typically enter the ballot. Many do not even have a particular bill in mind. Typically 20 'slots' are allocated in the ballot. Realistically, only those drawn in the top 10 have any chance of turning proposals into law: in 1999–2000, for instance, only five 'ballot bills' were turned into law. A Member who draws a 'high' number in the ballot will be inundated with draft bills from pressure groups and Parliamentary colleagues. This category of Private Members' legislation is associated with groundbreaking reforms, especially in the area of social reform: laws decriminalizing homosexuality, abortion and abolishing capital punishment originated in this route. But of the 147 ballot bills that became law between 1983 and 2001, most were on technical and uncontroversial subjects. While the leaders of the major parties – especially the governing party – often prefer to leave to Private Members' legislation highly sensitive issues that divide parties internally, this very sensitivity makes passage difficult. This is because there are so many opportunities to delay legislation when party controls are relaxed that any controversial legislation is likely to be ambushed on its passage through both Houses.

*Source*: Information from HC Information Office (2003).

⮕ The most precious commodity in Parliament is time. Parliamentary time is controlled by the governing party which controls the Executive; time allocated to Private Members' bills is very limited. This makes proposals – even when they enjoy the support of a majority of members – immensely vulnerable to delaying tactics by opponents. It is easy to 'talk out' a proposal by debating with real or specious points. A member lucky enough to come high in the annual ballot, to maximize the chances of getting a Bill into law, should choose a technical and non-controversial measure. If a contentious measure is chosen, it is only likely to succeed if it has the implicit support of the government of the day (a feature of the famous measures of social reform such as decriminalization of homosexuality referred to in the box).

vital in all kinds of ways. Above all, it obliges ministers to be present to defend government policy and actions against opposition. It means that those government backbenchers who have not been recruited to office still have a vital governing function: their votes ensure that government business carries through the Commons; their voices will be heard in arguments supporting the government of the day. This last role is in turn central to a second important function that we now examine: fighting the adversarial battle between the parties.

### Fighting the partisan battle

Normal people only occasionally view the House of Commons at work, and then usually on high-profile occasions, such as the weekly 'joust' at Prime Minister's Question Time between the Prime Minister and the official Leader of the Opposition. Normal people are often shocked at the atmosphere of debate: the point scoring, and the apparent lack of interest in reasoned exchange where arguments would be conceded and modified. Were we to observe this style elsewhere – say, in a university class or in a business meeting – we would undoubtedly think that these were peculiar, dysfunctional people in a peculiar, dysfunctional world. But this is to miss the point in respect of the Commons: partisan point scoring is the very essence of Commons life because it is a party-dominated institution, and because the conventions of party life stress adversarial confrontation. This is not an inevitable consequence of party organization: other democracies have legislatures, with parties, where there is much more stress on consensus and accommodation of different views. But for better or worse the history and culture of the British House of Commons has implanted this adversarial style. The House works best either when what it does can be easily accommodated to this style, or when for some reason the style is totally suspended. Suspension is most likely to happen in two almost entirely opposite circumstances: when some great national crisis (such as war) unites all in a common purpose; or when the issues are so technical and detailed that it is hard to convert them into partisan form. We shall see later that this latter style can be observed in some of the work of Select Committees. But even in times of national crisis, or when faced with a technical question, MPs usually instinctively look for a partisan 'spin' on the issue.

## Scrutinizing legislation

Much the most common way of scrutinizing the details of proposed legislation is through the institution of the committee, notably the small Standing Committee (see Documenting Politics 10.3). In these committees some of the culture of party adversarialism is modified, for reasons that are not hard to understand. Business is done less formally than in the Chamber. (On some occasions the whole House transforms itself into committee mode

as a 'Committee of the Whole House', and here too formality is diminished.) Smaller numbers, the more intimate atmosphere of a committee room, diminished public attention, the often grinding detail of working through the clauses of a bill: all encourage a more normal exchange of views. Committee stages also fulfil other purposes: for the ambitious backbencher this is an occasion to impress the Whips with a grasp of detail and therefore increase the chances of promotion to the front bench. But the process is still dominated by the fact of partisan organization: the members almost always in the end vote on party lines; the object of the exercise for the majority is to report the bill out for further progress to the statute book; and amendments will not pass unless the minister responsible for managing the bill is convinced.

## Scrutinizing the executive

The more general scrutiny of the operations of the executive has historically been an important function of Parliament. It is partly constrained, and partly enabled, by the adversarial battle across the floor of the Commons. As a general rule, the more the scrutiny of the actions of the executive involves the high politics of the government of the day, the more likely it is to be dominated by the pursuit of that adversarial party battle. The most extreme version of this is provided by Prime Minister's Question Time which, while nominally about holding the Prime Minister to account, is now dominated by a virtually gladiatorial, personal battle between the Prime Minister and the Leader of the Opposition. The process can, by chance, wring information and accounts out of the government of the day, but this is virtually an incidental side effect. Nobody pretends that the occasion is seriously about holding the executive to account; it is about measuring the calibre of the two gladiators. Although it is doubtful that the performance in the battle by either the Prime Minister or the Leader of the Opposition makes any significant impact on public opinion, it is intensely followed within the Commons: prime ministers invest significant time in preparation, and the fate of the Leader of the Opposition can hang on whether opposition back

**DOCUMENTING POLITICS 10.3**

## THE YEARLY WORK OF A COMMITTEE: EXTRACT FROM A REPORT ON THE YEARLY WORK OF THE EUROPEAN SCRUTINY SELECT COMMITTEE

EIGHTH REPORT

'The European Scrutiny Committee has agreed to the following Report:

THE COMMITTEE'S WORK IN 2002

1. In our Report on *European scrutiny in the Commons*, we said that we intended in future to follow the practice of other select committees in producing an annual report on our activities. This is the first such report. Since the tasks of the Committee are set directly by its standing order rather than being elaborated in the list of core tasks for select committees drawn up by the Liaison Committee, it does not follow the Liaison Committee's template for annual reports.

2. Our core task, on behalf of the House, is to examine each EU document deposited and to assess the legal and political importance of each and whether it should be debated. 1220 documents were examined during 2002, 535 were deemed of legal and/or political importance, and 86 were recommended for debate (nine on the floor of the House). 33 debates took place in standing committee (in some cases covering several documents), and two on the floor of the House. The latter were on the Single European Sky proposals and reform of the Common Fisheries Policy. We used our power to seek an opinion from a departmental select committee in respect of one document relating to overseas aid.

3. We conducted a major inquiry into *Democracy and accountability in the EU and the role of national parliaments*, and also carried out the first re-examination of the Commons' European scrutiny system since 1998 (*European scrutiny in the Commons*). Reports other than our weekly reports examining documents included those two and three others: *Appointment of parliamentary representatives to the Convention on the future of Europe, Reform of COSAC* and *Scrutiny reserve breaches*. In addition, we agreed two reports on individual documents on which we had taken oral evidence and which deserved greater than usual prominence – *European Arrest Warrant* and *Animal testing and cosmetic products*. We agreed 30 weekly reports, containing 536 sections on documents or groups of documents.'

➲ This extract from an annual report of the committee concerned with the scrutiny of EU legislation is both a good example of the style and range of the work of a committee; it also illustrates an area – the workings of the EU – where the Westminster Parliament has found the exercise of effective scrutiny particularly problematic.

benchers feel their leader is doing well in the public jousting across the floor of the House. The single most important reason why Iain Duncan Smith was deposed as Conservative leader in 2003 was his failure to beat the Prime Minister in these gladiatorial exchanges.

The further the scrutiny of the executive gets from this adversarial struggle – which in part means the further it gets from the floor of the House – the more it indeed recognizably looks like an attempt at scrutiny: to examine the actions of the executive; to extract information from the executive; and to pass judgements on the executive. The most effective instrument for all this is the House's system of specialized Select Committees. Although in composition these attempt to mimic party strength in the wider House, the culture of the committees often suppresses much of the partisan debate and unites members in the common pursuit of scrutiny. Some of the most important of these committees are in direct descent from an age of executive scrutiny in the nineteenth century when party ties were weaker than now, and the assertiveness of backbenchers greater. But the system was considerably strengthened by reforms at the end of the 1970s that established a stable system of committees which, despite some changes in name and jurisdiction over time, have since then established that every significant department of state is 'shadowed' by its own Committee. (See Briefing 10.2 p. 197).

The significance of these committees derives from three features:

- They have real power to call witnesses and demand documents both from departments of state and from a wide range of other public agencies. While officials and ministers often wriggle out of producing evidence and giving straightforward testimony, the committees have an impressive record in this kind of scrutiny.
- The committees represent substantial areas of specialist expertise. Although their numbers of permanent staff and specialist advisers are tiny by comparison with the resources of departments and public agencies, they nevertheless represent a considerable accumulation of information and expertise, at least by the modest historical standards of expertise available to backbenchers (Documenting Politics 10.4).
- The committees have gone some way towards solving a perennial problem in a partisan Parliament. We saw earlier that a prime function of the Commons was, simply, to provide a pool of talent for both government office and the Opposition front benches. What does an MP do who fails to make it to the front bench? For MPs of talent who have failed to progress, or whose front-bench careers are over, the committees have created an alternative Commons career. In particular, chairing a committee offers a rewarding and often well-publicized public role.

## Representing interests

Interest representation is built into the very nature of the Commons. Territorial representation is at the heart of the member's life, and this naturally stretches to representing the economic interests of the territorial constituency. A member for, say, a constituency with a large car plant within its boundaries becomes a natural, and legitimate, voice for the interests of the automobile industry. A more troubling link connects members of the House to the world of functional representation described in the last chapter. Historically, members were virtually expected to speak for functional interests: the Labour Party, for instance, began as a parliamentary group speaking for organized trade unionism. Members were not even paid a salary until 1912. In this era before the payment of a salary a pattern developed of MPs combining their seat in the Commons with outside economic interests, either in the form of employment or property ownership. That pattern, though changing, still persists. Indeed in the last generation it has been expanded and systematized by the spread of consultancies, through which members hire their knowledge and connections to outside interests. (This is a development connected to the rise of professional lobbying which we also described in the last chapter). Since the 1970s a Register of Interests has tried to keep track of, and to put into the public domain, all the payments received by MPs from outside interests (see Documenting Politics 10.6, p. 206). A series of scandals in the early 1990s, when some MPs were revealed as willing to ask parliamentary questions in return for covert payments, led to the establishment of a Committee on Standards in Public Life.

On the committee's recommendation there is now an Office of the Parliamentary Commissioner for Standards. The workings and powers of the Commissioner have been the subject of much controversy (in 2002 the incumbent Commissioner was in effect forced from her post at the end of her first period of office as a result of conflict with powerful groups of MPs). These controversies

**DOCUMENTING POLITICS 10.4**

## THE EUROPEAN REGULATION MOUNTAIN

A Selection of Endorsements for Consideration by the House of Commons on Saturday, 28 June 2003

*DOCUMENTS REFERRED TO EUROPEAN STANDING COMMITTEE A*

| Date referred | Document | Progress |
| --- | --- | --- |
| 30 Jan 2002 | Community Strategy for Dioxins, Furans and Polychlorinated Biphenyls (13438/01) | Resolution reported, 14 Jan 2003. Resolution agreed to in the House, 20 Jan 2003. |
| 6 Feb 2002 | Greenhouse gas emission trading (14394/01) | Resolution reported, 21 Nov 2002. Resolution agreed to in the House, 26 Nov 2002. |
| 3 Jul 2002 | Reform of the Common Fisheries Policy (COM (02) 181, COM (02) 185, COM (02) 187, COM (02) 190, COM (02) 180 and COM (02) 186) | Referred, 14 Nov 2002. |
| 3 Jul 2002 18 Dec 2002 | Allocation of slots at Community airports (10288/01); and (14205/02) | Awaiting consideration. |
| 23 Oct 2002 | Sustainable use of pesticides (10665/02) | Resolution reported, 26 Mar 2003. Resolution agreed to in the House, 31 Mar 2003. |
| 6 Nov 2002 | Trans-European Networks (12817/02) | Awaiting consideration. |
| 18 Dec 2002 | Quality of bathing water (13789/02) | Resolution agreed to in the House, 16 June 2003. |
| 30 Apr 2003 | Identification of sheep and goats (15829/02) | To be considered, 9 July 2003. |

➲ Documenting Politics 10.4 reproduces only a tiny extract from much longer list, but it reinforces the comment made on the preceding box: it shows the astonishing variety, and complexity, of EU rule-making to which Parliament assents, and why the Commons has such difficulty in understanding, let alone realistically scrutinizing, its content.

*Source*: www.parliament.uk/commons.hsecom

touch on fundamental differences about the function of MPs in representing interests, and go well beyond issues about personal honesty or publicity of payments. MPs are now paid a handsome professional salary with liberal 'perks', such as very generous pension arrangements. This leads some to argue that paid connections with any special interests should cease (see Documenting Politics 10.5), and that the member should become solely a full time professional representing only the interests of the

territorial constituency. Others argue that this violates the historically important role of the Member of Parliament. As we shall see later, this argument connects to a fundamental uncertainty about the purpose of the modern House of Commons.

Interest representation is a central function of the Commons, but what this means for the daily behaviour of members is plainly disputed. There is more agreement on the final function, below.

**DOCUMENTING POLITICS 10.5**

## SOME RESOLUTIONS OF THE HOUSE OF COMMONS RELATING TO THE CONDUCT OF MEMBERS

**Lobbying for Reward or Consideration**
*Resolution of 2nd May 1695*
*Against offering Bribes to Members*

'The Offer of any Money, or other Advantage, to any Member of Parliament, for the promoting of any Matter whatsoever, depending, or to be transacted, in Parliament, is a high Crime and Misdemeanour, and tends to the Subversion of the Constitution.'

*Resolution of 22nd June 1858 Rewards to Members*

'It is contrary to the usage and derogatory to the dignity of this House, that any of its Members should bring forward, promote or advocate, in this House, any proceeding or measure in which he may have acted or been concerned for or in consideration of any pecuniary fee or reward.'

*Resolution of 15th July 1947, amended on 6th November 1995 and 14th May 2002*
*Conduct of Members*

'It is inconsistent with the dignity of the House, with the duty of a Member to his constituents, and with the maintenance of the privilege of freedom of speech, for any Member of this House to enter into any contractual agreement with an outside body, controlling or limiting the Member's complete independence and freedom of action in Parliament or stipulating that he shall act in any way as the representative of such outside body in regard to any matters to be transacted in Parliament; the duty of a Member being to his constituents and to the country as a whole, rather than to any particular section thereof and that in particular no Member of the House shall, in consideration of any remuneration, fee, payment, reward or benefit in kind, direct or indirect, which the Member or any member of his or her family has received, is receiving, or expects to receive –

advocate or initiate any cause or matter on behalf of any outside body or individual, or urge any other Member of either House of Parliament, including Ministers, to do so, by means of any speech, Question, Motion, introduction of a Bill or amendment to a Motion or Bill, or any approach, whether oral or in writing, to Ministers or servants of the Crown.'

➲ Parliamentary concern with standards of behaviour is nothing new, as these resolutions, separated by over 300 years, illustrate.

*Source*: www.parliament.uk/comm/hecom

## Protecting individual constituents

A historically well-established function of the member of the Commons lies in protecting individual constituents. This 'casework' aspect of the MPs role is constantly growing. As the 'back office' support has become more sophisticated, casework has become increasingly important, not least in trying to establish the member's reputation and visibility among the constituency electorate. It comprizes a range of work enormous in its variety and significance. The institution of the 'surgery', where an MP is freely available at set hours in an office in the constituency, remains central to the lives of most members. (Indeed, some members now try to reach out further by holding regular surgeries in places such as supermarkets.) This fairly unrestricted public access means that MPs hear everything, from the ravings of barely sane cranks to accounts of the most grievous miscarriages of justice. The office business of any efficient MP is dominated by chasing this casework, especially in the first instance by correspondence with the relevant public agency. Down the line, if correspondence does not produce a satisfactory resolution, lie more public means of pursuit: a request for a written parliamentary answer from a minister; raising the issue in a direct oral question to a minister on the floor of the Commons; even employing the device of an adjournment debate, when backbenchers can use a short debate to raise a particularly serious case.

At the end of this chain of mechanisms for protecting constituents lies one that dates from the founding of the Parliamentary Commissioner for Administration (the 'Ombudsman') in 1967. The Ombudsman has extensive powers of investigation in cases where a citizen's grievance is thought to be the result of abuse of administrative powers. While the report and recommendations of the Ombudsman in a finding of maladministration are not binding on a department, the weight of the report is hard for even the most arrogant of departments to ignore. The connection with the role of MPs is that the MP is the 'gatekeeper' to the Ombudsman; an investigation by the Ombudsman requires the approval of the complainant's MP. That rule makes the backbencher important in the processing of grievances from the individual citizen. It is also an added weapon in the hands of the backbenches, since the mere threat of referral means that a department is faced at the very least with considerable potential extra work in the event of an enquiry by the Ombudsman. The Ombudsman system is part of wider mechanisms for the redress of citizens' grievances (something examined more closely in Chapter 23, where the idea of 'maladministration' is also explained more fully).

## The House of Commons and the changing Westminster system

The House of Commons is the best-known symbol of the Westminster system of government, and the pressures to which it is subject are reasonable indicators of the strains on that system. Three issues have proved especially troublesome: of legitimacy, of professionalism, and of purpose.

### Issues of legitimacy

Had we looked at the Westminster system as recently as the 1970s we would have noticed that the House of Common stood alone in one key respect: it was the only elected legislative chamber in the UK. In a system of government that claims to be democratic, and where a key mark of democratic legitimacy is popular election, that was an important mark of distinction. Now it is faced by a clutch of elected assemblies: for instance, the European Parliament, directly elected since 1979, and the Scottish Parliament and Welsh Assembly (dating from 1999). As we shall see in a moment, some reform proposals would also face the Commons with a directly elected House of Lords. None of these developments has yet supplanted the legitimacy of the Commons: turnout in European elections is low and the public visibility of MEPs slight; the Scottish and Welsh Assemblies have had their own problems of legitimacy and popular support (see below). But the Commons can no longer claim the special, definitive mark of democratic legitimacy as it once could.

### Issues of professionalism

Historically the Commons was a very 'unprofessional' institution: that is, it rejected the notion that its members should be full-time, professional legislators. Paying a salary of any kind is, we saw above, a practice which is less than a century old; paying a conventional professional salary is less than a generation old. Partly in consequence, the House historically organized itself as a kind of social institution. Its hours of work (typically beginning in mid-afternoon, usually stretching into the late evening, and often lasting overnight) were very different from those of any conventional professional body. That was in part because many members had occupations (for instance, in law) that they practised earlier in the day. The odd hours of business encouraged the development of an intense social life, where the politics of the Commons were mixed up with dining, drinking, gossiping, conspiring and fornicating. Conventional office facilities were among the poorest in any legislature across the democratic world. Overwhelming domination by men reinforced the atmosphere of a club.

More conventional styles of professionalism have for at least a generation chipped away at this self-conscious 'unprofessionalism'. The salaries of members are now comparable to those of other middle-class professionals, such as doctors or university professors. A declining proportion of members tries to combine being a member of the House with an outside profession. Indeed, for most politics *is* their profession; we will also notice the rise of the professional politician when we come to Chapter 18 on leadership recruitment in British government. As we saw above, the 'back office' support for the member – secretaries, personal assistants, research assistants, the latest IT – has recently improved greatly. The occupations of members before entering the House are increasingly preparations for the parliamentary life (for instance, as researchers, or advisers to senior politicians). The rise of Select Committees means that, outside the Chamber, much formal business is now done at conventional business hours, in morning hearings. In 2002 reforms were even introduced to reschedule the sittings of the Chamber to allow a more conventional professional timetable, with fewer late sittings. The fact that parliamentary sessions still reflect the old rhythms of political life has if anything strengthened some aspects of this professionalism. It has encouraged MPs to use the greatly improved back office facilities to pursue their 'casework' function, in turn raising their profile in the constituency. But the rise of this professionalism has itself raised important issues, and these go to the heart of the modern meaning and purpose of the Commons.

## Issues of purpose

The most important functions of the Commons are to provide a pool of talent for the front benches, especially for the government of the day; and to provide an arena where the adversarial battle between government and opposition is fought out. But this latter function in particular developed before the rise of the 'professional' ideal in the Commons, in an age when being an MP was for many a part-time occupation to be fitted in with other social roles, such as a career in business or the professions, or local prominence as a landowner. The rise of professionalism raises questions about the adversarial function, because the professional ideal stresses a very different approach to political life: an approach that emphasizes the importance of the dispassionate scrutiny of the details of government. For the modern backbencher with no obvious hope of serving on the front bench, acting as a cheerleader for the front bench or as an abuser of the opposition often does not seem a tremendously rewarding long-term career; hence the pressure to develop professional career patterns such as service on Select Committees. For traditionalists, however, the rise of this kind of professionalism seems a betrayal of the traditional ideal of Commons life – the triumph of an arid, bureaucratic, technical model over the notion of the House of Commons as a jousting arena where the great conflicts of national life are played out.

## The House of Lords: structure, influence, reform

We noted at the start of this chapter that Britain has what is technically known as a bi-cameral legislature, consisting of the House of Commons and the House of Lords. Bi-cameralism is normal among democratic nations (and some undemocratic ones), but the British version of bi-cameralism has three features which have shaped the modern relationship between the Commons and Lords: there is a history of tense relations between the two Houses; in modern times the House of Commons has been by far the dominant chamber; and the tensions,

**DOCUMENTING POLITICS 10.6**

## DECLARING INTERESTS: EXTRACTS FROM THE REGISTER OF INTERESTS

**BLAIR, Rt. Hon. Tony (Sedgefield)**

6.  **Overseas visits**
    October 2002, my wife and a family group stayed for a week at Government House, Bermuda, following a conference she was asked by the Bermudian Government to address in her professional capacity. The Bermudian Government paid her airfare: all the other expenses of the group were met by her, including payment for their accommodation at the standard rate fixed by the Bermudian Government. (*Registered 31 October 2002*)
    3 January 2003, the Egyptian Government provided my family and I with a single flight from Sharm-el Sheikh to Cairo for security reasons. (*Registered 14 January 2003*)

8.  **Land and Property**
    Two flats in Bristol for which rental income may be received.

**HAGUE, Rt. Hon. William (Richmond (Yorks))**

1.  **Remunerated directorships**
    AES Engineering, Rotherham.

2.  **Remunerated employment, office, profession etc.**
    Parliamentary adviser to the JCB Group. (*£45,001–£50,000*)
    Member of the Political Council of Terra Firma Capital Partners. (*£65,001–£70,000*)
    Contract with Harper Collins Publishers to write a book about William Pitt The Younger and a contract with Knopf Publishing Group, New York, to publish the book in the United States.
    9 March 2002, speech for Computer People. (*£5,001–£10,000*) (*Registered 17 July 2002*)
    14 March 2002, speech at Legendary Dinner. (*£5,001–£10,000*) (*Registered 17 July 2002*)
    2 May 2002, speech for the Institute of Chartered Accountants, Corporate Finance Faculty. (*Up to £5,000*) (*Registered 17 July 2002*)
    15 May 2002, speech for Bell Pottinger. (*£5,001–£10,000*) (*Registered 17 July 2002*)
    23 July 2002, speech for Marks and Spencer PLC. (*£5,001–£10,000*) (*Registered 2 August 2002*)
    12 September 2002, speech for Primary Capital Partners. (*£5,001–£10,000*) (*Registered 14 October 2002*)
    4 October 2002, speech for the British Sugar Federation. (*£5,001–£10,000*) (*Registered 14 October 2002*)
    17 October 2002, speech for Safeway PLC. (*£5,001–£10,000*) (*Registered 14 October 2002*)
    11 November 2002, speech for the Lighthouse Club. (*Up to £5,000*) (*Registered 8 January 2003*)

**DOCUMENTING POLITICS 10.6**   (continued)

28 November 2002, speech for the Institute of Financial Services. (*£5,001–£10,000*) (*Registered 8 January 2003*)

11 December 2002, speech for 100 Property Club. (*£5,001–£10,000*) (*Registered 8 January 2003*)

25 February 2003, speech for Bloomberg. (*£5,001–£10,000*)

March and April 2003, series of speeches for Grant Thornton. (*£15,001–£20,000*)

4.  **Sponsorship or financial or material support**
    The following people and company make financial support available to my office:
    Lord Ashcroft KCMG
    Lord Harris of Peckham
    Lord Kirkham
    Mr Howard Leigh
    Mr Malcolm Scott
    Mr Christopher Shale
    Dr Leonard Steinberg
    Flowidea Limited (investment company)

5.  **Gifts, benefits and hospitality (UK)**
    Until 31 March 2003 I had the occasional use of a Range Rover provided by Lord Coe OBE. (*Registered 12 July 2002*)
    Complimentary membership at Champney's, Piccadilly, for me and my wife. (*Registered 8 January 2003*)

6.  **Overseas visits**
    27 June–1 July 2002, to Morocco, flights and accommodation for my wife and me paid for by Le Cercle, a political group which organizes conferences. (*Registered 17 July 2002*)

9.  **Registrable shareholdings**
    (a)  100% of share capital of Canyon Research Limited; company established to receive income and make payments relating to my forthcoming book on William Pitt The Younger and related or similar activities.

---

➲ This extract from the Register of Interests for two leading members of the House of Commons, pursuant to the resolutions in Documenting Politics 10.5, is revealing in four ways:
• The way the rules now oblige the declaration of the even the most minor interests – note the entry for Mr Hague's (at the time of writing) unwritten life of Pitt.
• The way the demands and rules of office strip a figure such as Mr Blair of outside interests.
• The way, conversely, Mr Hague's resignation as Leader of the Conservative Party in 2001 opened up generous income-enhancing opportunities.
• The way Mr Hague's interests show how outside interests are now a function of Parliamentary office, whereas a generation ago outside interests were the result of careers or property independent of a parliamentary role.

*Source*: www.parliament.uk/comm/hecom

combined with Commons domination, have now combined to destabilize this part of the Westminster system to the point where the Lords has not only been radically reformed, but its very existence brought into question (see Timeline 10.1). We examine each of these features in turn.

## The history of a tense relationship

The House of Lords was originally the dominant chamber in Parliament. Before the rise of industrialism it contained the greatest holders of economic power, titled aristocrats who owned landed estates. The balance shifted after the nineteenth century for two reasons: the Industrial Revolution meant that other kinds of wealth, notably those based on manufacturing, became more important; and the extension of the vote to, eventually, virtually the whole adult population meant that the House of Commons became the dominant voice in a system of government which claimed to be democratic. At first, however, the decline in the relative power of the Lords largely happened by custom – the Lords came to accept that there were limits to the extent to which it could obstruct decisions of the House of Commons. But the difficulty with customary understandings was that they were likely to be challenged in any crisis. That potential for crisis was engrained in the social and political nature of the House of Lords.

By the end of the nineteenth century almost the whole of the landed aristocracy supported the Conservative Party, and the Lords was a perennially Conservative institution. The first great crisis of the twentieth century therefore occurred in 1909 when a reforming Liberal government introduced a Budget which was too radical for the Conservative-dominated Lords. Despite a convention that the Lords did not 'block' budgets approved by the Commons, the Lords did exactly this. A profound constitutional crisis culminated in the passage of the Parliament Act of 1911: this abolished the Lords' veto over money bills and gave it only a delaying power on most other legislation. The Labour government elected after 1945 reduced the delaying power to, in effect, a single year, in the Parliament Act of 1949. These restrictions still left the Lords

with significant influence and left ample potential for tension in the relationship between the two chambers. The need to pass legislation through both debates in the full chamber, and through a committee stage in the Lords, gave the Lords, if it chose to threaten it, considerable control over one of the scarcest commodities in Parliament: time. In a crowded legislative timetable, even delay can kill a bill given the present convention that a proposal must pass all stages in a year.

## The competition for supremacy between Lords and Commons

While the House of Lords consisted only of hereditary peers it had very weak claims in any struggle over supremacy with the House of Commons. For almost the whole of the twentieth century the system of government gave primary legitimacy to elected representatives such as those in the Commons, but the Life Peerages Act of 1958 subtly changed the long-term balance of advantage. The Act provided for the creation of peerages that would not be inherited (hence the life term peers). The creation of a large body of life peers diminished the importance of the in-built Conservative majority derived from hereditary peers in the Lords. Before the reforms of 1999 described below, over one-third of all peers were life peers, and active members of the House were almost always life creations. The life peers broadly formed two groups. The first were those nominated by the leadership of the political parties, overwhelmingly Conservative and Labour. These were often distinguished former Commons members, and many became active 'working peers' for the parties in the Lords. They were particularly important in augmenting Labour support, because the Party could count on the support of few hereditaries. The second group of life peers were created on the basis of distinguished service (in business or the professions, for example). Many, though not all, were 'cross-benchers', declining any party allegiance. The in-built Conservative majority provided by hereditary peers still existed, and could occasionally be brought out to win a vote, but now the most able and industrious members of the House were increasingly the life peers.

## TIMELINE 10.1   THE LONG ROAD TO LORDS REFORM

| Date of measure | Proposal | Comment |
| --- | --- | --- |
| 1911 | Parliament Act | Lords effectively loses veto over any money bills; and veto over other legislation abolished, replaced by ability to delay Commons' leglisative proposals to two years. |
| 1922 | Government proposal for election of some peers to Lords | Proposal dropped after criticism. |
| 1929 | Viscount Elibank introduces first bill to create life peers | Withdrawn after Second Reading. |
| 1949 | Parliament Act | Reduces Lords delaying power over Commons legislative proposal to one year. |
| 1958 | Life Peerage Act | Allows addition of peers created for life to existing hereditary peers; and leads to creation of women peers for first time. |
| 1963 | Peerage Act | Allows hereditary peers to disclaim their title following campaign by heir of Lord Stansgate, who disclaims his inheritance, adopting instead the title 'Tony Benn'. |
| 1969 | Labour Government Reform Bill | Agreed in Lords, but dropped after opposition in Commons from an alliance of left-wing Labour radicals and right-wing Conservative traditionalists. |
| 1999 | House of Lords Act | Abolishes hereditary entitlement to a seat in the Lords; 92 hereditary peers selected by their hereditary peers to continue sitting in House as a transitional measure. |
| 1999 | Royal (Wakeham) Commission on reform of second chamber appointed | Commission reports in 2000. Proposes largely appointed upper house, but with small minority of elected members; 15-year tenure to replace tenure of life peers; representatives of other faiths to be added to existing Anglican bishops in House. Proposals not adopted. |
| 2001 | White Paper, *The House of Lords: completing the reform* | Proposes a minority of elected peers (120) but 480 to be appointed. Proposals not adopted. |
| Feb. 2003 | Free votes in both Houses on range of options | No option on offer in Commons secures majority. Leader of House (Robin Cook, advocate of an elected House) advises MPs to 'go home and sleep on it'. |
| Mar. 2003 | Second Gulf War | Robin Cook, main advocate of radical reform inside government, resigns from Government in disagreement over British participation in Second Gulf War. |
| Mar. 2004 | Reform plans postponed | Secretary of State for Constitutional Affairs announces indefinite postponement of further reform in face of anti-reform majority in Lords. |
| May 2005 | Labour Party Manifesto | No firm promise of fundamental reform. |

*Sources*: Adapted from Butler and Butler (2000); Cook and Stevenson (2000); www.scottishparliament.uk

'Lifers', by virtue of ability and achievement, were far from compliant with either the Commons or the governing party. There were numerous occasions in the 1980s and 1990s when the Lords amended legislation in defiance of majorities in the Commons, and this only reflected the tip of the iceberg of the Lords' influence: the mere threat to amend and delay legislation obliged governments with a majority in the House of Commons to pause. In part this assertiveness came from a strengthened sense of legitimacy. The life peers greatly strengthened the technical capacity and the authority of the Lords, for many of the life peers could (and can) speak with great authority on policy: in fact they could often speak with greater technical knowledge when the issue touched their area of expertise than could most members of the Commons (see People in Politics 10.1).

The historically tense relationship between the two chambers, then, was based on a clash between the principles of election and the principles of inheritance. The tension was magnified because the hereditary peers, although most were inactive, nevertheless gave the Conservative Party an in-built majority, and also created a majority which occasionally could be mobilized against radical measures. But by the last two decades of the twentieth century this tension had receded into the background. The governing party in the Commons that had most trouble with the Lords was the Conservatives when they were in power from 1979 to 1997. It suffered defeats in the Lords in every one of its Parliamentary sessions, and in some years there were more than 20 occasions. This reflected the growth of new potential sources of legitimacy that were used to challenge the right of governments to make policy on the basis of their elective majority in the Commons, and led to new sources of tension. This new claim to legitimacy derived from the Lords' claim to shape law by virtue of experience and knowledge – attributes that were often superior to those of the Commons. It also amounted to a claim to legitimacy by virtue of a principle of representation which we examined in the last chapter: by virtue of speaking on behalf of some great interests in the community, such as the professions, industry and even universities.

Attempts to reform the Lords are dominated by this tension between competing sources of legitimacy, as we shall now see.

## Reforming the Lords

In the decades after the introduction of life peers the House of Lords became increasingly effective in three areas:

- In performing a classic function of a second chamber: scrutinizing the details of legislative proposals and amending them
- Through its own specialist committees, akin to the Select Committees of the Commons, but with members who were often genuinely authoritative experts in examining both policy problems and government actions
- Through debates in the Chamber of the Lords. Whereas the Chamber of the Commons is dominated by the language of the adversarial party battle, debate in the Lords has been very different in style: less adversarial, more directly addressed to the problem at issue, and at least conveying a sense that the issue in question was being debated on the merits of the case. Normal members of the public would immediately find Lords' debates more appealing and recognizable than they would those in the Commons.

This growing effectiveness did not protect the Lords from fundamental change after the return of Labour to office in 1997; indeed, it may have helped endanger the Lords by making the Lords/Commons relationship tenser. The new Labour government was committed to the most radical programme of Lords reform ever (see Image 10.2). That commitment had two origins. First, there was an engrained historical tension between the Lords and the Labour party because, despite the life peers, there was still a huge in-built Conservative party in the Lords provided by the hereditary peers. Second, in its long years of opposition in the 1980s and 1990s the Labour party became converted to the view that British political institutions generally needed reform – that they were archaic, conferred excessive power on the central executive and hampered democracy.

Reform of the Lords was therefore part of a larger programme (notably the devolution reforms which will be examined in Chapter 11).

Two problems faced Labour in achieving reform, one short term and one that continues to dog all reform efforts. The short-term problem was that, if the reform was to be achieved reasonably swiftly, the majority of peers had to vote for their own extinction: the hereditary turkeys had to vote for a constitutional Christmas. This led to complex

---

## *People in politics*

### 10.1   THE IMPORTANCE OF EXPERTISE IN THE HOUSE OF LORDS

Cartoons: Shaun Steele

**Baroness Warnock** (b. 1924, created 1985): a Cambridge don and principal of a College, she chaired (or served on) most of the leading official committees concerned with laboratory experiments on humans and animals in the last two decades of the twentieth century, notably the Advisory Committee on Animal Experimentation and the Inquiry into Human Fertility. In 2003 she was a member of the Lords' Committee on Animals in Scientific Procedures.

**Lord Soulsby** of Swaffham (b. 1926, created 1990): one of the leading academic researchers into animal diseases in Britain in the twentieth century. A distinguished research career culminated in a period as Professor of Animal Pathology, University of Cambridge, 1978–93. In 2003 he was chairing sub-committee 1 of the Select Committee on Science and Technology, investigating the control of infectious diseases in the UK.

**Lord Wilson of Dinton** (b. 1942, created 2002). He exemplifies an important source of talent in the Lords: the senior civil servant whose public life is prolonged after formal retirement. Beginning as an Assistant Principal in the old Board of Trade (the point of entry for high fliers) in 1966, his career culminated as Cabinet Secretary and Head of the Home Civil Service, 1998–2002. He entered the House of Lord with an unrivalled knowledge both of the machinery of government and the personalities involved.

➲ It is now rare for members of the House of Commons to have any significant experience in any other occupation than politics, and the most successful have usually been full-time politicians from early adult life. But the creation of life peers after 1958 brought into the House of Lords distinguished (if usually elderly) figures from all walks of life in Britain. The result is that, while any witness before a Commons Committee can be fairly certain that the Committee consists of nothing more than quick-witted amateurs, in the Lords anyone appearing as a witness is likely to be facing a world expert in the subject in question. The three figures profiled here are entirely typical of the expertise at the Lords' command.

**Image 10.2**
**The stubborn persistence of the dignified constitution: the Lord Chancellor at work**

Photo: PA/EMPICS

➲ In this chapter we have discussed the long and still inconclusive road to reform of the House of Lords. The photo crystallizes one of the difficulties. Mr Blair's second Lord Chancellor (Lord Falconer) wished to reform the Lords and to abolish the office of Lord Chancellor itself, replacing it with that of a modern Secretary of State. Thus far, he has been unsuccessful in his efforts, so is obliged, reluctantly, to turn out in full ceremonial robes on occasions like that pictured here – the State Opening of Parliament.

bargaining, notably with the leadership of the Conservative peers. It explains the shape of the only reform presently achieved. The House of Lords Act 1999 abolished the voting rights of almost all hereditary peers, but, as an interim measure, in order to put together a majority for the reform in the Lords, the initial proposals were amended to allow the retention of 92 hereditary peers. All but two of these were elected by a very special constituency, composed of fellow hereditary peers. The reform has nevertheless drastically changed the composition of the Lords: the number of hereditaries was cut from over 750 to 92.

All parties publicly agree that this is only an interim solution, and the fact that after 1999 the reform process was becalmed arises from problems more fundamental than the tactical difficulties just discussed. The government established a Royal Commission to examine reform options. Its report is, however, now only one of a number of reform proposals being debates. The most important are summarized in Briefing 10.4.

It is impossible to say which of these models of reform will triumph – or, indeed, if any will. The sheer difficulty of arriving at a conclusion is the single most revealing feature of the whole process. (In Chapter 11, we will see a marked contrast since the fundamental changes involved in devolution to Scotland and Wales were executed with clinical swiftness after 1997.) The difficulties arise because modes of reform are connected in a complex way with different views of the proper functions of a second chamber.

The immediate difficulty involves agreeing a principle of selection by which a reformed House should be constituted. The issue is difficult because the principle of selection in turn affects the legitimacy of the institution itself. In other words, it resurrects the great historical source of tension between the Lords and Commons. Any principle of selection creates problems. A fully appointed House – an option publicly supported by Tony Blair – is widely opposed on the grounds that it puts too much power into the hands of the government, and especially of the prime minister. Election on the basis of territorial constituencies – a commonly supported option – raises a key issue: how would differences between two democratically elected Houses, Commons and Lords, be resolved? A very different principle of selection has been advocated historically, for instance, by the great Conservative statesman, Winston Churchill, in the 1920s: that the Lords could become a chamber of 'functional' representation in which the great interests in the community – industry, commerce, labour, professions – were given a voice. As we saw in the last chapter, the idea that functional interests have a legitimate right to representation is embedded in the way the interest group system works. But there are obvious and formidable problems in the way of working out this principle in the Lords: how selection in practice would be made; how the different interests would be numerically balanced; and, once again,

# Briefing 10.4

## REFORMING THE HOUSE OF LORDS: THE OPTIONS

| Option | State of play after February 2003 Parliamentary debates and votes |
| --- | --- |
| All appointed House | Secures only 78 votes from MPs in Commons vote of 4 Feb. 2003; no vote in Lords. |
| 60% of House elected | Secures 227 votes in Lords, but only 63 votes in Commons. |
| 80% of House elected | Secures 246 votes in Lords (best supported option) but only 3 votes in Commons. |
| 100% of House elected | Secures 223 votes in Lords, but only 17 in Commons. |
| Abolish Lords | No vote in Lords; secures 218 votes in Commons. |

➲ Attempts to reform the House of Lords now date back nearly a century, but by the start of the twenty-first century the reform process had reached stalemate. In a series of votes in February 2003 no option, from the most radical to the most piecemeal, received a majority in either House. Two separate forces were at work: fear of expanding the patronage power of the executive, and fear in the Commons of creating a rival in democratic legitimacy. The former killed off attempts to weight the reform in the direction of a House dominated by appointees; the latter killed off attempts to install an elected majority, or even a fully elected, Lords.

how any clash between elected territorial representatives and representatives of functional interest would be resolved.

These difficulties in settling a principle of selection are formidable because they either implicitly or explicitly rest on competing views of the proper functions of a second chamber. There is no settled agreement about these functions, and the difficulty of arriving at an agreement is compounded by the practical evolution of the functions actually performed by the present Lords. The present House performs a variety of almost accidentally acquired functions, not all of which are easily compatible. We can see this by considering four of the most important.

*It represents interests.*   The House of Lords is not a chamber of industry and the professions, but many of the life peerage creations of the past 40 years have been designed to give a voice to leading industrialists, professionals and trade unionists. In many public debates, therefore, there are members of the Lords who can plausibly claim to speak for particular interest groups, by virtue both of their individual expertise and by virtue of their careers.

*It scrutinizes legislation.*   Scrutinizing the details of legislation is a common function of second chambers, notably of those which, like the House of Lords, are clearly subordinate to another chamber. A large amount of parliamentary time in the Lords is indeed spent on this function, and the absence of an adversarial party culture means that attention to proposals on their technical merits is easier than in the Commons. But how much 'added value' this creates is uncertain. Members of the Lords often bring considerable expertise to bear on policy proposals, but the extensive process of consultation with interest groups which, as was noted in Chapter 9, accompanies policy making means that proposals will already have been subjected to the expert scrutiny of the affected interests well before they reach the Lords. More commonly, the Lords' stages provide an opportunity for interests that have not had their way in earlier consultations to make a more public attempt at exercising influence – and, occasionally, a successful attempt to delay a measure.

*It prolongs distinguished public lives.*   Membership of the Lords via the life peerage route has provided an extended coda to the public lives of senior public figures, notably distinguished politicians. It has become almost universal for successful Commons MPs to have a peerage conferred on them at retirement (see Political Issues 10.1). Since retirement from the Commons does not always come at a normal retiring age – members are at risk of losing their seat at any election – this function has often extensively prolonged the lives of public figures.

POLITICAL ISSUES

## 10.1   PARLIAMENT: WORKPLACE OR CLUB? REFORMING THE WORKING HOURS OF THE COMMONS.

The working hours of Parliament, though apparently a narrowly technical matter, actually touch on key issues about parliamentary role and style. The House of Commons is a particularly good instance of this. It was famous for its unusual working hours, these practices dating from the pre-democratic past when it was a kind of club for the ruling classes. Until the start of the twenty-first century it was routine for the Commons to sit and debate till late into the evening, often overnight. The real business of the Chamber did not typically begin until about 4 p.m. – a time when many 'conventional' jobs are actually coming towards the end of the working day. In October 2002 the House agreed, after strenuous debate, an experiment involving sitting on Tuesdays, Wednesdays and Thursdays from 11.30 a.m., with Chamber business concluding at 7 p.m. on Tuesdays and Wednesdays, and at 6 p.m. on Thursdays. MPs are divided on the experiment, and a review is taking place at the end of the Parliament elected in 2001. The original pressure for change came partly from the large number of new women MPs returned in Labour's victory of 1997, who wanted more 'family friendly' hours. Some reformers now want to shift all Friday business to earlier in the week, making Friday a 'constituency' day. Critics, on the other hand, complain that the change has damaged the social atmosphere of the House; more immediately, the large numbers of MPs from constituencies outside London (who live apart from their families while the House is in session) are now at a loose end in the evenings.

The case raises four issues:

- The contrast between the Commons and the new Parliaments in the UK: the Scottish Parliament, for instance, typically sits for 'office hours', from about 9 a.m. to 6 p.m.
- The clash between competing conceptions of what the House of Commons is for: is it essentially a place to do business according to conventional notions of efficient office working, or is it also a social institution for governors?
- The related clash between different conceptions of the 'professional' role of MPs. It has been traditional for many Members to combine the role of MP with outside jobs. 'Normal' office hours make that increasingly difficult.
- The pressure to compress the Parliamentary week still more raises the issue of where a back-bencher's prime role lies: as a representative in the Chamber in London, or as a public figure in the territorial constituency?

*It provides a source of patronage for party leaders, especially for the governing party.* Prolonging public lives is a particular aspect of a wider function that the life peerage system has made important. This function is patronage. Peerage creations are largely in the control of the parties, and are especially closely controlled by the party of government. The social prestige of a peerage means that it is often a cheap way of rewarding a party functionary: for instance, this is the route by which Lord Archer, a peer who became infamous as a convicted perjurer, arrived in the Lords. It has sometimes been used as an inducement to members of the Commons to vacate their parliamentary seats at short notice, thus allowing some favoured candidate of the governing party a run at the vacancy. And it has become

# DEBATING POLITICS

## 10.1   DO WE NEED A SECOND CHAMBER AT WESTMINSTER?

| We need a second chamber because | Abolish the Lords and work with a single Commons chamber because |
|---|---|
| ■ A check is needed on the power of the executive majority in the House of Commons, where the governing party is usually in control of a majority. | ■ No workable principle of selection can be devised that does not either extend executive patronage (appointment) or challenge the democratic legitimacy of the Commons (popular election). |
| ■ Modern legislation is so complex that a second chamber is needed to review the detailed implications of legislative proposals. | ■ Scrutinizing the details of legislation is what a serious Committee stage in the House of Commons should already do. |
| ■ Virtually every successful democracy in the world has a second chamber, suggesting that it is a functional necessity of good democratic government. | ■ In the devolved Assemblies we already have elected counter-weights to the House of Commons. |
| ■ A second chamber, however selected, will widen the range of talent that participates at the highest level of national political life. | ■ Checking the power of the executive majority is most effectively done through the wider groups of civil society, such as mass media and pressure groups. |

important as a means of recruiting talent to the governing party, and indeed to the ranks of the government. While it is rare to find more than two members of the Lords in the Cabinet (the Lord Chancellor and the leader of the governing party in the Lords), there are many fascinating and well-paid ministerial posts below Cabinet level. Able potential ministers who cannot, or will not, run the gauntlet of democratic politics by contesting a seat in the House of Commons can find this a painless route to ministerial office. Typically in recent years up to 20 per cent of ministers have been peers, though peers have in the main held comparatively junior posts. (But, for some examples of glittering careers, see People in Politics 18.1, p. 392).

## The Westminster Parliament: renewal or decay?

Great constitutional changes transformed the Westminster Parliament in the first quarter of the twentieth century. The power of the House of Lords was greatly reduced through the Parliament Act of 1911. The general election immediately after the First World War returned the first Commons to be elected on something close to universal suffrage. Home Rule for the Irish Free State in 1921 removed a large body of Irish members from the Commons chamber. For virtually the rest of the twentieth century the Commons was utterly dominated by two disciplined party blocs, Conservative and Labour. The functions and power structures of Parliament were also set for many decades.

Since the 1970s, however, the Westminster Parliament has seen great changes, some swift and dramatic, some slow moving but fundamental. In the House of Commons backbenchers are more independent minded, and more willing to defy the front-bench leadership than was the case up to the 1970s. The Commons as an institution is better equipped to scrutinize the executive, through more effective systems of specialized committees, and through the provision of better 'back office' facilities for backbenchers. Modest changes in procedure have made the Commons a more businesslike place. The long-term effect of the life peerage reforms has revitalized the House of Lords.

This summary points to an optimistic interpretation of recent parliamentary history: it suggests that we have been living through an era of renewal. Pessimists view recent history very differently. The Westminster Parliament is now surrounded by democratic rivals, in the European and Scottish Parliaments and the Welsh Assembly. It is no longer an unchallenged democratic giant. Reform

## REVIEW

The dominant themes in this chapter have been:

1 The overwhelming importance of party on the functions, powers and style of the House of Commons;
2 The way changing ideas of political life, and the changing ambitions of the party politicians, have called into question traditional ways of doing business at Westminster;
3 The way the impasse over reform of the House of Lords has dramatized both the tensions inherent in the two-chamber Westminster system, and highlighted also the wider tensions to which that Westminster system is subject.

of the Lords is presently in a cul-de-sac, and such reform as has been achieved has strengthened the role of executive patronage in its composition. The Commons is turning into an institution where backbenchers immerse themselves in the detail of policy in Select Committees, to the neglect of the Chamber as the cockpit of national debate.

As this summary shows, whether we are optimists or pessimists depends on more than the facts of what has been happening to Parliament; it also depends on our judgements about what are the proper functions of Westminster Parliamentary institutions in a democratic political system (see Debating Politics 10.1).

## Further reading

The most important modern academic stiudy is Judge (1993); see also Judge (1999). Norton (1981), though dated, is still the most comprehensive statement by the most distinguished modern student of Parliament. Russell (2000) very helpfully sets the debates about reform of the Lords in longer term, comparative perspective. Cowley (2002) is the latest instalment in a growing literature on the voting behaviour of MPs.

CHAPTER 11

# The devolved systems of governance

## CONTENTS

## AIMS

This chapter:

❖ Establishes how and why the devolution reforms that were introduced by the Labour Government after 1997 are so important

❖ Describes the 'roads to devolution' in Scotland, Wales and Northern Ireland

❖ Describes the institutions of devolution

❖ Describes the practical experience of devolution since their establishment

❖ Pays special attention to the experience of Northern Ireland but stresses that the province is part of the wider experience of governing the United Kingdom

❖ 'Sets' the devolution experience into our wider understanding of the shift of the UK governing system in the direction of multi-level governance.

**Images 11.1 and 11.2**
**Images of devolved government**

Image 11.1   'Traditional'

Image 11.2   'Modern'

➲  The face that government presents to the public is immensely important symbolically, and devolved systems are no exception. Here are two different 'faces'. Image 11.1 shows the original Parliament building at Stormont for Northern Ireland. (It is also the home of the Assembly established after the Belfast Agreement.) It was intended to convey an image of permanence and tradition; actually, construction began in 1922 and the building was finally opened in 1932. Inside, the Chamber has the look of a Masonic temple, which is hardly surprising since the Protestant rulers of Northern Ireland after 1922 were enthusiastic Freemasons. Image 11.2 shows the Scottish Parliament still under construction in May 2004. (It was finally opened in September 2004.) It is a strikingly contemporary design with state-of-the-art facilities, to project Scottish identity as modern. Unfortunately, construction was plagued by huge cost overruns, long delays and acrimonious arguments about the design.

## Devolved government and multi-level governance

A key theme of this book is the transformation of a once settled system of government in the United Kingdom. It has been labelled the Westminster system, in recognition of the extent to which its institutions and powers are heavily concentrated in a small part of central London. This chapter examines one of the most important ways in which the Westminster system is being changed: by the rise of newly devolved systems of government beyond the capital city. (Chapter 12 describes a similar process at work through political innovation in local and regional government.) Although these developments have taken different forms in different parts of the United Kingdom, they are nevertheless sensibly considered as a piece (see Images 11.1 and 11.2). One reason for this is that they came to a head at more or less the same moment – after the return of

the Labour party to government following the long years of Conservative rule between 1979 and 1997. The three key changes described here are the institutional reforms in Scotland, Wales and Northern Ireland. The devolved systems in Scotland and Wales are described in tandem because both were part of the same package of institutional reform introduced by Labour. There are similarities to the Scottish and Welsh cases, but also, as will become clear, important differences. That is why, though they are examined as a pair, the emphasis is on sketching both the similarities and differences.

The institutional changes in Northern Ireland are considered separately, for a number of important reasons: because the forces that shaped the politics of the province, and therefore the possible solutions to those problems, were very different from the Scottish and Welsh cases; because the institutional reforms introduced by the Belfast Agreement of 1998 (more commonly called the Good Friday

Agreement) were also highly distinctive; and because the aftermath of institutional reform has been very different in Northern Ireland. But I have deliberately placed the examination of Northern Ireland into this chapter on devolution rather than, as is conventional in texts on British politics, allocating a separate chapter to something called the Northern Ireland 'problem'. This is because to treat Northern Ireland as a distinct problem on its own is to misunderstand the Northern Irish case. There is no Northern Ireland problem. The problem concerns the 'unity' of the United Kingdom, of which Northern Ireland is the most extreme manifestation. The devolution packages for Scotland and Wales, and the peace process and Belfast Agreement in Northern Ireland, are all attempts to manage the fundamental problem of how to maintain the unity of the United Kingdom. The effects of the reforms are helping transform Westminster government into a multi-level system of governance.

## Scotland and Wales: similarities and contrasts

### The forces leading to change

The immediate forces leading to the landmark devolution reforms of 1998 are similar in the cases of Scotland and Wales (see Timelines 11.1 and 11.2). But the more fundamental historical forces creating pressure for devolution are subtly different in the two countries, and these differences help explain important differences in the form taken by devolution. Scotland and Wales both experienced the consequences of the great centralization of government that occurred over most of the twentieth century in the United Kingdom. We saw in Chapter 2 that the beginnings of modern democratic politics in Britain can conveniently be dated from 1918, the year when the First World War ended. The election fought at the end of that year was the first to be contested on something close to universal adult suffrage, and it produced a pattern of two-party rivalry between the Labour and Conservative parties that dominated the system of government for half a century. That era was one of great centralization in British politics, the

high point of what we have called in this text the 'Westminster system'. That centralized Westminster system was subject to serious challenge from the latter part of the 1960s. At the end of that decade, as we shall see later in this chapter, there was a full-blown nationalist revolt in Northern Ireland. A nationalist party committed to full independence for Scotland (the Scottish National Party) won a seat in the Westminster Parliament in 1967; since then there has been continuous Scottish Nationalist representation in the Westminster Parliament. In the 1997 general election – following which the devolution measures described below were introduced – the Nationalists won 6 seats and over one-fifth (22 per cent) of votes cast in Scotland. Plaid Cymru, the party of Welsh nationalism, also achieved a Westminster breakthrough in the 1960s, winning its first ever seat in 1966. While its advance was not as great as that of the Scottish nationalists, by the 1997 election it was able to win four seats and almost one tenth (9.9 per cent) of the Welsh vote.

The most obvious reason for the success of this nationalist challenge was the persistent failure of Westminster governments successfully to manage the British economy, and the way Wales and Scotland bore much of the brunt of economic decline. By the end of the 1970s the challenge was so strong that the Labour government in 1979 attempted, unsuccessfully, to implement devolution in the two countries. The fall of Labour in 1979 led to 18 years of Conservative government and this intensified the consequences of centralization of power in Westminster. In this era of Conservative dominance a wide gap developed between the political colour of Westminster, which was dominated by Conservative majorities, and of Wales and Scotland, where the Conservatives lost popular support. Thus for much of the last two decades of the twentieth century Wales and Scotland were ruled by a government which would not have been elected had the vote been in these two countries alone. This experience connected to a wider movement for constitutional reform in the United Kingdom that influenced, but was not confined to, the Labour party. That movement traced the wider problems of the United Kingdom to the highly

## TIMELINE 11.1    THE ROAD TO DEVOLUTION IN SCOTLAND

**1928**
National Party of Scotland founded.

**1934**
Merger with Scottish Party (founded 1932) to create Scottish National Party (SNP).

**1945**
SNP wins Westminster seat at by-election in Motherwell; loses seat in general election three months later.

**1953**
Scottish nationalists remove 'stone of destiny' – ancient symbol of Scottish kings – from Westminster Abbey on eve of Coronation and hide it in Scotland.

**1957**
Establishment of Scottish Standing Committee to examine committee stage of Scottish Bills in House of Commons.

**1967**
SNP wins seat in Hamilton by-election to Westminster Parliament, beginning period of continuous SNP presence at Westminster.

**1970**
Exploitation of North Sea oil supports argument that an independent Scottish economy is viable.

**1970**
Conservatives commit to a measure of Scottish devolution; Labour opposes.

**1973**
Kilbrandon Commission on the Constitution recommends foundation of a Scottish Assembly.

**1975**
Major parties perform somersault: Labour now supports, Conservatives now oppose, devolution.

**1976**
Labour government introduces Devolution Bill but abandoned after failure to guillotine debates in House of Commons.

**1979**
New Labour bill falls after failure to secure special majorities of 40 per cent of all Scottish electorate in referendum, a clause inserted by Labour anti-devolutionists at Westminster.

**1979**
Election of Mrs Thatcher begins 18 years of Conservative government during which Conservative Party support in Scotland drains away.

**1989**
Campaign of mass disobedience to Westminster Parliament's poll tax (new form of local authority taxation) begins.

**1989**
Scottish Constitutional Convention begins extended national debate about form of devolved government.

**1994**
Labour in Scotland changes name to Scottish Labour Party.

**1996**
Labour commits to post-election devolution in Scotland and Wales.

**1997**
Labour wins landslide victory in general election; referendum on principle of devolution and giving tax-raising powers to a Scottish Parliament gives majority for both.

**1998**
Scotland Act puts devolution into law.

**1999**
First Scottish Parliament elected, first Scottish Chief Minister (Donald Dewar) appointed, first (coalition) Executive formed.

➲ Devolution in Scotland did not suddenly burst on to the British political scene in the 1990s; it was the product of a long period of evolution and struggle, dating back to the 1920s.

*Sources*: Adapted from Butler and Butler (2000); Cook and Stevenson (2000); www.scottishparliament.uk

## TIMELINE 11.2   THE ROAD TO DEVOLUTION IN WALES

**1925**
Plaid Cymru formed to campaign for Welsh independence.

**1951**
Appointment of Minister (outside Cabinet) for Welsh Affairs in Westminster.

**1962**
Formation of Welsh Language Society to campaign for the Welsh language frees Plaid Cymru to concentrate on wider political issues.

**1964**
First ever Secretary of State for Wales appointed by incoming Labour government.

**1966**
Plaid Cymru wins first Westminster Parliamentary seat in by-election.

**1970**
Plaid Cymru claims 11.5 per cent of Welsh vote in general election (the highest percentage before or since).

**1979**
Only 12 per cent of the Welsh electorate (20 per cent of those voting) supports the Labour government's devolution proposals. Return of Conservatives for 18 unbroken years of government ends this first stage of attempts to secure Welsh devolution.

**1993**
Welsh Language Act in law and Welsh Language Board established to foster the language.

**1995**
Plaid Cymru becomes Wales' second largest party, after Labour, in local government elections.

**1997**
Labour landslide in general election; referendum approves principle of devolution.

**1998**
Government of Wales Act provides for institutions of devolution.

**1999**
Welsh Assembly elections; Labour forms administration as largest party but without a majority of seats; Alun Michael is First Minister.

➲ The devolution movement in Wales, though following a similar timeline to that in Scotland, has had to struggle against a much less receptive political environment. Note, however, the common origins of modern Scottish and Welsh separatism in the 1920s: both are in part a response to the success of Irish nationalist separatism which is discussed later in this chapter.

*Sources*: Butler and Butler (2000); Cook and Stevenson (2000); www.wales.gov.uk

---

centralized nature of the Westminster system. In Chapter 19 we shall see that there has been a long history of policy failure in Britain. If this failure was due to excessive centralization of institutions in London, an obvious remedy was to decentralize through devolution to political units such as the separate nations of the United Kingdom. The connection between centralization and policy failure is, we should note, one which can be contested; for present purposes we only need to know that it was an argument that influenced thinking about constitutional reform.

Thus Wales and Scotland share a common long-term experience, the weakening of the Westminster system of centralized rule; and share also the short-term experience of being ruled for the closing years of the twentieth century by a government that relied for majorities on English voters.

However, there are big differences in the nature of nationalism in the two countries. The most important source of distinction lies in different conceptions of national identity. Welsh nationalism has been focused on defending and encouraging the Welsh language, and by extension defending and encouraging the cultural distinctiveness of which language is an expression. In Scotland, by contrast, the language has been a much less central issue; indeed, there are only about 60,000 Gaelic speakers left in the whole country. In part this difference in cultural emphasis has also been reflected in the social bases of support for the two movements: the original core of Welsh nationalism lay in rural, Welsh-speaking communities; the rise of Scottish nationalism encompassed a significant part of urban Scotland, especially the belt that links the two most important cities, Glasgow and Edinburgh.

These distinctions have also been accompanied by differences in support for forms of devolution that fall short of independence. Electoral support for nationalism has been higher in Scotland than in Wales, and correspondingly there has been more Scottish enthusiasm for devolution when it has been tested in referenda. A glance at Figure 11.1 shows these differences. Support has been consistently higher in Scotland than in Wales: when a referendum on proposals was held in 1979 Scotland was markedly more enthusiastic, and this pattern was repeated in the referendums which led to the devolution reforms of 1998. This higher level of Scottish enthusiasm in part reflected the already greater distinctiveness and autonomy of Scottish institutions. A separate Scottish Office with its own administration based in Edinburgh dates from 1892; a Welsh Office with a Secretary of State for Wales in the Westminster Cabinet was only established in 1964. These differences in pre-devolution governing arrangements reflected wider differences between the two countries. Unlike Wales, Scotland has a long established, and separate, legal system; a separate and distinct education system, stretching from elementary schools to universities; and while both countries have their own mass media, Scottish newspapers are more distinctive and better established than are those in Wales. Wider patterns of popular culture mirror these differences. For instance, in professional football the most powerful Scottish teams play in their own league, while the most powerful Welsh ones – Cardiff and Swansea – play in the English-dominated football league. Some parts of Scotland, indeed, barely feel British in any conventional sense: any visitor to the Shetland Islands, for instance, soon feels the proximity of Norway, and sees signs of a long Scandinavian presence. This is hardly surprising: a glance at an atlas will show that Lerwick, the

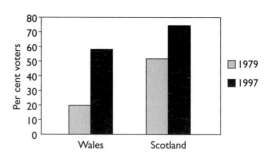

**Figure 11.1** Popular support for devolution in referenda in Wales and Scotland (percentage voting yes)

➲ The electorates in Wales and Scotland have been given two opportunities to vote on devolution proposals offered by the Westminster government: on both occasions the percentage voting 'yes' – the figures summarized here – have been higher in Scotland than in Wales. The proposals fell in 1979 through lack of popular support. The differences are also reflected in turnout: in both 1979 and 1997 turnout in Scotland was higher than in Wales.

'capital' of the Shetland Islands, is closer to Oslo than to London.

The pattern of similarity and contrast persists with the institutions of devolution themselves.

## Scotland and Wales: the institutions of devolution

Devolution in Scotland was introduced by the Scotland Act 1998. It provided for the election of a Scottish Parliament with devolved powers to make laws over a wide range of policy, and for the nomination by the elected Parliament of a First Minister (formally appointed by the Queen). The First Minister in turn selects the Ministers that compose the Cabinet of the Executive, again subject to agreement with Parliament and approval of the monarch. In parallel the Government of Wales Act 1998 provided for the election of a Welsh Assembly. The Assembly inherits the powers exercized before devolution by the Secretary of State for Wales. That last office, we saw earlier, dated from 1964. The Assembly elects a 'First Secretary' to serve as leader of a government, and the First Secretary in turn appoints Assembly Secretaries, who cover important policy areas such as agriculture, and who compose the Cabinet.

In chronology and bare structure the devolution arrangements in the two countries are similar. But small differences of language – a Scottish *Parliament* but a Welsh *Assembly* – hint at more substantial differences which will be examined more closely below. However, the election arrangements for the Assembly and Parliament are strikingly similar; they mark an important break with the prevailing arrangements for Westminster, and therefore should be highlighted. One common departure is that both institutions are elected for fixed terms of four years. By contrast the Westminster Parliament is elected for a maximum period of five years, but within that prime ministers can request a dissolution from the Queen virtually at their own calculation. The devolved arrangements therefore immediately change a critical element of the rules of the game by comparison with Westminster: it is impossible for devolved administrations to try to spot the most electorally opportune moment to call an election, which is a key part of the strategy of any governing party in Westminster.

The rules of the political game by comparison with Westminster are also fundamentally changed by the mode of election to the Parliament and the Assembly (see Briefing 11.1). We shall see in Chapter 17 that Westminster uses the 'first past the post' single member constituency system: a single member elected for each separate territorial constituency, chosen by which candidate secures simply the largest number of votes. Both in Scotland and Wales the devolved system uses different, virtually identical arrangements. Each elector has two votes to cast. One of these is used to select the single representative for the territorial constituency in which the voter is registered, the winner being, Westminster fashion, the candidate who receives the largest number of popular votes. For these purposes Wales is divided into 40, and Scotland into 73, constituencies. The second vote is cast to indicate a preference from party lists of candidates grouped regionally: Wales is divided into five, and Scotland into eight regions. In Wales this

method selects an additional 20, and in Scotland an additional 56 members. This Additional Member System selects according to the proportion of votes received across the whole regions. This familiar form of proportional representation is intended to redress one of the best known defects of the 'first past the post' single member constituency system: the inability of candidates from parties with minority but significant support that is widely dispersed geographically to gain representation in the elected institution.

The first elections to the Parliament and the Assembly were held in 1999, and the second in 2003. Both sets of elections showed how the different election arrangements had produced a profoundly different political arrangement by comparison with the Westminster system. Four important effects could be observed.

## Simple majorities rare

Although Labour emerged from the 2003 Welsh Assembly elections with a small majority of seats (see Briefing 11.2), achieving this is much more difficult than in the Westminster Parliament. The very large majorities enjoyed by majority parties in the House of Commons are virtually impossible. Scotland has been ruled by coalition since 1999. In Wales, for a year after the first Assembly elections in 1999 Labour tried to govern alone as a minority, but was obliged in 2000 to enter a formal coalition with the Liberal Democrats. It has now returned to sole control of government on the back of its small 2003 majority. The initial attempt to govern alone in 1999 without a working majority is a sign of the problems Labour endured while trying to abandon the working assumptions about single party government formed by nearly 80 years' experience of the Westminster system. In Scotland, from the beginning Labour was obliged to be constitutionally more radical: devolved government in Scotland has involved a continuous coalition between Labour and the Liberal Democrats, stretching to the sharing of ministerial posts and the development of joint policies. By contrast, there has not been a single coalition government in the Westminster Parliament since 1945, and only brief periods when

# Briefing

11.1

## THE ELECTORAL SYSTEM UNDER DEVOLVED GOVERNMENT IN SCOTLAND AND WALES

The elections to the Scottish Parliament and the Welsh Assembly are governed by essentially the same method, a mix of the 'simple majority' method that also elects MPs to the Westminster Parliament, and the Additional Member System.

- A majority of seats (40 in Wales, 73 in Scotland) elect on a simple majority system: the single candidate with the largest number of votes is declared elected, even if that candidate wins only a minority (less than 50 per cent) of votes cast. The constituency boundaries are the same as those for elections to the Westminster Parliament.
- In Wales 20 seats, and in Scotland 56, are held by 'Additional Members': hence the label. In both cases the countries are divided into regions (five in Wales, eight in Scotland) with seats divided equally between the regions.
- Voters have two votes: one for the 'single member' simple majority constituency selection, and a second cast for a party. The second vote is used to 'top up' a party's representation from candidates on a party's list, to bring the party's total representation in a region as close as possible to its proportion of the popular vote. This explains why (see Figure 11.2) Labour in 1999 in Wales had only one additional member, while Plaid Cymru had eight: Labour had almost achieved its full proportional allocation via those returned in single member single majority contests in the constituencies. The system also greatly helped the Conservatives: they won no 'single member' seats in Scotland, for instance, but gained 18 members under the Additional Member system in 1999.

⮕ The electoral system for devolved government marks a major innovation in the governing system. As we see at several points in the text of the chapter it has enforced a more consensual governing style very different from the partisan, adversarial system that we saw embedded in the Westminster system in Chapter 10. And as we shall see later it has also helped widen the range of political talent recruited to political leadership.

governments relied on the votes other than those of their own backbenchers. Recall that in describing the Westminster Parliament we emphasized the extent to which its culture was shaped by the need to support, or to oppose, a single governing party with a majority: for instance, in developing a particularly extreme form of adversarialism in political exchange. We can see immediately that the electoral arrangements for the Scottish Parliament and Welsh Assembly foster a very different culture of cross-party accommodation. The culture of the new institutions is shaped by the realization of all parties that they face a high probability of having to cooperate with a rival party either in a formal coalition, as presently in Scotland, or in some more informal arrangement to support the single party in office.

## A more 'proportional' allocation of seats

The Additional Member System achieved the objective of ensuring a closer correlation – though not an exact one – between the proportional allocation of seats for parties in the Parliament and Assembly, and their shares of the popular vote. This greater 'proportionality' also ensured that minority radical voices that would not be heard in a body elected under the first past the post system are represented under the devolved arrangements. The most spectacular example was the election to the first Scottish Parliament under the Additional Member System of Tommy Sheridan as the single representative of the Scottish Socialist Party, a radical alternative to Labour in Scotland. Mr Sheridan first came to prominence in the 1980s and early 1990s as a leader of civil disobedience against the then Conservative government's 'poll tax', a failed attempt to reform local government finance. He actually served a prison sentence for this defiance. In 1999 he famously substituted a clenched fist salute for the more conventional form of assent when members were sworn in as members of the new Parliament. Mr Sheridan used the solitary seat for the Scottish Socialist Party so effectively that in 2003 the Party's numbers increased to six, all garnered from the Additional Member list (see People in Politics, 11.1, p. 230).

# Briefing                                    11.2

## THE DISTINCTIVE WORKINGS OF ELECTIONS UNDER DEVOLVED GOVERNMENT: AN ILLUSTRATION FROM WALES, 2003

|  | Per cent of votes cast | Seats won |
|---|---|---|
| Conservatives: single member constituencies | 20.44 | 1 |
| Conservatives: Additional Members | 19.15 | 10 |
| Labour: single member constituencies | 39.54 | 30 |

*Source*: Calculated from Electoral Commission data.

➲  This example examines the fate of the two leading UK parties in the Welsh Assembly elections of 2003, and it shows how the electoral system that governs devolution (the same applies in Scotland) produces very different outcomes from those that apply in UK elections for the Westminster Parliament. (See Briefing 11.1 for details of the election system.) The first and third rows show how the parties fare under a version of the 'first past the post' Westminster type system: despite securing over one-fifth of the popular vote in the constituencies the Conservatives won only one territorial constituency. A minority in Wales, their vote is spread geographically. Despite securing more than half Labour's proportion of the popular vote, they received 1 seat (as against 30 Labour seats). But now look at the second row, which summarizes the results for the regional districts where seats are allocated by proportion of votes cast: here slightly less than one-fifth of the second votes cast yields 10 seats for the Conservatives. Labour has no regional allocation because it has already 'won' its proportional allocation of seats in the Westminster-type territorial constituencies. The Conservative allocation of 1 seat to the territorial constituencies is a good measure of the likely outcome had the election been fought under 'Westminster' type rules.

## Distinctive electoral calculations

The new electoral system has greatly altered the electoral calculations of the parties, probably in the direction of strengthening their official central

organization. This is because election under the Additional Member System, by allocating seats proportional to a party's popular vote, makes one factor critical for the ambitious candidate: where he or she is in the party's ranked list of candidates. (We shall see in a later chapter that this works in an even more imperative way in the case of European elections.) Ambitious candidates therefore in principle have two routes into the Parliament or Assembly: via adoption as a constituency candidate, or via the party list under the Additional Member System. In practice use of the latter has already allowed party leaderships to ensure the election of favoured candidates. The best-known example of this was the return under the list of Alan Michael, the founding First Secretary in Wales. Mr Michael was 'parachuted' in from the Westminster government at short notice when Ron Davies, the architect of Welsh Devolution, was obliged to resign at very short notice because of private troubles. Mr Michael had a weak political base in Wales, was adopted for no territorial constituency in the Assembly, and could only serve as First Secretary via election on the Additional Member list.

## A more modern parliamentary style

We saw in Chapter 10 that the Westminster House of Commons is dominated by a traditionally engrained adversarial culture. This owes a great deal to the way the electoral system has for over 70 years produced a chamber dominated by two opposing parties who have only cooperated in government during the crisis of war. The cultures of the devolved Parliament and Assembly are different. For example, procedures in the two elected bodies are self-consciously 'modern', by contrast with the studied cultivation of the ancient that we observed in the case of the Westminster Parliament. Members are allocated individual desks in the chamber, and voting is electronic, by contrast with the Westminster practice of actually walking through separate lobbies for the purposes of counting the vote. There is also a greater attempt to at least appear to practise more open government: for instance, Westminster Cabinet Minutes are only officially made public after a gap of 30 years, but minutes of the devolved government are published more or less immediately on the web. How much this contributes to open government the reader can judge by looking at the extract from the minutes of the Welsh Cabinet reproduced on p. 234. As a further expression of modernity, both the Scottish Parliament and the Welsh Assembly have commissioned self-consciously modernist designs for new buildings to house their proceedings (see Image 11.2). Both building projects have been bedevilled by huge cost overruns and delays in construction, but both indicate a statement of departure from the practices of the old Westminster model.

The new institutions of devolution have in important ways therefore created a common Welsh and Scottish departure from the prevailing politics of the Westminster system. In particular, they have begun to embed a style of governing and political debate which departs radically from the adversarial culture of Westminster, stretching as far as the prospect of long-term coalition government; they have allowed the representation of minority voices not capable of being heard in the House of Commons; and they have changed some of the calculations which ambitious candidates must make in trying to build a successful political career.

There nevertheless are important differences between the two devolved systems. These chiefly concern the different powers and scope for independent action of the institutions, and the differences in turn arise in part from the different political histories of the movements supporting devolved government in the two countries.

The single most important contrast is immediately clear from an examination of the formal powers of the Scottish Parliament and the Welsh Assembly. In two critical respects the powers of the Scottish Parliament are markedly greater (see Briefing 11.3). First, Parliament is empowered to pass its own legislation which, having passed through three stages, receives the Royal Assent in the manner of laws passed by the Westminster Parliament. Second, the Scottish Executive has power to vary the base rate of income tax by up to

33p in the pound. The Welsh Assembly, by contrast, has no power independently to pass legislation, and no tax-raising authority. These formal differences are substantial and have undoubtedly produced different experiences of devolution in the two countries; but, as we shall now see, while the differences are important, it is also striking how similar have been some of the experiences.

## The experience of devolution

We have seen that the formal design of the institutions of devolution in Scotland and Wales provides a mixed picture of similarities and contrasts. The most important source of contrast is that the extent of devolution in the Scottish case is self-consciously greater than is the case in Wales; but examination of the experience of devolution since the first elections in 1999 indicates that the similarities in experience are more evident than the contrasts. Six marks of similarity should be highlighted, because they all represent the continuing divergence of the new Scottish and Welsh systems from the Westminster model of government. These years, for all the particular problems encountered by the institutions, have seen them settled as secure parts of the British political landscape and increasingly important alternatives to the governing world represented by Westminster. The six marks of similarity examined here concern:

- Policy outcomes
- The stability of the governing institutions
- The problem of achieving popular success
- The development of distinctive careers and policy networks
- The importance of Europe in the workings of the new institutions
- The evolving role of the most senior political figure, the Chief Minister in Scotland and the Welsh First Secretary.

### Policy outcomes

The Scottish Parliament, by contrast with the Welsh Assembly, acquired the power to pass legis-

# Briefing

## THE SCOPE AND LIMITS OF DEVOLVED GOVERNMENT IN SCOTLAND

*Devolved issues include:*

- Health
- Education and training
- Local government
- Social work
- Housing
- Planning
- Tourism, economic development and financial assistance to industry
- Some aspects of transport, including the Scottish road network, bus policy and ports and harbours
- Law and home affairs, including most aspects of criminal and civil law, the prosecution system and the courts
- The police and fire services
- The environment
- Natural and built heritage
- Agriculture, forestry and fishing
- Sport and the arts
- Statistics, public registers and records.

*Reserved issues include:*

- Constitutional matters
- UK foreign policy
- UK defence and national security
- Fiscal, economic and monetary system
- Immigration and nationality
- Energy: electricity, coal, gas and nuclear energy
- Common markets
- Trade and industry, including competition and customer protection
- Some aspects of transport, including railways, transport safety and regulation
- Employment legislation
- Social security
- Gambling and the National Lottery
- Data protection
- Abortion, human fertilization and embryology, genetics, and vivisection
- Equal opportunities.

➲ The scale of devolution reflects the strength of the movement for separation in Scotland, and the pre-existing strength of Scottish institutions.

lation, and it has indeed used this power to create policies that are in some respects distinctive both from the Westminster Parliament and from Wales. The examples range from the symbolic to the outstandingly important. Hunting with dogs was outlawed while the Westminster Parliament continued to struggle with the issue. Two other issues affect millions and involve substantial resources: the Scottish Parliament, as one of its first measures, abolished the fees for higher education imposed by the Westminster government; and it has likewise departed in important ways from the Westminster policy of charging for care of the aged.

These differences with both Westminster and with Wales are important, but they should not be allowed to obscure the very real departures on policy which have been possible in Wales. The

Assembly, though wielding no power to pass legislation, inherited the range of powers wielded by the old Welsh Office. As Briefing 11.4 shows, it is striking how wide ranging has been policy innovation in all three devolved jurisdictions. (We return to the case of Northern Ireland later in this chapter.) It seems that the formal differences between the powers of the Parliament and the Assembly may matter less in the actual practice of making distinctive policy.

### Instability of government

Both the Scottish and Welsh system share a very important common experience: it has proved much more difficult for governing parties to manage the Parliament and the Assembly than has traditionally been the case with the Westminster system. A

# Briefing                                                                11.4

## THE DIFFERENCE DEVOLUTION MAKES: DIFFERENT PUBLIC POLICIES PURSUED IN SCOTLAND, WALES AND NORTHERN IRELAND FOLLOWING DEVOLUTION

| *Scotland* | *Wales* | *Northern Ireland* |
|---|---|---|
| ● Free long-term personal care for the elderly | ● UK's first Children's Commissioner | ● Abolition of school league tables |
| ● Abolition of up-front tuition fees for students in higher education | ● Creation of 22 Local Health Boards | ● Establishment of a commissioner for children |
| ● Three-year settlement for teachers' pay and conditions | ● Homelessness Commission, and extending support for the homeless | ● Decision to provide a Single Equality Act, consolidating legislation on religion, sex, race and disability with new provisions for sexual orientation and age |
| ● Less restrictive Freedom of Information Act | ● Abolition of school league tables. | |
| ● Abolition of fox hunting. | ● Free medical prescriptions for those under 25 and over 60 | ● Free fares for the elderly |
| ● 'One stop shop' for Public Sector Ombudsman | ● Free bus travel for pensioners. | ● Introduction of bursaries for students |
| ● Abolition of ban 'promoting homosexuality' by repeal of Section 2A of the Local Government Act ('section 28' in England). | ● Free school milk for those under seven | ● Decision on the abolition of the 11+ examination in secondary school selection. |
| | ● Six weeks' free home care for the elderly after discharge from hospital. | |

*Source*: Complied from information in Economic and Social Research Council (2004).

⇨ This chart, drawn from a briefing research paper on devolution commissioned by the Economic and Social Research Council, shows how far there is a distinctive policy dynamic on the ground in the devolved administrations. It reinforces the argument of the chapter that devolution has created a set of distinctive political systems within the UK.

simple index of this is the turnover of first ministers: since 1990, when Mrs Thatcher fell, there have only been two prime ministers in Downing Street, and of course Mrs Thatcher's was the longest peacetime occupation of Downing Street in the twentieth century. By contrast, thus far since 1999 there have been three First Ministers in Scotland and two in Wales. In part the difference is just due to human misfortune: the first Scottish First Minister, Donald Dewar, sadly died in office. But it also reflects a more turbulent parliamentary atmosphere where it has been much more difficult than in the Westminster Parliament to create stable governing majorities. This problem was the direct cause of the downfall of Alan Michael, the first Welsh First Secretary, who resigned after suffering a motion of no confidence.

## The problems of commanding popular support

The extent of deep popular support for the devolution project is uncertain in both countries. On the one hand, over 75 per cent of those who voted in the referendum on the principle of devolution in Scotland in 1997 supported the proposal for a Scottish Parliament. But, on the other hand, turnout in both Scotland and Wales was low by the historical standards of UK-wide general elections: just over 60 per cent of Scottish voters, and just over 50 per cent of Welsh voters, turned out. Even this modest level of popular engagement has proved hard to sustain. Turnout in the 2003 elections, the second in the history of the Parliament and the Assembly, was 49 per cent (Scotland) and 38 per cent for Wales, lower even than the historically low turnout in the 2001 UK general election. Part of the difficulty has been (as we shall see when we come to examine participation in Chapter 13) that the foundation of the institutions coincided with an apparent fall in commitment to established forms of political participation such as voting, and the rise of a generally sceptical popular attitude to politicians and to established institutions more widely. But part of the difficulty has also been specific to the new institutions. Some problems are probably short term: for instance, in both Scotland and Wales the impressive modern buildings intended to symbolize the new political order have been costly fiascos. There have been serious construction delays and large cost overruns, and at the time of writing nobody even has a clear notion of what the eventual costs will be. This fiasco has contributed to a sense that the new institutions are expensive and wasteful. In the Scottish case, the leading party – Labour – has also been dogged by a series of scandals, one of which, involving official expenses, forced the resignation of the second First Minister. In the Welsh case, part of the problem has lain in the more limited powers assigned to the Assembly, and the growing argument, heard even within the ruling Labour party, that the existing devolution settlement is inadequate and unstable.

It is hard to imagine that devolved government, now established, will not endure as a long-term feature of the UK system of government, but the continuation of the present arrangements is less certain. Both sets of devolved institutions have had difficulty establishing public enthusiasm, have been afflicted by a lack of public confidence, and contain within them many voices who already wish to alter the arrangements.

## Careers and networks

One reason we can be reasonably confident that some form of devolved government will endure is that even after only a few years of operation highly distinctive political communities have developed around the new institutions. In Wales and Scotland distinct political careers are being made separate from those offered by the Westminster

system. Although the most ambitious Welsh and Scottish politicians still gravitate towards Westminster, there have been some notable cases of individuals – the best known of which was the founding First Minister of Scotland, Donald Dewar – abandoning a Westminster career for one in the new institutions (see People in Politics 11.1). The simple fact of a separate career line is not in itself novel: there is a long tradition of powerful politicians establishing both a career and a power base in local government, as we shall see in the next chapter. But whereas for ambitious politicians local government careers are typically a 'jumping off' point for a Westminster career, there is no sign of this developing in the case of Wales and Scotland. In some instances politicians who felt 'blocked' at Westminster diverted to the devolved institutions: that was the case with, for instance, the second Welsh First Secretary, Rhodri Morgan. After filling Westminster front bench duties for Labour in opposition, he was passed over for office when Labour returned to government in 1997, and made a successful alternative career in Cardiff. Thus ministerial office in Cardiff and Edinburgh now offers a long-term paid alternative to a Westminster career.

Neither is this just a matter of the careers of individuals. Distinct governing networks are being created or, where they previously existed, are being strengthened. The establishment of departments with substantial policy-making authority has developed exactly the kinds of networks that exist in London. Interest representation through the kind of lobbying that we described in Chapter 9 has developed around the new institutions: consider the example of the Scottish Retail Consortium described in Documenting Politics 9.1, p. 166. In this way the devolution of government institutions has been followed by the devolution of the activity of interest representation, for the very good reason that important decisions have shifted from the Westminster system to the institutions in Cardiff and Edinburgh. The devolution reforms of 1998 are therefore having effects well beyond the institutions of government; they are stretching into a wider reshaping of the nature of political action and of the way policies are made.

*People in politics*

## 11.1    ENRICHING THE POLITICAL GENE POOL: HOW DEVOLUTION EXPANDS THE RANGE OF AVAILABLE POLITICAL TALENT

Cartoons: Shaun Steele

**Rhodri Morgan** (1939–), First Secretary for Wales, 2000–. Former senior civil servant, Labour MP in Westminster Parliament 1987–2001, front bench spokesman on Welsh affairs, 1992–7; not retained on front bench after Labour's election in 1997; unsuccessfully challenged Ron Davies for post-Devolution Welsh leadership; vetoed as potential Chief Secretary by Downing Street; succeeds as Welsh Secretary when Alun Michael falls to a vote of no confidence; leads coalition government in Cardiff, 2000–3, forms single-party Labour Administration following 2003 Welsh Assembly elections.

**Tommy Sheridan** (1964–). Member of Scottish Parliament, 1999–, elected on Additional Member list of Scottish Socialist Party (see Briefing 11.1). Local councillor for Pollok, Glasgow, 1992–. Elected from prison cell, serving six-month sentence for preventing a poll tax warrant sale; leader of Scottish anti-poll tax campaigns. Symbolic protests include boycotting the formal opening of the Scottish Parliament in 1999 in favour of picketing the event in protest against introduction of student fees in higher education. Advocate of policies long abandoned by New Labour, such as universal provision of free school meals.

**Brid Rogers** (1935–). Social Democratic and Labour Party (SDLP) member of the (suspended) Northern Ireland Assembly. Former member of the Senate of the Republic of Ireland; long-term civil rights campaigner, and chair of the SDLP talks team that led to the Belfast Agreement. Minister of Agriculture and Rural Development in the (now suspended) Northern Ireland Executive, where she won wide support for her management of the great foot and mouth crisis, a crisis that in mainland Britain became a byword for catastrophe and government incompetence.

➡ In Chapter 18 we will see that the range of political recruitment in the Westminster government is narrowing: politics is increasingly dominated by professional politicians with similar backgrounds and social experiences. These three examples show how the devolved institutions are allowing space for those who would be excluded in the Westminster system. The three cases stand for the more general widening of the pool of available political talent: for instance, the Welsh Assembly elected in 2003 is the first nationally elected institution to have a (small) majority of women members.

## Europe

Relations with the EU mark a common and permanent point of departure from the traditional routines of Westminster government. We have already seen that over 30 years of membership of the European Union reshaped the Westminster system in profound ways – indeed, so profoundly that we can no longer easily speak of separate British and European government. The role of the devolved governments marks a further important development in that reshaping: in effect it involves a devolution of the role of the EU itself away from Westminster. Although European Union relations do not formally come within the competence of the devolved administrations, in practice they are deeply involved in policy and negotiations over policy. Since the devolved administrations are responsible for implementation of much policy agreed at EU level, it has been felt sensible to involve them also in its negotiations.

Both Wales and Scotland also have powerful direct incentives to lobby in Brussels because of the interests at stake. For example, Scotland is more dependent than any other part of Britain on the Union's Common Fisheries Policy, while Wales is in receipt of over £1 billion in EU funds under the Union's programme of Structural Funding in the period 2000–6; and both are deeply affected by the Union's Common Agricultural Policy. Devolution was quickly followed by the separate establishment of Brussels-based offices. Though both the Welsh and Scottish Offices in Brussels liaise with the (Westminster) government's Permanent Representative in Brussels, they are dominated by the need to serve the devolved administrations. Both are integral parts of the devolved administrations, and are designed both to provide intelligence for ministers in Edinburgh and Cardiff, and to lobby for national interests. The Scottish case shows particularly independent activism. 'Scotland House' provides a public face for the new government in Brussels, and Scottish representatives in Brussels have made strenuous efforts to create alliances with other regional groups across the Union (see Briefing 11.5, p. 232).

## Role of the chief minister

The chief minister (the First Minister in Scotland and the First Secretary in Wales) is naturally thought of as the equivalent of the Prime Minister in Westminster, yet much of what we know already suggests that the roles are evolving in ways very different from the Westminster pattern. The most important source of difference arises from the limits on the authority of a chief minister in Scotland or Wales imposed by the very different patterns of party strength. Every prime minister in Westminster since 1945 has been able to run a single party government, and for almost the whole of that period has had the cushion of a large Commons majority. Managing a governing party in Westminster, as we saw in earlier chapters, cannot be done in an authoritarian way, and every prime minister has to conciliate party rivals and party factions. Nevertheless, the two parties that have alternated in government in Westminster – Labour and the Conservatives – have generally offered a stable base of support for the prime minister and the prime minister's government. The absence of secure majorities for the largest party in Scotland and Wales turns the First Minister in those countries into a figure who has to be much more concerned with bargaining and compromise, and with 'brokering' deals in order to win support in the Assembly and Parliament.

The skills to be called on are different in all three countries. The Scottish First Minister and the Welsh First Secretary are not at all in the same position. In particular, the situation facing the Chief Secretary has been much more fluid. The lesser powers assigned to the Assembly compared with those devolved to the Scottish Parliament mean that the future of devolution in Wales is much more open. The first four years of the Assembly were as much about trying to work out this future as about actually exercising the devolved powers. Is devolution in Wales to be of a significantly lesser order than in Scotland, or is the present extent a staging post to devolution on at least a Scottish scale? The role of the two first Secretaries so far encapsulates the choice. The first, Alan Michael, was very close to the Westminster

# Briefing

## DEVOLVED SCOTLAND IN EUROPE

*Devolved Scotland: key issues*

- Fisheries: EU Common Fisheries policy vital to Scottish fishing industry
- Agriculture: reform of Common Agricultural Policy impacts on (mostly poor) Scottish farming
- Environment: EU environmental policy impacts on pollution by Scottish industry, problems of acid rain and desire to protect wilderness for tourism
- Regional policy: European Structural Funds are major source of financial support for infrastructure development (such as roads).

*Devolved Scotland: the tactics*

- Ministers attend some meetings of the EU Council of Ministers
- External Relations of the Executive in Edinburgh oversees Scotland's external relations with the rest of the world, including the EU
- Scotland provides eight MEPs
- Scotland Europa, headquartered in Scotland House, an alliance of public and private bodies, promotes Scotland as a business location, speaks with a European voice for non-governmental Scottish interests.

*Devolved Scotland: the bigger picture*

- Scotland looks to other small successful national economies in the EU, including Ireland, as a model of small nation success in the EU
- The revival of Edinburgh as a significant centre of government also recalls the historic place of Scotland as a centre of the European Enlightenment (the key intellectual movement in the making of modern European identity)
- Scotland House also promotes connections with other parts of Europe with strong regional and national identities, such as Catalonia.

➲ Devolution did not of itself make Europe relevant to Scotland, nor lead to the invention of Scottish lobbying in the European Union. As we will see in the next chapter, the non-devolved local governments of England have also been active. But the creation of the Scottish Executive gave an institutional resource to organize a Scottish presence in Brussels; the system of devolved elections for the Parliament gave Scottish politicians an extra incentive to recognize the issues where Europe impinged on Scottish economy and society; and the sense of rediscovered national identity ('the bigger picture') led to a search for allies among other small European nations and regions.

executive. Although a Westminster MP for a Welsh (Cardiff) seat he was a Home Office minister who was 'parachuted' at short notice into the leading role in Welsh devolution politics. Mr Michael then had rapidly to be found a seat in the new Assembly via the Additional Member System described above. His time in office was devoted to establishing and managing the existing devolution arrangements. He resigned in 2000, essentially because he could not command majorities for policies in the Assembly. His successor, Rhodri Morgan, though also a Westminster MP, enjoyed no office at Westminster, and from the start pitched himself as intent on maximizing Welsh distinctiveness and autonomy from the Westminster system (see People in Politics 11.1).

## Northern Ireland: before and after the Belfast Agreement

### Before the Belfast Agreement

The role of Northern Ireland in British politics is the most extreme sign of a problem that goes to the heart of the nature of the United Kingdom: what should be those boundaries of that entity, and how can its boundaries be maintained? In 1800 an Act of Union abolished the Irish Parliament in Dublin and united the whole island of Ireland under the British Crown. In 1922 an Irish Free State came into existence with the same degree of independence enjoyed by other members of the Commonwealth, such as Canada and Australia. This followed a Treaty which brought to an end five years of military conflict between the British state and Irish Republican nationalists. But the new Irish state only covered 26 counties with an overwhelmingly Roman Catholic population. The remaining six, in the north of the island, dominated by a Protestant population that supported continued union with the Crown, was granted a high level of devolved government within the United Kingdom. That devolution lasted 50 years. The degree of devolution was unusual in an otherwise highly centralized political system, and was the result of a great clash about the identity of the United Kingdom. The independence settlement involved partitioning the island and incorporating the six northern counties as a component part of the United Kingdom, but one with its own legislature, executive and extensive control over its own domestic affairs.

The devolved system that survived in Northern Ireland contained features that eventually led to its collapse. It was designed from the start to ensure a permanent majority for a 'Unionist' party which, as the name suggests, stood for unity with the rest of the United Kingdom. This party also overwhelmingly drew its support from Protestant denominations in the Province. Although its numerical majority ensured perpetual rule, it reinforced this with a variety of discriminatory measures – for instance in drawing electoral boundaries – against the minority, Catholic, population. This minority population was indeed highly distinct in religious affiliation and political allegiance: it was dominated by practising Catholics, and a large minority did not accept the legitimacy of the political settlement that had been arrived at in 1922. In this latter conviction it was supported by the new Irish State in the south, which for almost all of its history had the aspiration of a united Ireland as at least a formally expressed aim.

The Northern Ireland system collapsed in a few short years at the end of the 1960s. A movement for civil rights reform (largely aimed at removing discriminatory measures against Catholics) caused deep divisions within Unionism, between those who wanted to conciliate and those who wanted to suppress reform. By the end of the 1960s the authorities were unable to ensure public order (and in some cases unable to ensure that their own police force did not breach public order by attacking civil

rights demonstrators). In 1969 the British government despatched troops to police the province. In the Catholic community this was rapidly followed by the rise of a new kind of radical Republicanism: as a party it took the form of Sinn Féin, and as a military group took the form of the Provisional IRA (Irish Republican Army). Within three years there had been a large-scale breakdown of public security in a three-way struggle between Republican paramilitaries, the British Army and Protestant Unionist paramilitaries. In 1972 the separate institutions of Northern Ireland were finally abolished, to be replaced by direct rule from Westminster through a Secretary of State with a seat in the British Cabinet. For over 20 more years military struggle, rather than orthodox democratic politics, shaped the politics of the province. Just under 3,500 people have been violently killed. The cost in wider human suffering, economic decay and social dislocation is almost incalculable. The majority of the dead were victims of military Republicanism, but many were also victims of the armed forces and of protestant paramilitary forces. The majority too were the victims of 'sectarian' violence (that is, attacks on Catholics or Protestants by those of an opposing religious and nationalist loyalty); but many were also the victims of violence within their 'own' communities.

Numerous attempts were made in these decades to construct institutions and settlements that would restore some kind of 'normal' democratic politics resembling the politics of the rest of the United Kingdom. All failed until the 1990s (see Timeline 11.3, p. 236). From 1990 the main republican groups and the British government began secret (and widely denied) negotiations. In December 1993 the British and Irish governments issued a joint 'Downing Street Declaration' that was intended to reassure both Nationalists and Unionists: the former by holding out the prospect of unity if a majority, both north and south, supported the idea; the latter by stressing, precisely, that no union would take place without the support of a separate majority in the north. Early in 1994 the Provisional IRA announced a ceasefire, followed shortly by the unionist paramilitary groups. A difficult, prolonged series of public and private negotia-

## DOCUMENTING POLITICS 11.1

## EDITED MINUTES OF THE WELSH CABINET

Welsh Assembly Government

Minutes of a meeting of the Cabinet

Monday 13th January 2003

**Present:** Rt. Hon. Rhodri Morgan AM, First Minister (Chair)
Michael German OBE AM
Andrew Davies AM
Jane Davidson AM (Items 3–9)
Sue Essex AM
Edwina Hart MBE AM
Carwyn Jones AM (Item 1)
Jenny Randerson AM
Sir Jon Shortridge, Permanent Secretary
Lawrence Conway, Cabinet Secretariat
Paul Griffiths, Special Adviser
Bridget Harris, Special Adviser
Lesley Punter, Special Adviser
Steve Pomeroy, Head of Cabinet and Constitution Unit
David Rich, Cabinet Meetings Secretary
Dr Ron Loveland, Head of innovation and Sustainable Growth Division
Apologies were received from Jane Hutt AM

**Item 1: Forward Business Look**
1.1 The Minister for Open Government outlined the forward business look up to the Easter recess.

**Item 2: Minutes of the previous meeting**
2.1 The minutes of the previous meeting were approved subject to an amendment.

**Item 3: First Minister's Items**

*ELWa*
3.1 The Auditor General's report into unauthorized spending by ELWa was due to be published on Tuesday 14th January.

*Defence Orders*
3.2 Ministers welcomed the recent defence contracts announced by Oshkosh in Llantrisant and Cogent in Newport.

## DOCUMENTING POLITICS 11.1    (continued)

*Llandarcy*

3.3  Ministers noted the launch of the major scheme to develop an urban village on the site of the former oil refinery at Llandarcy.

*Airbus*

3.4  Orders for the A380 were still being placed, the most recent coming from Malaysian Airlines.

*Allied Steel and Wire*

3.5  Ministers noted that Celsa had completed the purchase of the former Allied Steel and Wire site at Cardiff.

*Royal Gwent*

3.6  The report into orthopaedic waiting times in Gwent by Professor Brian Edwards was due to be published at the end of January.

### Item 4: Requests for use of the Executive Procedure

4.1  Cabinet considered three requests to use the executive procedure to make subordinate legislation:

The Sheep and Goats (Identification and Movement) (Wales) (No. 2) Order (SAGIMO) 2002
The Allocation of Housing (Wales) Regulations 2003
The Local Authorities (Executive Arrangements)(Discharge of Functions)(Amendment)(Wales) Regulations 2003

*Cabinet agreed all requests for the use of the executive procedure.*

### Item 5: Business and Environment Action Plan for Wales CAB(02-03)34

5.1  The Minister for Economic Development introduced the paper and the draft Business and Environment Action Plan. The draft had been finalised following wide consultation. There was substantial support in the responses that had been received. The purpose of the action plan was to make businesses more sustainable. The plan also emphasized wider aspects of sustainability that were not related to resource management.

5.2  Ministers made a number of comments on the draft. In particular Ministers discussed the WDA's role as the lead co-ordinating body. There was a need to ensure that the expertise and skills of other organizations were retained and utilized, and Ministers requested regular reports to Cabinet to monitor this.

➲ From the beginning the devolved governments have been more open in their practices than is common in the Westminster system. Cabinet minutes in the Westminster core executive are not normally publicly available until 30 years have elapsed. In the case of the Welsh Cabinet there is virtually immediate availability. Of course, this has consequences for the meaning and form of what is recorded: it is one thing to know that what one has said will be revealed in 30 years' time, when it is virtually certain that one will not be in active politics, and another to know that comments will be publicly available in a few days.

*Source*: Edited from www.assembly.wales.gov.uk/cabinet/minutes

## TIMELINE 11.3    THE ROAD TO GOOD FRIDAY 1998 – AND THE ROAD AWAY FROM GOOD FRIDAY

**1920**
Government of Ireland Act creates separate Northern Ireland Parliament with extensive devolved powers and creates 'Westminster' constituencies in the Province.

**1922**
Remainder of Ireland becomes effectively independent as the Irish Free State.

**1937**
New Irish Constitution contains clauses making explicit commitment to reincorporating Northern Ireland into a united Ireland.

**1965**
Historic exchange visits between 'modernizing' Northern Irish Prime Minister, Terence O'Neill, and his Republic of Ireland counterpart, Sean Lemass, begins brief period of attempts to conciliate between the South and North and between Unionists and Republicans in North.

**1967**
Northern Ireland Civil Rights Association established to campaign for reform of housing, employment and electoral laws.

**1969**
Attacks on civil rights marchers and riots in Derry and Belfast leads to despatch of British troops to province. Split in Republican Movement leads to formation of Provisional IRA.

**1972**
Paratroopers shoot 13 marchers to death on 'Bloody Sunday' in January. Northern Ireland government suspended and direct rule via Secretary of State in Westminster Cabinet introduced.

**1974**
Peace talks lead to formation of 'power sharing' executive; abandoned following general strike of Protestant Ulster Workers' Council, followed in turn by reimposition of direct rule and extension of IRA bombing campaign to British mainland.

**1981**
Death of IRA hunger strikers leads to riots that cause over 50 deaths.

**1984**
IRA bomb at Grand Hotel, Brighton narrowly misses the Prime Minister, Margaret Thatcher, and kills five people.

**1985**
Meeting of Thatcher and the Irish Taoiseach (Prime Minister), Fitzgerald, at Hillsborough produces the Anglo–Irish Agreement: sets up Intergovernmental Conference to discuss all Irish issues and states aim of reconciling the two 'traditions' of nationalism and unionism on the island. Provokes furious and widespread Unionist opposition.

**1993**
John Hume (Social Democratic and Labour Party or SDLP) and Gerry Adams (Sinn Féin) begin exploratory talks for a settlement; British government admits to several months of secret negotiation with the IRA.

**1994**
IRA declares ceasefire, quickly followed by ceasefire declaration by Unionist paramilitary groups.

**1995**
First official meeting between IRA and a British government minister for 23 years.

**1996**
IRA ends ceasefire with bombing of Canary Wharf in London, killing two. American Senator George Mitchell chairs (not quite) all-party talks: Sinn Féin excluded.

**1997**
Labour general election landslide; IRA and Unionist paramilitary ceasefires resumed; Sinn Féin readmitted to all party talks.

**April 1998**
The Belfast Agreement concluded on Good Friday after intense negotiation involving direct participation of all parties and indirect external pressure from the US government and the European Union.

**June 1998**
Elections for Northern Ireland Assembly

**TIMELINE 11.3 (CONTINUED)**

**July 1998**
Meeting of 'shadow' assembly, and David Trimble (Ulster Unionist) and Seamus Mallon (SDLP) selected as First Minister Designate and Deputy First Minister Designate respectively. Difficulties in moving from 'shadow' to 'real' government focus on police reforms and IRA decommissioning.

**July 1999**
Collapse of attempts to progress further implementation of Belfast Agreement, principally because of differences over police reform and decommissioning of IRA weapons.

**November 1999**
Assembly meets, and first Executive selected.

**2 December 1999**
Power devolved to Assembly and Executive.

**February 2000**
Westminster Secretary of State suspends devolved government because of dissatisfaction with progress of IRA weapons decommissioning.

**May 2000**
IRA offers concessions on inspections of its arms dumps and Assembly and Executive restored.

**May 2001**
Mr Trimble announces that he has signed and lodged with Assembly Presiding Officer a letter resigning as First Minister from 1 July, unless IRA weapons decommissioning begins.

**July 2001**
David Trimble resigns as First Minister.

**August 2001**
Secretary of State suspends Assembly for one day – a device to allow an extra six weeks to reach agreement and reselect the First Minister and Deputy First Minister.

**September 2001**
Secretary of State suspends Assembly again for one day, to buy more time for an agreement.

**October 2001**
David Trimble renominates his Ulster Unionist colleagues as Ministers.

**November 2001**
David Trimble and Mark Durkan (SDLP) elected as Minister and Deputy respectively, following procedural manipulation to create majorities.

**October 2002**
Suspension of devolved government, following allegations of security breaches and alleged Sinn Féin spies in the Secretary of State's Office. David Trimble threatens to resign if Sinn Féin not excluded; Secretary of State opts for suspension as least bad alternative.

**November 2003**
Assembly elections finally held; Democratic Unionists opposed to the Good Friday Agreement win largest number of seats in the Assembly; Sinn Féin displaces SDLP as largest nationalist party.

**May 2005**
David Trimble loses Westminster parliamentary seat; hard line Unionists and Republicans gain at expense of rivals.

➲ The timeline is deliberately distorted here in favour of a close summary of events since the Belfast (Good Friday) Agreement of 1998. The tortuous attempts to implement the Agreement and to create 'normal' politics in Northern Ireland have been obstructed by two substantive issues: the progress of policing reform, and the progress of the decommissioning of IRA weapons. The numerous twists and turns of David Trimble, the First Minister, arise both from the threat to his party of the rival Democratic Unionists, who opposed the original Good Friday Agreement, and from within his party from members who believe he has been too conciliatory in his working of the Agreement. At the time of writing the key institutions within Northern Ireland established by the Agreement are in suspension, direct rule is once again practised from Westminster and 'low level' violence – for instance punishment beatings administered by illegal paramilitary groups – is common.

*Sources*: Butler and Butler (2000); Cook and Stevenson (1983 and 2000); Northern Ireland Office (2003).

tions failed in February 1996 when the Provisional IRA spectacularly resumed bombing operations at Canary Wharf in London. When Labour returned to office in May 1997 it reopened a new round of all-party talks and announced a deadline for the completion of negotiations of May the following year. In July 1997 the IRA renewed its ceasefire. The ensuing negotiations involved the very highest reaches of both the British and Irish governments (prime ministers), influential foreign institutions (such as the European Union and the US government), and an elaborately put together collection of the many different political forces at work in the province. That led to the Belfast Agreement, which was concluded on Good Friday 1998; hence its better-known alternative name.

We examine the content and aftermath of the Agreement in a moment. But whatever its final fate, there is no doubt that a sea change took place in the politics of Northern Ireland in the second half of the 1990s. At the very least it produced a dramatic reduction in the level of violence, though not its elimination. Four important changes lay behind this development.

*Northern Ireland changed.* The Northern Ireland of 1969 – when the Troubles first seriously erupted – was very different from the Northern Ireland of the Good Friday Agreement nearly 30 years later. New generations of political leaders had developed: for instance, the young Republicans who had fought on the streets in the early 1970s were leaders, in Sinn Féin, of a nationalist political party which could claim to be the most rapidly rising party on the whole island from the 1990s onwards. Religious affiliation, which was very strong by mainland British standards in the late 1960s, had declined greatly in intensity. Nearly 30 years of reform had created policies and institutions designed rigorously to outlaw any sign of discrimination on religious or other grounds.

*The Republic of Ireland changed.* The hostility of a Nationalist, Catholic state in the south had been overwhelmingly important in the fate of Northern Ireland for 50 years after 1922. Whether governments in Dublin were really serious about wanting a united Ireland is uncertain; but the aspiration for unity, and the fact that it was enshrined in the Republic's Constitution, was a real source of fear to Unionists. In 1973 the Republic joined the (then) European Economic Community. Over the next quarter of a century Ireland was transformed: 'European' identity in substantial degree supplanted traditional Irish identity; Catholicism largely lost its popular hold; the economy boomed from the late 1980s, so that prosperity in the once impoverished Republic outstripped a Northern Ireland economy wrecked by the decades of violence; and the country became increasingly urban and self-consciously modern in its attitudes. Although the aim of a united Ireland was still in the Constitution, by the 1980s no leading politician in government seriously pursued it.

*Britain changed.* The Conservative Party styled itself the 'Unionist' Party, but for nearly 50 years from the early 1920s all leading British politicians were unionists, in the sense of not questioning the domination of the Westminster system. By the 1990s the Conservative party was, at first secretly and then openly, negotiating the end of this domination of Northern Ireland; and as we saw earlier in this chapter, the unionism of the Labour party was greatly weakened during its years of opposition, 1979–97. In the year of the Belfast Agreement Britain also marked 25 years' membership of the European Union – years that had also seen a great change in the political environment of the institutions of the Westminster system.

*The international environment changed.* The international environment of 1998 was radically different from that of 1969, when the violent years began. The European Union was now both a major institution – playing an important role in the negotiations that produced the Belfast Agreement – and an important new source of political loyalty and identity. The collapse of the Soviet bloc, described in Chapter 2, ended the Cold War. As a result it turned American attention to managing many smaller conflicts that had been relatively neglected. That helps explain why pressure and conciliation from the United States played so large a part in brokering the Belfast Agreement.

## The Belfast Agreement and the peace process

The Belfast Agreement (see Briefing 11.6) was designed to create peaceful devolved government in

# Briefing                                                                    11.6

## THE BELFAST (GOOD FRIDAY) AGREEMENT

### Principles
- Change in the constitutional status of Northern Ireland can only come about with the consent of a majority in the province.
- The Government of Ireland Act, claiming British jurisdiction, to be repealed.
- The Irish Government to hold a referendum to amend articles of the Constitution of the Republic, which claim jurisdiction over Northern Ireland.

### Implementation
There are three strands, as outlined below.

*Strand One: the 'North' dimension*
- A 108-member Assembly to be elected by proportional representation
- Rules to ensure that the Assembly cannot be dominated by a simply majority
- 'Cross-community' majorities required to elect the First Minister and Deputy First Minister
- The First Minister and Deputy First Minister to head an Executive Authority with up to 10 ministers with departmental responsibilities; ministerial posts to be allocated on a proportional basis.

*Strand Two: the 'North-South' Dimension*
- A North–South Ministerial Council to be be established under legislation at Westminster and in Dublin for consultation on matters of joint interest and to create cross-border initiatives
- Council decisions to be made consensually
- Annual meeting of full council and regular 'bilateral' meetings between Northern Executive Ministers and their counterparts in the Republic.

*Strand Three: the 'East–West' dimension*
- A British–Irish Council to be established consisting of representatives of the British and Irish Governments, and devolved institutions in Northern Ireland, Scotland and Wales, the Isle of Man and the Channel Islands; summit meetings twice a year, and more frequent meetings of particular policy sectors
- British–Irish Intergovernmental Conference to be established, providing the formal machinery for cooperation and joint action at the highest levels (up to British Prime Minister and Irish Taoiseach) of the two sovereign governments
- European Convention on Human Rights to be incorporated into Northern Ireland Law.

### Key issues
- Weapons decommissioning: participants in the Agreement agree to work with an Independent Commission on Decommissioning and 'to use any influence they may have to achieve the decommissioning of all paramilitary arms within two years following endorsement in referendums North and South of the agreement'; the British Government in turn commits to removing security installations and forces and to normalize levels of security in the province
- Independent Commission on Policing to be established to report on future policing arrangements by the summer of 1999.

➡ This summarizes what the parties signed up to in 1998. Later boxes, and the text, examine the fate of these commitments.

the province, replacing the direct rule from the Westminster government put in place over a quarter of a century before. As we shall see shortly, this attempt thus far has largely failed. There has been no resumption of terrorist violence on the scale that existed before the ceasefire, but the institutions created by the Belfast Agreement were from the beginning periodically interrupted by suspensions, and have been in permanent suspension since October 2002. The second Assembly elections, held in November 2003, led to the emergence of the Democratic Unionists, the most important critic of the Good Friday Agreement, as the largest Unionist party (see Figure 11.3, p. 244).

To make sense of the Agreement's troubled history since 1998 we need to understand the obligations it created for all the parties to the peace process. The failures since 1998 are due to the fact that not all parties have been able, or wanted, fully to meet those obligations.

*Obligations for the paramilitaries.* Participation in the talks that led to the Agreement entailed a range of obligations for paramilitary organizations (both those that supported a united Ireland and those that supported union with Britain): they would disarm completely; they would commit to peaceful politics via democratic elections; they would renounce all violent activities, including 'punishment beatings', a form of vigilante 'justice' administered by the paramilitaries within their own communities; and they would abide by the terms of any agreement endorsed in democratic elections by the voters of the Province.

These obligations have not been met. On the part of the Provisional IRA the main issue has involved decommissioning of all arms which, despite some measures, has yet to be fully implemented. Vigilante 'punishment beatings' have continued widely on both sides of the Unionist/Catholic divide. Membership of, and support for, some of the unionist paramilitary organizations has actually grown since the Belfast Agreement, and there has been strong, and often violent, rivalry between different factions of paramilitary unionism. Paramilitary violence therefore continues to be widespread despite the Agreement, though it now generally takes a 'low intensity' form,

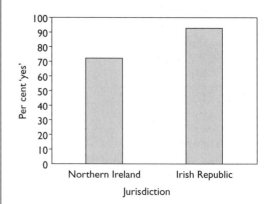

**Figure 11.2**  Support for the Good Friday Agreement in Northern Ireland and the Irish Republic (percentage voting 'yes' in referenda on acceptance)

➲ These figures show impressive support for the Good Friday (or Belfast) Agreement in the referenda in 1998 that followed its conclusion: 94.4 per cent voted yes in the Irish Republic, and 71.1 voted yes in Northern Ireland. But the bald figures hide some important features. The two populations were in effect voting on different substantive issues: in the case of the Republic, for instance, the most important was amending the Constitution to introduce clauses more conciliatory to the unionist majority in Northern Ireland. Participation was exceptionally high (81 per cent) in the North and low (55 per cent) in the Republic, the latter indicating widespread indifference to Northern Ireland. More important still for the future of the peace process, while a large majority of voters identified as Catholic voted yes, voters identified as Unionists were roughly equally divided.

rather than the widespread terrorist bombing spectaculars of the years before the ceasefires of the 1990s. Nevertheless, nearly 100 people have been killed by paramilitary violence since the signing of the Agreement. One of the greatest terrorist attacks in the whole history of the Troubles indeed came shortly after Good Friday 1998, when 29 people were killed in a bombing attack in Omagh, County Tyrone, in August of that year. This attack was mounted by the 'Real IRA', a group that had split with Sinn Féin and the Provisionals over the issue of taking part in the peace process.

*Obligations for the Irish Government.* We have seen that an important shaping historical influence on both the Catholic and Protestant communities in the province in the half-century after 1922 was the existence of an independent Irish state in the rest of the island, with the proclaimed ambition to incorporate Northern Ireland into a united Ireland. These ambitions were expressed in clauses of the Constitution of the Republic dating from the 1930s. In the Belfast Agreement the Irish Government committed itself to put to the electorate of the Republic in a referendum on an amendment to the Constitution, a commitment that brought overwhelming support in the ensuing referendum (see Figure 11.2). The critical wording of the new clause now reads: 'a united Ireland shall be brought about by peaceful means, with the consent of *the majority of the people, democratically expressed, in both jurisdictions in the island*'. (I have added italics to emphasize that this wording was explicitly designed to reassure Unionists in the north that the south would never rely on its numerical superiority in the whole island to enforce unification.)

*Obligations on the political parties in Northern Ireland.* This was one of the most contested parts of the Belfast Agreement, because the very diversity of political parties encapsulated the difficulties that had stood for so long in the way of a peaceful settlement. The status of some of the parties as potential participants in constitutional politics was denied by other participants. The Democratic Unionist Party (one of the two main Unionist parties) was from the outset opposed to the Agreement, in part on the grounds that Sinn Féin remained an unconstitutional wing of a terrorist organization, the Provisional IRA. The Ulster Unionist Party, which provided the first Chief Minister in the person of David Trimble, was a reluctant and protesting participant, partly on the same grounds. Nevertheless, assent to the Agreement did entail an obligation to work the institutions which it created, and this is an obligation which the parties have only partly been able to meet.

This obligation entails willingness to work what is technically a 'consociational' form of government. Consociationalism is a widespread device employed in societies trying to practise peaceful democratic government in conditions of extreme religious or ethnic division. It involves election procedures, rules for forming government, and rules for the making of policy, which try to maximize the range of groups included in government, and which give groups the power to veto decisions, thus ensuring that any numerical majority cannot use that numerical dominance to impose its view on minorities.

The marks of consociationalism in the system of government created out of the Good Friday Agreement are threefold.

First, the system used to elect the Northern Ireland Assembly is designed *to support consociationalism.* The Assembly consists of 108 members, elected for multi-member constituencies. There are 18 constituencies in all, each with six members. Voting is by a variant of proportional representation, the Single Transferable Vote (for details, see Briefing 11.7). The voting system marks a sharp break both in rules and intent with the system used for nearly a century for the dominant (Westminster) Assembly. As we noted earlier in this chapter (and see also Chapter 17), the 'first past the post' election system for Westminster is designed to produce single party majorities, while the system adopted in Northern Ireland is designed precisely to frustrate this outcome. The Assembly has a deliberately larger proportion of elected representatives to electors than the Westminster Parliament, to improve the chances of all shades of opinion being represented. There is an average of one elected member per 11,000 voters; the contrasting figure for the Westminster Parliament exceeds 60,000. The variant of proportional representation used in Northern Ireland is designed, by obstructing the emergence of any single majority, to compel the parties to compromise. This is reinforced by an additional measure. On election all Assembly members have to register themselves as Nationalists, Unionist or 'other' and, as we shall now see, this is critical to how decisions are taken within the Assembly. This is a much more radical departure from the Westminster rules even than that adopted for the new institutions in Wales and Scotland.

Second, the composition of the Executive Committee – in effect the government composed of ministers – is likewise designed *to reinforce consociationalism.* The devolved government is headed by a First Minister and a Deputy Minister who *jointly*

# Briefing

11.7

## THE SINGLE TRANSFERABLE VOTE IN NORTHERN IRELAND

The Single Transferable Vote is used as follows in Northern Ireland Assembly elections:

- The province is divided into 18 constituencies, each with six Assembly members.
- Each party puts forward a list of candidates, up to a maximum of six.
- Voters cast votes by expressing numerical preferences for as many or as few candidates as they prefer: thus, 1, 2, and so on.
- In counting, the total number of ballots is counted, and that total then divided by the number of seats to be filled; this figure, plus one, is the 'quota' (the required number of votes needed for election).
- Any candidate with enough votes to reach the quota is declared elected; any unused portion of their vote ('surplus') is transferred to the voter's second preference. If unfilled seats remain after all first preferences have been allocated, the candidate with the lowest number of votes is eliminated and their votes transferred to their voters' second preferences. The process of elimination and reallocation continues until all seats are filled.

⟳ One theme of this chapter has been devolved government as a laboratory of innovation. Britain is often described as having a 'first past the post' election system (see Chapter 17), but virtually its polar opposite has existed for over 30 years in local government in Northern Ireland, and we have seen that a kind of hybrid exists in the elections for the Welsh Assembly and the Scottish Parliament. The Single Transferable Vote System has two advantages for Northern Ireland: it is very good at ensuring the proportional representation of minorities; and the calculations it encourages in voters' choices can help counter attachment to one party or one confessional persuasion.

head the Executive Committee. The two must stand for election jointly and, to be elected, must have cross-community support: a majority of those members who have designated themselves Nationalists, a majority who have designated themselves Unionists, and a majority of the whole Assembly, must vote for their joint candidature.

The individual ministries are then allotted in proportion to party size in the Assembly, the total size of the ministry being decided by the First Minister and the Deputy Minister acting jointly. As an additional incentive to consociationalism, ministers are only eligible to take office if their nominations are supported by three designated Unionists and three designated nationalists.

Third, the rules of decision within the Assembly are also designed *to build consociational arrangements*. Virtually all decisions require a simple majority support from both the designated 'Unionists' and 'Nationalists', and in some important instances they require a special majority of 60 per cent of those voting.

The fundamental presumption of the Belfast Agreement is that all the political parties have an obligation to work in institutions that are built on consociational principles: on the principle of power and institution sharing, and the rejection of the adversarial politics that, as we saw in the last chapter, is the dominant feature of the Westminster Parliament.

*Obligations on the British Government.* The continuing peace process in Northern Ireland has been likened to riding a bicycle, where to cease pedalling forward is to risk falling off. The main obligation on the British Government is to provide the pedal power. Some of the impetus has been supplied in formal measures arising directly out of the Belfast Agreement: for instance, in the repeal of the original Government of Ireland Act. But the main impetus has been provided by the British government's management of both the process of institution building and the process of further reform in the province. In this the continuing presence of a Northern Ireland Secretary with a seat in the British Cabinet that symbolizes this obligation – and the tensions between the different Northern Ireland Secretaries and the different parties have symbolized the problems of managing the process. The single most important issue has concerned policing and security. This is unsurprising. Security issues dominated the politics of the province for nearly 30 years. The main domestic arm of policing, the Royal Ulster Constabulary (RUC), had a profound symbolic importance: for Unionists it represented a bulwark against terrorism; for Nationalists, the historical association of the RUC with the old Unionist domination of Northern Ireland, and the fact that membership of the force was dominated by Protestants, made it symbolic of Unionist political domination. The chief attempt to resolve the problem has arisen out of the Patten Report (see Briefing 11.8). This has led to both symbolic and substantive changes: changes in name, and in the symbols of authority worn by officers; changes in accountability arrangements to make the force accountable to a new board with wide cross-community representation; and changes in employment practices designed to recruit larger numbers of Catholics. For many Unionists these have been a betrayal; for Nationalists they are too little, too late.

The British government's central obligation as manager of the peace process has proved critical for a reason we now examine: the aftermath of the Belfast Agreement has been immensely difficult.

## The development of the peace process

Setting up the new institutions in the wake of the Belfast Agreement was itself a protracted business. Elections to the Northern Ireland Assembly took place in June 1998, but the designation of new Ministers was not completed until November of the following year. Issues like those that traditionally concern government elsewhere in the United Kingdom rapidly emerged: for instance, the new (Sinn Féin) minister responsible for education began to reform the school system to introduce comprehensive schooling in the province. If we look back at Briefing 11.4 we will see that there have been substantial, long-lasting and important instances of policy innovation under devolved government. Two features are striking about the Northern Ireland entry in that briefing: how far innovation concerns 'normal' politics, to do with social policy issues, instead of the usual Northern Ireland 'headline' issues to do with security; and how a province historically notable for bigotry and discrimination now has the most comprehensive anti-discrimination regime in the whole of the UK.

Nevertheless, the institutions established out of the Belfast Agreement have proved fragile and unsta-

## Briefing                                    11.8

### REFORMING POLICING IN NORTHERN IRELAND: THE PATTEN REPORT OF 1999

The Patten Commission set out 175 proposals that would transform the RUC, both to attract more Catholic recruits and to create legitimacy for the new police force in the eyes of the Catholic community. The main proposals were a mixture of symbolic changes and more substantive changes in practices:

- The force to be renamed and neutral badges and symbols introduced
- Officers originally from the North and currently serving in the Gardaí or forces in Britain to be encouraged to join the new Northern Ireland Police Service
- Current full-time staff of 11,400 to be reduced to 7,500
- Three interrogation centres in Belfast, Derry and Armagh to be closed. Power to use plastic bullets will remain, but alternatives are to be researched
- Gaelic Athletic Association (in the Republic) to be asked to repeal rule preventing security force members in the North from joining its organization.
- A Police Board to replace the current police Authority and two of the 19 members could be Sinn Féin representatives.

➲ The Patten Commission (chaired by Chris Patten, former Conservative Cabinet minister, and European Commissioner) resulted from a commitment in the Belfast Agreement to produce reforms to the policing service in Northern Ireland. The Service has been one of the most difficult and contentious of institutions in the province. For much of the history of Northern Ireland the Service was identified with the Unionist majority. In recent years it has increasingly been caught between the two conflicting communities, but has experienced little success in attracting Catholic recruits. The Report of the Patten Commission tried to navigate a middle course between Nationalist and Unionist views; so far, it has failed to satisfy either.

ble. Failure to reach agreement on the decommissioning of IRA weapons led almost immediately to suspension of all the institutions of devolution and the reimposition of direct rule by the Secretary of State. Since then there have been a series of suspensions of the institutions, periodic threats to withdraw from the institutions by the Ulster Unionist Party, the party of the Chief Minister, and resignations by the Chief Minister himself. The process is immensely complicated both by the lack of trust between figures who were for three decades sworn enemies (such as Sinn Féin and Ulster Unionist members of the Assembly and Executive) and by personal rivalries within both Nationalism and Unionism, notably within the latter. But these short-term factors have only been important because of more fundamental difficulties, of which three are especially important.

*The fragmentation of Unionism.* Unionism is deeply divided along a variety of lines. There are two major Unionist Parties: the Ulster Unionist Party and the Democratic Unionist Party (DUP), the latter led by the Reverend Ian Paisley. While the DUP has periodically taken its allotted posts on the Executive it has from the very beginning been hostile to the Belfast Agreement and to a peace process which incorporates Sinn Féin into parliamentary politics. It still regards Sinn Féin as simply the political wing of Nationalist Republican terrorism. In turn, the Ulster Unionist Party is internally deeply divided between opponents and supporters of the new institutions, and fear of being 'outflanked' by the Democratic Unionists has made the leaders of Ulster Unionism intensely aware of anything that seems like a compromise with nationalism. Beyond the constitutional unionist parties there is a growing world of paramilitary unionism, in part overlapping with gangsterism.

*The popular weakness of consociationalism.* The Belfast Agreement was overwhelmingly supported in a referendum of the Northern Ireland electorate – though even then Catholics were more enthusiastic than Protestants (see Figure 11.2). But since then the popular tide has swung away from groups that favour the conciliatory politics of consociationalism. On the Nationalist side Sinn Féin, the most radical nationalist party, has gained at the expense of its main rival, the Social Democratic and Labour Party (SDLP). On the Unionist side, as we have seen, the big advance has been by the Democratic Unionists, root and branch opponents of the Belfast Agreement. In the communities, while large scale terrorist attacks have been rare, daily violence has

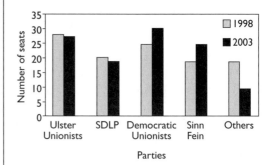

**Figure 11.3**    The rise of hard line parties in Northern Ireland, 1998–2003 (seats won in 1998 and 2003 Assembly elections)

➔ Two parties were central to the Good Friday Agreement, the Ulster Unionist Party (UUP) and the Social Democratic and Labour Party (SDLP). As a sign of this, they provided the first Joint First Ministers in the devolved government, David Trimble (UUP) and Seamus Mallon (SDLP). This reflected their established numerical dominance in Northern Ireland elections. The figure summarizes the decline of this dominating position. It reflects a decade of wider declining support for the major supporters of constitutional politics and the aims of the Good Friday Agreement. Note the advance of the Democratic Unionist Party, critics of the Good Friday Agreement, and the main rivals of Ulster Unionism, and the rise of Sinn Féin, the main rival to the SDLP for the non-Unionist vote. The 2005 general election confirmed this: Democratic Unionists won four extra seats, and Sinn Féin one new seat.

been widespread, especially in the form of vigilante punishment beatings and shootings (see Political Issues 11.1). Street confrontations over processions, parades and even routes walked by children to school have been numerous. There has been a sharp rise in the membership of Unionist paramilitary groups, though most of the resulting violence has been between Unionist groups, chiefly taking the form of rival criminals struggling for control of markets in illicit goods (such as drugs). While these struggles do not match in scale the old sectarian violence of the Province, they provide a poisonous atmosphere in which to try to build a consociational politics of compromise and power sharing.

*The weakness of the British Government.* The British government, as we have seen, is the key to the success of the peace process because it is the most important 'manager' of the process; it manages all

## POLITICAL ISSUES

### 11.1   NORTHERN IRELAND: THE PARA-MILITARY WARS

Following the Belfast Agreement of 1998 the 'Peace Process' was supposed to shape Northern Ireland politics. A big issue has been: just how much peace in reality is there in the province? The International Monitoring Group set up under the Belfast Agreement to oversee the Peace Process reported in May 2004 that in the preceding year murders had been running at the rate of nearly one a month – much lower than at the height of the Troubles, but only the most brutal sign of a wider atmosphere of violence and intimidation. Much of this violence is due to the continuing activity by paramilitary groups. On the Nationalist side, the Provisional IRA not only coerces many with 'punishment beatings' as a substitute for the rule of law, but is also engaged in a struggle with groups such as the Real IRA and the INLA (Irish National Liberation Army) who reject the Belfast Agreement. But the most brutal struggles have been between two 'Loyalist' groups, the Ulster Volunteer Force (UVF) and the Loyalist Volunteer Force (LVF). The former is the larger, allied to an even more shadowy organization, the Red Hand Commandos. The Loyalist Volunteer Force was created by a split within the Ulster Volunteer Force in 1996, over an unauthorized sectarian murder, which led the UVF to 'stand down' one its most notorious leaders, Billy Wright. Wright in turn was assassinated in the Maze Prison in 1997 by three members of the Irish National Liberation Army – a murder that itself continues to raise unanswered questions about the nature of security within the jail. But most Loyalist paramilitary violence has been self-inflicted, because since the original split in 1996 the two main groups (UVF and LVF) have traded assassinations and lesser violence with each other. Part of the violence has been fuelled by struggles for commercial competition, both legal and illegal. From the 1970s all paramilitary groups funded their operations from drinking clubs and from drug dealing. Competition for drug markets has been particularly intense since the 1990s.

The issues raised are:

- How real is 'peace' and how far is it only that high-profile terror has been succeeded by low-profile violence?
- How is this 'grassroots' sectarian violence reconcilable with popular support for a peace process?
- Why has there been apparently so much more internal strife within Unionism than within Nationalism?

the developments that were supposed to come from the Belfast Agreement. But the tangible resources at the command of the government are quite limited, especially once the institutions described above were brought into existence. It can threaten to suspend the institutions, and has actually issued the threat and put it into effect. But in many cases this merely coincides with the short-term calculations of the very parties that it is trying to influence. It can implement some key reforms, notably of the police

service, as we saw above, and it finds itself then caught between the widely different expectations of Nationalists and Unionists. Its success as a manager of reform therefore depends very heavily on the time and effort it invests in managing the process, and in the skill with which management is conducted. It has tended to address the first of these by bursts of negotiation involving participants at the very highest level, such as the British and Irish prime ministers. The best example of this is the intense sessions that

# DEBATING POLITICS

## 11.1   DEVOLUTION: THE ROAD TO RUIN OR THE SALVATION OF THE UNITED KINGDOM?

| Devolution begins the break-up of the United Kingdom | Devolution is a stable reform of an overcentralized political system |
| --- | --- |
| ■ The devolution settlement is unstable as shown by the lack of consensus about the existing arrangements for Wales.<br><br>■ The existing devolution is embedding distinctive political systems in the different countries of the United Kingdom.<br><br>■ Ireland has been the pace-setter in the break-up of Britain, and the history of the Belfast Agreement shows that there is no settled devolution in Northern Ireland.<br><br>■ Devolution awaits its first great test: the election of a separate nationalist party to office in Scotland or Wales. | ■ Devolution prevents the unbalanced and biased system that existed for much of the 1980s and 1990s.<br><br>■ The electoral system in the devolved governments in Wales and Scotland makes compromise between parties virtually certain; domination by a nationalist party is therefore unlikely.<br><br>■ Embedding distinctive political systems in the UK is far from a disaster: many successful states have this kind of variety.<br><br>■ The notion of a single, sovereign UK focused on Westminster is already an anachronism in a system of multi-tiered governance within the European Union. |

produced the Belfast Agreement itself, but there are obvious limits to this approach. The most obvious of all is that prime ministers are beset by numerous preoccupations and can only give short-term attention at a high level of intensity to Northern Ireland. This means that the quality of the daily management of the process, especially by the Secretary of State for Northern Ireland, is crucial. But every Secretary of State since the Belfast Agreement has been viewed with mistrust by either Nationalists or Republicans. One measure of the difficulty here is simply turnover: since 1998 there have been five different Secretaries of State; the aftermath of the 2005 general election produced yet another change.

In 1998 the Belfast Agreement was intended to begin establishing 'normal' politics in Northern Ireland. In other words, political argument would begin to concentrate on issues familiar in both the Republic of Ireland and mainland Britain: issues to do with economic management, the organization of education, the management of public transport and so on. The establishment of the Executive, and the appointment of ministers with portfolios responsible for the usual areas of government, began that process; but the periodic suspensions, and the fundamental problems with the peace process of which those suspensions are symptomatic, have so far greatly obstructed the emergence of this 'normal' politics. At the time of writing the results of the second Assembly elections of November 2003 (see Figure 11.3) have meant that the two most irreconcilable party groups (the Democratic Unionists and Sinn Féin) are respectively the biggest unionist and nationalist groups in the Assembly. Under the Belfast Agreement (which the Democratic Unionists in any case want renegotiated), the First Minister and the Deputy First Minister must come from these two, which at the moment is an almost inconceivable possibility.

## Devolution: towards multi-level governance

Of all the subjects in this book, the future development of devolution is most uncertain. As Debating Politics 11.1 shows, it can be interpreted as a way of stabilizing the pressures on the unity of the United Kingdom or, very differently, as a large first step to the break-up of Britain. Yet even after a few years, and even allowing for the special uncertainties in Northern Ireland, we can be sure that devolution is here to stay, and that it is producing large scale changes in the politics of the separate nations of the UK and in the Westminster system itself. Most of this chapter has been about what devolution is doing to the internal workings of these different systems. We can now stand back from the particular national effects and summarize what the changes are contributing to the system of government as a whole. It is immediately clear that they are reinforcing a development which recurs through the pages of this book: they are a further significant step in embedding multi-level governance in the United Kingdom.

- They are helping establish arrangements where the governing institutions are dispersed at different levels of the political system.
- Authority and control over policy has to be shared between those levels.
- A premium is placed on success in coordinating the different policy processes and policy outcomes at these different levels.
- The most important actors have to put a large amount of time and energy into calculating how different actors at different levels of the multi-level system will respond to their manoeuvres.
- Those same actors put a large amount of energy into managing their careers so as to exploit the opportunities opened up by multi-level governance.

We see here that the impact of devolution is part of a wider set of influences that are shaping the governing system. We have observed parallel effects arising from membership of the European Union: policy making becoming split between different institutions at different levels, in London, Brussels and other centres; resources invested in managing the coordination of policy at different levels;

## REVIEW

The most important themes of this chapter have been:

1 The diversity of the devolution experience in the different component parts of the United Kingdom;
2 The particularly highly conditional nature of the changes introduced in Northern Ireland following the 1998 Good Friday (Belfast) Agreement;
3 The nevertheless irreversible nature of the shift to a devolved system of government and the way this has created new governing networks in the different component parts of the UK;
4 The way the devolution changes represent a further large step in a wider process: the transformation of British government into a system of multi-level governance.

demands on political actors to develop new diplomatic and managerial skills effectively to operate in a world of multi-level government. Thus the government of the United Kingdom, once focused on a centralized set of institutions clustered in central London, is now being 'stretched' outwards and downwards.

## Further reading

The subject of this chapter has produced one classic study, though its argument is probably wrong: Nairn (1981); and for an extended afterthought, Nairn (2000). Bogdanor (1999) was a first attempt to discuss the devolution reforms; Hazell has since produced an annual 'audit', the latest being Hazell (2003). The single most important study of Northern Ireland is O'Leary and McGarry 1996 (at the time of writing a revised edition is promised).

**CHAPTER 12**

# The worlds of local and regional government: multi-level governance in action

## CONTENTS

## AIMS

The aims of this chapter are:

❖ To describe the evolution and present organization of local government

❖ To describe the institutional webs – local, regional and national – within which local authorities operate

❖ To show how the workings of this part of the system of government are a prime example of multi-level governance in action.

# Local government and multi-level governance

When we discussed how government and the state could be defined in Chapter 1, one feature stood out: any definition has to encompass the fact that states govern territory, an identifiable physical space. The spatial nature of government is at the heart of this chapter. As soon as we recognize the territorial face of the state we see also that government is about much more than nationally organized institutions (even institutions nationally devolved to Wales or Scotland). The local is intensely important, both as far as governing structures and processes are concerned, and as far as the wider political life of the community is concerned.

This recognition of the local also reveals another key aspect, not just of the character of 'local' government but of the wider system of government in Britain. Even the most superficial glance at the territorial world of government beyond national capitals such as London and Edinburgh soon shows that there is no simple separation in Britain between the 'local' and the 'national' or central. The territorial world, indeed, illustrates to perfection one of the key themes of this whole book: that Britain has a multi-level system of governance. This means more than the simple observation that there are

indeed multiple levels at which governing institutions operate; it means that that these levels interact in numerous, often complex ways. On occasion the relations are hierarchical: national government commands, or at least seeks to command. But more commonly, networks of governing institutions are joined in more subtle ways: they are obliged to cooperate with each other, to bargain with each other, and often to try manipulate each other. The government of a locality cannot therefore be viewed in isolation. Local governments are embedded in webs of relationships: with other local governments; with national institutions; with regional bodies. Even the most schematic outline of the local government system soon reveals this layered, multi-level character, as is shown by the simple example in Table 12.1.

That is why this chapter describes four linked aspects of the multi-level system:

- The local world of local government, which examines the institutions of local government itself
- The national world of local government, meaning the important institutions that give local government a nationally organized presence
- The regional world of local government, where we discuss the emergent attempts to create, in

**Table 12.1** Divided responsibilities: who keeps England clean?

| | Met/London authorities | | | | Shire/unitary authorities | | |
| --- | --- | --- | --- | --- | --- | --- | --- |
| | Joint authorities | Metropolitan counties | London boroughs | Greater London Authority | District Councils | Unitary Authorities | County Councils |
| Waste collection | | X | X | | X | X | |
| Waste disposal | X | | | X | | X | X |
| Environmental health | | X | X | X | X | X | |

*Sources*: Data from Local Government Association (2003b); Wilson and Game (2002: 117).

➲ Although the precise details of the division of labour in local government matters tremendously for citizens and for those who work in local government, for our purposes this matters less than the single overwhelming impression conveyed in this table: of a system which consists of an immensely complicated series of layers of responsibilities, some very hard to disentangle. (Notice the separation of waste collection and waste disposal in the 'two tier' authorities, for example.) This pattern imposes the biggest single problem for local government organization: coordinating the workings of these often overlapping layers of organizations.

England, a regional level of government that partly parallels the devolved worlds of government in Wales and Scotland described in Chapter 11

● Local government and the web of governance, which refers to the extent to which local authorities are embedded in networks of quasi-government agencies, often appointed, that span policy fields like health, education, land use planning and protection of the environment.

## The local world of local government

Local government cannot be understood without knowing the long trajectory of its development. Two linked features are important: for much of the twentieth century local government was in a long decline; but in recent decades there has been a substantial process of reinvention and revival. These two features provide the centrepieces of what follows.

### The historical decline of local government

The nineteenth century was a golden age of local government (see Image 12.1, p. 254). A succession of measures reformed the organization of the system, replacing often corrupt and amateurish local bodies with professionally organized authorities, and with councils elected on an increasingly wide franchise. Democratic government was pioneered at the local level. Two important Acts (in 1888 and 1894) established a structure of county and borough councils; an Act of 1899 did more or less the same job for London. Thus by the end of the nineteenth century a structure was established that mostly lasted into the 1970s (see Timeline 12.1).

The vitality and creativity of local government in the nineteenth century made it an important source of national political leadership for the new system of government that was being created in the world's first industrial society. For instance, the most important radical figure of the second half of the nineteenth century, Joseph Chamberlain, came to national prominence from a power base in local

government in Birmingham. Local government pioneered provision of public services in a period when national government offered little beyond traditional functions such as defence against external attack. By the start of the twentieth century virtually all the services that were later associated with the nationally organized welfare state were already being provided by many local authorities: school education, policing, public health, hospital care, road maintenance, water supply and sewage disposal, public transport, child health care and welfare, gas and electricity supplies, public libraries. Local government not only pioneered the welfare state: it was also highly entrepreneurial, running successful businesses to supply, for example, gas and electricity. 'Municipal socialism' – providing public services at a local level – was a common description of important local government bodies of the nineteenth century, such as Birmingham City Council, even when they were run, as was Birmingham, by businessmen who were horrified by socialism.

Much of this importance in service delivery remains. The one public service that visits virtually every British household weekly, for instance, is the local authority run, or contracted, refuse collection service. But over the course of the twentieth century the development of local government was essentially a history of declining importance and independence. There were a number of signs of this: money, functions, independence, stability.

*Money.* Money is often the key to power in government, and the ability to raise money is a particularly sensitive indicator of power. Over the long term local government became increasingly dependent on central government for its resources. Local authorities had historically raised money in two main ways: by charging for services; and by imposing local taxes, of which the most important were taxes on domestic property and on business property. Over the last century central government has increased its own taxation capacities, principally by drawing more and more workers into the net of income tax payers (see Chapter 21 for a longer account). By contrast, local property taxes have provided a poor yield. After the catastrophe of the poll tax (see Briefing 19.4, p. 431) that yield fell still further: as Figure 12.2 shows, at the end of the

## TIMELINE 12.1 LANDMARKS IN LOCAL GOVERNMENT HISTORY

**1834**
Poor Law Amendment Act: establishes Boards of Guardians as special purpose parish authorities to administer new workhouses.

**1835**
Municipal Corporations Act: establishes directly elected boroughs in place of self-selecting medieval corporations.

**1888**
Local Government Act: establishes 62 elected county councils, including London County Council, and 61 all-purpose county borough councils in England and Wales.

**1894**
Local Government Act: revives parish councils and establishes 535 urban district councils, 472 rural district councils and 270 non-county borough councils.

**1899**
London Government Act: establishes 28 metropolitan borough councils in London and the Corporation of London.

**1929**
Local Government Act: abolishes Poor Law Guardians (set up 1834) and transfers functions to local government.

**1963**
London Government Act: creates 32 London boroughs and a Greater London Council.

**1972**
Local Government Act: removes county borough councils, reduces number of county councils in England and Wales to 47, establishes six Metropolitan county councils and 36 metropolitan district councils, and replaces urban and rural district councils with 334 district councils.

**1980**
Local Government Planning and Land Act: establishes Compulsory Competitive Tendering and Urban Development Corporations.

**1982**
Local Government Finance Act: establishes Audit Commission (operational 1983).

**1984**
Rates Act: establishes system of rate-capping.

**1985**
Local Government Act: abolishes Greater London Council and the six metropolitan councils.

**1988**
Local Government Finance Act: replaces domestic rates with community charge (poll tax).

**1992**
Local Government Finance Act: replaces poll tax with council tax.

**1992**
Local Government Act: begins further structural change; by 1998 some 46 new unitary authorities created in England.

**1994**
Local Government (Wales) Act: creates 22 Unitary Authorities responsible for all services in the Principality.

**1998**
Government of Wales Act: sets up National Assembly for Wales, and establishes statutory Partnership Council between Welsh local government and the Assembly.

**1999**
Local Government Act: introduces 'Best Value' as regulator of competitive tendering

**1999**
Greater London Authority: establishes directly elected Mayor and Assembly for capital, effective 2000.

**2000**
Local Government Act 2000: gives local authorities power to promote social, economic and environment well being of their area, and duty to review and make new arrangements separating executive and scrutiny functions.

**2003**
Legislation provides for referendums on issue of creating elected assemblies in selected English regions.

**2004**
Proposal for elected regional assembly in north east defeated by margin of over 3 to 1.

*Source*: Adapted from Local Government Association (2003a).

**Figure 12.1** The decline of local financial independence: sources of revenue funding

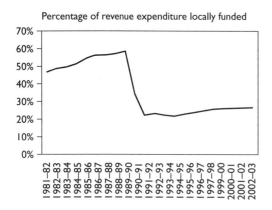

Percentage of revenue expenditure locally funded

**Figure 12.2** The decline of local financial independence: balance of funding

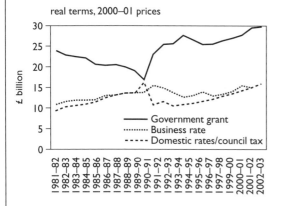

real terms, 2000–01 prices

£ billion

—— Government grant
·········· Business rate
- - - - Domestic rates/council tax

*Source*: Department for Local Government, Transport and the Regions (2002: 10).

➲ The figures here refer to only one part, but an important part, of spending: revenue expenditure, which excludes spending on capital projects. They also refer to England alone. But they make three points clear. First, as Figure 12.1 shows, central government grants have risen hugely in importance, providing a striking indicator of the declining independence of local government. Second, there has been a pronounced fall in the historically important tax on domestic property, and the sharpest fall coincides with the fiasco of the council tax at the end of the 1980s and beginning of the 1990s. Third, as Figure 12.2 shows, the overall outcome is a large fall in the contribution of locally raised resources.

1980s local government raised over half of its revenue spending from local sources; now the figure is barely more than a quarter.

The upshot is that grants from central government are the most important source of local government income. The three main sources of financing are:

● Central government grants, providing about roughly half of all revenue.
● A tax on business property, which yields about a quarter of revenue. The rate of this tax is, however, effectively set by central government.
● A locally imposed tax on domestic property – the so-called council tax – that raises just over one-fifth of revenue.

A small amount of money, covering the remainder, is also raised by charging for services at the point of consumption: for instance, parking meter or pay and display car park charges. But as the figures show, local government, once financially independent, now largely depends on central government for money.

*Functions.* Local government is still a major deliverer of services, but the range of services it truly controls has narrowed over the long term. In addition to losing a large part of its financial independence because it now depends on central government for most of its money, local government was also stripped in the course of the twentieth century of many of the functions it performed. For instance, local authorities lost most of their roles as providers of 'utilities' (services such as gas and electricity) as long ago as the 1940s. Likewise, the establishment of the National Health Service (NHS) in 1948 transferred ownership of local authority hospitals to the NHS and stripped local government of responsibilities for other health services. This loss of function has continued remorselessly. Until the 1980s local government was the dominant provider of public housing – so dominant that 'council housing' was the colloquial description of all publicly owned dwellings; but since the 1980s over 1.25 million local authority dwellings have been sold to sitting tenants under 'right to buy' policies of successive governments.

This has obviously greatly reduced the size of the housing stock administered by local government. In addition, the remaining estates are now gradually being taken from local government control and transferred to independent trusts, often controlled by tenants. The last large service that local government controlled – primary and secondary education – is today under threat: in the last couple of decades there has been a steady transfer of control over budgets, for example, direct to individual schools. Both the Labour and Conservative parties would like to strip more responsibility in education away from local government.

*Independence.* The freedom of local authorities to act independently has also been reduced, especially in the last couple of decades. This has happened in a number of ways. As the case of the Audit Commission (Briefing 12.1) shows, central government increasingly inspects how money is spent – not surprisingly, since it provides most of that money. One reason it increasingly provides the money is that it has also, over the long term, intervened to limit the taxing freedom of local government (for instance, by periodically putting ceilings, or threatening to put ceilings, on local property taxes). Central government has also tried to attach increasingly specific conditions to many of its grants, linking them to particular projects, to competitive schemes for which authorities have to 'bid', and by demanding co-financing from private sector sources.

*Stability.* The great late nineteenth-century reforms of local government lasted until well into the second half of the twentieth century. The map of local government in the early 1960s did not look very different from the map in 1900. Local government enjoyed stability and continuity. But look back at Timeline 12.1 for a moment, It has a striking feature: there is no entry for a major reform of the local government system between 1929 and 1963, when the government of London was reorganized. By contrast, the 40 years since then are littered with reorganizations. They range from major redrawing of the historic boundaries of local government (such as the reforms introduced by the Local government Act of 1972) to the local government consequences of the Labour Government's devolution reforms in

## Briefing 12.1

### THE RISE OF THE AUDIT COMMISSION AS A CONTROL AGENT

The audit of local government can be traced back to 1846, when the District Audit Service was first established. But the-nineteenth-century notion of audit focused on establishing that money had been spent in a properly authorized way; it took little notice of the efficiency and effectiveness of spending. This narrow conception of audit lasted into the twentieth century. A sea change occurred with the founding of the Audit Commission in 1983. The rise of the Audit Commission is marked by three features:

- The Commission is a regulatory arm of central government charged with the oversight of both local government and a range of other public bodies (see below).
- The Commission's functions range well beyond traditional audit, into a comprehensive responsibility to review the performance of local authorities.
- During the 1990s the Commission's responsibilities widened to encompass other locally active bodies. It now has audit responsibility for NHS Authorities and Hospital Trusts, and is part of the 'joint inspectorate' for social services with the Social Services Inspectorate.

*Source*: Based on information from www.audit-commission.gov.uk

➲ In Chapter 8 we saw that there has been a major expansion in the regulatory responsibilities and resources of the state in Britain in recent decades; the rise of the Audit Commission is a sign of the rise of this 'regulatory state' in local government.

Scotland and Wales. This is symptomatic of a great change in attitude: until the 1960s local government organization (and reorganization) was 'off limits' to central government, as it was considered a settled part of the constitution; since then, virtually every government, of whatever political persuasion, has felt free to impose reorganization, sometimes of a fundamental nature, and sometimes involving tinkering with the system.

## The reinvention of local government

All the changes summarized above amounted to the long-term decline of a particular 'model' of local government: the model that presumed that the individual local authority was a kind of miniature kingdom, able to fund its own activities, deliver the services that it chose to deliver, and deliver them without much interference from any outside agency. But the decline of this model has not extinguished the importance of local government; rather, it has led to its reinvention. One important aspect of that reinvention is examined in a later section of this chapter, when we look at the rise of the 'national world of local government': at the increasing extent to which nationally organized local government bodies are important in, for example, lobbying over policy. But there has also been a substantial process of reinvention at the local level itself. The result has reinforced the extent to which local authorities are embedded in 'multi-level governance': part of extended networks that stretch both upwards to regional and national level, and horizontally into partnerships with private sector organizations. This also anticipates a theme to which we will return later in the penultimate section of the chapter: the theme of local government and the web of governance.

The process of reinvention can be seen in four particularly important ways:

- The rise of the 'business-like' local authority
- The acquisition of new roles by local authorities
- The development of new Europe-focused lobbying activities
- The rise of local government as a centre of political innovation.

*The 'business-like' local authority.* The 'business-like' local authority is a phrase that summarizes important changes in the functioning and the culture of local government. This has involved local authorities working in much closer cooperation with the private sector, and modelling many of their internal practices on the private sector. One of the best established of the new business forms lies in the spread of *contracting out*.

**Image 12.1**
**The confident world of nineteenth-century local government**

Photo: Michael Moran

⮞ Manchester Town Hall (completed 1877) is one of the great icons of local civic pride in nineteenth-century Britain. Designed by Alfred Waterhouse after a national competition, it expressed the confidence of what was then the greatest industrial city in the world. The stylized design is medieval 'gothic' but that had a highly modern political purpose: it echoed the design of great civic buildings of independent city communities of medieval Europe and therefore emphasized Manchester's claims to a greatness independent of the capital in London. The statue in the foreground is a further expression of local pride and independence. It is a figure of John Bright, one of the leading radicals of the nineteenth century, and one strongly identified with the economic interests of Manchester at a time when it was the greatest cotton manufacturing city on earth.

Throughout the 1980s the then Conservative governments widened the range of *compulsory competitive tendering*, in effect obliging local authorities to put a range of services (from cleaning to waste disposal) out to open tender, thus inviting bids by private firms. The effect of this reform was muted in a variety of ways: many of the contracts were awarded 'in-house' to existing council departments; after 1997 Labour fine tuned competitive tendering to make it depend less on price competition and to remove the compulsory component. Nevertheless, the total impact has been great, even when tenders have been awarded in-house. There is in principle nothing novel about contracting with the private sector for goods and services; it is something entirely traditional in local government. The novelty lies partly in the way the pressure of competitive tendering obliges councils to organize their own departments so as to allow effective competition with potential private sector providers. It also lies in something subtler: in the way it turns the state at the level of the local authority into a 'contracting state'. In other words, a prime responsibility of elected bodies becomes the awarding and monitoring of contracts for service delivery. Only a small number of authorities (principally under Conservative Party control) have attempted to realize the full form of the 'contracting local authority', which would involve awarding and monitoring contracts to private firms for all major services. Nevertheless, the spread of contracting-out has involved a historic reinvention: the local authority becomes responsible for ensuring the delivery of services, and monitoring delivery quality, rather than doing the job directly. There is a weekly example of this: the local authority is responsible for the collection of household waste, but will often have contracted the job to a private firm. (Try looking at the name on the refuse disposal wagon that visits your street.) The shift to contracting is not only a matter of involving commercial firms: many services are contracted to non-profit making bodies, such as charities (a common arrangement in the case of many social services, such as care for the elderly, for which local authorities are responsible).

This 'turn' to business styles and practices has taken a particularly important form in local authorities that have troubled local economies. Here, there has been a spread of public–private partnerships, often with the aim of regenerating declining local economies and modernizing infrastructure, including public transport. In some instances this has involved formally organized large scale joint ventures with business, especially to fund and

## Briefing 12.2

### REINVENTING PUBLIC TRANSPORT AT LOCAL LEVEL: THE CASE OF THE MANCHESTER TRAM

Metrolink is the formal name given to what is colloquially called the Manchester tram system. Technically not a tram but a form of light rail network, the first part of the Manchester system came into operation in 1992. It pioneered a new kind of light rail transport, and has been followed by the development of 'supertram' networks in many other parts of the country, notably Sheffield and the West Midlands. But the pioneering aspect of Metrolink goes beyond tram technology; it also pioneered a way of uniting the public and the private sectors to build and manage large, expensive public infrastructure projects. The infrastructure and assets (such as the tram network itself and the trams) are owned by the Greater Manchester Transport Executive, itself a consortium formed out of the local authorities in the area covered by the tram network. The first phase of the tram system was built, and operated, from 1992 to 1997 by Manchester Metro Limited, a private consortium formed from a mix of large construction companies, builders of trams, and the Greater Manchester Transport Executive. Later phases of the tram network have been built and operated by still more private consortia.

Technologically the 'tram' systems pioneered in Manchester are 'hybrids' – a cross between traditional tram and rail. It is therefore fitting that they are also owned and run by hybrids – a cross between private and public organizations.

⮕ The case of the Manchester trams illustrates a whole series of themes from this section of the chapter: local government as a promoter of technological innovation, and innovation in public service provision; local government as a partner in investment with the private sector; and local government as the contractor in service delivery.

deliver big public investment projects. In the last couple of decades, for instance, many large English cities have built ambitious new tram networks in joint ventures with private operators, while operation of the London Underground is now a public–private partnership (though one only reluctantly accepted by London's elected mayor). Briefing 12.2 illustrates a particularly important example of these ventures.

Finally, the rise of the business-like local authority has begun to affect the internal organization of authorities, especially the role of democratically elected representatives. The dominant form of organization has hitherto involved committees of elected councillors covering the main functional responsibilities of local government. The Local Government Act 2000 was based on the premise that this system was cumbersome and outdated, poorly adapted to the need for swift and decisive policy making. It offered local government a choice: to move to a system of popularly elected mayors, or to a 'cabinet' system with an executive leader. As we will see in a moment the first option has led to some important innovations, but most local authorities have opted for the cabinet with an executive leader – a kind of 'chair of the board' model in part inspired by the organization of private firms.

*The acquisition of new roles.*   Local government lost many of its important historic functions over the course of the twentieth century, especially in the second half; but the reinvention of local government has involved the discovery of new roles for local authorities. The most important of these we have already touched on: the role of local government in the process of local economic development (a role that is now officially enjoined on local authorities in the Local Government Act 2000). The assumption of these new roles in economic development and regeneration was a response both to the problems of local economies and to the changed structure of the economy. Many local communities suffered acutely from the great problems that the British economy experienced in the 1970s and 1980s (see Chapter 3). This was especially true of the areas that had been at the heart of the old Industrial Revolution, such as South Wales and the north east of England, where the industries of coalmining, shipbuilding and steel production had been important. In these districts the British economic crisis produced the collapse of whole local economies, very high rates of unemployment, and

often desperate poverty. Faced with these problems local authorities were forced into attempts at economic innovation. The problems were compounded by the wider structure of the economy, notably by the importance of mobile multinational companies to local employment. Thus local government was compelled to pursue an active policy of trying to attract, and then retain, branches of multinationals.

Some of the novel consequences of this activist role in trying to promote local economic development include: the leading position taken by local authorities in helping to raise finance for large scale projects designed to improve local public services, such as the transport case profiled in Briefing 12.2; partnerships with private developers to bring new commercial and residential developments to inner city areas; and partnerships with local business to try to create new sources of employment in depressed districts, such as that profiled in Briefing 12.3.

*The rise of EU lobbying.*   These innovations in turn have stimulated the development of the local authority as a lobbyist, notably in lobbying for resources from central government and from the European Union. When in Chapter 9 we discussed lobbying in British politics we focused in the main on the lobbying activities of the private sector, but public bodies are also important lobbyists. Local government has always lobbied to try to influence other levels of government, especially central government. As we shall see later, in our discussion of the 'national world of local government' the many well organized national associations representing local authorities and those who work in local government have this kind of lobbying as one of their jobs. In recent years we have also seen the individual local authority, or the individual local authority in a consortium with a number of others, become an increasingly committed lobbyist. Probably the most important object of this lobbying is the European Union, especially the Commission in Brussels. A large number of local authorities have now appointed staff whose sole function is liaison with the European Union (see Documenting Politics 12.1); many have arrangements for direct representation in Brussels, either through their own employees or by using one of

# Briefing    12.3

## NEW ROLES IN ECONOMIC DEVELOPMENT FOR LOCAL GOVERNMENT: THE CASE OF CLEETHORPES

Cleethorpes is a small seaside resort on the Lincolnshire coast. In common with many other traditional resorts it has been hard hit by the rise of mass package tourism to sunnier parts of Europe. Yet tourism is integral to both the economic well being of the town and to the wider area: in the local government area of which Cleethorpes is part, tourism was estimated in 2002 to support 4,500 jobs. The efforts of the local council (North East Lincolnshire Council) illustrate both the new active roles in promoting economic development taken on by local government, and the way local authorities have to work with an alphabet soup of local, national and even supranational organizations – the living embodiment of the networks of governance which we will explore more analytically later in the chapter.

The organizations include:

● The Yorkshire Tourist Board, of which the Council is a constituent member
● Yorkshire Forward, the Regional Development Agency, which has to fit any strategy to revive Cleethorpes into its wider responsibility for regional development local service
● The Department for Culture, Media and Sport, because the efforts to promote Cleethorpes are part of the Council's wider strategy for Cultural Regeneration in north east Lincolnshire
● The Commission of the European Union, which is a source of funding (see below) to invest in improved tourism facilities
● Voluntary bodies, such as hoteliers' associations, whose members are targeted in attempts to improve the quality of local facilities.

The practical impact includes the following: the Council negotiated a grant of £140,000 from the EU to invest in improved tourism facilities and a grant of £290,000 from Yorkshire Forward to regenerate the Cleethorpes sea front. The 'on the ground' benefits include paying up to £6,000 towards the costs of new brochures for individual boarding houses, in return for investment in improved facilities, such as renovated bedrooms. The degree of EU intervention is striking: its grants even prescribe the size of double beds in guest rooms.

*Sources*: Information from North East Lincolnshire Council (2002); Wainwright (2003).

⮕  The role of local authorities in promoting local economic development is often far from glamorous, as this briefing shows. It involves trying to put together packages from a disparate range of organizations, in an institutional chain stretching from the immediate locality to Brussels. The Cleethorpes story, however, is only a sample; it is repeated, not only in numerous tourist resorts, but in virtually every local authority in Britain.

the numerous professional lobbying firms that have grown up around the institutions of the European Union; and many have formed partnerships with like-minded local governments in other EU regions. The single most important reason for this development is that the Union, especially the Commission, is an important source of money, especially money for the kind of large scale investment in local public services – buildings, roads, public transport systems – which have been important in the attempts to regenerate local economies. (Look back at Image 6.2 for a significant practical example.)

In summary, in the last quarter of a century local government, faced with the decline of many of its historically established functions, has undergone a substantial reinvention. This has involved:

## DOCUMENTING POLITICS 12.1

## REINVENTING LOCAL GOVERNMENT AT EUROPEAN LEVEL

Virtually every local authority in the UK of any size now tries to have an organized lobbying presence in Brussels. The biggest have their own separately organized offices: the Greater London Authority, for example, has established 'London House' in Brussels. But most authorities are too tiny to run a full-time operation, and rely heavily for EU representation on the Local Government International Bureau. This is how the LGIB describes its operations:

'The Local Government International Bureau, often simply known as the LGIB, acts principally as the European and international arm of the Local Government Association for England and Wales (LGA). We also represent the Northern Ireland Local Government Association. We promote the Associations' interests to policy makers in the EU and international organizations, and support councillors appointed to the [EU] Committee of the Regions and other bodies. We provide a wide range of services for local authorities, updating them on European and international issues ... assisting them in their international links and partnerships, and drawing attention to interesting practice from other countries ... We act as the all-UK partner of the Council of European Municipalities and Regions, a pan-European association of national local authorities ... LGIB's services are delivered by 21 staff in London ... and a Brussels office, where we have 3 staff.'

➲ It has long been commonplace to talk about a national world of local government (see Briefing 12.6), but the super-ficially parochial world of local government increasingly has a more international (and especially a 'European World') aspect, centred on the EU (see also Briefing 12.3).

*Source*: www.lgib.gov.uk

- Closer, more formally organized partnerships with the business community
- Shifting from direct delivery of services to contracting out those services
- A growing role in the development of local economies
- And, partly as a result of local economic initiatives, a growing involvement with the institutions and rules of the European Union.

*Promoting political innovation.* Historically local government was one of the most innovative parts of the British system of government. In the nineteenth century it was in the vanguard of democratic reforms. It was also a leader in management practices. Many ideas to which central government only came much later – for instance, the importance of

employing senior officers with specialized skills in areas such as engineering – were pioneered by local authorities. And as we saw above, the intervention-ist central state of the twentieth century was pre-figured in the 'gas and water socialism' of local government in the nineteenth century.

In recent years local government has rediscovered this capacity for innovation: indeed, this role was expressly recognized in the Local Government Act of 2000. Many large local authorities – Birmingham is a good example – have reorganized their modes of service delivery to encourage more effective local communication and responsiveness: for instance, by decentralizing their delivery operations so that offices in services such as housing are much nearer the point of delivery. Local government has also been at the forefront of attempts to combat a problem that we will discuss at greater length in Chapter 17: low electoral turnout. This pioneering role is not surprising. Turnout in local elections has been low, even by the standards of elections to the devolved assemblies and the most recent figures for Westminster elections. A variety of procedural innovations has been experimented with, all designed to make the actual act of voting easier, in the hope that this will encourage electors to vote. Innovations such as electronic voting through PC terminals and mobile text messaging have already been piloted in selected local authorities (see Briefing 12.4 for more details).

A potentially even more important innovation is the creation of elected mayors in selected local authorities, an option in the Local Government Act 2000. Only a few local authorities have even contemplated this innovation, and of these only a minority has actually proceeded with the innovation. The measure requires approval in a local referendum, and nearly two-thirds of the 30 authorities where it has been put to the vote turned the idea down. What is more, in those authorities where it has been instituted the impact of an elected mayor is restricted by the continuing presence of longer established forces. For instance, mayors formally cannot set a budget without the support of a majority of elected authority members, which in practice often means the support of the dominant political party. However, even here, the fine detail of the procedures allows a shrewd mayor to create more freedom of manoeuvre than the letter of the rules would imply.

The introduction of elected mayors – in a dozen authorities so far – does show how this idea can change the balance of political forces, and in turn produce policy innovations which are hard to push through in national government. The most spectacular illustration is provided in London. The first elected mayor, Ken Livingstone, ran on an independent ticket having failed to secure the nomination of the Labour Party, of which he was a long-serving member. He was also a Labour member of the Westminster Parliament. Mr Livingstone was able to use the mayor's office, and the publicity opportunities which it creates, to build a political following in London independent of his

## Briefing                                    12.4

### LOCAL GOVERNMENT AS A LABORATORY OF INNOVATION: TRIALLING ELECTRONIC VOTING

As we shall see in Chapter 17, the apparent fall in turnout in national elections, notably in the 2001 general election, led to widespread official concern, and an attempt to experiment with new forms of voting in an attempt to raise turnout. It was to local government that the responsible official body, the Electoral Commission, turned to conduct these experiments. In the local government elections of May 2003 the Electoral Commission launched the largest ever trial of electronic voting in Europe. Over 1.5 million voters in 18 council areas were covered. The methods trialled included:

- Use of text messaging via mobile phones to vote
- Internet voting via voter-owned PCs
- Internet voting via specially constructed High Street kiosks
- Voting via digital televisions.

The effectiveness of these methods is discussed further in Chapter 17.

*Source*: Information from www.electoralcommission.org.uk

➲ In the nineteenth century local government was the test bed for the great political innovation of the time: widening the franchise to allow all adults to vote. In the twenty-first century it is the centre of attempts to use the most advanced technology to combat perceived decline in electoral turnout.

former party, in the process administering a number of embarrassing blows to Labour (not least the dismal performance of the official Labour candidate in the first mayoralty election). The new political constellation in London has led to a major policy innovation – the introduction of congestion charging as a way of managing traffic – which no other organized level of government in Britain has been able to introduce (see Briefing 12.5). So spectacular was Mr Livingstone's political and policy success that in 2003 the Labour party, facing the prospect

# Briefing                                                                12.5

## ELECTED MAYORS AND POLICY INNOVATION: CONGESTION CHARGING IN LONDON

Managing traffic congestion is one of the most intractable problems facing government. In May 2003 the new Greater London Authority, under the leadership of Mayor Ken Livingstone, introduced a major and highly successful innovation: the introduction of a special charge on cars entering a central 'congestion' zone in the capital. The scheme is now acknowledged to be a highly successful policy innovation. Why was London able to innovate when central government – superficially much more powerful – could not bring itself to introduce any comparable systems of charging? The answer lies in the new political system created by the reforms of London government involving a directly elected mayor and an elected London-wide Greater London Authority.

- The leading runners for the office of Mayor were political outsiders. The most spectacular outsider was the eventual electoral victor in 2000, Ken Livingstone. A maverick backbench Labour MP, Livingstone reacted to the blocking of his attempt to secure the Labour party candidature by running as an independent. His official Labour opponent, Frank Dobson, was left in third place behind Livingstone and Steven Norris, the Conservative Candidate.
- The ability of maverick candidates to run so prominently reflected the rise of a distinctive style of campaigning, where the organizational resources of traditional party machines could be counterbalanced by shrewd use of the mass media to generate publicity.
- An innovative electoral system also had distinctive effects. In place of the 'first past the post' system used in Westminster and most local government elections hitherto (described in Chapter 17), the Mayor was elected by the Supplementary Vote electoral system. This allows voters to rank two candidates in order of preference. This electoral system thus helps free voters from the crude choice between totally supporting, or totally abandoning, one party.
- Innovation was not confined to the mayoral election. A London Assembly elected at the same time was chosen by the Additional Member system: voters had two votes, one for a 'constituency' representative and one for a party list. The party list vote was used – as in the case of the devolved assemblies in Wales and Scotland – to correct disproportionality: the Liberal Democrats and the Greens won no 'constituencies' but were allocated 4 and 3 seats each respectively to reflect their share of the list vote. Thus the electoral system again widened the range of representation beyond the two traditionally dominant parties.
- Because politics is so focused on individual personalities, there are great incentives for leading politicians to promote policy innovations in the hope of being associated in the voters' minds with successes. This gave a huge incentive to Livingstone to risk introducing congestion charges in 2003.

➲ Congestion charges are not just a story about London. They show how new forms of organization at local level are creating opportunities for policy innovations too risky for Westminster government to contemplate.

of humiliation in the 2004 mayoral election, was obliged to readmit him on his own terms and adopt him as its official candidate for the mayoralty. He duly won again, running on a platform often highly critical of the Blair government, in 2004.

The case of London is always special because of the scale and prominence of the capital, but established parties have been similarly undermined in the other authorities where there have been mayoral elections. Half the contests so far have been won by independents or by rebels from the established parties, such as Livingstone. A variety of eccentrics and political outsiders have defeated candidates from the official parties, including in one case the mascot of the local football team (a figure dressed in a monkey suit). But as the case of congestion charging shows, behind the gimmicks lies something serious: a change in the balance of political forces at local level which is weakening the old party machines and creating space for important policy innovations.

The impact of the innovation of elected local mayors is due to a variety of factors, some special to local government, and some to do with the weakening relationship between voters and parties. The latter is examined in Chapter 17. As far as local government is concerned, the innovation of the elected mayor happened in local political systems where voter interest in traditional elections was very low. And while in Westminster elections there has been a long history of voters turning out governments, many local authorities have been dominated by a single party for decades (and even generations in a few instances). 'Mavericks' running for office therefore offer voters a way of rejecting the dominant party in their locality. That this reflects a more deep-seated rejection of the established political parties at local level seems to be suggested by the wider history of independent candidates in local government elections. Throughout the twentieth century independent candidates for council elections without a formal party affiliation declined in importance. Councils became increasingly dominated by one of the two major parties, with occasional incursions by the Liberal Democrats. But independents are once again on the rise, and have been accompanied by the rise of a wide range of minority parties, such as the Greens.

## The national world of local government

It is natural to identify local government with the local, but a striking and increasingly important feature is the extent to which local government has an important national presence. Look at Briefing 12.6 and you will begin to get some sense of this presence, and also an inkling both of why it exists, and why it is becoming more important.

Local government for long had national organizations (for instance, associations representing county and district councils), but the scale and coverage of national organization has grown greatly. Briefing 12.6 encapsulates three forces that are driving this creation of a nationally organized world.

### The rise of local government as a nationally organized lobby

Earlier in the chapter we documented an important historical change in local authority finance: the rise of central government as by far the single most important source of money for local authorities. One obvious effect of this development was to 'nationalize' issues of local authority finance. The financial health of an individual local authority no longer depended on how well it husbanded its own local resources, but on how well groups of local authorities did in a complex bargaining game with central government. Different groups of local authorities have different interests in this game, but all have a common interest in ensuring that in bargaining with central government the voices of local government are clearly heard. This increasingly pressing need helps explain the comparatively recent creation (1997) of the single most important national organization, the Local Government Association (LGA), out of an amalgamation of three separate bodies: the Associations of County Councils, of District Councils, and of Metropolitan Authorities. The LGA is not only the national voice of local government; it is also a significant provider of research and consultancy services to the organizations in its membership. This process of 'nationalizing' local government has not just been the result of initiatives from local level; it has been encouraged by central government, which has an interest in bargaining with a single nationally organized representative association.

### Professionalism in local government

One of the striking features of local government is the extent to which it is 'professionalized'. At the top of the official hierarchy in the Westminster system are 'generalist' civil servants offering no particular specialized professional skills. But the dominant tradition in local government has given the most prominent roles to chief officers with specialized professional qualifications: sanitary and highway engineers, chartered accountants, public health inspectors, social workers. The professional organizations of these groups of workers transcend the boundaries of individual authorities. The national

# Briefing

## THE NATIONAL WORLD OF LOCAL GOVERNMENT: SOME IMPORTANT ASSOCIATIONS

| Association | Membership | Main functions |
| --- | --- | --- |
| Local Government Association | Over 500 organizations, principally local authorities, but also including authorities responsible for fire, transport and regulation of National Parks. | Leading voice of local government in all public debates, including negotiations over resources and policy with central government, and major provider of information and lobbying services for local authorities. |
| Society of Local Authority Chief Executives and Managers (SOLACE) | Senior strategic managers working in the public sector. | Represents the views of senior managers in policy debates and provides training and consultancy services. |
| Society of Personnel Officers in Local Government (SOCPO) | Senior personnel professionals in local government and in fire, police and probation services. | Lobby to influence public policy; provides a forum for discussion of personnel function between members. |
| Society of Procurement Officers in Local Government (SOPO) | Over 1,300 members concerned with the procurement function at local government level. | Lobby to make members voice heard in debates, promote better carrying out of the procurement function. |
| Employers' Organization for Local Government | Main nationally organized local government employers groups. | Provides voice for local government employers and provides research and advice services to employers. |

⮕ Briefing 12.6 is only a sample of the alphabet soup of nationally organized associations for local government. It nevertheless shows how dense is the national network for local government, and to what extent institutional resources are invested in organizing local authorities as a nationally significant lobby.

professional bodies provide a natural way in which specialized policy issues are 'nationalized': the professions provided forums where issues can be discussed, standards worked out, and the interests of the professional groups represented in both central and local government. A good example of this is provided in Briefing 12.6 by the case of SOCPO, the Society of Personnel Officers in Local Government. This looks highly esoteric, but it goes to the heart of local government. The personnel function – the recruitment, training and management of people – is increasingly important in all organizations, and with

its rising importance has gone the rising importance of the trained professional personnel officer. The example of SOPO (Society of Procurement Officers in Local Government) is another apparently esoteric example of the same process at work but, far from being a backwater, the procurement function is vital in local government, because as a major deliverer of public services, local government is also a large-scale purchaser of goods and services from the private sector. The 'procurement function' thus raises big issues about the most efficient way to buy, and issues to do with professional and ethical standards among a group of professionals who have the authority to spend large sums of public money. SOPO provides both a lobbying voice for procurement professionals nationally, and a series of meeting places where the issues facing procurement officers can be debated.

These specialized cases are samples from a wider world of national professional organization in local government, covering the important occupations of social work, housing officers, accountants and highway engineers, among others. They form a dense, often overlapping series of networks linking the local, the regional and the national.

## Local authorities as employers

Over two million people work in local government, far more than are employed by the Westminster civil service (about 500,000) or by the devolved administrations in Scotland and Wales. The working conditions of these employees – their pay, hours and so on – are only marginally locally determined. Working conditions are mostly the result of national negotiations. On the side of workers, nationally organized unions representing local government employees are among the best organized group of British unions, and are a major part of the 'national world of local government'. This national union organization has been an important stimulus to the national organization of local authorities as employees (something reflected in the last example provided in Briefing 12.6). Another important stimulus has come from central government itself, on two grounds. As it is the chief financier of local government – which means the chief funder of pay, easily the biggest item in local authority spending – it naturally tries to intervene to shape the outcome of negotiations. In addition, pay and conditions obviously bear on the issue of the efficiency with which local government works so, as central government has become increasingly concerned with more efficient public sector organization, it has tried to shape pay negotiations to produce efficiencies. In some cases, settling pay has been so difficult that central government has tried to take it out of collective bargaining altogether,

handing responsibility to independent review bodies to make recommendations (a solution, for instance, to the troublesome question of the pay of teachers).

This does not diminish the importance of national local authority organization, however, for the local authority employers are still major actors in the negotiations: in submissions to the pay review body, and in arguments with central government about the precise method of funding pay awards. Even where local authorities are nominally independent negotiators, central government in Westminster often intervenes to transform the process into a national one. This was the case, for instance, with the long firefighters' dispute that lasted from 2002 to 2004, the first in the fire service for over a quarter of a century. Although a consortium of local authorities nominally negotiated for the employers, central government intervened both publicly and privately in the bargaining. It did this in part because it knew that the level of settlement would be part funded from central resources, but its intervention also reflected a determination to use the pay negotiations to introduce new, cost saving working practices into the service.

The national organization of local authorities as employers is a particularly striking instance of the 'national world of local government'. Although the issues involved are vital to the daily workings of each local authority, they are almost all debated and decided through national level institutions. And in negotiations about pay and conditions the nationally organized world of the local authority is matched by the continuous intervention of national, central government itself and nationally organized trade unions. This is one particularly important area, in other words, where we just would not understand local government if we tried to make sense of it only at the level of the individual local authority.

The national world of local government is nothing new, but its rising importance reflects three themes that are central to this chapter. The first is what we earlier called the 'reinvention of local government': the extent to which local authorities realized that they had to carve out new roles by various forms of collective organization. The

**POLITICAL ISSUES**

## 12.1    REGIONAL GOVERNMENT IN ENGLAND

The creation of devolved governments in Scotland, Wales and (until suspended) Northern Ireland has highlighted a key feature of governing arrangements in England: it remains the one part of the United Kingdom where the old Westminster-style system of extreme formal centralization on London still persists. Some local elites have argued that 'devolution-style' reform is now needed in England. As we see in this chapter, a kind of prototype for regional government has already been created across Greater London. Shadow regional assemblies, though unelected and with no power, also exist across the English regions. The Labour Government published a White Paper in 2002 outlining enhanced proposed powers. It also intended to hold referenda in three regions in 2004 on the question of whether to create elected regional assemblies to exercise these enhanced powers: the North West, Yorkshire and Humberside, and the North East. In July 2004 it published a draft bill outlining the proposed powers of the Assemblies, principally focused on roles in economic development and environmental control. But at the same time it announced that referendums in the North West and Yorkshire and Humberside would be cancelled. It had been intended to ballot by postal vote alone, and the reason given for cancellation was that there was concern about the postal voting system following the local and European elections of June 2004. (For more details, see Briefing 13.2, p. 285). However, the postal referendum was held in the North East on the grounds that there was strong support for all-postal voting in the region, though the basis for this assertion was not clear. In the event, the turnout was 48 per cent and the proposal was defeated, 78 per cent to 22 per cent.

The case raises the following issues:

- The true extent of the demand for a new tier of devolved government in England. The reliance on postal balloting was itself due to lack of confidence that there was public interest in the issue, and the fear that turnout in a referendum would be embarrassingly low. The cancellation even of the postal ballots in two of the selected regions reflected this continuing lack of confidence in public interest.
- The decision to ballot the North East reflects both a strength and weakness in the argument for devolved regional government in England. Whatever the limits of Scotland, Wales and Ireland as governing systems, it is undoubtedly the case that in all three populations there is a powerful and distinct sense of identity. Nothing like a corresponding sense of regional identity exists in the English regions, with the possible exception of the North East.
- If elected Assemblies with significant powers are introduced it will strengthen one feature which is stressed in this chapter: the development of multi-level systems of governance. But it will also require extensive consequential changes to manage multi-level governance in England, including, probably, the abolition of at least one existing level of local government.

second is the extent to which local government in Britain has to be considered within the framework of multi-level governance, for it is in the nationally organized worlds – for example, over pay negotiations – that some of the most complicated strategic games are played between the different levels. There is, for instance, now usually an annual row over the funding of a pay award for some group of local authority workers. This row is invariably part of the manoeuvring between local and central government over exactly how the award is to be funded. Finally, the numerous overlapping national networks sketched here – lobbying organizations, professional institutions, employers' bodies – anticipates a theme we will encounter later: the extent to which the world of local government is, precisely, a world of networks of organizations which have to cooperate with each other. But before we turn to this theme, we will see that to the national world of local government we have to now add an increasingly important regional world.

## The regional world of local government

We instinctively identify local government with local authorities such as county and district councils, but there is another face of local government, the regional, and it is becoming increasingly important, especially in England (see Political Issues 12.1). Local government has long had a regional face. The birth of the welfare state, for example, created a 'National' Health Service in which the building blocks of the national system were actually regional organizations. Likewise, both before and after water privatization the provision of this absolutely vital good has been organized partly along regional lines. This regional 'dimension' is an important contribution to what later in the chapter we will be describing as the pattern of *governance* at local level: in short, it makes policy decision and delivery at local level heavily dependent on coordinating networks of organizations, including those organized at the regional level.

Since 1997 the issue of the regional organization of government has become more pressing still, as a consequence of the devolved institutions introduced by the Labour government into Wales and Scotland (measures that were described in Chapter 11). The case for devolution rested in part on the importance of the distinctive identity of Wales and of Scotland, and partly on the argument that a decentralized system of government would be more effective and more democratically responsive than the hitherto dominant Westminster system. But these two arguments cannot be limited to the case for national

devolution. If they are right, they also amount to a case for regional devolution in England. Some parts of England – such as the north east – claim a distinct sense of regional identity, and without some form of regional devolution England, unlike Scotland and Wales, is left under the centralized Westminster system.

Following the introduction of devolved government, therefore, there has been a slow inching in the direction of regionally devolved government in England. The Labour government in 1997 inherited a system of regional offices, in effect 'outposts' of the Whitehall executive, charged with trying to manage issues at the regional level that cut across both the responsibilities of separate Whitehall departments, and the limited territorial boundaries of elected local authorities. There have been persistent attempts since the return of Labour in 1997 to try to augment the role and the visibility of these offices, and for the moment this has resulted in the existence of three kinds of regional institution.

- Government Regional Offices, originally established in 1994, charged with implementing the regional aspects of a wide range of central government policies, stretching from advisory (providing business support) to disbursing public grants
- Regional Development Agencies, established in 1999, appointed and controlled from the centre, and charged with preparing an economic strategy for their regions
- Regional Chambers (alternatively called Regional Assemblies), made up largely of local authority elected representatives, whose only formal function is to comment on the economic development strategy produced by the Regional Development Agencies.

What is most obvious about this regional structure is the extent to which the two arms that have any resources and 'clout' – the government offices and the Regional Development Agencies – are basically part of the field administration of central Westminster government. In 2003, however, the government edged further down the road of

# Briefing

## MULTI-LEVEL GOVERNANCE IN ACTION: THE CASE OF THE HUMBLE WHEELIE BIN

Virtually every British reader of this book makes regular journeys with the contents of the kitchen waste bin to the household refuse bin, typically a 'wheelie bin'. That bin in turn is usually emptied weekly. We never think of the institutional system that disposes of our household waste, but the reality is that behind this mundane service lies a classic example of the complex, multi-layered reality of multi-level governance:

- Responsibility for the weekly collection of household waste is the responsibility of the *district council*.
- Under the central government obligation to open household waste collection to competitive tendering, some district councils will have introduced a private actor – *a commercial firm* – into the process by awarding it the contract to collect waste. In this case the district authority's responsibility extends to awarding and monitoring the performance of the contracted firm.
- The waste has to be disposed of. Responsibility for the provision of waste disposal sites lies with the *county council*. Thus so far three sets of institutions – *district councils, private contractors* and *county councils* – are involved in disposing of our household waste.
- The county council in turn may contract responsibility for the management of waste sites to private firms: if you turn up at your local authority 'refuse amenity site' – the euphemism for the rubbish tip – you will almost certainly find it managed by a private firm.
- But the county council cannot simply decide arbitrarily to locate a waste disposal site where it chooses. *The Environment Agency* – central government's main agency for regulating protection of the natural environment – licenses waste disposal sites.
- In turn, the Agency cannot simply decide to locate a new site at its whim. Any proposal for a new site will enmesh all the parties in planning regulations, widening further the range of public and private actors. The location of rubbish tips provides some of the most contentious land use planning cases.
- The Agency's system of licensing in turn involves implementing a wide range of regulations governing what waste can be tipped, and what must be recycled. These regulations in turn are the result of entanglement with yet another layer of government: with the negotiations that produce *European Union* Directives governing waste disposal and transportation.

➲ Disposing of household waste is multi-level governance in action: we see an institutional trail stretching from the household kitchen to the European Commission headquarters in Brussels.

regional devolution when it announced referendums in three of the regions – the north east, the north west, and Yorkshire and Humberside – on the issue of whether or not to create elected regional assemblies to, in effect, wield the powers now vested in the Regional Offices and the Regional Development Agencies. The delicacy with which government is approaching the issue of English regional devolution is shown by the decision to fund both opponents and supporters of devolution in the proposed referendums. The outcome was a catastrophe for  supporters of regionalism. The referendums in the north west and Humberside were abandoned nominally on

technical grounds, but in reality because public interest and support was embarrassingly low. The north east's referendum produced a huge defeat for regional devolution proposals: the suggestion was defeated by 78 per cent to 22 per cent in November 2004.

There are three reasons why deciding on regional devolution via elected assemblies is proving immensely difficult. The first is that there are *powerful entrenched interests* whose very existence would be threatened by such assemblies. The creation of a regional tier of elected government would almost certainly lead to an attempt to abolish one tier of local government in those parts of

England where there presently exist two tiers (see below). In practice, the most endangered institutions are probably the county councils.

A second difficulty lies in *identifying the governing principles for defining a region*. At present the regional boundaries used to define the nine English regions covered by the Regional Offices and the Regional Development Agencies are for the most part based on administrative conventions. While some regions – such as the north east – are believed to have a high sense of identity and distinctiveness, others plainly are no more than administrative inventions. An alternative principle to that of relying on the administrative conventions of regional boundaries might be to base regional assemblies on 'city regions', on the grounds that both economic structures and a sense of identity are more easily centred around the cities at the heart of the large conurbations in England, such as Manchester, Birmingham and Newcastle. Indeed there is one practical form of elected regional government already in existence, for that in reality is what the Greater London Authority amounts to (for details, see Briefing 12.8). But the achievement of establishing the Authority also hints at the limits of the model for the rest of England. Whatever arguments there might be about the appropriate boundaries of Greater London, or about the division of local responsibilities within the capital, it is unarguable that London is distinctive. As we saw in Chapter 3, it has a highly distinctive economy, based in particular on the importance of finance, commerce and government itself as an employer. As a uniquely large conurbation (by English standards) it has unique resources and unique problems. How far this model might be 'transplanted' to other metropolitan areas is uncertain.

Finally, any new system of government, to be legitimate, has to *arouse some public interest and support*. All the evidence is that there is neither public interest in, nor enthusiasm for, regional government in England.

Whatever the future of regional reform in local government, the regional face of local government brings home clearly how far the best known institutions of local government – elected local authorities – are embedded in extended networks of organiza-

---

## Briefing 12.8

### THE GREATER LONDON AUTHORITY AS ONE MODEL OF REGIONAL GOVERNMENT

**Functions**
The Authority has key direct governing roles: it controls most aspects of public transport, most strategic planning and most provision of fire services. It has a promotional role: to attract investment to the capital, and to foster London as an artistic centre.

**Structures**
There is an elected executive Mayor and a 25-member elected Greater London Assembly, the latter charged with oversight of the former. (See also Briefing 12.5.)

**Money**
It receives 70 per cent of its income in grants from central government; the remainder comes as a mixture of direct charges for services and a slice of the council tax levied by its constituent boroughs.

⮞ The Greater London Authority is important in its own right as a key player in the government of the capital, a leading world city and one of the world's leading financial centres. But it may also be important as a possible template for further regional devolution in England.

---

tions. This is, too, a main theme of the next section of the chapter.

## Local government and the web of governance

Local government is big business. When the state touches our lives in Britain, as it does in a thoroughly pervasive way, it more often than not does it through local rather than central institutions. Local authorities in England and Wales alone employ over 2 million staff, and account for about 25 per cent of all public spending. The range and scale of the services delivered has produced a complex and highly variegated institutional pattern. Two aspects of this complex pattern are particularly important: the pattern of organization and the pattern of governance.

## The pattern of organization

There is no single pattern of local government organization, and there is no stable agreement on what a single pattern might be. The basic principles of organization are different in England and Scotland. In Scotland there is only one level of local government, services being delivered across the country by 29 authorities. In England, by contrast, there exists no such single principle of organization. Most of the large metropolitan areas have single-tier authorities, but outside these a system of two-tier authorities prevails, with divided responsibilities for district and county councils. What is more, even in areas covered by unitary authorities there are specialized bodies covering fire prevention and transport services that are in effect 'consortia' of individual local authorities. Just how complex is the resulting division of responsibilities we saw schematically at the very beginning of this chapter, in Table 12.1 p. 249.

The consequences of operating this complex system are not difficult to see. There is no 'natural' way to divide responsibilities between different local government systems, so the appropriate division of labour is a constant source of debate. Neither is it obvious that unitary and two-tier systems are superior or inferior to each other; the choice tends to be made as a result of lobbying and struggles of interests between different groups in the local arena. This explains why the most distinctive feature of local government organization in recent decades has been its instability. The present pattern is in part the result of organizational changes introduced by the Labour government after 1997, the most important of which was the wholesale reorganization of the local government of the capital. It is very possible that the existing pattern will soon be outmoded. If the proposals to create elected regional assemblies with substantial governing powers are realized, it is likely that something akin to the Scottish/Welsh system of unitary authorities will have to be created. Experts on local government agree on very little, but they do agree that the simple addition of yet another layer of regional government to the existing two-tier system would be a step too far.

There is agreement on this because plainly one of the great costs imposed in a multi-tier system is the cost of efficiently coordinating these levels. Indeed, coordination is one of the great problems in local government. Even where there exists a unitary system there are still big problems of coordination, between those authorities and the other levels of multi-level government: in the devolved institutions in Cardiff and Edinburgh, in central Westminster government, and increasingly of course in the institutions of the European Union. The simple story of the 'wheelie bin' told in Briefing 12.7, p. 266 illustrates the reality of these issues of coordination, but this problem of coordinating the formal institutions of government is itself only part of a wider feature of local government, and perhaps its most important feature: that it is part of a broader system of governance.

## The pattern of governance

In the opening chapter of this book we encountered the idea of *government*, and saw that it was closely connected with the exercise of hierarchical relations of power and authority. This notion is encapsulated in Weber's famous definition of the state (see Briefing 1.1, p. 9): 'a human community that [successfully] claims the monopoly of the legitimate use of physical force within a given territory'. But if we think about the workings of local government in Britain, this emphasis on force does not really ring true – or at least it seems to be only part of the picture. It is hard to imagine the delivery of the wide range of services in local government, and the coordination of the institutions of delivery, working effectively solely through hierarchy and the threat of physical sanctions. This realization explains why it is increasingly common to think of government at the local level as a series of interconnected networks that require management and coordination, rather than as a hierarchy that needs to be subject to command and control. *Governance* is the name we commonly give to this process of network coordination. If government is, in the last resort, about using the state's monopoly of coercion, *governance* is about recognizing the limits to what can be done with the 'monopoly of the legitimate use of physical force'. It is about seeing the everyday reality of making policy and delivering services as fundamentally a cooperative activity between institutions that somehow must live together to have a chance of achieving their objectives. Weber's picture of the state invites us to think of it as a kind of military hierarchy; *governance* invites us to think of it as a partner in a kind of polygamous marriage, albeit an often very unhappy marriage.

A summary idea of the huge population of institutions that interact at local level was given in Table 12.1. The table conveys the often minutely complicated patterns of the divisions of responsibility at the formal level of local government organization. But even this table only gives a partial sense of the reality of governance – of the reality that making and putting policy at the local level into effect is about coordinating networks of organizations. It is

---

**Table 12.2**   Local government and the web of governance: numbers and variety of institutions operating at local level

| Type of institution | Number |
|---|---|
| Higher education institutions | 166 |
| Further education institutions | 511 |
| Foundation schools | 877 |
| City technology colleges | 15 |
| Training and enterprize councils (England) | 72 |
| Local enterprize councils (Scotland) | 22 |
| Career service companies (Scotland) | 17 |
| Registered social landlords (England) | 2,074 |
| Registered social landlords (Wales) | 92 |
| Registered housing associations (Scotland) | 255 |
| Registered housing associations (Northern Ireland) | 40 |
| Housing action trusts | 4 |
| Police authorities (England and Wales) | 41 |
| Joint police boards/unitary police authorities (Scotland) | 8 |
| Health authorities (England and Wales) | 99 |
| NHS trusts (England and Wales) | 373 |
| Primary care groups (England and Wales) | 434 |
| Primary care trusts (England and Wales) | 40 |
| Health boards (Scotland) | 15 |
| Special health boards (Scotland) | 8 |
| Acute NHS trusts (Scotland) | 14 |
| Primary care trusts (Scotland) | 13 |
| Integrated acute and primary care trust (Scotland) | 1 |
| Health and social services trusts (Northern Ireland) | 19 |
| Health and social services councils (Northern Ireland) | 4 |
| Health and personal social services boards (Northern Ireland) | 4 |
| Advisory committees on JPs (UK) | 119 |
| Dartmoor Steering Group (Ministry of Defence) | 1 |
| Total | 5,338 |

➲ This table, taken from an invaluable examination of the 'local quango state' by the Select Committee on Public Administration, was intended by the Committee to illustrate the extent to which local bodies consisted of non-elected, and largely non-accountable, figures. But it also reinforces one of the main themes of this chapter: that the territorial world of local government is part of an astonishingly dense network of institutions. As we see, over 5,000 are identified in this (almost certainly incomplete) census alone. Some are comparatively specialized, though important: the 119 Advisory Committees on JPs, for instance, advise the Lord Chancellor on appointment of Justices of the Peace. But some are central to the workings of the welfare state: for instance, the 373 National Health Service Trusts in England and Wales in effect control the hospital system. Neither these Trusts, nor the local authorities in whose territory they operate, can work effectively without good coordination mechanisms with local government. 'Governance' has been coined as a way of describing these complex, extended networks. 'Government', as we learnt in Chapter 1, relies heavily on hierarchy, power and authority; but 'governance' is a matter of trying to coordinate institutions that necessarily have to cooperate together, but whose operations are too complicated to be coordinated by any straightforward hierarchical exercise of power or authority.

*Source*: Select Committee on Public Administration (2001): table 6.

partial because it only includes the world of formally organized local government. But in truth local government is 'set' in something even bigger and more complicated, and some better hint of this is conveyed by looking at Table 12.2. The most important lesson of this table derives from a simple, but profoundly important, fact: local governments operate in a definable territory, but they do not monopolize service provision in that territory. They have to work alongside institutions such as universities, the health service and the machinery of justice, which are all delivering services in the same territory covered by local government units. The table was originally created to show the existence of a 'local state' dominated by non-elected institutions, but it serves to stress the reality of governance as a process of network coordination. It also highlights another important feature of governance at local level: not all of these networks of organizations are in the 'public sector' as conventionally defined. Some lie in a kind of undefinable 'borderland' between the private and the public: for instance, the more than 250 registered housing associations identified in Scotland alone. Some are private companies, or individual private entrepreneurs, who provide some public service under a system of 'franchises' or licences: consider in the table, for instance, the more than 2,000 registered social landlords in England.

Viewing the local as an arena of governance has a number of important implications for how we make sense of local politics and of the wider system of governance in the United Kingdom. It immediately alerts us to one of the key features of both the local and the national: the multi-level character of governing arrangements. It is at the local level that we can see this most clearly. This is not only because the local is the 'bottom' of the multi-level ladder, thus having to coordinate with institutions 'higher up'; it is because so much of the local is dominated by service delivery. It covers most of the services that as citizens we could expect to call on frequently throughout our lives: from education – the single biggest service delivered at local level – to the weekly household waste collection. In our own daily lives we constantly find that performing some service depends critically on coordinating

what we do with others. Even units as small as families or student households only run efficiently if members cooperate with each other in mundane tasks, including doing the washing up and emptying the waste bin. Magnify the task to the kind involved in delivering care for the old, education for the young, or waste disposal for us all, and we see immediately the immense importance of coordinating different networks of organizations. The only effective way to make policy work at the local level is to manage the governance arena: to manage, in other words, a local system where the formal institutions of local government are necessarily embedded in a dense network of both state and non-state organizations.

## The decline and rise of local government

For most of the twentieth century local government was in decline. It relied increasingly on central government for money. Local councils were colonized by the two leading nationally organized parties, so that the turn of electoral fortunes at the local level was largely a reflection of national political trends. Over the course of the century local authorities lost many of the responsibilities which they had played a pioneering part in establishing in the latter part of the nineteenth century, such as the delivery of utilities (gas, electricity, water) and the provision of services such as health care.

Much of this decline is irreversible: for instance, there is no prospect of local government ever again becoming important in the delivery of basic utilities, and there are no signs that local government has the capacity to diminish significantly its reliance on grants from central government as a main source of revenue (see Debating Politics 12.1). But three long-term changes are reducing the long historical subordination to Westminster government.

### Devolution

Devolution has reshaped the relationship between local and central government in Wales and

# DEBATING POLITICS

## 12.1 LOCAL GOVERNMENT: MORIBUND OR RENEWED?

| Local government is moribund | Local government is being renewed |
|---|---|
| ■ Turnout in local government elections is lower than for any other public elections, and is among the lowest in Europe.<br><br>■ Local authorities are run by parties that have few members and little popular support.<br><br>■ Local government has lost most of its financial independence, relying on the centre for grants.<br><br>■ There has been a century-long loss of functions by local authorities, to central government and the private sector. | ■ The decline of the old parties is allowing new groups and parties to enter local government.<br><br>■ Local government is a renewed source of experimentation and innovation, as illustrated by the London congestion charge.<br><br>■ The decline of the central Westminster system is creating new spaces for local action.<br><br>■ New functions in local economic renewal are being acquired by local government. |

Scotland, and it has the potential to do it in England if the elected regional assemblies become a reality. The experience of London shows the possibilities, where the elected mayor has become a major source of opposition to Whitehall government over issues such as the funding of the London Underground system, and a source of one important policy innovation, the introduction of traffic congestion charging.

## The decline of national parties

Party in local government is no longer just a reflection of national struggles. As the two main parties have lost their hold over the loyalties of electors, the effect has been felt most clearly at the local level. The growing diversity of the party system, with the rise of many different third parties, is more accurately reflected in the composition of local councils than in the composition of the Westminster Parliament. There now exists party representation spanning the Greens at one end and the quasi-Fascist British National Party at the other. And the weakening of national party controls has, especially in mayoral elections, helped elect 'mavericks' to office: they range from serious dissenters against the two-party system, such as Ken

Livingstone in London, to mavericks such as the monkey-suit wearing football mascot elected as mayor of Hartlepool.

## The shift to governance

Paradoxically, perhaps the most important reason for the revival of local government lies in the growing realization that local authorities cannot behave like little monarchies in their own

### REVIEW

The most important themes of this chapter have been:

1 The fall, and then the reinvention, of local government;
2 The importance of national and regional organization of local government institutions;
3 The growing connections between the private and the public at local level;
4 The way local government has evolved into *governance*.

territories: they are part of the extended networks of organizations described earlier in this chapter. Local authorities have been obliged to recognize that the need to work cooperatively in these networks sets limits to authority and autonomy; but by the same token the shift to governance puts the local authority – the deliverer of major public services such as education and transport – at the centre of governance networks.

## Further reading

Wilson and Game (2002) are standard on the whole system. Stoker (2004) integrates the latest 'governance' language into the study of the subject. Two books by Rhodes are pioneering studies of the modern approaches (1988 and 1999). Pimlott and Rao (2002) are authoritative on the very important 'exceptional' case of the government of the capital city.

CHAPTER 13

# How citizens participate

## AIMS

This chapter has the following aims:

❖ To explain the central importance of popular participation to democratic politics

❖ To sketch the main forms of participation in Britain

❖ To examine the factors that influence who participates, and who does not

❖ To describe how patterns of participation are changing in Britain, and to show how our conventional notions of what participation amounts to are being challenged.

## Participation and British democracy

Every theory of democracy involves some notion of *popular participation*. The roots of the word democracy itself derive from the Greek term for the people, anglicized as 'demos'. But the original history of the concept of Greek democracy shows how complicated the connection between participation and democracy can be. The theory of Greek democracy was based on the notion of direct democracy: of rule through the participation of all citizens in an open assembly taking decisions. But 'citizens' here did not mean all adults, because citizenship was actually confined to a minority of male adults: among those excluded were slaves, a large part of the population, and women, an even larger part.

Even the limited original Greek notion of direct participation has been of little importance in Britain. The dominant theories of British democracy have given a marginal role to mass participation, which has mostly been confined to participation in elections for the Westminster Parliament, where all entitled to vote can have a say in choosing governors. Obviously we could hardly expect a country of over 50 million people to organize Greek-style forums where all the adult population gathered in a particular place to meet and debate, but the practice of democratic participation in Britain has been limited by more than these practical considerations.

We can see some of the limits to democratic participation in Britain if we look at practices abroad. Some rural parts of the United States, for example, have a long-established system of town meetings, where communities try to recreate some of the conditions of the democratic 'forum' for all citizens. British democracy has also been more reluctant than many other democracies to use the opportunities offered by mass voting. Until recently, voting in Britain mostly meant choosing on two occasions: in general elections to select representatives to the Westminster Parliament; and in local elections to select representatives – councillors – for local government. By contrast, in the

United States a much wider range of public office is decided by election. In addition, it has been common there for many important policy questions (for example, concerning the setting of local and state taxes) to be the subject of popular votes in referendums. In many countries where the head of state is, unlike Britain, a president rather than a hereditary monarch, voters at large make the choice: the examples range from the United States and France, where the president is a real executive head of government, to Ireland, where the president performs the symbolic roles fulfilled in Britain by the monarch.

The formal organization of participation in Britain has therefore given comparatively restricted scope for mass participation. But as the chapter unfolds we will see that two important changes are coming over political participation in Britain:

● The formal opportunities to participate have been significantly widened in recent years
● The form and meaning of participation have changed greatly.

This second point provides a natural introduction to the next section of this chapter, where we begin by looking in detail at what might be called political participation 'old-style': the kind of participation that was in its heyday when the Westminster system of government was dominant, and when the Westminster Parliament was held to be the main means of channelling the popular will.

## The range of participation: 'old-style'

The evidence from the most comprehensive study of political participation in Britain now dates from the 1980s. It is therefore, as we shall see, to some degree historically dated, but precisely for that reason is an invaluable guide to the forms and levels of participation that were developed under the old Westminster system.

As we might have expected from the theory of democracy and participation in Britain, political

**Figure 13.1** The pattern of participation in Britain, old-style (% of population who claimed to have engaged in different forms of participation at least once)

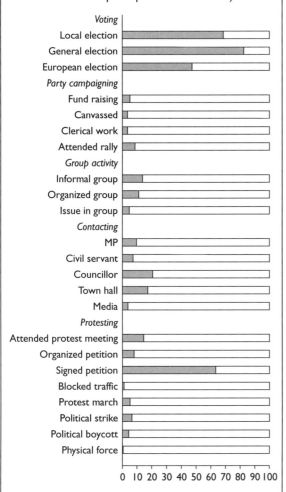

*Source*: Data from Parry, Moyser and Day (1992: 44).

➲ Figure 13.1 is labelled 'participation old-style' because, as we shall see later in the chapter, there is mounting evidence that some of the acts of participation performed most frequently here – such as voting – are in decline, and some new kinds of participation may not have been detected by our older notions of what constituted participation in politics. Although the publication from which the information is drawn dates from the early 1990s, the fieldwork on which the figures are based is older, dating from the 1980s. The work of Parry and his colleagues is the most thorough study of participation ever conducted in the UK, and it stands as our definitive picture of participation 'old-style' from the age when most people were still content to participate in conventional ways allotted to them by the Westminster elite, such as voting.

participation was dominated by taking part in elections, especially the infrequent general elections that cover all the United Kingdom. Other forms of participation, even very sporadic ones were in this picture confined to a quite small minority. Democratic participation in this world was a minority sport or hobby, rather akin to train spotting, playing snooker or listening to opera. Even the figures in Figure 13.1 almost certainly overstate the extent of participation in Britain, since they tell us about *reported* participation – what people in a survey told social scientists about their participation. Since participation in politics, unlike playing snooker, is in general viewed as a virtuous thing, it is almost certainly the case that reported levels exaggerate true levels. We can see this, indeed, when we cross-check against measures of actual participation. Figure 13.2 shows levels of participation in elections across Britain; we can see that participation in elections is lower than reported.

Not everyone participates, and not everyone participates equally. The evidence in Table 13.1 conveys a truth that the passage of time has not altered: there exists only a tiny minority of totally committed activists for whom politics is an all-consuming activity. To some extent, this is a matter of random taste: there are obsessive political activists just as there are obsessive train spotters, or people with an all-consuming interest in rock climbing, or rock music. This is the minority that runs political parties at local level, for instance, or that devotes all its waking hours to organizing for a particular cause, be it animal welfare or opposition to new road building. The people in this category are on the fringes of a group we will consider in Chapter 18, the full-time politicians, and often they actually aspire to join that group. But just as we would find that train spotters and rock climbers are not a random sample of the population – train spotters are mostly male, rock climbers tend to be the young and fit – so participation is not randomly distributed. The two most important factors affecting the propensity to participate are not at all mysterious, and are briefly summarized here.

**Figure 13.2** Participation in general (Westminster) elections in the UK, 1945–2005 (turnout as percentage of electorate)

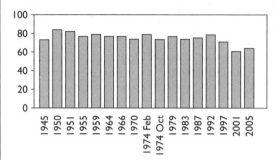

*Source*: Calculated from standard sources.

➲ Figure 13.2 charts turnout in all general elections since 1945. It may be premature to decide that there is a crisis of electoral participation. But the turnout for 2001 represented a marked fall, and there had already been some sign of tailing off in 1997. Turnout recovered slightly in the 2005 general election. But this is mostly explained by the new ease of postal voting, not by re-engagement with 'old' politics; and unprecedented geographical variations have developed.

**Table 13.1**  Politics as a hobby, compared with other hobbies

| Activity | % of population claiming to participate |
|---|---|
| Swimming | 14.8 |
| Darts | 5.6 |
| Gardening | 48.0 |
| Dressmaking, needlework, knitting | 22.0 |
| Voting in general election | 82.5 |
| Canvassing for a party | 3.5 |
| Organizing a group | 11.5 |
| Contacting MP | 9.7 |
| Taking part in a protest march | 5.2 |

*Sources*: For politics, Parry, Moyser and Day (1992); for hobbies, *Social Trends* and *Annual Abstract of Statistics*.

➲ Table 13.1 compares what Parry and his colleagues found about frequency of political participation with frequency of participation in a range of leisure 'hobby' activities. Parry's data are from the late 1980s, and that for leisure for the mid- and late 1990s. I choose one activity from each of the main Parry categories, extracted from Figure 13.1. In fact the 'test' for leisure activities is harder than for politics: Parry and his colleagues asked only if respondents had ever done any of these; the surveys of leisure require participation in the four weeks before the survey. Although voting is well ahead of leisure activities, the table puts 'old-style' politics in the lives of citizens into perspective: a bit more popular than darts, but less popular than dressmaking or gardening.

## Education and class

There is a powerful link between formal education and likelihood of participating. All other things being equal, the rate of participation rises the longer an individual has spent in education. There are many possible reasons, but one of the most obvious is that formal education provides the resources and skills that make participation most effective and satisfying. In Britain participation is for the most part a cerebral activity. There are forms of participation that are far from cerebral – for instance, attacking the agents of the state or burning cars and buildings – and as we will see these can be very important. But for most people, most of the time, participation is a matter of talking, writing and organizing – skills that some people have naturally, but that are undoubtedly fostered by education.

Education is also closely associated with likelihood of participation because it in turn is associated with other important life features that help participation. The better-educated people are more likely to have white-collar and professional jobs, high levels of income and high levels of consumer affluence. They have the leisure and other resources that make it easier to take part in politics. Consider, for example, how something as obvious as owning a car makes participation easier. There is thus a powerful bias in the participation system: at every level, *participation rises with occupational class*.

Education and class are two of the keys to variations in levels of participation in Britain, but there is still one overwhelmingly important point that we should keep in mind: high political participation is a *minority activity*. Although there is indeed a powerful connection between education and class, nevertheless even within the groups most likely to participate, political participation beyond the most episodic kind, such as voting in a general election, is still confined to a minority. To take an example: more university professors than university porters participate intensively in politics. University professors have all the advantages: high formal education, leisure and money. But among university professors themselves, still only a minority participate in politics. If we thought of politics as a hobby (Table 13.1), we would find that even among university professors it occupied a lower place than sport, opera or gardening.

Does this mean that actually participating in politics is in the end an arbitrary matter of taste, akin to a taste for going to the opera or to rock concerts? The answer is no, and part of the clue lies in observing the contrasts between different kinds of participation. The most obvious feature of the commonest kind of participation – voting, especially in general elections – is that the means to do it are periodically provided, and in ways that make this kind of participation easy to perform. To vote, all you have to do is take the trouble to stroll down to a polling station on election day – and, as we shall see, recent reforms are designed to make voting easier still. But suppose you want to do something more sustained, such as promote animal rights or advocate the release of political prisoners? To do this, you will need either to find a group or to found a group.

## Group networks

Group participation is particularly important. Working alone – just voting, or writing to your MP – is not going to make much of a difference to what governments do. We saw in Chapter 9 that some people have the energy and skill to bring groups into life when they feel strongly about an issue. But most of us do not have the qualities to be this kind of successful political entrepreneur. We depend heavily on the prior availability of groups. Their vitality – how efficiently they are run, whether they are rising or declining – is therefore critical for whether people can realistically participate, and for whether their participation can make a difference. Imagine, for example, that you are a Muslim with strong views about how education should be organized in Britain – favouring, as many Muslims do,

public financial support for Islamic schools on the same terms as are presently offered to those run by Christian denominations. If you live in Bradford or North Manchester you have a ready-made network of groups – centred on the mosque and on the local community – in which to participate to help advance those views. But imagine living on Orkney, where you would be part of a tiny minority; there is no such network. You either have to participate ineffectively (say, by writing to your Parliamentary representative) or you actually have to build a group.

The pre-existence of strong social networks is therefore a vital influence on the opportunity to participate, and to participate in an effective way. When we turn to examine changing forms and levels of participation we will see that changes in these networks have a big influence on the way participation is itself changing in Britain. Being lucky enough to have ready access to groups and networks therefore deeply influences what might be called the quality of political participation that citizens in Britain can enjoy. But there are also more blunt influences at work. Some factors have worked simply to exclude some groups from participation in political life. In addition, some methods of participation are symbolically excluded: in other words, they are not considered compatible with participation in the normal procedure of democratic politics in Britain. These two sources of exclusion are examined next.

## Participation and political exclusion

The rules of democratic politics in Britain provide a wide range of familiar ways of participating in politics, all of which we have seen at some stage above: they range from the one opportunity every four or five years to vote in a general election to the intense, all-consuming commitment to political life of a tiny proportion of the population who are political activists. This model of democracy presumes that everyone who really wants to take part in politics can do so if they have a sufficiently strong inclination. It also presumes that the means of participation are sufficiently effective so that any group that has a serious interest or grievance can effectively make its voice heard.

**POLITICAL ISSUES**

## 13.1   EXCLUSION FROM POLITICAL PARTICIPATION: THE CASE OF PRISONERS AND THE VOTE

In 1870 all those held in prison lost the right to vote. Until recently this total prohibition held. This is internationally unusual: 19 states in Western Europe allow prisoners to vote. Under the impact of rulings from the European Court of Human Rights in Strasbourg, and the incorporation into domestic law of the European Convention on Human Rights, this has now begun to change. The UK has lifted the ban on remand prisoners and a few others voting and made it easier for the unsentenced held in prison to register. But this still leaves at least 50,000 prisoners without a vote. A case supported by the Prison Reform Trust – from whom these details are taken – has begun the process of challenging this following the passage of the Human Rights Act. (For more details of the Human Rights Act and the European Convention on Human Rights, see Chapter 23).

Three issues are raised by this case:

- What should count as an entitlement to vote: mental capacity or moral worth?
- Is the right to vote an inalienable human right, as challenges under the Human Rights Act would suggest?
- What are the proper boundaries of the 'people' in a democracy? If prisoners can vote, why should not those presently disqualified by age or nationality?

*Sources*: Information from Prison Reform Trust (2000); and www.prisonreformtrust.org.uk

We have already had to modify this picture by recognizing that some of the costs of persistent participation are higher for some groups than for others, depending in part on whether they have ready access to pre-existing social networks. But there are also significant groups in the community who are, or until recently were, consciously excluded from political life (see Political Issues 13.1). That exclusion can take the form either of open rules barring participation, or of social pressures and a hostile climate of public opinion that makes participation all but impossible.

### Participation: excluded groups

There is a long history of overt, formal exclusion of groups and individuals from political participation in Britain. This was particularly important in the era before the development of modern institutions of democratic citizenship, such as universal suffrage.

The rules of exclusion included: property and gender qualifications that regulated qualification to vote; and laws forbidding the entry of many religious groups, including Jews and Catholics, into civic life. It was not only the avowedly religious who were excluded: only after a long struggle in the nineteenth century was it possible for atheists to sit in the House of Commons without disavowing their atheism. Achieving universal adult suffrage in 1928 – when women and men finally achieved formal equality of entitlement – was a sign that the theory of British democracy was now based on an inclusive notion of the right to take part in the political life of the community. The development of anti-discrimination legislation since the mid-1970s helped tackle some of the residual exclusions practised by institutions in politics and in the wider society. Nevertheless, in modern Britain exclusion from many forms of participation is still practised. Six grounds of exclusion are particularly important.

*Age.* The rules of participation openly discriminate against the young. That is because of the principle, sometimes voiced and sometimes implicit, that full participation in political life requires the maturity and experience of adulthood. Where the boundary to adulthood is set is in part conventional, depending on the assumptions of particular epochs.

**Image 13.1**
**Mass protest as participation: the memorial to the Kinder Mass Trespass**

Photo: Michael Moran

⮕ Image 13.1 reflects a feature of political participation in Britain which is emphasized again in Timeline 13.1: the extent to which participation has involved defiance of the law. The plaque in the photograph commemorates a mass trespass by hikers across the mountain of Kinder Scout in the Derbyshire Peak District in 1932. The deliberate breach of the law on right of way was a protest against the use of state power defending the rights of landowners to exclude walkers from crossing their property. The results of the protest included skirmishes with gamekeepers and police. Identified ring leaders were arrested and jailed. Many 'moderates' condemned the trespass tactic. Seventy years on the aims of the trespassers are part of the accepted rights of walkers and, as the plaque shows, the trespassers have achieved respectability. The trespass is part of a long history of participation as defiance of the law; the modern descendants of the trespassers include eco-warriors blockading big construction projects such as roads and airports.

Until 1969, the boundary was set at 21 – the qualifying age to appear on the electoral register. The infrequency of general elections meant that this most common single act of participation could often be exercised only in the mid-twenties. Now the qualifying age of registration to vote, and standing for elective office, is 18. Of course, voting in general elections, although the commonest form of participation, is not the only one, and almost all others are in principle open to those under 18. Nevertheless, exclusion from the full rights of citizenship makes the alternative forms of participation less valuable. Many of the organized opportunities for participation for the young are viewed as pre-political: as a kind of practice for adult participation, in the form of school councils, debating societies and the development of a citizenship curriculum in schools. Just how far the age barrier depends on conventional notions of what constitutes 'adulthood' is shown by the increasingly common debate about the possibility of reducing the qualifying age for voting to 16.

*Religion.* Historically, as we saw above, religion was openly used to create legal barriers to participation. As we saw in Chapter 11, the exclusion of Catholics was a central organizing principle of the state in Northern Ireland until the late 1960s. On the mainland of Britain, the law now forbids the open creation of barriers of grounds of religion. Because open discrimination is illegal, there is an obvious motive to hide it, and that in turn makes estimating the extent of residual exclusion difficult. The growing indifference to organized religious practice in Britain is, in truth, probably the greatest influence in destroying these residual barriers and such barriers to participation as are raised probably now exist more as a by-product of wider ethnic discrimination. Jews, for example, are almost certainly not welcome in some local political parties, but actually attending a synagogue probably does not make the barrier to participation higher.

*Ethnicity.* There exist powerful barriers of exclusion against immigrants. For first-generation immigrants these barriers may exist because they lack the resources that, as we saw earlier, are important in participation: English may not be their first language, for example. While the economic history of migrants is highly diverse, in the first generation at least there is a necessary focus on work and economic security above participation in the wider society. Nationals of other states residing in Britain also have limited participation opportunities, but the most extreme forms of exclusion relate to asylum seekers and illegal immigrants. There is an increasing flow of people across borders, especially as the poorest, and those fleeing war and persecution, try to reach the comparative security and prosperity of countries such as Britain. For obvious reasons (because they want to escape detection) there is an unknown, but substantial, population of illegal immigrants in Britain, whose status means that they can neither exercise formal rights to participate, such as voting, nor realistically participate by other means.

*Poverty.* One powerful additional barrier to participation which immigrants and asylum seekers share with many of the 'native' population is poverty. As we saw earlier, participation generally is linked to the possession of economic resources. At the most extreme levels of poverty, this is more than a deterrent: it is an absolute barrier. This kind of poverty is increasingly identified with the notions of 'social exclusion'. The significance of being poor extends beyond obvious material deprivation: poverty also excludes many of the poor from meaningful participation in the life of the community. The exclusion can be extreme – as in the case of homelessness – or more subtle, as when poverty just makes the daily round of life incredibly difficult: the rural poor without access to their own transport, for instance, are often trapped in isolation because of poor public transport provision. It is easy to see that social exclusion and political exclusion often go together. The homeless provide the most obvious case; until recently, the homeless could not even register to vote, and the lack of a permanent abode is plainly a powerful barrier to political participation.

*Deviance.* British liberal democracy presumes an entitlement to participate in political life on the part of all adult citizens. The 'liberal' in 'liberal democracy', as we saw in Chapter 1, refers in part to the toleration of a wide range of views and practices. But no liberal democracy has been able to tolerate everything, and a key issue in any liberal democracy is the possible range of toleration. What range of views and practices will be viewed as intolerable, and what intolerable views will result in exclusion from the participatory entitlements of citizenship? The boundaries of exclusion are drawn around various groups and various methods of participation.

In Britain, convicted criminals who are serving jail sentences have highly curtailed citizenship entitlements. Some social practices are so vilified that any attempt to participate in politics in their defence is in practice impossible. Thus, while in principle a group could form to campaign for the repeal of existing laws against paedophilia, any attempt to do so openly would soon produce intense popular hostility and, probably, police intervention. The range of people whose views and practices are labelled so deviant as to ensure their exclusion from participation in political life changes over time, as society and its cultural understandings change. For example, until the late 1960s gay people were viewed much as paedophiles are now. Any attempt to mobilize gays into political activity would have provoked both popular hostility, and – since all male homosexual relations were criminal until 1967 – intervention by the police.

*Gender.* We know that historically gender was an important ground of open, legal exclusion from some important forms of participation: we only have to recall the history of the suffrage to see that. The most important legacy of that history, as we shall see in Chapter 18, is to be found in patterns of leadership recruitment rather than in patterns of participation. But the story is not just one of waning barriers to exclusion. Newly important immigrant groups, which themselves suffer exclusion, also have their own internal barriers which exclude women in some immigrant groups from the opportunity to take part in politics.

## Participation: the excluded methods

Exclusion thus raises barriers against participation by different social groups in British political life. But exclusion also works by establishing barriers against certain methods of political participation. Three kinds of participation have proved especially problematic even though, as we shall see, they have deep historical roots and are still common.

*Violence.*    Violent protest is an important tradition in Britain (see Timeline 13.1). Some of the most important moments in the historical development of British politics were accompanied by, and partly caused by, violence. They include the civil war in the seventeenth century which led to the execution of the King and the destruction of the claims of the monarchy to exercise special, divine authority; violent public demonstrations that accompanied the campaign to change suffrage in the nineteenth century; and an armed uprising across what was then the Irish part of the United Kingdom after 1916 which resulted, in 1922, in the foundation of a separate Irish state. Violence continues to be a tactic used by some radical groups, normally targeted against particular institutions and personalities: radical animal rights groups have, for example, targeted both firms and researchers who are believed to be involved in experiments on animals. A more pervasive form of violence, one that shades into general criminality, is a well-established pattern of racial attacks. But it is disputes about the territorial boundaries of the state that have provoked the longest violent campaigns in modern British politics. As we saw in Chapter 11, the political life of Northern Ireland since the late 1960s has been marked by persistent violent political participation. This has included mob attacks and intimidation (for instance, to force evacuation of housing); the use of the traditional tactics of terror, such as large-scale bomb blasts in urban areas designed to cause both random loss of life and extensive economic damage; targeted violence against the agents of the state by both Republican and Loyalist paramilitary groups; and targeted violence by the agents of the state themselves against, in particular, known Republicans and parts of the wider Catholic community.

Violent forms of political participation are, therefore, an engrained part of the British political tradition. But violence is problematic since it plainly runs counter to the expectation that politics will be pursued in a 'constitutional' way: in other words, by employing argument and the ballot box to advance policies and interests. So while violence is common, it also attracts both widespread disapproval and a hostile response from the agencies of the state charged with maintaining public order.

*Civil disobedience.*    Civil disobedience consists in a refusal to obey the legal commands of the state. It is typically a tactic adopted when those commands are believed to lack moral authority. Like violence, civil disobedience has a long history in Britain. By far the most important and successful campaign of civil disobedience in recent decades was the campaign that destroyed the poll tax (see Briefing 13.1, p. 284). But civil disobedience can stretch well beyond the 'can't pay, won't pay' tactic of refusing to pay a tax. The workings of a modern economy are highly complex, demand for their effective functioning the cooperation of large numbers of people, and are easily disrupted. A wide range of tactics has been used in recent years by a variety of groups to exploit this vulnerability, including blockades of the transport network and physical blockades (for example, of proposed new roads) designed to prevent or delay the completion of work.

*Industrial action.*    Industrial action is not illegal, and in most instances is not a form of political protest at all; it is just part of a normal process of bargaining between groups (workers and employers) in the modern economy. But precisely because of the nature of a modern economy, where effective working demands cooperation by many different groups, it can have a devastating effect, and therefore can be an effective weapon by disaffected groups. In the last quarter of the twentieth century many attempts were made by unions of manual workers to use the strike as a weapon of political protest. National industrial action by coalminers in 1972, 1974 and 1984-5, though in part about employment conditions, were also protests against the government of the day.

Political violence, civil disobedience and industrial action are well-established modes of political participation. But they occupy a problematic position in democratic politics in Britain, which for so long has given a pre-eminent position to voting, and assigned a kind of supreme moral as well as legal authority to the decisions taken by governments

## TIMELINE 13.1    VIOLENT POLITICAL PARTICIPATION: AS BRITISH AS BARNSLEY BITTER

**1715**
Attacks on dissenting (non-conformist) chapels in Midlands and the north west leads to passage of first Riot Act.

**1736**
Porteus riots in Edinburgh, when crowd lynches a commander of troops who had opened fire on a demonstration.

**1763–5**
Violent machine breaking by weavers in London.

**1780**
Gordon Riots in London, with over 300 people killed in anti-Catholic demonstrations.

**1791**
Riots and destruction of property of non-conformist dissenters in Birmingham.

**1795**
King's coach attacked in huge demonstration against war with France.

**1797**
Naval mutinies at Spithead and the Nore.

**1800–1**
Widespread food riots.

**1811–12**
Widespread machine breaking by gangs protesting against new technology across the Midlands and the north of England.

**1819**
Reform demonstration in Manchester; 11 killed in 'Peterloo massacre.'

**1820**
Attempt to assassinate Cabinet uncovered in 'Cato Street conspiracy'; conspirators executed.

**1830–3**
'Captain Swing' riots across south of England: hundreds of demonstrations, riots, machine breaking.

**1842**
Riots, and Chartist general strike in north of England.

**1852**
Riots between Catholics and Protestants near Manchester; Catholic churches sacked.

**1866**
Demonstrations for electoral reform lead to widespread damage to property.

**1867**
Illegal demonstrations for electoral reform; Fenian (Irish nationalist) gunpowder attack on Clerkenwell Prison.

**1868**
Anti-Catholic riots in Manchester.

**1886**
Unemployed riot in West End of London following demonstration in Trafalgar Square.

**1893**
Two killed in clashes between troops and striking miners in Yorkshire.

**1909**
Sectarian (Catholic/Protestant) riots in Liverpool.

**1911**
Strikers shot in clashes with troops in Liverpool and in south Wales.

**1914**
Threats of armed revolt against Irish Home Rule by Ulster Unionists, with the complicity of leading Conservatives in Britain, averted only by outbreak of First World War.

**1916–21**
Uprising in Dublin in Easter 1916 leads to civil war, ended only by the establishment of a separate Irish Free State.

**1919**
Police/strikers clash in Glasgow general strike; police strike in Liverpool is followed by riots in the city.

**1931**
Widespread clashes between unemployed and police in cities in England and Scotland.

**1932**
'Hunger march' on London by unemployed followed by clashes with police; serious riot in Dartmoor prison.

## TIMELINE 13.1    (CONTINUED)

**1936**
Police and anti-fascist demonstrators clash in 'battle of Cable Street' in London's East End.

**1937**
113 arrested and 28 injured in illegal fascist march through East End of London.

**1947**
Anti-Semitic demonstrations in Liverpool and Manchester.

**1958**
Race riots in London and in the Midlands.

**1961**
'Sit-down' demonstrations by campaigners against nuclear weapons designed to force government policy change by causing social disruption.

**1968**
Clashes between police and anti-Vietnam War demonstrators at US Embassy in London.

**1969**
Widespread violence in Northern Ireland leads to 25-year civil war in which over 3,000 people die.

**1968–71**
'Angry Brigade' bombs public buildings, banks and home of Cabinet Minister before being apprehended in 1972.

**1974**
Demonstrations in Red Lion Square in London between fascists and opponents; one man killed.

**1976**
Disturbances at Notting Hill Carnival; Hull Prison wrecked in riot.

**1977**
Clashes between police and pickets in strike at Warrington, Lancashire.

**1979**
Race riots in Bristol.

**1981**
Race riots in London, Liverpool and Manchester lead to large scale (Scarman) public inquiry.

**1984–5**
Series of confrontations between police and mass pickets of miners in prolonged miners' strike; two people killed and over 12,000 miners arrested.

**1985**
Riots by football supporters culminate in Heysel stadium disaster when 38 fans were killed in riots between Liverpool and Juventus supporters; race riots in London and Birmingham, resulting in three deaths.

**1986**
Prolonged confrontations between police and striking print workers in London; wave of riots across British prison system following prison officers' strike.

**1990**
Anti-poll tax demonstrations across Britain culminate in rioting following demonstration by 300,000 in Trafalgar Square; Strangeways Jail in Manchester wrecked in riot.

**1991**
Arson and looting as youths battle police in wave of summer riots in English and Welsh cities.

**1992**
Repeat of 1991 riots, spreading to smaller towns.

**1994**
Riots in London against Criminal Justice and Public Order Act.

**1995**
Race riots in Bradford and London; clashes between police and animal rights activists over exports of live animals.

**1995**
Anti-capitalist demonstrations in City of London cause £1 billion of damage.

**2001**
Race riots in Bradford.

**2002**
Race riots across towns of north of England.

➲ The rules of liberal democracy stress peaceful political participation, and official versions of the British constitution stress its importance. But we have arrived at our present condition by a route that involved large-scale violence both by the state and against the state. Violence and political participation are woven together in the British political tradition.

*Source*: Adapted, with additions, from Cook and Stevenson (1983 and 2000).

# Briefing

## A SUCCESSFUL CASE OF MASS CIVIL DISOBEDIENCE: THE POLL TAX

The community charge (commonly known as the poll tax) was legislated in 1988. It replaced a system of 'rates', local authority taxes which were levied on historic rateable values attributed to owner-occupied houses. The poll tax, by contrast, was a fixed charge in each local authority area which was applied to all. Two features provoked widespread resistance: the spread to all of what had been a selective tax confined to houseowners; and the shift from a variable levy linked, at least notionally, to house values to a flat-rate charge. Resistance was intensified by one tactical decision by the government: it introduced the charge a year earlier in Scotland (1989/90) than in England (1990/1). Scotland already produced anti-Conservative majorities in elections, so the charge was 'trialled' in uniquely hostile territory. At first opposition took the form of conventional methods, such as public demonstrations. This soon spread to passive civil disobedience: large numbers declined to pay the tax; larger numbers still simply ceased to register on the electoral register, the main source used by the authorities to track down occupants of houses. The Prime Minister, Margaret Thatcher, had identified closely with the original legislation, and pictured resistance as a challenge to established, legitimate authority. Encouraged by the Prime Minister's support, enforcement of the charge increasingly relied on the full force of the law, notably through court orders, property seizures and prison sentences. Passive resistance soon grew to large-scale organized public demonstrations, and then to violent confrontations with the police, notably during a protest in London on 31 March 1990, when 300,000 took part. The resistance campaign divided the Labour party between those who wanted to stay within the conventional bounds of constitutional resistance, and those who favoured passive, or even violent, resistance. But the consequences for the Conservative party were greater, indeed catastrophic. As it became clear that the poll tax was unenforceable over large parts of the country, leading figures in the party began to fear that the issue would cost them victory in the next general election. This contributed to the fall from office of Mrs Thatcher in November 1990. Her successor, John Major, appointed the man most responsible for Mrs Thatcher's fall, Michael Heseltine, as Secretary of State for Environment, with a brief to replace the poll tax. Its successor, the council tax, was rapidly introduced. The new council tax closely resembled the old system of rates that the poll tax had been designed to sweep away.

⇨ The history of the poll tax echoes features summarized in Timeline 13.1 above. It is in a long tradition of non-constitutional resistance to laws passed by government. The problem of how to draw the line between 'constitutional' resistance, passive civil disobedience and violent resistance has run through the history of these campaigns and deeply divided the Labour movement especially as regards the poll tax. The official national leadership took the position that law, once passed, had to be obeyed, until a new Labour government could repeal it; some Labour local authorities in effect refused to enforce the tax, joining the civil disobedience camp; and some activists allied with anti-poll tax campaigners from the militant left outside the Labour party actively to obstruct the implementation of the Act (for instance, by blocking court officers attempting to serve enforcement orders on poll tax defaulters). The poll tax is thus an object lesson from several points of view: for government, in illuminating the limits of enforcement when a measure is viewed as objectionable; for those who resisted, in illuminating the problem of deciding when resistance had gone beyond the pale of constitutional action; and for the Labour party, in continuing a long tradition of not knowing where to draw the line between 'constitutional' and 'unconstitutional' protest.

produced by voting. Challenges to government by violence, strikes or civil disobedience therefore call into question understandings central to the workings of established democratic politics. But as we will now see, changes in both institutions and in wider social values are themselves altering the relationship between political participation and democracy in Britain.

## Political participation: 'new-style'

We can begin our survey of change with the most commonly noticed 'headline' change in participation in recent decades. In the general election of 2001, turnout was sharply down on the average levels recorded in general elections over the years since the end of the Second World War in 1945, and this fall seemed only to confirm hints of decline which could

# Briefing

## EVALUATING INNOVATIONS DESIGNED TO INCREASE PARTICIPATION, 'OLD-STYLE'

The sharp fall in turnout in the 2001 general election, coupled with other signs of falling participation in tradition-ally established institutions such as political parties, led to a variety of experiments designed to increase electoral participation. The Electoral Commission, the regulatory body charged since 2000 with the regulation of parties and elections, has evaluated the effectiveness of these. It found:

- Making postal voting available to all had the most dramatic effect in raising participation, but the extent of the rise was heavily influenced by the class make-up of the district and whether there was a tradition of postal voting
- Multi-channel and electronic voting (via Internet access and mobile phone technology) was popular with voters but appeared to have no significant effect in raising participation
- Experiments with postal-only balloting in local and European elections for regions covering 14 million voters in June 2004 were a shambles, with delayed delivery of ballot papers, much voter confusion and allegations of wide-spread fraud. The Commission has recommended that in future no ballot should be confined to postal voting alone, and that much more preparatory work needs to be done to make the system more efficient and effective.

*Source*: Information from Electoral Commission (2002a and 2004).

➲ We will see later in this chapter that much of the crisis in political participation is actually a crisis in particular, tradi-tional forms of participation. But since these forms are the ones most valued by the Westminster political elite, the fall in this kind of participation has produced significant 'official' attempts at experimentation. The Electoral Commission cited here is a good example of the way the political elite is responding to the decline of the forms of participation it most values.

be gleaned from general elections in the 1990s. The official response was to treat this fall as a sign of a serious problem in democratic participation in Britain, and to introduce reforms designed to counter the fall. We have now seen experiments involving placing polling booths in more accessible places (pubs and supermarkets) and rules easing the conditions for voting by post (see Briefing 13.2).

Whether there is a serious problem of democra-tic participation is, however, not certain. *Patterns* of and *opportunities* for participation have undoubtedly changed, but all these changes have by no means been in the single direction of weakening democra-tic participation, as we can see if we survey some of the most important forms of participation.

## Voting

The case of voting shows how complex the true picture is. Beyond the individual case of the spec-tacular fall in turnout in the general election of 2001 there is a consistent pattern of low turnout (by

traditional general election standards) in the 'new' elections that were created in the closing years of the twentieth century: for instance, direct elections to the European Parliament (beginning in 1979) and elections for the Welsh and Northern Ireland Assemblies, and the Scottish Parliament (from 1999). But there is nothing novel in this disparity between general election turnout (see Briefing 13.3) and turnout elsewhere. As we saw in Chapter 12, there is also a long-established pattern in local government of turnout that is much lower than for general elections. The 1990s were remarkable, indeed, for the way they increased opportunities to vote in a political system that had, as we noted at the start of this chapter, been very restrictive by the standards of other democracies such as the United States. For instance, by the end of the 1990s voters in Scotland, once restricted to voting only in local government and general elections, were now able to select the European, Westminster and Scottish Parliaments, and had been able to vote for or against the principle of devolution.

# Briefing 13.3

## PARTICIPATION IN THE 2005 GENERAL ELECTION

Turnout across the United Kingdom was marginally up in 2005 on the catastrophic fall in levels recorded in 2001. But this hardly indicated any serious re-engagement with 'old style' politics. Turnout still remains well below the levels recorded as recently as the 1990s. The UK wide figures for the last four elections now read: 1992: 77.7 per cent; 1997: 71.4 per cent; 2001: 59.4 per cent; 2005: 61.3 per cent. The small rise in 2001 was more than accounted for by much relaxed (and open to serious abuse) postal voting rules. The most striking feature of participation reflected a wider feature of the electorate and of the political system: its growing fragmentation. There were sharp regional variations: turnout in the south west was 66.6 per cent, in the north west, 57.1 per cent. The differences between individual constituencies were even starker: Liverpool Riverside had a turnout of only 41 per cent; Taunton in Somerset registered a figure of 69.7 per cent. In part the disparities reflected differences in the perceptions of the marginality of contests: Riverside is safe Labour country, Taunton a wafer thin Liberal Democrat gain from the Conservatives. But it also reflected the wider fragmentation of a system of politics where the Westminster elite are well attuned to the politics and economics of London and the south of England, and less well attuned to wider, increasingly diverse society that is the United Kingdom.

This last example, of a referendum, is a striking instance of the widening range of participation. The first major referendum in modern British politics was held in 1975, on whether the terms of membership of the EEC that had been renegotiated by the Labour government returned in 1974 should be accepted (they were). At the time, there was extensive debate about the very principle of submitting a major issue to the test of a referendum, some arguing that that it contradicted the responsibilities of Cabinet government. But in the 1990s there were, as we saw in Chapter 11, referendums on devolved government proposals in Scotland and Wales, and on even bigger issues to do with govern-

ment in Northern Ireland. In 2004 there was a referendum in the north-east on the principle of regional government. In the same year the Blair government reversed a long-established position and promised a referendum on the terms of a new constitution for the European Union, and a referendum preceding any British adoption of the Euro (the common European currency) is also promised by all major parties. Three decades after that original 1975 referendum on membership of the EEC referendums seem to have become an established, if sporadically employed, method of popular decision.

In the case of general elections, because Britain has over 80 years of experience under conditions approximating universal adult suffrage, we can discern long-term trends in participation; it is precisely because the 2001 result was such a drop on the trend that it both stands out and rings alarm bells among those who think voting is important. But precisely because so many of the voting opportunities now on offer are novel it is hard to decide whether turnouts are 'high' or 'low'. Most are low by the historic standards of general elections, though when an issue is of historical importance (as in the case of the referendum on the Belfast Agreement) the turnout could actually better general election levels (see Briefing 13.4).

## Participation in parties

The evidence of participation provided by political parties is similarly mixed. One important measure of party participation is indeed unambiguous: the total membership of parties has fallen sharply over the last half-century. (In Chapter 14 we examine the institutional significance of this fall; here we are concerned only with what it means for the bigger participation picture.) Although historic measures are not totally reliable, it seems well documented that in the early 1950s the leading parties truly had mass memberships: individual membership of Conservative party associations in constituencies probably exceeded 2.8 million and the corresponding total for the Labour party was probably just over 1 million. (In addition, Labour had a huge 'affiliated' membership exceeding 5 million at national level that mostly derived from the trade unions, but this simply represented

# Briefing                                                           13.4

## NEW PARTICIPATION OPPORTUNITIES: THE CASE OF REFERENDUMS

| Year | Electorate | Issue | Turnout |
|------|-----------|-------|---------|
| 1973 | Northern Ireland | Constitutional status of Northern Ireland | 58.1% |
| 1975 | United Kingdom | UK's continued membership of the (then) European Economic Community | 63.2% |
| 1979 | Scotland | Devolution for Scotland | 63.8% |
| 1979 | Wales | Devolution for Wales | 58.3% |
| 1997 | Scotland | Devolution and tax powers for Scotland | 60.4% |
| 1997 | Wales | Devolution for Wales | 50.1% |
| 1998 | Greater London | Assembly and Mayor for London | 34.0% |
| 1998 | Northern Ireland | The Belfast (Good Friday) Agreement | 81.0% |
| 2001– | Referendums in over 30 separate local authorities | Establish elected mayors in individual local authorities | Range from 64% (Berwick-upon-Tweed) to 9.8% (Ealing) |
| 2004 | Referendum in north east of England region | To decide for or against elected regional assemblies | 48.0% |

*Source*: Adapted with additions from Magee and Outhwaite (2001).

➲ It can seem that referendums in Britain are a bit like the proverbial London bus: you wait for ages for one, and then a bunch turn up at the same time. The table shows a small bunch in the 1970s, and then a large one after the return of Labour to office in 1997. At least two more are promised, with date unspecified: to decide whether the UK will replace the pound with the Euro; and to endorse a constitution for the European Union. The permanent place of the referendum in Britain is also shown by the fact that regulation of referendums is now one of the statutory tasks of the Electoral Commission established in 2000.

the size of financial subscriptions to the party, a mechanism that is described in Chapter 14.) The youth wings of both the main parties also had large memberships; there may perhaps have been as many as 250,000 Young Conservatives. These figures are all expressed as orders of magnitude because neither party kept precise membership records.

The figures for the early 1950s, however, probably also represented an historic high point of party membership. (In other words, it we had accurate figures for earlier decades for the parties as a whole we would almost certainly record lower membership levels). What is undisputed is that even by the mid-1970s this mass membership was melting away: an official inquiry into party finances put Conservative membership at about 1.5 million – a loss of more than a million in just over 20 years (Houghton 1976). By the 1990s, the figures had fallen further. A

membership campaign after the election of Tony Blair as Leader in 1994 produced a brief rise in individual Labour party membership, but it has since fallen away, to about 250,000. There is an even more serious crisis in the Conservative party: individual membership is probably at about the same level as in the Labour party, but the age of the members is high and participation in politics through Conservative party membership does seem to be literally dying out. There has been some compensation for the whole party system in the form of increased participation through other parties: for instance, the Scottish National Party (SNP) and Plaid Cymru were tiny institutions 50 years ago.

Accurate measurement of membership levels is difficult because parties are not very efficient institutions and there are almost certainly large errors in the figures they report. But the reported decline is of such an order of magnitude that we can be certain that it corresponds to real changes. Overall, there are probably about three million fewer party members in Britain than there were in 1950, with the two leading parties, Labour and Conservative, suffering the worst damage.

As we shall see in Chapter 14 on parties and their organization, this is a serious matter for the parties. But it is less certain that it is a serious matter for the health of political participation, still less for the health of British democracy. Much depends on what participating in a party meant in the past. It is almost certainly the case that in the early 1950s, membership of the Conservative party, for instance, had more a social than political meaning: the party, especially through its well-organized network of Conservative clubs, was a part of middle-class social life. This partly helps explain the decline in membership. One undoubted reason for the fall is, for instance, the shift in occupational patterns among women. In the 1950s it was common for professional women to interrupt, or even abandon, their careers to rear children. The grassroots of the party relied heavily on these women, who by the 1990s were typically too busy juggling careers and family to devote time to local Conservative social activities. So at least part of the change in participation through parties is a reflection of wider patterns of social life.

Membership for social reasons was very important to the parties – as we will see in Chapter 14, these 'social members' of the Conservative party, for example, were crucial to fund raising. But social participation was not the same as political participation, and over time, especially in the 1990s, all the major parties increased the opportunities for participation offered to their members. We shall examine this in more detail in Chapter 14. Here, one important example will suffice. In the 1950s both the Labour and Conservative parties insisted on reserving the right to select the party leader to their respective parliamentary parties – in short, to an electorate composed of a few hundred, mostly elderly, men. Indeed, in the case of the Conservatives there was not even an open 'parliamentary' election until 1965; before that, leaders 'emerged' by a mysterious process of soundings among the parliamentary elite. Now, as we shall see in more detail when we consider the rules

in Chapter 14, membership of the two major parties (and most of the minor ones) gives to individual members the right to cast a vote in selecting the leader. While the 'quantity' of participation in parties has fallen, the quality, in the sense of an opportunity actually to take a meaningful part in important internal decisions, has actually become richer. Thus while there has been a substantial long-term withdrawal from membership of the major political parties, the effect of this on participation is not as disastrous as the bald figures might suggest. This is in part because the fact of party membership cannot simply be equated with political participation. A much higher proportion of party members than in the past are now members because they want to have a say in policy and party leadership, and the increasing need felt by parliamentary parties to share choices with rank-and-file members is a sign of this. We saw in the case of the electorate at large that opportunities to participate through elections have widened in recent years; and we can say the same thing of the internal political life of major political parties.

## Group participation

In the 1990s the American political scientist Robert Putnam prompted a great debate about democracy in the United States by arguing that a long-term decline in the stock of what he called 'social capital' had occurred. (His most extended statement is gathered in Putnam 2000.) One measure of social capital for Putnam was participation in associational life, and part of his argument was that figures showed a long-term decline in membership of all kinds of associations, many not directly connected with politics in any way. This gave him the riveting title of his main work, *Bowling Alone*, which referred to the decline of organized club competition in (ten-pin) bowling in the United States.

If a parallel decline has happened in the United Kingdom, the implications for democratic participation are gloomy (see Table 13.2). Participation in nominally 'non-political' institutions, such as churches, can be very beneficial for democratic participation. This is partly because even non-political institutions, (such as churches) intervene in political debates, giving their members a chance to have a say; and partly because participating even in non-political associations can help foster the skills, and access to social networks, that allow citizens to participate more formally in politics. One institution that undoubtedly did have these beneficial effects – the political party – has lost its power to attract a mass membership. A key question for democratic participation in Britain, therefore, is whether any groups have developed to compensate for this loss.

It is easy to show that some other important institutions have to a degree shared the fate of parties. Two obvious examples, which were briefly discussed earlier, are some Christian denominations and some trade unions. It is also easy to show that other groups have advanced in membership in recent decades. Not all religious groups have declined: among the fastest growing are the evangelical churches of Afro-Caribbean immigrants and their children, and Islam and Hinduism which are strong among groups of immigrants from the Indian sub-continent. In Chapter 9 we saw striking evidence that another field of group life – organizations such as the National Trust and the RSPB that cater for the growing interest in the environment – have seen huge membership growth in recent decades (see Table 9.1, p. 174).

It is all too easy to swap examples of groups that have declined or advanced in membership. But deciding whether Putnam's gloomy view also applies to the United Kingdom requires a more systematic comparison over time. This makes the evidence summarized in Table 13.2 valuable. It suggests that long-term, associational membership is healthy in Britain, and it also shows how important immigrant groups may have been to the renewal of associational life.

Of course, counting the numbers either of organizations or their members tells us only a limited amount. Paying a subscription to the National Trust is no more significant a form of political participation than was baking cakes for Conservative coffee mornings in the 1950s – though both activities can be important because they help fill the coffers of the organization. It is when we reflect on, and investigate, the social meaning of group membership that the connection with changes in participation becomes clearer. Here, the picture is mixed. The

**Table 13.2**  Has social capital in Britain depleted? (Associational life in a big British city: two snapshots in time of numbers of voluntary associations in Birmingham)

| Type of association | Number in 1970 | Number in 1998 |
|---|---|---|
| Sports | 2,144 | 1,192 |
| Social welfare | 666 | 1,319 |
| Cultural | 388 | 507 |
| Trade associations | 176 | 71 |
| Professional | 165 | 112 |
| Social | 142 | 398 |
| Churches | 138 | 848 |
| Forces | 122 | 114 |
| Youth | 76 | 268 |
| Technical and scientific | 76 | 41 |
| Educational | 66 | 475 |
| Trade unions | 55 | 52 |
| Health | 50 | 309 |
| Not classified | – | 75 |
| Total | 4,264 | 5,781 |

*Source*: Reproduced by permission of *Political Studies* from Maloney, Smith and Stoker (2000: 805).

➲ Debates about participation in the UK have often taken a historical turn: they concern arguments about what has happened over time. The influence of the theories of social capital associated with the American political scientist, Robert Putnam, sharpened the arguments. Putnam showed that there had been a long-term decline in associational life in the United States (Putnam 2000). An obvious question was: had the same thing happened in the UK? The great value of the study by Maloney and his colleagues is that it allows us to compare two snapshots of the same scene – associational life in the second city, Birmingham – at two separate moments in time. What is striking is not only the continued vitality of associational life, but the way some features run counter to our conventional expectations. For instance, the UK is supposed to be a society where religion is declining in influence; yet one of the most rapidly growing categories is churches. Notice also that, contrary to some theories that society is dumbing down, there has been a huge growth in the number of associations devoted to education. One factor helping account for these unexpected developments is the influence of mass immigration into Birmingham, and into other big British cities: in Britain, immigrants are usually more religious than the natives, and are keener on education.

biggest losers have probably been white manual workers and their families. The decline of trade unions has come disproportionately in traditional industries that employed manual workers; the buoyant unions are those that organize white-collar and professional workers. Similarly, the big decline in church membership and attendance has hit denominations that were important in the lives of manual workers: the non-conformist denominations such as Methodism, for example. These two instances show the subtle connection that exists between group organization and political participation (see Briefing 13.5 for more detail). Both often provided practical examples of democratic control at the lowest local level. Both offered the chance to acquire some basic skills – such as speaking in public and running meetings – that 'transfer' easily into the more formal political arena. Both provided important social networks that anyone wishing to engage in overt political activity could use. The decline of

# Briefing                                                        13.5

## THE DECAY OF TWO WORKING-CLASS NETWORKS OF PARTICIPATION: METHODISM AND THE MINERS

*Methodism*'s founder, John Wesley, was born in 1703. Methodism began as a part of the established Church of England, attempting to reach the faithful by a more direct and colloquial style than was practised by official religion. But by the start of the nineteenth century it was a fully independent denomination, and by the start of the twentieth century it had reached its peak, with nearly a million members of Methodist congregations in the UK. A century later membership was only just over 300,000 and falling rapidly, principally because that membership was itself old. It is likely to die out, literally, within a couple of decades. Methodism was a key institution in encouraging working-class participation in politics, especially in the early decades of the history of the Labour party. The faith was particularly strong among the manual working class created by industrialism. In an age when formal education for workers was limited, the Bible and the great hymns of Methodism were an important contribution to the literacy and general culture of workers. Methodist congregations are largely self-governing, so the life of chapels provided a training ground in politics and organizing skills. And the direct inspiration of the Bible, especially the New Testament, was an important source of the commitment to social justice in the new Labour party. With the decay of Methodism, all this – the organizing base and the Christian inspiration – has greatly weakened. Paradoxically, the decay of British Methodism has coincided with its rise globally: there are 33 million Methodists across the globe, and prominent Methodists include George Bush (US President 2000–) and Nelson Mandela.

*The National Union of Mineworkers* (NUM) was formed in 1945 by an amalgamation of the different regional parts of the Miners' Federation of Great Britain. It then had 533,000 members. Miners were the pioneers of working-class political activism. Miners' unions were the first to send their own officials into the Westminster Parliament; the acknowledged founder of the Labour party, Keir Hardie, was a union officer in Ayrshire; and until the 1980s the union was a powerful voice in the Labour movement and an important means by which this group of manual workers exercised direct control in the party (for instance, by continuing to send into Parliament members who had actually worked as miners). As recently as the mid-1980s, over 190,000 people worked in mining – almost all belonging to unions. The latest official records (2003) show that the National Union of Miners has just over 5,000 members. The catastrophic decline is due to two linked factors: a disastrous, defeated strike in the mid-1980s, and the almost total disappearance of deep coalmining as an industry in Britain. The NUM not only provided a direct channel into politics; just as Methodism imparted political and organizing skills, running the union at pit level was often the way future mining politicians acquired the skills needed for effective participation. All this has now disappeared.

⭕ The decay of Methodism and mining unionism has been catastrophic for working-class participation in politics. In some instances the impact has been redoubled because the two were historically linked: some of the greatest centres of working-class Methodism were in the coalfields, such as the now vanished coalfield communities of South Wales.

the unions and non-conformist churches has therefore made political participation by groups in the population who already suffer disadvantage more difficult. By contrast, the health of religious institutions among new communities of immigrants is important in providing a voice for those who, for other reasons, find conventional political participation difficult: because in the first generation they may lack fluency in English, and because, as the poorest, they have least leisure to engage in politics.

The rise in membership of environmental groups hints at another beneficial consequence of group change for political participation. These groups, too, even when they are not overtly formed to press for changes in public policy, can provide networks for those wishing to become active in changing policy: for instance, local Ramblers' Associations – who hardly exist primarily for purposes of political participation – have been an important means of allowing individuals to group together to lobby for the opening of public footpaths and more general 'rights to roam' over large parts of the countryside. (For a historical example, look back at Image 13.1.)

This last example illuminates an important feature of the changing relationship between group organization and political participation. All our examples so far have been of formally organized groups; but many of the groups in question shade off into more informal social movements, and help create the networks that allow these movements to operate. These movements are perhaps the single most important influence on the changing nature of political participation.

## Social movements and direct action

A 'social movement' is a broad and imprecise category; but this lack of precision is understandable because we are dealing with a broad and imprecise category of social organization. We have already encountered the idea of these movements when we examined group representation (in the form, for example, of the many groups concerned with the defence of the physical environment). The new movements have considerably widened the range of public participation beyond conventional lobbying of government. They create conditions for flexible, rapid and often unpredictable mobilization of large numbers of people, often around particular issues that have appeared suddenly on the political agenda. Three examples show the possibilities:

- In the autumn of 2000 government was taken completely by surprise by mass blockades of fuel depots, mostly by farmers protesting against the level of fuel tax. (The example is described in more detail in Chapter 9, p. 179.)
- The 'Countryside Alliance', a loose alliance of a very wide range of rural interests, mobilized up to 250,000 people for a protest march in London against a ban on hunting with dogs (see Image 13.2).
- An even larger series of mass demonstrations – possibly exceeding 1 million people in London alone – protested early in 2003 against the imminent war on Iraq. This was probably the largest single public demonstration of political protest in modern British history.

These are only the most spectacular and widely reported instances of countless demonstrations that take the form of direct action: in other words they bypass conventional lobbying of policy makers and public representatives in favour of the direct expression of (usually) hostility to some government policy. They stretch from demonstrations about the largest historical issues – such as war – to the most local, such as opposition to particular road-building schemes. They also stretch across the full range of forms of participation. Most involve the peaceful, passive mass expression of opinion, perhaps by marching and banner carrying; but some also involve active forms of civil disobedience – for instance, passive obstruction of large building projects such as roads and airport runways by occupying the land to be built on. And, on occasions, as in a series of protests against high finance and globally organized corporations, they have stretched to sabotage and other attacks on property.

There is an irony surrounding these new forms of participation. Though undoubtedly 'new' in the setting of modern British politics, they actually resurrect an old tradition of political participation in Britain that disappeared for much of the

## Image 13.2
## Political participation 'new-style' in action

Photo: Maurice McDonald/PA/EMPICS

➲ The photo shows a pro-hunting demonstration against the Bill which eventually outlawed hunting with dogs in 2005. The picture shows demonstrator Daisey Crutchley, a name that might have come from a bucolic soap opera such as *The Archers*. The anti-hunting demonstrators were a striking instance of the capacity of 'new-style' political participation to by-pass old institutions such as parties, and to mobilize on to the streets young demonstrators who in a previous generation would have been indifferent to politics, or who would have been quietly baking cakes for Conservative party coffee mornings. The 2005 general election showed that the anti-hunting lobby was electorally unimportant; but these young people flexed their muscles in the student vote.

twentieth century. Many of the great constitutional and humanitarian reforms of the nineteenth century – such as the abolition of slavery and the extension of the franchise – were accompanied by spectacular public demonstrations, sometimes accompanied by violence and destruction of property. The revival of direct action of this kind thus shows that while there may be a decline in some forms of participation, other forms are rising. In particular, participation that is channelled through the institutions that are most closely tied to Westminster politics – such as voting, and membership of the traditionally dominant parties that fight each other in Westminster – is being displaced by this direct action. The participation that we earlier labelled 'old-style' is therefore not all that old: it is mostly a characteristic of the decades in the twentieth century when the Westminster system of government was utterly dominant in the United Kingdom. Moreover, the participation that we have labelled 'new-style' actually often has a long historical ancestry.

Many reasons help to account for the rise of direct action. One of the most obvious is, simply, the declining hold of the established political parties: 50 years ago, most people who wanted to express their political views beyond the act of voting joined a political party, and took it from there – and

taking it from there hardly ever meant direct political action. All the parties were agreed that the point of political action was to change policy by changing government, and this meant succeeding in Parliamentary elections. The fact that the politically active no longer automatically absorb themselves in party activity has opened up opportunities to by-pass the party route in favour of trying to change policy by more direct means.

Numerous social changes have accelerated these developments. Many readers of this book will have direct experience of one: the creation of a mass system of higher education. In the 1960s about 5 per cent of the 18–21 age group attended university; now over 40 per cent of the same age group are in higher education. Most large British cities have areas dominated by student populations: in Manchester, for instance, there are well over 50,000 full-time students in higher education at any one time. These areas, and the universities themselves, provide ready-made networks for mobilizing people into direct participation.

However, while it is possible to see the influence of this student group in mass participation in movements focused on peace, the environment and animal rights, this cannot be the whole story. For instance, while it was reported that some fox-hunting public school boys had supported mass

## DOCUMENTING POLITICS 13.1

### NEW STYLES OF PARTICIPATION: AN ANTI-GLOBALIZATION MOVEMENT IN ACTION

'About Us

*Jubilee Research* is building on the work of the hugely successful Jubilee 2000 [see below] debt cancellation campaign, and in particular its reputation for providing up-to-date, accurate research, analyses, news and data on international debt and finance ... We are not just an economic think-tank. We are a think-and-do tank. We encourage our readers to undertake advocacy and campaign action. *Jubilee Research* continues to work closely with the campaigning groups around the world which have taken over the mantle of the Jubilee 2000 campaign ... Jubilee 2000 grew from small beginnings to become an international campaign that brought great pressure to bear on G7 leaders to 'cancel the unpayable debts of the poorest countries by the year 2000, under a fair and transparent process'. By the end of the campaign, 24 million signatures had been gathered for the Jubilee 2000 petition, the first-ever global petition. There were Jubilee 2000 campaigns in more than 60 countries around the world.'

➲ These passages are edited extracts of the main web page of the campaigning group, Jubilee Research. In Britain the group started in the run-up to the millennium as Jubilee 2000, a mass campaign to persuade governments, including Britain's, to cancel the debts of poor countries. After the millennium, as the text makes clear, the campaign was converted into a wider campaign aimed to mobilize anti-globalization groups from many sources: the radical political left, Christian and other churches. Two particularly important features should be noted: the way the movement uses the technology of the web to link networks of groups, partly by the simple device of providing links to other web addresses; and the way this British group is embedded in a global network of groups – once again, partly courtesy of the web.

*Source*: www.jubilee2000.org

demonstrations by the Countryside Alliance, it is unlikely that there were many university students on their marches. To political changes (such as the decline of political parties) and social changes (such as the rise of mass higher education) we should add the importance of changes in technology. One historical advantage the state had over protest groups was its own well-organized communication systems: armies and police forces usually, for instance, had their own radio communication systems. For most of the twentieth century the state in Britain was also the monopoly owner of the network for landline telephone communication. Newer technologies have tilted the balance of advantage towards citizens wishing to organize at short notice. The spread of mobile phone ownership and of Internet access have both been important contributions, making the swift, cheap organization of new networks much easier. The

rapid fall in the cost of powerful desktop computing since the 1980s has also reduced the costs of organizing for participation. A PC costing less than £500 can store and process data that at the start of the 1980s could be stored only on a huge, expensive mainframe computer. It is now possible, for example, to store, exchange, retrieve and use the database of contacts of large numbers of supporters and potential supporters of an organization for purposes such as mail shots, circulars and newsletters. Cheap, easy-to-use desktop publishing packages have also transformed small group publishing, making it much easier than in the past to produce attractively laid-out minority interest newspapers, newsletters, magazines and pamphlets. Finally, the spread of global networks linked by Internet communication means that states find it hard to control and censor international communication. (For an example, see Documenting Politics 13.1.)

**Figure 13.3**   Political participation, new-style (percentage who said they had undertaken the action in the previous 12 months)

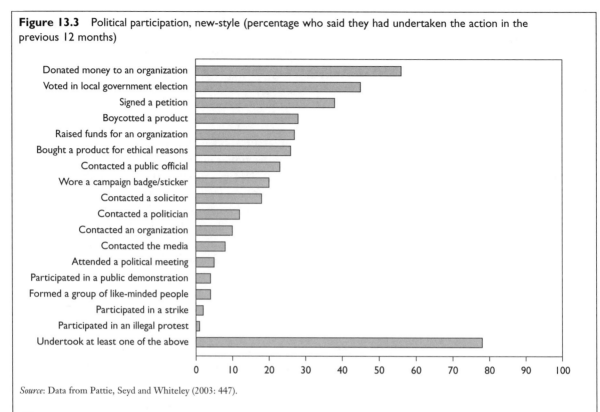

*Source*: Data from Pattie, Seyd and Whiteley (2003: 447).

These figures come from a national survey dating from autumn 2000. It is instructive to compare the findings with Figure 13.1. The differences are partly due to methods of enquiry. Pattie, Seyd and Whiteley actually impose a 'harder' test because participation must have taken place within the previous 12 months. But despite this, and despite the perceived crisis of participation, the overall result actually suggests high levels of engagement. But this engagement is no longer so focused on established institutions such as parties, but is highly individual: the best symbol is the figure of 26 per cent who bought a product for ethical reasons (for instance, choosing a 'Fair Trade' brand). This is undoubtedly a political act, but one typically practised in the supermarket, not in any more obvious political forum.

## From group to individual participation: summing up changing patterns of participation

Some of the social networks that were once important in encouraging political participation – such as working-class Methodism – are in serious decline. Conversely, we have many new technologies that make group organization easier. These two unconnected developments may help explain why the very latest research tells us that participation is actually very much more common than we may conventionally assume, but that it does not take the forms that we have come to expect. Participation is happening: we have just not been looking for it in the right

places. In particular, while there has been a decline in some important forms of group participation, such as activism in political parties, individual acts of participation are in truth very common, and may be becoming commoner. By individual acts are meant those that we can take as single individuals: signing petitions, writing letters, spontaneously attending demonstrations. A year-long study of a sample of the population conducted over 2000 found that three out of four people (or 33 million adults) engaged in one or more political activities. These included: 29 million who had given money to a citizen's organization; 22 million who had signed a petition; 18 million who had boycotted some products in their day-to-day shopping; and 2.5

# DEBATING POLITICS

## 13.1   HAVE CHANGES IN PATTERNS OF PARTICIPATION BENEFITED OR DAMAGED THE HEALTH OF BRITISH DEMOCRACY?

| An age of apathy is damaging British democracy | Participation has changed, not declined, and changed for the better |
|---|---|
| ■ The institutions that were at the heart of the development of modern British democracy – notably the mass political parties – have lost their mass membership. | ■ The decline of institutions such as mass parties is no loss to democracy: they were just means by which metropolitan elites exploited a large rank and file to raise money and to fight elections. |
| ■ 'Conventional' politics – the politics at the core of the state machine, such as voting to elect government – is what really shapes our lives and this is the kind of politics in which citizens are losing interest. | ■ Much of the supposed decline in participation is due to the fact that we have not been looking in the right places: we have had too narrowly conventional a view of what is participation. |
| ■ Though some kinds of participation are widespread, they are typically sporadic, and focused on single issues which arouse great emotional fervour and then rapidly fade away. | ■ New technologies and new social attitudes have produced a huge growth in new kinds of participation. |
| ■ Political participation has turned into an isolated, individual activity, rather than a sustained form of group commitment. | ■ The new participation is much healthier for democracy than was the old, because it allows the more direct expression of citizen concerns than did hierarchical institutions such as mass parties. |

million who had taken part in a demonstration (for more information, see Figure 13.3). These findings immediately make sense of the some of the features we noticed earlier in the chapter, including the sudden rise of mass demonstrations focused on single issues, whether they be fuel costs or foreign wars.

Not only does this research oblige us to be cautious about picturing ours as an age of apathy; it also calls into question our conventional notion of what constitutes political participation. A more expansive notion of participation can turn a visit to the supermarket into an act of participation: if you buy Fair Trade Coffee in preference to Tesco's own brand because you believe it offers a fairer deal to coffee farmers, then you are engaged in a political act. This is not politics as it was understood in the great days of the mass party, when participation was channelled into party membership and party activism, but it could hardly be said to be an inferior or less effective form of democratic participation. Is it less political to boycott the coffee rather than to

brew the coffee? Who is the more serious political activist: the boycotter of coffee products, or the foot soldiers in the mass party who 40 years ago were used by the party elite to raise money by coffee mornings, to stuff envelopes and to get out the vote every four or five years?

## Participation and Westminster democracy

Political participation brings us to a paradox about the nature of the governance of Britain. We live under a system of democratic politics. At the heart of the idea of democracy – contained even in the root of the word – is the notion of popular rule; yet genuinely popular participation in the system of government has been confined to rare moments, most obviously voting in fairly infrequent general elections. What is more, popular participation has been organized through institutions – such as elections and the dominant political parties – focused on the political struggle in the Westminster system. Numerous mechanisms excluded from this established world a variety of social groups, and viewed as problematic forms of participation such as civil disobedience and industrial action (see Debating Politics 13.1).

In the domain of participation, as in other domains examined in earlier chapters, the established routines of the Westminster system are now under pressure. There has been a withdrawal of much popular participation from the established channels: the evidence includes the decline in turnout for general elections and, most striking of all, the virtual collapse in the membership of the major political parties. This is, however, not a crisis of participation, but rather a crisis in one form of participation. The opportunities to participate, even in elections, have expanded as the Westminster system has been reformed; and while turnout in elections for the newly devolved governments is lower than has been usual for general elections, we need to bear in mind that even at these lower levels we are witnessing participation which simply did not exist as recently as a decade ago. Moreover, new forms of participation are drawing groups into political action in fresh, and often unexpected, ways. Much of this change is renewing traditions of participation that declined in the heyday of Westminster-focused politics. The great modern campaigns, such the campaign for the relief of Third World debt profiled in Documenting Politics 13.1, echo some of the great campaigns of the nineteenth century, such as those against slavery and the evils of alcohol. There is therefore a problem of participation in Britain only if we insist on putting a special value on forms of participation that focus on Westminster, and if we imply that the new patterns are either only of marginal importance, or are in some way threatening to democratic government.

## REVIEW

Four themes have dominated this chapter:

1 The restricted notions of popular participation that characterized British democracy in the era of the domination of the Westminster system;
2 The numerous barriers to participation that excluded, and still do partly exclude, a wide range of social groups;
3 The decline of the classic forms of mass participation that were at the heart of the Westminster system;
4 The renewal of a tradition of mass political action as a result of a mix of social and cultural change.

## Further reading

The classic study of participation in Britain, and the essential starting point for any study of participation and British democracy, is Parry, Moyser and Day (1992). At the time of writing, results are still coming out from later studies of new forms of participation, but Pattie, Seyd and Whiteley (2003) is an important source. Putnam (2000) created a sensation when it appeared, and while it concerned the United States it aroused wide interest in the United Kingdom. The importance of Maloney, Smith and Stoker (2000), referred to in the text of this chapter, is that it suggests a considerably brighter condition for social capital than might be inferred from Putnam. Cain, Dalton and Scarrow (2003) is an important collection of comparative essays which describes the wider social forces reshaping participation, and thus illuminates a key theme of this chapter – that participation has not declined, but changed.

CHAPTER 14

# Parties and their organization

## AIMS

This chapter:

❖ Explains why party organization is important

❖ Introduces the historical development of party organization

❖ Sketches the organization of the main parties in Britain

❖ Shows how and why the mass party is in decline

❖ Describes how this decline has changed the nature of parties and how they are regulated

❖ Examines the argument that parties are not in decline but have evolved into new kinds of 'cadre' parties.

## Why parties organize

Organized political parties are a universal feature of all modern democracies – indeed, of almost all modern political systems. They have been at the centre of British politics for over two centuries, although the nature of their organization has altered greatly over that time. Parties organize because in Britain they have a central role to play in vital aspects of the system of government. If parties did not exist we would have to invent them, or invent some other way of carrying out the functions for which they are organized. Four of these functions are particularly important.

### Fighting elections

Competitive elections are the single most important defining feature of democracy, and in Britain the competition is overwhelmingly between parties. As we shall see when we turn to our chapter on elections, it is now almost unknown for anyone to enter the Westminster House of Commons, or one of the new devolved assemblies, without the nomination of one of the major parties. Styles of fighting elections are changing all the time, but they still depend heavily on party organization. At local level the party remains the key unit of organization to canvass voters, distribute propaganda material and try to persuade electors to vote on election day. At national level, which is increasingly the most important arena for election competition, parties are the dominant unit of organization: an election campaign for the Westminster Parliament or for one of the new national assemblies introduced under devolution is largely a contest between nationally organized party machines.

### Raising money

Politics costs money, and fighting elections in particular can cost large amounts: for instance, in the general election of 2001 the two big parties, Labour and the Conservatives, declared combined national spending of over £23 million (Fisher 2003). Parties use all levels of their organization to raise this money: individual members contribute subscriptions or, sometimes, larger donations; local branches of parties hold numerous fund-raising

---

**Images 14.1 and 14.2**
**The historical residue of the mass party**

Image 14.1    A Conservative Club

Image 14.2    A former Liberal Club

⊃ The two photographs convey the physical face of the political party from the age of mass party organization, and show how anachronistic it now is. The first image is of a Conservative Club, the second of what was once a Liberal Club, both in a small northern industrial town. They incarnate the ambitions of parties with a mass membership, and when built they were among the most imposing buildings in the town centre. Notice the balcony feature on both, designed to allow triumphal party proclamations. The Conservative Club now functions solely as a drinking club; the Liberal Club has long since been turned into a theatre (the advertisement for the latest production can be seen).

functions; at national level immense effort is put into cultivating rich individuals and institutions for donations. Fund-raising activities have been an important catalyst in recent years for changes in party organization, as will become clear later in this chapter.

## Representing interests

There exists an elaborate network of specialized interest representation in Britain, but parties are also important in interest representation, and their organization is often shaped by this fact. The clearest instance is provided by the Labour party, which was first founded as an arm of the trade union movement, and whose internal organization, as we shall see, still bears testament to these origins.

## Recruiting political leadership

The most direct way, though not the only route, to the top in British politics is via membership of a political party (see Chapter 18). Above all, parties in Britain organize to provide the most important of all group of political leaders: those who occupy governing positions, at all levels of the multi-level of system of governance in Britain. Party is key to leadership recruitment in all the assemblies we have examined so far in this book: in the Westminster Parliament, in the new devolved assemblies and in the European Parliament. And while there is some sign that the grip of party over leadership recruitment is weakening a little in the newer local government institutions (notably the new elected mayoralties), even in local government party remains the key organizational funnel through which most potential leaders have to pass. Were parties to be abolished tomorrow, we would have to find some different organizing process through which political leaders generally, and governments in particular, could be selected in Britain.

Parties organize, then, because if they did not we would have to invent them, or invent some other means of doing what they presently do.

## The historical development of party organization

Parties have deep historical roots in British politics (see Images 14.1 and 14.2). Groups claiming the label party were already exceptionally influential in the parliaments of the eighteenth century. But the modern history of party organization has been closely shaped by the developing history of the British system of government. The parties that grew out of the eighteenth-century parliament were what are commonly called *cadre* parties in their organization, meaning that they mostly consisted of a small cadre (group) of leaders at the centre. Indeed, until well into the nineteenth century parties were not much more than labels worn by factions inside Parliament: they had little internal discipline, were rarely united by any coherent political principles, and had only loose links with wider interests in the society.

That situation was transformed by changes in the size and role of the electorate in the nineteenth century. Beginning with the Great Reform Act of 1832, the size and social range of the electorate grew: before the Great Reform Act of 1832 there were just over half a million voters; by the reform of 1885, the last great extension of the nineteenth century, there were over 5.5 million. In 1832, the vote was restricted mostly to a small range of property owners. Less than a century later, in 1918, after periodic relaxations of the property requirements, it was finally opened up to all adult males and most adult women. Inevitably, parties now had to organize to represent an increasingly wide range of social and economic interests.

Mass party organization was also prompted by changes in rules governing elections. Until 1872 ballots were cast in public, and electors could thus be bribed or intimidated into voting for particular candidates. The introduction of the secret ballot in that year, especially when coupled with the increase in the size of electorate, made these weapons largely redundant. Some other way had to be found of appealing to the loyalty of large numbers of voters.

The development of the franchise throughout the nineteenth century therefore presented parties with two connected problems: how to organize an electorate that grew in size and social range; and how to attract the votes of this electorate when the secret ballot meant that it could not could not be directly bought or coerced. Cadre parties, made up largely of factions of Westminster parliamentarians, were useless at solving these problems. The two parties that dominated British politics from the middle of the nineteenth century until the end of the First World War in 1918 – the Liberal and Conservative Parties – both shifted from being cadre to mass parties in response to this problem. The connection between party organization and the new electorate is shown by the fact that the great spurt in party organization in the country at large happened soon after the passage of the 1867 Reform Act, the first piece of reform that not only expanded the electorate greatly but, for the first time, gave votes to sizeable numbers of manual workers.

Although there were differences in the organization of the Conservative and Liberal parties, they shared important features:

● They both aimed to recruit a mass membership.
● In order to provide an incentive to members to join, they established bodies which claimed to give members a say in how the party was run, and in particular a say in the policies which the party put before electorates.
● They formed local organizations based on Westminster parliamentary constituencies, since the most important function of the new mass membership was to help convince electors to identify with the party, and then turn out to vote for it on election day.
● As a further incentive to local organization they gave these local parliamentary associations a big say – in many cases the dominant say – over who would be selected as the party's parliamentary candidate, and thus gave an early say in leadership selection to local activists.
● They used mass organization to raise money, both by direct subscriptions and by encouraging local party activists to raise funds.

By the end of the nineteenth century a model of party organization that lasted through much of the twentieth century was thus already established. The rise of the Labour party, which displaced the Liberal party as the main opponent of the Conservatives after the First World War, gave the mass party an extra dimension. Because the Conservatives had first existed as a parliamentary faction, and then only created a mass party to solve the problems this faction faced in managing the new mass electorate, the party organization in the country had always been subordinate to the parliamentary leadership. But the Labour party was mostly created outside Parliament, and already had a fully-fledged national party structure with its own constitution and conference before Labour became a significant parliamentary force. Labour developed a theory of party organization which, on some readings, gave the party in the country, and notably its annual party conference, the dominant voice in deciding party policy. At the party conference all the extra-parliamentary interests in the party were represented: notably, the trade unions and the individual members organized into constituency Labour parties. Just how far this theory can be made to work, as we will see, has been a long-term problem for the Labour party.

The rise of Labour ushered in the age of the mass party, an age that lasted over half-a-century. The mass party flourished in a period when leaders had to reach millions of electors, and when the only direct means of doing this was through personal contact. Election campaigns turned on contacting voters personally, and addressing as many as possible in public meetings and by canvassing. All this demanded masses of volunteers. But the rise first of radio, and then (in the 1950s) the increasing importance of television in contacting voters, changed styles of campaigning and made the mass party progressively less important. Leaders now began to appeal directly to voters through news and current affairs broadcasts. The mass meeting and direct canvassing of voters became just a subsidiary instrument: a means of providing 'sound bites' for radio and television. By the 1990s the mass party had even ceased to be important in reaching individual voters. Parties could do the job by centrally organized telephone canvassing; they could gauge public opinion by increasingly sophisticated polling methods; and they could try to persuade electors by expensive advertising campaigns. These develop-

**Figure 14.1** From giants to pygmies: the declining membership of the Conservative and Labour parties

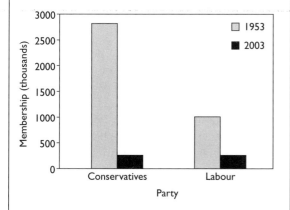

*Sources*: Figures for 1953 from Butler and Butler (2000: 141, 158); 2003 figures are estimates from party sources.

➲ Estimating the individual membership of parties is an inexact art, so the numbers on which this figure is based are approximations. But the orders of magnitude are not disputed. In the early 1950s both main parties had huge individual memberships: that is, real people who paid their own subscriptions for membership. The Conservatives also had more than double the individual membership of the Labour party. By the start of the twenty-first century both parties probably had about the same number of members – around 250,000 each – but the Conservatives were probably in a weaker condition because they had an older membership.

ments help explain a feature we noticed in Chapter 13: the fact that since the 1950s the total membership of parties has fallen by well over two million (see Figure 14.1).

This does not mean that party organization, especially party organization outside Parliament, has become irrelevant; on the contrary, as we shall shortly see, all the major parties have been making increasing efforts to involve their members more closely in party government, especially in leadership selection. Parties have not viewed the decline in their membership with indifference: both Labour and the Conservatives have launched periodic campaigns in the last decade to recruit new members. Leaders worry about the health of the mass party because, for all the changes that have occurred in campaigning styles, the party still carries out important functions. Thus while local

campaigning by party members is now only marginal to results, these margins can decide elections: in the 2001 general election ten seats were won by a margin of fewer than 400 votes. Constituency parties also still have a dominant say in selecting candidates for parliamentary elections (and both below and above that, party members have a large say in selecting council candidates, and candidates for European constituencies). Party leaders worry that if they do not have a large and local active membership it would be easy for the selection process to be controlled by a small faction. And for all the changes that have come over the mass party, one factor that was critical to its birth remains as vital as ever: money. The new styles of campaigning, though no longer as demanding of people power, are even more financially demanding.

We will see when considering the individual parties themselves that their organization reflects the legacies and problems of the age of the mass party.

## The Conservative party: organization and power

The Conservative party, we saw above, originated as a Parliamentary faction, and only created itself as a mass organized party to cope with the demands of fighting elections under the secret ballot and expanded suffrage in the nineteenth century. This gave the organization of the party a distinctive character. Above all, it ensured that the party in Parliament, and especially the parliamentary leadership, was the dominant component. But this by no means consigned the rest of the party to insignificance. Above all, the parliamentary party's control was limited by the decentralized structure of the wider party. The party in the constituency – the Constituency Association – was the key unit of organization in the mass party. It was impossible to join a national Conservative party because the Conservative party nationally was just an assembly of these different constituency organizations.

The importance of this mass organization was heightened by the fact that it was very successful. The Conservatives were easily the best organized mass political movement in twentieth-century Britain. There were around 250,000 Young Conservatives in the golden years of the early 1950s; it is possible that there are now only 5,000 of their contemporary equivalents. These figures are approximate for a reason that is itself revealing: the party has always been haphazard about recording and retaining its members. Historically, this reflected the fact that party organization in the country was as much social as political. The vitality and numbers derived in part from the fact that the party was an important institution in middle-class social life, but this integration between party organization and middle-class culture made the mass party even more significant.

The decentralized nature, and the social character of the party in the country, provided the clues to how party organization in practice functioned – better clues than lie in any formal organization chart. For instance, formally the party outside Parliament had no more than an advisory role in making policy. Thus the event called colloquially the Conservative Annual Conference was actually just an Assembly of the separate autonomous constituency associations with only an advisory role on policy. In practice, relations of influence in the party were more subtle than this simple organization model suggested. Decentralization into highly autonomous constituencies put several powerful cards into the hands of local constituency activists. It gave them a very high level of control over the selection of parliamentary candidates and therefore, in safe seats, control over who would be returned as Conservative MPs. It gave them a large say over finance in the party, since the party's wealth – which was great – depended heavily on the funds raised by the constituencies. When the party had a mass of members these constituencies were formidable fund-raising machines. And in part because of their role in parliamentary candidate selection, local associations had a direct, if informal, line of communication with the Parliamentary leadership on matters of policy and political strategy.

These generalizations are in the past tense because the Conservative party is in a period of great change. The forces prompting change include a catastrophic fall in constituency membership; the huge defeats suffered by the Conservatives in the general elections of 1997 and 2001; and the question mark placed over Conservative party organization in Wales and Scotland by dismal results for elections to the Westminster Parliament and the development of the distinct patterns of devolved politics following the devolution reforms in those two countries. Eighteen years in government (1979–97) had led to neglect of party organization. The election of William Hague as party leader in 1997 following the party's landslide defeat at the hands of Labour provided the occasion for institutional reform. Plainly influenced by the example of Labour party leaders from Kinnock to Blair in reshaping their party institutions, Hague quickly produced a series of proposals for reform. These reforms (see Briefing 14.1 for details) showed the impact of a new creed of managerialism in the party. (Hague's one proper job outside politics had been a spell as a management consultant with the world's leading management consultancy, McKinsey.) An attempt was made to trim the size of some of the more unwieldy old institutions, such as the Executive Council, which had a theoretical membership of nearly 1,000! A Management Board was established with the object of unifying what had been formerly two separate institutions, the party organization controlled by the Leader and the National Union of Constituency Associations in the country at large. An attempt was made to spell out clear lines of responsibility between the components of the party. In short, an attempt was made to replace the decentralized, rather ramshackle structure that had grown up since the nineteenth century.

Perhaps even more significant than the institutional changes themselves was the manner of their introduction. In an echo of a tactic used by Tony Blair when he became leader of the Labour party, Hague organized a plebiscite of party members through a postal ballot to give a verdict on his proposals. (They were overwhelmingly endorsed.) This attempt to draw in the wider membership was also reflected in the new rules for selecting the Leader which Hague also introduced in 1998. As Timeline 14.1 shows, this continues a long-established widening of the group entitled to a say in choice of party leader.

# Briefing

## THE CRISIS OF CONSERVATIVE PARTY ORGANIZATION

Although the Conservative party historically had a reputation of being a tightly controlled hierarchy, it was anything but. Indeed it was a highly fragmented institution in which local constituency associations had great autonomy, and the representative bodies were often huge and chaotically run. This worked fairly well when the culture of the party was deferential, the parliamentary elite was left to get on with its job, and the so-called Annual Conference could be used as a big social occasion and for propaganda purposes. But in the 1980s and 1990s membership declined catastrophically, and at the same time activists began to demand a greater say in policy making. The 'Hague reforms' of 1998 were partly modelled on reforms already made in the Labour party, and partly reflected Mr Hague's experiences as a management consultant. They established:

- *A Board* to meet monthly, charged with overall responsibility for all aspects of party management beyond the parliamentary party in Westminster
- *A National Convention* to meet twice yearly, mostly with the job of channelling grassroots views to the Leader
- *A National Convention Executive*, a small body with executive responsibilities, reporting to the Board
- *Policy Forums*, an idea copied directly from Labour. These are networks of ordinary members, to be consulted on policy documents and issues. This is an attempt to damp down the increasingly difficult-to-manage Annual Conference.

*Sources*: Information from Kelly (1999 and 2001).

➲ The organization of the party is in crisis: membership is falling catastrophically, and settled agreements about the division of responsibilities between the parliamentary leadership and the rank-and-file membership are under challenge. The changes summarized above are an attempt to move from the informal, often chaotic, structures of the past to a more formally organized institution.

These reforms in part 'empower' the party in the country more formally than in the past, but they also attempt to organize it on more centralized lines. This has made the position and organization of Central Office, the party's central headquarters, more prominent and contentious. ('Central Office' is forever associated with the party's historic, imposing headquarters in Smith Square, just round the corner from the Palace of Westminster. In a sign of the fallen fortunes of the party, its headquarters are now housed in offices over a Starbucks in Victoria Street. I retain the traditional usage here.) Central Office, like any bureaucracy, has its own distinctive culture, interests and feuds, but the most distinctive feature of the national organization is the extent to which it is put at the disposal of whoever happens to be leader of the party at any particular moment. The leader has the power of hiring and firing, and while this obviously cannot be

done capriciously, in practice the leader does have a large say over key personnel appointments. Perhaps the single most important organizational appointment made by the leader is that of chairman of the party, for the chairman can be, and in recent cases almost always has been, the main 'manager' of the party on the leader's behalf. As a result appointment of, and dismissal of, the Party Chairman has often been a public signal of internal power struggles in the party.

The role of Central Office, and its relationship with the parliamentary leadership of the party, depends heavily on whether the party is in government or opposition. Not surprisingly, when the party was in its long occupation of government from 1979 to 1997 it was more marginal, rising to prominence at key moments such as general elections. But the Central Office machine nevertheless has key enduring functions in the party regardless of

## TIMELINE 14.1  THE EVOLUTION OF CONSERVATIVE LEADERSHIP SELECTION METHODS

### 1922–65

Conservative leader 'emerged' by a secret, informal process of consultation involving leading Conservatives, mostly in the House of Commons. In this period every change of Conservative Leader took place while the party held office and a name was forwarded by the party leadership to the monarch of a figure who was to be invited to invited to form a government.

### 1965

Leader to be elected by secret ballot of all Conservative MPs. Failure to produce majority winner (50 per cent of all votes cast and margin of 15 per cent over second candidate) leads to second ballot; if still no clear winner, 'run off' between the two top candidates. Leaders elected under this method were Edward Heath (1965–75), Margaret Thatcher (1975–90); John Major (1990–97); William Hague, (1997–2001). All but John Major were elected while the party was in opposition.

### 1975

Provision for annual re-election introduced, allowing leader to be challenged. Procedure invoked by Margaret Thatcher in her successful challenge to Edward Heath, 1975; by Sir Anthony Meyer against Margaret Thatcher, unsuccessfully, in 1989; and by Michael Heseltine in November 1990, leading to Mrs Thatcher's displacement, but by John Major, not Mr Heseltine.

### 1998

William Hague introduces new rules with two provisions:

- Annual re-election rule abolished. Provision for (maximum of one) no-confidence vote per year, to be triggered by call for ballot of Conservative MPs supported by at least 15 per cent of MPs. Passage of no-confidence vote triggers leadership election.
- Leadership election in two stages: if more than two candidates, MPs vote to eliminate all but top two, bottom candidate being eliminated in each successive round. Remaining two candidates contest for simple majority of all members of the Conservative party in the country.

### 2001

Iain Duncan Smith elected Conservative Leader by this method in 2001, following resignation of William Hague after general election defeat.

### 2003

Michael Howard 'crowned' as Leader, 2003: Conservative MPs agree among themselves on a single candidate, and the wider Party electorate is left merely to endorse their choice.

### 2005

Howard annonces that he will stand down after a gap allowing reconsideration of election method.

➲ The history of Conservative leadership election methods since the mid-1960s is essentially one of 'broadening the franchise', to the present point where the critical choice is formally in the hands of rank and file Conservatives in the country. The significance of starting the timeline at 1922 is the following: while before then the 'emergence' of leaders after informal consultation took place, 1922 marks the date of the beginning of formal organization by all Conservative backbench Members of Parliament. (For the history of the 1922 Committee, see text.) But, as the 'crowning' of Michael Howard in 2003 shows, the wider membership can still be deprived of the opportunity to make a choice.

whether the Conservatives are in office or opposition. It is the backbone of the machine at the leader's disposal for fighting elections. It controls an important gateway to Parliament, because eligibility for selection as a Conservative parliamentary candidate depends on being on the Central Office-approved list of candidates. It is the main machine by which the party seeks to raise funds, either from the constituency parties at large in the country, from the donations of companies or from wealthy individuals. Above all, the Central Office machine is an important means by which the leader attempts to manage the wider party in the country.

This brief summary highlights one overwhelmingly important contingency: the biggest single influence on the practical working of Conservative party organization is whether the party is in opposition or government, and this contingency makes the role of the parliamentary party uniquely sensitive, if only because, as we saw earlier, the party began as a parliamentary group which created its own mass organization.

The whole group of Conservative MPs is commonly called 'the 1922 Committee', after a famous meeting in 1922 when a meeting of all Conservative MPs led to the fall of a government. The 1922 meets weekly when Parliament is in session, and has itself a network of special committees covering some of the most important responsibilities of government. But its most important mechanisms of influence and control are informal. The number of Conservative MPs is never large: even after the great Conservative landslides of the 1980s there were fewer than 400, and after the 2001 general election there were only 166. MPs mix in the enclosed, intense social world of the Westminster Parliament that was described in Chapter 10. The most important mechanisms of control and influence are therefore informal. The 1922 Committee has its own elected officers, the most important of whom is its Chairman. The chairman shoulders important responsibilities, mostly exercised informally: in particular, informing the leader about the sentiments of backbenchers, and especially warning the leader of dissatisfaction on the backbenches. In extreme cases the chairman and officers of the 1922 Committee may have the responsibility of telling leaders that support is so low that they should step aside. This last role has led to the development of a great legend about the role of the 'men in suits', the 1922 Committee, in quietly telling leaders to step aside (the political equivalent of inviting a disgraced fellow officer to retire to some quiet corner with a loaded revolver). In practice leaders are so attached to office that they rarely take these gentlemanly hints: in the last 30 years Conservative leaders have only been removed after bruising public leadership contests (Heath in 1975, Thatcher in 1990, Duncan Smith in 2003) or have resigned after leading the party to electoral disaster (Major in 1997, Hague in 2001, Howard in 2005).

One reason changes of leadership in the party are so bloody is that traditionally Conservatives have given unusual authority to the leader – in formal terms, probably more authority than in any other democratic party in Britain. As we shall see when we turn in Chapter 18 to leadership recruitment, this formal authority has been strengthened by the leaders' prominence in the wider struggle for political leadership in Britain. This makes the changes in recent years in the method of selecting the leader all the more important. Until the middle of the 1960s the leader of the party just 'emerged': when a new leader was needed some senior older figures in Parliament informally canvassed MPs, giving special weight to the leading MPs. That secretive process, which dated from pre-democratic days, became increasingly anachronistic in a democratic political system. From the mid-1960s to 1998 the Conservatives worked with the same system, subjecting it to only minor modifications. This system essentially allowed the 1922 Committee to select the leader. In the 1990s the Conservatives' main opponents, the Labour party, gradually widened their own 'franchise' for electing the leader to give a more direct say to individual members, as we shall see below. After William Hague's election in 1997 he moved rapidly to do the same (see Timeline 14.1 for details). In 2003 the party, exhausted by bitter factional battles during the brief leadership of Iain Duncan Smith (2001–3), arranged a 'coronation' in which Michael Howard emerged as the sole candidate for the leadership after negotiations within the parliamentary leadership. When Mr Howard announced his impending resignation following the 2005 general election this also offered the chance to reconsider the scale of franchise.

## The Labour party: organization and power

By contrast with the Conservatives, the Labour party first emerged in the early decades of the twentieth century as a mass organized movement in the country before Labour became a serious parliamentary force. The formal establishment of the modern party, in 1918, in fact coincided with the emergence of Labour as the Conservatives' main opponents in the general election of the same year. The Constitution on which the party settled in that year created Labour not as a single entity, but as a federation of 'affiliated' organizations. Affiliation meant that organizations such as trade unions and individual constituency parties subscribed financially to the party, and enjoyed voting rights in the party's key national institutions in rough proportion to the size of their subscriptions. Thus Labour developed as a mass party organization before it emerged as a great parliamentary force, and the voting power of the components of this organization was heavily influenced by financial 'muscle' in the party. These historically inherited institutional features explain the key tension in the organization of the party, a tension that has periodically threatened to pull it completely apart: the tension between a Party that is a federation of organizations in the country at large, and a parliamentary leadership that is concerned with winning majorities in Parliament and with governing when in office.

Like the Conservatives, therefore, Labour was for much of its history a truly mass party, and the history of this mass character in part mirrored the history of Conservative development. 'Individual' membership of the party has generally been equated with membership in the individual constituency Labour parties. These levels of membership never matched those achieved by the Conservatives, but they have shown a similar pattern of decline: they peaked at just one million in 1952, and their recorded levels by the close of the twentieth century were below 400,000, though the true figure may now may be as low as 250,000. The only departure from this pattern occurred in the aftermath of Tony Blair's election as leader, when a national recruitment campaign produced a short-lived influx of new members.

The most impressive nominal measure of mass membership historically was provided by the affiliation figures for the most important institutional component of the party, the trade unions. At its height at the end of the 1970s trade union affiliation to the party was measured as the equivalent of over 6.5 million members. But this was an institutional fiction, produced by a financial mechanism. The figures did not represent real people who had made a decision to link with the Labour party. Unions created their own separate political funds, from a small additional levy added to the individual subscription of each union member. After 1946

union members had to 'opt out' of paying this levy and, since the amount is trivial, few did so. The fund could be used for a variety of purposes, but for unions affiliated to the Labour party it funded the union's affiliation. The size of the subscription paid by the individual union decided the nominal number of members it had affiliated. This financial mechanism put the unions at the centre of party organization for two reasons: historically, it made them the main sources of party finance; and since the size of affiliation fees converted into the size of the vote which a union could cast in key party bodies, it often gave them a predominant voice in any forum where decisions were made by vote. Of these, the most important, and most contentious, was the Annual Conference.

The power of the Annual Conference of the party was historically contested, because in the way that power was exercised was the key to how Labour solved the tensions inherent in its organization: the tensions in a federated party where one element, the unions, provided most of the money and commanded most of the votes at Conference; and other tensions, cutting across these, between the mass organization outside Parliament and the parliamentary leadership created by the rise of Labour as the Conservatives' main rival. Some official accounts pictured Conference as the 'Parliament of the movement', implying that it had supreme decision-making power. But this created two kinds of problem: where the use of the union 'block vote' carried decisions that overrode the votes of individual members from the constituencies; and where conference decisions opposed the policies of the parliamentary leadership – which claimed, by virtue of fighting democratic parliamentary elections, to represent a different, (and wider) constituency in the country at large (see Briefing 14.2).

Throughout much of the party's history after 1918 these tensions were contained by a variety of means. In part they were suppressed when the party was in government, because the parliamentary leadership then had especially strong grounds for either calling on the loyalty of the mass party, or ignoring its views. The parliamentary leadership was also able, for much of its history, to create alliances with parts of the trade union leadership, thus using part

# Briefing

## THE BLOCK VOTE AND THE FEDERAL NATURE OF THE LABOUR PARTY

The 'block vote' is a direct outcome of the Labour party's federal structure and has been wielded by all affiliated organizations. But historically it mattered most in the case of union votes because unions had by far the largest voting 'blocks'.

The 'block' originates in the case of unions from the mechanism of affiliation. All unions are permitted to establish a separate 'political fund' which is financed by a small levy on individual members. To avoid paying the levy members must 'contract out'. Few do so, and few are even aware that they are paying this supplement. This fund can be used for many political purposes. Some unions (for example, the Association of University Teachers) have a political fund, but are not affiliated to the Labour party. At the time of writing 22 unions are affiliated to Labour, including some of the largest, such as the Transport and General Workers Union. They pay affiliation fees from the Political Fund (at the time of writing, £2.50 per member). Some members 'affiliate' up to their whole membership; some up to the proportion of members who pay the political levy, or less. Thus the affiliation is not connected to the choices of real individual members. Each 'affilation' carries one vote in, for example, voting at the Annual Conference: thus a union that pays (at current rates) £2.5 million annually is 'buying' one million votes. With individual membership at less than 250,000, this gives big unions a potentially dominant voice in votes. But a number of features moderate the impact of the union block vote:

- Even at the height of union influence in the party, the split between unions and other affiliated organizations at the Annual Conference was only 70:30
- Unions even at the height of their power were divided and often 'cancelled out' the block vote of each other
- Since reforms introduced in 1993 unions have been obliged to divide their 'block' vote at conference between each individual union delegate, who votes separately. In practice, though, most unions will vote together
- In the electoral college for choosing the Leader of the party unions are obliged to ballot their members, and to cast their 'block' in proportion to the choices made by the individual members.

➲ The 'block vote' has commonly been pictured by opponents of the Labour party as an undemocratic mechanism. Whether undemocratic or otherwise, it arises out of a consistent, and historically deep rooted, theory of party government.

---

of the union block voting power to carry its own views. These mechanisms broke down at the end of the 1970s when the party lost office to the Conservatives after a difficult spell in government, 1974–9. The years in office strained relations between the unions, the parliamentary leadership and many constituency parties to breaking point. Something close to civil war broke out in the party. The 1980s were a decade of struggle, both about the content of policy and about the focus of authority in the party. The struggle resulted in two major changes to party organization: in the structure of party policy making; and in the method of leadership selection.

The main change in the organization of policy making was first introduced in 1990. It was an attempt to 'dethrone' the Annual Conference, the formerly sovereign policy-making body whose role in reality for decades had proved a source of contention. Below Conference was established a series of 'policy forums' where larger numbers of individual party members could simply turn up and contribute to debates about policy. This was strengthened by reforms introduced in 1997, with the creation of a National Policy Forum with 175 members, hearing and considering reports from eight separate policy commissions. The whole process is in effect a rolling policy review, with the

**TIMELINE 14.2   THE EVOLUTION OF LEADERSHIP SELECTION IN THE LABOUR PARTY**

**1922–81**

'Leader' means leader of the Parliamentary Labour party, elected at the beginning of each parliamentary session. In the rare contested elections, the winner was the candidate gaining an absolute majority of votes (if necessary through a second ballot of the best two supported candidates). First leader elected by this method was J. Ramsay Macdonald, 1922; last, Michael Foot, 1980.

**1981–93**

1981 special conference decides the Leader (and Deputy Leader) will be re-elected each year by Annual Conference. Conference to form an electoral college, with 40 per cent of votes allocated to unions, 30 per cent to Parliamentary Party, and 30 per cent to constituencies. Neil Kinnock (1983) and John Smith (1992) elected by this method.

**1993**

Party Conference changes balance of votes in electoral college to equal (one-third each) for union, parliamentary party and constituencies; and unions and constituency parties obliged to ballot individual members on their choices, and divide their votes according to the expressed preferences of their members. Tony Blair (1994) elected under this method.

➲ For most of the twentieth century both big parties gave control over leadership choice to their parliamentary representatives. Labour was the first to share control with the Party outside Parliament, but it took some years before the party gave individual members a direct vote in leadership selection.

---

object of considering the full range of policy over the lifetime of a single Parliament. The National Policy Forum in turn commends policies to the Annual Conference, which is thus often faced with a 'take it or leave it' choice.

The second major organizational change produced by Labour's internal turmoil in the 1980s was a transformation of the party's method of selecting its leader. The details of the development of Labour leadership selection methods are given in Timeline 14.2, but the direction of development can be simply summarized: for over 60 years following the rise of Labour as one of the two main parties the parliamentary party entirely controlled leadership selection; but since the early 1980s it has had to share control over the choice with individual rank-and-file members and with the trade unions.

We can sum up the recent development of Labour party organization as follows. Imagine someone who fell asleep at a Labour party meeting in 1979 (all too easy to do) and suddenly woke up 25 years later. Our character would soon notice three big changes in the way the party is run that have affected the historical building blocks of Labour party organization.

## The parliamentary party

This has simultaneously become more influential but less independent. Institutional changes in the way party policy is formulated have allowed the parliamentary leadership increasingly to control policy debates. The party Conference is stage-managed by the parliamentary leadership: it has become a kind of annual assembly organized for publicity purposes, with carefully choreographed leadership speeches and announcements of new policy initiatives geared to provide sound bites for broadcasting. It is hard to know how enduring this ascendancy will be, because it largely dates from the 1990s. In other words, it dates from the period when all the major components of the party decided to sink their public differences in the attempt to get back into office after the long years of Conservative ascendancy; and since 1997 it coincides with Labour's occupation of government, a condition that has always helped the ascendancy of the parliamentary leadership. But it has been buttressed by longer-term changes which have, for instance, increased the control of the leader of the party over the party's own central administrative machinery.

The parliamentary Labour party's autonomy has, however, been diminished by two long-term changes. Even at the end of the 1970s Labour MPs in safe seats virtually had a job for life, or for as long as they wished to stay in Parliament. Since then, re-selection as the party's candidate has become far from automatic, and the spread of 'one member, one vote' in candidate selection has opened up the process of candidate selection to many more individual party members in the constituencies. The numbers of 'deselected' MPs are not great, but a few examples help make all sitting MPs sensitive to this possibility and therefore careful to cultivate their local parties. The second long-term change we have already described: the parliamentary party has lost its monopoly over the choice of party leader.

## The trade unions

The unions' influence has declined. It is true that the electoral college mechanism for selecting the leader has given unions a secure place in selection, but in other respects organizational changes – not to mention the drift of policy itself – have left them increasingly marginalized. But this shift in organizational arrangements has only magnified the tensions at the heart of Labour's federated party structure. As institutional changes have made the block vote less effective, and the content of policy in government has often drifted completely out of control of the unions, voices have increasingly been questioning the point of continuing as major paymasters of the party. The party relies less on the unions for funding than it did a couple of decades ago; but the unions also get less for their money than they did a couple of decades ago (see Table 14.1 for more information on funding).

## The territorial organization

The most important aspect of this is obviously the organization in the constituencies, which has become increasingly divided along national lines. One of the most important forces causing this is the devolution measures passed by the government after 1997. The existence of new governing institutions in Wales and Scotland, and the need to fight

**Table 14.1** Money in the parties: the influence of the election cycle

|  | 2002 | 2001 |
| --- | --- | --- |
| Labour's total income | £21.2 million | £35.5 million |
| Labour's income from donations | £4.6 million | £16.0 million |
| Conservatives' total income | £9.9 million | £23.2 million |
| Conservatives' income from donations | £5.7 million | £17.7 million |

*Source*: Calculated from electoralcommission.org.uk

Note: The figures are only comparable for approximate orders of magnitude. The Labour figure for 2002 is for the whole of the calendar year; the Conservatives' for the last nine months; Labour's 2001 figure is for the calendar year; the Conservatives' for the calendar year beginning 1 April 2001.

➲ The most important features of these figures are not the monetary differences between the parties, which can be affected by a variety of reporting conventions, but the way income jumps in the year of a general election, and the extent to which both parties rely on donations to stock their 'war chests'.

separate elections to control those governing institutions, created quite distinct institutional forces in those two countries, and has led to the increasingly separate organization of the party in the separate countries of the UK.

## Challenging two-party dominance: alternative models of party organization

'Third parties' used to be virtually a residual category in discussion of the British party system because the Labour and Conservative parties were so overwhelmingly important, but we have already seen that this is now far from the case. In the devolved governments 'third parties' are often no longer in third place: in Scotland the Liberal Democrats have been in coalition with Labour since 1999, and the Nationalists have been the largest opposition party; in Wales Plaid Cymru is the largest opposition party. As we will see in

Chapter 17, in elections to the Westminster Parliament the domination of Labour and Conservative has been in long-term decline (see People in Politics 14.1).

These third parties vary in electoral significance, but that significance is often great and is almost universally growing. The Nationalists and the Liberal Democrats by now have established a secure hold within elected national assemblies and, in the case of the Liberal Democrats, in governing

## *People in politics*

### 14.1    PARTY LEADERS BEYOND THE 'MAGIC CIRCLE' OF LABOUR AND THE CONSERVATIVES

Cartoons: Shaun Steele

**Alex Salmond** (1954–), MP for Banff and Buchan in the Westminster Parliament, 1987–; educated St Andrews University; civil servant, economist with Royal Bank of Scotland, 1980–87. Convener (leader) of Scottish National Party, 1990–2000. Resigned as Leader in 2000, but following the fall of John Swinney (see Political Issues 14.1) stood again for the leadership and was elected in September 2004 with a huge majority of the vote of members.

**Gwynfor Evans** (1912–), educated University of Wales, Aberystwyth, and St John's College Oxford. President Plaid Cymru, 1945–81, Honorary President, 1982–; MP, Carmarthen, 1966–70 (returned as first ever Plaid Cymru Westminster member) and 1974–9. He became in old age a fully integrated member of the Welsh political establishment, but was a key figure as an outsider in creating the uniquely 'cultural' character of Welsh nationalism.

**Charles Kennedy** (1959–), educated University of Glasgow; 1983–97, MP for Ross; Skye and Inverness West, 1997–. First elected as Social Democrat MP, 1983; switched to Liberal Democrats on merger of Liberals and SDP, 1988. Succeeded Paddy Ashdown as Liberal leader, 1999. Had he opted for the Conservative or Labour parties he could have expected only a slow route to the top; the smaller world of Liberal Democratic politics catapulted him in youth into national prominence.

➲ The rise of third parties created some political careers that would have been difficult in the two major parties. Two of these figures are pioneers: Salmond's success cast a long shadow over his successor, John Swinney, who resigned in 2004; Gwynfor Evans, a cultural nationalist and pacifist, is the dominant figure in modern Welsh nationalism. Charles Kennedy was elected to the Westminster Parliament almost on graduation from University, and the Liberal Democrats skipped a political generation in electing him Leader in 1999. His career suggests a risky, but potentially rewarding, strategy for any ambitious young politician: join a small party on the brink of a surge of support.

institutions. Others, such as the Greens, have made periodic though unsustained breakthroughs at national level, but have a more permanent presence in local government. We shall see in the next chapter that these parties are highly varied in their ideologies but, as regards organization, they show important common features which amount to a departure from the historically engrained nature of the two dominant parties. The two dominant parties have been deeply marked by their Westminster Parliamentary histories – by the fact that since 1918 in the case of Labour, and for much longer in the case of the Conservatives, they have been focused on the Westminster battle, and the battle in particular to occupy (and, when occupying, to keep) office in the Westminster system. The history of, and forces shaping, organization in the other parties have been very different, and this is what makes them important as alternative models of party organization. These third parties have either had to create themselves as extra Westminster parliamentary forces or, in the case of the Liberal Democrats, to recreate themselves as such.

The Liberal Democrats are the modern result of a fusion between two political forces of unequal weight and with different organizational histories. The party was created in 1988 when the Liberal Party fused with the Social Democratic Party (SDP). (The original name, Social and Liberal Democrats, was changed to the Liberal Democrats a year later.) The SDP was originally the creation of a Westminster parliamentary faction. It was born in 1981 when four leading members of the Labour party announced the formation of a new party in reaction to what they alleged was the capture of Labour by militant socialism. The Social Democrats rapidly attracted a large electoral following, and a large membership. Between 1981 and 1987 they fought elections as part of an Alliance with the Liberal party (see below). This produced disappointing results, notably in the 1987 general election, as the rapidly acquired SDP electoral support and membership melted away almost as rapidly. The disappointment of 1987 was followed by a proposal from the Liberals for merger (a takeover in all but name). After some infighting this

was accomplished, as we saw above, in 1988. The SDP brought little institutional originality to the marriage, because it was part of the old Westminster world: it was the product of a disappointed faction within the Labour Westminster parliamentary leadership. The Liberals, by contrast, had a considerably more innovative institutional history.

The Liberals were one of the two dominant parties in the United Kingdom until 1918, when they were supplanted by Labour. By the 1950s they had shrunk to parliamentary insignificance. The lowest point came in the general election of 1951, when the Party returned only six Westminster MPs with 2.5 per cent of the popular vote; and then again in the 1970 general election it returned six members. Since then, as we shall see in more detail in Chapter 17, the decline of Labour and the Conservatives as electoral forces has been accompanied by the revival of the Liberal Democrats, especially in the Westminster and Scottish Parliaments. This long, half-century road to revival has largely depended on extra-parliamentary organization, and this has been reflected in the structure of party policy making and leadership selection. On the latter the Liberal Democrats pioneered leadership selection through one member, one vote, and still remain distinct in this way from Labour and Conservatives: from the former in not operating an electoral college which gives votes to constituent organizations; from the latter in not using the election in the parliamentary party as a 'filter' to select candidates to put before the membership. On methods of internal policy making the party has been similarly pioneering. For instance, while devolution has in effect forced Labour and Conservatives to develop a federal party structure to reflect the new devolved governments, the Liberals historically operated as a federation of the separate national parties. But the amalgamation with the Social Democrats reinforced UK-wide organization, making the UK-wide annual assembly, for example, the sovereign policy-making body in the party.

Organizationally, then, the Liberal Democrats represent the fusion of two very different traditions of party organization: that of a centralizing parliamentary cadre (the original Social Democrats) and that of a party recreated from the ground up after being virtually wiped out as a parliamentary force. But parliamentary organization has probably strengthened in recent years, because parliamentary representation has become stronger. As we saw in Chapter 11, the Liberal Democrats are now a major (indeed a governing) force in the Scottish Parliament, and also in the Welsh Assembly. There has been a also been a sharp rise in Westminster parliamentary representation in general elections since 1997: 46 MPs were returned to the Westminster Parliament in that year 52 in 2001; and 62 in 2005.

The importance of extra-parliamentary organization is even stronger in the case of Nationalists (for more on Nationalism in general, and Scottish Nationalists in particular, see Political Issues 14.1). Indeed, as we also saw in Chapter 11 on devolved government, the origins of the nationalist parties are very far removed from parliamentary politics, still less from the particular politics of Westminster: in the case of Plaid Cymru the origins lie, for example, in a movement to defend the language and the traditional culture which it supports. Some, admittedly minor, elements in nationalism have even flirted with overt anti-parliamentarianism, of the sort brought to full, violent development by parts of the Republican movement in Northern Ireland. The founding figures of these nationalist parties have no Westminster parliamentary pedigree, and for virtually the whole of their history their Westminster parliamentary wings have been tiny factions, nominally there to agitate for the separation of their country from the United Kingdom. The extra-parliamentary weight of the parties has been reflected in both their formal structures and in their modes of leadership selection. Whereas the two big parties, Labour and the Conservatives, have in recent years had to adapt to allow their extra-parliamentary wings a bigger say, the newly successful nationalist parties had their structures well established before the emergence of an established parliamentary group.

We saw in the case of the organizational history of the Labour party that Labour also originated in this fashion, developing a vigorous national organi-zation before becoming a parliamentary force. And we saw also that the party's subsequent emergence as a force in Westminster created a powerful tension between its parliamentary and extra-parliamentary components. The creation of the Welsh Assembly and the Scottish Parliament, in which for the first time the two nationalist parties have significant representation and a genuine possibility of capturing government, means that the potential for this history of tension is being recreated within nationalism. It is, however, still too soon to say whether this potential is being realized.

As we survey the parties that have emerged to challenge the domination of Conservative and Labour we move along a spectrum in which extra-parliamentary party organization is increasingly important: this is more true in the case of nationalists than in the case of the Liberal Democrats, and even truer in the case of the Greens. This is partly, perhaps, because the Greens have yet to make the breakthrough of winning even a single seat in the Westminster Parliament, and have only a tiny representation even under the more proportional electoral systems choosing members of the Scottish Parliament and the Welsh Assembly. But it is also because the Greens have sought to develop a distinctive philosophy of organization, which emphasizes the internal control of the party by members. Two distinctive signs of this are leader-ship selection and the formal methods of policy decision: until now, the Greens have insisted on a collective leadership rather than identifying a single figure as leader; and they stress the impor-tance of party conventions involving large numbers of members as the crucial mechanism of policy choice.

## The regulation of political parties

Until the 1990s, in describing the organization of political parties, we could content ourselves largely with describing their own internal systems of orga-nization. They were essentially voluntary institu-tions that governed their own affairs, but the Elections and Political Parties Act 2000 greatly changed the environment in which almost all

## POLITICAL ISSUES

### 14.1    THE FALL OF JOHN SWINNEY: DILEMMAS OF NATIONALISM

In June 2004 John Swinney resigned as leader of the Scottish National Party, having served as Leader since September 2000. The short term reasons for his resignation arose from personal rivalries at the top of the party – one leading Member of the Scottish Parliament had been suspended for criticizing Swinney's leadership – and poor electoral performance: the SNP fared disappointingly in the elections for the European Parliament in 2004 and, crucially, dropped eight seats in the elections for the Scottish Parliament in 2003. But beneath these short-term issues lie more fundamental ones which create great strategic dilemmas for nationalist parties that seek independence by peaceful, constitutional means in the new devolved British system of government. Two sets of issues are critical. First, what is the ideological colour of nationalism? The aim of independence can unite people of very different political philosophies, and the struggle for independence encourages them to sink their differences. But the existence of the Scottish Parliament with significant legislative powers posed the question: how radical or conservative was the SNP? Was the SNP's best electoral strategy to exploit radical dissatisfaction with Labour? The fact that the SNP lost nine seats, while the Scottish Socialist Party and the Scottish Greens between them picked up 11 seats in the 2003 elections, suggested that such a strategy was not viable. Alternatively, should it try to totally supplant the Conservatives as the Scottish party of business and the middle class? The second issue is: what should the attitude of nationalists be to devolved institutions? John Swinney's strategy was to work the devolved institutions, aiming to convince sufficient voters to make the SNP the governing party in the devolved system and then to offer a referendum on independence. But for many in the party this involved working with institutions that were patently designed to kill off the possibility of independence by permanently establishing the compromise of devolution. The election of Alex Salmond to the post of Leader, from which he had resigned in 2000 (see People in Politics 14.1, p. 310) puts the SNP into the hands of a leader with more proven capacities, but does not eliminate the great dilemmas of nationalism. The SNP recovered a little ground in the 2005 general election.

The fall of John Swinney thus highlights three sets of issues for all constitutional nationalists in the United Kingdom, not in Scotland alone:

- What distinctive social philosophies, left or right, should nationalists adopt?
- How far should they cooperate with non-nationalist parties?
- How far should they try to ensure the success of devolved institutions that are intended to frustrate their long-term aim of independence?

political parties operate. For the first time it created a framework of state regulation for the operation of many aspects of party life, notably to do with party finance and campaigning (see Briefing 14.3).

The immediate origin of the Act lies in the Fifth Report of the Committee on Standards in Public Life. It will be recalled that we summarized the content of this report in Chapter 5 (see Briefing 5.2, p. 86). The Committee's investigations in turn were prompted by scandals connected to party financing in the early 1990s. However, its report covered much more than the narrow area of party financing itself, and the Act of 2000 has also been correspondingly wide. It does four particularly important things.

# Briefing

## THE ELECTORAL COMMISSION: A NEW REGULATOR FOR POLITICAL PARTIES

The Electoral Commission is an innovation in British politics: for the first time, political parties (and the conduct of elections) are subject to a statutory regulatory body. The Commission's powers derive from the Political Parties, Elections and Referendums Act 2000 (PPERA).

The Boundary Committee for England – formerly the Local Government Commission for England – became a statutory committee of The Electoral Commission in April 2002. Thus the only statutory body hitherto concerned with the regulation of elections is now incorporated into the Commission.

The Commission's main legal duties are:

● to keep a register of political parties under the 2000 Act without registration, an organization cannot now be named as a political party on any ballot paper (though individuals are still free to stand)
● to ensure that applicants for registration comply with the registration and financial regulatory requirements of the Political Parties, Elections and Referendums Act 2000
● to ensure that, once registered, parties comply with the statutory reporting requirements of the PPERA and the relevant parts of the Representation of People Act 1983
● to regulate the conduct of any future referendums in Britain.

Beyond its strict statutory duties, the Commission is now the main institution offering guidance on the workings of the 2000 Act, and it has a wider responsibility to review the functioning of competitive elections in Britain.

*Source*: Information from Electoral Commission.

➲ The establishment of the Electoral Commission in 2000 was an epoch-making event in the history of political parties in Britain. It signals a decisive change in the official view of parties: they are no longer private associations, but public bodies who must be regulated as to their organization and finances. For a discussion of what this means for the nature of parties, see the last main section of this chapter.

## It sets rules for giving and accepting party donations

This is the aspect of the new regime of regulation that most directly arises from the scandals of the 1990s, when the two main parties were revealed as accepting donations from questionable sources, and suspicions existed that party policies, and government policies, were being adjusted to the interests of big donors. Now, all gifts in excess of £5,000 nationally and £1,000 locally must be declared.

## It 'caps' the cost of general election campaigns

It sets the limit that can be spent on a national campaign at £30,000 per constituency, which means that parties contesting virtually all seats (as Conservative and Labour do) are limited to just under £20 million per campaign.

## It establishes a wider set of rules for the registration of political parties

This is potentially the most far reaching consequence of the 2000 legislation. The Electoral Commission (see below) is a body with statutory power to register a political party – and registration is a condition of fighting elections under a party label (see Documenting Politics 14.1). In considering whether to register a party, the Commission has to inspect and approve a party's scheme for regulating its financial affairs, such as the officers it appoints and the reporting arrangements it devises. This also

## DOCUMENTING POLITICS 14.1

## REGISTERING A NEW POLITICAL PARTY

**Application To Register A Political Party In Great Britain & Northern Ireland** — The Electoral Commission

RP1 UK

*Important: the accompanying Guidance Notes (RP1UK/GN) should be read before completing this form, which can be used to register a party in GB and NI.*

**1  Declaration to register**

The party named below is applying to be a registered party in accordance with the requirements of Part II of the Political Parties, Elections and Referendums Act 2000.

I declare that the _____ [name of party]

intends to contest one or more relevant elections in Northern Ireland and one or more such elections in Great Britain and is accordingly applying to be registered in both the Northern Ireland register and in the following part(s) of the Great Britain register:

England ☐
Scotland ☐
Wales ☐

**2  Signatures**                    GB Party

**Proposed Registered Party Leader/Nominating Officer** (delete as applicable)

I declare that I am authorised to sign this application on behalf of the above named party.

Signed _____
Printed name _____  Date _____

**Proposed Registered Treasurer**

I declare that I am authorised to sign this application on behalf of the above named party.

Signed _____
Printed name _____  Date _____

**Proposed Campaigns Officer** (if applicable)

I declare that I am authorised to sign this application on behalf of the above named party.

Signed _____
Printed name _____  Date _____
Checked by: _____

Date of Receipt _____
Date Entered in Database _____
File Reference Number _____

**Great Britain Party**

**3  Party Name**

English _____
Welsh _____
Other language & English Translation _____

**4  Address**  (Party Headquarters or for correspondence if no HQ)

_____
Town _____  County _____
Post code _____
Telephone number _____
Fax number _____
Website/E-mail address _____

**5  Emblems**

Details of emblems submitted on separate sheet(s)?  Yes ☐  No ☐ (enter number)

**6  Party Leader**

Dr/Mr/Mrs/Ms/Miss/Other ___  First Name(s) ___  Surname ___
Name _____
Home address _____
County _____  Post code _____
If Leader for a particular purpose, please specify _____

**Nominating Officer**

Dr/Mr/Mrs/Ms/Miss/Other ___  First Name(s) ___  Surname ___
Name _____
Home address _____
County _____  Post code _____

**Additional Officer** (if necessary)

Dr/Mr/Mrs/Ms/Miss/Other ___  First Name(s) ___  Surname ___
Name _____
Home address _____
County _____  Post code _____

**Treasurer**

Dr/Mr/Mrs/Ms/Miss/Other ___  First Name(s) ___  Surname ___
Name _____
Home address _____
County _____  Post code _____

**Campaigns Officer** (if applicable)

Dr/Mr/Mrs/Ms/Miss/Other ___  First Name(s) ___  Surname ___
Name _____
Home address _____
County _____  Post code _____

➲ The document illustrates how far the formation and regulation of parties has now become a state function in the United Kingdom, and how far as a result the rules governing parties have become complex. The document is only an *extract* from the whole. Registering a party now involves completing a ten page form, downloadable from the Electoral Commission website. This also includes an appendix requiring details of all separate accounting units in each party (such as women's sections, constituency parties, etc.). Completing the form also involves use of detailed accompanying guidance notes.

*Source*: Extracted from: Electoral Commission, Form RPUK1, 2003.

extends to a system for regulating 'third parties': in other words, registered, approved donors to parties.

### It establishes a permanent, highly active regulator not only for parties, but for elections and referendums

It does this in the form of the Electoral Commission. The Commission's statutory (legally prescribed) duties relate in part to issues summarized above. In particular, it registers political parties (over 120 registered thus far) and it receives and scrutinizes reports on the sources and size of political donations. In effect, it is the main scrutinizer of the financial affairs of all registered political parties. But it does much more: it is now the main public body concerned with the regulation of elections – including referendums – in the widest sense. The range of these duties is impressively wide. It includes:

- Preparing and publishing a report on administration of all relevant elections, including all referenda
- Keeping under review and reporting on electoral boundaries of constituencies for both national parliaments and local government
- Reviewing and reporting on all political advertising via electronic media
- Keeping under review and reporting on the registration of political parties and their income and expenditure.

These statutory duties relate to the actual conduct of elections and of the main institutions that fight them, political parties. But the Commission also has wider responsibilities designed to improve the capacities of parties to contribute to the democratic process. These include:

- Developing and administering policy development grants to political parties
- Promoting public awareness about the electoral process in Britain
- Regulating the wording of any referendum bill introduced in the United Kingdom.

## The changing organization of parties: from mass parties to cartel parties?

Throughout the twentieth century political parties were institutions vital to British democracy. They provided one of the main mechanisms by which the people at large could express political views and, in particular, support competing political programmes. In principle they were thus a key means by which popular choices could be made between alternative policy preferences in government. They were also key institutions in the system of interest representation, because the two-party system that dominated British government after 1918 allied the two main parties to competing interests in Britain: the Labour party to organized trade unions and a large section of the manual working class; the Conservatives to large parts of the business community and of the middle class. The parties were also important institutions of direct participation in politics because they both had a mass membership, but the nature of this mass participation showed that parties not only facilitated democratic participation, they also defined its limits. Labour and the Conservatives utterly dominated the party system and both, despite their different histories, were in turn heavily dominated by parliamentary leaderships which operated to a substantial degree independently of the party at large (see Debating Politics 14.1).

Important changes in organization, changes that now stretch back over more than two decades, are altering the structure of parties and the way they function, and in so doing they are contributing to the changing character of democratic politics. The mass party is a thing of the past, as antiquated as the manual typewriter and the roneo duplicator (two technologies, incidentally, that it used very effectively). This change is partly due to changed patterns of campaigning, which now demands much less by way of huge numbers of active supporters on the doorsteps of individual voters. Parliamentary parties are no longer so independent of the wider party organization. This is partly because the parties that have risen to challenge the supremacy of Labour and the Conservatives – such as the Nationalists and the Liberal Democrats – have much stronger traditions of engagement between their parliamentary leadership and the party in the country. But, as we have seen, there have also been changes in the organization of Labour and the Conservatives, and these changes have given the party outside Parliament a bigger say in party government. The best 'headline' sign of the change is the way the choice of party leader is no longer the monopoly of Labour or Conservative Westminster parliamentarians. The role of the party in interest representation has also changed. There has been a weakening of links in the case of the Conservatives and Labour between the party and the big interests to which they were historically close: business and the trade unions. In part this separation is the work of the party leaderships, as they calculated that they needed to widen their electoral base, and to do this they needed to distance themselves from sectional interests. That has been an important feature of the reshaping of the union–party relationship in the Labour party in recent years. In part it has been due to the organized interests. As we saw in Chapter 9, functional interests are increasingly well organized in their own specialist institutions, and close alliance with political parties increasingly looks like a very blunt instrument of interest representation. Why not cut out the middleman – the political party – and do the job directly through interest group organization?

The decline of mass membership; the increasingly distant connection with special interests; the

# DEBATING POLITICS

## 14.1 POLITICAL PARTIES: ENEMY OR FRIEND OF BRITISH DEMOCRACY?

| Parties are vital to the health of British democracy: | Parties damage the health of British democracy |
|---|---|
| ■ Elections are at the centre of the democratic process, and parties are the way choice is offered at elections. <br> ■ Parties remain open, voluntary bodies through which citizens can participate in politics. <br> ■ Parties have become increasingly democratic in their formal organization, and increasingly transparent in their financing and regulation. <br> ■ Parties are vital institutions of democratic interest representation, complementing interest groups and catering in particular for groups that find formal interest organization difficult. | ■ The choice parties offer voters in British parliamentary elections is limited and crude and fails to allow significant, discriminating selection. <br> ■ Parties have lost huge numbers of members in the last generation, and have become moribund institutions dependent on state handouts and rich backers. <br> ■ The adversarial style practised by the main British parties produces crude, aggressive debate which alienates most citizens. <br> ■ Behind a rhetoric of common interest parties are tied to sectional interests and parliamentary factions. |

staggering cost of the new styles of campaigning; all these factors have combined to create serious financial problems for political parties. It was these financial problems that lay behind the scandals of the 1990s and the reforms of the legislation of 2000 described above. They thus explain the final important organizational change described in this chapter: the increasing regulation of political parties by a public body, the Electoral Commission.

The summary we have provided so far suggests that parties are declining institutions. But there is another way of reading change: that while a particular kind of mass party is in decline, this is not true of party as a political phenomenon. The influential theory of the *cartel* party suggests that we are seeing not decline, but transformation (Katz and Mair 1995). The theory of the cartel party suggests the following. Parties are increasingly providing functions for the state – such as supplying leaders in government – rather than functions for the wider society. As state servants they are decreasingly reliant on money or membership from that wider society. They are *cartel* parties because, rather like firms that can 'rig' a market by colluding in a cartel, they manipulate the political marketplace to protect

the position of established parties against outsiders.

It is plain that the marks of 'decline' in the British mass party, notably the fall in membership, can be read as a shift to a 'cartel'-like character. The appearance of a state regulator, in the form of the Electoral Commission, is also consistent with the cartel party thesis. The history of state funding of parties also 'fits' the thesis. State funding began in 1975 as a quite modest subsidy to opposition parties in the Westminster House of Commons, to help provide some research support. In the 1990s it was first extended to the House of Lords and then, in 1999, was increased greatly in scale (threefold, in fact). Funding of opposition parties is plainly a significant step to transforming the party into a state institution.

Despite this evidence, it is doubtful that the 'cartel' party thesis fits Britain well. (It does fit parties in some other European states better.) There are two reasons for this. First, while the scale of state funding has indeed grown, the parties still rely tremendously on the wider society to provide them with the funds to fight elections. Second, the evidence of party support does not support the 'cartel' thesis, or at least suggests that, if these are cartel parties, they are pretty hopeless at rigging the political marketplace. The history of party support, as we have seen in this chapter and will see in even more detail in Chapter 17, is a history of declining support for the dominant institutions in the 'cartel'. Outsiders – Liberal Democrats, nationalists – have gone a long way to busting the cartel.

## REVIEW

The main themes of this chapter are as follows:

1 Parties organize for many reasons, and these different motives often import great tension into the internal life of parties
2 The single most important long-term change to affect party organization in the last generation is the decline of mass membership parties
3 The party's role in interest representation has been partly supplanted by the rise of specialist pressure groups
4 Parties, once largely private association that ran their own affairs, are being increasingly regulated by public rules.

One further reason the established parties are an ineffective cartel takes us back to a key theme of this book: the reality of multi-level governance. Devolution has accelerated the spatial fragmentation of the parties. The different logics of electoral competition under different electoral systems in the devolved governments, and the different pressures created by those governing systems, have all undermined the parties as 'United Kingdom' institutions. Thus not only is the mass party in decline; parties that maintain a UK-wide cohesion are also becoming increasingly hard to sustain.

## Further reading

Webb (2000) is the most important modern study of parties. McKenzie (1963), the great classic study, is a 'must' for any serious beginner on the organization and history of parties. Pinto-Duschinsky (1981) is a great study of finance, with implications that go well beyond finance, and the work of Fisher (for instance, 2003) always keeps the story up to date. Whiteley and Seyd (2002) are authoritative on party activism.

# CHAPTER 15

# Parties and their ideologies

## CONTENTS

## AIMS

This chapter has the following aims:

❖ To describe the meaning of ideology

❖ To sketch the ideologies of the parties that have been historically dominant in British politics

❖ To sketch challenging and marginalized ideologies

❖ To summarize the changing role of ideology in British party politics.

## Ideas, ideologies and party politics

Like many key concepts in the study of politics, 'ideology' has been given many different meanings. These can range from the particular to the general. 'Ideology' can be reserved for political views that are expressed as an elaborate, consciously worked-out political doctrine; or it can refer to the broad world view of a group or individual, often consisting of little more than a set of implicit assumptions. It is perfectly possible for a political party to disavow ideology in the former sense; but in the latter sense all institutions, and indeed even all individuals, operate with some kind of ideology. The meaning employed in this chapter is closer to the latter, more general view. We are concerned to explore the broad view of the political world expressed by parties. The reason for adopting this approach is that it allows us to explore some important distinctions: notably, between parties that do indeed have an ideology that consists of an elaborate set of doctrines, and those that reject this approach to politics, operating instead with ideologies that involve only fleeting and implicit assumptions.

Just as there are different views of the meaning of ideology, so there are also contrasting views of the role of ideologies in political parties. A simple but helpful distinction is between the *instrumental* and the *idealistic* view of ideology.

The *instrumental* view does not deny that parties have ideologies, but sees them primarily as instruments for other purposes: notably, in a democracy, the purpose of winning elections. We can find this view of ideology both in the formal academic literature and in common everyday views of the parties in Britain. In academic studies, one of the most influential bodies of theory is derived from *rational actor models*. In rational actor models, parties (to be more precise, those who really control them) are thought to be primarily engaged in winning elections or, even, maximizing the vote of the party. Hence the label, because these actors have an overriding goal – vote winning – to which all other goals are subservient. (The classic study which popularized this view in political science is Downs 1957.) Thus party ideology will be adopted, modified and discarded according to its ability to win votes; it is

Image 15.1

**The case of the red rose: image as marketing ploy or sign of ideological identity?**

➲ The Labour Party's adoption of the red rose as its 'logo' was the work of Peter Mandelson who served as the Party's Director of Communications, 1985–90 – the exact period, we shall see later in this chapter, when the foundations of 'New Labour' were laid. Its adoption illustrates particularly well the debate about the significance of ideology in British politics. It can be viewed in diametrically opposed ways. One sees it as a self-conscious marketing gimmick by Mandelson, the party's genius of presentation. Red is the traditional colour of the left, and its most important symbol is the red flag which has waved above numerous demonstrations. The new logo retained the colour but absorbed it into the quintessentially English symbol of a rose. But a different view points out that the changes that occurred in the 1990s were not mere marketing developments: they did indeed coincide with substantive changes in ideology. Thus the new logo could be given an alternative interpretation, as more than a marketing device, symbolizing a real change in the ideological identity of the party. (Labour rose logo © The Labour Party)

really just part of the 'brand image' the party uses in the political marketplace (see Image 15.1). This formal academic view is often echoed in everyday 'cynical' views of parties and politicians, which suggest that they just adopt policies without any guiding principle.

The *idealistic* view gives a much more powerful influence to ideology. It sees parties as shaped at least as much by the ideas of their leading members as by either the interests they represent or the demands of attracting votes. Party ideology is part of the core identity of the party and understanding any party demands understanding both what party members themselves say are the principles of the party, and what sort of view of the world we can deduce from what they say. One of the most important academic studies of British politics published in the last 50 years, Beer's *Modern British Politics* (1969/1982), is largely about the changing ideologies of the two main parties. It takes ideology seriously, and assumes that understanding the parties means understanding their ideological identities. The idealistic view does not dismiss the importance of interests, including an interest in winning votes, on what parties think. But it does work on the assumption that we should take ideas in parties, and what parties say are their ideas, seriously.

## Conservatives and their ideologies

### The myth of a non-ideological party

We begin with the Conservative Party for a simple reason: it has been the most important party in British politics. A simple measure of this is tenure in office. Although the party has experienced electoral hard times since 1997, viewed over the long term the Conservatives are easily the most successful party in British politics. In the period since 1918 – the date when the modern party system first emerged – Conservatives have been in government, either alone or as the dominant coalition partner, for over 50 years. And that reflects in turn the fact that some of the most powerful interests in British society have traditionally allied themselves with the Party: for instance, most of the business community, large and small; and the great mass of middle-class voters, especially those working in the private sector. What Conservatives believe, and what they think they believe, is of utmost importance to the study of British government, and to the wider understanding of British society. Even were the Conservative party to disappear tomorrow, understanding Conservative ideology would be vital, because the party has left indelible marks on British government and society.

The distinction between what Conservatives believe, and what they think they believe. is important, because Conservatives have a persistent self-image that dismisses the importance of ideology in the party. In political arguments they are fond of picturing themselves as the 'common-sense' party by contrast with the impractical theorists in the Labour party. This is more than a bluff in political argument. If we glance at Documenting Politics 15.1 we will see some examples of this from classic statements of Conservative principles.

This self-image of the Conservatives as a 'non-ideological' party does express important truths about the nature of Conservatism, notably the unwillingness to be drawn into elaborate, extended statements of what the party stands for. But as an argument that Conservatism is a non-ideological party it is both psychologically and historically untenable. It is psychologically untenable because it implies that Conservatives are some special breed of political animal free from the commitment to ideas that marks all others in politics. In the general sense of ideology that we are using, Conservatives are as governed as anyone by broad assumptions about the nature of the political world in which they operate. It is historically untenable because, as we shall discover when we turn to the reality of Conservative politics, the party has indeed often been ideological in a more narrow sense: it has been guided by highly specific political doctrines.

### The reality: the richness of Conservative ideology

The most striking feature of the Conservative party is not that it is bereft of ideology, but that it is very rich in ideological traditions. This is hardly surprising, because the party has been around for a very long time and, over that time, it has acquired successive traditions and interests. Conservatives can trace their lineage back to seventeenth-century Britain when a 'Tory' faction emerged to defend strong monarchy against the claims of those who wished to elevate Parliament at the expense of the Crown. 'Tory' was then an abusive term that originally referred to Irish bandits; but most modern Conservatives are happy to accept 'Tory' as a slightly slangy short label for their party. The long history of the party means that examining its ideologies is a bit like undertaking a piece of political archaeological research: the long history of the party has left successive layers of ideas.

## DOCUMENTING POLITICS 15.1

## CONSERVATIVES ON CONSERVATIVE BELIEF (BURKE, DISRAELI, HOGG).

*Edmund Burke on the reach of the state*: 'The state ought to confine itself to what regards the state, namely the exterior establishment of its religion; its magistracy; its revenue; its military force by land and sea; the corporations that owe their existence to its fiat; in a word, to everything that is *truly public and properly public* – to the public peace, to the public safety, to the public order, to the public prosperity.' (1795)

*Benjamin Disraeli on the role of the Tory Party*: 'The Tory party is only in its proper position when it represents Tory principles. Then it is truly irresistible. Then it can uphold the throne, and the altar, the majesty of the empire, the liberty of the nation, and rights of the multitude. There is nothing mean, petty or exclusive, about the real character of Toryism. It necessarily depends upon enlarged sympathies and noble aspirations, because it is essentially national.' (1862)

*Quintin Hogg on Conservative attitudes to politics*: 'Conservatives do not believe that political struggle is the most important thing in life. In this they differ from Communists, Socialists, Nazis, Fascists, Social Creditors and most members of the Labour Party. The simplest among them prefer fox-hunting – the wisest religion.' (1947)

⮕ The striking feature of statements of Conservative principles is not only their variety, as illustrated here, but also how far they are the product of particular circumstances – a feature of which Conservatives themselves are proud. Edmund Burke (1729–97) is generally agreed to be the greatest of 'British' Conservative philosophers (he was actually Irish). What is striking about his account of the state is how wide are its potential functions: peace, safety, order, prosperity. The passage was written in 1795, however, at the height of the struggle in revolutionary France. Benjamin Disraeli (1804–81) was the greatest Conservative of the next century: novelist, opportunist, statesman and creator of modern Conservatism. The passage shows Disraeli's political prescience: even before the extensions of the franchise to encompass the middle and working classes he is 'positioning' the party as a national party. Quintin Hogg (1906–2001) wrote his account in the most influential statement of Conservative principles produced since the end of the Second World War. Its importance is magnified by the fact that Hogg later spent over 40 years at or near the top of the Conservative party. The passage is a reaction against nearly a decade of 'total politics' when private life had indeed been dominated by public events, notably war and the threat of war, and when collectivism managed by a highly interventionist state seemed the most likely future. Compare Hogg on private life with similar sentiments from Anthony Crosland, a leading Labour party figure, in Documenting Politics 15.3, p. 331.

*Sources*: Passages quoted from White (1950: 81, 226 and 31).

Although Conservatives can trace a line back to the seventeenth century, the modern party originated in the nineteenth century from a great split over a mixture of principles and interests. In 1846 the leader of what was then known as the Tory party, Sir Robert Peel, repealed the Corn Laws: this legislation had prevented the import of cheap corn, protecting British agriculture from competition in the process. The Corn Laws were opposed by an alliance of industrial capitalists and workers, who both wanted cheaper food; they were opposed by farming interests who wanted to exclude foreign competition. In opting for repeal Peel was therefore deserting the traditional interests of the old Tory party, but the ideological inheritance of the split in the party that resulted was complex. The modern party was born out of the group that split from Peel, and its most important voice was Benjamin Disraeli, the dominant figure in the party in the second half of the nineteenth century (see Documenting

## DOCUMENTING POLITICS 15.2

### 'CIRCUMSTANCES PRODUCE THEORIES': CONSERVATISM AS TRADITIONALISM AND PRAGMATISM

'The great object of our new school of statesmen ... is to form political institutions on abstract principles of theoretic science, instead of permitting them to spring from the course of events, and to be naturally created by the necessities of nations. It would appear that this scheme originated in the fallacy of supposing that theories produce circumstances, whereas the very converse of this proposition is correct and circumstances produce theories.' (Benjamin Disraeli, 1835)

➲ This passage from the greatest of nineteenth-century Conservative politicians, Benjamin Disraeli (1804–81) introduces two recurrent themes in Conservatives' own accounts of what they stand for: common-sense opposition to the fancy theorizing of their opponents (Liberals in the nineteenth century, Socialists in the twentieth and twenty-first); and a pragmatic fashioning of policy to meet immediate circumstances.

*Source*: White (1950: 36).

Politics 15.2). Disraeli began fashioning a distinctive ideology for the Conservatives: by picturing them as the opponent of the new industrial society that was developing in Britain; by opposing the doctrines of free trade abroad and minimal government at home that were advocated by the new industrial interests; and by picturing the Conservatives as a party that would unite society under the leadership of a traditional, landed aristocratic elite, protecting the poor against the insecurity and poverty produced by industrialism.

By the time of Disraeli's death in 1881, however, the party had been transformed once again. It had now made its peace with the Industrial Revolution and was the most important party of the wealthy and powerful in Britain. It was closely identified with the great new Empire that Britain had acquired in Africa and India. It accepted free trade, and was increasingly the natural home of the great industrialists. Disraeli's greatest successor, the Marquess of Salisbury, fitted the old mould in coming from a great traditional aristocratic family; but he had been an opponent of even the limited social reforms that the Conservatives under Disraeli had actually pursued. By the turn of the century the party was the home of the most orthodox defenders of minimal government and free trade. Thus while Peel and his followers had split from the old Tories

over exactly these issues in 1846, the inheritors of the Peel tradition in the next generation had migrated back to the Conservative party. At the same time, the great struggles over the national identity of the United Kingdom had added another dimension to its ideology. Faced with campaigns for Home Rule in the Celtic nations – especially Ireland – it invented itself as the 'Unionist' party, the defender of the union of the United Kingdom under the monarchy. This was strengthened when it became the home for the faction in its main rival, the Liberals, that opposed Home Rule for Ireland promoted by the Liberals' greatest leader, William Gladstone.

At the start of the twentieth century, therefore, the Conservatives stood for three broad principles:

- An economic system based on free markets
- Imperialism
- The supremacy in the British Isles of the political institutions based in London – the Westminster Parliament and the English Crown.

Lord Salisbury, leader of the party from 1885 to 1902, died in 1903 (see People in Politics 15.1). Were he to be resurrected a century on he would be astonished, and probably appalled, at some of the ideological changes in the party, but he would also approve some of the principles it still defends. Support for imperialism has disappeared: indeed, it was Conservative governments in the 1950s and early 1960s who dismantled much of the Empire. All that remains is a broad conviction among some Conservatives that Britain has a vital role to play on the world stage – a conviction that, we shall see shortly, is important in the party's attitude to the European Union. Lord Salisbury would also be appalled at the party's attitude to the domestic

## *People in politics*

### 15.1    THREE MAKERS OF CONSERVATIVE THOUGHT

Cartoons: Shaun Steele

**Edmund Burke** (1729–97) typified the Conservative approach to political thinking in uniting a career as a practical politician with the life of a philosopher. The event that crystallized Burke's conservatism was the French Revolution (1789). His *Reflections* on the Revolution argued for a peaceful, aristocratic constitutionalism, piecemeal change, and the importance of recognizing that institutions were rooted in their past and should not be radically torn from that past. Though for much of his life he was an active reformer, his reputation rests on this classic statement of Conservatism.

**Earl of Salisbury** (1830–1903) was also a typical Conservative: though an intellectual by inclination he never systematized his political thought into a definitive statement. But, especially in his two longest periods as Prime Minister (1886–92 and 1895–1902) the core of the ideology that shaped Conservatism for nearly a century evolved: a vision of Britain as a world power, notably as an Imperial power; a vision of a United Kingdom, under the Crown; and economic and social policies designed to unify traditional aristocratic interests with those of the growing suburban middle classes.

**Friedrich von Hayek** (1899–1992) was an Austrian philosopher who spent much of his working life in Britain. Hayek disavowed Conservatism, and supporting a systematic philosophy defending free markets and government restricted by explicit constitutional rules. But after Mrs Thatcher became Leader (1975) the Conservative elite became much more interested in systematic doctrines, and Hayek exercised both a direct influence on Mrs Thatcher and, more indirectly, on the whole Thatcher generation that dominated the Conservative party in the 1980s.

➲  These three figures illustrate the variety of Conservatism, both in ideas and sources. They encompass a rigorous systematic theorist, Hayek, and in Salisbury a typical instinctive Conservative who worked his philosophy out in political practice. They also encompass an establishment figure (Salisbury was from one of England's great aristocratic families); a semi-outsider (Burke was Irish and depended all his life on aristocratic patronage); and a complete outsider (Hayek was Austrian by birth, Central European by cultural inclination, and never a Conservative).

Union. The party still calls itself 'Unionist' but, after a rather perfunctory opposition to the Labour government's devolution reforms, it now accepts the devolved assemblies in Wales and Scotland. More important still is its abandonment of Unionism in the Irish case, the great historical issue that forged Conservative identity. Until the 1960s the Ulster Unionist Party MPs returned to the House of Common used to vote as a block with the Conservative party. That alliance ended a generation ago. Under John Major the party abandoned the claim to distinctive British sovereignty in Northern Ireland whilst in government. It has also, albeit with some grumbles and hesitations, accepted the great limits on British sovereignty now in place in the peace settlement negotiated in 1998 (the details of which were examined in Chapter 11).

The one key component of Conservative ideology that Lord Salisbury would recognize is the party's continuing defence of the free market economy. Over the last century the Conservatives have nevertheless sometimes deeply qualified this defence. In the early years of the twentieth century the party was internally divided over the issue of how far it should abandon free trade, which was finally abandoned at the start of the 1930s. After 1945, for a generation, it supported large scale nationalization and a large state-provided welfare system. But, compared with its main opponent, the Labour party, even at the height of its support for state intervention, it was still the more 'market friendly' party. In the last two decades of the twentieth century this defence of free markets became, as we shall see, much more prominent.

This present state of affairs is in large part the product of a great upheaval in Conservative ideology, which took place under the leadership of Margaret Thatcher (1975–90).

## Modern Conservative ideology: the Thatcher legacy in ideology and policy

Margaret Thatcher became leader of the Conservative Party in 1975. She replaced Edward Heath. Under Mr Heath's leadership, especially in his years as Prime Minister (1970–4) the party departed from many traditional Conservative positions.

- It abandoned any affection for the old Empire, becoming instead the leader of pro-European opinion in Britain. It successfully negotiated British membership of the then European Economic Community in 1973, in the face of opposition from the dominant section of the Labour party.
- It not only accepted large scale public ownership and a large scale welfare state, but actually expanded both in its period of office.
- It spent its last two years in office attempting to run a full scale system of state control of pay and prices, backed by law.
- It tried, albeit unsuccessfully, to manage the economy in partnership with the trade unions.

By contrast, by the time Mrs Thatcher was deposed as leader and Prime Minister in 1990, the Party occupied very different positions.

- It had established the free market as the entirely dominant mechanism in fixing pay and prices.
- It had broken with the unions, reducing their power greatly by changing the law and confronting them in large scale strikes.
- It dismantled almost all the nationalized industries, selling off most state enterprize to the private sector.
- It had established itself as the most 'Euro-sceptic' of all the major British political parties.

These revolutionary changes in policy will be explored later in this book and need not be examined in detail here. What matters is the change in ideological assumptions that made Thatcherism such a break with the past. While Thatcherism often invoked some of the party's ideological traditions – for example, support for free markets – it was novel both in its approach and in the scale of the changes it introduced. The novelty of Thatcherism as a Conservative ideology lay in five features (see also Briefing 15.1).

*It was self consciously 'ideological'.* Conservatism had always been ideological but, as we saw earlier,

# Briefing

## THE CONTRADICTIONS OF THATCHERISM

'Thatcherism' is a rarity: a political creed named after a British prime minister. (There is no corresponding 'Blairism' or even 'Churchillism.') But Mrs Thatcher never claimed to be a political philosopher, and so we have to infer the meaning of Thatcherism from what her governments did in office (1979–90). And what they did pointed in contradictory directions.

On the one hand, they dismantled many state controls:

- Sold numerous state enterprizes to the private sector
- Withdrew state aid from many ailing industries
- Decisively turned away from state regulation of prices and incomes
- Obliged many institutions that remained part of the state (education, health, local government) to 'contract out' many of their functions by competition to private firms.

But in the Thatcher years, there also occurred:

- Increased central control over numerous parts of the public sector, such as local government and the education system
- More central control and direction of policing
- The active use of the law and other kinds of central state power to curb the power of forces in the wider society (such as the trade unions)
- The active use of state power to oblige firms to combat cartels and price fixing in the economy.

Was Thatcherism just opportunistic, or incoherent? The most convincing answer, given by Gamble (1994) was that it was neither: building a free market demanded also more central control – 'a free market and a strong state'.

⬤ Debates about whether Thatcherism has any ideological coherence are part of a wider tradition, of debating whether Conservatism has any ideological coherence. But this particular debate is of outstanding importance, because Thatcherism reshaped all British politics, not just Conservatism.

the party rarely liked to talk much about it or to expound ideas systematically, preferring to pick and mix from the various traditions as the occasion suited. Thatcherism presented itself as a self-conscious, coherent philosophy (even when in practice it was much less systematic). The most important theorist of Thatcherism among practising politicians, Sir Keith Joseph, was deeply and openly influenced by some of the great economic theorists of the free market, including the Austrian economist Friedrich von Hayek; even Mrs Thatcher herself claimed to be so influenced.

*It was radical in its ambitions.* Before Thatcherism, Conservative leaders had normally liked to say that they 'conserved' – in other words, they accepted change, but rarely initiated it. (Indeed, this was one of the main reasons why the great inspiration of Thatcherism, Professor Hayek, rejected conservatives: he argued that conservatives usually ended up accepting the socialism and collectivism of their opponents.) Thatcherism was not 'conservative': it set out to make fundamental changes in economy, society and government.

*It radically changed the role of markets in the British economy.* The single most important way Thatcherism was radical in thought and deed was that it fundamentally altered the role of markets in the British economy. Thatcherism believed in free markets. Though many of the great reforms of the years of Mrs Thatcher's period in office were the result of on-the-spot tactical decisions rather than some long-term strategy, nevertheless Mrs Thatcher and her supporters practised what they preached. By the time the Conservatives lost office in the 1997 general election Britain had, as a result of government reforms, transformed the market's role compared with the situation inherited by the Conservatives in 1979. Labour markets had become among the freest from trade union restrictions in Western Europe. It had sold off about 40 per cent of what had been in public ownership at the end of the 1970s, including industries central to the old industrial economy (for instance, steel) and those central to the new high technology economy (for instance, telecommunications).

*It radically changed the role of the state.* Radicalism about markets involved withdrawing the state from some areas, but it also meant radically empowering the central state in others. Thatcherism greatly centralized state authority in Britain: it used the law to subject a whole range of interests (ranging from local government, to trade unions, to universities) to central state control. It did so for a reason spelt out most compellingly by Gamble, the leading analyst of Thatcherite ideology: because remaking free markets in a radical way could only be done through a strong state that would defeat and control those who opposed free markets (see Gamble 1994).

*It believed Britain's future lay with globalization.* The high point of Thatcherism coincided with a surge in the amount of integration in the global economy, and Thatcherism believed in exposing Britain to that surge. In the Thatcher years the economy of the south-east of England, especially in finance and commerce, was integrated into this wider global economy, and Britain as a whole became the most important centre in the EU for inward investment by multinational companies. In this commitment lay another feature of Thatcherism that became increasingly important during the later years of her Premiership: its scepticism about the EU. Although only a tiny minority of Conservatives advocate withdrawal from the European Union, a growing majority in the party became increasingly hostile to further European integration. This hostility was partly due to the belief that an integrated economy also meant the creation of a powerful European state which would intervene in free markets, but it also reflected a belief in the wider importance of global markets and a suspicion that the European Union was designed to create a 'fortress' within which the European economy would trade with itself.

Mrs Thatcher was forced from office by her party in 1990, but that made no material difference to the triumph of Thatcherite ideology in the party. The 'remaking' of the party after its election defeat in 1997 has also made no difference. Indeed, some elements – especially scepticism about the European Union – have, if anything, become stronger.

Thatcherism transformed the dominant ideology of the Conservative party irrevocably. But its achievements were even wider: it also had profound effects on the Conservatives' main rival in the Westminster system, shown below.

## The Labour Party ideology: history, crisis, remaking

### The origins of Labour's ideology

The Labour party has always been more self-consciously at ease with ideas in politics than has its Conservative opponent. 'Intellectuals' in Britain in the twentieth century were more inclined to left-wing than to Conservative politics; and the party itself has always contained a high proportion of 'ideas workers' among its activists: teachers among local activists, and university lecturers and journalists among national leaders. The party's Conservative opponents often tried to exploit this by picturing Labour as a party of socialist dogmatism, and of hare-brained professors weaving wildly impractical theories. In practice, Labour was almost as ideologically fluid as were the Conservatives before the rise of Thatcherism.

Labour was finally created as a national party in 1918, the moment being marked by the adoption of its constitution. That constitution certainly seemed to mark the party as Socialist. The famous Clause IV, which was reprinted until the 1990s on the membership cards of all party members, committed the party to 'common ownership of the means of production, distribution and exchange' (see Documenting Politics 15.5, p. 333).

However, this 'socialist' constitution was adopted at an unusual moment: a rare high point of revolutionary ferment in Britain as the shock waves of the 1917 Bolshevik Revolution in Russia swept westward across Europe. That wave soon receded, and in reality the 1918 Constitution created a federation containing very different ideological traditions. The most important traditions came from the following groups.

*Christian Socialists.* Such socialists, especially those brought up in highly democratic Protestant denominations (for instance, Methodism), were prominent. There is indeed a long tradition of Christian political radicalism in Britain that pre-dates Labour and which it partly inherited. In some cases this takes the form of a full-blown vision, mainly derived from the New Testament, of a 'new heaven and a new earth' – of a society remade in the image of a Christian community, where the equality of souls before God is matched by equality in political power and economic resources. Some of the most important figures in the party's intellectual history, including R. H. Tawney, have been products of this tradition. (see People in Politics 15.2).

## People in politics

### 15.2   MAKERS OF LABOUR PARTY THOUGHT

Cartoons: Shaun Steele

**Sidney Webb** (1859–1947) began life as a radical Liberal – a characteristic of many early Labour thinkers. He helped define 'Fabianism', a doctrine that capitalism could be reshaped gradually from within by well-informed experts armed with detailed research. This gradualism deeply influenced the practice of Labour governments. Webb also helped draft the original Clause IV of the Labour Party Constitution (see Documenting Politics 15.5 below.) Most of his intellectual and practical work was done in partnership with his wife, Beatrice (1858–1943).

**R.H. Tawney** (1880–1962), both an academic historian and a polemicist, he profoundly shaped 'ethical' socialism – a particularly British version rooted in religious commitment which looked back to older radical movements, such as the 'Levellers' in the seventeenth-century civil war. He stressed the importance of social and economic equality, and also the importance of democratizing the practice of government. The commitment of many contemporary Labour leaders to a version of Christian socialism echoes Tawney's ethical influences.

**George Orwell** (1903–53), novelist and journalist. Though long a columnist on the Labour-supporting journal *Tribune*, Orwell was no orthodox Labour supporter. But his writings deeply influenced Labour intellectuals in the second half of the twentieth century. Two influences are important: his widely-read satires on Soviet Communism helped the Labour left line up against the Soviets in the Cold War, and made it deeply hostile to violent revolution; and his explorations of English identity helped define a perceived 'British' kind of socialism.

➲ Labour party thought resembles that of the Conservative party in its avoidance of systematic theory. The mix of 'practical' policy work (Webb), ethical argument (Tawney) and sharp polemic (Orwell) catches its diversity.

*Social reformers.* Social reformers overlapped with the Christian Socialists. The single most important group in making the Labour party was the trade unions, who were already well organized and politically influential before the party ever appeared. Not surprisingly, the trade unions had their eyes on immediate bread and butter reforms, such as working conditions. Social reformers did not want to revolutionize Britain in the manner of Socialists; they wanted to use the power of the state to reform society so as to curb the effects of free markets. This tradition in the Labour party was greatly strengthened by a historical coincidence. The great source of social reform in the early years of the twentieth century was the Liberal party, whose government introduced reforms such as old-age pensions and health insurance before the First World War. But the Liberal party was destroyed by internal divisions during the First War and Labour inherited much of its social reform tradition, and indeed some of its social reform activists. From this group Labour also inherited a tradition of radical dissent about foreign policy. There had been an important wing of the Liberal party that opposed Imperialism at the height of empire, and supported pacifist, or pacifist-leaning, foreign policies. Many from this tradition of dissent migrated into Labour after the collapse of Liberalism.

*Fabian reformers.* These were small in number but disproportionately important. Indeed, the 1918 'socialist' constitution was drafted by a Fabian, Sidney Webb. The Fabian Society was founded in 1884 and throughout its history has mostly been dominated by small groups of London-based intellectuals. Fabianism took its name from the Roman general, Quintus Fabius Maximus (died 203 BC), nicknamed the Delayer for his characteristic method of wearing down his opponent, Hannibal, by ultra-cautious military tactics involving indirect engagement, harassment and small skirmishes. (The connection shows another link in the Labour chain of historical ideas: the influence of the classics on the educated Victorian mind.) Fabian ideology was based on the gradual transformation of capitalism by long-term reform. It blended easily with social reform, because the Fabians believed above all in the power of the state – especially of the central state machinery – to reform the wider society. From the Fabians the Labour party drew its faith in central state intervention: for instance, via nationalized industries and the National Health Service.

*Marxist socialists.* These were briefly important in the party because the party constitution was promulgated at a brief revolutionary moment in Britain: the point at the close of the First World War when the impact of the Russian Revolution of 1917 spread a wave of revolutionary support across Western Europe. But most British Marxists were soon organized into separate movements, and Marxism became a minority influence in the party.

## The development and crisis of Labour ideology

We can see that from the beginning the Labour Party contained many different ideological traditions. The task of national leadership was to maintain some sort of unity between these. Great national crises often split the Party. This is what happened in the economic crisis of 1931, when Labour was in government. It led to a catastrophic general election defeat and a position of opposition and political weakness throughout the 1930s. But during and after the Second World War the different ideological traditions in the party were more or less unified around a common programme. All could sign up to the public ownership of important industries, and to the creation of important institutions of the welfare state such as the National Health Service (1948). But different groups signed up for different reasons: for socialists, this was a staging post to a transformed society; for social reformers, it was part of the means by which capitalism would be controlled and humanized. Labour lost three successive general elections in the 1950s and the attempt by the party leader, Hugh Gaitskell, to remove the 'socialist' Clause IV of the party constitution exposed these differences: for reformers such as Gaitskell Clause IV was an embarrassing, meaningless symbol; for socialists it was the guarantee of the party's long-term commitment to the transformation of capitalism.

Gaitskell's campaign was defeated, but in the 1980s the party's ideology was convulsed and then transformed by a great crisis. This crisis had its origins in Labour's experience of government, especially between 1974–1979. When Labour lost the general election in 1979 it had enjoyed the lion's share of government in the preceding 15 years. But the experience satisfied none of the main ideological groups in the party: socialist radicals saw only a failure to make any significant change in the nature of British capitalism; social reformers and Fabians saw, especially in the 1970s, a succession of failures in the task of efficiently managing and humanizing the market economy. The party then suffered a series of electoral disasters: it lost four successive general elections (1979, 1983, 1987 and 1992) to the Conservatives; two of these (1983 and 1987) were huge Parliamentary defeats, and Labour's share of the vote in 1983 was its lowest since 1918. Labour had been defeated in a run of elections before in the 1950s, but that was by a Conservative party that won mostly by copying the Labour party. The Conservative governments of the 1950s accepted most of the radical changes introduced by the Labour governments of 1945–51: they accepted the welfare state, large scale public ownership and the responsibility to manage the economy so as to achieve full employment. But the victorious Conservatives of the 1980s were moved by a very different ideology: the Thatcherism that we described earlier. As the Conservatives' radical policies unfolded, Labour was faced with the twin problems of how to counter them in elections, and what, if anything, to do about reversing them if it was ever returned to government.

A triple crisis – of policy failure, electoral failure and the spectre of successful Thatcherism – dominated Labour ideology for the last two decades of the twentieth century. It led to the transformation of ideology and the emergence of the self-styled 'New Labour' (see Documenting Politics 15.3).

## New Labour: ideology remade

The Labour party's early efforts to respond to its crises in the 1980s involved reasserting its radical socialist traditions. It fought the 1983 general elec-

tion on an economic policy which advocated radical reversals of Thatcherite policies and the creation of a centrally planned, socialist economy in Britain. The greatest electoral defeat in the party's history, in 1983, forced a rethink. The party led by Tony Blair (1994–) is normally thought of as 'New Labour'. In reality the most important changes in official Labour ideology happened in the 1980s under the leadership of Neil Kinnock (1983–92), especially in the period between 1985 and 1987 when the party established a commission on policy to examine comprehensively what it stood for (see Documenting Politics 15.4).

This process produced a wholesale transformation of the ideology of the Labour party, though the change took some years to complete. Labour began by abandoning the policies influenced by the socialist traditions that had been advocated in the electoral disaster of 1983. Then, as the Conservatives' privatization programme became more bold and sweeping in the 1980s, Labour moved through a succession of conciliatory responses. It had begun with total opposition to privatization and a commitment to renationalize what the Conservatives had sold to the private sector. It then moved to a position of abandoning a return to nationalization in favour of some notion of 'social ownership'. Next, it adopted a position of reluctant acceptance of the new status quo that the Conservatives had imposed. Finally, under the leadership of Tony Blair it attempted to outbid the Conservatives by planning to privatize enterprizes that even radical Thatcherism had not got round to, such as the country's air traffic control system.

These changes also entailed institutional and symbolic reforms. As we saw in the last chapter, a powerful historical influence on the ideology of the Labour party had been the party's close links with the trade unions. Throughout the 1980s and 1990s a series of internal institutional reforms – such as in the running of the annual conference – reduced union influence in the party, as we saw in the preceding chapter. At the same time the Conservative government's changes in the law governing industrial relations had greatly reduced the power of the unions in the wider society. These changes made easier a further great adaptation by Labour: it

## DOCUMENTING POLITICS 15.3

### THE PREDECESSOR OF NEW LABOUR? ANTHONY CROSLAND ON 'SOCIALISM'

Anthony Crosland's *The Future of Socialism* was published in 1956, and it greatly helped stimulate debates in the Labour party about whether the party's traditional version of Socialism was now historically relevant. Crosland argued that many of Labour's traditional beliefs were outmoded: that capitalism had now been transformed into a system where the profit motive was controlled by the state and the autonomy of professional managers; and that public ownership, to which the party was attached as a mark of socialism, should actually be viewed pragmatically as one means of control among many. His arguments heralded much of the content of 'New Labour' in the 1980s and 1990s. But Crosland in *The Future of Socialism* was a figure very different from a new Labour politician. He differed in three key respects:

- *In objectives*. He argued that the Party should pursue greater equality, and in this connection argued for higher and more 'progressive' taxes, and reform of institutions such as public schools and grammar schools.
- *In values*. He favoured maximum freedom in private life, covering matters such as divorce, sexual preferences and the organization of family life: all these are far away from New Labour's moral concerns with preserving traditional family values, and were highly radical in the 1950s.
- *In style*. He thought that modern organizational politics were actually unimportant, and was thus far removed from the modern politician who is obsessed above all with politics: 'The time has come for a reaction: for a greater emphasis on private life, on freedom and dissent, on culture, beauty, leisure, and even frivolity. Total abstinence and a good filing-system are not now the right sign-posts to the socialist Utopia: or at least if they are, some of us will fall by the way-side.'

➲ Crosland's book was the most intellectually distinguished attempt to restate socialism in the decades after the Second World War. But its importance is reinforced by Crosland's own career: he was a Labour MP, and a leading figure in Labour cabinets of the 1960s and 1970s, until his early death in 1977.

*Source*: Quotation from Crosland (1956/64: 357).

accepted all the important changes in labour law introduced by the Conservatives that had been designed to weaken the ability of unions to exercise power in collective bargaining. Labour also accepted much of the transformation of central state power under the Conservatives: increased controls over local government; more central control over the education system; and more centralization in the direction of parts of the welfare state and of the agencies of public order, including the police.

Most of these changes had occurred in substance before Tony Blair became leader. But after 1994

Labour also changed its symbols to match the substance of ideological change. A tiny but telling symbolic change came with the adoption of the red rose as the Party's 'logo': red is the traditional colour of left-wing socialism, and the rose is a highly traditional symbol of England. The new symbol thus cleverly fused traditional 'socialist' and 'English' symbols (see Image 15.1). The language used by the Labour leader also stressed the importance of the market. The party embraced another important ideological element in Thatcherism: it accepted the view that globalization of the world

**DOCUMENTING POLITICS 15.4**

## THE PARTING OF THE WAYS: NEIL KINNOCK'S 1985 CONFERENCE SPEECH

'With impossible promises you start with far fetched resolutions. They are then pickled into rigid dogma and you go through the years sticking to that, outdated, misplaced, irrelevant to the real needs. You end in the grotesque chaos of a Labour council hiring taxis to scuttle round the city to hand out redundancy notices.'

Neil Kinnock, Leader of the Labour party, speech to Labour Party Annual Conference, 2 October 1985

➲ If there is one moment that can be said to mark the birth of New Labour it is this speech, and not the election of Tony Blair as Leader in 1994. Neil Kinnock had been elected Leader in 1983 as the great hope of the Labour left. The speech was an attack on the hard left militant faction which controlled, among other things, Liverpool City Council (the 'city' referred to in the speech). But it provoked a walk-out in mid-speech by Eric Heffer, a leader of the old left in the Party with whom Kinnock had in the past been in alliance. And the same 1985 Conference established a policy review which over the next two years abandoned most of the distinctive socialist economic policies on which the party had fought the 1983 general election.

economy limited what any British government could do. All this culminated in a change that had been beyond Hugh Gaitskell as leader: the removal of the old socialist Clause IV in the party constitution, and its replacement by a 'market friendly' clause (see Documenting Politics 15.5).

Labour remade its ideology, therefore, to accommodate the Thatcher revolution. It largely accepted Thatcherism's radical departures: towards a freer market; towards a stronger central state to manage this freer market; and towards integrating Britain into a globally competitive economy. But this did not mean that Labour became simply a clone of Thatcherism. In two important areas it developed highly distinctive positions: on the constitution, and on Europe.

Since the 1920s the two big parties had largely shared the same constitutional ideologies: they defended the 'Union' of the United Kingdom and they defended the supremacy of the Westminster Parliament. But in the 1990s Labour worked out radical constitutional policies, the content of which we have already summarized in earlier chapters. These included the devolution of important responsibilities to directly elected assemblies in Wales and

Scotland, which were implemented after 1997 (see Chapter 11). They also included the radical (if not yet complete) reshaping of the Westminster Parliament by virtually abolishing the position of hereditary peers in the second chamber, the House of Lords. This constitutional radicalism was partly the product of the need to differentiate the party from the Conservatives after it had accepted most of Thatcherism's economic policies. It was also partly the product of discontent in the Celtic nations with a political system that imposed Westminster governments upon them against the wishes of their own electorates: had Wales and Scotland been able to vote separately for governments after 1979 the Conservatives would never have ruled beyond England. The upshot was that New Labour rediscovered an old strand of Labour ideology: a constitutional radicalism that had been strong in the Labour movement in the early decades of the twentieth century but which disappeared when Labour rose as a party of government in Westminster.

The reshaping of Labour's policy on Europe, though less historically radical, was also exceptionally important. Until the 1980s, of the two major parties Labour had been the less enthusiastic about

## DOCUMENTING POLITICS 15.5

### OLD 'SOCIALIST' CLAUSE IV AND NEW LABOUR'S 'MARKET FRIENDLY' CLAUSE IV

**Clause IV of the Labour Party Constitution, 1918–1995:**

'To secure for the workers by hand or by brain the full fruits of their industry and the most equitable distribution thereof that may be possible, upon the basis of the common ownership of the means of production, distribution and exchange, and the best obtainable system of popular administration and control of each industry and service.'

**Clause IV of the Labour Party Constitution, 1995–**

'The Labour Party is a democratic socialist party. It believes that by the strength of our common endeavour, we achieve more than we achieve alone so as to create for each of us the means to realize our full potential and for all of us a community in which power, wealth and opportunity are in the hands of the many not the few, where the rights we enjoy reflect the duties we owe, and where we live together, freely, in a spirit of solidarity, tolerance and respect.

To these ends we work for:

A dynamic economy, serving the public interest, in which the enterprize of the market and the rigour of competition are joined with the forces of partnership and co-operation to produce the wealth the nation needs and the opportunity for all to work and prosper, with a thriving private sector and high quality public services, where those undertakings essential to the common good are either owned by the public or accountable to them.'

➲ The simplest contrast between the two clauses is length: the 1995 version is much wordier, even in the abbreviated version quoted here. There is a revealing reason for this. It is not necessarily that the drafters of the new clause were more verbose than the old: it reflects their attempt at a compromise between the old and the new. While the new Clause IV abandons the old socialist rhetoric of common ownership, it still tries to gesture towards traditional symbols of the party, such as solidarity and community. But it also contains radical new ideas such as commending the market enterprize and competition, which were viewed with hostility in the party that felt at home with the old Clause IV.

Britain's membership of the European Union. The Conservatives had negotiated British membership in 1973 and Labour only accepted this after much internal division. But from the 1980s Labour reinvented itself as a 'Europhile' Party, thus opening up a gap with the increasingly 'Eurosceptic' Conservatives (see Political Issues 15.1). In part this change happened as the result of the long years of Thatcherite domination, because in those years the institutions of the European Union often seemed to offer a source of influence which could be used by many of the groups opposing Thatcherite policies.

By the 1990s the ideological spectrum spanned by the two main parties was growing narrower. But at the same time the ideological diversity of the rest of the party universe became greater, as we shall now see.

## Liberal Democrats and Nationalists: alternative ideologies

### The ideology of the liberal democrats

The Liberal Democrats are the product of a long history, and their ideology reflects this. 'Liberal' is an echo of the historical origins of the party: it is the descendant of the Liberal party which before the First World War was the main party in British politics opposing the Conservatives. The Liberals were the governing party which took Britain into that war, and they emerged from it divided, soon to be replaced as the Conservatives' main opponents by the new Labour party. The War was catastrophic

POLITICAL ISSUES

### 15.1  EUROSCEPTICISM: A NEW FORCE IN BRITISH PARTY IDEOLOGY

The 2004 elections to the European Parliament produced sensational gains for the United Kingdom Independence Party (UKIP): it won 12 of the 78 available United Kingdom seats, increasing its numbers by 10 on the previous result, and pushing the Liberal Democrat share of the vote into fourth place (16.1 per cent, UKIP; 14.9, Liberal Democrats). Labour and the Conservatives, though still the two leading parties, both registered their lowest share of the vote in a UK-wide election for over a century.

UKIP originated in 1991 as the Anti-Federalist League, acquiring its present name in 1993. Its main aim is simply stated: to withdraw Britain from the European Union, at least as it is presently constituted. The emergence of UKIP is potentially significant because it suggests the emergence of a key issue now able to move voters, and may create a new line of ideological division in the British party system. The electorate in Britain has long been among the most 'Eurosceptic' in the European Union, but the two main parties, though often divided internally, have been committed to Britain's continuing membership of the Union for over 30 years.

The Conservative government in 1986 passed in the Single European Act the most important advance in European integration since Britain's original accession, but since the 1980s the party has become increasingly hostile to fresh forms of integration, such as the introduction of the Euro currency and the creation of a consolidated constitution for the Union. But no leading Conservative has ever yet publicly advocated withdrawal from the Union. Faced with loss of voters to UKIP the Conservative leadership in 2004 sought to position the party as pursuing a middle way between the 'extremes' of more integration (allegedly championed by Labour and the Liberal Democrats) and withdrawal (as championed by UKIP). Three sets of issues are raised by the emergence of UKIP:

- Whether the 2004 results were a single act of protest unlikely to be repeated at a general election: turnout at 38 per cent was very low, and voters were perfectly aware that the result had no direct impact on how Britain was governed. UKIP indeed was trounced in the 2005 general election.
- How far the Conservatives could move to pre-empt the position of UKIP. The Party has for over a decade been riven by internal dissension over Europe, and to the extent that the leadership tries to 'outbid' UKIP in hostility to the Union it risks internal revolts by the pro-integrationists who are a well organized faction in the party.
- How far the Labour government dare risk commitment to two measures on which it has promised referendums: entry of Britain into the Euro currency zone; and adoption of a freshly negotiated Constitution for the EU.

for the Liberals for reasons that still throw light on the nature of Liberal ideology. By 1914 the Liberal party contained two very different ideologies: a traditional radicalism which was suspicious of the state, whether it was involved in social and economic intervention at home or armed intervention abroad; and a new 'social reform' liberalism, which viewed the state as an instrument for the pursuit of welfare reform at home and the defence of national interest abroad. The crises of war produced irreconcilable tensions between the two, broke the party into pieces, and consigned it for the rest of the twentieth century to the margins of British politics (literally to the margins in most cases, since after the Second World War its small Parliamentary representation tended to come from the Celtic margins of Britain).

That history has left two marks on the modern ideology of the party, however. There is still a tension in the ideology of the Liberal Democrats between a desire to use the power of the state and a suspicion of state power. Throughout the modern history of the party it has remained committed to its social reform tradition. Some of the most important figures in the creation of the modern welfare state were active Liberals in the period between the two great World Wars. They included, for example, the economist John Maynard Keynes (1883–1946), on whose economic theories were built policies of extensive state intervention in the economy; and William Beveridge (1879–1963), who produced a famous official report (1942) on which some of the most important features of the modern welfare state were built. Indeed, since the end of the Second World War Liberals have been consistent supporters of the welfare state. The devolved government in Scotland gave the Liberals their first taste of participation in government for nearly 80 years, when they entered coalition in 1999 with Labour. They have been consistent supporters of active state intervention in Scotland.

Thus the ideology of modern Liberalism has adapted to a world of large scale state intervention in social and economic life. The modern party is at ease with a big state, but elements of the different tradition of liberal individualism and suspicion of the state, which once dominated the party, still also

exist. The historical tradition of individualism is most obvious at the grassroots level of the party. Surveys show Liberal activists to be unusually strongly committed to the defence of civil liberties. The party has long claimed to be a supporter of more decentralization in Britain. And, trying to practise what it preaches, much of the modern revival of the modern party has been achieved by stressing 'grassroots' political activity: taking the most local issues, such as the immediate quality of everyday lives, as the starting point for political campaigning. On foreign policy issues, too, the Liberal radical tradition that is pacifist by inclination has been influential: the Liberal Democrats in the Westminster Parliament opposed the commitment to war in Iraq in 2003, against majorities in both the Labour and Conservative parties.

Thus the modern Liberal Democrats simultaneously support big government in the cause of economic management and social reform, and are suspicious of big government and centralized institutions. This is obviously a complex, often contradictory, ideological inheritance. Its complexity was magnified by the history of the party system in the 1980s. At the beginning of that decade, as we saw in the preceding chapter, a group of leading members of the Labour party (the 'Gang of Four') broke away from Labour to form a separate party, the Social Democrats. The new party principally catered to those who were enthusiastic supporters of Britain's integration into the European Union (at the time, the Labour party was officially sceptical) and who opposed Labour's move in the early 1980s to a radical policy of extensive state intervention in the economy. This put the new party very close ideologically to the Liberals. The two parties fought a number of general elections in a succession of alliances. Following the 1987 general election, as explained in Chapter 14, the two fused (hence the Liberals' change of name to Liberal Democrats). A brief attempt to keep the Social Democrats in existence by their last leader, David Owen, soon failed. The relevance of this history to the modern Liberal Democrats is that, in the remnants of the Social Democratic party, the Liberals incorporated a party with a very different tradition from the old individualistic, decentralized Liberalism. The Social

Democrats were an elitist creation, the product of the ambitions and strategies of a small number of disillusioned Labour party politicians, and their focus was on the politics of Westminster government. The incorporation of the Social Democrats therefore marginally strengthened the ideological elements in the Liberal Democrats favourable to strong state controls over the individualists and decentralizers; and it also strengthened those with a 'Westminster' focus over those more interested in non-metropolitan politics.

## Nationalist ideologies in the UK

There are presently three important groups in the UK which advocate various degrees of nationalist separation from the present British state: the Irish, Scottish and Welsh.

*Irish nationalism* is by far the most successful of the separatist nationalist ideologies. It has already secured one break-up of the United Kingdom (the secession of the largest part of the Ireland as the Irish Free State in 1921). Irish nationalists fought a guerrilla campaign (chiefly through the Provisional IRA) for nearly a quarter of a century after 1970 to secure the integration of the six counties of Ulster into the Republic of Ireland. They accounted for the overwhelming majority of the 3,000 plus murders in the province in those years. The new political institutions in the north (which were described in Chapter 11) substantially weakened the sovereignty of the British state in Ulster. Nationalism in the north – whether committed to armed force or to peaceful means – has principally had been supported by sections of the Catholic community, especially the Catholic working class and a small Catholic middle class principally employed in the public sector. This social base has meant that all the different nationalist factions have advocated extensive government intervention in social and economic affairs. *Sinn Féin*, the leading party of separatist nationalism, has often used the language of socialism, but during its brief participation in government following the Good Friday Agreement it was associated with reforming rather than socialist radical policies: for example, attempting to replace selective secondary education in the province by comprehensive schooling.

*Scottish nationalism* is the most successful brand of nationalism on mainland Britain. Though its ideological origins looked back to a traditional rural Scotland, the SNP that now is so important in Scottish politics offers a modern vision of Scotland. Its aim is full independence, but full independence within the membership of the European Union. The models it offers point to other small, successful economies in Europe (including the Dutch) and it emphasizes the 'modern' side of Scottish life, such as Scotland's importance as a modern European economy.

By contrast with Scottish nationalism, *Welsh nationalism* has long been, and continues to be, 'cultural' in character. Plaid Cymru, the Welsh Nationalist Party, has its roots in movements to protect and foster the Welsh language. (Scottish Nationalists have by contrast shown much less interest in Scots Gaelic). Socially and economically it also draws on long traditions of Welsh radicalism, and has become a natural home in Wales for economic and social radicals who, for whatever reason, do not feel able to support Labour in Wales. It also draws on a tradition of radicalism in foreign affairs that has roots in the radicalism of Welsh nonconformist Protestantism. Thus *Plaid Cymru*, like the Liberal Democrats, opposed the 2003 Iraq war.

As we saw in Chapter 11, the environment of nationalism is changing rapidly in Britain. For the first time nationalists have participated in government; and in the new political environment the old 'British' parties, notably Labour and Conservative, are changing their strategies. Nationalist ideologies are therefore among the most fluid in modern British politics.

## Ideologies of the marginalized: racists, Marxist and Greens

The British political system, like any other, has parties that have dominated political life and others that remain at its margins in the sense that they command little popular support. It is important not to lose sight of these marginalized groups, however. The 'marginal' of one decade are often central in another: a book on British politics written in the early

1960s would have treated Scottish and Welsh nationalism as little more than historical curiosities. What is more, importance lies in more than numbers. Ideologies that are marginal in the sense of enjoying little overt popular support can nevertheless have a big impact on mainstream parties: we will shortly see that this is true both of racism and Green ideology. Finally, the very fact that an ideology is marginalized may tell us something very revealing about the wider political system: we will see that this is true of the position of Marxism.

A word of caution is needed here. The ideologies discussed here are grouped together because they share a common fate – they have enjoyed little popular support. This grouping is not meant to suggest that they are morally equivalent.

## Racism

Racist ideologies are based on the twin claims that some races are innately superior to others and that nations should be racially homogeneous, even if this means expelling or otherwise eliminating 'inferior' races. Racism thus defined was a great influence in European politics in the twentieth century, and it continues to be important in many European countries (see Briefing 15.2). One of the big puzzles of British political history is why an important party supporting racism never managed to establish itself in the United Kingdom: parties with a racist ideology have never managed to gain more than a tiny minority of the popular vote. There seem to be two reasons for this. First, racist parties suffer the same handicaps as any other minority party under the Westminster electoral system. Second, for the past 50 years the issue most likely to gain support for racists, the immigration and settlement of large numbers of people from different races and cultures, has been appropriated by the two big governing parties. Since the first appearance of overt large scale hostility to immigrants in the 1950s the two governing parties have competed with each other to impose ever more strict immigration controls; in this sense they have suppressed racist parties by adopting one of their most important policies. At the same time both parties have supported the general idea that everybody already

in Britain should be treated without discrimination, and have put onto the statute book laws outlawing racist discrimination, and racist abuse, in the work place and the housing market.

# Briefing 15.2

## RACISM: AS BRITISH AS ROAST BEEF AND YORKSHIRE PUDDING

In twenty-first century Britain racism is treated as a marginal, un-British phenomenon. Yet racism has deep historical roots in Britain, and at various times its fundamental tenets have been widely accepted by political leaders and by established political parties. The core of racism has two components:

- That some social groups are genetically superior to others (for instance, in intelligence).
- That Britain should be preserved as a racially homogeneous society, notably as a homogeneous white society.

Among powerful traces of racism in the recent past are the following:

- The belief that the British 'race' had a special civilizing mission was central to the creation and maintenance of the British Empire.
- The belief that selective breeding to improve the racial 'stock' – technically, eugenics – was widespread among politicians of both the left and right well into the twentieth century.
- Large scale public hostility to foreign immigrants, on the grounds that they threaten the homogeneity of society, are a commonplace in Britain. They span public hostility to the Irish, to Jewish immigrants from Eastern Europe, and to immigrants from the so-called 'new Commonwealth' countries such as Pakistan and India.

Parties such as the British National Party, which argue for the creation of a racially homogeneous Britain, are not therefore 'un-British': they are instead systematizing, and expressing publicly, a strand of the British political tradition.

➲ Political ideologies are complex phenomena. They crop up in the most surprising, and often inconvenient, ways as this case of racist ideology shows.

## Marxism

Marxism covers a broad spectrum of beliefs, all inspired originally by the work of the German revolutionary and social thinker, Karl Marx (1818–83). At its core is the argument that conflict between classes is the driving force that shapes societies. In Britain, a developed capitalist society, this means conflict between capitalists and labour, a conflict that must finally result in the transformation of society and the establishment of a socialist order where labour rules. The most striking feature of Marxist ideologies in Britain is their popular weakness. Even before the fall of Communism in the Soviet Union and Eastern Europe after 1989, Britain was unusual in this respect. For most of the twentieth century countries such as France and Italy had large, well supported Communist parties based on a Marxist ideology of class conflict between an exploited mass of workers and a small elite of capitalists. The Communist party of Great Britain never enjoyed more than trivial popular support (except perhaps for a brief period in the Second World War when Britain allied with the Communist Soviet Union against Nazi Germany). In turn the Communists in Britain had a large number of fierce rivals in the form of tiny factions offering alternative variations on Marxist ideology. After the fall of Communism in Eastern Europe the Communist party itself fragmented into a number of even tinier factions. But Marxist ideology has been more important in Britain than formal organization or support for the Communist party would suggest. As we saw above, it has been a minority but well established tradition in the Labour party. Communist party activists were important out of all proportion to their numbers in the British trade union movement. And in a more general way, Marxist ideas have been important among various groups of British intellectuals: among many creative writers, for instance, and in the history of social science in Britain. These examples show how important it is not simply to assume that a political ideology is identical with a particular political institution. This is a point we will also notice with our next ideology.

## Environmentalism

Concern with the protection of the physical environment is at least as old as the Industrial Revolution: there is a long tradition, dating from the nineteenth century, of laments about the impact of economic development on nature. In this broad sense environmental ideologies are well embedded in the main political parties; but a distinct ideology of environmentalism, with its own party, the Greens, is very new in British politics. The Green Party was founded in 1985, as an institution with a more user-friendly name than its predecessor, the Ecology party. The most important feature of Green party ideology is its claim to be dealing in a new kind of politics. It claims, in other words, to be about more than environmental protection. The old ideologies, according to this view, are still obsessed with economic growth. Green ideology is concerned with a wholesale reconstruction of the economy so that it can be run in a way that does not depend on the continued pursuit of an economic growth that damages nature. Within Green ideology, in turn, there are varying shades of radicalism. 'Deep Greens', for example, advocate more than environmentally-friendly public policy: they argue for a wholesale revolution in the nature of society's culture and institutions. This attempt to practise a 'new' politics stretches beyond policy. As we saw in the preceding chapter, Greens reject traditional party hierarchies, favouring collective leadership over a single leader. This failure is connected to issues raised in the next section of the chapter.

## British party ideology: the rise and fall of consensus

If we look back over half a century, there is a clear pattern to the development of party ideology in Britain. In the first half of the 1950s there were two distinct features to the pattern of ideology:

- The two leading political parties, Labour and Conservative, shared common assumptions about how the economy should be run and how the government of Britain should be organized.

# DEBATING POLITICS

## 15.1   IDEOLOGY: FIG LEAF FOR INTERESTS OR CORE OF PARTY IDENTITY?

| Ideology is merely a 'cover' for the interests that a party represents | Ideology has an independent power of its own |
|---|---|
| ■ It is usually very hard to make a clear link between what parties do in British government and what they profess ideologically.<br>■ The big parties are closely linked to economic interests and could not survive without serving those interests.<br>■ Politicians are driven people, and what drives them is the desire to get into, and stay in, government.<br>■ Modern politics is so dominated by marketing that deep-seated beliefs are pushed to the margins of politics. | ■ Leading politicians are no different from the rest of us: they need something to believe in.<br>■ For most politically active people politics brings few material rewards, and attachment to an ideology is the only credible explanation for their activism.<br>■ The parties do not always deliver on their promises, but what parties promise is still a remarkably good predictor of what they do in government.<br>■ Politicians inside parties constantly fight about ideas, so the ideas must be important to them. |

● Once Labour and Conservative ideology had been described, one had virtually the full ideological picture. Other ideologies were marginal and marginalized.

Some observers of British political history have challenged these generalizations, notably the generalization that there once existed a consensus between the two leading parties. It is undoubtedly possible to exaggerate the extent of agreement between the parties in the 1950s. For instance, while the Conservatives indeed accepted most of the reforms of the Labour governments of 1945–51 (such as the introduction of the National Health Service) they often did so reluctantly, and consistently thought of themselves as the party that more instinctively understood the market economy. In the 1950s there were also deep and bitter differences over foreign policy: for instance, the Labour party strongly opposed the British government's attempt to invade the Suez Canal in Egypt in 1956. (We might contrast this with the consensus between Labour and Conservatives over the invasion of Iraq in 2003.) In the late 1950s there also developed, partly from the socialist wing of the Labour party, a mass movement favouring a highly radical policy: unilaterally abandoning Britain's nuclear weapons in order to set a moral example for world nuclear disarmament.

There is never complete consensus – complete agreement – in any political system, so measures of consensus are bound to be relative, and it is relative to what came later that a decade such as the 1950s appears to be an age of ideological consensus. Two big changes have occurred over the years. First, the old consensus about economic management between the two leading parties has been destroyed. In the 1980s the Thatcherite reforms described earlier in the chapter radically broke with the established understandings about how the economy should be run. By the 1990s there had, indeed, been created a new consensus between the parties, because by now Labour had largely accepted the Thatcherite revolution: accepted large scale privatization of nationalized industries; accepted reforms in the law designed to control trade unions; and symbolically accepted the primacy of market forces in governing the economy, as illustrated by its new 'Clause IV' described earlier. But now there were new areas of dissensus. The settled agreement about how to govern the United Kingdom, which had existed since the 1920s, broke down, as Labour moved to introduce its radical devolution proposals after 1997. An increasingly wide gap also opened up between the two big parties over the issue of Britain's relations with the European Union – an issue of critical and growing importance as the pace of European integration increased in the 1990s, and as Britain's economy and society became increasingly entangled with that of the Union.

The decline of the old consensus therefore refers in part to what divides the two big parties in the world of Westminster government, but there is a more fundamental change still in the nature of ideological consensus. In the 1950s the two big parties dominated the political system, and consequently their ideologies were also dominant. Both were coalitions bringing together different ideological traditions, and the range of ideologies encompassed by those coalitions encompassed most significant ideological traditions in Britain. Ideologies such as Scottish Nationalism seemed simply to be quaint anachronisms, and ideologies such as environmentalism were virtually invisible.

The situation is now very different. Not only are there vigorous and rising ideologies that challenge Labour and the Conservatives; ideology flourishes outside the whole party system itself (see Debating Politics 15.1). A kaleidoscope of political movements exists, often with little or no organized connections to established parties of any kinds. Two important examples, which were encountered in Chapter 9, are environmentalism and feminism. Although environmentalism is partly organized in the Green party, it is much wider than the Greens, and takes numerous forms in a whole host of locally inspired manifestations. Partly for this reason it has also been appropriated by the big parties, if only opportunistically and rhetorically. Feminism, meanwhile, has also influenced all the political parties, but has most of its organizational and ideological life outside the formal boundaries of party organization. The world of political ideology in Britain used to be comparatively one-dimensional, capable of being summarized in the differences between Labour and Conservative. Now it is highly diverse, multi-dimensional and only partly incorporated inside the formally organized party system.

## REVIEW

Five themes have dominated this chapter:

1 Ideology can either be considered as just an instrument that parties use to manage their 'brand identity' in the political marketplace, or as a key to their essential identity;

2 Party ideology in Britain is overwhelmingly shaped by the fact that two parties, Labour and the Conservatives, have dominated British politics for nearly a century. Understanding party ideology is to an important degree a matter of understanding the ideology of these two parties;

3 Both Conservative and Labour ideologies were transformed in the last two decades of the twentieth century: the Conservative version by the rise of Thatcherism; the Labour version by the need to respond to the challenge of Thatcherism;

4 Party ideologies once thought of as little more than historical relics, such as nationalism, are growing in importance in British politics;

5 The nature of political ideology in Britain is changing fundamentally. Parties are of decreasing importance in expressing ideology, as movements beyond organized parties, and often beyond formal organization at all, rise in importance.

## Further reading

The most important work on the ideology of modern Conservatism is Gamble (1994). Gamble (1974) ranges back in the history of Conservative ideology. Beer (1969/1982) is a classic on both Conservative and Labour ideology. Furious historical debates on the character of Labour ideology are best explored via Howell (1980). A pithy statement of the character of New Labour can be found in Coates (2000b).

**CHAPTER 16**

# How political communication happens

## AIMS

The aims of this chapter are:

- ❖ To sketch the main forms of political communication

- ❖ To describe the main forms of mass political communication, in the printed word and in broadcasting

- ❖ To describe the regulation of political communication, and the main issues this creates

- ❖ To summarize what we presently know about the impact of bias in mass political communication

- ❖ To summarize how new technologies are affecting political communication in Britain.

## Political communication and British democracy: the forms and significance of communication

Political communication is vital to the workings of any system of government, but it is particularly important in a country such as Britain, a democratic political system attempting to govern a territory with a large population (nearly 60 million people). We only have to reflect for a moment on the simple fact of the size of population to see that communication between governors and governed is not something that will happen automatically; it has to be organized. This chapter is about *how* it is organized.

Faced with the phrase 'political communication' most of us will instinctively think of the world of party communication in the mass media, of debates on television between party leaders or news reporting in national papers; but that is only a part of political communication. There are actually four overlapping forms of communication that have to happen if democratic government is to be conducted at all effectively:

- *Communication from the people to the government.* There are many theories of democracy but all at root involve the assumption that the people's voice is heard and that government listens. Most theories of democracy assume that the people 'speak' decisively at election time but, as we shall see, there are numerous other opportunities for government in Britain to 'listen' to the people.
- *Communication from the government to the people.* A first condition of effectively conducting the business of government is that the population at large actually knows what the government wants to do, and what it requires the population to do. So government has to put a large amount of energy into communicating with the people. Take something that is part of the daily life of every motorist: obeying the speed limit. Obedience depends critically on something elementary: knowing what the limit is. Thus an elaborate network of road signs throughout the country alerts motorists to this. (See Images 16.1–3, p. 346 for an illustration.)

- *Communication from the political parties to the electorate.* This overlaps with the second form of communication above, because parties in office often deliberately mix up the wider job of communicating with citizens for the purpose of governing with the narrower job of communicating their own partisan message. But of course all political parties, in office or out of it, also have both to get their message across and to persuade voters that their message is convincing enough to merit support at elections. This kind of communication is therefore vital to democratic political competition.
- *Communications between the people.* It is important not to identify political communication only with what we might call 'vertical' communication: messages going up and down between political leaders and the people. Citizens also communicate with each other about politicians and about government in a whole host of ways and, when we turn near the end of this chapter to look at new technologies of communication, we will find that this sort of communication may be becoming more important.

How does each of these forms of communication happen? See Timeline 16.1 for an introduction to the historical development of mass political communication.

### From people to government

*Elections.* In most theories of democracy 'the people speak' at elections. Winning parties, for example, will claim that their votes give them a mandate to do what is in their 'manifesto', the document typically prepared by all parties at election time summarizing the programme they propose for government. The assumption is that a vote for a party is also an expression of support for the party's programme. In fact there is plenty of survey evidence that this is not so: often voters are unaware of the small print (or even the large print) in a party manifesto. And even when they are, a single vote can hardly be taken as assent to a whole complex programme: an elector may vote for a party because they strongly approve of its policy on taxation in

## TIMELINE 16.1    HISTORY OF THE DEVELOPMENT OF MASS POLITICAL COMMUNICATION IN BRITAIN

**1702**
First daily paper, *Daily Courant.*

**1712**
Stamp Act effectively puts a tax on newspapers.

**1771**
First free reporting of parliamentary debates allowed.

**1814**
Steam presses first used to print *The Times*, greatly increasing speed of newspaper production.

**1837**
Invention of electric telegraph allows rapid news gathering.

**1855**
Repeal of stamp duty allows development of cheap popular press.

**1896**
*Daily Mail*, first mass circulation newspaper, founded.

**1901**
First transatlantic radio message broadcast.

**1922**
Radio broadcasting begun by privately owned British Broadcasting Company (BBC).

**1924**
John Logie Baird transmits first television pictures.

**1926**
BBC established as public monopoly for radio broadcasting.

**1936**
First regular television service.

**1939**
Television transmissions discontinued for duration of war.

**1946**
Television transmissions resume, with BBC monopoly.

**1953**
Press Council established as self-regulatory body controlled by newspaper industry to adjudicate on complaints against newspapers.

**1955**
First commercial television stations begin broadcasting in competition with BBC.

**1973**
First commercial radio stations begin broadcasting in competition with BBC.

**1982**
*Mail on Sunday* becomes first photocomposed newspaper, replacing centuries of physical type setting.

**1986**
News International moves operations for its major titles (*The Times*, *The Sun*, etc.) to new site at Wapping. Breaks power of print unions, fully adopts technology of photocomposition, and is soon followed by all its national competitors.

**1989**
First satellite television transmissions begin in Britain from Rupert Murdoch-owned Sky TV.

**1991**
Press Complaints Commission replaces Press Council (see 1953 above) in attempt to make self-regulation by newspaper industry more effective.

**2003**
Report on Iraq on BBC Radio 4 *Today* programme leads to Hutton Inquiry and crisis in BBC–government relations (see Political Issues 16.1).

**2004**
OFCOM (Office of Communications) established as single regulator for all broadcasting media.

➲ The history of the mass media communications in Britain is a mixture of technological change and regulatory change. The key technological innovations for the newspaper industry were already made before the twentieth century; for radio and television made early in the twentieth century. There has been another burst of innovation, associated with IT, in both newspaper production and broadcasting, in the last two decades.

*Source*: Adapted, with additions, from Cook and Stevenson (1983 and 2000).

spite of the fact that they disagree with its policy on control of immigration. Elections are therefore an important form of upward political communication, but are also a highly imperfect form.

*Polling.* These imperfections help explain why many other ways of detecting the popular voice have developed. Over a period of more than 60 years scientifically drawn surveys have evolved into a method of continuously monitoring the views of the population on almost every conceivable political issue, from judgements about personalities to views about the most complex policy problems.

*Focus groups.* One of the drawbacks of polling by mass surveys is that they usually only gather a view hastily expressed to a stranger who puts a series of quick questions. (Questions about political issues are often mixed up with quite unrelated questions of market research for products, giving an even more fragmented character to responses.) There is rarely opportunity to express more complex views and judgements, and it is consequently not possible to be confident that conventional polling tells us much about the deeply held views of the people at large. Focus groups are an attempt to remedy this problem. They literally 'focus' on a narrow range of issues or personalities. The groups are encouraged to discuss in depth their views and feelings about a whole variety of matters, ranging again from their reaction to personalities to their feelings about policies. Focus groups originally developed in commercial marketing but are now (see Briefing 16.1) a key method of 'listening' used by the political parties.

An elaboration of the 'focus group' approach, less tied to marketing, occurs in various forms of organized 'deliberation'. These are attempts at enriching the quality of popular reflection. Typically a cross-section of the population is assembled as a kind of 'jury' to deliberate on an important issue demanding government decision. It hears evidence (for instance, from expert witnesses) and engages in extended discussion of the issue in question. At the end of the process, it is hypothesised that the views formed better reflect the true quality of popular opinion than, for instance, do instantaneous responses to conventional opinion surveys. Government is increasing the use of these jury-style mechanisms, (for example, to try to gauge popular

# Briefing 16.1

## HOW FOCUS GROUPS WORK

For over half a century political parties have used their own private polls to try to 'listen' to the electorate. The poll asking questions of a representative sample of the population is a powerful and efficient way of tracking opinion, but it has some obvious defects: it provides only a superficial snapshot of opinion, and is hard to use to explore deeper feelings about either policies or people. The 'focus group' originated in marketing as a way of exploring views more deeply:

- A focus group will typically involve 6–10 participants. A 'moderator' will guide the discussion, encouraging discussion between members. This group communication is a key distinction between the focus group and the conventional survey, where an interviewer poses questions.
- Parties present a variety of features to focus groups for discussion: they can 'trial' hypothetical policies, in the manner of a manufacturer trialling new brands; they can explore the 'image' of their leaders; and they can also explore the images associated with the party in general.

Focus groups communicate much more subtle information about popular views than do conventional surveys. But they also present problems:

- They are an expensive way of gathering information, and since the groups are tiny there is every possibility that they are an inaccurate guide to what people at large think.
- Their origins in market research make some defenders of democracy uneasy, since they seem to suggest that leaders should shape policies and personalities as if they were 'brands' in the marketplace. This seems the very opposite of 'conviction' politics.

➲ Political communication flows in all directions in a modern democracy. Focus groups are one of the most sophisticated means of channelling communication between leaders and people. For a defence of this method in democratic politics, see Documenting Politics 16.1.

opinion about issues such as how access to health care should be rationed).

Elections, sample surveys, focus groups and deliberative juries have this in common: the terms on which the communication takes place tend to be set by political leaders, who are in a position to ask the questions and raise the issues. Indeed focus groups, which look at first glance like the most serious attempt to listen to the people, originated as a market research technique designed to help firms design and sell products more effectively. But there are other, more direct and less controlled forms of upward communication.

*Written direct communication.* These can range from individual letters to organised petitions that attract millions of signatures. For instance every member of the House of Commons has a large postbag, particularly from constituents, on every conceivable matter. Politicians seem to attach particular weight to these individual communications, presumably on the grounds that anyone prepared to take the trouble to write has strong feelings on a subject. The spread of the web has supplemented 'snail' mail communication with e-mail: virtually every MP can now be e-mailed, though how far the messages are read and digested depends on the efficiency of each member's office.

*Direct action.* Communication does not have to be in writing. It can take the form of a physical presence, peaceful or otherwise. Marches, blockades, gathering in large public assemblies: all are established and normally peaceful ways in which groups of citizens make their views known. But direct action need not only be peaceful: sometimes public demonstrations that start out as peaceful direct action can turn into violent confrontation, perhaps with the police. And some groups decide from the outset that direct action of a violent sort is the only effective way of communicating. Some militant groups have combined written with violent communication, by mailing letter bombs to public figures. The Provisional IRA strategy of 'the armalite and the ballot box' that was practised in Northern Ireland also joins the peaceful and violent in communication (the armalite is a sniper's gun).

## From government to people

In a democracy communications by government to people very often have a partisan purpose: the governing party wants to impress its record on voters. But there is much more to it than this: British governments address three very important forms of communication to the people.

*Commands.* Government has equipped itself with a vast array of powers over all our lives, and these powers are embodied in law and backed by powerful resources, such as the police force. However, such command is of little use if it is not communicated. We live our lives surrounded by these communicated commands from the state. Just consider something as trivial as getting into the car to drive to the supermarket. Our journey will be shaped by commands: road signs that dictate the maximum speed at which we can drive over different stretches of road; traffic lights that forbid us to progress if they show red; national billboard advertising campaigns, especially at particular times (say Christmas), reminding us of the penalties of driving after consuming alcohol.

*Information.* Over the last century government in Britain has vastly expanded the range of services and benefits that it delivers to the population. The entitlements to these services are often governed by complex rules and there is no need to assume that we will be familiar with these. So government puts considerable resources into trying to communicate this information throughout the community: the latest available figures, for 2001, show a budget in excess of £270 million. A ten minute trip to the nearest post office will illustrate what is going on: you will find a rack of leaflets and brochures covering everything from details of the savings scheme offered by government to information about housing benefit entitlements.

*Advice and warnings.* If you are a smoker, look at your cigarette packet now. You will see on it the following stark warning: 'Smoking Kills'. This is an example of a very common communication that government addresses in countless numbers to millions of citizens: warnings about what it is unsafe to consume, or advice about what is the best style of life. As we have all become increasingly sensitive to risk in modern life, this form of advice and warning has become more common. The example of warnings on cigarette packets is particularly relevant. The National Health Service, we shall see in a later chapter, is one of the biggest of all public spending programmes, and government has developed an increasing interest in communicating advice about healthy lifestyles in an attempt to contain demands on health spending.

## From political parties to the electorate

Communications from government to the people are often semi-concealed efforts by parties to get messages across to the electorate: announcements of new welfare programmes, for instance, are implicitly boasts about the achievement of the governing party. But parties also have to put huge resources into communicating more openly with electors. Small, poorly supported parties have to do this in traditional ways long established in Britain: by holding public meetings and demonstrations, or 'canvassing' voters on their doorstep. Well supported, rich parties do this too, but most of their effort to communicate with their electorate consists of sophisticated political marketing: the conscious design of 'packages' of policy and personalities to appeal to groups of electors, and the conscious selling of those packages. Marketing like this involves the use of techniques of communication often borrowed from commercial market research and selling. Parties intensively survey the electorate, and use focus groups of the sort described above, in order to explore what policies will have most appeal to which groups. Rather like advertisers marketing a commercial good, groups are often 'targeted', with the message adapted to the target. A party may want to send a message to its 'core' support (those who can be expected to be more or less automatically sympathetic). Very often, however, parties can take their core support for granted so packages are put together and marketed to 'swing' voters, who can be detached from other parties. Victory in elections, as we will see in Chapter 17 on voting, can turn on the votes of relatively small proportions of these 'swing' voters.

In marketing their packages parties have learnt to use the most advanced forms of communication technology. Large advertising budgets mean that, especially at times of elections, many of the conventional tools of marketing, such as billboard

**Image 16.1–3**
**Government communicates with the people**

Image 16.1    Advice and warning

Image 16.2    Information

➦ Government communication is all around us, as these three everyday images connected with motoring show: the first conforms to 'advice and warning'; the second is straightforward information; and the third is a command backed up by the threat of monitoring by speed camera technology.

Image 16.3    Command

Photos: Michael Moran

campaigns, are used intensively. As we saw in Chapter 14, the two main parties in the past have recently been spending over £20 million in a general election year. A combination of sophisticated surveys and modern means of electronically storing data means that parties can also target particular groups of voters with 'mail shots', letters and leaflets designed to communicate with particular groups of voters. The existence of rich collections of data about particular groups in the electorate, coupled with the fact that virtually every

## DOCUMENTING POLITICS 16.1

## A DEFENCE OF MODERN POLITICAL MARKETING

'The public want leaders who lead, they want governments that tough it out. But they also want to be heard. Of course, governing with principles and yet in a continuous dialogue with voters is complicated. But modern politics is complicated. The electorate is more demanding and is right to be so. It is up to us to meet the new challenge. I do not just see focus groups and market research as campaigning tools; increasingly I see them as an important part of the democratic process: part of a necessary dialogue between politicians and people, part of a new approach to politics.'

➲ Philip Gould is the most successful 'marketer' in modern British politics, the key influence on the 'relaunch' of the Labour Party as 'New Labour'. This extract from the most considered statement of his philosophy shows how self-conscious has been the adoption of the newest marketing techniques, and how far Gould is prepared to go in arguing that their use strengthens democratic communication.

*Source*: Gould (1998: 328).

household in the country now has a telephone, means that parties can contact large numbers of key voters inexpensively by ringing intensively from a single call centre. This sort of rapid, intense phone polling can be used quickly to test voter reaction to particular packages, and to try to stimulate support among them. The Internet has given parties an extra set of instruments; all the parties have their own well-designed websites, and increasing numbers of individual MPs also have their own web pages.

The single most important feature of the communication between parties and the people is that it is a highly self-conscious activity, best summed up in the idea of marketing (see Documenting Politics 16.1). We will see in the next section why this gives the mass media such an important part in communication.

### From people to people

As we have noted, political communication is not all 'vertical' (up and down between people and government); communication can also be 'horizontal': that is, between people. Survey researchers long ago discovered, for example, that we get a large part of our information and opinions from each other: for

instance, by talking to friends and family. Consider Figure 16.1 for example, which reports what people told researchers about their sources of political information. One of the most important (75 per cent) was indeed 'friends and family'. This means that the kind of community in which people live has a big effect on the form of political communication. Imagine living as part of a big family in an isolated fishing community, for instance, and contrast that with living alone in a bed-sit in a big city: the communication possibilities are plainly very different in the two. This kind of people to people communication can be tremendously important in either reinforcing or subverting messages that politicians are trying to put across. Since most people do not take an intense interest in politics, information picked up in 'non-political' ways – listening to family at the meal table or to friends in the pub – can be very important, but obviously is not subject to much control. Surveys repeatedly show that large numbers of people simply do not have correct information: they put leading politicians in the wrong parties and ascribe the 'wrong' policies to parties. Half-an-hour spent listening to people talk about politics in virtually any bar in Britain will also show that people communicate a whole folklore about politics to each other: gossip and rumour, some of it true, some untrue, about the private lives of political leaders; conspiracies by government, and about government; disasters to which government has supposedly not owned up.

In recent years new technology has helped this people to people communication: the spread of unregulated Internet news sites, and the possibilities offered by mobile phones to allow rapid, easy communication between demonstrating groups are only two obvious examples. We look at the significance of these new forms of communication later in the chapter. (Indeed, we have already glanced at its possibilities in Chapter 9: look back, for example, at Documenting Politics 9.2, p. 173.)

## Political communication and the mass media

The most important feature of political communication in modern British politics is that it does not just happen; it is *managed* by politicians in and out of government to try to have the maximum effect (see Documenting Politics 16.1). Of course politicians cannot manage all communications. Events – disasters, mistakes, scandals – get in the way of control. But one of the biggest obstacles to management is that the politicians do not effectively control the most important institutions of mass communication: newspapers, television and radio. (This is a contrast with many other national political systems: even in some democratic political systems on continental Europe it is common for individual television and radio stations to be under the control of particular political parties.)

Television, newspapers and radio are vital to political communication: that much is clear from Figure 16.1. They are vital precisely because much important communication has to be on a mass scale. With a population of nearly 60 million, and an electorate of over 44 million, politicians can hardly expect to communicate by direct face-to-face contact: contrast the situation before the first great electoral reform of 1832, when there were only just over 500,000 voters in all. But these institutions of mass communication cannot be considered as a single group. There are big differences in how they

operate and in the relations they have with politicians. The most important divide is between newspapers, on the one hand, and radio and television on the other.

### The newspaper industry and political communication

National newspaper readership in Britain is high by international standards, but it is declining. Although there is a separate, highly distinctive press in both Scotland and Northern Ireland, in England and Wales the newspaper industry is dominated by papers edited from London. These nationally circulating newspapers have a number of important characteristics that affect their political roles.

*Papers are business enterprises.* All the papers have to survive in an atmosphere of intense competition, both for readers and (just as important) advertising revenue. In addition, most of the newspapers are themselves now no longer independent enterprises; they are part of larger corporations, many of which are multinational in scale and operating across a whole range of industries. For instance, as we can see from Table 16.1, the most successful tabloid of recent decades (*The Sun*) and one of the most prestigious broadsheets (*The Times*) are both controlled by News International, a worldwide corporation with interests across all media – print, broadcasting and film. Lord Beaverbrook, a newspaper magnate famous in the first half of the twentieth century, once claimed that he ran newspapers purely for propaganda. But whatever the propaganda ambitions of modern newspaper tycoons, in the end they have to be worked around running papers as profitable enterprises.

*Papers are partisan.* We will shortly see that there are detailed rules intended to ensure 'balance' in television and radio broadcasting. No such rules exist for newspapers. No political party owns a newspaper, but most papers have a long-term sympathy with one of the two major parties. Because papers are business enterprises, and because they are nowadays often part of large business corporations, there has been a tendency for papers to be partisan in favour of the Conservative party, but this is hardly an iron rule. *The Sun*, for

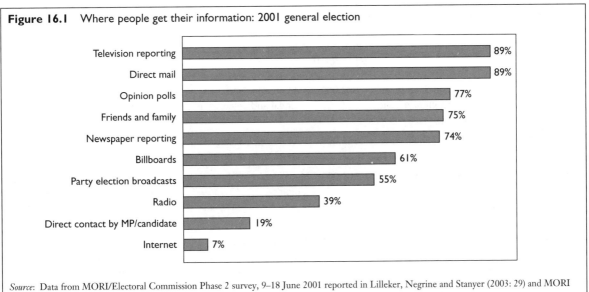

**Figure 16.1**    Where people get their information: 2001 general election

*Source*: Data from MORI/Electoral Commission Phase 2 survey, 9–18 June 2001 reported in Lilleker, Negrine and Stanyer (2003: 29) and MORI website.

➲ The figure draws on survey research done by the polling organization MORI for the Electoral Commission, and shows the commonest sources of information cited by the public about election issues. It shows that while the organized mass media, especially television, are very important, 'face to face communication' with friends and family is also very important.

long a supporter of the Conservative party, deserted it for Labour during the general elections of 1997 and 2001. One reason for its desertion is precisely that papers are businesses operating in a competitive world; they will not want to be too closely attached to a party if large numbers of their readers are deserting that party. They also do not want to fall out too seriously with a party if it is likely to form the next government, precisely because they have other economic interests to defend. For instance, the big business corporations that typically own newspapers in Britain often also have commercial interests in broadcasting which are affected by regulations made by government.

*Papers are competitive.*    Even when papers incline to a political party – the *Daily Telegraph*, for example, has usually faithfully supported the Conservative Party – the parties cannot control what the papers publish. Papers will routinely report both news and comments that are damaging to 'their' party. One reason they do this is that a force stronger even than partisan loyalty drives them: competition. Journalists compete for stories;

newspapers compete to be first with news. The competition is especially intense in the mass market for 'tabloid' newspapers. As a glance at any issue of *The Sun* or the *Daily Star* will show, these papers are neither produced nor read primarily for their political content. They are dominated by sport, show business, scandal and 'human interest' stories; politics is incidental. Political reporting just has to fit around the competitive reporting of other parts of life. If a damaging political scandal sells papers, it will be reported regardless.

*Papers are weakly regulated.*    We will soon see that there are powerful legal controls governing both entry into television and radio broadcasting, and regulating the content of what is broadcast. These controls are absent in the case of newspapers. There is no obligation to provide 'balance' in a story. The only formal regulatory body is the Press Complaints Commission, a 'self-regulatory' body controlled by the industry itself and with no power beyond administering admonitions to offenders. A more powerful control, true, is provided by the libel laws in Britain, which on occasion have meant that

**Table 16:1**  Ownership, circulation, journalistic style and political sympathies of main daily and Sunday newspapers

| Name | Ownership | Circulation (April 2004) | Publishing style | Partisan sympathies |
|---|---|---|---|---|
| Daily Express | Northern and Shell (part of publishing empire built on porn magazines) | 882,000 | Tabloid, specializing in scandal and celebrity news | Has supported Labour, but sympathies unreliable |
| Sunday Express | Northern and Shell | 866,000 | Tabloid, specializing in scandal and celebrity news | No firm partisan sympathies |
| Daily Star | Northern and Shell | 901,000 | Most 'down market' of the tabloids | No firm partisan sympathies, and will never allow any political loyalties to get in the way of a good scandal story |
| The Sun | News Corporation (multinational media corporation controlled by Murdoch family interests) | 3,345,000 | Tabloid which pioneered modern style of scandal, soft porn and celebrity exposés | Has supported both Labour and Conservative in recent elections; loyalties influenced by business interests of News Corporation |
| News of the World | News Corporation | 3,829,000 | Historical pioneer of sex scandal journalism now following modern tabloid styles | Unreliable |
| Sunday People | News Corporation | 1,033,000 | Tabloid specializing in scandal and celebrity news | Has supported Labour, but no reliable affiliations |
| Daily Mail | Daily Mail and General Trust PLC (publishing corporation controlled by Harmsworth family, historical pioneers of tabloid journalism in the UK) | 2,305,000 | Tabloid, with mix of scandal, celebrity exposes and substantial news reporting. | Conservative |
| Mail on Sunday | Daily Mail and General Trust PLC | 2,322,000 | Sister paper of Daily Mail | Conservative |
| Daily Mirror | Trinity Mirror (controller of large publishing empire) | 1,888,000 | Tabloid with large doses of scandal and celebrity news | Labour leaning, but cannot be relied to present party line |
| Sunday Mirror | Trinity Mirror | 1,562,000 | Tabloid, specializing in exposés of celebrity scandals | Labour leaning, but unreliable |
| Daily Telegraph | Bought by Barclay Brothers from Hollinger International in 2004. | 879,000 | Broadsheet with extensive coverage of politics. | News content aims to be impartial, but strong Conservative editorial sympathies |
| Sunday Telegraph | Barclay Brothers – see Daily Telelgraph. | 678,000 | Broadsheet replicating style of sister paper. | Strong Conservative editorial sympathies |
| Guardian | Scott Trust (charitable trust designed to ensure independence of paper from business interests) | 354,000 | Broadsheet with extensive coverage of politics | Reliable supporter of 'left' and 'liberal' causes, but unreliable supporter of Labour |

⇨

**Table 16:1**    (continued)

| Name | Ownership | Circulation (April 2004) | Publishing style | Partisan sympathies |
|---|---|---|---|---|
| Observer | Scott Trust | 422,000 | Sunday broadsheet, now virtually sister paper of Guardian | Reliable supporter of 'left' and 'liberal' causes, but unreliable supporter of Labour |
| The Times | News corporation (Murdoch controlled corporation which also owns tabloids like The Sun) | 613,000 | Broadsheet content, but with a tabloid format edition, with extensive coverage of politics | News coverage aims to be impartial; editorially, an unreliable supporter of Conservatism, but opinion columns cover a very wide, often unpredictable, range |
| Sunday Times | News Corporation | 1,373,000 | Now virtually a sister paper of The Times | News coverage aims for impartiality; editorially, an unreliable supporter of the Conservative Party |
| Financial Times | Pearson PLC (multi-media publishing corporation) | 422,000 | Broadsheet; the leading specialist business newspaper but with increasing range of 'general' news | Not aligned with any party; strong commitment to impartiality in news coverage; editorially, supports interests of business, where identifiable |
| Independent | Independent News and Media PLC (controlled by the family interests of Tony O'Reilly, Ireland's leading businessman) | 227,335 | Broadsheet 'content' but now a tabloid format, with extensive politics coverage, trying to market itself as paper that specializes in European news | Reliable supporter of 'liberal' causes, but no party alignment |
| Independent on Sunday | Independent News and Media PLC | 179,000 | The sister paper of The Independent | Reliable supporter of 'liberal' causes, but no party alignment |

*Source*: Author's files.

➲ There is a widespread belief, especially among Labour party supporters, that the London-based press which dominates British newspaper publishing is pro-Conservative and hostile to Labour. But this figure shows a more complex picture. There are very few publications with truly reliable partisan affiliations. The reason, paradoxically, is that most newspapers are closely tied to business: only the *Guardian* and the *Observer* are controlled by charitable trusts. The single most important business interest, especially among the tabloids, is maintaining and increasing circulation. The result is that, whatever their nominal partisan loyalties, these newspapers will never spurn a story that sells copies, no matter how damaging the revelations are to a particular political grouping. Among the broadsheets, their internal 'cultures' mean that the editorial line of the paper is often contradicted by their star opinion columnists, a state of affairs tolerated because of the realization that readers more readily buy a broadsheet for the stimulation of a star columnist than for the content of the editorial leader.

juries have awarded huge damages to individuals judged to have been libelled by stories in newspapers. All national newspapers have teams of lawyers on duty to read content before publication and to warn of possible libel, and rich and powerful people can use the threat of libel to prevent publication of stories. But even this is not a very powerful restriction on political reporting. Most of the really big libel awards have been about non-political stories (such as those concerning the private lives of show business stars). The two most spectacular political libel cases in recent years (involving the Conservative politicians Jeffrey Archer and Jonathan Aitken) eventually resulted in both Archer and Aitken serving jail sentences for perjury. The competitive pressure to publish is a powerful force countering the inhibiting fear of a libel suit.

There is a second sense in which the weak regulation of newspapers is important: the regulation of entry. If you or I decide to broadcast our own radio station without a licence, technically a quite simple matter, we will be closed down and prosecuted. (From January 2004 the issue of licences is the responsibility of a regulatory agency, the Office of Communications – see Briefing 16.3). But no licence is needed to publish a newspaper or magazine. There are indeed powerful barriers to entry, but they are mostly economic: establishing and running a national newspaper, for instance, demands the investment of tens of millions of pounds before any income is received. That explains why in the last twenty years only two new nationally circulated daily newspapers (the Independent and the Daily Star) have appeared and survived – and these two are among the weakest on the national scene. But entry at a lower level – for instance through a weekly with a low circulation aimed at a target audience – is much easier. Every conceivable shade of political opinion has its own weekly paper, most with tiny circulations. More important, there are well established magazines of opinion and comment which, while having small circulations, are read by the most active and politically committed: the joint circulation of *Prospect* and of the *New Statesman* is below 50,000, but readership of the most interested and committed gives these magazines an importance beyond that which the mere figures would suggest.

Some small circulation independent magazines have had effects well beyond their small proportions. The satirical fortnightly *Private Eye*, for example, has often printed stories which the national press has been too timid to publish for fear of libel, but which have subsequently been widely publicized.

## Broadcasting and political communication

When we turn from newspapers to broadcasting we see immediately several important contrasts.

*A mixed economy.* Newspapers are commercial enterprises. The structure of broadcasting is more complex. The longest established broadcaster, the British Broadcasting Corporation (BBC) is a publicly owned corporation. Its biggest single source of finance is the licence fee, a state-imposed levy that every household in possession of a television must pay. The Corporation's output of programmes is huge: two national 'terrestrial' television channels; a growing number of specialist channels than can be received by non-terrestrial satellite-based communication; dedicated specialist channels for Wales, Scotland and Northern Ireland; regional divisions producing news and specialist interest programmes for their region; five national radio stations and a range of digital specialist stations; and 37 local radio stations. The Corporation's role in political communication is immense, and understanding that role depends in part on understanding the history of the 'mixed economy' of broadcasting.

The Corporation originated as a commercial company to exploit the new technology of wireless in the 1920s, but it became a nationalized corporation in 1926. It had a complete legal monopoly of all broadcasting for the first 30 years of its history, and of radio for over 40 years: the first commercial television broadcasts were in 1955 and commercial radio was not allowed before 1973. For much of its history it had a powerful 'public service broadcasting' culture. It produced its programmes 'in-house' rather than buying in from other providers. It relied overwhelmingly for its income on the licence fee. It not only rejected commercial advertising but also took strenuous steps to ensure that no commercial advertising appeared accidentally in its broadcasts. It operated on the principle that its role was to

# Briefing 16.2

## POLITICAL COMMUNICATION IN THE 2005 GENERAL ELECTION

Political communication in 2005 illustrated a wider long-term feature of the mass media system. The centralization and professionalization of communication continued, via the reliance on targeted mailing, targeted phoning from party controlled call centres, and 'staged' events designed to attract newspaper and TV publicity. Yet this only emphasized the growing disjunction between the communication system and the wider governing system and, indeed, the wider society. The UK has become increasingly diverse; non-metropolitan Britain has become increasingly distinctive; and the system of government has responded by shifting to less decentralized multi-level systems of governance. All these trends are emphasised in this book. But the system of communication has if anything become more centralized on control from London-based institutions – institutions that are themselves often part of global conglomerates. The distinctiveness of regional television broadcasting has declined; local electoral communication has been superseded by communication from centrally controlled communications 'warehouses'; the only distinctive national press outside London – the Scottish – is in decline. This helps explain a key feature of the 2005 campaign: that the issues focused on, notably by mass media, reflected disproportionately the concerns of the booming economy, and distinctive society, of London and the south-east.

broadcast programmes that would be freely available to anyone with a receiver. Since radio receivers soon fell to a price that almost everyone could afford, BBC programmes soon approximated what in Chapter 21 we call a 'public good': a free service available virtually to all on demand.

There has in recent years been some relaxation of this public service culture. Programmes are increasingly 'bought in' from programme makers in the marketplace and the selling of BBC products is an increasingly important source of revenue. But the public service broadcasting culture nevertheless largely shapes how the BBC reports politics. The content and style of reporting resembles more the 'broadsheet' than the tabloid press. While news reporting includes a diet of human interest and celebrity stories, it is dominated by reporting of public events. There are elaborate rules designed to ensure balance in reporting, especially balance in reporting the debates between the main political parties. On important national occasions – a public disaster, or a general election – the BBC's self-image as a provider of a public service for the whole nation shapes how it reports events. Much of this has to do with the Corporation's history, and in particular the fact that for much of the twentieth century (including the critical years of the Second World War), it did indeed have a monopoly in broadcasting to, and on behalf of, Britain.

There is a mixed economy of broadcasting because alongside the BBC there has grown up, since the foundation of the original commercial television stations in the middle of the 1950s, a large and diverse commercial sector. This includes three national commercial television services (though the first of these is composed of a federation of stations licensed for different regions of the UK); an increasingly important commercial sector which broadcasts programmes via satellite that can reach across many different national boundaries; a growing number of national radio stations mostly specialising in offering one kind of output, such as light classical music; and over 250 local stations which mostly specialize in various styles of pop music mixed with short news broadcasts usually dominated by local information. Although regulation has meant that much of the 'public service' culture is important in the commercial sector, these stations are nevertheless very different from the BBC. Commercially they are more like the newspaper industry. They are often part-owned by large corporations where commercial broadcasting is only part of the business; in many cases these corporations are also major owners of newspapers; as with newspapers they are competitive because they survive in the main on the income from commercial advertising and (increasingly, in the case of television) from subscriptions paid by viewers. Because they have to survive by commercial competition, they often specialize to attract particular audiences. Since the audience for serious, large scale reporting of public events is neither large nor lucrative this means that much of the commercial sector barely reports politics (this will be obvious to any reader who is a regular listener to the local pop music commercial station).

*Broadcasting is impartial.* Newspapers, we saw, make no bones about bias: most have an open commitment to one or other political party, and most write major news stories around their partisan commitments. Broadcasting aspires to be impartial in two senses. First, no broadcasting channel admits to supporting either a particular political party or a particular political outlook. (This singles out Britain from other countries: in the USA commercial stations often have a marked political bias and, across mainland Europe, even when publicly owned, they are often controlled by a political party.) Second, in the actual broadcasting of news and current affairs all follow rules designed to ensure neutral reporting of events and balanced reporting of different view-points. How far this aspiration is achieved is something we will examine in a moment.

*Broadcasting is regulated.* The aspiration to impartiality is a direct result of probably the single most important contrast between newspapers and broadcasters: public bodies regulate the latter. Regulation comes in two forms. First, commercial broadcasters can only broadcast legally on receiving a licence. Whereas anybody with the resources can launch a newspaper, only somebody with a legal licence can launch a broadcasting service. This control over entry has many causes, but originally technology was very important: some controls were deemed necessary over access to a limited range of broadcasting frequencies. (Technology is in turn undermining this control over entry, as we will see below.) This regulation of entry in turn leads to the second form of regulation. The licence is granted by a public body, from 2004 the new Office of Communications described in Briefing 16.3. It is for a fixed period; is usually granted after a competition between several proposers of new services; is based on a prospectus supplied by applicants, in effect a picture of the kind of service they propose to offer; and continuation of the licence is conditional on observing regulations, some of which are designed to ensure political impartiality. As we see from Briefing

## Briefing                                                                    16.3

### A NEW REGULATOR FOR THE BROADCASTING COMMUNICATIONS' INDUSTRIES

We have seen that there is a 'mixed economy' of broadcasting in Britain: a mix of private and public ownership which, combined with the development of new broadcasting technologies, also developed a very mixed system of regulation. Until 2003 there were six important regulators for broadcasting: the Broadcasting Standards Commission; the Independent Television Commission; OFTEL, the telecommunications regulator; the Radio Authority; the Radiocommunications Agency; and the Board of Governors of the BBC. The Broadcasting Act of 2003 changed all that. It established a single independent Office of Communications (OFCOM), run by a Board with legal powers and replacing all but one of these regulators. (The exception concerns the BBC, details of which are given later in this chapter.) OFCOM is an independent regulatory commission with powers that run across the whole range of broadcasting. It also now wields powers hitherto exercised by regulators covering other important parts of the communications industries, such as OFTEL, the regulator for telecommunications. This 'stretch' reflects in part the way new technologies, such as the Internet, are breaking down the traditional distinctions between different communications markets, such as those covered by broadcasting and telephone technologies. The establishment of OFCOM as a single regulator also, however, puts pressure on two other parts of the regulatory system described in this chapter: on the system of self-regulation in the print industry, controlled as it is by the industry itself; and on the BBC's own independent regulation via the Corporation's own governors.

➲ The regulation of broadcasting in Britain is in flux, and the new Office of Communications is a sign of this. At the time of writing the Office is barely established and we do not have a clear idea how the regime for governing broadcasting will develop.

16.3 the regulation of broadcasting is now in the process of being much more heavily centralized in one body, the Office of Communications. And as Briefing 16.4, shows, this is in turn throwing up questions about the traditionally separate method of regulating the BBC.

The contrast sketched here between the two wings of mass communication – a largely unregulated press, and a historically closely regulated world of television and radio – corresponds to two sets of problems created by the system of mass communications in government. These are the problem of regulation, and the problem of bias. We examine each in turn.

## Political communication: the problem of regulation

There are problems of regulation in both newspapers and broadcasting, but they are different. In newspapers, as we have seen, beyond the wider law of the land there is no specialized public regulation; there is only self-regulation in the form of the Press Complaints Commission (see Briefing 16.5). The Commission originated over 40 years ago in the Press Council, and its present form dates from a reorganization at the start of the 1990s which was designed to make self-regulation more effective than hitherto. The main role of the Commission is to adjudicate on complaints about press coverage received from members of the public, against a standard of a voluntary code of conduct by which all members agree to be bound. It is this voluntary character that has proved the most controversial aspect of press regulation. The sanctions of the Commission amount to admonition. The most severe penalty is to oblige an offending publication to publish a critical Commission judgement prominently. Precisely because newspapers are commercial enterprises that are highly competitive, the temptation to breach any code in the search for an exclusive story has often proved great. The political effect is twofold: first, there is now a long

## Briefing                                                              16.4

### REGULATING THE BBC

Despite the changes in broadcasting regulation documented above, the BBC has managed to retain its own distinctive system, separate from other means of public regulation. At the heart of this success lies the fact that the BBC operates under a Royal Charter. Each issue of the Charter is for a limited period (the present Charter expires in 2006) and each renewal is typically accompanied by arguments as to whether the Corporation's distinctive arrangements effectively secure public accountability. At the heart of the BBC's independent system of regulation lies a board of 12 governors. These are part-timers appointed by the Queen on the advice of ministers. Until recently the appointment process was secretive, and posts were largely in the gift of senior ministers. More recently vacancies have been advertised. Governors set the broad objectives of the Corporation, and appoint the most senior executives, including the Director General. They formally discharge their accountability responsibilities through an annual report and by being the main point of report by the Corporation's senior operational managers. This means that it is the governors who are primarily responsible for providing safeguards against activities that breach the Corporation's obligations, such as those requiring editorial impartiality. As we shall later, this proved a point of serious difficulty in the Kelly affair (see Political Issues 16.1, p. 359).

➲ The means of regulating the BBC in the interests of public accountability is now, in the wake of the establishment of OFCOM, unique in broadcasting: while all other broadcasting media are regulated by an external regulatory agency the BBC continues to do the job 'in-house', through its Board of Governors. As Political Issues 16.1 shows, this has now attracted considerable criticism.

# Briefing

## THE SYSTEM OF PRESS SELF-REGULATION IN BRITAIN

Self-regulation is what the modern newspaper industry has so far offered as a compromise between the need for regulation and the fear of subjecting the press to state controls. Efforts at independent self-regulation go back over 40 years, but the present system, organized by the Press Complaints Commission, dates from the early 1990s.

- The Press Complaints Commission is a permanent body funded by the newspaper industry. It administers a Code of Conduct originally drawn up by the industry in 1991, and subsequently amended over 30 times.
- Any member of the public can complain in writing to the Commission that a publication has breached the Code. The Commission aims for conciliation before issuing a judgement: it advises all complainants in the first instance to seek an agreement with the editor of the offending publication; if it takes up the complaint it tries to secure an agreed settlement between the editor and the complainant; and only then, if the Code has been breached, does it issue a judgement against the publication.
- The Commission's only sanction is publicity: an offending publication is obliged to publish the Commission's judgement, giving it 'due prominence'.

The industry argues not only that self-regulation protects a free press from the dangers of state control; it also argues that the Commission's procedures are fast and cheap, since they avoid the courts. Criticism of the Commission focuses on three arguments: that it is reactive, only responding when it receives complaints; that it has no effective sanctions against powerful newspapers; and that its most powerful members are typically editors of the leading national newspapers (typically the most serious offenders against the Code).

➲ By contrast with the regulation of broadcasting, the regulation of the print media has hitherto been conducted by the industry itself, through systems of self-regulation. Outside the special circumstances of war, the only enduring special legal restraints have been provided by the courts, in the form of libel laws. Following the passage of the Human Rights Act in 1998, a number of attempts have been made to establish a law of privacy that would set legal limits to the right of the press to report on private individuals; but they have so far had very limited success with the courts. For more details of PCC organization and operation, see pcc.org.uk

established debate about whether the law should step in to replace voluntary regulation; second, many of the problems of the voluntary code have involved figures that are part of the state. One of the most sensitive issues in press regulation concerns how far newspapers can claim that it is in the public interest to report on the private lives of public figures, especially if the reporting is salacious. Reporting about leading members of the Royal Family and leading politicians in these terms has proved problematic in recent years.

Press regulation is a highly sensitive issue in part because the wrong sort of regulation could threaten the freedom of the press to report on events and people, and press freedom is one of the defining features of democracy. This sensitive issue also

arises in the case of broadcasting. As we have seen, public regulation (both of access to broadcasting bands and of what is broadcast) has been an established feature since the first technology, radio, became popular in the 1920s.

The regulation of broadcasting is faced by two diametrically opposed problems: that it may be too effective, and that it may be of declining effectiveness. The first exists because there is a difficult line to walk between regulation and state control of broadcasters. There have been times in the history of the BBC when it has clearly taken the side of government in disputes with sections of the community: thus in 1926 the BBC explicitly supported the government against the trade unions who called a general strike in that year. All politicians try to pressurise broadcasters about both the content and style of broadcasts. The fact that government exercizes control over the issue of commercial licences, and that it also controls the level of the licence fee and thus the income of the BBC, means that when a governing party puts pressure on, that pressure is not innocent: the broadcasters cannot help but be aware of the sanctions that lie behind it.

By contrast, technological change in recent years has actually reduced the ability of governments to regulate some broadcasting services. The most obvious example is the growth of satellite broadcasting channels which can easily broadcast across national boundaries and which can therefore reach subscribers without the authority of national government. Across the world this has had many beneficial effects, not least because it poses problems for dictatorships in controlling what their populations view and listen to. But it also means that the long-term ability of regulation to impose public interest regulation – for instance in the interests of public decency or political balance – is weakened. Technological change in broadcasting is creating, for the moment only at the fringes, a sector that resembles the press in its freedom from regulation.

Regulation is typically conceived to be a problem because it is widely believed that the content of the mass media matters. Thus there is a connection between the problem of regulation and the second problem we have identified: the problem of media effects.

## Political communication and the effects of the media

There is no doubt that politicians both in and out of government are convinced that the media do matter in shaping the opinions of citizens. That is why they spend an immense amount of time alternately criticising and cultivating the media. Both commercial broadcasters and the BBC are the frequent and common object of complaints that their reporting is biased, and these complaints come at various times from virtually all political parties, and with great

frequency from the Labour and Conservative parties (see Political Issues 16.1). And whereas politicians complain about bias among broadcasters, they positively encourage it among newspapers. The party leaderships put a lot of time and effort into cultivating the owners of the leading national newspapers, and their editors. They do this in the hope that newspapers will actively support them, especially at election times. The quickest way to be invited for tea at 10 Downing Street is to buy a national tabloid.

All these complaints and efforts at cultivation only make sense on two assumptions: that media bias does indeed exist; and that it has some effect on the way political judgements are formed. In the case of newspapers there is, as we have already seen, no argument about the existence of bias, but the issue of whether there is bias in broadcasting is more complicated. Regulation itself is designed to prevent biased reporting of one party over another. This is reinforced by the professional assumptions of many broadcasters, who conceive of their role in precisely these neutral terms. But bias can operate in more subtle ways than open partisanship, and it is likely that these more subtle biases in broadcasting do shape reporting. One important way this can happen is in the way issues are 'framed': in other words, in the way they are presented as policy problems in political reporting. The technologies and production values of broadcasting can be important in this respect, even when everyone concerned is trying hard to be impartial. Television provides some obvious examples. The visual character of the medium puts a premium on reporting which can be supported by images: this gives a powerful implicit bias to the reporting of politics in terms of personality because political leaders obviously provide ready pictures. And most television reporting, especially news reporting, has to be done in a very short time: even the debate of a complex political issue will typically be compressed into a few minutes. In these circumstances, subtlety, uncertainty and ambiguity are casualties; all those involved in the debate are forced, if they are not to be lost in the shouting, to take up clearly defined, simply expressed positions.

Bias, both open and subtle, therefore exists; whether it has any effect is one of the most debated issues in research on political communication.

Three common views about the effects of this media bias illustrate the variety of possibilities.

## The manipulative view

This view gives great power to the media. It stresses the persistent bias in the printed media, and the more subtle biases in broadcasting, coupled with the fact that in Britain broadcasting is consumed on a huge scale: the British are among the most avid television watchers in Europe, for instance, and are also great national newspaper readers. The constant stream of biased material, coupled with the fact that the mass media are a critical channel through which most of us receive political news and political comment, surely could not but shape political views and political choices. Politicians are a good sign of the power of this view. As we have seen they endlessly cultivate newspaper editors and owners, so they obviously believe in the manipulative view. They have powerful incentives to form a correct view of the effects of the media on political opinion as their jobs depend on getting that view right.

## The reinforcement view

The reinforcement view accepts that bias exists but gives a more modest role to the manipulative power of the media. It partly rests on a large body of evidence, some of it from social psychology experiments which show that people come to the media with well formed views, that these views help them filter out biases that do not correspond to their own, and that they mostly pay attention to biases that do indeed correspond to their own. Newspapers are very biased but most of us spend no more than a few minutes a day reading them, and most of us read them for sport and show business gossip rather than for politics. What could be more reasonable than to expect us to be shaped by communicating with friends and family – who plainly matter more to us than does the *Daily Mail*?

We might summarily say that the manipulative view sees the media as exploiting us all, and the reinforcement view sees us all as exploiting the media. One of the difficulties in resolving these competing accounts is that it is hard to isolate media effects from other forces that shape our views: adults consuming newspapers and television obviously have already been subject to decades of other influences; and even in the short term we consume the mass media alongside a range of other influences that might be shaping what we believe. We could only disentangle media effects, if they exist, by very carefully designed research. This research has indeed now begun to uncover media effects and lies behind the third view described here: I call it the *marginal but critical view*.

## Marginal but critical

Most of us do choose to consume newspapers and broadcasting that fit our existing views, and most of us reject hostile media. A strong Labour party newspaper reader will use the *Daily Mail* for nothing more than wrapping fish and chips. Professors spend more time listening to Radio 3 than to Radio 1, and this affects the way they receive news, since the style of news broadcasts varies even between different BBC radio stations. But a minority of people do systematically use media biased against their own views. Labour supporters might read the *Daily Mail* because they like its show business coverage, or just because through historical accident it is the paper that has long been bought in the family. (Remember that for most people choosing which newspaper to buy is a trivial act of consumption, which is probably about as engaging as choice of brand of hair shampoo.) A Liberal Democrat tabloid reader has no choice but to read a hostile paper: no national tabloid supports the party. People who consume media biased against their views are a very interesting group, because if they change their views over time that does suggest that something more influential than mere 'reinforcement' is going on. And indeed there is evidence that this is so: if we track the views of this minority in the population they do seem to modify their views and loyalties to fit with the biases of the media they consume. There is thus some 'manipulation', but only of a minority.

Media bias may therefore have only a marginal effect, but at the margins it can be critical. Take the particular case of effects on voting, the reason politi-

## POLITICAL ISSUES

### 16.1 THE HUTTON INQUIRY, THE BBC AND THE KELLY AFFAIR

The Hutton Inquiry convulsed government in the latter part of 2003 and the early months of 2004. It both revealed, and intensified, the arguments about 'spin' in government: the common accusation that government media managers were now so skilled and sophisticated that they routinely manipulated information. It began with a classic accusation of spin: reports in May and June 2003 by a BBC reporter Andrew Gilligan, claimed that in the run-up to the Iraq War of 2003 intelligence reports that Iraq could fire weapons of mass destruction within 45 minutes had been 'sexed up' under pressure from the Prime Minister's chief spin doctor, Alistair Campbell, to make the case for war more convincing. The enraged Campbell initiated a search for the source of the story within government. In July Dr David Kelly, a government scientist, was 'outed' as Gilligan's source. On 18 July Dr Kelly committed suicide. The Prime Minister established an independent judicial inquiry under Lord Hutton into the circumstances surrounding the death, amid competing accusations that Dr Kelly had been hounded to his death by pressure from the government and the BBC. Lord Hutton's inquiry produced close accounts both of how intelligence material was gathered and assessed, and of BBC news gathering methods. His *Report*, published in January 2004, produced another sensation. Expected at best to criticize both the Government and the BBC in equal measure, it entirely exonerated Mr Campbell and the Government, and laid the blame almost entirely at the door of the BBC. The Chairman of the BBC's Board of Governors and the Director General both resigned.

The controversy surrounding the Kelly Affair and the Hutton Inquiry has ramifications for British government (see Political Isues 22.1, p. 489 for the intelligence-gathering consequences). For the purposes of this chapter it highlights three issues:

- *The regulation of the BBC.* The aftermath has led to a fundamental review of the role of the Governors, since one conclusion arising out of Hutton was that they had not performed their checking and regulating roles effectively. (See also Briefing 16.4.)
- *The ethics of reporting.* The humiliation of the BBC after Hutton could be interpreted as a reverse for a journalistic culture which valued the adversarial confrontation of government over accurate reporting; or it could, on the contrary, be interpreted as an attempt to impose unrealistic standards of accuracy on reporters who have to work against tight deadlines and against secretive governments.
- *The power of media managers.* Though Hutton exonerated Mr Campbell, it also showed that he was much more than a communicator of government policy: he played a central role in negotiating the content of that policy (for instance in respect of the use of secret intelligence).

cians so assiduously cultivate owners and journalists: at the 2001 general election, as we noted earlier, ten seats were won by a margin of fewer than 400 votes – indeed four were won by fewer than 100 votes. Changing the votes of this tiny proportion of the population can have a big effect on outcomes: in six

general elections since the Second World War the winning party has had a majority over all other parties of less than 30 – in other words, winning a few of the most marginal seats determined which party entered office. The claim by *The Sun* newspaper after the general election of 1992 that 'it was

The Sun wot won it' is now part of the folklore of British politics. This is probably an exaggeration; but, if the 'marginal' effect argument is correct, The Sun can claim a big part of the credit, because the Conservatives' majority over other parties in that election was only 21 seats.

This discussion of bias, insofar as it has concerned newspapers, has concentrated on the effects of what might be called 'partisan' bias: that is, the effect newspapers have on party loyalties and voting. But there are other forms of political bias, and they are growing in importance. For instance, the newspaper industry in Britain in the last three decades has become increasingly 'metropolitan' – London-focused – in its operations. Newspapers have tended to scale down, or even close, their regional reporting operations, and to centralize in London. This has had a paradoxical effect. It has made the cultures of the leading newspapers more London-focused than in the past; yet as we have seen time and again in this book, the wider shape of both the society and the governing system is producing challenges to the old system of centralization based in London. This lack of 'fit' between more decentralized social and political networks and the cultural centralization of newspapers may help explain why newspaper readership is in long-term decline. New forms of communication, based on innovations in electronic technology, are displacing the metropolitan-focused press in political communication, and in other forms of communication. We examine these new forms of communication next.

## New forms of communication: the electronic revolution and communication

Technological change and political communication are bound together and always have been. *Mass* communication of the kind that we now take for granted is itself the product of earlier technical revolutions. The mass circulation newspaper delivered to millions of breakfast tables daily only became possible in the late nineteenth century with the invention of telegraphic communication which allowed rapid news gathering, and of power-driven printing presses which allowed print runs of millions to be produced in a few hours. Radio and television are, of course, the product of twentieth-century technologies, so it is not surprising that political communication is continually reshaped by new technologies. That it is indeed reshaped, and will continue to be reshaped, is just about the only thing of which we can be sure. The case of earlier technologies suggests, for instance, that we do not accurately appreciate the political implications of technologies such as the worldwide web, which has only been accessible to wider populations in the last decade. For instance, at the dawn of both radio and television neither was conceived primarily for what they have become: technologies for mass popular communication. Almost certainly, therefore, we do not now at all understand the implications of the latest technological changes.

We can nevertheless make some educated guesses, and these guesses suggest four kinds of effect: on regulation; on parties and voters; on 'horizontal' communication, people to people; and on surveillance of people by the state.

### Undermining regulation

Technical change is undermining the ability of government to regulate access to, and the content of, mass communication. The most obvious example of that is broadcasting. For most of the twentieth century the state in Britain controlled what the people could hear and see, by its control of licences giving access to the airwaves. The growth of satellite-based broadcasting has destroyed the monopoly of government-based regulation in Britain. Internet-based communication is weakening it even further. The rapid spread of Internet access (see Figure 16.2) has created a system of mass communication that is very weakly regulated. Individual access requires only a PC, which is constantly falling in price, and a telephone connection. Control of the content of sites on the web varies from weak to non-existent. The implications are most profound for dictatorships that depend heavily on control of mass communication to determine what their peoples hear about politics. But even in democracies the effects are far reaching. The sort of state monopoly of broadcasting which was the norm in Britain for most of the twentieth century is now impossible. Technical change is also making regulation through censorship more difficult. One sign is the difficulty of operating traditional state controls over pornography in the world of the globally organized websites and satellite television broadcasting. A more obviously political example is the difficulty of censoring material on grounds of national security: in a number of recent cases bans on the publication of books held to be damaging to the security services have been circumvented by simply posting the material on a website available to millions. Websites may also be undermining the ability of the rich and influential in Britain to use the libel laws to control their privacy: the sort of allegations that no national newspaper will dare to print frequently turn up on the web.

## Parties and voters

In the second half of the twentieth century technology had already revolutionized the way parties communicated with voters, especially at elections. Traditional methods, such as mass meetings addressed by powerful orators or face-to-face mass canvassing, became less and less important. Direct appeals via television, and manipulated contacts through organised 'photo opportunities' – staged meetings with selected members of the public that were then televised – replaced these direct personal contacts. The development of cheap and powerful computers is probably the next great phase in this evolution. At this early stage much of what is going on is passive rather than active. Parties are using the new technologies to make material quickly and easily available. As we noted earlier, all the main parties have well-designed websites, and the same is now true of an increasing number of MPs. All this is 'passive' in the sense that it simply tries to use the new technologies to communicate material that would have been less efficiently transmitted by older methods, such as 'snail mail'. But more active strategies are also developing. Large amounts of data about

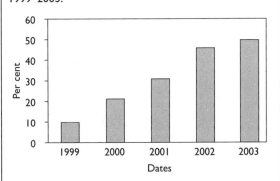

**Figure 16.2** The spread of Internet access in the UK: percentage of UK homes with Internet access, 1999–2003.

*Note:* Yearly figures from the following months: 1999: January; 2000: January; 2001: February; 2002: February; 2003: August.

*Source:* Calculated from OFTEL (2003).

➲ The growth of Internet access in UK homes has been astonishing rapid in recent years. The figures do not, however, convey one important feature: there are marked social inequalities in access. Access correlates strongly with high levels of income and formal education.

targeted groups of voters can now be retrieved and used rapidly; hence mail shots to these targeted groups, with the content aligned to what the parties know to be the preoccupations of particular groups. Even backbench MPs can now do this, such are the facilities offered by even a cheap laptop. I guarantee that if you write to your own MP about an issue – say, Third World debt – you will receive regular messages updating you on what the MP and the party are doing about it. Targeted telephone canvassing of voters, using computer-assisted dialling for speed, is now also common. Technology is bringing down the cost of frequent mass communication: the most obvious case is the use of standardized e-mail lists by the parties to pump out messages to the growing numbers of voters on e-mail, and the use of text messages to mobile phone users.

## People to people

All our examples of the impact of the new technology so far have been 'vertical' (up and down

## DOCUMENTING POLITICS 16.2

### HOW SINGLE-ISSUE GROUPS EXPLOIT NEW TECHNOLOGIES: THE CASE OF THE MOVEMENT AGAINST THE IRAQ WAR IN 2002–3

#### 'ACTIONS

**Wednesday 5 November:**
**REMEMBER REMEMBER THE FIFTH OF NOVEMBER DECEPTION, URANIUM AND SPIN!!**

Whalley Range Stop the War are collecting letters urging Manchester's Chief Constable to arrest Tony Blair. They are meeting on 5th November in Albert Square at 12 noon and proceeding to Bootle Street Police Station at 12.30. If you would like the text of the letter sent to you as an attachment, contact Rick at wrasccals@hotmail.com now.

**Wednesday 5 November**
**BRITISH POLITICS AT THE CROSSROADS**

George Galloway, the MP recently expelled from the Labour Party for his views against the war on Iraq, will speak in Manchester next Wednesday, debating British Politics at the Crossroads with Salma Yaqoob, chair of Birmingham Stop the War Coalition; John Rees, Socialist Alliance exec, and a striking postal worker from London.

**Saturday 9 November**
**WALL DOWN DEMONSTRATION AGAINST THE APARTHEID WALL BUILT BY ISRAEL**

Market Street, Manchester City Centre, 1–3 pm.

between leaders and people), but the potential of the new technologies to affect 'horizontal' communication between the people at large is particularly intriguing (see Documenting Politics 16.2). We touched on this in Chapter 9 when we examined interest mobilization. Until recently this kind of communication – for instance, to organize mass protests – was cumbersome and traditional: it relied heavily on word of mouth and the distribution of written material, the latter often expensive and difficult to print and distribute. But many British protest groups are now part of loosely coordinated networks that regularly organize demonstrations on big international issues, such as the trading policies of the rich nations and the treatment of the debts of

Third World countries. Communication through these networks via the technologies of e-mail and interactive websites is now cheap and can be accomplished almost instantaneously. Even the adaptation of older technologies helps: the most obvious case is the spread of mobile telephone ownership. Until recently in public demonstrations the police had a distinct advantage because, unlike demonstrators, they had their own mobile radiotelephone communication system. In recent years the fact that demonstrators can use mobiles to communicate rapidly with each other has altered the balance of advantage. The speed with which technologies are spreading means that we are probably only barely appreciating the importance of these technologies

**DOCUMENTING POLITICS 16.2** (continued)

### SEND A LETTER TO THE PRESS!
Send an email. Write to letters page – to the local press and media.

Manchester Evening News: postbag@mcr-evening-news.co.uk;
asiannews@gmwn.co.uk;
news@metro-news.co.uk;
granada.tonight@granadamedia.com;
stockportexpress@gmwn.co.uk;
City Life (Letters@citylife.co.uk);

### THAT WAS THE DEMO THAT WAS
For pictures of the 8 March Manchester demo, click HERE, the 19 March school students demo and blockades of 21 March click HERE or HERE the various events of 20–23 March click HERE.) the 29 March demo at the BBC click HERE.) the 1 April Blair's A Fool demonstration HERE the most recent London demonstration HERE and recent Manchester mobilisations against the BNP HERE.'

➲ This reproduces part of the web pages from the Manchester Coalition against the Iraq war. Virtually any large city in Britain will have a similar movement and web presence. Notice three features:

• The movement against the war involved massive mobilization over the short term, and the publicity and communication resources of web technology were vital to this. Web-based technology means that once the material is posted 'distribution' is costlessly accomplished by the process of logging on.
• Links, and the publication of e-mail addresses of key broadcasting and press organizations, encourage supporters to exploit the communication possibility of the new technology further.
• The 'crossover' with different, though related movements: note the publicity for the campaign against important aspects of Israeli policy.

*Source*: www.manchesterstopthewar.org, accessed 5/11/03.

in allowing people to people communication: in the mid-1990s about 15 per cent of British homes had a mobile phone owner; the latest figures I have suggest that the figure is now approaching 80 per cent, and growing.

## Surveillance of the people

The extent to which government operates surveillance over us is one of the most tense and difficult questions in democracy. This is what is best conceived of as 'unobtrusive communication': we communicate information about ourselves without ever realizing or intending to do so. Surveillance is needed, long established and accepted. The creation

of an organized system of policing in the early part of the nineteenth century was exactly such a system, designed to provide security in the new cities of the Industrial Revolution. Over time surveillance has involved the adaptation of each new technology: thus the bobby pounding his beat became the bobby on the bicycle, then in the police car and, most recently, in the control room at the football match watching different parts of the ground on banks of television monitors. The new technologies are vastly expanding the possibilities for unobtrusive surveillance. Take an example given earlier: the use of speed cameras to detect motorists who break the law. So far these have been inefficient and slow to communicate and process information. The newest

## DEBATING POLITICS

### 16.1    MODERN TECHNOLOGIES OF COMMUNICATION: FRIEND OR FOE OF DEMOCRACY IN BRITAIN?

| Modern technologies of communication make democracy healthier because: | Modern technologies of communication endanger democracy because: |
| --- | --- |
| ■ They cut the costs of political mobilization and organization.<br>■ They undermine the monopolies over mass communication traditionally organized by the state.<br>■ They promote communication between, and organization of, large numbers of physically dispersed citizens.<br>■ They promote open debate, and can allow electronic referendums giving all a potential voice in policy making. | ■ They encourage a 'marketing' mentality on the part of political leaders.<br>■ They give the state new means of surveillance over the population, and thus strengthen hierarchical control.<br>■ They allow the combination and storage of masses of information about private citizens.<br>■ They discourage the face-to-face communication and debate which has traditionally been central to democratic life. |

generation of digital cameras allows both much more reliable and comprehensive surveillance and, via a link with a central national computer, much more rapid detection. (In the old technology, for instance, the cameras were often not functioning and the film had to be manually loaded and unloaded.) New technologies of surveillance can also be a counter to the new opportunities offered to the people at large: for instance, unless e-mails are encrypted (coded) it is technically a straightforward matter for authorities (either within firms, or within the state) to monitor their content.

Much of the discussion of the political impact of new technologies is premised on the view that in reshaping communication it will also reshape democracy. Some accounts stress the dangers to British democracy: for instance, through the new opportunities opened up to political parties to manipulate us with their sophisticated marketing, and the opportunities opened up to the state to spy on us. (The latter issues are examined from a different angle in Chapter 22.) Some, by contrast, stress the way democracy could be extended. For example,

a standard justification for electing a House of Commons periodically to pass laws on our behalf is that it would never be possible to gather together over 40 million electors to choose directly what policies they prefer. But we are now almost at the point where every voter has access – for instance, through a telephone keypad – to the means to register electronically their policy preferences. In principle we could realise the dream of direct democracy, cutting out the 'middle men' (and women) in the House of Commons (see Debating Politics 16.1).

We do not know whether these visions will be realized. The one lesson from the recent history of mass communication technology is that we almost certainly do not understand the implications of present technological change for political communication. At the dawn of 'wireless' and television hardly anybody predicted the two great uses of these technologies, for mass entertainment and political communication. Technologies can develop and be discarded with great speed. In the 1980s 'citizens' band radio' – a system of short-wave radio communication – was briefly supposed to transform our lives. The mobile phone made it redundant. As a child in a remote west of Ireland village in the early 1960s I witnessed the widespread use of the

The most important themes of this chapter are that:

1  The 'flows' of political communication are wide-ranging and complicated;
2  Mass communication via newspapers and broadcasting raises very different issues for politics and politicians;
3  Media bias is probably of critical importance in political communication, but is critical only at the margins;
4  Technology has always reshaped political communication, and the only thing we can say with certainty about the potential impact of the latest technologies is that we almost certainly do not really understand what their long-term effects will be.

telegraph: a system of communication based on landline wires and a special code, the so-called 'Morse code' (devised by an American, Samuel Morse, in the nineteenth century). It is unlikely that any reader of this book has seen the system outside a museum.

## Further reading

Seymour-Ure (1996) is the best historical overview of the development of the mass media system. Bartle and Griffiths (2001) is a collection focused on change. Mughan (2000) examines the connection between media effects and governing styles. The complex and difficult issue of media effects, on which this chapter draws, has been explored in several landmark papers by Newton and Brymin: see Newton and Brymin (2001) and Brymin and Newton (2003).

CHAPTER 17

# How elections are decided

## CONTENTS

## AIMS

The chapter has the following aims:

❖ To summarize the roles of elections in the system of government, especially their relevance to the functioning of democratic government

❖ To describe elections, electioneering and the campaigning strategies of the parties

❖ To describe what influences the choices electors make, and to summarize how these influences are changing

❖ To explain how election outcomes happen in Britain, and especially how the rules of the electoral system shape these.

## Elections and British democracy

Elections are central to the theory and practice of democracy in Britain. As we saw in our chapter on how citizens participate in politics, going to vote is just about the most widespread act of participation. And while most of this chapter is about general elections – the UK-wide elections that happen, at a minimum, once every five years – many citizens have opportunities to participate in other elections, and these opportunities have grown in recent years. They are:

- Elections in local government. In London the range of these has now grown to encompass direct election of a London-wide assembly and a directly elected mayor; the innovation of an elected mayor has spread to some other local authorities.
- Elections to national assemblies in Scotland, Wales and Northern Ireland, which occur every four years.
- Elections to the European Parliament, which occur every five years.
- Outside government itself elections by secret ballot have become increasingly common: for instance, the reforms of trade union law in the 1980s greatly increased the use of secret ballots in choosing trade union officials and in opting for industrial action.

Britain thus has a voting 'culture'. Most of the elections summarized above have been discussed in earlier chapters, and partly for this reason the focus here is on general elections. However, general elections also deserve a separate chapter for a number of additional reasons:

- Despite the introduction of elections in other arenas, such as the Scottish Parliament and the European Parliament, general elections still remain those that are most likely to bring citizens to the polling booth. Although turnout in general elections seems to be falling it is still much higher than in any other elections in the United Kingdom.
- Despite the devolution of power downward within Britain, and the transfer of power upward to European institutions, the Westminster Parliament remains exceptionally significant. On the outcome of Westminster elections turns the identity of which party will control central government in Whitehall.
- Elections generally, and general elections in particular, are central to the theory and practice of British democracy. There are many theories of democracy, but all assign some important place to choice by the people at large through competitive election. There are also many different views about how British democracy actually functions: they range from the view that Britain is, by world standards, a highly democratic country to the view that democracy in this country is a sham. But all these views turn in part on judgements about the effectiveness of general elections as means of giving the people a voice in government.

Elections are about choice, but that simple statement conceals a powerful tension, a tension that runs underneath this chapter and surfaces at the end. We make choices all the time, notably as consumers in markets. One obvious way to think about electoral choice is therefore in the language of consumerism. That is an increasingly popular mode of thought both among politicians and electoral analysts: among politicians because they use marketing techniques to sell the party brand; among analysts because they picture the voter as a calculating shopper in the political marketplace. But there is a very different way of thinking about voting. The history of struggle for the vote in Britain was not expressed in the language of the market. When the suffragettes demanded votes for women they did not demand the right to shop alongside men in the electoral marketplace; they demanded the vote as an expression of human equality and common citizenship. The 'brands' in the market – the parties – continue to move voters to depths of feeling that Tesco or Sainsbury's cannot evoke, whether the feelings concerned be loyalty or fury. When they vote, are electors shoppers or citizens? And are the changes coming over voting behaviour changing the balance between citizenship and shopping? These questions are examined more closely at the end of the chapter.

## Election rules and election outcomes

The rules governing the conduct of general elections in Britain were historically one of the flashpoints in the struggle to widen democracy in Britain. Chapter 2 showed that one of the most enduring political struggles for most of the nineteenth century and the early decades of the twentieth century concerned election rules. The most important points of struggle included the following:

● Who should be entitled to vote? How should voting be conducted – in secrecy or publicly?
● What kind of inducements, if any, should politicians be allowed to offer voters to secure their votes?

One result of this long struggle is that elections in Britain, and particularly general elections, are now conducted under elaborate rules, the most important of which are contained in statute law. (It is actually fairly unusual for political life in Britain to be so regulated by law.) Four particularly important sets of rules concern: eligibility to vote; the calling of elections; the conduct of elections; and the outcome of elections.

### Eligibility to vote

The great struggles of the nineteenth century were partly about removing property ownership (of various levels) as a condition of entitlement to vote. There is now a universal franchise, but that does not mean everyone is entitled to vote. Property qualifications may have disappeared, but the law still retains other important qualifications.

The clearest of these is age. The qualifying age was set at 18 in 1969. Strictly, this is the qualifying age for admission to the electoral register, a roll of names of all those entitled to vote. This exposes another important qualification: entitlement to vote in a general election is only an entitlement to vote in the constituency (one of the 646 territorial divisions of the UK) where the individual citizen is entered on the electoral register (see Briefing 17.1). Failure to register disbars an individual from voting.

This is not a formality. There are many reasons for failure to register, but the most important are connected in some way or another with the way people are housed. Until recently the homeless could not register, and although this restriction has now been eased it is certainly the case that the homeless will include few voters. Beyond the homeless, it is known that many of the very poorest – who often of course have precarious housing conditions – also do not register. The short-lived community charge (poll tax), since it was levied on all those listed on the electoral register, also led to large numbers of de-registrations, and it is probable that many of those have not returned. (The charge was first introduced in Scotland in 1989, and then in England and Wales in 1990; its abolition was announced in 1991, and it was finally replaced in 1993). At the end of the 1990s Weir and Beetham estimated that as many as 3.5 million voters were disfranchised at any one time (Weir and Beetham 1991: 41).

Until recently, even for the registered, casting a vote could often be difficult. Voting could – except in unusual circumstances, such as illness – only be done in person, at a particular location (a polling station, usually a local public building such as a school), for particular candidates in a particular parliamentary constituency. The apparent fall in turnout in recent general elections – which is documented below – has led to some experiments designed to ease these restrictions. For instance, it is now comparatively easy to vote by post; the opening times of polling booths have been extended; and experiments have been attempted in locating booths at more accessible locations, such as in supermarkets.

### The timing of elections

Unlike many countries (and unlike the European Parliament and new assemblies created by devolution), there is no fixed minimum term for the life of the House of Commons. The law stipulates that the life of a particular Parliament shall not exceed five years. The five-year maximum is a fairly firm constitutional convention of the kind we discussed in Chapter 5. In principle, a government with a

# Briefing

## REGISTERING AND VOTING: EASING THE RULES

Voting is voluntary in the United Kingdom and for nearly a century we have had 'universal suffrage' – the presumption that virtually all adults have an entitlement to vote. But exercising that entitlement traditionally was closely connected to the historical notion of the link between voting and representation which was a territorial link, since the vote was cast for the representation of a locality. This imposed two restrictions:

- To register, voters had to establish permanent residence in a parliamentary constituency on a fixed registration date. This effectively ruled out registration by groups such as the homeless.
- To vote, electors had to present themselves in person to a particular 'polling station', between fixed hours, on election day. Voting by proxy (for instance by post) was only allowed in exceptional circumstances. This made voting often very difficult for some (frequent house movers, those forced unexpectedly to travel on election day).

There is a long-term trend in favour of easing both registering and voting rules, particularly as concern has grown about falling electoral turnout. They include the following:

- Voting innovations as described in Chapters 12 and 13: they include making postal voting available virtually on demand, introducing experiments in proxy electronic voting (for example, via the web), extending voting hours, and placing polling stations in more accessible places, such as supermarkets.
- The Representation of the People Act 2000 eased the rules for electoral registration. In place of evidence of permanent residence, certain groups can make a 'declaration of local connection', allowing groups such as the homeless, remand prisoners and those in mental hospitals (other than the criminally insane) to be placed on the electoral register.
- The Act also provided for 'rolling registration': in place of once a year registration it is possible to apply at any time of the year, enabling those who move to a new district to register in their new place of residence, for instance.
- The Electoral Commission is now conducting a wider review of electoral law.

*Source*: Information from www.electoralcommission.org.uk

⮕ The long struggle to establish universal suffrage left a legacy of assumptions about the vote even when the struggle was won. One of the most important and subtle was that voters had to claim their entitlement to vote (a residue of the age when voting was a privilege of the few). Efforts actively to encourage voting, and to remove institutional obstacles, in part reflect fears about falling turnout, but also a change in assumption – voting is now a right whose exercise should be actively encouraged.

simple majority in Parliament could by a change in statute extend the period beyond five years. In practice the only time in modern British history when this has happened has been with all-party agreement in the great national crisis of the Second World War (an election would normally have been due by 1940, but was delayed until the end of the war in 1945). The legal prescription that Parliament have a maximum life of five years is therefore one of the most deeply rooted conventions of the constitution which can only be breached in the greatest

national crisis. But there is no legal minimum life: the House of Commons elected in 1992 almost ran its full length, until May 1997; conversely, there were two general elections (February and October) in 1974.

Formally an election is called when the monarch agrees to a request from the prime minister for a dissolution of Parliament. In practice, there is not a single instance in modern British politics of monarchs declining such a request (though we do not know, since the archives are not always available, how far a monarch might have demurred, or even dissuaded a prime minister). Prime ministers in effect decide when general elections are held; indeed, deciding when to 'go to the country' is among the single most important decisions that prime ministers make, though of course they would be foolish to make the decision without getting the best advice possible. It is rare for a Prime Minister to let a Parliament run its full legal life. Prime ministers have occasionally asked for a dissolution because their government could no longer command a working majority in the House of Commons: that was the case with James Callaghan in 1979. But more commonly, they calculate what is the most favourable circumstance for fighting an election that will return their party with a majority large enough to form a government. Among the most important skills needed by prime ministers are those that lead to shrewd choices of election dates.

## The conduct of elections

The details of the conduct of elections are elaborately prescribed. They begin with precise rules governing the nomination of candidates, whose papers must be filed by a specified date and supported by prescribed numbers of nominees from registered electors. In addition, all candidates must post a non-trivial deposit (£500) which is not returned if the candidate fails to secure 5 per cent of the votes cast. Over the course of the campaign, spending by individual candidates is also subject to strict, and in the main rigidly enforced, limits (see Briefing 17.2). The conduct of the ballot on election day is also strictly regulated. Balloting is secret and anonymous. Elaborate precautions are taken to ensure that no individual's ballot paper can be identified. Once the polls close various arrangements are in place to ensure that counting is efficient and honest. Independent officials – returning officers, mostly local government officials – organize the counting. Candidates are allowed scrutineers who observe the process, and who can – for instance, if the result is very close – demand a recount to ensure that the outcome is not produced by counting error. These detailed (and important) legal safeguards reflect the historical struggle to create fair elections

in Britain: as was explained in Chapter 14, until 1872 balloting was open and therefore subject to bribery, intimidation and social pressure. Although there is a folklore of electoral fraud, especially in Northern Ireland, it is probably the case that the formal conduct of elections in Britain is free of any serious corruption.

However, the fact that the law governing the conduct of elections has largely been shaped by nineteenth-century problems has left it struggling to regulate the changed conditions surrounding election campaigns. The two most obvious instances are the national financing of elections (as distinct from financing in separate constituencies) and the national reporting of elections in the broadcasting media that became so important in the second half of the twentieth century. We look at each of these in turn.

## Finance

The stringent restrictions on spending by individual candidates were until recently not matched by limits on a much more important source of spending, that by parties nationally in their campaigns. The expense of modern campaigning means that all the parties, and particularly the Labour and Conservative parties, devote enormous energies to fund raising, and their efforts have prompted serious concerns about the way rich interests can exercise influence over government. Following a series of scandals about sources of funding, and a set of recommendations for change by the Committee on Standards in Public Life, new statutory ceilings have now been set, administered by an institution discussed in Chapter 14: the Electoral Commission. The short-term impact of these limits is slight, since they have been set by reference to amounts spent in the most recent general election campaign, and thus they still allow the parties to commit historically substantial amounts of money (and commit the parties to raising that money). But they are part of an important trend which we saw in Chapter 14: the growing degree to which party organization and party competition are being governed by legal codes administered by the Electoral Commission (for details, see Briefing 17.2).

# Briefing

## THE RULES ON LIMITS TO CAMPAIGN SPENDING

| Election | Regulated period (ends with the date of the poll) | Determination of spending limit |
|---|---|---|
| Westminster £540,000 NI | 365 days | £30,000 per constituency contested |
| Scottish Parliament | 4 months | £12,000 per constituency contested plus £80,000 per region contested |
| National Assembly for Wales | 4 months | £10,000 per constituency contested plus £40,000 per region contested |
| Northern Ireland Assembly | 4 months | £17,000 per constituency contested |
| European Parliament | 4 months | £12,000 per constituency contested plus £45,000 multiplied by the number of MEPs in each region contested |

*Source*: Information from www.electoralcommission.org.uk

➲ Limits on campaign expenditure by individual candidates in constituencies have long been in place, but in the age of expensive national campaigns constituency spending became a small part of the total. The new limits introduced by the Political Parties and Referendums Act of 2000, and administered by the Electoral Commission, are an attempt to 'cap' total spending during the defined 'regulated period', in the wake of widespread concerns about the cost of election campaigning and related worries about the lengths to which the big parties were prepared to go to fund their expensive campaign habits.

## Reporting

The framework of the law governing election campaigns was established before the advent of the most important forms of mass communication, notably television. For the first 40 years of mass broadcasting, following the establishment of the original BBC in the 1920s, the Corporation interpreted its duty of impartial reporting to mean that the actual conduct of campaigns should not be reported. Election broadcasting was confined to 'party political broadcasts' prepared by the parties, entitlement to air time being approximately proportionate to the number of candidates fielded. The rules governing party political broadcasts still exist, but from the late 1950s the restrictions on news coverage of elections were removed. General elections now attract saturation coverage in the broadcast media, but are still surrounded by rules concerning the balance of attention given, for instance, to separate candidates in individual constituencies.

## The outcome of elections

General elections are fought in 646 constituencies. (The major parties feel obliged to fight in virtually all constituencies even when they patently have no hope of victory. By convention the Speaker of the House of Commons is not challenged.) But 'winning a general election' is the outcome of a complicated (in effect, two-stage) counting process. Within each constituency, for general elections, the United Kingdom still determines the single winner by a 'simple majority', or colloquially the 'first past the post' system: the candidate declared elected is the one who secures the largest number of votes. This is only one of a number of possible electoral systems, and in recent years there has been continuing debate about its possible reform; as we now

# Briefing

## TYPES OF ELECTORAL SYSTEMS IN USE IN THE UNITED KINGDOM

| Title | How it works | Where used |
|---|---|---|
| Simple Plurality, Single Member ('first past the post') | One representative per constituency; victor is candidate with largest number of votes. | Westminster Parliament; most local elections other than Great London Assembly |
| Supplementary Vote | One representative elected. Voters have two votes, ranking candidates in order of preference. If one candidate fails to win 50% of first preference votes, all but top two are eliminated. Any second preference votes for top two cast by voters for eliminated candidates are distributed accordingly. Winner is candidate with most votes. | Mayor of Greater London |
| Additional Member System | Electors have two votes. Proportion of seats allocated to single member constituency contests settled by simple plurality (see above). Second vote is cast for a party list of candidates; remaining seats allocated according to share of votes cast, 'topping up' any seats won within constituencies so as to ensure share of all representatives is as close as possible to proportional share of popular vote. | Scottish Parliament Welsh Assembly; Greater London Assembly |
| Single Transferable Vote (STV) | Constituencies have multiple members (up to five). Voters 'rank' their preferred candidates in numerical order. A 'quota' of votes necessary for election is calculated, based on a division of total votes by number of seats. Successful candidates' surplus votes are allocated to the second choice candidate of their supporters. At each successive stage, if nobody has reached the quota, the bottom candidate is eliminated, until all the seats in the constituency have been filled. | All elections in Northern Ireland |
| Regional Party List | Electors vote for a party in constituencies covering large regions, with multiple members. Seats awarded to parties in proportion to their share of the popular vote; parties rank their candidates in advance, thus determining the likelihood of a candidate actually being allocated a seat. | Elections to European Parliament |

➲ Britain is sometimes summarily described as the home of the 'simple majority' or 'first past the post' electoral system. It is not; as Briefing 17.3 shows, there are now a wide variety of electoral systems in use. And the system is in flux: at the time of writing, a bill is before the Scottish Parliament to introduce STV for local elections.

know from earlier chapters very different systems exist for elections to the devolved parliaments. (See Briefing 17.3 for a summary.)

Beyond the outcome in a single constituency, 'victory' in a general election is decided not by the letter of the law, but by conventional understandings – widely shared understandings, but nevertheless, like all understandings, sometimes unclear at the margins. The clearest and commonest case of 'victory' is when a single party ends up with a workable majority of the 646 seats in the House of Commons over all other parties. Here is an obvious case where conventional understandings give only a partial guide. Mr Blair had clearly won the general elections of 1997 and 2001 (see Table 17.1), with majorities over all other parties of 240 and 195 respectively. But parties have continued in government even when not commanding a majority, by creating an informal alliance with another party sufficient to command a majority in the Commons. (We have not had a formal coalition at Westminster of the kind that has ruled Scotland since 1999 since the dissolution of the wartime coalition that ruled Britain from 1940 to 1945).

Thus emerging as a winner with a 'workable majority' can depend on something other than simple arithmetic, and it can mean something that can only be tested by practice: does it 'work' in the sense of allowing a government to carry on its everyday business, get important legislation passed, and survive any motions of no-confidence? A majority that at the moment of a general election looks perfectly workable may over time degenerate into something very fragile. The Conservatives emerged from the general election of 1992 with a majority of 21 over all other parties, in normal circumstances workable enough to form a government. But deaths and resignations over the life of the 1992 Parliament meant that the party had to defend a succession of seats in by-elections (one-off elections to fill a single parliamentary seat). It failed to retain a single one, and in the meantime became increasingly bitterly divided over the issue of relations with the European Union. The upshot was that in the closing months of the Parliament the government was often only able to continue in

**Table 17.1** Proportionality and disproportionality in Westminster Parliamentary elections: the example of 2001

| Party | % popular vote | % Westminster Commons seats |
| --- | --- | --- |
| Labour | 40.7 | 62.5 (412) |
| Conservative | 31.7 | 25.2 (166) |
| Liberal Democrat | 18.3 | 7.9 (52) |
| Scottish and Welsh Nationalists | 2.5 | 1.4 (9) |
| Others* | 6.2 | 3.0 (20) |
| Green Party | 0.6 | 0 (0) |

* Mainly Northern Ireland parties.

*Source*: Calculated from Butler and Kavanagh (2002: 261).

➲ 'Proportionality' – the extent to which seat allocation mirrors popular vote distribution – is not the only test of an electoral system, but it is an important one. As the figures show, the Westminster system performs poorly by this standard. The winning party, Labour, has a seat allocation in the House of Commons out of proportion to its popular support. Labour's 'lead' here is also exaggerated by the fact that it is deriving some short-term advantages from the present drawing of constituency boundaries. It is this pattern which helps explain the adoption of a variety of different electoral systems at other levels of the system of government (see Briefing 17.3).

office with the tacit support of minority groups such as the Ulster Unionists.

The lesson of this is that rules governing the outcomes of general elections are not hard and fast. (And as we saw earlier, this is even truer in the very different electoral systems that now operate in elections to the Scottish Parliament and the Welsh Assembly.) Nevertheless, it will be obvious that the outcome of a general election is crucially determined by what the election produces in terms of parliamentary seats. That outcome is a complicated product of the interaction between the behaviour of millions of individual electors and the way the electoral system results in their views being counted. Later in the chapter we will look at each of these factors in turn; but first, we need to complete our account of the actual business of fighting elections by looking at the campaigns themselves: at electioneering, in other words.

## Fighting elections

The day of a general election in Britain – by convention always a Thursday – is the culmination of an intense period of open electioneering usually lasting around four weeks. It follows the acceptance by the monarch of the existing prime minister's request for a dissolution of Parliament. This period is frenzied, intense, often hysterical and sometimes fun, for the candidates, for their active supporters, and for the voters at large who are the object of all the frenzy. In this period virtually every parliamentary candidate, and certainly every leading figure in the major parties, spends each waking hour consumed by the elections – and, as polling day nears, usually cuts down on even the fairly small amount of sleep that leading politicians normally allow themselves. Ministers of the existing government remain in office but attend only to the most pressing business themselves; much of the running of government is left in the hands of civil servants.

Although electioneering is conducted in a frenzy it is not completely chaotic. There are clear patterns, and these patterns are changing systematically over time (see Documenting Politics 17.1). Four long-term changes of particular importance concern the length of campaigns, the role of manifestos, the significance of national campaigning relative to campaigning in separate parliamentary constituencies, and the changing role of electronic campaigning. Each of these will be examined in turn.

### Length of campaigns

The formal length of general election campaigns (the gap between dissolving Parliament and election day) has not changed since the end of the First World War. But electioneering is not confined to these campaigns, and the extent and depth of campaigning has extended over time. In an important sense electioneering is now continuous. As soon as one election is over parties start to prepare

**Image 17.1**
**Personality campaigning in modern elections**

Photo: Chris Radburn/PA/EMPICS

➲ The photo here was actually taken at a by-election, but it perfectly illustrates the character of modern election campaigning by the Westminster elite. It is all the more striking because it depicts a party leader, Charles Kennedy, who might be expected to depart from that metropolitan style. On the contrary: Kennedy, like the leaders of the Labour and Conservative parties, practises a style that puts the individual leader right at the centre of staged events designed to create photo opportunities. The local candidate stands behind Kennedy; but the most important figure in the photograph, apart from Kennedy himself, is the TV cameraman recording the event for the sound-bite in the evening TV news.

for the next. All the major parties now invest in tracking the demands and perceptions of voters. They closely monitor published polling results and commission a constant stream of private polling. In recent years all the major parties have invested in focus groups, of the sort that was described in Chapter 16. This adaptation of a commercial marketing technique is designed to allow parties to acquire a more subtle picture of how electors view the parties and the political world generally. Thus, in the sense of continuously probing what the electorate feels, and in adapting their message to the findings, parties can now be said to be in continuous electioneering mode. This has been accentuated by

**DOCUMENTING POLITICS 17.1**

## ELECTIONEERING FEVER, OLD AND NEW

The *Daily Mirror* reports on Prime Minister Attlee's style of campaigning across the country, 1951:

'While his wife drives, Mr Attlee puts on his glasses, rests on a brown and green folk-weave cushion, and does newspaper crosswords … If their car is held up at a level crossing Mrs Attlee gets out her knitting … Like a good wife, before they set out every morning, Mrs Attlee puts a crease in her husband's trousers with a portable electric iron.'

Prime Minister, John Major, on his victorious general election campaign of 1992:

'My election schedule … had been agreed before the campaign began. The aim was to shuttle me across the country, with the twin intentions of highlighting our predetermined themes and visiting constituencies … I woke each morning at about 6.30, usually to find an already alert Sarah Hogg waiting edgily for me to approve a statement for that morning's press conference. Then I would scan documents briefing me on live issues of the day, gather up ministers due to appear with me, and head off over to Central Office.' [for the daily press conference]

➲ The big contrast between these two campaigns 40 years apart is not how hard the two prime ministers worked (Attlee had an exhausting schedule of public meetings) and neither is it a contrast in efficiency: John Major's account in his autobiography emphasizes the chaos of campaigning. It is a contrast between Attlee's style, involving little administrative support and attempting to reach as many voters as possible in mass meetings; and the style a generation later which is geared to creating photo and broadcasting opportunities.

*Sources*: *Daily Mirror*, quoted in Harris (1982: 491); Major (1999: 298–9).

the proliferation of elections. Local, devolved assembly and EP elections are important in their own right but are also now integrated into the permanent campaigning mode of the parties.

### Role of manifestos

As electioneering has spread beyond the formal election campaign, so the shape and functions of manifestos has changed. Formally, manifestos are the documents issued early in a campaign that outline authoritatively what the different parties stand for; but hardly anybody reads manifestos. This is sensible, because they are not intended to be read; they are intended to be reported, and to be culled selectively by the party's campaigners during the campaign. Nobody pretends that many voters read manifestos, still less make up their minds about voting after reading them; but they are nevertheless important. They form the heart of the theory of the mandate: the theory that support in a general election means that voters have assented to what a party stands for, and therefore that a winning party has the legitimate right to put into effect any commitments in the manifesto. Detailed research indicates, indeed, that parties in practice take mandates seriously: a large amount of comparative evidence indicates that the content of election manifestos is a surprisingly good guide to what parties actually do in government (Klingemann, Hofferbert and Budge 1994). They therefore form a kind of contract with the electorate, even if most of those involved – electors – never bother to read the contract. Just as electioneering generally has now spilled beyond the formal campaign, manifesto-making has expanded. The major parties typically prepare a 'pre-manifesto' a couple of years before an anticipated election (an outline draft, in other words). The technique partly markets the party by highlighting its main commitments without the clutter of detail, and partly tests commitments in the political marketplace: any that look unpromising can be quietly dropped in the final version. Parties have also elaborated the idea of the manifesto as a contract by culling the main manifesto for what are believed to be a few of the most attractive commitments and issuing them as separate highlighted pledges: for instance, in the 1997 general election campaign the victorious Labour party gained extensive publicity for ten pledges which it extracted from the larger manifesto and 'marketed' as the party's 'contract with the people'.

## Rising importance of the national campaign

Historically, election campaigning in Britain developed primarily as a struggle in individual constituencies. But now all the important action takes place at a national level. The daily rhythm of campaigning is largely dictated by the schedules of nationwide broadcasting, television and radio, and of national newspapers. Party leaders host daily early morning press conferences designed to put a 'spin' on particular issues, sometimes chosen as part of an overall strategy, sometimes picked up at short notice to exploit a weakness in a rival party. Rapid transport – flying, or racing around the motorway system in 'battle buses' – means that most leading figures can combine being present in London for press conferences with extensive touring. But touring, although it looks superficially like old-fashioned 'meet the people' campaigning, is largely designed with the media, especially television, in mind. A set speech in the open air, a visit to a work place or a home, or a 'walkabout' in a shopping centre: all have the same purpose, which is to create a reporting opportunity – a good photo and story for newspapers, or a 30-second slot in the evening television and radio news. At the centre of this style of campaigning will be the individual party leaders themselves. They are party leaders because they are

specially gifted at this kind of activity. Most normal people, faced with meeting a succession of total strangers, would be tongue tied. But good politicians are expert at converting casual acquaintances with total strangers into a 30-second exchange suitable for a television broadcast. They are also skilled at summing up their party policy, or denouncing their opponents', in a short sound-bite suitable for radio and television; at surviving hostile questioning by reporters; or (now virtually mandatory in general elections) at fielding questioning from 'cross-sections' of the public in television forums. There is a film clip dating from about 1950 of Clement Attlee, the prime minister and leader of the Labour party. A reporter asks Mr Attlee if he has a message for the electorate. Attlee, famously monosyllabic, replies simply 'No'. A party leader who conducted himself in this way now would soon be replaced.

## Rise of electronic campaigning

As the above suggests, there is increasing use of the most modern technology in election campaigning. Not only do parties now rely heavily on television and mass advertising to reach voters, but they also increasingly use electronic technology to contact 'target' voters – groups of voters who might vote for the party, but whose support needs to courted. Modern computing technology, allied to the use of social survey databases, allows parties quickly to identify these target groups of voters, and the technology also makes it easy to send 'personalized' letters to them from the party leader in mail shots. Modern telephone technology, coupled with the fact that telephone ownership is now almost universal, means that target voters can also be contacted personally. During elections the big parties now run what are in effect call centres to do this. Finally, the use of websites (see Table 17.2) and e-mail is becoming increasingly common (a mode of communication examined in Chapter 16).

In summary, election campaigning in Britain is turning away from attempts to reach voters en masse in public places, such as in election rallies, and relying more and more on attempts to contact targeted voters directly and privately. A century ago a visitor to Britain during an election campaign who had no English would nevertheless soon realize that something momentous was going on: there would be numerous very public activities, including parades, rallies, mass meetings and impromptu open air speeches. A visitor now who had no English might well miss the campaign altogether: campaigning, though more frenzied than ever, is much more targeted and delivered by mass communication and modern electronic technology.

❖   ❖   ❖

A great deal of debate has taken place about how far campaigns actually influence election outcomes. This issue is bound up with what we examine next in looking at what determines election results.

## Going to the polls

As voters we have to take two separate decisions: whether to vote; and, if we decide to turn out, who to support. We know a great deal about how voters make the second decision and rather less, as we will see in this section, about the first.

### Deciding to vote

If voting were considered strictly in terms of its costs and benefits almost none of us would bother to turn out. Since the reforms of the nineteenth century we can no longer expect to be bribed. The chances of our single vote determining the result are virtually nil. The result of the 2001 general election was typical: the smallest majority recorded was 33 votes (for the Liberal Democrat candidate in Cheadle) and only four seats were decided by majorities of less than one hundred. Thus even a group (of friends or a family) let alone one individual could not realistically think that their votes alone would decide a result; yet millions of us continue to turn out.

What we must conclude from these figures is that voting is about something more complicated for the individual voter than cost of voting and the benefit of winning:it is about an affirmation of some kind of identity. Since our sense of identity is formed by our

**Table 17.2** The race to establish an electronic presence by the parties (dates of first web site launch).

| Party name | Date established |
| --- | --- |
| Labour | October 1994 |
| Plaid Cymru | April 1995 |
| Alliance Party (Northern Ireland) | August 1995 |
| National Democratic Party | September 1995 |
| Conservative | October 1995 |
| Ulster Unionist Party | November 1995 |
| Social Democratic and Labour Party (Northern Ireland) | January 1996 |
| Scottish National Party | February 1996 |
| Scottish Liberal Democrats | March 1996 |
| Democratic Unionist Party | April 1996 |
| Scottish Conservative Party | May 1996 |
| Referendum Party | September 1996 |
| UK Independence Party | September 1996 |

*Source*: Extracted from Ward and Gibson (1998: 94).

 Ward and Gibson's study emphasizes that the earliest efforts to use a web presence for campaigning purposes were primitive. But what is most striking about the table is the way the technology of the web was adapted so rapidly by the parties.

own complicated life histories, and our understanding of those life histories, we each turn up in the polling booth with histories that give us very different identities to affirm. For a quite small minority, those who are deeply committed supporters of a particular party, the vote is an opportunity to affirm their partisan identity and they will do it regardless of the likely outcome. These partisans would vote even if they suspected that they were the only supporter in the constituency; indeed, that might be an added incentive to vote, since the affirmation of identity would be especially visible. For a larger group of voters the identity that is affirmed is an identity as citizens exercising their lawful entitlement to cast a ballot. Few people would actually use the formal language of citizenship, but the sense, however weak, that we have a duty to use our ballot is what carries large numbers of people with no great interest in politics to the polling station. And once there, the actual choice can involve affirming all kinds of contingent identities, from the deepest –

such as a lifelong loyalty to a party – to the most immediate, such as dislike of the personality of the prime minister of the day, or even dislike of a physical trait, such as the prime minister's tone of voice. (Worries that voters found Mrs Thatcher's tone too strident in the 1980s led to coaching designed to move her voice down the register.)

## Deciding not to vote

We saw earlier that there are millions of potential voters who are disqualified because they do not register as voters, but there are also millions who, despite being properly registered, decide not to vote. For much of the twentieth century these non-voters were a fairly small minority of the population at general elections. What is more, the little we knew about them suggested that they were 'sporadic' non-voters: in other words, they formed a floating group who shifted from voting to non-voting at different elections, rather than forming a distinct group who had withdrawn completely from electoral participation. (They were, however, a large majority in elections in local government, as we saw in Chapter 12.) It seems that a long-term decline in voter turnout in Westminster general elections is taking place. Some of the reforms in voting procedure – such as making postal voting easier – are designed to try to reverse this trend. It also seems that non-voting is no longer 'sporadic'. It is consistent with other evidence we have discussed in earlier chapters. Voting in general elections is associated with support for one of the old-established political parties, notably Labour and Conservative; and we saw in our discussions of party organization, and of political participation (Chapters 13 and 14), that there has been a long-term withdrawal of active support for these parties. The rise of non-voting in general elections, though it is too recent a phenomenon for us to understand fully, may therefore indicate a permanent withdrawal on the part of large numbers of people, from the kind of politics conventionally associated with competition between political parties for votes at general elections for the Westminster Parliament.

The dramatic fall in turnout in the 2001 general election seems also to support this view because it

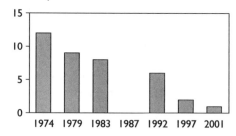

**Figure 17.1**    The disappearing gender gap in voting (Conservative lead over Labour among women voters 1974–2001)

*Source*:   Data from Worcester and Mortimore (2001: 199), from MORI sampling data. The figure for 1987 is zero, so invisible.

➲ The distribution of women's votes at any moment will reflect the wider pattern of electoral choice. This figure compares the electoral choices of women and men: it measures the Conservative lead over Labour among women minus the Conservative lead over Labour among men. Thus a positive figure means that women are more likely than men to support the Conservatives. Historically, women were predisposed to the Conservative party; as the figures show, that historical predisposition has virtually disappeared over the last three decades.

was most pronounced among young voters. Research reported by the Electoral Commission shows that among 18–24 year olds, turnout fell from 68 per cent to 39 per cent between the two elections of 1997 and 2001: a fall three times greater than among the whole population (Electoral Commission 2002b).

As we will see in a moment, this is also consistent with evidence that the strength of identification with the parties among the electorate is declining (for more on the eroding link between women voters and the Conservatives, see Figure 17.1).

## At the polls: casting a vote

The evidence of turnout at elections suggests that voters are changing in their behaviour and loyalties, and this suggestion is strengthened when we look at how electors actually cast their votes (see Figure 17.2). There seems to be growing volatility in voter behaviour. However, this volatility is relative; in other words, it shows up against the background of well known, long-established, stable trends in behaviour. The best way to understand the new volatility is to begin first with a sketch of these old-established patterns.

## Party voting

If we wanted to predict how a group of voters would vote in a forthcoming election, and we were allowed to have only one piece of information about them, one of the most useful bits of information to have would be how they voted last time. Voters do change, but the majority still have fairly settled loyalties to parties. This is not surprising when we consider both that voting is about affirming identity, and that in most other areas of life – even trivial ones, such as the beer we consume – we tend to settle for particular brands.

But the way this party link works, and the way it is changing, also provides an important clue to the way the landscape of voting is changing. Perhaps the most important reason why voters are so often willing to vote time after time for a party is that they have tended to organize their political loyalties through the psychological mechanism of party identification. Students of electoral behaviour explore this by examining responses to questions that ask voters if they feel attached to a party, and if so, how strongly they feel attached. A minority have a very strong identification, and these are a bed-rock of support that a party can rely upon even in bad times. But even quite weak identification can help a party: if we only weakly identify ourselves as Scottish Nationalist or as Conservative, that never-theless makes us a bit more receptive to the party's claims, and a bit more sceptical about those of its opponents. How party identification is formed has been the subject of intense investigation and debate – hardly surprising, since we are talking here about a quite complex mental process. One of the most important features is what is sometimes called the 'cohort' effect: different generations of voters, with common experiences, often show distinct patterns of identification. The most famous example is the generation that entered the electorate in the years

**Figure 17.2**  Combined Labour and Conservative share of the vote in Westminster elections, 1950–2005

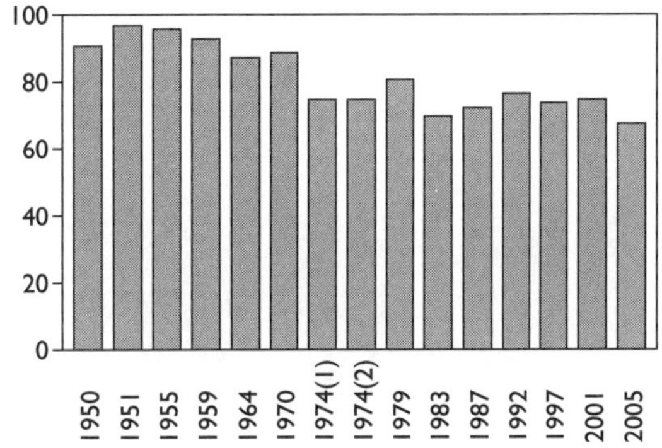

➲ The two major parties, Conservative and Labour, dominated elections to the Westminster Parliament from 1950 to 1970; since then, the separate parties have had varying fortunes, but the combined effect has been a steady erosion of their popular support in general elections, a trend continued in 2005.

up to 1945, containing large numbers of Labour loyalists, and contributing to the Labour party's landslide victory in 1945. This was a highly distinc-tive cohort marked by the experience of economic depression in the 1930s and common struggle in the Second World War.

The changing nature of party identification is one of the important clues to electoral change in Britain. The most important change is summarized in Figure 17.3. The changes summarized there are subtle, but consistent: there is a waning in the strength of party identification. There is also a modest rise in the proportion of voters who reject any party attachment.

We have already now identified three key features of electoral change in Britain:

- In Westminster elections there has occurred a pronounced fall in turnout, and in the new elected bodies created by devolution turnout is even lower.
- Votes for the two historically dominant parties, Labour and the Conservatives, are declining.
- Identification with political parties, especially with the two main parties, is weakening.

**Figure 17.3**   The declining attachment to political parties (% of electorate professing a 'very strong' attachment to party, selected dates, 1964–2001)

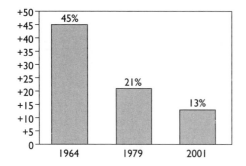

*Source*: Data from Clarke *et al.* (2004: 41).

➲ These figures summarize responses in a series of nationwide surveys of electors. Answers to single surveys have to be treated with caution: the views expressed can often be heavily affected by the particular timing of a survey. Trends over time are therefore much more revealing. The trends revealed here show a dramatic loosening of the hold of party over the minds of voters.

There are many reasons for these changes, but one probable source is the changed nature of class relations in Britain.

## Class

The two-party (Conservative/Labour) system dominated British elections for half-a-century after the First World War and reached its peak at just about the mid-point of the twentieth century. This system was closely bound to the wider British class structure. There was a historically high level of 'class solidarity' among voters: middle-class voters, however defined, were very likely to vote Conservative, and working-class voters, however defined, were likely to vote Labour. A generation ago a leading textbook on parties and elections said: 'Class is the basis of British party politics; all else is embellishment and detail,' (Pulzer 1967: 98). That, we shall also shortly see, is no longer true, but class location still remains a very important influence over how we vote. 'Class' is itself a complicated concept, but in the context of voting behaviour it

usually means occupational class: the location in the class hierarchy identified by occupation. It traditionally referred to the divide between manual and non-manual workers, but as the divisions in the labour force have become more complicated and subtle, that simple divide is no longer quite so revealing. It is still not difficult to see why some measure of occupational class would be electorally significant. Occupational class is important to our perceptions of our economic interests, and our judgement about which party would be most likely to defend those interests.

The connection between class and voting is changing over time, but why it is changing is a matter of some debate. The simplest indisputable reason for the change is that one class that was at the heart of the old class-based voting system has declined greatly in numerical importance. These are male manual workers and their families, especially those employed in the old important industries of the Industrial Revolution. A glance back at Figure 3.1, p. 42 will show just how dramatic was the change over the course of the twentieth century – from an overwhelming majority to a minority, and a minority that continues to decline. The symbol of the change is the virtual disappearance of deep coal mining as an occupation in the last two decades, and the consequent disappearance of one of the most powerful and best organized parts of this old working class. The Labour party, which depended so heavily on the support of this old working class, has had to adapt its appeal beyond this working-class heartland. But it may be more than a matter of changing numbers: the culture of classes has altered greatly in the last half-century. This is partly a matter of superficial changes in styles of dress, entertainment and accent, but superficial changes that may nevertheless be symbolic for class identity. More systematically documented are changes in really significant material circumstances. The rise of car ownership has shrunk the proportion of the population that now depends solely on public transport – in other words on a good provided or regulated by the state. The rise of home ownership, and the decline of 'social' housing such as that rented from local authorities, is another important long term change, again involving a decline in a key good provided or regulated by the state. This is not only breaking up the cohesion of groups such as manual workers, but it may also be elevating in importance a feature that we next examine: sectoral location as an influence on the vote.

The last quarter of the twentieth century was the critical period when parties realized the threats and opportunities opened up by the changing social structure. Figure 17.4 illustrates what was going on by taking the key case of the Labour party, the institution most threatened by the shrinking size of the traditional manual working class. It simply compares the class composition of the Labour vote at the two moments when it was victorious in a Westminster Parliament election (though by very different margins). It shows that by the end of the century Labour's vote was coming less and less from its class 'core' and more and more from beyond the old working class – the result in part of a 'New Labour' strategy that included, as we saw in Chapter 15, the abandonment of many of the policies and ideological symbols to which Labour had been traditionally committed.

## Sector

All economies are divided into sectors: the publicly owned and privately owned sectors, for example, or the manufacturing and service sectors. As far as voting behaviour is concerned, the public/private divide is particularly important. Even taking into account other influences on the vote, such as occupational class, private sector workers have long been more likely to vote Conservative, and public sector workers more likely to vote for the Labour party. We could interpret this difference in terms of a rational calculation of interests: especially after the rise of Mrs Thatcher and her radical economic ideas in the Conservative party, Conservatives were viewed as more likely to defend the interests of private sector employees than of public sector ones. Or we could interpret the difference in identity terms: that in important parts of public sector employment, such as health and education, there are distinctive cultures which are more likely to favour the values of the Labour party than of the Conservative party. The example of employment is

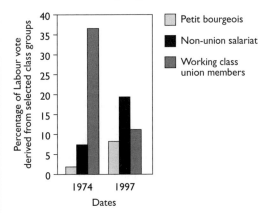

**Figure 17.4**    The changing place of class and voting: the case of the Labour party, 1974–97

*Source*: Data adapted from Heath, Jowell and Curtice, 2001: 139.

➲    The figure is adapted from the analyses of Heath and his colleagues, the most complete long-term survey of voting change. It is important to know that the figure is highly selective. To illustrate the long-term change I select only the beginning and end points; their original table includes figures for all the intervening elections. (The 1974 figure is for the election of October of that year.) The figure also does not present the full composition of the Labour vote. For illustration again, I select the contribution of three key groups. 'Petit bourgeois' refers to employers and the self-employed; the 'salariat' refers to salaried professionals, managers and administrators; working-class refers to manual workers, and union members from this class are the traditional 'core' of Labour support. The fall in the contribution of this group did not happen because it deserted Labour, but because it fell sharply in size – a fall which forced Labour to reach out to groups not traditionally aligned to the party.

only one instance of the influence of sector on the vote. Housing tenure – especially whether we own, or rent publicly owned houses – and extent of reliance on public transport can all affect the kind of calculations we make as voters about where our economic interests lie.

## Territory

The influence of territory on the vote is marked, and also seems to be explicable in terms of an 'identity' interpretation of voting. In some cases these territorial variations are striking and could not be explained by, for instance, variations in the class composition of particular parts of Britain. The most vivid example was provided by the 1997 general election result. That was the culmination of a period of nearly two decades when the electorates of Wales and Scotland became increasingly alienated from rule by Conservative-dominated governments in Westminster. The culmination of this alienation was the failure of the Conservatives to return a single MP in the two Celtic countries. In one part of the United Kingdom, Northern Ireland, the pattern of voting is shaped by identities which are virtually unique in Britain: the competing parties are distinctive to the province, and are expressions of national and religious identity, Irish and British, Catholic and Protestant. With devolution, the influence of territory may be growing, as the distinct nations develop their own separate cultures and constellations of interests.

## Religion

Religion used to be a powerful influence on voting across the whole of the United Kingdom: broadly, Anglicans were disproportionately Conservative; non-conformist Protestants and Catholics voted for non-Conservative parties (in the nineteenth century the Liberal party, and then increasingly for the Labour party). The waning of organized Christian religion in the second half of the twentieth century in Britain has left only a faint echo of this once powerful divide. Indeed, as far as the institutions of religion themselves are concerned the social thinking of the Church of England became hostile to the sort of Conservatism represented by the governments that ruled between 1979 and 1997. But religion has reappeared in another form to which we now turn.

## Ethnicity

Ethnic identity – the identification with some racial, national or culturally distinctive group – was always important: Irish Catholicism in all parts of the United Kingdom, for example, tended to be hostile to Conservatism, probably because it was associated with defence of the Union against,

**Image 17.2**
**We have ways of making you vote**

Photo: Michael Moran

➲ We have seen at several points in this chapter and earlier that there is now widespread 'official' concern about electoral turnout, and that a new agency – the Electoral Commission – has been created to regulate elections and parties. The image unites the two features: it shows a billboard campaign by the Commission to boost voter registration. The photograph was taken in Northern Ireland, where voter registration and participation is especially sensitive.

among others, Irish nationalists. Successive waves of immigrants over a period of more than a century have reinforced ethnicity as an influence on the vote. The most important present influence is among immigrants from the 'new Commonwealth' – the former colonial possessions of the Indian subcontinent and the West Indies – and their descendants. There are two striking features of voting among the most recent waves of ethnic minorities, at least those that originated from the 'new Commonwealth'. One is that there is markedly strong support for the Labour party – marked even when we try to take into account long term social features, such as class location, and short-term features, such as the overall strength of parties at particular moments. However, when we do the arithmetic new Commonwealth immigrants and their descendants are Labour voters (see Figure 17.5). But the second is that black and ethnic minority voters participate in voting much less than the population as a whole. An Electoral Commission study suggests that this is due to a variety of causes. Factors such as language often hinder registration (an essential condition, as we saw earlier, of actually casting a vote), but there is also evidence that for many black and ethnic minority voters there is a feeling that the parties do not stand for the policies they would like to support (Electoral Commission 2002c).

## Gender

There have long been marked gender variations in voting, though they have changed over time. Hard evidence about individual patterns of voting behaviour has only become available since the rise of systematic mass surveying in the last generation. It nevertheless seems to be the case that, for at least a generation after adult women first received the vote in 1918, women disproportionately supported the Conservative party. That pattern persisted into the age when we have fairly good survey-based evidence about voting behaviour (see Figure 17.1, p. 378). But the special Conservative gender lead has been fading away in recent decades. The reasons for this are many, but probably the most important is that the life experiences of women and men are becoming more similar. How and why this is happening will be described in the next section.

## The outcome: winning and losing elections

So far we have what might be called a 'voter's eye' view of elections: a view of the influences that shape the individual voting decision. But parties are interested in a bigger picture: how do all these separate votes add up to an election outcome? This section is about this bigger picture. What determines the rise and fall of a party's election fortunes? We can divide the determining factors into three: what might be called the long waves of change in the wider society; the short-term intervention of critical historical events; and the policy performance of governing parties and their opponents.

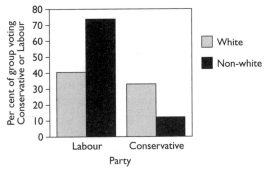

**Figure 17.5**  The ethnic vote is a Labour vote (Labour and Conservative share compared in 2001 general election)

*Source*: Calculated from Worcester and Mortimore (2001: 5).

➡ The figure is based on MORI sampling data, relying on what voters told pollsters about how they voted in the general election of 2001. The simple categories 'white'/'non-white' are crude, but the figures confirm a long documented pattern: a far higher proportion of ethnic voters supports Labour than supports the Conservatives.

## The long waves of change

A glance back at the development of British society over a long period – say, over the last half-century – shows that there are some clear long-term changes, often taking place quite slowly, which fundamentally alter the social structure. These alterations in turn affect electoral fortunes. We have already discussed these in some detail in painting a 'voter's eye' picture of voting, so we can summarize them briefly.

Easily the most important is the long-term alteration to the class structure. In 1950 British politics was dominated by two parties which had their roots firmly in occupational classes (that was especially true of the Labour party). Since then the size of the manual working class has shrunk. Were Labour to rely on its old manual working 'heartland' it would never win elections, and those occasions in recent decades when it has performed disastrously – for instance, in the 1980s – were marked by such a reliance. Indeed, shifts in the occupational class structure have not only affected the fortunes of the

Labour party. The growing size of the middle class in the *public* sector – among teachers and health care workers, for instance – has worked against the Conservatives.

The second big long-term change concerns gender. For a generation after women were enfranchised the female vote favoured the Conservatives: at any given point in the class structure, for instance, women were more likely than men to vote Conservative. This persistent gender gap has disappeared, to the disadvantage of the Conservatives. Many possible reasons explain this, all connected to long-term social change. Women now go out to paid work in much larger proportions than 50 years ago: they made up just over 29 per cent of the workforce near the start of the twentieth century (1911) and just over 44 per cent by the end of the century (see Gallie 2000: 292). From a point where they barely entered higher education, they now outnumber men. In short, the job and educational experiences of women are no longer as different from those of men as they once were, and in consequence their electoral behaviour is losing its distinctiveness.

A final long-term change concerns the electoral impact of the Christian religion. Even though church attendance for most of the twentieth century was declining, religion still exercised a strong cultural influence, so that, for instance, the large working-class vote that the Conservatives gained was an echo of working-class Anglicanism (the Protestantism of the state church). Much of Labour's working-class support echoed earlier non-Conformist and Catholic connections. The influence of Christian religion on election outcomes has faded to a distant echo. (However, in the case of non-Christian religions, notably Islam and Hinduism, there is a different story.)

The outcome of elections is therefore in part the result of long-term, slow changes such as those sketched above. The composition of the electorate gradually alters by the succession of generations. At one end large numbers of people leave through the graveyard and crematorium. If they disproportionately represent a particular social formation – say, manual workers, or practising Anglicans – that can materially affect the chances of a party winning an election. At the other end, large numbers join as

they reach the age of 18 (see Political Issues 17.1). These figures are so large that they can dwarf more short-term swings in opinion. Around 500,000 voters a year join as they reach the qualifying age to register; the number obviously varies with the birth rate 18 years before. Likewise a roughly similar number leave through death (and a smaller number through such factors as emigration). The 'turnover' in the electorate over a five-year life of a parliament, therefore, is around 2.5 million. These changes often lie behind historic election upheavals: Labour's landslide victory in 1945, for example, owed a lot to the fact that war had postponed the election, and since the previous one in 1935 there had been massive change in the composition of the electorate.

However, if long-term social change were the only important determinant of election outcomes, we would expect parties to rise and fall slowly. They do not; they often have dramatic changes in electoral fortunes because of the intervention of great historical events.

## Critical historical events

Consider three general election results from the twentieth century: the result in 1918, the first occasion when the Labour party decisively displaced the old Liberal party as the main alternative to Conservatism in Britain; the 1945 result, which produced a huge Labour majority, broke the Conservative hold on government which had been almost continuous for nearly 30 years, and led to major reforms in economic policy and to the creation of the welfare state; and the 1979 result, which led to an unbroken 18 years of Conservative government and radical changes in economic policy (including a huge privatization programme which forced the Labour party to recast most of its social and economic policies). All these results were critical in the exact meaning of that word: they were great turning points in the electoral history, and in the history of policy. They represented decisive breaks with the past and, while they were connected to long-term social change, they were also a response to great historical turmoil: to the great stresses of the First World War (1918); to the

POLITICAL ISSUES

### 17.1 VOTES AT 16

The qualifying age for voting was reduced to 18 (from 21) in the Representation of the People Act of 1969. The 'Votes at 16 campaign' advocates a further reduction in the qualifying age. It argues the case partly on grounds of consistency: at the age of 16 young people have many of the obligations of citizenship, such as liability for tax, and therefore should have its entitlements. It also argues on moral grounds, claiming that the exclusion of those under 18 is similar to earlier historical exclusions, such as those barring women and the working class. The campaign now has a wide support base, ranging from established political parties (the Liberal Democrats and the Greens) to important groups in civil society, such as Charter 88 and the YMCA. In April 2004 an Electoral Commission Report rejected changing the qualifying age from 18. The Liberal Democrats' support is strategic: by opposing tuition fees and the Iraq War they benefitted greatly from the 'post-18' student vote in the 2005 general election. For more on the campaign visit *www.votesat16.org.uk*.

equally great events of the Second World War (1945); to the deep British economic crisis of the 1970s (1979). Thus the three most significant election results of the twentieth century were due to great historical dramas, and not simply to long-term social change. A party can be destroyed as a major national electoral force as a result of a historical crisis, as was the Liberal party in 1918; or it can be so badly damaged that it only recovers electorally after a long and painful transformation of its organization, policy and ideology, as was Labour's experience after 1979.

### Policy performance

This leads to an obvious conclusion: parties cannot rely on the long tide of social change to carry them to office; but, equally, they do not have to submit to fate. In the 1960s there was a widely held theory that the Conservatives were doomed to permanent opposition because of the graveyard effect: Conservative voters were older than average, so they were disproportionately dying off. Yet between 1970 and 1997 the Conservatives were the governing party for all but five years. Many short-term factors can affect a party's electoral fortunes, such as the skill of its leaders in marketing policy, and the

internal unity of the party. But in the last generation one overwhelmingly important influence has become clear: electors' perceptions of policy performance, especially economic policy performance. As the word 'perception' indicates, the connection between the judgements voters make, the state of the economy, and the government's contribution to the state of the economy, is complex. For voters, a powerful influence is their sense of the way the economy is affecting their fortunes: do they, for instance, feel optimistic about their prospects over the coming months? It is possible for governing parties to do much to shape perception: they can manipulate tax and spending policies to put money into the pockets of voters; they can use allies in the press, when they have them, to 'spin' a picture of an economy in prosperity. But no amount of 'spin' can detach the perceptions of voters from the underlying experience of policy performance. Labour lost office in the critical election of 1979 because, either through bad luck or bad judgement, it ran the country when the economy was marked by very high inflation, successive currency crises and hugely disruptive industrial disputes. But perception and performance are linked in complex ways. The Conservatives suffered the landslide defeat in 1997 despite four years of economic growth. What

**Figure 17.6** 'Black Wednesday' and electors' judgements about the economic competence of the two main parties.

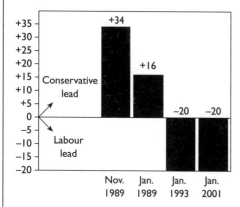

*Source:* Calculated from Clarke *et al.* (2004: 62–3).

➲ Using a model developed by David Sanders and colleagues at Essex University, the data represented here from the British Election Study of 2001 subtly explores the connection between voters' perceptions and actual economic performance. But the central lesson of this figure is simple: a single catastrophic episode of mismanagement can damage a party for years. The figure charts responses to a question put over the years to a sample of electors: 'With Britain in economic difficulties, which party do you think could handle the situation best – Labour or the Conservatives?' The figures show the percentages that prefer the Conservatives, minus the percentage that prefer Labour: when the bars are above zero, the Conservatives lead. As the figure shows, the Conservatives lost a comfortable lead in 1992, when under a Conservative Chancellor the country humiliatingly left the European Exchange Rate Mechanism, and they never recovered it.

seems to have done for them was a single policy disaster: the episode of 'Black Wednesday', 16 September 1992. On that day, after a public humiliation at the hands of currency speculators, the Conservative Chancellor of the Exchequer was obliged to suspend Britain's membership of the European Exchange Rate Mechanism, then central to monetary management in the European Union. Before that episode voters' perceptions – as reported in polls – had generally pictured the Conservatives as more competent economic managers than Labour; after it, Labour was consis-

tently seen as more competent. (See Figure 17.6 for more details.)

## Winning and losing: the parliamentary result

It is one thing to win the popular vote; it is another to convert those votes into seats won in Parliament. The connection between popular votes and seats differs in the various election systems now working in Britain: Chapter 11 described the Welsh, Scottish and Northern Irish systems, so here we focus on the Westminster Parliament in so-called general elections.

Earlier in this chapter the bare bones of the system for electing the Westminster House of Commons were described but, although there are mechanics to election systems, the effect of election rules on Parliamentary majorities is not mechanical. The rules combine both with the perceptions of voters and the distribution of voters to shape outcomes.

The system for producing parliamentary representation at Westminster has two features:

- It is based on separate territorial constituencies with single-member representatives. The size of the popular vote within each separate constituency is critical. There is no provision – as there is in the arrangements for the Welsh and Scottish Assemblies – for taking some account of the wider popular vote in calculating numbers of legislative representatives.
- Within constituencies the 'simple majority' rule prevails: it is a winner-takes-all system, in which the candidate with the largest vote, irrespective of whether this truly represents a majority of all votes cast, is declared elected.

These features produce a number of well known effects. The system systematically exaggerates movements in the popular vote at the parliamentary level. The Labour party's share of the popular vote between 1992 and 1997 rose from 34.4 per cent to 43.2 per cent; its share of Westminster seats rose from 41.6 to 63.4 per cent. This is precisely the result of the 'winner takes all' character of the

# Briefing                                                                17.4

## VOTING BEHAVIOUR IN THE 2005 GENERAL ELECTION

The 2005 general election confirmed trends now well established in British voting behaviour, and introduced some striking new features. Superficially, it represented a reassertion of some older patterns. There was a small increase in turnout over the 2001 election and, more important, this seemed at last a reversal of what appeared a perpetual trend towards lower participation. The sharp reduction in Labour's majority, which nevertheless left it with a sizeable lead over all other parties, also seemed to represent a reassertion of more 'normal' parliamentary politics than was provided by the huge Westminster majorities generated by the unprecedented landslides of 1997 and 2001. The age of Blairite domination of politics was plainly coming to an end. Yet the slight rise in participation was largely illusory, a product of eased rules governing postal voting. Voting by post rose hugely, as did, almost certainly, electoral fraud through the postal system. There was no significant re-engagement with the style of politics – turning out on election day – favoured by the Westminster elite. The result also confirmed the continuing dissolution of the two party system. The Liberal Democrats continued their advance in popular support, an advance only partly reflected in parliamentary seats because of the workings of the Westminster electoral system. Numerous other minor parties, ranging from the Greens to the racist British National Party, all recorded significant popular advances. Three independent MPs were returned – a tiny number, but the highest of the modern era. The Conservative party advanced in Parliamentary seats, but continued almost to 'flatline' in popular votes. Most striking of all, Labour was returned with a safe Westminster majority on a share of the popular vote – 35.2 per cent – which was the smallest for a winning Westminster party since the early 1920s. Viewed as a whole, the most striking feature of the behaviour of the electorate as a whole was its diversity of behaviour; and viewed individually, the most striking feature of electors was their growing tactical shrewdness in exploiting the electoral system. The outcome of these two features was to produce great variety in local and regional outcomes. London and the south-east emerged as particularly distinctive. An opponent of the Iraq War, the former Labour MP George Galloway, overturned a huge Labour majority in an east London constituency. But this was just a sign of something more general, the way the booming, but hugely unequal, south-east economy produced its own highly distinctive concerns: an unusual sensitivity to a foreign policy issue, Iraq; and intense competition, not for traditional goods like jobs, but for scarce social goods like housing, land, and a wide range of services in education and health. In London and elsewhere, the vast expansion in higher education since the early 1990s meant that student interests – chiefly in tuition fees and in foreign policy – were important in shaping many results. The Liberal Democrats shrewdly tailored their appeal to this new, privileged, social group. Overall, the outcome emphasized that it makes decreasing sense any more to speak of a single 'United Kingdom' system of politics, still less of a single system of electoral politics.

counting system: a party can lose its constituency majorities, and therefore its seats, on fairly modest swings of support. For the same reason the system has a tendency to exaggerate the majority of the largest winning party, a feature well illustrated in Table 17.1, p. 373.

The system also to tends to underrepresent – relative to their popular vote – minority parties whose support is geographically dispersed rather than concentrated. For much of the period since the end of the Second World War the Liberal party (and their successors the Liberal Democrats) has suffered in this way. Again, this effect is produced by the combination of a simple majority rule and the counting of votes in separate territorial constituencies. But the big parties can also be penalized in parts of the United Kingdom where their vote sinks to the level of a small minority: that is how the Conservatives in Scotland failed in 1997 to return a single MP to the Westminster Parliament despite securing over 17 per cent of the popular vote; in 2001, they secured only one seat with 16 per cent of the vote.

There now seems to be a growing tendency for both some voters and the parties to learn strategic

# DEBATING POLITICS

## 17.1   ELECTIONS: SHAM OR KEY TO DEMOCRACY?

| Elections promote effective democracy: | Elections fail to promote effective democracy: |
|---|---|
| ■ Voting remains one of the commonest forms of political participation. <br> ■ Voting outcomes make a difference: parties seriously try to implement their manifestos. <br> ■ The 'voting culture' is strengthening in Britain because of widened opportunities to vote. <br> ■ Voting is among the simplest and least costly forms of participation; reforms such as electronic voting and easier postal voting are making it even simpler and cheaper. | ■ Though common, voting is declining in popularity. <br> ■ The mandate to implement a manifesto is a fiction: voters hardly ever read manifestos and are forced to accept party policies as a 'job lot'. <br> ■ New campaign techniques mean that election campaigns are really extended exercises in marketing and manipulation. <br> ■ Nobody's single vote alone determines an electoral outcome so the very act of voting is based on a fiction. |

lessons from these features of the electoral system: in other words, they adapt their behaviour to exploit its features. Among some voters the concept of the 'wasted vote' has long existed: the notion that it is pointless to vote for the party they would ideally prefer because it is unlikely ever to win. This is only a step away from a consciously strategic vote: supporting the candidate nearest the preferences of the voter who has the most realistic chance of winning. The result is a tendency for minority parties in separate constituencies to be squeezed out. The Liberal Democrats seem to be particular beneficiaries: in constituencies where Labour has traditionally done badly, with large Conservative majorities, strategic Labour voters switch to the Liberal Democrat candidate; and, vice versa, where Conservatives are weak in strong Labour constituencies, strategic Conservative voters switch to the Liberal Democrats.

The rational strategy for the two leading parties is to exploit this by pacts with the Liberal Democrats in individual constituencies. But there are huge obstacles to this, not least the problem of persuading local activists to give up their chance of even a hopeless contest. Nevertheless, the parties as organizations have begun to adapt. The Liberal Democrats' adaptation is simplest: they concentrate

resources in constituencies where they are already in second place. On the part of Conservative and Labour the expectation that virtually all parliamentary constituencies will be fought inhibits this. Nevertheless, both parties now concentrate their national resources on groups of target winnable constituencies, leaving 'hopeless' constituencies relatively neglected.

## Electors and democracy in Britain: citizens or shoppers?

Competitive elections are central to British democracy. Historically, the struggle to establish democratic politics in Britain was dominated by the struggle to create a democratic franchise – to create an electorate that included virtually the whole adult population. In recent decades the democratic significance of elections in Britain has grown, if only because the range of electoral opportunities has widened. As recently as 30 years ago voters had only two opportunities to cast their vote: in local council and Westminster Parliament elections. But in the intervening three decades significant new voting opportunities have been created, and more will probably be created in the future. The opportunities include: the widened use of referendums to settle particular policy choices; new electoral opportunities in local government, notably to choose mayors; new electoral opportunities in the form of choices for membership of the devolved Assemblies; and the opportunity to elect members of the European Parliament. At the same time, what was once a highly uniform electoral system, dominated by the 'first past the post' method of selection, is now much more varied in the electoral systems used in different elections. All these developments can be seen as an expansion of the citizenship possibilities of voting.

However, the contribution of elections to democratic politics in Britain has also become more problematic. This partly reflects some healthy developments in British democracy. In particular, the growth of mass group campaigning, as documented in Chapters 9 and 16, means that citizens no longer rely so much on voting every three or four years to make their voices heard. But the power of elections to mobilize citizens democratically also seems to be waning. The new electoral opportunities are typically grasped by only a minority of voters. The poll that historically had shown great effectiveness in mobilizing voters – the UK-wide general election – dramatically lost its drawing power in the election of 2001 (for 2005's results, see Briefing 17.4).

The changing character of elections and the electorate in British democracy have also influenced the way voting behaviour is analyzed. In the 1960s and 1970s electoral analysts tended to view the voter as a social animal: as one moved by collective identities and group solidarity. Identification with party was pictured as a critical psychological mechanism shaping the vote, and consciousness of class interest as a critical source of group solidarity. These two features lay at the heart of the first great study of voting behaviour in Britain (Butler and Stokes 1974). But the waning of party identification and the weakening of class identity has helped shift the focus of electoral analysis to the individual voter as a calculating animal. The shift has also been encouraged by fashions in political science, notably the rise of 'rational actor' models of behaviour – models that idealize political men and women as moved in their

behaviour by close cost-benefit calculations of the consequences of choice. Thus the voter, once rooted in rooted in loyalty to class and party, now turns into a kind of 'shopper' in the electoral marketplace (see, for instance, Clarke *et al.* 2004; and also Debating Politics 17.1.)

## REVIEW

Four themes dominate this chapter:

1  The UK-wide general election is the 'kingpin' of the British system of elections, but it has been joined over recent decades by a variety of other electoral opportunities;
2  Although the franchise is formally virtually universal, allowing all adults to vote, in practice many are excluded from voting, and many more have withdrawn;
3  A wide range of social and economic factors helps to explain the pattern of electoral choice, but long-term change seems to be weakening what was once the overwhelming influence of occupational class on voting;
4  In consequence, voting is becoming less an affirmation of citizenship and more a form of political shopping.

## Further reading

Denver (2002) is authoritative, up-to-date, and wonderfully clear – ideal for the beginner. Butler and Stokes (1974) was the first great study of voting behaviour and set the intellectual agenda for decades. Clarke *et al.* (2004) introduce both survey evidence and political science models, in a subject which has been more subject to political science professionalization than most. Farrell (2001) is best on electoral systems.

# CHAPTER 18

# How leaders are selected

## AIMS

This chapter has the following aims:

❖ To explain the connections between leadership recruitment and the theory of British democracy

❖ To show that for elected office the political party remains the all-important gateway to the top

❖ To describe how elective office is being increasingly dominated by career politicians

❖ To summarize how two alternative methods to election – bureaucratic selection and patronage – work in Britain

❖ To assess how far leadership selection is done by merit, and discuss how far it should be meritocratic.

## Leadership recruitment and British democracy

Choosing and dismissing political leaders is one of the keys to any successful system of government, and countries (such as Britain) that claim to be democratic set themselves exacting standards. Choosing and dismissing political leaders is in modern Britain a largely peaceful business, though Northern Ireland is a partial exception to this generalization. Managing peaceful selection and dismissal of leaders is a great achievement, and just how great can be seen by glancing at less fortunate countries. Over large parts of the world, as our morning newspaper will usually confirm, people regularly lose their lives and are driven from their homes because they live in countries that are unable to choose and dismiss political leaders peacefully. But we take peaceful choice and dismissal for granted in Britain and demand more: that the people at large should determine who become their leaders; and that all of us, as citizens, should have a fair chance of realizing an ambition to reach the top in politics. No actual democracy fully meets these stiff standards, and there are often good reasons why this is so. But we should keep the ideal claims of democracy in mind in assessing leadership recruitment in Britain, and we will return to them at the close of this chapter. Some, though not all, theories of democracy entail views about the social structure of political leadership. In other words, it is thought to be a problem if, for example, democratic methods lead always to the selection of leaders from among those who are already rich and powerful. That is why the last main substantive section of this chapter looks at the social structure of leadership in Britain.

There is no single path to the top in Britain, any more than in any complex system of government. Indeed, one of the things we will discover is that over time the routes to the top seem to be becoming more diverse. But there are three main paths and they are each examined in this chapter.

● *Competitive election.* The best known is the method that is characteristically associated with democratic choice: selection for top positions as a result of competitive election. That is the route that the most publicly prominent political leaders – such as the prime minister and other members of the Cabinet – have to follow, although as we shall see the mechanism of election is mediated in a number of important ways.

● *Bureaucratic selection.* 'Bureaucracy' is a word with unfavourable connotations for many: it conjures up images of rigid, inflexible officialdom. But bureaucratic selection in its precise form has accompanied the development of democratic and accountable government in Britain. Bureaucratic selection means selection and promotion by merit or ability – as measured, for example, by success in a range of standard tests. It is an important method of selection in numerous large organizations in Britain, in both the public and private sector. It was developed in the second half of the nineteenth century as the characteristic method of selecting and promoting one key political group in Britain: the higher civil service that advises ministers on the making and imple-mentation of policy. It remains, we shall see, an important route to the top, and possibly one that is growing in importance.

● *Patronage.* This is one of the most important paths to the top in Britain, and also one of the most controversial. It is perfectly possible to achieve positions of great influence in British government without ever having contested an election, or passed any qualifying selection test, by virtue of being chosen by a powerful patron (see People in Politics 18.1). It is plain why this is also controversial: it is hard to fit with our notions of democratic selection.

Election, bureaucratic selection and patronage are the three main routes to the top in Britain. Notice some that are, by omission, assumed to be unimportant: buying office and inheriting office. Buying office is openly prohibited and, while there are often allegations that large donations to political parties are suspiciously connected to some appoint-ments, it is probable that purchase of office is rare. This is historically fairly novel. As recently as the early nineteenth century public office – for instance, in the armed forces – could be openly bought, and

## *People in politics*

### 18.1   PATRONAGE: HOW TO GET TO THE TOP WITHOUT FIGHTING ELECTIONS

Cartoons: Shaun Steele

**Lord Irvine of Lairg**, b. 1940; educated Glasgow and Cambridge Universities; barrister, then Deputy High Court Judge, 1957–97; Lord Chancellor, with seat in Cabinet, 1997–2003. A mentor of the Prime Minister (he gave him his first start as a young lawyer) he remained a trusted adviser, and was catapulted to the highest law office in the state, and a place in the Cabinet, by his protégé, Tony Blair, in 1997. As a peer he did not have to compete electorally for a seat in Parliament.

**Lord Falconer of Thoroton**, b. 1951; educated Cambridge University; barrister; created a peer 1997; successive ministerial posts, culminating in Lord Chancellor 2003 with responsibility for abolishing the office, reforming the system for the administration of justice and reforming the House of Lords with the aim of removing the remaining hereditary element. A close personal friend of the Prime Minister who appointed him to ministerial office in 1997. As a peer, he did not have to compete electorally for a seat in Parliament.

**Alistair Campbell**, b. 1957; educated Cambridge University; journalist 1980–, culiminating as political editor, *Daily Mirror*; Press Secretary to the Leader of the Opposition, 1994–7; Prime Minister's Official Spokesman, 1997–2001; Director of Communications Strategy, 2001–3. Recruited by Mr Blair when he became Leader of the Opposition, Campbell was probably the Prime Minister's closest adviser, 1997–2003, and one of the most powerful people in government.

➲   Many features unite these three figures: all went through an elite university, Cambridge; all made their career in the overlapping London worlds of media and law; all owed their career to the patronage of one figure, Tony Blair. But the most important commonality is that they show how, with a powerful patron, it is possible in Britain to ascend to high powerful office without either having to undergo either bureaucratic selection or democratic selection via competitive election.

it was widely assumed that the purchaser could expect a return on the investment. In other words, purchase and the corrupt enjoyment of office were directly connected. Until the secret ballot was introduced in 1872, bribing electors was a useful additional tactic in winning a parliamentary seat. The inheritance of office has taken longer to die out. Indeed, it still exists in a residual form in the hereditary monarchy, and even in the presence of a small group of hereditary peers in the House of

Lords. (See our discussion of Lords reform in Chapter 10.)

## Elections and leadership recruitment

Suppose you were asked by an ambitious young person for advice about starting off on a successful career as an elected politician. What is the best advice to give? The answer is actually fairly straightforward: get a university education; join a political party as soon as possible; forget any career other than politics; and get elected into office – preferably in the Westminster House of Commons – as young as possible.

We can put flesh on this general advice by considering the examples of the two most successful elected politicians in Britain in the last decade: Tony Blair, leader of the Labour party since 1994 and Prime Minister since 1997; and his Chancellor of the Exchequer, Gordon Brown, acknowledged to be the second most powerful figure in government by far and the longest-serving Chancellor of modern times.

At first glance these two look opposites. The Prime Minister, the leader of the party historically associated with the working class, was educated at Fettes (Scotland's most prestigious public school, commonly called the Scottish Eton) and St John's College Oxford, a college that is a by-word for wealth and privilege even by Oxford standards. His Chancellor looks much more like traditional Labour leadership material: the son of a Church of Scotland minister, educated at state schools and the University of Edinburgh.

In fact the two have a huge amount in common and their commonalities provide clues to how to get to the top in Britain. Both have the formal mark of the modern middle-class professional: a university education. Even more important, both have been virtually nothing in their adult lives but professional politicians. Though Blair was briefly was a lawyer, and Brown briefly a university teacher and television researcher, these were just waiting rooms before they entered full-time politics as members of the House of Commons. Both did so – coinciden-

tally at the same general election, 1983 – while still in their early thirties. Both were hugely active in the Labour party and focused on a parliamentary career by their early twenties, Brown indeed a little earlier as an undergraduate. Both were elected for seats with large Labour majorities, making their place in Parliament secure from any temporary dip in their party's wider electoral fortunes.

Of all the different advice the examples of Blair and Brown would suggest to the politically ambitious, one is overwhelmingly important: join a political party. In the electoral route to the top in Britain parties provide the only realistic route. Until recently, the advice could have been even more exact: join the Labour or Conservative parties. As we know from our discussion of devolved government and local government (Chapters 11 and 12) these two parties do not quite monopolize leadership as much as they once did. But wherever we look for the obvious sources of political leadership that are the result of election – in the Westminster Parliament, in the new Welsh Assembly, in the Scottish Parliament – we find them dominated by people with party labels. And although we will see later that a few of the top positions – for example, in the Cabinet in London – are occupied by people who have ascended by other means, such as patronage (see People in Politics 18.1), most of the top positions are dominated by people who began their ascent by winning elections under party colours. This is why, in examining paths to the top, we have to start with election to Parliament.

### Pathways to the Westminster Parliament

As we saw in earlier chapters there is considerable doubt as to whether individual backbench members of the Westminster Parliament exercise any significant influence over how Britain is governed. But these doubts do not deter large numbers of aspirants wanting to become MPs, and the single most important reason is that further success in political life is heavily dependent on being a member of Parliament – indeed of the House of Commons. The very top of the political ladder – the Cabinet – is dominated by MPs; it is now over a century since a prime minister was drawn from beyond the House

**POLITICAL ISSUES**

### 18.1    'TONY'S CRONIES': PERSONAL CONNECTIONS AND PUBLIC POLICY

'Tony's cronies' was a critical phrase that tripped off many tongues after the return of Labour to office in 1997. It referred to the supposed ease with which those enjoying personal connections to the new prime minister achieved positions of power and influence, or were able to shape policies in their own interests. It grew out of two very different features. First, the Prime Minister had a temperamental preference for direct personal dealings over working through formal structures. As Prime Minister, from the very beginning Tony Blair preferred to do business by informal meetings with small groups rather than through formally constituted committees: it played to his great strength in managing people. But a second feature was more institutional: the scale of prime ministerial patronage was large, and growing. The personalities profiled in People in Politics 18.1 are only the tip of the patronage iceberg. What is more, there were often striking connections – sometimes based on kinship and marriage – between those appointed to jobs under New Labour. Polemical journalism (see Cohen 2003) reinforced this with the argument that government policies, and even contracts, were suspiciously connected to donations to the Labour Party and direct access to the Prime Minister.

The 'personalization' involved in the phrase 'Tony's cronies' concealed important wider issues.

■ Surrounding himself with friends and acquaintances gave the Blair premiership the air of a 'court' around a monarch. But all prime ministers have created a court of this kind: the very pressures of the job mean that they only feel able to survive with friendly faces who can be trusted because their own personal ambitions do not challenge those of the prime minister.

■ The Blair premiership coincided with profound changes in the way patronage was exercised in British government, forcing appointments to be made more openly and impersonally (see Briefing 18.4). The 'issue' therefore may be less about Blair's style than the era in which he practised that style.

■ Individuals have always used their connections at the top to try to extract personal favours and concessions for the interests to which they are aligned. But this was made more pronounced under Blair by the huge growth in the professionally organized lobbying industry (see Chapter 9) and by the weakening of Labour's links with its main block of interests historically, the trade unions.

of Commons (Lord Salisbury, Prime Minister 1885–6, 1886–92, 1895–1902). Serving in the Scottish Executive and the Welsh Cabinet also demands election to the Parliament and Assembly respectively.

So it is here that the importance of party starts, for it is virtually impossible to enter either the House of Commons, or their Scottish and Welsh counterparts, without possessing a party label. (For more on the new national assemblies, see below.)

And while, as we saw in Chapter 17, on elections, voters are increasingly volatile in the choices they make, in practice a party's nomination for a seat is in the overwhelming majority of cases a guarantee of a seat in the Commons: in the last two Westminster parliaments there has been only one 'independent' MP elected for a constituency on the British mainland.

This makes the nomination and selection process, especially in the Labour and Conservative

Parties, a critical first step in making a political career. Both major parties operate with a centrally approved list of candidates. This list is centrally controlled and acts as a filter allowing the party nationally to rule out undesirables, whether on grounds of ideology or personal character. But the really important choices for the Westminster Parliament are still made by the parties in the individual constituencies. The party activists make these choices. There are some variations in method between the parties, but in most cases a short list of possible candidates is drawn up, usually by some executive committee of the constituency party. Those on the short list are then usually presented to an open meeting of members of the constituency party. Nominees normally deliver a short speech, and answer questions. The process puts a high premium on two things: public presentation and back-stage manoeuvring. On the day, it advantages those who have the ability to speak convincingly and to respond at short notice and at short length; but the nomination is very often sewn up before the big day, because the other quality that can clinch things is the ability to find supporters and patrons, especially in the leading members of the party. Even though there is now a strong expectation that anyone with parliamentary ambitions will first fight a hopeless seat, nevertheless parties with no chance of winning often find it difficult to find a reasonably competent candidate. In these cases a novice can still turn up and win on the day with a good public performance without having powerful connections. However, in safe seats the big day is always preceded by lots of lobbying and the making of connections.

This account holds in broad outline for how candidate selection to the Westminster Parliament works, although subtle but important differences between the parties have developed in recent years. In particular, candidate selection in the Labour party is more under central control than in the Conservative party, where local activists jealously guard their traditional control of the process. In 2002 the Labour government passed legislation allowing the imposition of women-only short lists (previous attempts had been ruled contrary to anti-discrimination legislation: see Briefing 18.1). This is

# Briefing    18.1

## WOMEN-ONLY SHORTLISTS

All the leading parties are committed to increasing the proportion of women parliamentary candidates, especially in winnable seats. Promotion, mentoring and training have all been tried, with modest results. The Labour party is the only leading party to try to change things by women-only short lists, which of course guarantee the selection of women as parliamentary candidates. An earlier attempt in the 1990s by the party to introduce women-only short lists was struck down after a successful challenge in the courts, the argument being that the practice breached anti-discrimination law. The Sex Discrimination (Election Candidates) Act 2002 removed this obstacle. It allows parties to introduce women-only short lists, to introduce special gender awareness training for party selection committees, and to introduce women-only training for potential women candidates and women's networks. The measure has often encountered strong local resistance: in the 2005 general election a male independent Labour candidate overturned a 19,000 official Labour majority in a South Wales seat in a protest against a woman official Labour candidate selected from an all-woman shortlist.

➲ The case of women-only short lists is important in its own right, but it also encapsulates a wider issue in selection for political office: how far should selection be made by some criteria of individual merit, irrespective of class, gender or ethnicity, and how far is the job of political selection to promote the political representation of some social groups?

a sign of a wider interest among the national Labour leadership in 'engineering' candidate selection. The reasons for this move have been various. As the 2002 legislation shows, one important aim has been to alter the gender make-up of the candidates' group and thus of Labour MPs – an aim shared by the Conservative leadership, but much more effectively accomplished because of greater central control over the process. In other instances, Labour has successfully engineered selection to head off the likelihood of adoption of potentially embarrassing or ideologically troublesome candidates, and to ensure the selection of candidates favoured by the national leadership.

Securing a safe seat in the House of Commons – the prerequisite for a political career at the apex of British politics – therefore demands persistence: willingness to fight a hopeless seat first; and spending time cultivating local supporters or a powerful patron at the top of the party. It is best to start young because, as we shall now see, entering the Commons before the age of 40 at a minimum is important to making it to the top in politics.

## Pathways to the front bench

The 'front bench', as we saw in Chapter 10, is where the members of the government, and their 'shadows' on the opposition benches, face each other in the Westminster parliament; it has become a widely used short-hand symbol for the Westminster Parliamentary leadership of the two parties. The most important frontbenchers of all are the (usually 20 or so) members of the House of the Commons who are in the Cabinet. In addition, government appoints up to an additional 80 ministers of various ranks. (As we see below, a small number of Cabinet members and of other ministers is drawn from the House of Lords.) Getting into government, and finally into the Cabinet, is for most MPs the whole point of a political career. Increasingly, it is precisely that: a career. In the fairly recent past there were many MPs who combined being an MP with other careers (for example, in business and the law), but the most successful politicians now – as with Mr Blair and Mr Brown, profiled above – have been full-time politicians for almost all their adult lives.

In fact, once a politician has managed to get into the Commons, the odds on getting a front bench position shorten dramatically. Even a government with a large parliamentary presence – as Labour had after both the 1997 and 2001 general elections – has to fill around 100 jobs. So even if the selection were random, the odds – with over 400 Labour MPs – would be close to four to one. But it is not random. A sizeable minority is already ruled out of selection by a mixture of considerations: their private lives are too chaotic, perhaps through drinking or shady business dealings, to risk entrusting them with a job; they have been tried in the past and found too incompetent; they are too old (it is now rare for any member of the Commons to be appointed to a first-time job after their mid-50s); they have powerful enemies at the top of the party, either because of their political views or because of some personal feud.

A prime minister forming a government therefore has even fewer options than the bare arithmetic of parliamentary numbers suggests, but other considerations also restrict choice. As we will see in a moment, at the level of the most important part of the front bench – the Cabinet and the Shadow Cabinet – at least party leaders work from close personal knowledge, but in filling the most junior ranks a prime minister will have to rely on others for advice and talent spotting. The Whips – who maintain discipline in the parliamentary parties and generally manage them – are very important in talent spotting. Many a successful career is started by catching a Whip's ear through a good speech in the chamber, a useful intervention in a committee, or a favour done: for instance, by asking a minister a helpful parliamentary question.

Apart from being hemmed in by lack of direct knowledge of many of the more junior candidates, prime ministers also have to 'balance' their selection; they cannot appoint on simple competence alone. Increasingly the make-up of governments is scrutinized, and criticized, for its gender and ethnic balance, the balance between different regions' representatives, and the balance between different factions in the party. Balancing factions is also linked to appeasing powerful rivals to the party leader. Ambitious junior MPs get ahead by acquiring a powerful patron (hitching their careers to a leading figure in the Cabinet, for instance). It is well documented that there have been avowed 'Brownites' promoted of necessity by Mr Blair as Prime Minister because of their powerful patron, the Chancellor. Since these powerful figures are always on the look-out for supporters – either to boost their status generally, or with an eye to a future contest for the party leadership – the network of patron and client is very important in all the parliamentary parties.

One lesson of this is that the business of picking front-benchers is a business full of chance and personal considerations, heavily shaped by the intense political life of the quite small communities that compose parliamentary parties. This mix of chance and personality is even more important in the bigger promotion: to the Cabinet.

## Pathways to the top: entering the Cabinet

A minority of Cabinet members is drawn from the House of Lords, but most come from the ruling party in the Commons and it is very rare for someone to be promoted directly to the Cabinet from the backbenches. In the promotion from a junior ministerial job many factors are at work. Since the Cabinet is a small group the prime minister will be able to rely heavily on direct knowledge of individuals, rather than, as in the case of the many junior posts in government, having to take advice from Whips or from powerful Cabinet colleagues pushing the claims of their clients. Getting into a Cabinet, and staying there, depends on a mixture of competence and luck (see Documenting Politics 18.1). But the competence needed to be a Cabinet minister is fairly specialized, and we got a glimpse of it in our account in Chapter 7 of life in the core executive. Almost everyone around a Cabinet table will be pretty intelligent, but brains are not the most important qualification for the job. Those who get right to the top will have enormous stamina, self-belief and ambition. Physically, the life of a Cabinet minister is punishing: the working day is spent in a hectic round of meetings, private and public. Paperwork – contained in the 'red boxes' into which by tradition civil servants put the papers to be read by ministers – is heavy and usually has to be dealt with in the late evening or early morning. A Cabinet minister constantly has to perform in a very wide range of settings: in official meetings, from Cabinet committee downwards, where the Department's interests and values have to promoted, often in fierce competition from equally self-confident and ambitious Cabinet colleagues; in debates and questions in the House of Commons, where the minis-

ter is constantly attacked by the Opposition, and often from the government side; and, increasingly important, on television and radio where interviewers now commonly see their job as being to cross-examine ministers in as aggressive a manner as possible.

A Cabinet minister will thus often start the day at the crack of dawn trying to catch up with paperwork while being driven to the office in the ministerial car; will have not a moment of free time during the day, moving rapidly between high-level appointments (most of which involve intense argument); will often have an official dinner or reception with a set piece speech to make in the evening; and can end up at 11 o'clock, while the rest of us are sipping our bed-time cocoa, being aggressively cross-examined by Jeremy Paxman on BBC2's *Newsnight*. The minister may then have to work for a couple of hours on ministerial papers at home to prepare for the next day's round. Any weakness – a shred of self-doubt, a physical illness – will soon be magnified by this life. To enter and survive in the Cabinet, it helps to be clever; but it is essential to be hugely self-confident, limitlessly ambitious, and have the physical stamina of a brewery dray horse.

Even all this is not enough: plenty of politicians with these qualities never get off the backbenches, or do not survive a Cabinet reshuffle. By the time the very top is reached in politics chance plays an important role. Prime ministers choose Cabinets not just by the personal qualities of colleagues, but on a host of other grounds: they need to balance the different factions in their party, and increasingly to seek some balance on lines of gender and region; they want to have their own allies in Cabinet, but also have to give jobs to powerful rivals, many of whom are potential candidates for the job of prime minister itself. Once in, a Cabinet career can be destroyed by bad-luck: the career of Chris Smith, who served four years in the first Labour Cabinet from 1997, and then disappeared into the obscurity of the backbenches, never recovered from his Department's responsibility for the disastrous project to build a Millennium Dome in London, even though he only inherited the project. Personal foibles also often destroy careers. Top politicians tend to be extrovert risk takers, and are likely to get

**DOCUMENTING POLITICS 18.1**

## AN UNUSUAL RESIGNATION: ESTELLE MORRIS'S RESIGNATION LETTER TO THE PRIME MINISTER, OCTOBER 2002

'Dear Tony,

I am writing to confirm my wish to resign as Secretary of State.

As I explained when I came to see you yesterday morning, I am proud of the role I have played in the Government, both as Schools Minister and as Secretary of State. In many ways, I feel I have achieved more in the first job than I have in the second. I've learned what I'm good at and also what I'm less good at. I'm good at dealing with the issues and in communicating to the teaching profession. I am less good at strategic management of a huge department and I am not good at dealing with the modern media. All this has meant that with some of the recent situations I have been involved in, I have not felt I have been as effective as I should be, or as effective as you need me to be.

You were kind enough to say you wanted me to think about it further overnight and be absolutely sure that this is what I want to do. I have done so, and it is.

I will look back with real pride at the role I have played in helping to raise standards in literacy and numeracy in primary schools, in the reform programme we now have for secondary schools, and indeed at all levels of education; and perhaps above all the enhanced status of the teaching profession. But I feel this is the right decision for me, and for the Government.

I also want to thank you personally for giving me the chance to serve in the Cabinet and also for being so considerate and understanding.

I believe passionately in what this Labour Government is trying to do and I will continue to support you in whatever way I can.

Best wishes,

Estelle Morris'

➲ Estelle Morris was Secretary of State for Education – the ministerial head of the Department – when in 2002 she created a minor sensation by sending the resignation letter reproduced above. The sensation lay in the grounds given for resigning: a feeling that, while she had been effective in a more junior post in the Department, she was not able to cope with the larger demands of being Secretary of State. Her reaction came during a period of intense criticism of her role, though no more intense than that commonly experienced by Cabinet ministers. In a profession where self-confidence is widespread, and where the public admission of any weakness or doubt is discouraged, it was an unusually frank declaration. Within a year of resignation she was back in the government, in a more junior, non-Cabinet role as Minister for the Arts; but retired from the Commons in 2005.

into more scrapes than, say, the average timid university professor. In recent times Cabinet resignations have more often happened because of these personal scrapes than because of policy failure. They include resignations for having a pregnant mistress; making love to a mistress while wearing a Chelsea football kit (allegedly); taking a huge secret loan from a colleague to buy a house; being robbed on a London common while allegedly cruising in the search for gay sex: all despite the fact that not a single one of these activities (not even wearing a Chelsea kit!) is illegal.

## Pathways to the top: becoming Prime Minister

Prime ministers require in abundance all the qualities demanded of Cabinet ministers, and an even more generous helping of luck to get to the top job (see Briefing 18.2). In the Westminster system for over a century now they have had to be leader of one of the two main parties, and for over 80 years the job has alternated between the leader of the Labour and Conservative parties. Though these are no longer quite as securely dominant as in the past, the best advice for the ambitious youngster wanting to end up as prime minister is probably still to join either Labour or the Conservatives.

The 'job description' for a prime minister is daunting. A necessary, but not sufficient condition, in modern times has been to achieve leadership of either the Conservative or Labour parties and, as we will see in the next section, doing that demands the support of an increasingly wide range of interests in their party. Prime ministers often get the job while their party is already in government. This was the case, for example, with Harold Macmillan (1957), James Callaghan (1976) and John Major (1990). But to hold on to the office they have both to win general elections, and to convince their party that they can continue winning. This last condition is critical. Mrs Thatcher, for instance, led the Conservative party to victory in every general election she fought (1979, 1983, 1987; see also Image 18.1). Yet three years after winning a landslide for the Conservatives in 1987 she was deposed in 1990 by MPs who feared that she would not be able to repeat the trick a fourth time.

Once in the job, the qualities demanded are a magnified version of those required of a Cabinet minister. Most of the problems a prime minister deals with are insoluble. A prime minister has simultaneously to be able to think and argue about issues of great complexity; be skilled at personal relations and handling others with huge egos (including Cabinet colleagues and other foreign political leaders); be able to take life and death decisions, and then move on quickly (every British Prime Minister since 1979 has had to fight a war somewhere); be good at every imaginable form of public presentation, from the set piece speech to an aggressive interview at the hands of a television or radio journalist. A prime minister who cannot excel at all this on a tiny amount of sleep is lost. Surrounded by supporters and courtiers, the prime minister is nevertheless also subject to a barrage of criticism. Several close Cabinet colleagues will usually think they could do the job better and will be waiting for an opportunity to depose their leader. The job is all-consuming, usually demanding attention for at least 18 hours a day, seven days a week. A prime minister who cannot perform at top level after a few hours' sleep will not survive. And finally, every bit of private life is increasingly scrutinized. Where prime ministers spend their holidays is argued over in the newspapers, and the immediate family dragged into the spotlight. Being prime minister is hard. Being the spouse or the child of a prime minister can be a nightmare: every personal foible, or even something as trivial as dress style, is jeered at by journalists and political opponents.

Even for the most ambitious, self-confident, tough and able politician, walking into 10 Downing Street as prime minister also demands a large helping of luck (see Briefing 18.2). Every British prime minister since 1979 has arrived unexpectedly, helped by chance. Mrs Thatcher quite unexpectedly became Conservative leader in 1975 (the precondition of becoming prime minister four years later) ahead of several better placed candidates, after her predecessor Mr Heath was destroyed by electoral failure. Mr Major emerged from obscurity in 1990, helped mostly by feuding at the top of the government which removed more likely successors to Mrs Thatcher. Mr Blair became Labour leader (and inherited Labour's electoral triumph in 1997) because of the early death from a heart attack of his predecessor in 1994. This accidental unexpected quality helps explain the rise of a 'non-standard' figure such as John Major, a school failure and the son of a circus performer. The one thing we can be sure of in speculating about future prime ministers is that, if we try to guess who the next prime minister will be, still less the next prime minister but one, we will almost certainly guess wrong.

# Briefing

18.2

## THE IMPORTANCE OF LUCK: HOW PRIME MINISTERS REACHED THE TOP, 1945–2004

| Prime Minister | Critical event that led to No. 10 |
| --- | --- |
| Clement Attlee (1945–51) | Leader of victorious Labour party in 1945; originally became leader in the 1930s when huge electoral defeats removed stronger Labour leadership candidates from Parliament. |
| Winston Churchill (1951–5) | An excoriated outsider for most of the 1930s, he originally became Prime Minister and Leader of the Conservatives because of the great war crisis of 1940. |
| Anthony Eden (1955–7) | A rare case of the 'heir apparent' succeeding to the job. |
| Harold Macmillan (1957–63) | Emerged from an informal process of consultation when the expected successor, R.A. Butler, was found to have too many enemies at the top. |
| Alec Douglas-Home (1963–4) | Emerged as totally unexpected winner from a mysterious and secretive process to choose the leader of the ruling Conservative Party. |
| Harold Wilson (1964–70) | Leader of ruling Labour party, from 1963, elected when the party's leader, Hugh Gaitskell, died unexpectedly after an apparently routine operation. |
| Edward Heath (1970–4) | Won leadership of Conservative party in 1965 in first open election for office; led Conservatives to unexpected victory in 1970 general election. |
| Harold Wilson (1974–6) | Unexpectedly returned to office in general election of February 1974. |
| James Callaghan (1976–9) | Won election for leadership of Labour party after sudden, unexpected resignation of Harold Wilson. |
| Margaret Thatcher (1979–90) | Won general election as leader of Conservatives in 1979; elected as Conservative leader in 1975 as 'dark horse' candidate ahead of more senior and powerful candidates. |
| John Major (1990–7) | Elected as Conservative leader and prime minister after Mrs Thatcher deposed by backbenchers. Another 'dark horse' who came through the field late in the day when better known candidates failed. |
| Tony Blair (1997–) | Elected as Labour Leader in landslide victory of general election 1997. In 1992 was a middle-ranking member of the Shadow Cabinet. Labour's unexpected loss of 1992 general election led to resignation of Neil Kinnock as Leader; in 1994, his successor died of a heart attack. Blair inherited a virtually impregnable Labour lead in the polls. |

➲ Politics is often now spoken of as a career, and it is indeed becoming more professionalized. But right at the top luck (including other people's bad luck) plays a huge role in deciding who gets into 10 Downing Street as prime minister. Though many of these prime ministers first entered the door of Number 10 as leaders of a victorious party in a general election, even most of these owed their leadership of the party to chance circumstances, often emerging quite unexpectedly as leader. Just about the only example in this list of an orderly expected succession involved Anthony Eden succeeding Winston Churchill in 1955 – and he lasted less than two years, destroyed by the catastrophically failed attempt to invade Egypt to control the Suez Canal in 1956. Another way of reading this table is as a study in how prime ministers lose office. We might expect, in a democracy, that prime ministers would vacate office on loss of a general election. But that is true of only six of the twelve postwar prime ministers: Attlee (1951), Douglas-Home (1964), Wilson (1970), Heath (1974), Callaghan (1979) and Major (1997). A 'palace coup' of the sort that toppled Mrs Thatcher is just as popular a way of ejecting prime ministers.

## Elective paths to leadership: changing trends

We now have a snapshot of the elected paths to the top in British politics, at least in the Westminster system, but these paths naturally evolve over time. Three changes are particularly important, especially the first since it is indeed modifying the significance of the Westminster route.

### Widening range of routes to the top

Until very recently getting to the top in British politics meant one thing: getting to the top in the Westminster system. This monopoly of political leadership is now being broken. The alternative of a political career in the European Parliament, though it does not compare in visibility with membership of the House of Commons, is increasingly attractive. It cannot lead to government position, but the pay and conditions are at least as good as Westminster, the opportunities to fiddle expenses greater, the burden of constituency case-work lighter, and the scrutiny powers of the European Parliament are steadily growing. Membership of the European Commission (there were two Britons, now reduced to one) is highly influential and very well rewarded. It is in practice in the gift of the British government and is presently occupied by those who fail to make it to the very top at Westminster, a consolation prize for missing out on ministerial office. It probably should therefore be considered part of the 'patronage' route to office examined below.

More significant alternatives still have been opened up by the devolution measures introduced by the government after 1997. The Scottish Parliament and Executive, and the Welsh Assembly and Cabinet, now offer alternative careers to anything available in the Westminster system, both as parliamentarians and as ministers. An equally significant development, as we saw in earlier chapters, is that both these systems of government have broken the hold enjoyed for nearly a century in Westminster by the Labour and Conservative parties: both have operated coalitions, and the electoral systems at work in Wales and Scotland suggest

**Image 18.1**
**The political leader as icon: the case of Margaret Thatcher**

Photo: Chris Young/PA/EMPICS

⮕ The photo shows Margaret Thatcher with the leader of the Conservative Party at the start of 2005, Michael Howard. Mrs Thatcher (leader, 1975–90) was an iconic figure for Conservatives: instantly recognisable; provoking admiration and hatred in almost equal amounts; hugely successful electorally; and the definer of a brand of Conservative ideology, 'Thatcherism'. Her four successors (Major, Hague, Duncan Smith and Howard) have all struggled in the giant shadow she cast. Howard recovered some of the party's parliamentary (but not its popular) fortunes in the 2005 general election, but not sufficient to retain the leadership. Yet another Conservative leader now has to try to escape the Thatcher shadow.

that coalition will be common in future. Finally, the introduction of directly elected mayors may diversify routes to the top even more. London already has a directly elected mayor in Ken Livingstone, an independent who deserted the Labour party, successfully defied it to win the popular contest, and then had to be reinvited back into the party on his own terms.

These diversified routes to the top are also exerting complex effects on the role of political parties in leadership selection. As we noted, in Wales and Scotland they are destroying the two-party Conservative/Labour domination that has marked Westminster for over 80 years. The pattern in the admittedly still small number of communities that have opted for an elected mayor also suggests that the elective mayoralty may become a career route that offers a real alternative to the monopoly of the established parties: non-party 'mavericks' seem to have a better chance of success than in the Westminster Parliament. But conversely, the election systems used in the European Parliament, and in the devolved national institutions, strengthen national party control over the chances of election, weaken constituency influence, and thus diminish the chances of returning members prepared to act independently of party.

## Widening range of selectors

An increasingly wide range of people is becoming involved in picking political leaders in Britain. The most important change we documented in Chapter 14: choosing the individual national political leaders. As shown in that chapter, Labour first involved members in leadership election in the early 1980s, the Conservatives late in the 1990s. The Liberals pioneered the widening of this franchise, electing David Steel through an electoral college representing all constituency associations as long ago as 1977. Now all three parties give a big say to individual members through secret ballot.

## Professionalization

The third and final trend is affecting all politicians, but especially those at the top of the Westminster and the devolved systems. *Professionalization* means that politicians who want to get to the top have to treat it as a lifetime career. The most successful (such as Tony Blair) have really never had another serious job: they enter Parliament young and their pre-Parliament job is either just to mark time or is directly linked to politics (for example, as a political adviser or researcher). A route that existed a generation ago in both the Conservative and Labour parties, carving out a successful career in business or in trade unionism before entering Parliament, has now almost disappeared. As a reflection of this shift, the real pay of politicians has been rising over the years. MPs, for instance, were first paid only in 1911, an annual salary of £400;

now the pay of a backbencher matches that of a very well paid professional, has numerous 'perks' for expenses, and a generous, non-contributory pension scheme. The professionalization of politics does not mean that politicians rely on their political income alone. The pay of an MP compares well with that of a university professor or a GP, but has nothing like the job security of these professions: redundancy and obscurity beckon at every general election. MPs supplement their salaries by lucrative short-term work: directorships and consultancies, where the MP is in effect a lobbyist for an economic interest; journalism; and speaking engagements, where the rewards for good speakers can be high. But this kind of work is very different from the kind of independent career common a generation ago; it is an extension of political professionalism.

## Leadership recruitment: the bureaucratic path

The higher ranks of the civil service, in the Westminster and the devolved systems, exert great influence over policy. Top civil servants do not enjoy the public recognition of politicians, but for a clever, ambitious 20-something, a career in the civil service is probably a more certain route to power and influence than running for elected office, with all the uncertainties described above. It also offers much more job security and, at the very top (for example, as the head of a civil service department) the financial rewards are better than those at the top in politics. In the most prestigious departments, such as the Treasury, exercising significant influence over policy need not indeed wait until the top has been reached. The Treasury is small and collegial in its working methods, and officials at formally junior levels often have access to the most important policy-making discussions.

Although changes are constantly taking place in the formal structure of the civil service, the bureaucratic route to influence has not fundamentally altered since the civil service was reorganized in the second half of the nineteenth century. These original reforms were designed to eliminate selection and promotion by personal connection and political favouritism. Under various guises since then the service has had a 'fast stream', recruits who normally enter in their early twenties and who are marked out for rapid promotion to the top (see Briefing 18.3). Most of those in the fast stream can expect by their fifties to be at a level where they are playing a large part in advising ministers and directing the implementation of policy, both of these being activities that confer great influence. A minority can expect to become Permanent Secretaries – the highest grade – heading a department and acting as the main adviser and close confidant of ministers. They always exit from these posts at the age of 60, when they can expect to have an active retirement supplementing a gener-

ous pension with lucrative company directorships or membership of quangos, exploiting the expertize and contacts built up during their working lives.

This is an attractive route to the top, avoiding many of the stresses and uncertainties of the elected route. Competition, especially to enter the fast stream, is intense; but the gate of entry is so narrow that, once in, competition is much less intense. Fast-stream applicants are virtually guaranteed a long career of rising influence. Most successful applicants will have enjoyed great success in formal education: until recently Oxford and Cambridge graduates dominated those recruited, and graduates of the leading universities are still disproportionately represented. This is hardly surprising because the

## Briefing                                                                        18.3

### THE BUREAUCRATIC PATH: THE CIVIL SERVICE SELECTION BOARD (CSSB) PROCEDURE FOR 'FAST STREAM' APPOINTMENTS

'Fast-stream' appointments to the civil service are the most desirable: they give early access to roles in providing policy advice to ministers, and mark appointees out for rapid promotion, culminating in the most senior civil service posts. Entrants are mostly new, or nearly new, graduates. The selection procedure is a refined version of 'bureaucratic' selection according to criteria which attempt to select impersonally – by marks of ability independent of any considerations of background or connection. Over the decades CSSB has refined the process into a three stage routine:

● First: a qualifying test which anyone can complete on-line. Candidates who meet a qualifying standard are then invited to the second stage.
● Second: a computer administered qualifying test consisting of three aptitude tests, taken at a regional centre and normally lasting about 3.5 hours. Candidates who meet a qualifying standard are shortlisted for the third stage.
● Third: short-listed candidates invited to a two-day assessment centre, run by the Civil Service Selection Board, involving written and group exercises, and interviews.

From this final group are drawn those offered fast-stream appointments. Some who narrowly miss the final offer are offered other posts in the service.

*Source*: Information from www.faststream.gov.uk

● The Civil Service Selection Board procedure, notably the third stage above, used to be widely caricatured as the 'country house weekend' method, in which it was often argued that candidates were being chosen by the social graces they displayed during the period of the selection exercise. Whether true or not, the Civil Service over the years has tried hard to move as close as possible to a 'bureaucratic', impersonal model of selection. How far methods of selection that emphasize the sort of skills tested by such methods as group exercises contain inherent cultural biases goes to the heart of the argument about what the civil service is, and should be, looking for in selecting the future administrative elite.

selection process advantages the academically gifted. The first stage and second stages involve a battery of written tests; the third and final stage a series of interviews and role-playing exercises, all of which are suited to the quick witted, the socially confident, and those educated at elite universities where education still relies heavily on small group discussions.

The method of recruitment reminds us that the civil service is a bureaucracy, because this kind of formally impersonal selection by some measure of ability is one of the classic marks of a bureaucracy. Promotion too depends heavily on these qualities. Top civil servants have to be able to do three things to a high standard: master the essence of a subject quickly, because they are generalists offering ministers advice about a wide range of issues; write quickly, clearly and concisely because a large part of the job is writing briefing papers for ministers who want rapid, easy-to-assimilate documents; and put views across orally, since much of a civil servant's life is spent in meetings, formal and informal.

These skills are akin to those of a lawyer, a journalist or possibly a university teacher. They are different, for instance, from the skills often required in business, such as the ability to sell, or to manage complex projects in a hands-on manner. The kind of skills needed to work in the prime minister's private office are very different from those required in managing a large scale building project such as constructing a new hospital or a bridge. Whether civil servants need these latter skills is at the heart of the long debate about the competence of higher civil servants, as discussed in Chapter 8. The 'hiving off' of agencies described in that chapter, following the Next Steps Initiative, was in part an attempt to value these latter skills more highly. Daily management of the Prison Service, or of the benefit system, does demand the ability to manage administrative operations of high social and technical complexity. Indeed, the creation of the Next Steps agencies has also involved some direct recruitment of top managers from the private sector.

As we saw in Chapter 8, the wisdom of creating agencies in this fashion is the subject of debate. But leaving aside these debates, the separation between department and agency has had one possibly unintended effect: it has actually made more valuable the traditional skills of the civil servant, for it has removed from departments the very tasks – managing delivery of administratively and technically complex policies – that stretched traditionally skilled civil servants. As the higher civil service specializes more and more in policy advice and strategic thinking, the traditional skills – intelligent quick wit, the ability to write and speak fluently – become even more important. The traditional bureaucratic route to the top thus remains largely unaltered.

## Leadership recruitment: patronage and networking

'Patronage' means selection for a position because one is a client, a favourite or a political ally of those who have the position in their gift. It can be contrasted with selection by some formal measures of ability (the method used for civil service entry) or competitive election. It has always been important in Britain and is becoming more so. It is becoming more important for three reasons. First, at the very heart of the constitution the reform of the House of Lords has now virtually abolished one traditional method of getting to the top, inheritance of an aristocratic title. Although the reform of the House of Lords is not complete, entry now is largely an act of patronage, principally by the leaders of the three major political parties in the Westminster system. Second, government both nationally and locally has increasingly resorted to a wide range of specialized agencies to carry out its functions. Some idea of the scale of this can be gained by looking at Table 18.1. Third, government increasingly relies on task forces and advisory groups to help it formulate policy, and membership of these task forces, often put together at short notice, is another important 'patronage' route to positions of influence.

Agencies, task forces and advisory groups of the sort covered in Table 18.1 are staffed by official appointment. 'Official appointment' here covers many forms. The most sensitive top positions – appointing the chair of a major public body such as the chair of the Governors of the BBC – rests heavily on personal knowledge among small groups

---

**Table 18.1**   The scale of patronage in British government (numbers of appointments available, 2001–3)

| Appointment | Number |
|---|---|
| Parliament (the reformed House of Lords, inc. hereditaries, law lords, archbishops and bishops) | 690 |
| Board members of executive and advisory non-departmental bodies, public corporations, etc. (central and devolved government) | 21,901 |
| Task forces, ad hoc advisory bodies, policy reviews | 1,895 |
| The courts (the judiciary throughout the UK; lay JPs, etc., except for district court service in Scotland) | 29,338 |
| Members of non-departmental public bodies/tribunals (not of social security and employment tribunals, etc.) | 11,572 |
| NHS (health authorities, primary care trusts, NHS trusts, other NHS bodies, commissions and tribunals) | 4,591 |
| Local public spending bodies (registered social landlords, training and enterprize bodies, board members of higher and further education institutions) | 47,647 |
| Local partnerships (statutory and on local authority initiative)* | 75,000 (est.) |
| Prison service (members of Boards of Visitors) | 2,002 |
| School governors** | 381,500 |

\* Members are elected to a few neighbourhood regeneration boards alongside appointed and co-opted members.
\*\* Includes parent governors who are elected to governing bodies alongside other categories of member.

*Source*: Select Committee on Public Administration (2003: Table 1).

➲ The table is taken from one of the latest in a series of investigations by the House of Commons Select Committee on Public Administration into the scale of appointed office in British government: into patronage, as used in this chapter. Not all these offices by any means are in the gift of the Westminster executive, never mind the prime minister. Not all are equally important, as will be obvious. But they do emphasize that the 'patronage' route to office is important whether we think of the importance of the jobs in question, or of the sheer scale of the appointment system.

---

of top people. Boastful self-promotion; getting a track record by already serving on successful bodies; being personally known to the right people; making the right political alliances; all these are important. But as the range of bodies to be filled has increased vastly, government has had to systematize the process. Dissatisfaction with the lack of transparency in the appointment process led the Committee on Standards in Public Life – a body encountered in Chapter 5 – to recommend new procedures and safeguards in the middle of the 1990s. The result is summarized in Briefing 18.4: the creation of the Office of the Commissioner for Public Appointments.

Patronage of the kind described here is fairly straightforward to chart because it ends up in formal appointment to top positions. There is, though, another route to the top that is more elusive, but nevertheless important. In summary it can be called 'networking': individuals exploit their personal skills, social contacts and organizational location to gain access to the very top level of government. Among the most effective networkers are 'fixers': figures who specialize in helping people at the top when they are, literally, in a fix, either because of a private or public problem. Lawyers tend to be among the most common 'fixers'. Ministers' lives mostly consist of one crisis after another, and they

# Briefing                                    18.4

## A LIMITED REFORM OF THE PATRONAGE SYSTEM: THE OFFICE OF THE COMMISSIONER FOR PUBLIC APPOINTMENTS

The Commissioner for Public Appointments was established in 1995 following recommendations of the Committee on Standards in Public Life. Appointment by the Crown is intended to signal independence of the Executive. The Commissioner is responsible for public appointments in England, and in the devolved administrations of Scotland, Wales and Northern Ireland. The Commissioner monitors, advises and reports on public appointments in health bodies, non-departmental public bodies (examples range from the Arts Council to the British Potato Council), public corporations, nationalized industries and the utility regulators. The Commissioner's jurisdiction covers over 11,000 public appointments. The Commissioner works mainly through a Code of Practice which stipulates a set of principles (such as appointment on merit, and openness in the appointment process).

*Source*: Information from www.ocpa.gov.uk

➲ The establishment of a Commissioner for Public Appointments was a response to the growth of patronage as a method of recruitment to public office, and is in effect an attempt to 'bureaucratize' the process: to subject it to a formal, standard procedure. The effect has been greatly to increase the openness of patronage appointments. But there remain two important restrictions: as the examples in People in Politics 18.1 show, at the very top the most politically sensitive appointments are exempted from this process; and quantitatively, although the Commissioner covers a huge number of posts, the sheer scale of the patronage state documented in Table 18.1 (p. 405) shows that even this large number constitutes only a minority of patronage appointments.

constantly need people who can help them respond. If there has been some catastrophic scandal or other policy failure in their department they often need a 'safe pair of hands' to chair an ad hoc committee of inquiry; if there is a delicate bit of negotiation they need someone reliable to have a quiet word in the right place; if they are in some personal difficulty they will need confidential advice about how to handle the problem if it becomes public, or even how to avoid the law. Since fixers often have to be found in a hurry, being well placed in easily accessible networks is a key to benefiting from this kind of patronage.

## The changing social structure of political leadership

### The traditional structure

Some systems of government in the past have occasionally selected political leaders by lottery, thus ensuring that they are a random sample of the people, but political leaders in Britain are anything but a microcosm of the population. Everything we have seen in this chapter shows that only those with unusual tastes and energy are likely to persist in the struggle to the top. It is hardly surprising, therefore, that when we look at the social characteristics of leaders they are also unrepresentative of the wider population. In both the colloquial and statistical sense of the word, they are not 'normal' people.

We can best understand the present by starting with a quick glance at the past. Until the middle of the nineteenth century there were two routes to the top in Britain: birth, since the country was ruled mostly by a hereditary aristocracy; and patronage, since an alternative route for the ambitious was to attach themselves to an aristocratic patron. Some of the most distinguished figures in the country's political history, such as the great Conservative philosopher and politician Edmund Burke (1729–97), relied on aristocratic patronage. The reforms of the senior civil service from the middle of the nineteenth century removed patronage from civil service selection, and opened up a bureaucratic route to the top for those able to satisfy the measures of ability used by the service in selection and promotion. The widening of the franchise in the second half of the nineteenth century, coupled with the introduction of the secret ballot, meant that increasingly the route to the top lay through successfully winning election to the House of

Commons. But, as we now know, this newly created electorate largely voted for parties, not individuals. This meant that the leading parties were the key institutions in shaping the social structure of political leadership. The Liberal party, the Conservatives' main rival until 1918, played an important part in modestly widening the social range of leadership recruitment: on the eve of the First World War, for instance, the Liberal prime minister was of modest lower middle-class origins, having made his way via university scholarships and a successful legal career; his Chancellor of the Exchequer (who became prime minister in 1916) was from a poor rural Welsh family, having made his way by qualifying as a country solicitor, and then forging a reputation in radical Welsh politics (see also Table 18.2).

The more socially inclusive nature of political leadership was accentuated by the rise after the First World War of the Labour party as the main opponent of the Conservatives. For instance, Labour's first nationally recognized leader (Keir Hardie, 1856–1915) began his working life as a miner; the first Labour prime minister (Ramsay MacDonald 1866–1937) was born illegitimate and into poverty.

Looking back over the whole span of the first half of the twentieth century two trends in the social composition of the political leadership can be seen:

● For the first time in the political history of Britain a significant section of political leadership had been born in families of manual workers.
● There was a steady decline in the once utterly dominant position of the aristocracy.

## The changing structure

The striking feature of long-term developments since then is the continued decline, to the virtual point of extinction, of aristocratic influence – but also the decline of manual workers as a source of political leaders. All the main parties now look remarkably alike in the social composition of their leadership: aristocratic 'grandees' are a curiosity in the Conservative party; working-class self-made politicians are a curiosity in the Labour party. With the decline of aristocrats and working-class recruits the social range of political leadership has become narrower: political leadership in both parties is dominated overwhelmingly by those from middle-

---

**Table 18.2**  Political leadership, 1904 and 2004

|  | Schooling | University | Gender |
|---|---|---|---|
| Prime Minister, 1904 | Fee paying | Cambridge | Male |
| Prime Minister, 2004 | Fee paying | Oxford | Male |
| Chancellor of the Exchequer, 1904 | Fee paying | Cambridge | Male |
| Chancellor of the Exchequer, 2004 | State school | Edinburgh | Male |
| Foreign Secretary, 1904 | Fee paying | Oxford | Male |
| Foreign Secretary, 2004 | State school | Leeds | Male |
| Leader of the Opposition, 1904 | State school | Glasgow and Cambridge | Male |
| Leader of the Opposition, 2004 | State school | Cambridge | Male |

*Note*: The Office of Leader of the Opposition did not exist in 1904. The figure referred to here is Henry Campbell-Bannerman, leader of the Liberal Party in the Westminster House of Commons, who became prime minister in December 1905 following the Liberal victory over the Conservatives in the general election.

*Sources*: Information from standard directories and from Butler and Butler (2000).

⮞ Analyses of the changing composition of the political class as a whole over the course of a century show some well documented changes, referred to in the text, such as the decline in aristocratic representation. But when we look right at the very top of the political tree the most striking pattern is continuity: continuity notably in the dominance of elite universities and in gender.

**Table 18.3**  The rise of the professional politician: the case of the Westminster Parliament of 2001

|  | Labour | Conservative | Liberal Democrat |
|---|---|---|---|
| Median age | 50 | 48 | 47 |
| % university educated | 67 | 83 | 70 |
| % public school educated | 17 | 64 | 35 |
| % from professional occupation | 43 | 39 | 52 |
| % business | 8 | 36 | 27 |
| % manual workers | 12 | 1 | 2 |
| Grand totals | 412 | 166 | 52 |

*Source*: Adapted from Criddle (2002).

➲ The case of the MPs elected to the Westminster Parliament shows that some of the historical differences between the parties are still faintly present: a higher proportion of Conservative MPs continue to be public-school educated, while there are still a few more Labour MPs who have been manual workers in their adult lives. But the most striking feature of the profile of the MPs from the three leading parties is their similarity. They are middle-aged university-educated professionals.

class families and by those who, insofar as they have ever had a job beyond politics, have pursued middle-class occupations.

The most important cause of this is something we have already noticed: the steady professionalization of politics (see Table 18.3). Politics is turning into a middle-class professional occupation like any other: quite well rewarded, demanding the skills acquired in a long formal education, and full time in its demands. Even a generation ago really rich men could combine managing their wealth with a political career, and trade unionists could make a career as union officials and then enter Parliament in late middle age. But as we have seen, successful political careers now demand early and total dedication. The most successful will now only have had a brief career before entering Parliament, and that usually related to their long-term political ambitions.

Professionalization therefore has the consequence of narrowing the social class range of politi-

cal leadership, but some other common signs of professionalization are helping widen that social range in other ways. The most important of these concerns the gender make-up of the political class. In professions at large the proportion of women has been rising, though often quite slowly. The slow rise is partly due to the persistence of factors that obstruct the recruitment and promotion of women, and partly due to the fact that, since at the top professions often reflect patterns of recruitment of 30 years earlier, it is taking some time for occupations to reflect the more recent advances made by women in the education system. These factors also operate in politics. One of the key first steps for an ambitious politician – being adopted as a party's candidate in a winnable seat – is still sometimes difficult for a woman because local parties are simply reluctant to select a woman candidate. (This is the origin of Labour's decision in some instances to impose women-only short lists at candidate selection stage.) Probably more serious handicaps to the ascent of women in political life are the tensions between family and motherhood, and career, created by the uniquely demanding nature of political life. Even something as mundane as the working hours of the House of Commons – until very recently stretching into the late evenings as a matter of routine – creates difficulties for women. But just as the gender make-up of other professions is changing, so there is some evidence that women are now becoming commoner at the top in politics, as we can see from Figure 18.1.

Widening the social range in other senses is much more problematic. Religious and racial minorities have long faced barriers to advancement. At various times in the nineteenth century Catholics, Jews and atheists were all openly barred from the House of Commons. Now there are no formal barriers to ethnic minorities but powerful, subtler barriers exist. Anti-Semitism and anti-Catholicism undoubtedly exist in some constituency parties, but are probably residual and declining, and are never openly acknowledged. Newer minorities resulting from more recent waves of immigration – particularly those descended from immigrants from former imperial territories in the Caribbean and the Indian sub-

**Figure 18.1**    The diverse routes to political office: the gender dimension (percentage of women in different kinds of public office in the UK, January 2000)

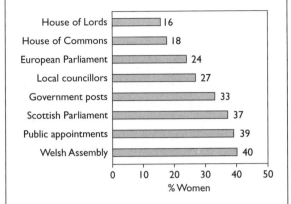

*Source*: Reproduced by permission of *Political Studies* from Lovenduski and Norris (2003: 85).

➲ Figure 18.1 shows how the growing diversity of institutions, especially elected institutions, is producing very different outcomes in selection for public office, using the example of gender. The figure is also changing over time. The paper from which this information is drawn also showed that there were actually fewer women members of the House of Commons in 1979 than in 1950, but that the numbers rose fivefold by the end of the twentieth century. The figures here date from 2000, and since then the new elected institutions have become even more distinctive: after the 2003 elections the Welsh Assembly had a majority of women members.

continent – are disproportionately under represented at all levels of the political class. Only in 2002 did we see the first member of the Cabinet from these groups: Paul Boateng, the child of an immigrant from Ghana, reached Mr Blair's Cabinet as Chief Secretary to the Treasury. There have been some well-publicized cases of crude discrimination on race grounds by the parties, and this probably reflects more deep-seated, subtle discriminatory practices. But there are also powerful economic forces at work. Communities descended from poor migrants are still themselves disproportionately among the poorest. The rare success of Paul Boateng helps make the point, for he is the son of professional parents. We have already seen that, by contrast with the position half

a century ago, it is now much more difficult for the very poorest to rise to positions of political leadership. The Labour party – the main channel of ascent – has increasingly professionalized its methods of selection. Perhaps the most striking feature of political leadership in Britain at the start of the new millennium is the absence of political leaders drawn from the very poorest in our society. Black, brown or white: they are all equally absent. In at least one important sense, this has made leadership selection less undemocratic. An important historical definition of democracy – dating from the Greek political philosopher Aristotle – pictured it as rule by the poorest. For better or worse the poorest in Britain no longer get close to political leadership.

## Is recruitment meritocratic?

The increasingly professionalized nature of leadership selection is, we have seen, partly due to the rise of a 'meritocratic' theory of leadership selection: to the notion that selection and promotion should depend on displaying 'merit' in the sense of ability measured by standards such as success in formal education. That selection and promotion should be by 'merit' is now a deeply engrained value in British society. This does not mean that it is always practised. In business, for instance, the route to the top for those from families who own a big share of a firm is much easier than for those who simply display ability. But the attachment to the value of 'merit' is now so strong that even in cases where family nepotism determines promotion, public justification will usually at least mention merit. In other parts of our society – for instance, recruitment of students to university – any apparent departure from strict meritocratic rules becomes a public scandal. This public attachment to the idea that we should be a 'meritocracy' has probably become stronger, even over the last half century.

Meritocratic selection does not abolish social exclusion. On the contrary; it can produce elites that are even more socially exclusive than those produced by other methods. For example, the abolition of patronage in civil service recruitment in

## DEBATING POLITICS

### 18.1   MERITOCRACY: CURSE OR BLESSING?

| Meritocracy is the best method of selecting leaders in Britain: | Meritocracy is a danger to British democracy: |
|---|---|
| ■ Selection by merit involves open rules equally known to all competitors.<br><br>■ Selection by merit involves choosing the most technically able people to fill positions of authority, and therefore is the best way of choosing competent government.<br><br>■ Selection by merit ensures that able people without connections or wealth will have the chance to rise to the top.<br><br>■ Meritocratic selection is 'blind' to the numerous grounds on which prejudice is now exercised in Britain: gender, race or religion. It therefore greatly increases the fairness of selection processes. | ■ 'Merit' usually means academic prowess, and ruling in a democracy demands a wide range of less easily measured talents.<br><br>■ A meritocratic hierarchy is still a hierarchy, although not one based on wealth or inheritance.<br><br>■ Because meritocratic tests so often select the academically gifted, meritocratic selection is socially unequal, because academic success is distributed in a socially unequal way.<br><br>■ Democratic leadership should be representative of all the people, and not just the most meritocratically gifted; a meritocratic elite is still an elite. |

Britain in the nineteenth century actually made the service more socially exclusive. There was no longer a place for the poorly-connected clients of rich aristocrats. The method of selection itself – largely by written examinations modelled on the syllabus of the ancient universities – virtually guaranteed domination of the service by those who had a privileged public school and university education.

Beyond the senior civil service, almost all the routes to the top examined in this chapter depart from formal notions of merit, though it is routine to invoke ability as the grounds for any selection or promotion. Ability is needed at the top, we have seen, but it is not primarily the sort of academically produced ability usually displayed in meritocratic selection. The qualities demanded are stamina, toughness and self-confidence. Making alliances, and cultivating powerful patrons, matters hugely. There has indeed been some growth of meritocratic influence, and as we have seen this has largely served to narrow the social range of political leadership: as politics has become more like a professional occupation where good formal education is demanded, those from both the very poor and the

traditional aristocracy have been excluded (see Debating Politics 18.1).

These meritocratic influences, although they help shape the general conditions of political selection, have to compete with very non-meritocratic influences. Democratic selection is not meritocratic selection: the characteristic way of winning in democracy is through election, not according to ability. More practically, recently in Britain there have been powerful expectations that recruitment should take into account not just achievement but what is sometimes called 'ascription': in other words, we should be concerned with the ascribed characteristics of our leaders, such as their gender or their ethnicity. This is what lies behind such initiatives as all-women short lists in selecting parliamentary candidates in some constituencies. This is a conscious departure from meritocracy in the interests of producing political leadership that is more socially representative of groups in the population. But this in turn produces its own complications. Because most successful politicians now also have high formal education, and because participation in higher education has been particularly low

**REVIEW**

Five themes dominate this chapter:

1 The importance of party in controlling the path to the top of elected office in the Westminster system;
2 The continuing domination of the two-party system as a route to the top in the Westminster system, but also the challenge to two-party domination, especially in the new devolved systems of government;
3 The importance of a bureaucratic route that is organized on formally meritocratic principles, and a very different system of patronage and networking, as alternative routes to the top for unelected leaders;
4 The rise of the professional politician which is having the effect of narrowing the social range of those recruited into politics;
5 The virtually total exclusion from elite positions of those drawn from the poorest and dispossessed in Britain.

among women from the families of unskilled manual workers and from some ethnic groups, consciously discriminating in favour of women actually reinforces the long-term trend towards middle-class domination of politics. Of course, in principle this problem can be solved, for instance by targeting selection on women precisely from these dispossessed groups.

## Further reading

Guttsman (1963) was a pioneering study, and is still unrivalled for its historical depth. Norris and Lovenduski (1995) and Lovenduski and Norris (2003) are essential on dimensions neglected in earlier work, notably gender. Theakston (1999) examines leadership in a key arena, while Leach and Wilson (2000) look at local leadership. Hennessy (2001) surveys the apex – the office of Prime Minister – for the post-war period.

CHAPTER 19

# Understanding policy under multi-level governance

## CONTENTS

## AIMS

The chapter has the following aims:

❖ To describe the special nature of policy making as a process

❖ To summarize important analytical frameworks as means of understanding that process

❖ To introduce the notion of multi-level governance as a means of understanding the British policy process

❖ To show that what is not decided can be even more important than the policy decisions actually taken

❖ To examine how far the British policy-making system is uniquely prone to failure and fiasco.

## Understanding policy

At numerous points in this book we have examined the substance of policy decisions in Britain (consider, for example, Chapters 11 and 12). In Chapters 20 to 22 we will be looking in more detail at separate important policy domains where government makes decisions: in other words, yet again at the substance of policy. This chapter has a different purpose: it is to help us make sense of policy making more widely by alerting us to the vocabularies that can be used in studying the policy process. And we begin at exactly that point: by asking what it means when we speak of policy making as a process.

### Policy as a process

To most of us, the policy that government pursues shows itself as a set of separate authoritative decisions: the Chancellor delivers his annual budget; the Secretary of State for Education and Skills announces a new initiative to widen the social range of students recruited to universities. Then everyone moves on to a different set of concerns, and a new set of decisions. The reality of policy in modern government is actually very different, and the difference is well caught in the image of policy as a process. This image conveys the two most important characteristics of the policies that all systems of government in Britain make and try to put into practice.

- Policy is not the product of a single decision but is the result of a continuous set of linked decisions.
- Different policies are not independent of each other, but constantly interact with other policies, sometimes beneficially and sometimes harmfully.

The first of these insights tells us to think of policy in government as forming a continuing stream (see Figure 19.1). There is thus rarely a moment when policy is 'made' in the sense of being finally concluded, whatever the publicity of ministerial announcements might suggest. This is not something we would ourselves intuitively anticipate, because in our private lives we constantly do make these kind of final decisions, from the trivial to the important: we can clearly say that the decision to go to one film rather than another, or even to go to one university rather than another, is made and concluded at a particular moment. But the decisions of government are rarely like that: the moment when a minister announces a new policy is often only the moment when the real work starts. Because decisions in government usually involve large numbers of people, and large numbers of institutions, they only happen when those people and those institutions start to get involved. Suppose, for instance, that the government announces a decision to recruit 5,000 extra new teachers over a fixed period (say, within the next 12 months). That decision in turn involves the cooperation of a whole range of institutions and of private citizens. Among institutions, both the Department for Education and Skills and the Treasury will have to be involved, the former as the Department with obvious responsibility for education, the latter as the Department that tries to controls the purse strings of government. Among individuals, the success of the policy will require the voluntary choices of 5,000 students not presently intending to enter the teaching profession to do so.

The simple insight that policy is a continuing process – a never-ending stream – means that, while

---

**Figure 19.1**　Policy as a never-ending stream

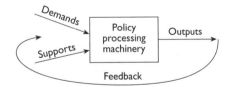

➲ The figure schematically reproduces one of the commonest images of the policy process, sometimes called a 'systems' image. It has two great merits: it shows that the production of policy is shaped by both demands, and by supports such as money and people; and it brings home the continuous nature of policy making by showing that policy 'outputs' feed back to introduce later 'inputs'.

politicians in making policy announcements often separate those announcements from actual delivery, in practice there is no clear line of separation. Policy making and policy implementation are intimately bound together.

The second insight offered by the image of process – that policies across government are inter-connected – has even more profound implications. The most obvious form of connection is through money, since government always has finite resources at its command. As we will see in the next chapter, in Britain these are huge by the standards of private citizens and even by the standards of other big organizations, such as business corpora-tions. But they are still finite, so each policy commitment that involves spending money – and most do – involves choices that affect other policy areas: £500 million spent on building new schools is £500 million not available for new defence equip-ment. But the interconnections go well beyond money. Pursuing one policy often complicates the pursuit of others. For instance, if government pursues a policy of restricting new house building in the south-east of England in order to protect the rural environment, the resulting shortage helps push up house prices. In turn, expensive housing makes it difficult to attract workers to public sector jobs (including teaching and nursing) in the south-east, thus frustrating an entirely different public aim of ensuring adequate staffing for public services.

## Theory and making sense of policy

The two features of policy just identified – that it comes in a continuing stream where making and delivery are inseparable, and that there are compli-cated connections between different policy areas – pose huge problems for government in producing effective policy. They also create problems for those who study policy. This is one reason why so much thought and argument has gone into trying to understand the nature of the policy process in the governance of Britain theoretically.

Why do we need to think theoretically about policy at all? A common-sense alternative would seem to be to observe examples of policy in government and draw conclusions from these case studies, but this approach has a number of obvious limitations. In the absence of theory, what would guide our selection of these cases or, indeed, guide our selection generally of what aspects of the huge canvas of British government on which to focus? Some kind of theory is therefore important, above all, in indicating to us what are the key policy processes to observe. Even when we have settled this difficult question, 'common-sense' observation of what we think of as 'the facts' of particular cases will not be enough. Even a single policy case in government will present us with a huge amount of material. Imagine writing an account, for example, of the history of British attitudes towards the Euro (the single European currency) and trying to draw conclusions about the policy process from that account. Even if we admit to no theory in writing the account, in practice we are going to have make a whole set of general assumptions in selecting what aspects of the case to highlight, and these general assumptions in turn will, without our even realizing it, imply views about the nature of the policy process. For example, if we write the history of a British decision on the Euro in terms of the struggles between leading figures in government – say, the Prime Minister and the Chancellor – we are implicitly committing ourselves to the view that policy is the product of human choice and human personality, rather than, for instance, more impersonal forces such as economic interests. It is far better to have these assumptions out in the open in the form of some general theoretical state-ments.

Even if we accept the argument for theory, however, we are still left with numerous problems. 'Theory' in the study of politics is very different from theory in the natural sciences. In the most highly developed natural sciences theories both guide, and are refined by, observations made under controlled conditions in laboratories. Typically, they take the form of generalizations about the rela-tions between various forces or elements. Statements about these relations then produce predictions whose accuracy in turn can be measured either in laboratory experiments or by observation of the natural world.

It is obvious that things are very different in the study of policy. We do not study our subject under laboratory conditions, and even if we could devise laboratory experiments they would not be very interesting: we want to understand how British politics functions in the here and now, not how it might operate if we made a whole set of assumptions that produced a simplified 'model' of politics. Observation and generalization have to take place under the messy circumstances of observing everyday reality where the relationships between forces at any one moment will be both highly complicated and difficult to disentangle. One result is that notions of what 'theory' amounts to in the study of politics are much less narrow than in the natural sciences. As we will see in some of the examples that follow, predictive theory as used in the natural sciences is rare. Theory is more often a looser framework, a set of assumptions about the world of policy, or even just a helpful image of the policy process – all designed to help us organize in some systematic way the otherwise impossible diversity that we can observe in the political world. This is why in the next section we examine only different 'images' of the policy process, because they rarely amount to anything that would be recognized as 'theory' by the standards of the laboratory sciences.

## Images of the policy process

### A rational and comprehensive image

Suppose we have to make a big decision in our private life, such as buying a house. Most of us will attempt to do this in a fairly systematic way: forming a picture of the house we really want given what we can afford, and then viewing as many possibilities as time and energy allows before making an offer for the one that most closely meets our demands. We attempt, in short, to make a rational choice: to match our final selection to our wishes and resources, and to make the choice after as comprehensive a scan as possible of the housing market in the area where we expect to live. This simple example encapsulates the essence of the rational and comprehensive image of policy choice (see Documenting Politics 19.1). One of the commonest ambitions of governments is to produce policy that is also the result of such a rational and comprehensive analysis of the available evidence and the available options. In presenting this image of the policy process, policy makers are working according to one of the oldest theories of the policy process, though they rarely acknowledge, or perhaps even realize, this fact. This is a *prescriptive* theory; in other words, it says what should happen, not necessarily what does, and what should happen

---

## DOCUMENTING POLITICS 19.1

### THE LIMITS OF RATIONAL ANALYSIS: TONY BLAIR ON 'JUDGEMENT'

'When people talk about me having suddenly changed, I suppose I have toughened, but there are some issues you believe in strongly that accord with the popular will, and others that don't. When I was young I paid more regard to intellect than judgement. As I've got older I pay more regard to judgement than intellect.'

⮑ Virtually every problem faced by a prime minister is either insoluble, or soluble only with the greatest difficulty. It is almost impossible to settle things by thinking out the most rationally desirable solution. After a few years experience of office at this level most prime ministers despair of 'rational', intellectually coherent solutions. They increasingly trust instinct, and like Mr Blair after six years of office 'pay more regard to judgement than intellect.'

*Source*: *Saga* (2003).

**DOCUMENTING POLITICS 19.2**

## THE RATIONAL-COMPREHENSIVE MODEL ENCOUNTERS POLITICS: MICHAEL HESELTINE'S EXPERIENCE WITH MINIS

The Management Information System for Ministers (MINIS) 'was designed to give Ministers a thorough understanding of what each activity of the Department cost by defining each task in detail and allocating the costs of the civil servants involved'. Heseltine presented a slide show on the system to Cabinet members and their Permanent Secretaries in 1981. The Prime Minister asked John Nott, Secretary of State for defence what he thought. He replied:

'Prime Minister, at the Ministry of Defence I am trying to come to terms with an overspend of billions of pounds. Is it seriously suggested that I should spend my time grubbing around, saving ha'pennies?'

Heseltine continues: 'The row that followed marked the end of any prospect of MINIS being adopted in Whitehall.'

⮡ Michael Heseltine was a leading member of Conservative Cabinets in the 1980s and 1990s. He was an advocate of rational planning models influenced by his business experience. He introduced MINIS into every department he headed, but could never convince the rest of the government to follow suit.

*Source*: Heseltine (2000: 190–3).

is exactly that policy production should be 'rational and comprehensive'. It should be the result of a clear picture of the objectives of policy; it should involve a full (comprehensive) analysis of the available options; and it should result in the choice of the option that most effectively realizes the objectives (see Documenting Politics 19.2).

Attractive as this theory looks, it rarely matches what happens, or what can happen. We can see this even in our private life. Numerous house buyers start out trying to use a rational comprehensive method, but notoriously they often then make a choice on some unanticipated instinctive ground (just because they like the garden or the fitted kitchen, say). The bigger the choice, the less likely we are to make it 'rationally'. Few people select a marriage partner rationally and comprehensively; they just stumble in and out of love, and we would think anyone who tried to make a 'rational and comprehensive' choice here a pretty odd and cold fish.

If even making single choices in private life is hard to make rationally and comprehensively, how

much more difficult is it to make in government. Take again the choice of whether Britain should 'join the Euro zone', and replace her domestic currency with the Euro and therefore become a partner in the European Monetary Union with the other member states in the EU. The core of the rational and comprehensive approach is that there exists a clear objective to which the means are adapted, but it is impossible to formulate a single list of objectives for the decision on joining the Euro. A Cabinet faced with the decision has to consider party, nation, special interests including business and labour – all with differing objectives, often conflicting. Individual members of the Cabinet, being only human, will also be calculating what the episode will do to their own careers. The comprehensive evaluation of evidence is impossible. Some relevant evidence – for example, about the state of the economy – may be fairly precisely measurable. Other evidence – for instance, about the state of the public's emotional attachment to the pound sterling as a symbol of British identity – may be highly intangible. And beyond all this there is the

# Briefing                    19.1

## THE SCIENCE OF MUDDLING THROUGH

'The science of muddling through' (see Lindblom 1959) is a classic article which influentially put the case for 'incrementalism' as both a way of understanding, and as a way of making, policy. Incrementalism proved especially popular among British policy makers because its central tenets appealed to the traditional culture of the policy-making elite. It stressed:

- Our limited knowledge about the future
- Our limited ability to store, recall and analyse our present knowledge
- The dangers of making large scale changes
- The importance of 'muddling through' by making incremental changes which could then be assessed before further change was introduced.

*Source*: Lindblom (1959).

➲ It is doubtful if many senior British politicians or civil servants have ever read Lindblom's classic paper but it precisely systematized their suspicion of rational models of policy making and their preference for making policy through piecemeal bargaining.

problem of trying to predict a highly uncertain future if Britain goes in, or stays out.

## An image of incrementalism

These problems lie behind the rise of an image that has challenged that of the rational and comprehensive: incrementalism. The *incrementalist* image of the policy process says we should recognize all the limits – technical and emotional – to rational decision, and recognize that in practice most policies are made piecemeal or incrementally, and amount to 'muddling through' (Briefing 19.1). Governments hardly ever have the resources or the time to engage in rational comprehensive analysis, so they typically do what we all do in our private lives: just plump for the nearest available short-term choice. A more analytical way of putting this is to say that policymakers typically 'satisfice' rather than 'maximize':

they cannot spend time fully analyzing all the evidence and options, so they do what they can given available resources and time – both of which are often in short supply. They are like the typical car buyer who, deciding that life is too short systematically to compare and test drive ten models, buys by a single rule of thumb: because the manufacturer has a reputation for reliability, or because there is a once and for all special offer on a particular model.

It cannot be disputed that 'muddling through' accurately describes the reality of most policy processes, just as it accurately describes much of our own private decision making. But the rational-comprehensive image still offers a serious challenge: since it is prescriptive rather than descriptive, it asks us how far we should accept the muddling through character of real policy making. As the frequent resort to the imagery of rational decision making in official accounts shows, it remains a powerful ideal in the minds of most modern policy makers. Incrementalism in government is particularly dangerous because of the sheer scale and diversity of government. If every bit of government is taking decisions incrementally, how can there ever be any coherence and consistency in what government does?

## Rational choice institutionalism: model building

The great power of the incrementalist model is that it seems accurately to describe so much of the messy reality of government. But what if we approached the problem of theoretical understanding by a very different route: by self-consciously building a deliberately simplified model of the policy process? The 'model' here is obviously not a simplified physical representation of reality, of the sort, for example, commonly used in engineering design; instead, it is a kind of mental experiment. This approach is the nearest we have in the social sciences to the controlled experimental conditions of the laboratory in the natural sciences. It is widely used, for example, in the study of economic behaviour. Economists build theories of how economies work by starting with a set of assumptions that simplify human behaviour and motivation. They then make deductions about how economic actors – either individuals or institutions, such as firms – would behave in different circumstances if they were so motivated. For example, in elementary economic theory it is common to assume that firms attempt to maximize profits at the expense of anything else. Nobody believes that real firms are driven just by this imperative, but the assumption that firms do want to maximize profits allows the economist to explore what this would mean in different market conditions: for example, what would happen when there are only a few powerful firms in the market, as in the market for automobiles, or when there are numerous small competitors, as in the market for second-hand books?

One of the most productive sources of models of the policy process comes from *rational choice institutionalism*. It is called *rational choice* because it is a close relative of the models built by economists, where rationality means the assumption that people are self-interested, have a few, clearly realized values that they want to maximize (say profits), and shape their behaviour to realize those objectives. *Institutionalism* recognizes that the choices are being made here in a world where institutions shape behaviour. It is possible to define institutions in many different ways, but a straightforward one is to picture the organizations that shape all our lives as institutions. It is then easy to see how a rationally self-interested individual would have to adapt to the way these institutions impinge on our lives. Imagine a student, for instance, who has a rational set of goals that include maximizing the amount of free time she has, while minimizing the amount of trouble she encounters from her teachers. Working out a strategy to achieve these twin aims will involve working within the rules and culture of a particular institution, the college: for example, knowing exactly what the attendance rules are and manipulating those rules. (If the rules say that students are reported after two consecutive absences, the rational student misses only alternative lessons.)

Rational choice institutionalism builds models of the policy process by beginning with a small number of simplified assumptions about what motivates actors who contribute to policy; identifies the main incentives, opportunities and obstacles that exist in any particular institutional setting, such as

the core executive in Britain; and then works out what are the most effective strategies for rationally self-interested actors in the light of those incentives, opportunities and obstacles.

Obviously a key question in this sort of model building is: what can we assume are the motives that drive self-interested actors? Early rational choice models assigned fairly simple values: for instance, politicians wanted to maximize votes, while bureaucrats (such as senior civil servants in Britain) wanted to maximize the budgets of their departments, because maximizing budgets was presumed to be a sign of maximizing prestige and power. But later versions applied to policy in Britain have assigned more complex values (see Figure 19.2). One variation is to see senior bureaucrats as actors who want to maximize job satisfaction: they want to retain in their own hands intellectually pleasurable and prestigious activities, such as advising ministers on policy; but they want to shift less prestigious and less intellectually pleasurable roles (the stressful job of actually delivering policy) on to other shoulders. This simple model proves to have remarkable predictive power: it would predict, for example, that senior civil servants would support a policy of 'hiving off' responsibility for actually delivering difficult policies (for example the daily running of prisons) on to specialized agencies; and that, as we saw in Chapter 8, is exactly what has been happening in the 'Next Steps' reforms that were introduced in the 1990s.

## Images of networks and governance

The twin theories of incrementalism and rational comprehensiveness are attempts to understand the intellectual process by which policy is made: how far it involves, or should involve, the careful evaluation of all possible choices in the light of all possible information. Models of rational choice institutionalism involve working out how rationally self-interested actors play the games of realizing their self-interest within the boundaries set by the institutions inside which they have to work. Our final set of images of the policy process offers us an overview of the whole experience of making policy, and has proved in recent years unusually influential

**Figure 19.2**    Dunleavy's illustrations of different kinds of budget

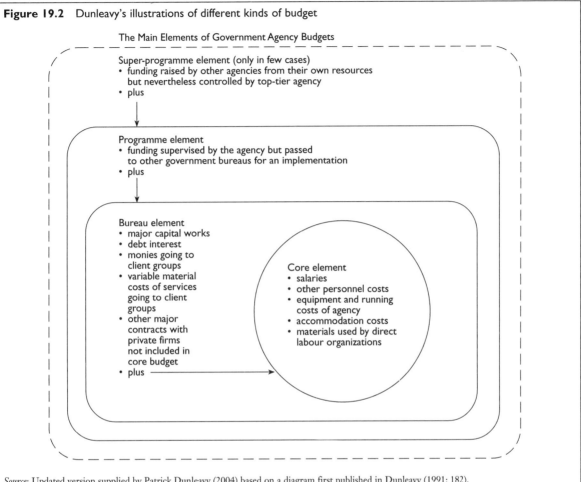

The Main Elements of Government Agency Budgets

Super-programme element (only in few cases)
• funding raised by other agencies from their own resources
  but nevertheless controlled by top-tier agency
• plus

Programme element
• funding supervised by the agency but passed
  to other government bureaus for an implementation
• plus

Bureau element
• major capital works
• debt interest
• monies going to
  client groups
• variable material
  costs of services
  going to client
  groups
• other major
  contracts with
  private firms
  not included in
  core budget
• plus

Core element
• salaries
• other personnel costs
• equipment and running
  costs of agency
• accommodation costs
• materials used by direct
  labour organizations

*Source*: Updated version supplied by Patrick Dunleavy (*2004*) based on a diagram first published in Dunleavy (1991: 182).

➲ Dunleavy's version of rational choice institutionalism gives this theoretical approach greatly added power. He retains many of the basic assumptions of the rational choice model, notably that actors try to calculate and if possible to maximize some preference. But hitherto the dominant assumptions had been fairly simple: for instance, that actors in institutions would want to maximize institutional budgets. Dunleavy's apparently elementary point in this diagram – that there are different kinds of budget elements in any institution – immediately opens up huge possibilities: different actors at different levels of an institution will have different strategies for different kinds of budget. And Dunleavy goes further. He argues that many key actors – such as senior civil servants – want to maximize not money but work satisfaction: for instance, they will want to control congenial roles (such as offering policy advice to ministers), and to 'hive off' difficult and tedious roles, (such as complex management tasks).

among both policy makers and those who study policy. These images are usually summed up under the label 'governance'.

The popularity of 'governance' imagery arises from changes that are taking place in the nature of modern government and society. These changes have greatly complicated the way policies can be made and put into effect. In the past, taking decisions by government was often a tightly knit, hierarchically organized affair. Putting those decisions into effect was typically done bureaucratically. 'Bureaucratic' here is used technically and neutrally, not as the pejorative term common in everyday speech, where bureaucracy is associated with

**Figure 19.3**    An example of a policy network: Reid's version of the tobacco policy network

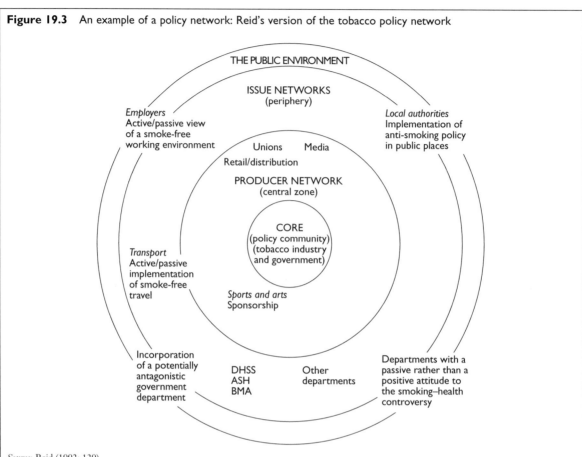

*Source*: Reid (1992: 129).

➲ Most representations of policy networks picture them as rather like wiring diagrams, with all the parts intercon-nected. Reid's representation of the tobacco policy network as a series of zones brings out something that can be lost in the 'wiring diagram' approach: that different parts of policy networks specialize in different things; that they vary in their centrality to the policy process; and that they vary in the amount of power exercised over the actual production of policy.

slowness and rigidity in taking decisions. It simply means that government is carried out by officials organized in hierarchical organizations where everyone has a defined task and a clearly identified place in the hierarchy. Matching this is a hierarchi-cal theory of how government itself works: the democratically elected government of the day decides policies, which are then carried out by bureaucracies (government departments) issuing orders to put policy into effect.

In practice hardly anything of the sort happens in government, and the history of British government in particular has for decades been one precisely of

policy failure: instead of policy being smoothly and efficiently put into effect there has often been resis-tance and policy fiasco. (Some of the most spectac-ular of these failures will be explored later in this chapter.) The governance approach springs from an attempt to work out why policy failures happen. The essence of the governance answer is that it is no longer possible, if it ever was, to make and imple-ment policy as if all that mattered was the issuing of orders, even when those orders come from a government that claims the authority of democratic legitimacy. Policy also has to be sensibly designed, and it has to take into account the views of those who share responsibility for putting it into effect. Policy has to be made and implemented, not in simple hierarchies (such as an old-fashioned army) but in organizations that are connected in complex ways which make them dependent on each other.

Thus, when we look at the structure of modern government in a country such as Britain, we see not simple hierarchies, but a pattern consisting of *networks* of mutually dependent organizations (see Figure 19.3). Effective policy making is about steering these networks of mutually dependent organizations. This becomes most obvious when we look at the attempts made to put policy into effect. Take the example of a Chancellor of the Exchequer making policies that are designed to affect the level of investment in the economy, or to raise the productivity with which labour is used. These policies, if they work, only do so when an extended chain of organizations – stretching down to individual firms – actually responds appropriately: the Chancellor can change the tax rules so as to make investment more attractive, but in the end individual firms have to do the investing; the Chancellor can introduce schemes for better training of workers to make them more skilful and potentially productive, but firms have to employ and use those workers so as to take advantage of their skills. When governments make policy, to be effective they cannot do so by issuing orders; their task is to participate in, and to try to manage, networks of organizations. Making effective policy is about bargaining, negotiation and compromise; about recognizing the nature of the networks in different policy areas; and about responding sensitively to the powerful organizations in those networks.

All this is summed up in the very language that shifts from 'government' to 'governance', a tiny symbolic shift with huge implications. 'Government' suggests a clear line between government and the rest of society, with government the independent source of authoritative orders. 'Governance' suggests that the act of governing in a modern industrial society such as Britain usually crosses the conventional line separating government from the rest of society. 'Governance' is not confined to the conventional institutions of govern-

ment, the central departments of Whitehall, but is a collaborative act that takes place in the extended networks which can be found in any policy area. What we usually think of as government is embedded in those networks. When we study policy making, therefore, we have to bear in mind a key question which is also central to the problems faced in making effective policy: since policies are made and implemented through separate, complex networks which only sometimes overlap, how can the workings of these networks be coordinated? Linking up separate networks is, in the governance approach, one of the key functions of government departments, and one of the key roles of people such as senior politicians and civil servants.

One reason for the growing popularity of the image of governance is that it seems to chime with the reality of the changing nature of government in Britain. A generation ago we would usually analyze policy making in Britain in terms of a centre in London making policies for everywhere else. Now, the only sensible way of picturing policy making is through images of multi-level governance involving extended networks.

## The multi-level governance of policy

### The rise of multi-level governance in Britain

The rise of multi-level governance is connected to institutional changes which are coming over the British system of government, all of which we have already encountered in various forms in earlier chapters. The most important are, in summary, as follows:

● *The rise of the European Union.* The rising importance of the institutions of the European Union, especially of the Commission and its policy-making world in Brussels, has been documented at many points in previous chapters. There is almost nothing done by way of policy making and implementation that does not have to take account of an EU dimension, something we saw clearly in Chapters 6 and 7.

**Table 19.1**   The web of multi-level and multi-agency governance: examples

|  | Public | Mixed public/private | Private |
|---|---|---|---|
| Global | WTO | International Air Transport Association | Pharmaceutical Manufacturers' Association |
| Regional European | European Commission | European Telecommunications Standards Institute. | Confederation of Food and Drink Industries of the EU |
| UK-wide | Core executive departments. | Privatized rail industry. | Confederation of British Industry |
| Devolved national | Scottish Executive | Scottish Enterprize | Scottish Retail consortium |
| Regional | Government regional offices | North West Development Agency | North West Regional Office of the Confederation of British Industry |
| Local | Local authorities | Greater Manchester Passsenger Transport Executive | Local chamber of commerce |

⮕ Table 19.1 simply tabulates the main levels at which institutions that can have a hand in policy operate, and creates a very simple classification according to how far they are private or public bodies. It illustrates the potential range and complexity of institutional actors in multi-level and multi-agency governance.

● *The growing importance of international organizations.* In many areas of policy Britain now subscribes to agreements that restrict the ability of British governments independently to make policy. For instance, as part of our membership of the European Union we are bound by the agreements negotiated on our behalf by the Union in the WTO, the leading international organization that negotiates trading rules between nations. But this is only the most visible example. Virtually every internationally traded good or service – from air transport to computer software to telephone traffic – is governed by internationally negotiated standards, more often than not settled between nominally private bodies, such as firms and trade associations (see Table 19.1).

● *Territorial devolution in the United Kingdom.* The devolution of policy authority to the new assemblies and executives in Wales and Scotland by the Labour government in its legislation of 1998, has, as we saw in Chapter 11, created critical new levels of policy making.

● *Institutional devolution in the United Kingdom.* All the above examples involve different *territorial* levels, above (the European Union) or below (devolved government in Scotland) the level of government in Westminster. But there is also 'devolution' in another dimension: privatization, and the creation of agencies of the kind described in Chapter 8, shift parts of the policy making out to institutions beyond the core executive, and even beyond the whole of the Westminster system.

There is nothing new in having different levels of government in Britain: the distinction between central and local government is precisely such an arrangement; and from 1922 to 1972 Northern Ireland had extensively devolved government, most issues of policing, welfare and economic policy being controlled from a government and a parliament within the province. But the new world of multi-level governance is novel in scale. Instead of operating at the margins of a fundamentally centralized system, it is now a defining feature of how policy is made and executed. The list of levels summarized above shows that we now have something more than the simple hierarchy of central and local government, or piecemeal devolution to particular parts of the United Kingdom. The range and importance of institutions involved, including the European Union; the fact that multi-level arrangements are now connected to thorough-going constitutional reform, as in the measures of territorial devolution: these features show that a multi-level system is now a defining feature of the system of government in Britain. British government was until recently thought of as 'unitary', involving a concentration of authority in one single centre, within Westminster; the new multi-level system has replaced that. The scale of multi-level governance shapes the whole nature of policy making in Britain. Now, policy cannot be made at the centre but is a matter of negotiation and coordination between the levels. The levels in the multi-level system are not independent of each other. On the contrary; they both have to share authority, and to make decisions in the knowledge that decisions made at one level of government can produce effects through the rest of the system. Multi-level governance is therefore changing the very nature of the problems that the British system faces. What these problems are we now examine.

## Policy problems of multi-level governance

Multi-level governance spread because the old centralized, hierarchical system created numerous policy failures. (In areas where that old hierarchical system persists it may still be manufacturing fiascos: this is a matter examined in Chapter 24.) But the multi-level policy system is creating its own special problems. The rise of multi-level governance is profoundly changing the political 'game' in Britain; policy makers have to learn new ways of solving problems that the new game produces. In summary, they are problems of authority; resources; 'turf'; and coordination.

*Authority.* The formal distribution of authority in the old unitary system was simple. Parliament was supreme: 'Parliament can make or unmake any law whatsoever', in the words of a famous constitutional authority on the old unitary system of government (see Chapter 5, p. 73). Now authority is distributed in a complicated way across many levels. Short of actually withdrawing from the European Union, the British government now has no option but to share authority over numerous important policy domains with the institutions of the European Union. And 'below' the level of government in Westminster and Whitehall, there are now three directly elected popular assemblies – in Scotland, Wales and Northern Ireland – which not only have allocated to them the authority to make policies directly on a wide range of issues but can also claim the authority which goes with direct election. Elected mayors in cities such as London are also now a growing source of authority over policy. Authority can no longer be *exercised* by Westminster; it has to be negotiated, and negotiated in a multi-level system where there is increasing diversity in decision-making arrangements and policy preferences. If we think back to Chapter 1, we can see that this wider distribution of authority also has consequences for legitimacy. *Authority* is important to any system of government because it is the most effective and economical system of rule: if authority is recognized, then it is voluntarily obeyed. But in the new multi-level system there is increasingly no one, obvious source of authority; the point of authority at any particular moment has to be negotiated.

*Resources.* The problem of authority is compounded by the problem of resources. The independent resource-raising power of government beyond Westminster is still small. The EU cannot tax citizens or institutions directly; the resources at its disposal have to come from the member states. Within the United Kingdom only the Scottish Assembly has independent tax-raising power, and this is comparatively marginal: it can raise or lower the standard rate of income tax by 3p in the pound, but has so far not used the power. In other words, a separation is growing up between the place where resources are raised and the place where policies that demand resources are decided. That is not in itself novel in Britain; in the old unitary state it was common for the Westminster government to pass laws that imposed obligations on local government without providing the money to meet those obligations. But in the new system of multi-level

**DOCUMENTING POLITICS 19.3**

## THE 'CONCORDAT' AS AN ATTEMPT TO SOLVE PROBLEMS OF COORDINATION AND 'TURF' IN MULTI-LEVEL GOVERNANCE: EXTRACT FROM THE SCOTTISH CONCORDAT ON PROCUREMENT

'Scottish Concordat on Procurement

CONCORDAT ON CO-ORDINATION OF EU, INTERNATIONAL AND POLICY ISSUES ON PUBLIC PROCUREMENT ...

**2.   Purpose**

2.1   This Concordat sets out the mechanisms between the UK Government and the Scottish Executive for the handling of EU and international policy issues on public procurement. Specifically it covers:
  * provision of information;
  * formulation of UK policy;
  * attendance at EU and international (eg WTO) meetings;
  * implementation of EU and international obligations; and
  * infraction proceedings.

2.2   It is intended to guide the actions of officials working on these matters in the Scottish Executive and the UK Government, in particular the joint HM Treasury and DTI Procurement Policy Unit (PP).

2.3   The general principles on which this Concordat is based are those set out in the overarching Concordat on the co-ordination of European Union policy issues.

**3.   General**

3.1   Relations with the EU on public procurement policy and the development of EC legislation and international agreements in this field are the responsibility of the United Kingdom, as member state, Parliament and Government. The development and application of public procurement policy in Scotland, however, is a devolved matter. The UK Government therefore wishes to involve the Scottish Executive as directly and fully as possible in decision-making on EU and international public procurement matters.

3.2   To ensure that non-devolved matters which may affect devolved areas and devolved matters which may affect non-devolved areas are considered fully, Ministers and officials of the Scottish Executive and the UK Government will maintain close working relationships and will inform each other at an early stage of any relevant proposals or other developments on procurement policy and legislation, including litigation and infraction cases of potentially wider significance.

3.3   Given the common aim of achieving value for money, normally through competition and having due regard to propriety, regularity and the costs of acquisition, the Scottish

governance the relationships are often reversed: the policy commitments are being made beyond Westminster. 'Above' Westminster lies the EU, in which of course the United Kingdom government exerts substantial influence but which produces an important flow of authoritative decisions that have to be incorporated into UK law and policy. Below it, especially in Scotland, lies a new system of

## DOCUMENTING POLITICS 19.3   (continued)

Executive will seek to ensure that the policy and legal framework for public procurement in Scotland complies appropriately with the UK's EU and international obligations and will not prejudice the UK's objective of seeking EU and international measures which are effective in opening procurement markets while not imposing any unnecessary burdens or constraints on purchasers or suppliers.

**4.    Consultation and Exchange of Information**

4.1   The parties confirm their commitment to consult and exchange information on matters of mutual interest in a timely and helpful manner. There will be regular consultation between officials from the Procurement Policy Unit (PP) and the Scottish Executive to ensure that there is co-operation between the two administrations and that the business of both operates effectively and efficiently.

4.2   To this end there should be a formal liaison meeting between officials at least twice a year. In addition, the Director of Procurement of the Scottish Executive will normally be invited to participate in the Procurement Policy Committee and its Sub-Committees. Similarly, the Head of PP will be invited to any equivalent Scottish meetings.

4.3   In accordance with the framework set out in the Memorandum of Understanding, advance notification of, and consultation on, policy initiatives and associated announcements will normally take place not less than one month prior to the announcement. In the case of legislative proposals, including subordinate legislation, advance notification and consultation shall normally take place not less than three months prior to the introduction of primary legislation and the making of secondary legislation.

4.4   Each party undertakes to ensure that policy statements, interpretative documents or guidance notes are copied in draft to the other. This shall normally be in sufficient time to allow the other party to give full and proper consideration to the draft. Officials of each administration shall also ensure that relevant officials in the other are included in the circulation lists for such material when finalized.

4.5   In accordance with the Memorandum of Understanding both parties will also encourage joint working. For example, by inviting officials of the other administration to join working groups which may be of interest to them.

4.6   In respect of the EC/WTO rules, information will be provided by PP in accordance with the overarching Concordat on Co-ordination of European Policy Issues.'

➲ 'Procurement' is short-hand for purchasing decisions by government. As the biggest customer in Britain, purchasing worldwide, government has to work out rules that satisfy all levels of government: local, the devolved administrations (the focus of this box), the European Union and global organizations governing world trade, such as the WTO, with whom Britain has agreements. Concordats developed particularly rapidly to try to manage multi-level government after the devolution reforms of 1999. This document illustrates their reach, and their complexity: less than half the document is reproduced here. The dense prose is worth sampling, because it gives a direct sense of the daily reality of policy making in multi-level governance.

*Source*: www.hm-treasury.gov.uk

government which is producing policies that not only differ from those coming out of Westminster but that have very different spending consequences from Westminster policies. As we saw in Chapter 11, although there are formal differences in the status of the Scottish Parliament and the Welsh Assembly, in practice the impact of devolution has been remarkably similar. (See Briefing 11.4, p. 228

in particular.) Control of a block grant from the Westminster government to administer a very wide range of domestic policy has allowed the devolved governments to make decisions, especially in the sphere of welfare policy, which are making Scotland and Wales increasingly different from England.

*Turf.* 'Turf' is a political image imported from America (and originally an image transferred from land distribution struggles). Struggles over turf are struggles between institutions in government for control over areas of policy. Recall our image in Chapter 7 of central government departments in Whitehall as struggling tribes: one of the main things the tribes struggle over is the right to have a say in particular policy issues, because this is sign of departmental prestige, and because the first condition of having a real influence over policy is that the department's right to a say in policy debates should be recognized. Inside any system of government 'turf battles' command the time of most of the important people, whether they are politicians or civil servants.

The newly created systems of government under devolution have their own internal turf battles, often of a complexity and bitterness unknown even in the Westminster system. For instance, as was explained in Chapter 11, the whole system of devolved government in Northern Ireland is organized around a very delicate allocation of responsibilities and jobs in the executive between representatives of the different communities. More generally, since these systems are still being built, they are still working out understandings about turf allocation: a striking example is provided by the struggles between government in Whitehall and the elected mayor of London, Ken Livingstone, for control over the management of the London Underground rail network.

However, the turf issue is not confined to the internal organization of the different levels in the multi-level system; it goes to the very heart of managing the relationships between the institutions of multi-level government. In laws, treaties and concordats we can read the formal description of how 'turf' is allocated (the description of the formal division of legal rights and responsibilities between different levels of government). Just how elaborate these can be is illustrated in Documenting Politics 19.3. But famously in government the letter of the law settles nothing, especially in allocations of turf. Struggles for jurisdiction over policy are built into the very nature of the multi-level system.

*Coordination.* Coordination of policy making and policy delivery is a problem in any organization, even in the simplest: think of the number of times (even among your friends and your family) that you have failed to coordinate properly, missing appointments, duplicating tasks or failing to sort out who was responsible for what tasks, so that in the end nobody did them. If this kind of coordination problem litters even our simple daily tasks, it is easy to imagine that it is even more acute in modern government: big organizations with lots of internal divisions charged with complicated tasks that involve the cooperation of lots of different people and institutions over long periods of time. If a group of students in a flat cannot sort out who is responsible for doing the shopping, how much less likely is it that big government will be able to sort out exact responsibility for the delivery of urban renewal or education policy?

This is to emphasize that the existence of coordination problems in multi-level governance is nothing new. But for a multi-level system the problem is more acute for the most obvious of reasons: the essence of multi-level governance is not just that the governing process is divided between different levels, but it has to involve a constant process of communication and bargaining over how policy is to be made and put into effect. It also in many cases deliberately builds in the possibility of producing policies that are inconsistent with each other, which is something that the older unitary system always sought hard to avoid. For example, in the old unitary system before devolution of authority to Scotland there existed a powerful principle in welfare policy, sometimes called 'universalism': the principle that in welfare policy the entitlements and obligations of citizens should be the same right across Britain. But by devolving responsibility for making important decisions about welfare policy to the Scottish and Welsh devolved governments, this principle has been modified. We already seen some important results: student fees in higher education have been abolished in Scotland while remaining in force in England and Wales; and charges for long-term residential care (for example, of the very old) have been abolished in Scotland while remaining in force south of the border. It is important to realize that the new multi-level governance entirely changes the character of coordination problems. For example, if we discovered that students from Lancashire were obliged to pay fees while those from Yorkshire were exempt, we would immediately identify this as a breach of the principle of universal entitlements and a serious policy coordination problem; but the growth of differences of this kind between Scotland and England has to be accepted as a normal consequence of the new system of government.

The issues raised by the development of multi-level governance in Britain are partly technical: any big, complex organization has to work hard at transmitting information and orders from one part to another, and has to work hard at trying to make sure that decisions made by different bits of the organization are consistent with each other. But the issues now go well beyond technicalities. Problems of authority, coordination, control over resources, and battles for turf show that the new system is fundamentally altering the relations of power within the British system. The rise of multi-level governance in Britain involves the transformation of an old Westminster-focused unitary system of government, where power was heavily concentrated in a small number of institutions and people at the centre in London, into a semi-federal system of government, where power and authority are distributed at many different levels, all of which have to invest a great deal of effort in communicating with, and bargaining with, each other.

## Positive decisions, negative decisions and non-decisions

Our discussion of the policy process in Britain has thus far had an important but unacknowledged bias:

we have discussed only cases where government actually takes decisions. But just as important are the decisions that government, for one reason or another, neglects to take. This is what we now examine (and see also Briefing 19.2).

### Power, decision and non-decision

It is natural to be interested in what government actually does – in the great debates that take place, in the policies that arise from these debates, and in the sometimes dramatic choices that follow, such as the decision to go to war. The great drama of historical events provides the stuff of politics. When we look back at Mrs Thatcher's premiership we soon fix on the great drama of the Falklands War of 1982, and likewise we think of the Iraq War of 2003 as a key episode in Tony Blair's term of office. But this focus on the things that happen can blind us to something that is equally important: the things that do not happen, either because it never occurred to anyone to do them, or because the likelihood of their happening has been suppressed. Power in government obviously partly consists in the ability to make things happen: to pass new laws or commit to a military campaign. But power can just as certainly come from the ability to suppress decisions.

The way we usually express this is through the image of an 'agenda' in government. The metaphor of an agenda is approximate but helps make the point more concrete. Imagine a committee meeting. Like most committees it will have a particular agenda – a list of items of business, usually in printed form, about which there will be discussion and decision. Influence in the committee partly consists in the ability to decide what decisions are made on each agenda item. But it is easy to see that even more influence could arise from the ability to make sure that issues for decision inconvenient to a powerful member never actually appear as an agenda item at all, and therefore never have to be defended. The metaphor of an 'agenda' in government is approximate because British government is too varied and complicated to work from a single committee-style agenda. But government at any one time will have its metaphorical agenda: policy issues

# Briefing                    19.2

● ● ● ● ● ● ● ● ● ● ● ● ● ● ● ● ● ● ●

## POSITIVE DECISIONS, NEGATIVE DECISIONS AND NON-DECISIONS: THE CASE OF FUEL TAXES

**Positive decision**: The duty on unleaded petrol for cars presently stands at just over 48p per litre. The duty for ordinary diesel (used for instance in heavy goods vehicles) stands at just over 51p per litre. The levels are uprated periodically, and in the 1990s an 'escalator' was introduced by the Treasury to ensure that the levels were increased automatically.

**Negative decision**: The duty on 'red diesel' stands at just over 3 p per litre. Red diesel is ordinary dyed diesel, available only to farmers for use on their vehicles in connection with farm work. It arises from a 'negative decision': to exempt this class of fuel from the levied duties described under 'positive decision' above, and in particular to exempt this fuel from the 'escalator' clause introduced in the 1990s.

**Non-decision**: Aircraft fuel presently attracts no national fuel duties. The decision dates from the 1944 Chicago Convention. Signatories (of whom Britain is one) are legally bound to exempt aircraft fuel (and some other goods and services used by airlines) from national duties.

● ● ● ● ● ● ● ● ● ● ● ● ● ● ● ● ● ● ●

➲ The distinction between positive, negative and non-decisions is helpful in making sense of why some issues are decided after intense public argument, and others just seem to 'happen'. But the decision is not hard and fast: even the case of the exemption of aircraft fuel from taxation was the result of a negative decision made long ago, and it is increasingly being challenged, notably by those who argue that air traffic is environmentally damaging.

that are thought to be in need of attention, and policy options from which a choice has to be made. Getting something on the agenda of government ensures that it will at least be debated; conversely, keeping it off the agenda means no debate, let alone decision, and no necessity for the interests that benefit from inaction to defend themselves.

There are two ways in which the agenda of policy

debate and decision is shaped: by 'negative decisions' and by 'non-decisions'. They can be hard to distinguish at the edges but nevertheless are worth separating, especially because negative decisions are the easier to identify.

## Negative decisions and the policy agenda

A negative decision happens when some group is sufficiently powerful to manipulate either the content of policy or the terms of political debate to ensure that a decision harmful to its interests is suppressed. In a democratic political system with an inquisitive press that can be a hard trick to pull off. It can usually only be achieved by some group which is especially well placed within the higher reaches of government. The best way to understand how it works is to consider two examples.

● *Taxation of the monarchy.* Although many powerful institutions and individuals hire tax experts to minimize their tax liabilities, or even to ensure that they pay no tax at all, only one individual – the monarch – has enjoyed exemption from the obligation to pay taxes on private income. It has not even been necessary to hire a smart firm of tax accountants to minimize tax liabilities, as other rich people do. This exemption dated from the 1930s, when taxes on income first began to become substantial. It was renewed in 1953 by a truly negative decision: not to extend obligation to pay tax on income to the new monarchy when the present Queen succeeded her father. It lasted until the early 1990s. The result was that the Queen and her advisers did not have to do what all other tax payers were obliged to do: give an account to the Inland Revenue of income, and pay the bill levied by the Revenue.

● *Farmers and planning law.* As anyone who has tried to build a porch on the front of their house knows, there are rigorous laws restricting the alterations we can make to our own houses, and even more rigorous laws restricting our entitlement to put up new buildings. These planning laws are justified on a number of grounds: safety, public health and aesthetics. However, many farm buildings are exempt from these planning regulations. The result is that in erecting new buildings that have agricultural purposes farmers do not, unlike other builders, have to engage in open argument in defence of their proposals.

The point of these examples is not to debate whether the negative decisions are right or wrong; readers can work out their own views. It is to show that decisions *not* to do some things can be just as important in shaping policy as positive decisions favouring a particular course of action. The examples also give us some idea of the conditions under which a 'negative decision' can shape policy. Producing a negative decision demands that the interest or group that it favours already be powerfully placed: the monarchy in the middle of the twentieth century had uniquely good relations with government and was surrounded with such a mystique that it was widely agreed that the monarch should be exempt from many of the rules that governed her subjects.

Negative decisions are not only most likely to favour the already privileged and powerful; they reinforce existing power and privilege. Once the negative decision has been made, the privileged interest no longer has to do what other groups find necessary: mobilize its resources in defence of its interests in open political argument. In some cases – as with the farmers' exemption from some planning law – the exemption is publicly known but is just conventionally accepted as part of the natural order of things. In others, such as the royal exemption from taxes, it was for long not known to the wider public at all.

Exercising power through negative decision is probably becoming harder to achieve. The monarch's exemption from income tax, for example, was abandoned in 1993, at a time when the funding of the monarchy in general was coming under increased public scrutiny. Why it is becoming harder connects to wider questions about the changing nature of democracy in Britain, and we look at those in our final chapter.

## Non-decisions and the policy agenda

Non-decisions are difficult to study. A negative decision, as we saw above, involves a choice at some moment not to do something, and even if the choice is kept secret – as in the case of the monarch's tax-paying obligations – historians usually eventually track it down. But a non-decision does not involve a choice to suppress a particular policy option; it consists of a persistent bias in the way both debates and institutions are organized such that some policy choices never get considered at all (usually because it never occurs to anyone that they are viable options).

This is what gives non-decision its elusive quality. By the definition of non-decision given above there is literally an infinite number of non-decisions 'not taken' at any one time, since the range of options that are *not* considered is numberless. More concretely, we could easily conjure up possible policy options that are never considered because they seem self-evidently absurd. In the last century, for example donkeys, which were once widely employed in farm work, have been made redundant by technological change. Were I to suggest that we should have a national policy for retraining donkeys to do alternative work, backed up with unemployment benefits for donkeys, I would be dismissed as absurdly eccentric. The failure to consider such absurd options tells us nothing about the connection between power, policy and non-decision. But we have to be careful in using the 'absurdity' criterion, because what seems absurd in one historical setting will be revealed as the exercise of power in another. For instance, had we lived at the start of the eighteenth century the notion that there should be policies backed by law prohibiting cruelty to donkeys would have seemed as absurd as paying unemployment benefit to animals. But now we see that failure to consider the possibility of anti-cruelty laws reflected a particularly brutal aspect of power: wielding dominion over helpless creatures in the animal world.

The example of historical change gives us some idea of how to explore the way non-decisions shape policy. Looking back at what was considered absurd, and what sensible, about the protection of animal rights is an exercise in comparison between our own times and some time in the past.

Comparisons of this kind can alert us to what 'non-decisions' to look out for. They can alert us to non-decisions that reflect power differences, as distinct from options that are not considered because they are truly absurd. Comparison is the key to understanding how non-decisions shape policy. Briefing 19.3 shows some of the most important forms of comparison that can illuminate non-decisions.

## Policy success and policy failure in Britain

Government, we now know from all earlier chapters, is a huge presence in all our lives: it literally follows us from the cradle to the grave. Naturally a vital question is therefore what makes government a success or a failure? There is increasing interest in exploring this question through examination of policy: why do some policies succeed and some fail? Most attention is focused on policy failure. There are good reasons for this: if we can isolate why some policies spectacularly fail, then in principle we can improve the chances of success by not repeating those mistakes, because policy failures in recent decades have inflicted huge costs and a great deal of human harm.

### The idea of policy 'failure'

The notion of policy 'failure' is not straightforward. In our private life 'failure' is often easy to identify, but things are more complicated in government, where the aims of policy are often unclear, and the measurement of the impact of policy decision often extremely difficult. Consider for a moment an episode that many of us experience in our private life: taking a driving test. When we take the test we can easily identify success or failure because the aim (to pass) is unambiguous, and the measurement of success straightforward (the decision of the examiner). But government hardly ever takes this straightforward kind of test; indeed, since identifiable failure in government is usually punished by public criticism and even loss of office, governments have a strong incentive to 'fudge' the aims of policy and the way success will be measured. But often

they do not have to 'fudge': ambiguity and uncertainty are built in. Consider an example of a great historic decision, Britain's entry into the original EEC (Common Market) in 1973. Depending on your point of view this either remedied an earlier policy catastrophe (the failure to join the original Common Market at foundation in 1957) or was itself a disaster because it led to the loss of Britain's historical sovereignty. And even measuring the 'impact' of entry in 1973 is very hard: separating out the impact of 'Europe' from all the other forces working on British government in the intervening years is a tall order.

The identification of 'failure' will therefore often be uncertain and controversial (see Briefing 19.4). Nevertheless, there are some important episodes in British government in recent decades which hardly

# Briefing 19.4

## THE MAIN KINDS OF POLICY FIASCO IN BRITAIN

| Type of fiasco | Why a fiasco? | Example |
| --- | --- | --- |
| Icon fiascos | Projects are designed by politicians to create an 'icon' – a prestige project. | Millennium Dome |
| Great Leap Forward fiascos | Named after disastrous 'Great Leap Forward' of Chinese dictator Mao Zedong. Policy tries to short-circuit careful, tedious preparation to achieve a revolutionary breakthrough. | Rail privatization |
| Confrontation fiascos | Power of state and control of Parliament used to 'steamroller' through radical change without consultation. | The Community Charge (also known as the 'poll tax') |
| Club fiascos | Policies are made by insiders in a cosy club without systematic evaluation or investigation. | Banking regulation – especially collapse of Barings Bank in City of London 1995 |
| 'Capture fiascos' | Policy dominated by one set of interests who have captured the policy-making process, to the exclusion of the wider public interest. | BSE (mad cow disease) |

*Source*: Adapted from Moran 2001.

➲ There are many different ways of making policy fiascos; Moran's simple classification tries to enumerate them.

anybody would dispute have amounted to catastrophes. They are also very important for a straightforward reason: they have been identified as catastrophes because the costs they impose (either in money, disruption or loss of life) are great. In other words, they reveal the importance of trying to avoid failure in government, because the scale of modern government means that failure can have huge consequences. Government ministers who make a mess of their private lives mostly damage only themselves and their families; a minister who makes a mess of economic policy damages millions of people.

Just how catastrophic policy failure can be is illustrated by some of the most spectacular instances in British government in recent decades. Public housing provides one well documented example. In the 1950s and 1960s local and central government demolished hundreds of thousands of modest terraced houses that were condemned as slums, and replaced them with high-rise flats. The new estates cost billions. Many were structurally unsound. Most were very unpopular with their residents, and many were social failures, becoming centres of crime, unemployment and despair. A huge number had to be demolished in turn and replaced with 'low rise' dwellings which were near-replicas of the very terraced dwellings they had originally displaced. (Dunleavy 1981 is a classic study of this catastrophe.)

Almost any attempt to travel by train in modern Britain provides another example of failure. Rail privatization was introduced by the Conservative government in the middle of the 1990s. It took a poorly functioning national rail system and turned

## Image 19.1
## The Millennium Dome: a policy catastrophe

Photo: Michael Moran

➲ The modern history of British government is littered with policy fiascos. The strange tent-like structure photographed here across a dreary urban landscape pictures one of the most farcical: the Millennium Dome. Planned as Britain's show-case symbol of the new millennium in 2000, it was a farrago almost from the start: poor project planning, poor cost controls, ludicrously over-optimistic business projections, and even a chaotic opening night. It cost in the end over £750 million of public money, and even now remains an embarrassingly visible symbol of policy failure.

it into a catastrophe. Train reliability declined at one stage to a point when there was effectively no reliable timetabled rail service over large parts of the country. The operator of the track established at privatization, Railtrack, subsequently went bank-rupt. Some other catastrophic policy failures are, mercifully, more short lived, but their costs are huge. For instance, the Millennium Dome, a specially constructed building in east London as Britain's commemoration of the year 2000 ended up costing the taxpayer £750 million, and remained empty for several years, an embarrassment to all connected with it. (see Image 19.1).

Thus we see that policy failure can destroy whole communities (see Political Issues 19.1), can irreparably damage national systems of communica-tion, and can land the tax payer with huge bills.

### Explaining policy failure

Why do these failures happen? There are, broadly, three competing explanations.

*Fatalism.* One obvious possibility is that failure is just inevitable because neither institutions nor people are perfect. There are plenty of examples from the past of disasters: industrial and traffic acci-dents that killed hundreds; military catastrophes that resulted in the death of hundreds of thousands, even millions; failure to protect the physical envi-ronment that resulted in fatal pollution and epidemics. This is often the view that is implicit in official enquiries into disasters: we can learn from disasters, but since the world is an uncertain and dangerous place we must expect disasters to occur in the future.

*The risk society.* Fatalism argues that catastro-phes are nothing new. By contrast, the *risk society* account argues that we are living in novel historical conditions that greatly increase the chances of policy catastrophes, and that these catastrophes in turn inflict harm on large numbers of people. Ours is a *risk society* because this kind of risk of cata-strophic harm is a dominant feature both of govern-ment and of the lives of us all. The scale and

## 19.1   BSE – MAD COW DISEASE

Bovine spongiform encephalopathy, or BSE, more popularly known as mad cow disease, was first recognized as a problem in the 1980s. The disease destroyed cattle's brains, causing them to stagger crazily (hence the vulgar popular name). For a long time, most scientific and official opinion minimized the importance of the disease, first picturing it as marginal to the cattle population, then as confined to cattle. By the mid-1980s it was clear that a huge proportion of the national herd was stricken; soon after, the responsible Ministry admitted that it could 'jump' the species barrier and could potentially infect those who consumed beef from affected cattle. Though never conclusively demonstrated, there is a strong suspicion that consuming infected beef is a source of the human variant of the disease, CJD. Thus far only slightly more than a hundred deaths have been traced to this deadly incurable disease. But the disease is known to have a long incubation period, and estimates of the final likely death toll range from a few hundred to several tens of thousands. An official inquiry, in its final report and in 17 volumes of evidence, traced the history of BSE, the way it grew out of industrialized intensive farming, and the way the meat in turn entered the human food chain. The 'facts' are therefore very well known, but the issue illuminates the diversity of theoretical themes that run through this chapter:

- The failure to recognize and contain the disease is one of the most spectacular instances of the policy failure for which British government is so well known (see Briefing 19.4).
- Despite the magnitude of the catastrophe not a single minister or official resigned or was punished for the failures, despite the fact that the report of the official inquiry documented a long history of official concealment. Perhaps the most notorious stunt involved a minister publicly feeding a beefburger to his daughter to demonstrate food safety.
- BSE illustrates one of the major recurrent issues in modern policy making, discussed in the accompanying section of this chapter: the central place of 'risk' in our modern experiences with big organizations. BSE grew out of many of the features that make society a 'risk society'. It involved processes and technologies unknown to lay people; it imposed risk collectively throughout society; and it involved the exercise of power by powerful coalitions of organizations in government and in the food and agricultural industries.

To read more of the evidence on BSE, see www.bseinquiry.gov.uk

geographical reach of modern technologies mean that when they fail they inflict catastrophic harm on large numbers of people who cannot, separately, do anything to protect themselves. The most obvious example is the threat from safety failures in nuclear power plants: the 'meltdown' at the Chernobyl nuclear power reactor in the old Soviet Union in 1986 spread radiation across wide parts of Europe. But the 'risk society' is not only about the objective

existence of risk; it is also about perceptions of risk. Rising levels of education, the spread of different forms of reporting in a wide range of mass media, and the increasing willingness of citizens to organize in defence of their interests means that there is growing sensitivity to risk and growing willingness to organize in response to the prospect of risk. Thus governments find themselves in a difficult position: they are increasingly likely to fail catastrophically in

# DEBATING POLITICS

## 19.1   POLICY FAILURES: ARE THE BRITISH UNIQUELY INCOMPETENT?

| Britain is uniquely prone to massive policy failure | There is nothing unique about the British experience |
|---|---|
| ■ The history of national decline in the twentieth century, especially of economic decline, is testimony to policy failure.<br><br>■ Huge misjudgements were made about matters of high policy, such as the decision to stand aside from the early stages of European unification in the 1950s.<br><br>■ From high-rise housing to Concorde to the Millennium Dome: virtually any policy area produces an example of a catastrophic project.<br><br>■ Excessive centralization, excessive secrecy, and weak management skills locked Britain into a cycle of failed decisions, preventing learning from failure. | ■ Fiascos are inevitable given the scale and complexity of modern government.<br><br>■ 'Failure' is often a contested judgement: it is not obvious that 'high politics' (such as attitudes to European unification) can be judged a failure.<br><br>■ Numerous examples can be found abroad of great policy fiascos: indeed, one commonly cited British fiasco – the decision to build the Concorde airliner – was shared with the French.<br><br>■ British policy performance, especially in economic policy, actually compares well with our big European neighbours over the last 25 years. |

making policy, but they face increasing demands from their citizens to protect against the consequences of failure.

*A British disease.*   Arguments that policy failure is just inevitable given the complexity of modern government, or is the product of a risk society, obviously assert that failure in Britain is not due to particular British conditions. But while all countries experience policy catastrophes, not all suffer the same levels and kinds of catastrophe: only Britain made a complete mess of running its rail network; and only Britain built the Millennium Dome. The suspicion is obvious: policy failure is a British disease (see Debating Politics 19.1). If the British are uniquely prone to policy failure, it could be due to a variety of factors. One is technical incompetence. Getting policy right in modern government demands a very high level of technical skill, stretching from a mastery of scientific and financial information in making a policy decision, to competence in managing complex projects to conclusion. Politicians hardly ever have these skills; and the tradition of the gifted amateur 'generalist' in the civil service for a long time undervalued them among permanent officials. A second culprit might

be overcentralization of the machinery of policy making. Before the devolution measures introduced by Labour in 1997, the United Kingdom had one of the most centralized systems of government among democratic countries. Centralization guarantees that one catastrophic policy decision at the centre – such as rail privatization – sends its effects widely across the whole society. The new systems of multi-level governance discussed earlier, for all the new problems they bring, may therefore be a way of reducing the likelihood of catastrophic policy failure.

A final source of policy failure may be secrecy. One way to try to avoid making wrong decisions in our everyday lives is by consulting and debating. Organizations that allow open criticism and scrutiny also raise the chances of learning from failure. But there is a long tradition of secrecy and concealment in British government. This culture of secrecy was strengthened in the twentieth century by the impact of war, and the threat of war. In Chapters 21 and 22 we will explore further what the

There have been five major themes in this chapter:

1 'Policy' in British government is rarely the result of one single decision; it is part of a continuous stream of choices;
2 A central problem of British policy making, therefore, is the problem of managing this continuous stream of choice so as to ensure some consistency in policy;
3 Problems of coordination have become more urgent with the rise of multi-level governance in Britain;
4 The visible face of policy choice is complemented by two other faces: of negative decisions and non-decisions, both of which exert great influence over the policies pursued by British government;
5 The search for policy success is imperative, because the costs of failure, human and financial, can be huge.

rise of national security did to the secrecy with which many parts of British government operates.

## Further reading

Rhodes (1997) is a very accessible introduction to theories of the policy process and multi-level governance. Parsons (1995) is comprehensive on theories of the policy process. The idea of non-decisions and negative decisions is still best described for the beginner by Lukes (2004). Moran (2001) introduces the debate about British policy failures. Hood, Rothstein and Baldwin (2001) explore the idea of risk and policy, and provide some good, concrete case studies.

# CHAPTER 20

# Understanding policy: framing policy controversies

## CONTENTS

## AIMS

The chapter has the following aims:

❖ To describe some of the most important policy controversies in British politics

❖ To show how these controversies do not arise randomly, and to demonstrate how they fit recurrent patterns of division; their recognition depends on how they are 'framed'

❖ To illustrate these recurrent patterns by describing some particularly intense modern policy controversies.

## Policy in the frame

We saw in Chapter 19 that policy making is a *process*, and the way that process is conducted has big consequences: it can shape the success or otherwise of policy. But most of us do not experience policy as a kind of disembodied process: we experience it as real live controversy that often moves us, sometimes to fury. In the chapters that follow this present one we will examine some of the big themes that are embodied in the policy process in Britain: themes such as how resources are raised and distributed (Chapter 21) and how the state uses its power over individual citizens (essentially the dominant concern of the final Chapters 22–24 of this book).

Policy is also about more immediate things, however, and they are the things that impinge on our lives whether we consciously take part in political activity or not. This chapter is about those things: it puts some 'flesh' on the otherwise general, disembodied processes and issues that move so many of us. It looks, in short, at key policy controversies, but it does this by setting these controversies in their contexts. If we follow politics through the media for even a short period of time one of the things that will soon strike us is how short can be the life of immediate controversies: issues rise and then disappear with bewildering rapidity. Politicians typically have a short attention span, and they need a short attention span because they live in a world where one controversy, and even one crisis, rapidly succeeds another. As students of the system, though, we cannot just live in this short-term world: we need some way of setting the short term in a wide context. That is what is done in this chapter.

A technical way of expressing this is to say that policy controversies have to be 'framed', put into a setting that is wider than that suggested by the immediate controversy. The idea behind framing is simple. If we consider how we frame the physical world – either literally in framing it in a painting or photograph, or by arranging physical objects in a certain pattern – the way we do the framing affects our perception of each element of the picture, and of the whole scene: we can change the meaning by altering the alignment of the frame, or the clustering of the objects in the frame. In an analogous manner, we can 'frame' the political world: we put some issues at the periphery of the picture, and can make new connections that create new 'clusters' of issues. Of course no 'framing' is definitive. Indeed, that is one of the lessons at the heart of this chapter. Although every controversy fits some kind of frame, *how* it is framed can change dramatically: over time; over the life of a policy controversy; and depending on who is doing the framing. Take the campaign to abolish (or regulate and restrict) fox hunting, an issue that we examine later in the chapter. This can be 'framed' as an issue of animal rights; or as a 'class' issue (because those against fox hunting commonly believe that hunting is a recreation of the traditionally wealthy); or as an urban versus rural issue (because in part it involves a split between different attitudes to nature held by those who live in the countryside and those – the majority of Britons – who live in cities and large towns).

We can see how changeable are policy 'frames' by thinking about things historically. Up until the early 1920s the great domestic controversies in British politics could be fitted into four big frames:

- Class politics: these were the huge struggles for control of wealth that, for example, divided organized labour and the representatives of business.
- Territorial politics: these were the highly divisive issues to do with the nature of the United Kingdom. Their most explosive manifestation was the Irish armed struggle for independence, 1916–21.
- Religious politics: these encompassed struggles for control of education, struggles over the power of the Anglican Church, and struggles over 'moral' issues such as control of the drink trade.
- Gender politics: the most important of these concerned the struggle for women's suffrage, substantially won by 1918.

This historical list is highly revealing because it alerts us once again to an important truth: policy frames are neither self-evident nor unchanging. For nearly half-a-century after the early 1920s three of these frames – territory, religion and gender – virtually disappeared from open political controversy. (This is not the same as saying that the policy *problems* to which they related were solved.) Virtually every big domestic controversy for half a century was framed as a 'class' controversy. This reflected the fact that British politics was dominated in these decades by two mass parties, Labour and the Conservatives; by the fact that these parties represented competing class blocs; and by the fact that the two parties fought each other over quintessentially class issues.

This last observation gives us a clue to why in recent decades the framing of policy controversy has changed, and why it is now so malleable. We know from our earlier chapters that these two giant political forces are in decline; we know that politics is increasingly organized around single-issue groups; and we know that these groups are constantly mobilizing and declining. The worlds of policy controversy are thus now highly unstable. This means that the 'frames' or contexts described in this chapter cannot be exhaustive or definitive; they are simply handy means at our disposal to make sense of everyday controversies. This in turn recalls one of the main themes of the preceding chapter: that issues can be important not only because they are the object of controversy, but often because they are not the object of controversy. Non-decisions and negative decisions can be critical both to the exercise of power, and to what government does. This chapter, which focuses on open controversy, should therefore be read bearing in mind our earlier discussion of the importance of the decisions that are not made, and the controversies that are not ventilated.

In what follows, seven frames for policy controversy are sketched, and some of the most immediate controversies in British politics are put into those frames. Some of these controversies will be short lived; they might even have disappeared from the front pages of newspapers by the time the present reader uses this book. But even if they have, the reader will have no difficulty in setting new controversies into these frames.

## Image 20.1
## The new face of issue politics in Britain

Photo: Fiona Hanson/PA/EMPICS

➲ The photo is of a young demonstrator on one of the many mass demonstrations against the Iraq War in 2003. The war mobilized hitherto virtually unrecognized groups. It crystallized the new face of issue politics in Britain – a politics that confounds established stereotypes, in the manner well represented by this young demonstrator. Notice the headband: in her own unique way the demonstrator has broadened anti-war protest into something wider.

## War and peace

Look back briefly at Chapter 2, notably at Image 2.1, p. 29. What this will bring to mind is how warlike the British have been for several centuries and how far the great world wars of the twentieth century (1914–18 and 1939–45) marked Britain, economically, culturally and even physically. Some of these wars – such as that against Nazi Germany, 1939–45 – were supported by the overwhelming majority of the country. Others (such as the war against the white Boers in South Africa, 1899–1902) caused deep political division between supporters and opponents of the conflict. Many intense policy controversies in Britain are thus framed by the context of 'war and peace'. A power-

---

## DOCUMENTING POLITICS 20.1

### WAR AND PEACE: THE OFFICIAL GROUNDS FOR THE INVASION OF IRAQ IN 2003

'In recent months, I have been increasingly alarmed by the evidence from inside Iraq that despite sanctions, despite the damage done to his capability in the past, despite the UN Security Council Resolutions expressly outlawing it, and despite his denials, Saddam Hussein is continuing to develop WMD, and with them the ability to inflict real damage upon the region, and the stability of the world … Gathering intelligence inside Iraq is not easy. Saddam's is one of the most secretive and dictatorial regimes in the world. So I believe people will understand why the Agencies cannot be specific about the sources, which have formed the judgements in this document, and why we cannot publish everything we know … What I believe the assessed intelligence has established beyond doubt is that Saddam has continued to produce chemical and biological weapons, that he continues in his efforts to develop nuclear weapons, and that he has been able to extend the range of his ballistic missile programme … And the document discloses that his military planning allows for some of the WMD to be ready within 45 minutes of an order to use them.'

➲ The text reproduces part of the Prime Minister's foreword to the key intelligence report which provided the grounds for British support for an invasion of Iraq in 2003: that the dictator had and was continuing to develop Weapons of Mass Destruction (WMD). The extract also contains perhaps the single most contentious assertion in the whole history of the war: that WMD could 'be ready within 45 minutes'. The force of events drove this issue of war and peace to the centre of the policy frame from 2003 onwards.

*Source*: www.number-10.gov.uk.output.page284.asp

---

ful example is provided by the Iraq War that began in 2003.

This war fits the the second category, that of deeply dividing wars. Its immediate origins lie in two sets of events. First, the Iraqi dictator Saddam Hussein invaded the small oil-rich state of Kuwait in August 1990. In November 1990 a UN Resolution sanctioned the creation of an Allied force to expel Saddam. The force was led by the United States and Britain was a leading participant. The Iraqis were expelled from Kuwait by February 1991; the subsequent ceasefire still left Saddam in power in Iraq.

The second set of events occurred on 11 September 2001, when planes hijacked by terrorists were deliberately crashed into the giant twin towers of the World Trade Center in New York, and into the Pentagon, the headquarters of the US Defense Department in Washington. More than 3,000 people were killed in the attacks, responsibility being claimed by Al-Qaeda, an organization in turn claiming to be led by a terrorist of Saudi origin, Usama Bin Laden. This attack provoked an American-led invasion of Afghanistan, with Britain playing a supporting role. The invasion was designed to remove a regime which was believed to harbour the terrorist organization claiming responsibility for the September 11 attacks. But in 2003 the attacks of '9/11' also provided the grounds for the second war against Iraq. Again, an American-led alliance, with significant British participation, secured a swift military victory, this time toppling the regime and sending Saddam into hiding until his eventual capture in December 2003.

The Iraq War has created the bitterest policy divisions in the history of modern British politics. Two members of the government, including the former Foreign Secretary, Robin Cook, resigned immediately over the decision to commit troops. (Another member of the Cabinet, Clare Short, resigned later.) Some 139 Labour MPs rebelled in the critical vote on commitment to war in March 2003. The Labour party in Parliament and beyond meanwhile has become increasingly hostile to the commitment. The popular anti-war movement has mobilized the largest demonstrations seen in modern Britain (see Image 20.1). The main opposition party in Westminster, the Conservatives, are divided over the war. Every other party, in both the Westminster and the devolved Parliaments, is opposed.

Division has focused on three issues. The first issue is the legality of the war. Opponents argue that it required, and did not receive, the formal authority of a UN resolution. The government argues that earlier UN resolutions, and Saddam's failure to comply with them, gave authority (but its own chief legal adviser in the Foreign Office resigned on precisely this point). Second, the war was fought on the claim that Saddam possessed weapons of mass destruction (WMD) and links to Al-Qaeda (see Documenting Politics 20.1). Opponents point out that neither of these claims has been supported, despite close postwar searches for supporting evidence. The Prime Minister has come close to apologizing for these 'errors' but insists that the removal of a brutal dictator still justifies the war. Third, the swift military victory has not been followed by peace. Opponents argue that Iraq is a more dangerous and unstable place than even under Saddam, and that 'peacekeeping' involves brutal encounters that actually encourage support for terrorist militants. The British and American governments argue that this is a necessary stage of instability while effective democratic institutions are created in post-Saddam Iraq.

## Britain and Europe

We have seen at numerous points in this book that membership of the European Union is a central feature of political life in Britain: reshaping government institutions, reshaping the way interests are represented, and reshaping the lines of political divi-

sion. Issues concerning the future development of the Union now rival traditional lines of political conflict – such as those between capital and labour – as the defining line of division in British politics. In short, many policy controversies are now framed in 'Britain and Europe' terms. This is what gives controversies involving the Union, whether large or small, such intensity. The most recent, and potentially most divisive, concerns a proposed new Constitution for the Union, the product of long debate in a constitutional convention presided over by the former French President, Valéry Giscard d'Estaing.

An agreement on a treaty for a Constitution was settled under the Irish Presidency in June 2004, and signed by member states in October 2004. The Constitution only comes into force, however, after ratification within individual member states, usually by a referendum. Blair's government has presented the Treaty and the Constitution as essentially a modernising and tidying-up operation, systematizing a range of procedures that have developed piecemeal over the longer history of European integration. It insists that it has drawn, and successfully defended, a series of 'red lines'. These lines mark key policy areas (including control of most taxation), thus defending Britain from the authority of the institutions of the European Union.

Blair's government originally declined to hold a referendum on acceptance of the new Constitution. This contrasted with its willingness to hold a referendum before any British adoption of the Euro in place of sterling. The justification was the familiar one that the new Constitution was only a modernizing, piecemeal measure of no great historical significance. In 2004, however, the Prime Minister announced, in a sudden and unexpected change of policy, that a referendum would indeed be held to ratify, or not, the new Constitution. Some viewed this about turn as a concession to the power of the press baron Rupert Murdoch whose publications, notably *The Sun*, are hostile to the Union and to any perceived extension of its powers. That accusation has been denied by both the Murdoch interests and the government. More immediately, the concession of a referendum attempted to match a commitment that the Conservative Party had already made (see Documenting Politics 20.2), and to prevent the

## DOCUMENTING POLITICS 20.2

## BRITAIN AND EUROPE: THE EUROPEAN CONSTITUTION MARKS A LINE DRAWN IN THE SAND BETWEEN THE TWO MAIN WESTMINSTER PARTIES

'In June 2004, Tony Blair signed Britain up to a European Constitution, even though most people in Britain oppose it. This Constitution will, in the words of the Belgian Prime Minister, be the 'capstone' of a 'federal state'. The EU will win new powers at Britain's expense. Decision-making will become less accountable and more distant for British voters … After a long campaign led by the Conservative Party, Tony Blair was forced to reverse his opposition to giving the British people a referendum on the European Constitution. Now the British people will have the final say in a vote that will have to be held by the end of 2006. Tony Blair wants to delay the issue for as long as possible … But now that the final text has been agreed, Conservatives believe that the British people should be given the chance to decide as soon as possible … So, if the Conservative Party wins the next general election, we will hold a referendum by October 2005 … Conservatives are opposed to the idea of having an EU Constitution: the EU doesn't need one. Countries have constitutions; nation-states make treaties between each other. The EU needs to become more flexible to meet the challenges of the 21st century. The EU Constitution would be bad for Britain and bad for Europe.'

➲ This extract ftom the Conservative Party's policy position on the European Constitution shows how EU issues are now critical to drawing a dividing line over policy between the two major Westminster parties. We see here the Conservative party trying to reframe political division in an entirely novel way.

*Source*: Conservative Party (2004).

government seeming to deny popular choice on the referendum issue. Conservative hostility has been reinforced by the rise of the UK Independence Party as a rival to the Conservatives for the 'Eurosceptic' vote (see Political Issues 15.1, p. 334 for an example).

The referendum on the European Constitution is thus part of a larger pattern. That pattern links to one of the main themes of this book: the degree to which membership of the EU is increasingly a defining feature of the lines of political controversy in Britain. The demand for a referendum, and the upcoming campaign, are only two skirmishes in a longer, larger battle. Thirty years of membership of the Union have helped create a large political bloc sympathetic to the aim of deepening and widening European integration, and another bloc deeply hostile to the institutions and practices of the European Union. This latter bloc is mostly lodged in the Conservative party, the UK Independence Party, and some sections of the business commu-

nity. But it is also present to a lesser degree in the Labour party and in some sections of the trade union movement. Thus even 'victory' in referendums(whether acceptance that the Euro should replace sterling or that the Constitution should be ratified) will never be final. Euroscepticism is now lodged as a permanent, organized feature of British politics. How far the Conservative party will become defined by its Euroscepticism – in the way that in the past it has been defined by its support for the market economy, or for the Union of the United Kingdom – will depend in part on how sustained is the electoral challenge of the UK Independence Party.

## People and animals

Human behaviour towards the natural world has provided a source of key policy issues for over two

## DOCUMENTING POLITICS 20.3

### PEOPLE AND ANIMALS: THE DIVISIONS OVER FOX HUNTING

'We cannot hide behind the pretence that the Bill is a private Member's Bill. It is the Bill of a Labour Government who propose to fly in the face of principle and the evidence. Two inquiries have been held, at vast public expense, and neither produced any evidence to justify a ban on hunting. A regulatory Bill was introduced, which my right hon. Friend the Minister said was based on principle and evidence. No fair or open-minded person could conclude that the evidence exists to justify this Bill or that it is in the public interest. My right hon. Friend the Prime Minister said on 1 September 2004 that he had identified seven key challenges for the future of this country. He said that he had a key test for legislation and that was whether it would in practical terms advance and improve the lives of Britain's hard-working families in the future. He must know that this Bill will not do that. In contrast to the opponents of hunting, the rural community has shown its reasonableness and openness to scrutiny. It has participated fully in the Government's inquiries and hearings and the hunting community has placed itself under an independent regulatory body.'

⮕ The extract is from a speech in the House of Commons in September 2004 on the latest attempt to pass legislation to outlaw fox hunting. It is remarkable for its bitterness, for the fact that it is a speech by an MP from an urban (London) constituency, and for the fact that it is by Kate Hoey, Labour MP, one of a tiny minority opposed to a ban. The bill became law in 2005 and the anti-hunting lobby was quite ineffective in the 2005 general election.

*Source*: HC Debates, 15 September 2004, col. 1413.

centuries, ranging from the earliest movements for the humane treatment of animals to campaigns to protect the natural environment from pollution and degradation. Thus the regulation of our relations with the natural world provides a ready frame for a wide range of contentious issues. The issue of banning fox hunting, which has been 'live' almost from the first moment of the return of New Labour to office in 1997, is the latest, and one of the most acrimonious, episodes in this history (see Documenting Politics 20.3). At the time of writing the government is threatening to invoke the Parliament Act to put on to the statute book a bill to outlaw hunting with dogs, a measure aimed primarily at fox hunting but that will also affect other sports, such as hare coursing. (The Parliament Act allows a government with a majority in the House of Commons to override the ability of the House of Lords to modify and delay measures that have passed through the stages of legislation in the House of Commons.)

The threat to invoke the Parliament Act – an almost unprecedented measure – has been provoked by the tortuous history of attempts to legislate, and by the deep divisions created by the attempt to ban fox hunting. Though the measure has been passed in the Commons in a free vote, without instructions from Whips, the reality is that attitudes to banning fox hunting neatly separate the two main Westminster parties, Labour and the Conservatives: only a tiny number of Labour MPs including Kate Hoey, oppose a ban; only a tiny number of Conservatives including Ann Widdecombe, support the measure. The Conservative party has pledged to provide Parliamentary time for its repeal under a future Conservative government, which in effect is a pledge to repeal, since a House of Commons with a Conservative majority would undoubtedly also have a majority opposed to the ban.

The fox hunting issue is important in its own right because it has proved one of the longest running, and most difficult to settle, since the return of Labour in 1997. But it has a wider significance. Opposition to the ban on fox hunting has been the single most important issue uniting the Countryside Alliance, a loose coalition that has organized some of the largest public demonstrations of recent years (demonstrations that in size are rivalled only by the campaign opposed to the Iraq War). The issue also shows how new styles of political campaigning are testing the boundaries of acceptable political protest. Anti-fox hunting saboteurs have for several decades gone to the very edge of legality, and sometimes beyond, in trying to stop hunting. Supporters of hunting have now threatened, if the sport is outlawed, that they too will hunt in defiance of the law.

There is an even wider significance to the issue. Campaigns for animal rights now go well beyond the issue of hunting animals for sport. They encompass the conditions under which animals are farmed and, most explosively in recent years, the use of animals in laboratory research, notably for purposes of medical research. Firms and universities that operate animal research laboratories have been, and continue to be, targeted by those who oppose experiments on animals. The targeting has spanned the full range of political campaigning, from the lawful holding of demonstrations outside research facilities, to picketing that verges on the unlawful, to full-scale unlawful intimidation, including the threat to commit acts of violence against individual researchers and their families. A generation ago debates over 'animal rights' were among the most genteel areas of controversy in British politics; now they are the issue where the boundaries of acceptable political pressure are constantly being challenged, both by supporters and opponents of restrictive legislation.

## Global and local

All the issues we have highlighted in this chapter so far have been the source of highly publicized campaigns and deep political division. But not all campaigns on policy issues in Britain are striking for their strength; some are striking because they are diffuse or weak. The tension between the global and the local – focusing on 'globalization' and its alleged defects – is a good instance. In recent years it has provided a powerful focus of political protest in many countries other than Britain; in short, a powerful 'frame' for many political controversies. 'Summits' of the leaders of the world's most powerful national economies – the G-8 group that includes Britain – have provoked widespread, often turbulent and violent, demonstrations against globalization, such as occurred on a large scale in Seattle in 1999. In some other countries of the EU, notably France, firms that symbolize globalization, such as McDonald's, have been the targets of physical attacks. Campaigns against globalization worldwide therefore seem to touch a deep chord.

The British experience is different. While individual public campaigns against globalization and its alleged defects have been important, the anti-globalization movement has never reached the cohesion and level of organization achieved in recent years by other campaigning movements: a level that, for instance, enabled the Countryside Alliance and the campaign against the Iraq War to organize public demonstrations on a historically unprecedented scale. There have indeed been some anti-globalization campaign in Britain. These include demonstrations in the City of London – a powerful symbol of globalization because of its role as a great centre of world financial trading – which have caused physical damage and disruption of trading. Some of the most important campaigning groups in the more orthodox world of pressure groups also invoke a language hostile to globalization: look back, for instance, at the example in Documenting Politics 13.1, p. 293 to see its use in a church-backed campaign against Third World debt. Piecemeal campaigns by particular groups are also often surrogates for campaigns against globalization. For example, demonstrations by farmers against large supermarket chains, involving claims that the chains use their power to cut prices paid at the 'farm gate', often involve hostility to the global sourcing of products at the expense of buying locally. But these different campaigns have never coalesced in the manner of anti-war or pro-countryside

**DOCUMENTING POLITICS 20.4**

## GLOBAL AND LOCAL: THE TWO TONYS ON GLOBALIZATION

Tony Blair:    'The alternative to globalization is isolation.'

Tony Benn:    'The big question today is: Will globalization allow democracy to survive? On the one side, we have the multinationals, the International Monetary Fund, and the European Union. I want to help redress the other side.'

⮕ Put 'quotations on globalisation' into Google and it yields over 41,000 results. (The number rises to over 102,000 if we use the z style of spelling.) These two are chosen because they illustrate the important fault line in British politics: within the left, between New and Old Labour. The Blair remark is from his speech to the Labour Party Annual Conference, October 2001; the Benn, from a BBC interview in March 2001 when he announced his retirement from the House of Commons. New Labour, and Mr Blair in particular, was critical in putting 'globalization' into the policy frame from the 1990s onwards.

movements. Comprehensive 'framing' has not been achieved.

There are two possible explanations for this state of affairs, and they involve diametrically opposing propositions. One is that anti-globalization protests are so well organized by specialist groups – charities campaigning against debt, farmers campaigning against global trade in agricultural goods, anti-war protesters campaigning against American global power – that there is no demand for an umbrella anti-globalization movement. In other words, it is not that anti-globalization campaigns are weak in Britain; it is that they are very strong, but are specialized in their targets. As we saw in Chapter 9, the world of pressure group organization now offers opportunities to organize on a mass scale for a huge variety of special interests and distinctive views, and these opportunities have been expanded by new technologies of communication and mobilization.

An alternative, opposing, explanation is that there is little demand for a full scale anti-globalization movement in Britain because Britain is a country peculiarly favourable to globalization: a country with the dominant global language (English) which exposes its culture to the full influence of cultural globalization; an economy which is peculiarly open to the investment and marketing by the biggest

globally organized corporations; and a government which is uniquely closely allied to the great power that is associated with, and promotes, globalization, the United States (see also Documenting Politics 20.4).

## Life and death

Issues of life and death have long been a source of policy argument and political campaigning in Britain. The abolition of the death penalty as an extreme punishment by the state in 1965 only came, for example, after a long public and parliamentary campaign. But three sets of policy issues have more recently proved highly charged and difficult to resolve; indeed, are becoming more and more difficult. They all show the importance of 'life and death' as a frame for policy controversy. All concern the circumstances when life can be legally brought to an end. One factor that links them is the impact of changes in both medical technology and cultural assumptions about the conditions under which life can be ended.

The first controversy concerns abortion – the termination of life in the womb. After a long campaign, abortion was legalized in 1967 under closely regulated circumstances. These circum-

## DOCUMENTING POLITICS 20.5

## LIFE AND DEATH: REACTIONS TO A COURT DECISION

The judge's decision in the Charlotte Wyatt case is in the 'best interests' of the child, the British Medical Association said.

Dr Michael Wilks, chairman of the BMA's ethics committee, said: 'It is unusual for doctors and parents not to agree about whether or not to resuscitate a very seriously ill baby but when no consensus can be reached, the only way forward is for the case to go to court.

'The BMA is confident that Mr Justice Hedley, after having heard all relevant information, has made the right decision in the best interests of Charlotte Wyatt.'

Mencap chief executive Jo Williams said: 'Doctors should not make assumptions about the quality of life of disabled children.

'These difficult decisions for doctors and parents of very fragile children must properly take account of the value of the child's life and whether prolonging it would lead to intolerable pain.'

➲ The box reprints reactions to the third 'life and death' issue described in the text: the decision of a court in 2004 defining the conditions under which medical treatment could be withheld from a seriously ill baby. Even these restrained comments show the intense, agonized feelings aroused by such cases. The first quotation is from the leading doctors' organisation; the second from the main charity representing the mentally handicapped. The issue shows how technology can force new issues of life and death into the policy frame.

*Source*: *The Journal*, 8 October 2004.

stances specify both time (the length of time after conception when abortion is permissible) and grounds (the circumstances, medical and otherwise, that provide the reasons for the termination of pregnancy). The original legislation of 1967 amounted to an attempt to settle the terms for permissible abortion, an effort to create a consensus around this highly charged issue. That consensus has been undermined by a mix of technical and cultural change: by changes in the technology of abortion which have made it a simpler and more easily available medical procedure; by changes in medical technology that have blurred the line between contraception and abortion; and by changed cultural assumptions that challenge the power of medical professionals to make judgements about the rights of women to decide whether or not to carry a child to term. The grounds for abortion occasion in Britain nothing like the deep political divisions that exist in the United States (where they

determine the votes of many electors), but the effort of the 1967 law to create a consensus has not succeeded.

The second life and death issue concerns life right at the other end of the age span, among the very old. A mixture of improved material conditions and new medical technologies has significantly lengthened the span of life in Britain. Most people live to a vigorous and healthy old age. A minority do not, and a smaller minority still wish to end their lives voluntarily: to commit euthanasia, in the language usually employed in this debate. Some EU jurisdictions – for instance, the Netherlands – have responded to the issue by creating carefully regulated circumstances where patients can be given medical assistance to end their lives. Britain has not created these conditions. A number of agonizing cases have come to the courts where, for example, elderly people have assisted in the deaths of their terminally ill, and suffering, spouses. Although a number of campaigning groups exist to legalise euthanasia under specified conditions, it is easy to see why political parties are highly reluctant to adopt a position on such a sensitive and highly divisive issue.

The third issue is equally sensitive and potentially divisive. Advances in medical care now mean that babies who, in a previous generation, would have died at or before birth because they suffer severe medical problems, now survive to and beyond birth, but with little or no prospect of living anything other than brief and painful lives. Medical professionals agonize about how far to intervene to prolong those lives, and what level of intervention constitutes 'aggressive' treatment (treatment that causes excessive suffering). The attachment of parents to their new-born babies means that they often oppose the ending of treatment, and so courts have had to settle such divisions in recent years (see Documenting Politics 20.5).

## Men and women

At least one of the issues summarized above – abortion – is 'gendered': that is, at its heart lie policy issues to do with the relations between men and women. The 'gendering' of the policy world is perhaps the most striking development to come over the substance of policy making in Britain in the last generation: it has affected issues as different as taxation policy, poverty policy and employment policy, as well as the more obviously relevant domains of sexual relations and control over conditions of conception and birth. It is thus a striking example of the power of 'framing' in shaping the way policy controversy is expressed.

One of the most important policy domains where gender has been critical to policy controversies concerns the family. In particular, the high rate of marital and partnership breakdown in Britain has made the issue of parental access to children a key source of contention. The campaigning group, *Fathers4Justice*, has in recent years mounted a series of highly publicized stunts (see Image 20.2) to publicize its case that in arbitrating between parents in access cases the courts and policy makers have

### Image 20.2
### Guarding the guardians: mobilizing the physical might of the state

Photo: Stefan Rousseau/PA/EMPICS

➲ The campaigning group *Fathers4Justice* is illustrated in Documenting Politics 20.6 of this chapter. The photo was taken in the wake of one of the most spectacular stunts mounted by the group in 2004: a protester scaling Buckingham Palace (to the balcony where the monarch usually acknowledges public demonstrations), dressed as a cartoon character. The ensuing panic showed a striking difference between the 'dignified' and the effective coercive power of the state. The Palace is nominally protected by Guardsmen; as the photo shows, however, when a real threat occurred it was necessary to call in police with sub-machine guns. In the photo the nominal guardians are themselves being protected. The image encapsulates many of the themes about state power which we drew from Max Weber in Chapter 1: the state as both a locus of coercion and of authority.

shown a distinct gender bias in favour of mothers. These stunts have included launching 'bombs' of dyed ink at the Prime Minister from the public gallery of the House of Commons; closing roads by climbing linking bridges; and invading Buckingham Palace, demonstrating on the balcony from which the monarch usually reviews public displays. In addition, the campaign has succeeded in gathering some 'celebrity' endorsements (see Documenting Politics 20.6).

---

**DOCUMENTING POLITICS 20.6**

## MEN AND WOMEN: BOB GELDOF 'GENDERS' PARENTAL CUSTODY ISSUES

'The intent is that the law should always act in the best interests of the child. We all agree with that. But the unspoken assumption is that the interests of the child are nearly always best served by the presence of the mother. This is simply wrong. Only in exceptional circumstances will a man be allowed to raise his children – something that outside the justice system and within society is assumed to be inalienable upon his child's birth. The law is creating vast wells of misery, massive discontent, an unstable society of feral children and feckless adolescents who have no understanding of authority, no knowledge of a man's love and how different but equal it is to a woman's. It also creates irresponsible mothers, drifting, hopeless fathers, problem, violent and ill-educated sons and daughters, a disconnection from the extended family and society at large.'

➲  The campaigning group *Fathers4Justice*, discussed in the text, received a celebrity endorsement from former genteel punk rocker and famine relief fund raiser, Sir Bob Geldof. Geldof's arguments, parts of which are reprinted here, are notable for the way they 'gender' the issue, and explicitly oppose the assumption that women are the primary, and appropriate, carers for children. This reframes gender issues in an entirely new way. In December 2003 *The Sun* newspaper announced a joint 'justice for dads' campaign with Geldof.

*Source*: Geldof (2003).

---

The *Fathers4Justice* campaign has to be understood in the context of the increasingly gendered character of policy controversy in Britain. Two features are particularly important. First, in court-arbitrated disputes about parental access to children, statistically the courts have tended to judge in favour of the mother. In the longer run, fathers have shown a high likelihood of losing contact with their natural children. Second, the campaign comes after a generation when campaigning, on gender issues has overwhelmingly focused on women-related issues – from abortion to inequalities in employment – on the grounds that the historical bias of institutions and policy has been overwhelmingly against the interests of women. *Fathers4Justice* therefore represents in part a male 'backlash' against this generation long trend. How far this can provide the basis of a more sustained political movement is uncertain. Some campaigners are attempting to generalize the issue into a wider campaign favouring a return to more traditional institutions and values, such as those represented by monogamy and stability in marriage. The Conservative party has shown some interest, though an uncertain interest, in supporting both the *Fathers4Justice* case and the more general campaign for traditional family values. But there are serious difficulties with this, as shown by an earlier 'Back to Basics' campaign launched by John Major during his period as prime minister in the 1990s. That was derailed by revelations about the marital irregularities of some of his own colleagues, and has subsequently been further ridiculed by the revelation that Major himself conducted an extra-marital affair with a fellow Conservative MP. Since the marital lives of leading politicians are no less chaotic than those of the rest of us, charges of hypocrisy are always a danger in any 'moral' campaign about the relations between men and women.

### Rich and poor

For most of the twentieth century the division between rich and poor underlay the most important

---

**DOCUMENTING POLITICS 20.7**

### RICH AND POOR: PETER MANDELSON ON THE ATTITUDE OF NEW LABOUR TO THE 'FILTHY RICH'

'We are intensely relaxed about people getting filthy rich.'

Peter Mandelson was one of the principal creators of 'New Labour', the version of the Labour party invented in the 1980s and 1990s to meet the challenge of Thatcherite Conservatism. Though obliged to resign twice from Mr Blair's Cabinets because of finance, and finance-related, scandals, he remained close to the Prime Minister, who ensured that he was the British nominee to the new European Commission that was appointed in 2004. Thus, his views on Labour and wealth are of some importance. This is a dramatic reframing of the terms of political controversy.

*Source*: *Financial Times*, 23 October 1998.

policy controversies in Britain, usually expressed in the language of division between social classes (see Chapter 3). In other words, 'class' provided a dominant frame for the expression of policy controversy. The ability of government to make a difference to the relations between rich and poor has been a kind of touchstone: a key test of how far public policy actually makes a difference to the lives of normal people. The reshaping of the economy under Conservative rule between 1979 and 1997 produced sharp increases in class inequality: cuts in the highest rates of taxation, coupled with deregulated markets, led to huge increases in both the incomes and the wealth of the very richest. (Whether this was a good or a bad thing depends on how far one believes inequality of this kind is needed to uncork the dynamism of a market economy.) Under New Labour since 1997 some of these market-generated income inequalities have continued to grow, while the limit on top rates of income tax has been untouched. The often quoted remark of Peter Mandelson, one of the Prime Minister's closest advisers, that New Labour is relaxed about the existence of great wealth (see Documenting Politics 20.7) seems to confirm the view that the gap between rich and poor is no longer a source of either policy controversy or policy innovation.

After two terms in office, there is now a sustained debate about the impact of 'New Labour' on economic and social inequality. The debate also goes to the heart of an even bigger issue: can government make a difference by the policies it pursues? For over 30 years following the end of the Second World War, governments in Westminster of both major parties were committed to 'progressive' taxation policies designed to take more from the rich than the poor, and to 'progessive' welfare state policies designed to counteract the inequalities produced by the operation of market forces. Yet at the end of the period (see Chapter 3) inequality between rich and poor was still a defining characteristic of British society. Much that New Labour has done since 1997 has been designed to strengthen those very market forces that – whatever their other benefits – do increase class inequality. New Labour has declined to reverse the deregulation of labour markets achieved by the Conservatives. It has preserved the Conservatives' privatization reforms, and indeed has sought to extend the influence of the private sector by, for example, increasing the importance of private sector investment in public sector projects, such as hospital construction. It has sought to strengthen competition and market forces in the public sector, and at the time of writing is seeking a major extension of this policy through the introduction of foundation hospitals, which will give increased financial independence to successful hospitals. It has breached the principle that higher education should be available free from charges, first by introducing a standard fee for undergraduates, and then by the introduction of variable student fees, designed eventually to allow different universities to set different fee levels.

The story is, however, not all one of helplessness in the face of inequalities generated by markets. Indeed, not all market-shaped policies deepen the deprivations of the poor. For instance, New Labour has overseen the achievement of historically unique low levels of unemployment, and a historically unique period of continuous economic growth. While neither success directly addresses issues of inequality, both certainly do impact in a beneficial way on poverty. This success, in a wider global economy often marked by instability and crises, is ascribed by most observers to two 'market-based' reforms: to the extensive deregulation of labour and other markets introduced by the Conservatives in the 1980s and 1990s; and to the decision immediately implemented on Labour's election in 1997 to turn control of short-term interest rates over to the Bank of England (a measure intended to reassure financial markets about government economic policy).

The period since 1997 has also witnessed the introduction of a range of measures consciously designed to address inequality, especially among the very poor who suffer its most extreme consequences. A minimum wage (of £5 per hour by 2005) provides a 'floor' for over 1.6 million of the lowest-paid workers. A working person's tax credit, designed to give additional income for the lowest paid, is intended both to supplement low incomes and to provide extra incentives for the unemployed to seek work. A 'welfare to work' programme addressed, in particular, to the young unemployed, has accompanied a huge fall in youth unemployment (although how far this is due to the measure, and how far to the wider long-term fall in unemployment, is uncertain). A 'Sure Start' programme is designed to provide resources for pre-school education, the period when, research shows, the critical inequalities in later educational performance are largely fixed. More generally, after observing inherited Conservative limits on public spending for the first two years of the life of the Blair government, later spending rounds have seen massive increases, notably devoted to spending on health and educa-

tion: the three-year round from 2002 committed an extra £60 billion alone.

## Making a difference

We showed in the preceding chapter that *how* policy is made is important to policy outcomes: the actual organization of the policy process can help determine whether the decisions taken by government are a series of policy catastrophes, or actually have intended beneficial effects. Thus quite technical issues about the organization of the policy process can affect the question of whether government makes a difference, for better or worse. What we see in this chapter, however, is that there is another dimension to the policy process: the content of what government does, and of what citizens at large urge it to do. Policy controversies of the kind sketched here are the main means by which most citizens are connected to the process of government in Britain. Most of us do not have a generalized commitment to participate actively in political life; that, as we have seen in earlier chapters, is an inclination shared only by a small, obsessive minority. The rest of us are connected to politics by our feelings about a whole skein of issues. The connection might only be fleeting and minimal: we may do no more than swear at the television screen when an issue is reported that arouses our fury. But the evidence about the changing nature of political participation in Britain (see Chapters 9 and 13 in particular) is that political controversies do much more than arouse activism of the fleeting and minimal kind: they often, as in the case of war or the banning of hunting, bring huge numbers onto the streets. Recall that the greatest mass demonstrations in modern British politics have occurred since the late 1990s: they were organized by the Countryside Alliance, primarily campaigning against restrictions on hunting with dogs; and by the campaign against the war in Iraq in 2003.

Whether government policy choices actually make a difference to social and economic outcomes is, we have seen above, truly a contested matter. But it is undeniable that policy controversies do make a difference in terms of arousing large numbers of citizens to political action. Indeed, with the decline of mass participation in political parties, this kind of mobilization around specific issues is coming to be the main way normal people participate in political life. Recall (again from Chapter 13) that this was the main theme of the description of political participation 'old and new': in the old, participation was dominated by the hierarchically organized parties controlled by a Westminster elite; in the new, campaigns mobilize large numbers of individuals around particular issues. Viewed in the flux of everyday political life it can seem that these issues have an almost random character: 'one damn controversy' succeeding another in the agenda of items reported by the mass media. However, what this chapter shows is that there is nothing random about these controversies, though there is a lot of uncertainty and accident about their appearance. The most detailed issues have a wider context. They arouse people because they can be 'framed' to fit a bigger picture: of war and peace, life and death, and so on. All we have done in this chapter is sketch some of the most intensely controversial current issues, and their framing.

The idea of 'framing' has dominated this chapter because it alerts us to an important truth about the changing nature of policy controversy in Britain. As recently as 40 years ago classifying policy controversy would not only have been pretty straightforward, it would have been simple: almost everything was framed in class terms. What is just one frame in this chapter – rich and poor – would have been dominant, and had been dominant for half-a-century before that. 'Class' framed almost everything. In recent decades 'non-issues', such as those concerning gender, have been widely rediscovered. But we have not simply gone back to the past. We now live in a more individualistic political culture. We saw in Chapter 13 how that produced new styles of political participation, involving individual engagement with a host of particular issues. The new world of individualistic political participation is thus connected to the world of policy controversy. Issues are framed in increasingly diverse and changing terms. New issues are constantly presenting

## REVIEW

Three themes dominate this chapter:

1 Policy is not only about process; it is also about content;
2 Policy controversies are often immediate, and sometimes temporary, in nature; but they always 'fit' into a wider frame of issues;
3 Policy controversies have to be framed to fit a wider picture, but the way they are framed is increasingly diverse and shaped by our preoccupations as individuals.

themselves as the source of policy choice, and new ways of framing are continually developing. In the recent past 'class' framed almost everything because the Westminster elite had a tight hold over the terms of the political controversy, and it thought in the language of class. The grasp of that elite has now weakened. And as it has weakened many new ways of framing political issues have been developed, and continue to be developed.

## Further reading

The idea of policy framing central to this chapter derives from one of the classics of policy analysis: Schon and Rein (1994). A key argument of the chapter is that the issues argued over in British politics are often short lived. The best way to pursue the chapter's themes is therefore to follow the everyday polemics that dominate policy debates, most obviously in a good newspaper. However, Jones (2004), from which some of the examples in this chapter are drawn, is a model of how to think about everyday policy controversies in their wider setting, while Robins and Jones (2000) show how political debates are central to our understanding of British politics. Pilkington (1998) is excellent in describing the traditional world of policy controversy which, I have argued, is increasingly being superseded.

CHAPTER 21

# Raising and allocating resources

## AIMS

This chapter:

❖ Explains why government seeks to influence the way resources are allocated

❖ Describes how British government raises and spends the key resource: money

❖ Examines the impact of spending and other forms of influence over resource allocation on social and economic inequality, emphasizing the issues of definition and measurement raised in the study of policy impact.

## The British state and the allocation of resources

In preceding chapters we examined competing accounts of how policy decisions are actually made – or avoided – in government. That examination was important because, as we saw, the mechanism or process of decision can have a large bearing on what is done. The most obvious instances concern 'negative' and 'non'-decisions, which can be critical to what government does, and what it decides it is not able to do. *Process* is therefore important because it helps settle the content of policy. But we need to go beyond this to look directly at the content of what government does, because this shapes lives. Traditionally government exercized power of life and death over all who lived in its territory, but the range of responsibilities that it acknowledged was comparatively limited. In the main it claimed to defend territory against external aggression, and to maintain law and order internally. But over the course of the twentieth century British government expanded its responsibilities widely beyond these traditional areas. In particular, it took on increasing responsibility for the regulation of economic life and for ensuring the provision of a wide range of welfare services (including health care and education) for citizens. (Image 21.1 depicts both a reservoir and pylons, part of two ambitious schemes for the public good.) It became, in short, critical to the allocation of resources. The subject of resource allocation is the concern of this chapter.

The new responsibilities for resource allocation were often prompted by a common purpose: to intervene so as to reshape the way resources were allocated by the economic system itself. This economic system was for the most part run according to the principles of supply and demand in the market. Government intervened, and continues to intervene, because while the principles of market capitalism are widely accepted in Britain, there are believed to be a number of important instances where it produces unacceptable outcomes.

In part, intervention is justified by a long-established argument: that there exist a category of goods and services, commonly known as 'public goods', that would not be provided at all, or would

Photo: Michael Moran

**Image 21.1**
**Ambitious commitments of public resources are nothing new: the example of reservoirs**

⊃ These reservoirs in Longendale, Derbyshire, were constructed by local government in the nineteenth century to provide water for Manchester, then the greatest industrial city in the world. They were the most ambitious programme of reservoir construction in the world of their time. Crossing the photograph can be seen a mark of another, later, huge scheme of public works: the pylons and wires of the electrification schemes that brought the electricity supply to virtually the whole of Britain in the 1930s.

be insufficiently provided, if market mechanisms were left to do the job. We can see why this might be so if we consider the essential defining feature of a public good: that if supplied at all it is necessarily supplied to everybody. Expressed technically, this is to say that the good is always *jointly consumed* and *non-excludable*. A classic example is the clean air produced by environmental controls such as those regulating emissions from factories: everybody breathes the same air, and nobody can be excluded from breathing it. Other examples include street facilities such as lighting and pavements, or public parks. If we relied on the market to supply these goods they would either not be supplied at all, or supplied insufficiently, or the mechanism for demanding payment would become impossibly complicated. Imagine waking up one morning and finding that the supply of clean air was now a commercial concern, and that we would be charged according to how much we consumed, just as we are charged according to how much beer we consume in a pub. The attempt to measure the comparative air consumption of different citizens would involve absurdities like implanting a measurement instrument in the lungs of everybody. That is why the state provides clean air free at the point of consumption, but does not provide beer free at the point of consumption. Notice the good is not 'free' but 'free at the point of consumption'. Any good or service has to be paid for. A distinguishing feature of a public good is that its supply involves using the coercive power of the state. In the case of clean air, the state passes and enforces laws regulating emissions; in the case of street lighting the state uses its coercive power to tax, and then allocates the money to the cost of lighting.

The term 'public goods' covers some of the services traditionally provided by government: for instance, the defence against invasion from abroad provided by the armed services is available to all alike. But the growth of state responsibilities over the last century reflected more than the belief that there was a special category of 'public goods' that should be provided by the state. It also arose from the belief that, even when markets could allocate resources, they had unacceptable distributive consequences: that they produced levels of inequality that were too extreme, and which needed to be moderated by state intervention to reallocate some of the wealth created by market mechanisms. Thus the state became committed to more than the provision of some services; it also became committed to the allocation, and thus to the redistribution, of resources. This was a great historical change. Before the rise of democracy government was usually conceived – at least by those with power – as a means of defending inequality, not as a means of moderation.

Even putting the issues in the simple terms used here exposes some of the debates to which state intervention has given rise. How 'public' are 'public goods' in reality? How true is it that, for instance, national defence could not be supplied commer-

cially? History contains numerous examples of mercenary armies which supplied defence, and offence, for payment. In Britain today the private security industry provides many services, from patrolling individual neighbourhoods to transporting money. Thus it is not even certain that the most traditionally established state functions should indeed be publicly provided. However, it is when we move beyond the sphere of public goods to resource redistribution that arguments become really intense. The use of the state to redistribute presumes that governments, if they intervene, really do produce more equality of outcome than markets can achieve – an assumption that has been widely debated. Even if that presumption is accepted there are a host of other areas of argument. What price do we pay by restricting markets in the name of more equality? Do we sacrifice efficiency and liberty in the process and, if we do, how big a sacrifice should we make? Given that very few people support the aim of using the state to achieve complete equality, what level of inequality is acceptable?

These are the issues that lie at the heart of this chapter. The chapter is built around three blocks: how the state raises resources; how it allocates resources; and what impact allocation has on the distribution of resources.

Notice in passing the significance here of the word 'resources'. It marks an important limit to the concerns of this chapter. The state also plays an important part in the allocation of values other than material values. Historically, the British state prescribed, for instance, the religious values that could be tolerated: at various times it sought to prohibit, or put barriers in the way of, creeds such as Judaism, Catholicism and Quakerism, and in the way of belief systems such as atheism. The rise of doctrines of religious toleration meant that the state withdrew from these attempts, though the fact that the monarch is the Head of the Established Church in England and Wales signifies a residue of that desire to allocate 'spiritual' values. In recent decades the state has also tried to use the law to promote some values at the expense of others: thus anti-discrimination and anti-racism legislation seeks to prohibit some doctrines and practices defined as racist or discriminatory, and to promote other values, such as toleration and respect for others of different ethnic or religious persuasions.

## How the British state raises resources

Although huge in scale and complex in structure, government can still be pictured as resembling a household: like a household, it receives income and is committed to spending. Indeed, study of the domestic economy of government was one of the earliest areas of specialized scholarship in the study of the state. But because government in Britain is large and complex, its sources of 'income' are much more diverse than those of any domestic household.

Traditionally governments have been able to raise resources in five ways, and all are still used by British government. They are discussed here in ascending order of importance.

### By fiat money

Fiat money refers to the state's monopoly of the right to create money, in the most immediate instance literally by printing and minting. This is obviously one source of revenue raising that is not open to us as private citizens; if we try it, the state prosecutes us for forgery. The presence of the monarch's head on coin and notes is a symbol of the state's monopoly of the right to create 'legal tender'. This partly explains why the proposal that Britain adopt the single European currency (the Euro) is so controversial. If adopted, the traditional right to create fiat money would have to be shared with all the other partners in the federal European Central Bank. Historically the creation of fiat money was vital to raising resources. It remains symbolically significant of state power, but has been outstripped by other ways of raising resources.

### By income from assets

British government has traditionally been a large property owner and this property, like any other asset, can generate income. Much of the property

was acquired in the distant past: for instance, government receives income from licences issued to companies extracting oil from the North Sea because exploitable minerals were historically the property of the Crown. With the growth of industrialism the state acquired some lucrative new assets. Thus until near the end of the twentieth century the provision of telecommunications services was a lucrative state monopoly; and until recently the monopoly enjoyed by the Royal Mail was also profitable. In principle the state can acquire fresh resources by confiscating the assets of private citizens or associations. Since Henry VIII dissolved the monasteries and distributed their property in the Reformation, this has been recognized as a significant way for the state to acquire assets; but in a democracy this confiscation, especially without generous compensation, is not easy to carry through on a large scale.

### By sale of assets

Historically governments often 'sold the family silver' when short of cash. In the last couple of decades of the twentieth century, however, government in Britain sold assets on a huge scale through the privatization programme. As Timeline 21.1 shows, this has produced huge returns in recent decades. But of course there is an obvious limit to how far revenue can be raised by selling assets: there comes a point where there is nothing of significance left to sell. The state in Britain has not, however, yet reached that point.

### By borrowing

For centuries governments have often borrowed on a large scale, and we shall see in a moment that this is also true of modern British government. Government can usually borrow on better terms than we can as private individuals. It can often borrow more cheaply than us (for instance, by appealing to the patriotism of private citizens to subscribe to national savings). In the great world wars of the twentieth century government raised large amounts by this kind of patriotic appeal. Government can also often borrow for much longer

| TIMELINE 21.1 | THE BRITISH PRIVATIZATION PROGRAMME, 1980–2002 |
|---|---|

**1981**
British Aerospace; Cable and Wireless 1

**1982**
Britoil 1; Amersham International

**1983**
Associated British Ports 1; British Petroleum; Cable and Wireless 2

**1984**
British Telecom 1; Associated British Ports 2; Enterprize Oil; Jaguar Cars

**1985**
British Aerospace 2; Britoil 2; Cable and Wireless 3

**1986**
British Gas

**1987**
British Airways; Rolls-Royce; British Airports Authority; British Petroleum; Royal Ordnance

**1988**
British Steel

**1989**
10 regional water companies

**1990**
12 regional electricity companies

**1991**
Electricity generating companies 1; Scottish Electricity; British Telecom 2

**1992**
Property Services Agency; Northern Ireland electricity generation

**1993**
British Telecom 3

**1994**
Coal industry; London Buses

**1995**
Electricity generating companies 2

**1996**
British Rail; British Energy; HMSO (The Stationery Office)

**2001**
National Air Traffic Services

**2002**
Defence Evaluation and Research Agency

➲ The British privatization programme was the most ambitious and extensive in the advanced industrial world. Privatized enterprizes ranged from huge utilities which had to be privatized in stages (the numbers against instances such as British Telecom indicate this) to small 'core' parts of the government, such as The Stationery Office. While not primarily undertaken to fund government, the receipts were so large that they made an important contribution to meeting the deficit in public accounts in a period when the public finances were under great pressure: the proceeds over this whole exceed £60 billion at 2002 prices. In other words, if we glance at Figure 21.1 below, we see that without privatization the national debt would have been around £500 billion.

*Sources*: Compiled from HM Treasury and other information.

than can private citizens. Loans stretching over 50 years are not unknown, whereas even the longest house mortgage term for private citizens is usually 30 years. If repayment becomes a problem, government can also default on its debts. Defaulting can have adverse consequences on future ability to borrow, but states do default and they can get away with it. If you or I default on our building society mortgage, in the end our house will be repossessed or we will be made bankrupt. It is hard to repossess

assets from a state, and virtually impossible to make a state bankrupt in the way private citizens or firms can be made bankrupt. An additional attraction of borrowing is that, when borrowing for a long period, governments can often spend the money more or less immediately and leave the problem of paying the debt to successors in the distant future. For democratic governments needing to work to quite short general election cycles of four or five years this is obviously an attractive option.

**Figure 21.1**   The scale of government borrowing

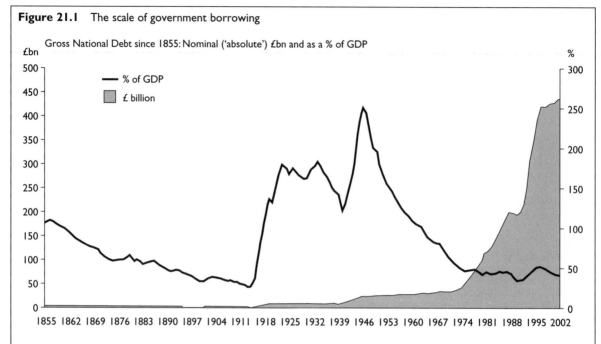

Gross National Debt since 1855: Nominal ('absolute') £bn and as a % of GDP

*Source*: National Debt Office, ndo.gov.uk

➲ The figure charts the size of government debt both in nominal terms and as a proportion of Gross Domestic Product, a standard measure of national wealth. It shows that while the monetary value of national debt has grown greatly in the last 30 years, when we take inflation and growth in national wealth into account – which is what the percentage figure actually does – the level of debt has proved remarkably stable, and is quite low by the standards of most of the last century. But the scale of the task of servicing existing debt, redeeming debt as it matures, and raising new debt is nevertheless so great that it can be done only through the financial markets, and requires a specialized agency, the National Debt Office, from whose website this figure is taken.

Borrowing is now integral to revenue-raising by government, and in recent decades the means of borrowing have been transformed by the development of more ingenious methods. Simple appeals to small savers to lend cheaply – either because of patriotism or because of the greater security of the state as a creditor – are decreasingly important. The financial markets now have huge and sophisticated markets in government debt, trading blocks of government bonds that vary in terms such as the rate of return and the date of redemption. In this way government does what no private individual could ever do: it perpetually extends, redeems and renews its debt from generation to generation. (See Figure 21.1 for more information on Britain's national debt over a period of almost 150 years.)

## By taxation

Governments have always taxed, and indeed disaffection with taxes has been one of the great dangers to rulers. Some of the greatest revolutions in history, such as the French Revolution, can be traced to tax revolts. And closer to home a huge revolt against a new form of local taxation in Britain in the late 1980s – the community charge or 'poll tax' – led to its abandonment and contributed to the fall from office of the then Prime Minister, Mrs Thatcher. (See Briefing 19.4.)

In the twentieth century taxation became the most important source of income for British governments, and it remains of primary importance. This happened because government developed powerful administrative techniques for levying taxes in ways that were hard to avoid. We can see the power of taxation by considering the main ways taxes are levied in Britain. Taxation comes from four main sources:

- Direct taxes on individuals' incomes, of which the most important source is the regular (usually weekly or monthly) deduction of tax at source on the incomes of the employed, usually called Pay As You Earn (PAYE).
- Direct taxes on the assets of individuals. Among the most important of these are various kinds of 'death duties' – taxes on the assets that individuals leave at death, and which in principle are targeted at the rich.
- Direct taxes on institutions, of which the most important are various taxes levied on business firms: for instance, the tax bill paid by the Royal Bank of Scotland in 2004, after a bumper profits result, was in excess of £2 billion.
- Taxes on goods and services, of which the most important is Value Added Tax (VAT). VAT is experienced by most of us as a tax on sales: the cost of the PC on which this book was written had 17.5 per cent added to it by VAT. VAT was instituted in Britain in 1973, replacing a variety of older sales taxes. It has proved to be a highly effective way of raising resources. But the principle of taxing a good or service is long established: historically, duties on goods such as alcohol and tobacco were an important source of Crown revenue, and remain important in contributing to the public coffers.

The importance of taxation dates from the middle decades of the twentieth century. Two administrative innovations already mentioned in passing explain why it became the centrepiece of resource raising.

The first innovation was developed during the Second World War in order to raise the huge resources needed to fight that war. It was the system of Pay As You Earn (PAYE) referred to above. The great administrative advance of PAYE was that, through its deduction of fixed amounts from the pay packet received by workers, it made taxation a routine and eventually almost universal experience

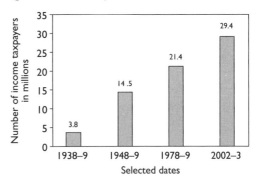

**Figure 21.2**   The spread of the income tax net

Number of income taxpayers in millions

1938–9: 3.8
1948–9: 14.5
1978–9: 21.4
2002–3: 29.4

Selected dates

*Source*: Data from Inland Revenue, 2004.

➲ The figures from selected dates show the number of income tax payers over a period of over 60 years. The jump in the decade after 1938 illustrates the importance of the introduction of PAYE as discussed in the text. Overall, the figures show that paying income tax has been transformed from an experience of a fairly wealthy minority to one experienced by virtually every adult.

for everyone in work. With rising incomes it meant that virtually everyone in work was drawn into the tax net and the state was provided with a hugely efficient source of tax revenue: there were fewer than 4 million income tax payers at the end of the 1930s, compared with over 29 million now (see Figure 21.2). In effect employers did the collecting by direct deduction from wages, and then simply transferred the money to the state, in the form of the department of Inland Revenue.

The second administrative invention, Value Added Tax, is more recent. It was introduced, as we saw above, in 1973. Although not in principle a new tax – in essence VAT is experienced by most of us as a sales tax, and taxes on the sale of goods have a long history – it is a uniquely thorough and subtle tax that is proving a hugely productive source of revenue. It is by far the most lucrative of the many levies collected by Customs and Excise, yielding nearly £60 billion in the financial year 2002–3 (the most recent financial year for which figures are available)

The importance of VAT is also indicative of an important shift in the balance of taxation in recent decades: a shift away from taxes on income to taxes on sales, good and services. One of the most important reasons for this is that governments in recent decades have come to believe that there is significant resistance to income tax, and that this resistance can be electorally damaging. Taxes taken from income are highly visible: every time employees look at a pay slip they see the size of the tax deduction. Taxes such as VAT, or duties on goods such as tobacco, by contrast, are partly concealed in the overall cost of a good or service (see Figure 21.3 for more information). In addition, there is evidence that taxes on consumption are less 'progressive' than income tax. By 'progressive' here we mean to describe, not make a value judgement. It is common to distinguish between 'progressive' and 'regressive' taxes. A 'progressive' tax extracts proportionately more from those with higher income; a 'regressive' tax extracts more from lower income groups. In principle income tax rates rise as income increases, and are therefore progressive. VAT is levied irrespective of income, and this is also true of an important category of taxes that more directly tax consumption: special duties paid on individual goods. The best documented example is the duty on cigarettes. Smoking is now disproportionately concentrated among the poor; thus raising money through duty on cigarettes is a 'regressive' rather than a 'progressive' way to raise resources. The shift to indirect taxation is therefore in part a response to the influence of organized interests: tax payers, especially higher rate tax payers, are better organized and more vocal than are the poor.

One of the main reasons why both PAYE and VAT are so important to revenue raising is that they are hard to escape, but the ability of individuals and institutions to escape the tax net is nevertheless a key problem for British government. Escape comes in two main forms, conventionally labelled tax evasion and tax avoidance. Evasion refers to illegal escape: businesses can falsify their books, thus escaping VAT and other tax obligations; workers can operate in the 'black economy', taking payment in cash without declaring it to the authorities. These problems explain why government has a big apparatus of tax surveillance: VAT inspectors raid firms; the Inland Revenue conducts spot checks on

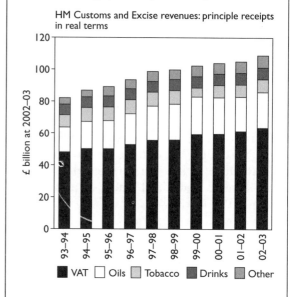

**Figure 21.3**   The different ways government raises resources: the legacy of entry into Europe

HM Customs and Excise revenues: principle receipts in real terms

*Source*: Customs and Excise (2004).

➲ Taxes on income are the biggest single source of government revenue. Even so, in recent years only about 55 per cent of central government revenue has come from the Inland Revenue. This figure shows how government spreads the net of taxation on goods and services widely to raise money. It also shows that Value Added Tax (VAT) is the most lucrative of these. VAT is a legacy of our entry into the original European Economic Community: it was introduced in 1973 in anticipation of British membership to begin harmonizing British tax regimes with those of our neighbours.

individual tax returns. It is hard to know how big is the loss of revenue by evasion, since the whole point of the operation is concealment. In some cases an additional reason for concealment is that the source of income may itself be also criminal: drug dealers prefer cash not only because they want to avoid paying income tax, but also because they want to conceal the very source of their revenue.

We use 'tax avoidance', by contrast, to summarize legal ways to minimize our tax liabilities. Most tax payers practise tax avoidance. When the Inland Revenue agrees to treat the cost of my annual purchases of academic books as an allowance against my tax bill, I am practising avoidance. This unsophisticated avoidance is dwarfed by the modern tax planning industry, run mostly by multinational firms of lawyers and accountants, who specialize in devising means for big corporations and the very rich to plan their affairs so as legally to minimize their tax losses. Thus while inheritance tax is incurred presently on estates valued at £263,000 or more, a quite modest threshold in the age of house price inflation, it is a very foolish or unlucky rich person whose estate pays duty on death: a good accountant will devise a trust to escape the liability. Similarly, big multinational corporations are skilled in channelling their revenue through tax havens and shelters: for an illustration see Political Issues 21.1, p. 468.

❖   ❖   ❖

Revenue raising by government is among the most technically complex areas of public life but, as this summary shows, it is also one of the most intensely political: success in revenue raising is vital for the effectiveness, and indeed the very stability, of government; and the struggles over where to lay the burden of revenue raising involve great clashes between different economic interests.

## How the British state allocates resources

In the previous section we looked at the 'income' side of the domestic economy of government; now it is time to look at the outgoings.

The rise of the state in Britain as a large-scale allocator of resources has taken the form of two very different kinds of spending programmes. The state can use the money it gathers in to fund services that it delivers directly. This is the characteristic feature of such important services as health care and schools education in Britain. It is natural instinctively to equate spending on direct provision with the state as an allocator of resources. But this is only half the picture and – as Figure 21.4 shows – quantitatively the less important half. Another large chunk of spending is accounted for by what are normally labelled 'income transfers'. Here government acts as

a channel taking money out of the pocket of some groups (for instance, wage-earning employees) and putting it into the pockets of other groups: for instance, the unemployed or pensioners. But the government is not a passive channel through which resources pass. Actually getting hold of the money, and then distributing it, requires large and expensive administrative machines. For instance, the Inland Revenue, the collector of taxes on income, employs over 75,000 staff; the Department of Work and Pensions has over 26,000 staff in two of its key benefit services alone (the Child Support Agency and in the Pensions Service). And the detailed rules of transfer – the entitlements that govern who gets what – are obviously critical to how the money is allocated upon transfer. As we will see in the next section, the way the resources for income transfer are raised, and the way they are distributed, are not just administrative technicalities; they go to the heart of how we view the purpose of government in Britain today.

Income transfers of the kind described here are obviously a very different way of allocating income from that operated by the market. Indeed, historically they were conceived as an alternative when the market 'failed': as 'income support', in circumstances when individuals could not command an income, or a living income, by sale of their labour. Thus the earliest large programmes of income transfer provided pensions for the old, and benefits for the sick; both groups, for different reasons, being unable to command wages in the free labour market.

The scale of resource allocation by British government is huge; it makes the state the biggest spender by far in British society. Understanding the history and recent composition of resource allocation is therefore vital, not just for the particular purpose of making sense of public spending but to understand the changing role of the state in Britain. Three features of resource allocation stand out.

### Public spending has risen greatly over the long term

In Chapter 1 (see Figure 1.1) we saw this trend illustrated. Over the course of the twentieth century there was a huge rise in the proportion of national

**Figure 21.4**   The importance of income transfers in public spending: the big programmes

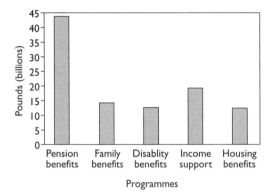

*Source*: Calculated from HM Treasury (2004). Figures relate to financial year 2001–2.

➲ Public spending is dominated by 'income transfer': the state raises money through means such as taxation, and then transfers the money as various kinds of monetary benefits to selected groups. These figures, taken from the total social protection budget, give an idea of the scale of transfer. The British state is virtually a pensioners' state: the bill for pensions is the biggest single item of public spending apart from the total bill for health care (£65.0 billion). The figures for income support have also grown hugely over recent decades, reflecting state intervention to supplement low pay in the labour market.

wealth that was taken, and allocated, by the state. And, as that figure showed, the two major boosts to spending occurred in the two world wars that the British state fought during the century. Indeed it was the demand for spending – to fund the great wars of the twentieth century, and to fund greatly expanded welfare programmes – that prompted great administrative inventions such as PAYE (as discussed in the last section).

## Total spending has been stable in recent decades

In the early 1970s a long period of sustained economic growth that had stretched back to the Second World War ended in Britain. At the same time political parties on both left and right began to argue that the growth in state spending had to be stopped. The Conservatives, who came to office in 1979, had the ambition of reducing the proportion of national income spent publicly (although note that in a growing economy this does not necessarily mean that total public spending has to decline). That ambition was very hard to realize, for reasons that we discuss below. But undoubtedly this new hostility to taxing and spending produced a new era of constraint on public spending, by contrast with the long history of growth over almost the whole of the preceding decades of the twentieth century.

## The composition of spending has changed over time

The kinds of measures we have been using above are handy, but crude, summaries: they simply measure the total volume of resources allocated by the state. Some of these changes have to do with great historical events. As Figure 1.1 showed, both world wars gave a huge boost to spending, but obviously that military-related spending declined radically when the great wars ended. Some changes have to do with the cycle of the economy: two very clear instances are provided by spending to 'service' public debt and spending on benefits for the unemployed. When the economy is booming, especially when unemployment is low, government budgets are often in surplus: the demand on spending for unemployment benefit is lowered; and tax returns are boosted by the expansion in the number of tax-paying wage earners. Conversely, economic recession usually puts pressure on governments to borrow. Thus when unemployment was falling rapidly in the late 1990s it was possible for the Chancellor of the Exchequer actually to repay significant parts of the 'capital' on the public debt, because the Treasury was getting a double benefit: falling demand for unemployment benefit, and rising tax revenues from those in work.

Totals of public spending that are stable over time can nevertheless conceal big changes in the composition of spending. Not all changes are due to big historical events, like war, or the cycle of the economy. They are due to political choices made by governments, and these choices are naturally influenced by the power of different groups of interests in society. Part of the reason why in the 1980s and 1990s politicians of most parties became hostile to increased public spending was that they were listening to powerful groups of tax payers who wanted their tax bills reduced. But the ambition actually significantly to reduce the overall level of spending was very hard to achieve. Most public spending is due to commitments that are hard to abandon, especially in the short term. A good example is the whole range of 'income transfers' that lie at the heart of the welfare state: these arise from legal entitlements to a range of benefits (child benefit, old age pensions, benefits for the disabled, unemployment benefit) that have to be paid out as a matter of law; only changes in the rules can cut or abolish these. The changes take time and naturally will be resisted by any threatened group powerful enough to organize effectively.

❖  ❖  ❖

These factors throw a lot of light on the changing composition of public spending. To cut spending governments have to cut commitments, and they will naturally look for the 'softest' targets: at spending on those social groups who are poorly organized politically, or who happen not to be obvious supporters of the party that is in power. Thus over the years of Conservative rule, while there was little change in the total levels of spending, some programmes were severely cut: for instance, investment on public housing was sharply reduced, a change confirmed by the policies of the Labour governments since 1997.

For the last 30 years struggles over public spending have essentially been about struggles for share of a 'cake' of more or less fixed size (by contrast with the era before that, when the 'cake' grew in size over the decades). A critical factor, then, has been the relative effectiveness of different social interests in protecting their share of the cake. This is only part of the larger political struggle of public spending, because obviously there is a similar struggle on the taxation side, as different groups try to minimize the amount they have to contribute to the public purse. As we saw earlier, over recent years there has been a shift from direct taxes on income, to indirect taxes,

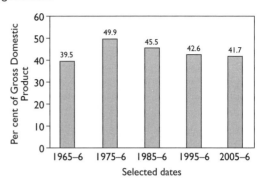

**Figure 21.5**  The levels of public spending in the last generation

*Source*: Calculated from HM Treasury figures: figure for 2005–6 is planned expenditure.

➲ The figures extract from Treasury figures the proportion of Gross Domestic Product accounted for by Total Managed Public Expenditure for decade intervals since the mid-1960s. (The 2005–6 figures are forecasts.) As with all summary figures, they can be interpreted in a variety of ways, but two points merit emphasis: there seems to be a long-term, though not radical, decline in the proportionate share of public spending since the mid-1970s; and the return of New Labour in 1997 seems to have made little difference to this. With growing national wealth, of course the absolute magnitude of resources devoted to public spending is much greater now than in the mid-1970s.

such as VAT, and the effect of this has been generally 'regressive': that is, it has meant that the poorest have paid an increasing share of the total tax bill.

There is therefore a close and delicate connection between the politics of resource allocation in government and the way the wider political system is itself organized. It is obvious that some groups are well placed to defend their interests in the struggle of taxing and spending and others have little or no means of their own. We need only look back to Chapter 9 at our discussion of the way interests are represented to see how and why these differences exist. This does not mean that those without resources of their own cannot have a voice: take the example of those suffering severe intellectual disabilities. They will often find it very hard to organize politically but, as the existence of groups speaking and lobbying on their behalf, (such as

MENCAP), shows, they need not be without a voice. How effective that voice can be raises questions that are central to the nature of democracy in Britain. As we will see in our concluding chapter, one (optimistic) view of democracy says that there is a wide range of different resources open to different groups, and that these can partly balance each other out. The arguments about this difficult matter we will examine there. But the issue shows that the whole area of public taxing and spending is far more than technical; it goes to the heart of the nature of democracy in Britain.

There is also another sense in which the technical details about resource allocation are of importance: they are relevant to large questions about the social impact of government in Britain. This is examined in the next section.

## The impact of the British state on the allocation of resources: evidence and debates

Until the start of the twentieth century government within Britain was mostly concerned with what we would now think of as narrow issues. These were chiefly to do with maintaining public order, especially with protecting property and people. The biggest single change that occurred in the twentieth century was that this narrow range of concerns widened greatly. The first half of the century saw the development of a welfare state. This involved the creation of a range of institutions and programmes where the state took responsibility for ensuring widespread access to services including health care, education and income support for groups such as the old and unemployed; a mix, in other words, of spending on direct provision and on income transfer.

Behind the rise of the welfare state lay the idea, which we have already encountered, that government needed to reallocate resources in such a way as to modify the kinds of allocations that would happen if the economic marketplace alone were allowed to do the job. This idea has provoked some of the most important debates about British government. In essence: can the state, or should the state,

seek to modify the market as a mechanism of resource allocation? And if it should, how radical should that modification be? One highly controversial but influential view – which lay behind the attempt made in the last couple of decades to cut back public spending – was that the attempt to modify the effects of the market had gone too far: for instance, that it required such high levels of taxation that it was undermining efficiency in markets, and therefore weakening the economy's ability to produce the wealth needed for reallocation in the first place. These views were originally associated with radical supporters of the free market, though now they are subscribed to even by the Labour government in power after 1997. An equally radical argument has come from some on the socialist left: that when we look closely at the efforts by the state to redistribute resources we find that it largely fails to modify the unequal distributions produced by the market (see People in Politics 21.1).

These debates are both politically contentious and intellectually complex. They are contentious and complex because they simultaneously raise three different sets of questions about the state and the allocation of resources.

- Who pays for state activity? Since the state only allocates resources after first raising them (through taxation, for example), any view about allocation has to depend in part on evidence about which social groups are paying the first place.
- Who is receiving the benefits of allocation? The theory of the welfare state was that those who for various reasons were badly placed to benefit from the market should receive the bulk of resources. But is this true? (See Figure 21.6.)
- What is the impact of allocation? This question raises some of the most difficult questions of all about the links between state activity and social and economic inequality. For instance, even if resources do go to the poorest, do these resources significantly moderate inequality?

### Who pays?

Earlier in the chapter we got a picture of the main sources of government revenue, but this only gives

**Figure 21.6**    Leaders and laggards in the public spending stakes

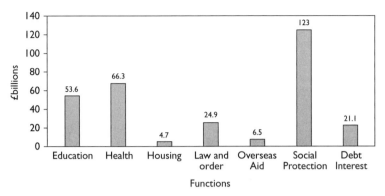

Functions

*Source*: Calculated from HM Treasury statistics (2004): figures for 2001–2.

➲ The figures are for selected public spending programmes, in terms of cash spending (in £ billions). They immediately show the huge ranges in scale of commitment: from housing at one end to social protection at the other. For an analysis of the social protection budget, see Figure 21.4.

us a very indirect idea of the identity of the payers. Until the twentieth century there was a well-established view on this matter. It was that taxation should be *regressive:* that is, every attempt should be made to ensure that the cost of government was borne by the poor rather than by the rich. This was because property was thought to be the foundation of the social order; it was therefore dangerous for government to tax it. But for over 100 years the dominant view has been that taxation should be *progressive*: more simply, the rich should pay more towards the upkeep of government than should the poor. Many of the formal rules of income and property taxation are designed with this in mind: the most obvious instance is provided by the rules for taxation of income, where the very lowest paid are exempted from taxation and the proportionate tax levy rises with income.

The formal principle that contribution to the cost of government should be on a progressive basis does actually very roughly correspond to the reality of the main sources of government income. Income tax is the most important source of revenue, and liability to pay rises with income. But the 'progressive' nature of contributions is only rough and ready, for a variety of reasons that we have already encountered in passing. The formal rules of *progres-*

*sive* taxation are often easily avoided. As we saw in the section above, there is a large industry of tax advice which is designed to ensure that the wealthiest individuals and institutions can do exactly this: in the jargon of the accountant, 'tax efficient' organization of both individual and corporate income considerably cuts tax liabilities (see Political Issues 21.1). In addition, the sheer size of the state's appetite for money in the age of big government has forced it to widen the tax net socially. At the end of the 1930s, for example, only a minority of the wealthiest earners paid any tax at all; now, as we saw earlier, the vast majority of wage earners have to pay (see Figure 21.2).

There has also been, as we saw above, a powerful trend shifting the bias of taxation from the *progressive* to the *regressive* in recent decades. This is due to the perception (right or wrong) that the limits of direct taxation on incomes have been reached. The result has been is a long-term shift to indirect taxes. The most obvious sign is the long-term growing importance of Value Added Tax and of special duties on targeted goods, of which the best known are cigarettes. Some of these taxes (as with excise duty on cigarettes) are direct taxes on consumption; and VAT also has many of the features of a consumption tax since the cost is in the end passed on in the final

## *People in politics*

### 21.1    THREE WHO SHAPED OUR ATTITUDES TO PUBLIC SPENDING

Cartoons: Shaun Steele

**Karl Marx** (1818–83) was a German philosopher and revolutionary, and founder of one of the most successful political creeds of the twentieth century. Marxism enjoyed little popular appeal in Britain, despite the fact that his most important work used Britain as a key case. But Marx's picture of the market economy as a generator of inequality and misery deeply influenced many on the left, strengthening the commitment to high public spending to combat market inequality.

**John Maynard Keynes** (1883–1946), the most famous British economist of the twentieth century, deeply influenced attitudes to public spending right across the political spectrum. Though an advocate of balanced budgets, Keynes popularized the idea that markets were not self-regulating, that active government economic management was needed, and that part of this would involve high levels of public spending. He supported the Liberal party, but his influence transcended party.

**Milton Friedman** (1912–) was an American economist, the most famous critic of high levels of public spending in the last quarter of the twentieth century. He argued that free markets were almost always superior to public provision, and that a large public sector was a threat to liberty. His ideas, summarized in his book, *Capitalism and Freedom*, deeply influenced the Thatcherite reformers who governed Britain after 1979.

price of the good. Consumption taxes need not be regressive. Indeed, one of the few historical exceptions to the principle that the poor should pay more than the rich in tax lay in so-called 'sumptuary taxation': the special taxation of luxury goods. Some of this principle is retained in elements of indirect taxation: food is exempt from VAT partly because it is obviously a necessity rather than any kind of luxury, while the taxation of tobacco and alcohol, though partly done to deter consumption on health grounds, also reflects the assumption that these are dispensable luxuries. Nevertheless, the bias of indirect taxation is regressive rather than progressive.

The way the costs of government are distributed cannot therefore be reduced to any simple sum. The most important reason for this is that there is a continuing struggle over who should bear these costs, and the losers and winners in this struggle form a complicated, and shifting, pattern. Much the same can now be said about the other side of the balance sheet: who benefits from what government provides.

## Who benefits?

We can identify four important kinds of goods and services that are provided by government. The importance of these variants is that each has a different distributional profile.

*Pure public goods.* The first are close to being pure public goods in the sense identified at the beginning of this chapter. Many of the 'benefits' of government spending are indivisible: once provided they are automatically available to all, are equally consumed by all and are equally worthwhile to all. Some of the classic traditional functions of government fall into this category, and they are further examined in the next chapter when we turn to the state and the maintenance of security: protection against banditry and thuggery is equally valuable to you and to me. An even better example we discussed at the start of this chapter: clean air. The Clean Air Act of 1956 introduced and policed more stringent restrictions over such emissions as fuel burning in fires in domestic homes. The Act is partly responsible for the fact British cities are no longer afflicted by the 'smogs' which had hitherto caused the deaths of significant numbers, and discomfort and filth for many more. The clean air resulting from the legislation is probably as close as we could find in the real world to the 'ideal' public good proposed in the models of economists: it is indivisible, in the sense that once available its consumption cannot be restricted to some members of the community, and therefore cannot be assigned to particular groups; and it is jointly and equally consumed by all. However, pure public goods are not the only kind of output of government.

*Universally available free services.* A second important kind of benefit has a more complex distribution. There is an important class of goods provided by government that is available freely and with little or no formality, but which is known to be unequally consumed by the population at large. One example is the free public library service. The free public library movement has its origins in the nineteenth century and, especially before the rise of mass education, was an important route to self-education for many. Public libraries still provide important benefits available equally to all in the community,

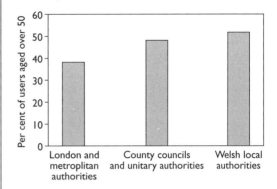

**Figure 21.7** The beneficiaries of a public service: who uses public libraries? (Age profile of users, 2000)

*Source*: Calculated from Audit Commission (2003: 9).

➲ The figure reports a survey of library users by the Audit Commission, the main government evaluator of public services. It illustrates a key point made in the text: that simply because a service is universally available, and is free, we cannot assume that it is equally consumed. The beneficiaries of public libraries are drawn disproportionately from older age groups. While no comparable figures were available for the class profile of users, there is a strong suspicion that similar class-related disproportional use also exists. No judgement is offered about the desirability or otherwise of this pattern; it is intended only to illustrate that 'public goods' are often not equally used by the public.

and using them involves the minimum of formalities: if you wish to join your local library you will have to do no more than provide a local address to be granted borrowing rights. But in fact libraries are only used by a minority, and this minority is not a microcosm of the population at large, as a glance at Figure 21.7 shows.

*Public services allocated by 'gatekeepers'.* The issue of the unequal consumption of the goods provided by government is central to this third category of benefits. Many of the services to which government commits large-scale resources are only available to those who can persuade a figure controlling access to the service to make it available. A good example is hospital care, which is available free but not to all of us on demand. Except in special circumstances, such as an emergency, none of us can turn up at a hospital and demand care. We have to be referred after consultation by our GP, who makes a professional judgement as to whether we need to be seen and treated in a hospital. The GP, in other words, is the *gatekeeper* to some of the most important parts of the NHS. Obviously, how the gatekeeper makes the judgement critically influences how the resource is allocated. GPs do not make capricious judgements in deciding which patients to refer to hospitals, but they do make discretionary judgements, and that discretion decides who consumes the resources of the hospital.

A striking example of the importance of gatekeeping is provided in Figure 21.8. It shows vividly for one important domain of public sector provision that expansion can actually redistribute resources away from the poor to the rich. During the 1990s British government vastly increased the scale of provision in higher education, leading to a great increase in the proportion of 18–21 year olds who entered colleges and universities. Though students in England and Wales pay fees, these nowhere near cover the cost; higher education is heavily subsidized by the state and is indeed one part of the welfare state that has expanded greatly in the last two decades. Higher education is, as many readers of this book will have experienced, only available to those admitted to a college or university. In a case such as this, the critical questions are: what rules do the gatekeepers to heavily subsidized higher education use to regulate entry, and what are the distributional consequences of the way the rules are applied? The evidence here is overwhelming: spending on higher education distributes public resources disproportionately to those from middle and upper income families; those from families in the very lowest income groups are very weakly represented in higher education. This is not because universities are biased against particular categories of applicants (though there is some evidence that universities that interview do fall victim to unconscious discriminatory practices); it is because the commonest rule that is applied – success in public examinations – produces a socially biased entry, simply because success in these examinations is closely correlated with the class background of candidates. As a consequence, public spending on higher education is 'regressive' rather than progres-

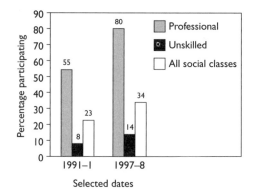

**Figure 21.8**   How the welfare state can benefit higher income groups: the case of higher education (percentage drawn from families of selected different social classes)

*Source*: Calculated from *Social Trends 1999*: (61).

➲   The greatest expansion of numbers in higher education for a generation took place in the early 1990s. The 'participation rate' – the percentage of the age group normally in higher education – jumped dramatically, as Figure 21.8 shows. As the figures show, the expansion mostly benefited students from privileged families. The figures measure the proportion from families where the main earner was either a professional or an unskilled manual worker. By the end of the period the proportion of students from the homes of unskilled manual workers had risen modestly; for the children of professionals, when the normal exceptions are taken into account, higher education was now virtually guaranteed. If we were to look at the most socially exclusive and prestigious universities – Oxford, Cambridge, Manchester or the LSE – we would find the disparities even more striking. This middle-class interest emerged as an electoral force, notably favouring the Liberal Democrats, in the 2005 general election.

sive: it disproportionately benefits students from better-off families. The expansion of provision in the 1990s therefore involved a significant increase in 'regressive' redistribution: from the poor to the children of the middle and upper income group families. (This is simply an observation about the evidence. It does not necessarily mean that subsidy to higher education is undesirable, or that the 1990s expansion was wrong. Justification is possible on a variety of grounds, ranging from the need to educate the most able to the desirability of supporting intellectual activity for its own sake, in the same way that opera is publicly subsidized as a 'useless' but valued art.)

*Targeted public services.* The case of higher education might be thought of as an unintended, or at least unstated, case of spending that allocates resources unequally. But the fourth area where government commits resources involves programmes that are openly targeted at particular groups. Distribution, in other words, is intended to be unequal, and not to be freely available to all. Some of the most important programmes in the welfare state are of this kind. The 'income transfers' that were discussed earlier provide some of the best examples: they are designed to support those who can no longer work, including the old, the unemployed or the physically disabled.

This simple fourfold classification of the different kinds of goods that are allocated by government leads to an obvious conclusion: it is not easy to draw up a balance sheet of who benefits most from the resources allocated by government. In our first case of pure public goods – such as the resources allocated to police clean air legislation – we should probably say that everyone in the community benefits. But in our second case of goods universally available free of charge (say, public libraries), unequal allocation is created by different rates of consumption. In our third case – goods available only after a decision by a 'gatekeeper' – the crucial issue is what rules, conscious or unconscious, the gatekeeper applies. And in the case of some of the resource transfers designed to maintain incomes of groups such as the sick and the otherwise unemployable, we can say that much of the allocation that is taking place is progressive, favouring the poorest in the community.

One helpful way to think about all this is to see government as a machine for transferring resources between different groups in the community. These groups can take a wide variety of forms: they could be the rich and the poor, those in work and those unemployed, the young and the old, the sick and the healthy. For example: when you and I reach old age

we hope to draw a state pension which has partly been funded by our own contributions during our working lives, but which will also rely on the taxes of those younger than us still in work; and if you or I are unfortunate enough to become seriously ill, we expect to be treated virtually free of charge by the National Health Service, funded by the taxes of the healthy who are in work. (Most of the money spent by the NHS is spent on patients in the last couple of years of their lives.) Wider arguments about the benefits of government spending, therefore, are also arguments about how that transfer machine is working: is it really seriously shifting resources from the poor to the rich, for example, or is it mostly transferring resources, regardless of wealth, between groups such as the presently sick and the presently healthy (in the case of health care spending) or between different generations (the case of old age pensions)?

## What is the impact of spending?

All we have discussed so far is about the way resources are allocated, but, in our own lives, when we lay out money we usually ask a further question, especially if we have spent a large amount: did the money give what we expected? The same kinds of questions are asked about government, usually in language of *impact*: do particular spending programmes achieve what they set out to do? Often a further question, sometimes not voiced, lies behind this: could the objectives have been achieved by a more cost effective alternative? These two questions are actually hard to disentangle, as we will now see.

We saw in the last chapter that there are numerous examples in British government of 'policy failure' (see Briefing 19.4), which is unsurprising. Even if we believed that British government was quite efficient at its job – something that is often disputed – the very scale and complicated nature of government would lead us to expect some failures, and some cases where spending was wasted. Researchers who specialize in particularly expensive areas, including health and defence, can provide long lists of wasteful, failed spending programmes: for instance, expensive weapons systems that end up vastly over their budget and are delivered several

### 21.1   TAX AVOIDANCE AND THE GLOBALLY ORGANIZED FIRM

We have seen in this chapter that over the course of the twentieth century various forms of taxation became the most important source of income for the state (see Figures 21.2 and 21.3, for instance). Virtually everyone tries to *avoid* these taxes, tax avoidance being the practice of organizing financial affairs legally to reduce the amount of tax one is obliged to pay. (*Tax evasion* is the illegal evasion of tax obligations.) For the rich and powerful, a large industry of tax accountancy has developed which takes legal tax avoidance to a high art. Most of the best known corporate names operating in Britain – Virgin, News Corporation (the vehicle for Rupert Murdoch's media empire), Microsoft – practise 'tax efficiency', which is the worldwide organization of their financial resources so as to minimize their tax bills to the British state. Mr Murdoch's enterprizes paid hardly any UK tax in the 1990s because they successfully practised tax efficiency. The commonest way to practise this is to create special trusts registered in 'tax havens' – jurisdictions which impose little or no taxation on trusts – through which profits are 'booked'. The transaction is purely a bookkeeping arrangement which legally avoids UK corporate tax. Well known 'havens' include the Isle of Man, Guernsey and Bermuda. But being tax efficient within the law is a highly complex business, and hence only those with the wealth to hire very skilled lawyers and tax accountants can realistically practise it. The phenomenon is worldwide, but Britain occupies an especially central place because most of the leading tax havens are Crown dependencies. Estimates of the amounts saved by corporate tax efficiency reach as high as £85 billion annually (nearly twice the annual cost of the NHS).

Tax avoidance is quite legal, but raises three important issues:

- It raises issues of fairness in the distribution of tax burdens, since loss of tax revenue to the financially mobile means that extra taxes have to be levied on those who do not have the ability to organize their financial affairs globally.
- Since corporate avoidance is very common, it raises the issue of whether, in a world of global accounting, British corporate tax rates may not be too high.
- It raises an issue at the heart of the operation of the global economy: whether national governments such as the British any longer have the capacity effectively to control the largest global corporations.

*Source*: Information from Sikka (2002).

years late. These are in effect studies of policy impact – and studies that conclude that the impact was at best a wasteful commitment of public resources. So it would be no surprise to find that public spending commonly did not achieve the objectives for which it was intended. The more difficult questions are: how frequent is this, and how far do these failures mean that we should doubt the ability of government to achieve the intended impact of spending programmes?

These questions are hard to answer. Asking whether a particular public spending programme has achieved its objectives assumes that we have a straightforward, measurable view of those objectives, but the reality is less clear-cut. Would we, for instance, measure the success of a programme to cut youth unemployment straightforwardly by its impact on measured levels of youth unemployment, or also by its impact on the electoral popularity of the government that introduced the programme?

# DEBATING POLITICS

## 21.1    THE WELFARE STATE: SUCCESS OR FAILURE?

| The welfare state is a success in redistributing resources | The welfare state is a failure in redistributing resources |
|---|---|
| ■ Most of the essentials of a good life, from education to health, are paid for by the welfare state.<br>■ Inequalities produced by markets would be much greater were it not for the way the welfare state modifies the impact of markets.<br>■ Welfare state services are vital for the most vulnerable, such as children and the disabled.<br>■ The commitment to redistribution by the welfare state expresses our obligations to each other as members of the community. | ■ Some of the most important beneficiaries of the welfare state are drawn from the prosperous and well organized.<br>■ Welfare state redistribution has failed to stem rising inequality in the last 25 years.<br>■ The welfare state produces large bureaucracies and hard-to-fathom rules about entitlements, consuming scarce resources in paying for welfare professionals.<br>■ The welfare state encourages a culture of dependence and undermines personal initiative and enterprize. |

Because government is a complicated business some programmes may actually have very different, and even contradictory, objectives: in pursuing housing policy, for example, government simultaneously usually wants to ensure cheap, affordable housing in the south-east, but also to ensure that house prices do not fall in the south-east.

Even where we are clear about the objectives of a programme, we also face the problem of deciding whether observed effects are actually due to the programme that interests us. Did youth unemployment fall because of a special programme, or because of some other improvement in the wider economy? Studying government cannot be like the studies of nature conducted in laboratories: we can never run controlled experiments in which we isolate the factors that interest us to observe their effects 'uncontaminated' by other forces. We can therefore never be sure that some other forces are not at work. The case of government spending on health provides a clear, well-documented example. Since the establishment of the National Health Service in 1948 the health of the people has, by any measure, improved immensely: we live longer, and our lives are freer from all kinds of pain and disabil-

ity than the lives of the generations who lived before the establishment of the NHS. Yet the connection between all this and spending on health is uncertain. Some significant improvements in health have to do with lifestyle changes: for instance, with better diet, more exercise, better control of pollution of the physical environment.

To take this last example: the comparatively modest cost of clean air legislation may be far more cost effective in curing chest diseases such as bronchitis than much larger health spending on respiratory care, and at this point in the debate the problem of identifying the objectives of a programme re-enters. The NHS, a huge, diverse and long established service, has had many different objectives ascribed to it. A common view is that it should be seen as having quite modest aims: not to make the population more healthy, but as a kind of national repair service, patching us up when we fall sick. On this last view, to measure how far spending is meeting objectives means looking not at measures of the overall health of the population, but at how quickly and effectively 'patching up' is being done: for instance, at how quickly the sick get medical attention or at how successful doctors are in 'patching up' (say, at success rates of hospital operations measured by the survival rate of patients). The one thing we cannot do is run a controlled experiment in which we 'simulate' the health history of the British people over the last 50 years with a different kind of health service, or no health service at all, to observe what difference the NHS has made. The measurement of impact is therefore a special case of an issue that we discussed in preceding chapters: the care we have to take in arriving at a judgement about the success or failure of a policy (see Debating Politics 21.1).

The case of health care also highlights another important feature of the measurement of the impact of resource allocation. Spending on the National Health Service is one of the largest programmes in what (for short-hand) we call the welfare state. Other large programmes have cropped up in this chapter: income transfer programmes such as old-age pensions; programmes of large-scale subsidy of services, such as subsidy for higher education; programmes that provide free services available on demand to all (free public libraries). All these, we have seen, have different patterns of usage, and therefore different potential impact. Debates about access to, and the impact of, the care provided by the National Health Service encapsulate the wider arguments about what impact we expect from the welfare state. Is it fundamentally about helping to make more equal the inequalities created by other social forces, such as the workings of the market? In that case we would judge it by how far its impact consisted in giving preferential care to the poorest in the community. Alternatively, is it fundamentally about providing a kind of public good similar to the clean air we all of us, rich and poor, can breathe? In that case we judge it by the quality of the service it provides for the whole community, and by the impact it has on the health of all, rich and poor alike.

## REVIEW

The main themes of this chapter are as follows:

1  The state raises resources in many ways but taxation is the most important;
2  Within taxation, government has a particularly important choice to make: whether to tax income or to tax sales, service or consumption, using methods such as VAT and excise duties. In recent decades it has shifted towards the latter, though income taxes remain the single most important source of revenue;
3  The way the state allocates resources has produced an extended debate about the vast scale of public spending in Britain, both about its purposes, and about how far those purposes have been, or could be, realized;
4  These debates also connect to wider debates about British society: notably about how social and economic equality can or should be promoted in a market economy.

## Further reading

A great study of the key place of taxation in resource raising is Steinmo (1993); it has the added merit of dealing with Britain alongside other leading nations. Thain and Wright (1995) remains the best modern study of public spending policy, but chapter 7 of Grant (2002), though short, is outstanding for the beginner. Goodin and LeGrand (1987), though now obviously dated, is still the best introduction to the vexed question of whether the provision of public goods contributes to equality.

CHAPTER 22

# The state, public order and security

## CONTENTS

## AIMS

This chapter:

❖ Explains the central role of the state in the maintenance of public order

❖ Summarizes the roles of the agencies and institutions in Britain concerned with the maintenance of public order

❖ Sketches the issues of efficiency and impartiality raised by the workings of these agencies and institutions

❖ Shows the development of recent attempts to cope with problems of efficiency and impartiality.

## The state and public order

In our everyday lives most of us look to the state for protection and security. If our flat is burgled, or we are threatened or physically assaulted, we expect the institutions of the state to act: we demand that the police catch the villains and that the courts punish them. If burglary or physical assault is at all common we complain that these institutions are not doing their job.

This everyday expectation springs from a key function of the state in Britain, and in many other societies: preserving public order and protecting the lives and property of all who live within the state's boundaries. Indeed most definitions of the nature of the state – such as those we examined in Chapter 1 – spring from the view that the preservation of order and security in society is one of its fundamental purposes. There we found (Briefing 1.1, p. 9) one of the most influential of all definitions of the nature of the state, offered by Max Weber: that it is 'a human community that (successfully) claims the *monopoly of the legitimate use of physical force* within a given territory'.

In Britain, in order to carry out the functions of preserving order and security we have a set of institutions which enjoy great power and which consume substantial resources in money and people. Some, such as the judiciary, are historically ancient, tracing their origins to medieval times. Some, such as a professionally organized police force, only date from the first part of the nineteenth century: the Metropolitan Police in London from the Metropolitan Police Act of 1829, and police forces elsewhere from the obligation in the Municipal Corporations Act 1835 requiring all boroughs to appoint a force of constables. Some, like MI6, the branch of the security services which spies abroad for the British state, are largely the product of the world wars that the state fought in the twentieth century.

When we experience threat or loss, the duty of the state usually seems straightforward. If we are attacked on the street we feel anger and outrage; we want the police to appear rapidly, to catch the assailants, and to bring them before the court for punishment. But in the wider organization of British society and government, the great power and resources given to the agents of public order raise issues that go the heart of the nature of democratic government. They are a main concern of this and the next chapter. Three are especially important.

### Public order and liberty

Since we live under a system of government that claims both to be democratic and to respect the liberties and rights of all, the great power and resources given to the agents of public order should be used in conformity with principles of democracy and liberty (see Images 22.1–3). But behind this simple claim lie complex and troubling issues. Observing the rules of democratic government implies, at a minimum, that institutions such as the police and the security services will be subject to control by the democratically elected government. But even if this is achieved that meets only the condition of democratic accountability (of control by, for instance, elected politicians): it does not in itself meet the condition that the agents responsible for securing public order and security will respect the liberties and rights of citizens. Democratically elected governments are quite capable of ignoring these. The maintenance of public order has to take place within a set of restraints additional to those of democratic control: it has to be limited by respect for the rights and liberties of all of us, whether we are the victims of crime or are those who commit it. But agreeing what rights we should have against agencies such as the police and the security services is not at all straightforward. Enforcing those rights is also difficult. Enforcing public order usually demands that we allow a large amount of discretion in daily operations. It is not practical continually to look over the shoulder of the policeman on the beat or the soldier on the streets of Northern Ireland, or to try to prescribe in detail rules for all security circumstances. We have to trust agents of public order to respond appropriately as situations arise. But how far they can or should be trusted is one of the big problems that has to be solved in maintaining public order while at the same time preserving liberties. These issues recur in this chapter, and are also a main focus of Chapter 23. They have become

**Images 22.1–3**
**The new technology of surveillance**

Photos: Michael Moran

Image 22.1    Supermarkets          Image 22.2    Moorlands          Image 22.3    Townscapes

➲ Closed circuit television cameras are everywhere: in supermarkets (22.1); guarding public spaces even in wild parts of Britain (22.2) – the photo was taken at over 600 metres above sea level in the Derbyshire moorlands; and guarding whole townscapes – Image 22.3 was taken on the streets of Belfast, a city where much of the new technology was pioneered.

even more sensitive since the terrorist attack on New York in September 2001, which dramatized the fact that states such as the British find themselves in a new and dangerous environment of terrorist aggression.

## Public order and efficiency

Providing public order involves providing a very special kind of public service because, as we saw above, it has historically been the core function of the state. But nevertheless, functions such as policing are, viewed another way, simply public services like health, education or rubbish disposal. Just as we can try to measure the efficiency of health care or education provision, so we can try to measure the efficiency of the agencies of public order and, if they do not seem to be performing satisfactorily, we can debate how to organize them better. This raises issues which have cropped up in different policy domains in earlier chapters: for instance, how far the state should itself directly 'deliver' the service of public security and how far it should contract out to private firms.

## The relationship between 'external' and 'internal' security

Traditionally the state operated with a clear distinction between the domains of 'internal' and 'external' security. We expected the armed forces to protect us from external threats, mostly from other (hostile) nations; and we expected agencies such as the police to provide defence against internal threats. We did not normally expect to see the army involved in policing on the streets of our cities. This division between the internal and the external is increasingly difficult to maintain. For 30 years from the late 1960s the army was mainly responsible for trying to maintain order on the streets of Northern Ireland, in cooperation with security services and with the civilian police. 'External' threats now often come not from other nation states, but from secretive, loosely organized terrorist networks which try to operate freely across national boundaries. Countering those threats demands close cooperation between all the agencies of public order in Britain, and with agencies in other states. As we shall see, combating terrorism is an exercize in multi-level (indeed, multi-dimensional) governance.

The issues raised here are wide-ranging and complicated, and recur in this and the following chapter. They will also be important in our concluding review of the nature of democratic government in Britain. In the sections that follow, merely for ease of description, we condense them into two: the efficiency with which institutions and agencies operate; and the extent to which they are even handed and impartial in the way they treat citizens.

## Courts, judges and public order

We saw in Chapter 1 that the exercize of authority in British government is in the main what Max Weber classified as 'rational-legal': that is, the claims for obedience that public bodies make on citizens rests on their decisions being made in conformity with agreed rules governing the powers of public agencies. The most important source of rational-legal authority is the law, and this is why judges and the courts are so important to the state's function in maintaining order. Five particularly important roles for the courts should be highlighted.

*Symbolizing the law*. Laws are among the most important expressions of state power, and thus both courts and judges are among its most visible public symbols. In the language of Walter Bagehot the courts perform important 'dignified' functions. Many apparently trivial aspects of the courts and judges, especially of the highest courts, are designed for symbolic effect: the historical practice of wearing arcane outfits (wigs, gowns); the use of a specialized language and procedures; the construction of impressive buildings to house courts, all these perform the function of 'dignifying' the power of the state expressed in law.

*Applying the law*. This emphasis on 'dignity' and symbols is designed to assist the courts in performing important 'efficient' roles, to use again the language of Bagehot from Documenting Politics 5.1, p. 72. In

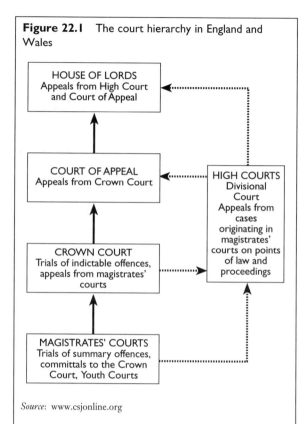

**Figure 22.1**  The court hierarchy in England and Wales

*Source*: www.csjonline.org

➲ The diagram of the court structure brings out a historically important feature of the system which may soon be superseded. At the very highest level the most supreme court is confusingly referred to for ease of reference as the House of Lords. In fact it consists only of the Lords of Appeal, lawyers of eminence appointed from among the judges of the Court of Appeal, who are appointed peers of the House of Lords and who sit as a court in the precincts of the Lords. The impending proposals for a separately organized Supreme Court, described in the text, would abolish this arrangement.

this respect the most important function of the courts is to apply the law: to convert the often general language of a statute passed by Parliament into an application in a particular circumstance, deciding whether the state's authority has been defied and, if so, what sanctions should be imposed. A good deal of what courts do consists of fairly straightforward application of the law. Over time there have developed standards of applicable evidence in deciding a verdict, a long history of cases which can be invoked as precedents to guide both verdict and sentence, and 'tariffs' which give guidance as to sentencing for particular categories of offence. This role of applying the law is particularly prominent in the lowest levels of courts, where magistrates – lay people who devote only part of the time to the role – hear cases on a wide range of less serious offences. But courts are far more than institutions for mechanically applying the law, and this gives to the remaining roles considered here a special importance, and a special political significance.

*Interpreting the law.* We noted earlier in this chapter that maintaining public order usually involves giving discretion to the agents of the state. The discretion to interpret statute is vital in the courts. No statute passed by Parliament can cover every eventuality, and for the most part statutes are very general in the language they use. Application of the law therefore in practice commonly demands interpretation. Indeed, this is the most creative role played by the courts, and especially by the highest courts. If we look at Figure 22.1 we will see that the 'supreme' court at the moment consists of the most senior members of the judiciary sitting in the House of Lords. The most important role of the 'Law Lords' is to hear appeals on points of law: in other words, precisely on whether the law has been properly interpreted and applied. The importance of interpretation immediately highlights the political sensitivity of judging as an activity, since it plainly raises the issue of how far interpretation is guided by ideological preferences, open or implicit. This is an issue we directly address later in discussing the impartiality of the courts, but it is also an issue in the way judges perform two other important roles that we now discuss.

*Making the law.* In the modern democratic state law is typically thought of as arising from legislation: from the law-making activity of a specialized institution, a legislature. Law making in this explicit way is becoming more important, as is shown by the historical increase in the volume of laws passed by parliaments both in Westminster and in Scotland. In addition, the European Union has emerged as an important source of law, through its Directives and regulations. But historically things were very different: until well into the nineteenth century the volume of laws passed by Parliament was small, and most law was the product of the 'common law'. The common law refers to a wide range of practices, including the historically established customs of the courts, covering both procedures and the rules of evidence, and the legal reasoning courts employ. A particularly important source of common law lies in judicial decisions on important cases. They become a source of authoritative precedents, guiding courts in the way they reason about later cases. When elected legislatures such as the Westminster Parliament were not highly active, passing by modern standards comparatively few statutes, judge-made common law was the most important source of law. Even today, the common law remains an important point of reference for courts both because of the binding power of precedent in particular cases, and because it provides a framework of customary assumptions about legal reasoning. It will also be plain that judge-made common law shades into the interpretation of existing statutes that we discussed above.

*Reviewing the application of the law.* Judicial review has in the past been of most importance in systems of government that have a written constitution (such as the United States or the Federal Republic of Germany). In those systems an important function of the higher level courts is to review the decisions of public bodies when there is a challenge to a decision on the grounds that it breaches the constitution. The doctrine of parliamentary sovereignty, discussed in Chapter 5, limited the role of judicial review in the United Kingdom, since that doctrine assigned to Parliament the power to make laws free of the restraints of a written constitution. Nevertheless, judicial review was still historically important. Judges retained and used the power to strike down decisions of public bodies, including decisions of ministers of the Crown, on the grounds of ultra vires: that the decision was made without the sanction of law. Since the original decisions were almost invariably made in the belief that they were indeed sanctioned by some existing statute, it is easy to see that judicial review of this kind was really a species of interpretation (courts taking a different view of the meaning of the law from that taken by the offending public body). The scale and scope of judicial review has grown greatly in recent decades (see Figure 22.2). This is due to three influences:

- It is a natural result of Parliamentary activism: the growing volume of legislation means that there are many more points where the powers of public bodies depend on (contestable) interpretations of the meaning of the law in statutes enacted by Parliament. This is likely to become even more significant with the passage of ambitious and far-reaching statutes such as the Human Rights Act (discussed in the next chapter) which confers on citizens a wide range of broad rights against the power of the state.
- There has been a huge expansion in the volume and range of what is usually called administrative law, administered by a quasi-judicial system of tribunals. (These are described in Chapter 23.) This area of law covers matters of tremendously complex detail, ranging from entitlements to the services of the welfare state to entitlements to migrate into the United Kingdom. The complexity of the issues is reflected in the complexity of the rules, and therefore there is constant pressure on the higher courts to arbitrate on the contested meaning of the administrative rules implemented by the tribunal system.
- Membership of the European Union has begun to introduce some elements of a superior written constitution. British government, and the courts, are bound in various ways by the Treaties creating the Union, such as the Maastricht Treaty of 1992; by the Regulations that the Commission of the European Union is empowered to make; and by the Directives which are made by, in the last analysis, the Council of Ministers. That is why the European Court of Justice has on occasions enforced judgments in advance of what would be claimable through domestically made UK law. The best known examples concern issues of equal pay between men and women, where the ECJ enabled employees to enforce rights against employers that went further than the Equal Pay Act 1970 and the Sex Discrimination Act 1975 (Bradley 2000: 43).

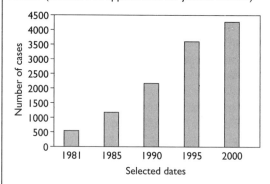

**Figure 22.2**  The growing importance of judicial review (numbers of applications for judicial review)

*Source*: Calculated from Sunkin (2001: 10).

⮕ One of the most striking features of the changing role of judges in recent decades is the huge growth in the volume of judicial review: cases where the courts review the legality of executive action. This change is partly a matter of supply: judges are increasingly willing to entertain judicial review as a key part of the judicial function. As Figure 22.2 shows, however, it is also a matter of demand: increasing numbers of citizens, and the organizations that represent them, are ready to challenge public power and the decisions made by the exercise of public power.

The wide range of judicial functions summarized here have raised in especially serious form the two major issues which we identified near the start of this chapter: those of impartiality and efficiency.

## Impartiality and the courts

The traditional image of Justice pictures her as a blindfold figure balancing truth in a pair of scales, to symbolize the even-handed character of the courts in weighing evidence. This claim to 'blindness' is also central to the claim of the modern state to base its authority on rational-legal grounds: that is, on impersonal rules that apply to all. But it is well documented that in the past justice was far from 'blind': for instance, it protected the rights of particular kinds of property, and until well into the twentieth century was hostile to some kinds of organized interests, notably trade unions.

Accusations that the modern judicial system fails the test of impartiality rest on two grounds. First, the social world of the law and the courts remains highly exclusive. The world of the lay magistrate; the world of the organized legal professions, solicitors and barristers; the world of the judiciary itself; all three show significant social biases, with a wide range of groups – women, members of ethnic minorities, those born to working-class families – strikingly underrepresented. A second ground for accusations of partiality concerns the institutional structure of the judicial system, notably organization at the highest levels. Unlike many other democratic states, the United Kingdom has not had a separately organized Ministry of Justice, or a distinct Supreme Court. The head of the judiciary (and the main 'manager' of the court system) was the Lord Chancellor, a political appointee who combined a role as a member of the Cabinet – and therefore partisan political commitments – with both a judicial role and roles in making key appointments in the judicial system. The highest supreme court, the Law Lords, not only included the Lord Chancellor but was composed of judges who also sat as members of the legislature, in the House of Lords. These institutional connections tied the leading members of the judiciary to the government not in any partisan sense, but in the sense that it led them to share some of the preoccupations of the governing elite in Whitehall. These included a shared predisposition to favour particular values, such as a preference for secrecy about the policy-making process.

The argument that the impartiality of the judicial system is compromised either by the social makeup of the judiciary, or because of institutional connections with the executive and the legislature, is strongly disputed. (See Briefing 22.1.) But, as we shall see shortly, it has seriously influenced important reforms in the administration of justice in recent decades. Before turning to these reforms let us briefly examine the second theme, that of efficiency.

## Efficiency and the courts

That the system of justice is slow and inefficient is a long-established belief: it is, for instance, the dominant theme of one of the great nineteenth-century

## Briefing 22.1

### JUDICIAL BIAS: FACT OR FICTION?

The modern debate about whether judicial bias was a problem was begun in the 1970s by Griffith (1977/1991). He argued that judges exhibited persistent class bias by virtue of their elite social origins, their training and the culture of legal institutions. Since the 1970s these allegations about class bias have been added to by arguments that the judiciary at all levels shows distinct gender and ethnic bias. Regardless of whether or not these arguments are sustainable, it is undoubtedly the case that they have produced institutional responses intended to guard against bias. Two important examples are:

● The Judicial Appointments Board was established in 1979 to advise the then Lord Chancellor on training at all levels of the judiciary, from magistrates to Lords of Appeal. Over the years it has developed extensive training programmes that go well beyond technical legal training: for instance, courses aimed at sensitizing the judiciary to a wide range of issues to do with gender and ethnicity.
● The Commission for Judicial Appointments was established in 2001 to review appointments of judges and Queen's Counsel (the most senior barristers) and to investigate complaints about the operation of those procedures. It reports to the Secretary of State in the Department for Constitutional Affairs.

*Sources*: www.jsb.gsi.gov.uk; www.ja-comm.gsi.gov.uk

➲ Arguments about judicial bias are particularly damaging in a system of government that relies heavily on the exercize of rational-legal authority, since the key claims are that authority is exercized impartially and within openly stated rules. The reforms summarized are part of a continually developing programme.

English novels, Dickens' *Bleak House* (1852) where the suit of *Jarndyce* vs *Jarndyce* makes a tortuously slow and ruinous progress. In recent years, however, the pressure for efficiency has become more intense as the New Public Management has penetrated the administration of justice. As we shall see below, similar influences are at work in other parts of the system for the maintenance of public order, notably in the police and prison services. Since 1995 the administration of the court system in England and Wales has been 'hived off' to an executive (Next Steps) agency, the Court Service, which employs over 9,000 people. (We discussed the general organization of Next Steps agencies in Chapter 8.) In the devolved system of the administration of justice, the Scottish Court Service is also an executive agency. The Court Service has the familiar marks of a Next Steps agency. Its relations with its governing department, the Department for Constitutional Affairs, are ruled by a framework agreement and by negotiated performance targets. It also publishes a Charter for users of court services describing the standards it expects to reach in delivering its services to clients. (For extracts from a typical framework agreement for an agency see Documenting Politics 8.3, p. 146, which details the example of the Prison Service.)

### Reforming the institutions of the justice system

Arguments about impartiality, and pressures for greater efficiency, have been important in producing reforms in the administration of justice. Under the Conservative government before 1997 many changes were introduced by Lord Chancellor Mackay, who was Lord Chancellor between 1987 and 1997. They have accelerated since the return of the Labour party to office in 1997. The reforms can be divided into three categories

- *Implemented.* The most visible of these have been the abolition of the Lord Chancellor's Department. In 2003 it was succeeded by a Department for Constitutional Affairs with a Secretary of State of Cabinet rank.
- *Continuing.* There are continuing reforms designed both to make appointments at all levels of the legal system, from lay magistrates upwards, more transparent in the appointment procedure and more inclusive in the social range of those appointed.
- *Impending.* These promise radical changes in structure. A Constitutional Reform Bill has been introduced to complete the institutional changes

involved in the creation of the Department for Constitutional Affairs by abolishing the office of Lord Chancellor. The successor office will be a Secretary of State for the new Department. In place of the existing highly confidential system of making judicial appointments there is proposed an independent judicial appointments commission with a lay chair, to propose names of appointees to ministers. More important still, it is proposed to create a Supreme Court to replace the present arrangement involving the Law Lords in the presently constituted House of Lords. In this way, the highest branch of the judiciary will be institutionally and physically separated from the legislature, and the practice of a member of the Cabinet – the Lord Chancellor – sitting as a judge will cease.

## The police and public order

Most of us obey the law most of the time quite voluntarily, but professionally organized police forces are nevertheless in the front line defending public order. Maintaining public order through policing is nothing new in Britain, but modern policing was created in the nineteenth century (see People in Politics 22.1). The Industrial Revolution, alongside its amazing technical and social advances, also brought huge social problems. The scale of cities, coupled with poverty, lack of education, and lack of even rudimentary social services, helped make crime rife. As we noted in the opening section of the chapter, most of the institutions that we now think of as traditional to British policing were created in this period, notably in the Metropolitan Police Act of 1829 and the Metropolitan Corporations Act of 1835. So rapid and complete was the development that by the start of the twentieth century the uniformed British 'bobby' was perhaps the most important authority figure representing the power of the state that most people came across in their daily lives. The connection with state power was emphasized by the particular status of the police officer. Although the organization of police forces was highly decentralized, the individual police officer was an officer of the Crown, bound by

## People in politics

### 22.1  GUARDIANS OF PUBLIC ORDER

Cartoons: Shaun Steele

**Sir William Blackstone** (1723–80), educated Charterhouse, University of Oxford; fellow of All Souls College 1744, Professor of Civil Law, 1753. Though a judge of the Court of Common Pleas from 1770, he was mostly an academic lawyer whose *Commentaries*, first published in 1765, became the most authoritative source in the eighteenth and nineteenth centuries for the content of the 'common law' in an age when Parliament passed few laws.

**Sir Robert Peel** (1788–1850), educated Eton public school and University of Oxford. Though chiefly known as the dominant figure in British politics from the 1830s until his death, associated with the repeal of the Corn Laws and the resulting division of the Conservative Party, one of his most significant acts was to reorganize the way London was policed, creating in 1829 a new Metropolitan police force – the terms 'bobbies' and 'peelers' echo his importance.

**Lord Denning** (1899–1999), educated University of Oxford, Law Lord, 1957, Master of the Rolls, 1962–82. Probably the best known judicial figure of the twentieth century, his tenure as Master of the Rolls allowed him to make many landmark judgments. His interventionist approach – 'The judge should make the law correspond with the justice that the case requires' – was applauded by some, and denounced by others as a usurpation of Parliament.

➲ These are three key figures in the history of law. The differences over the centuries are great. But note one striking commonality: all were educated at the elite University of Oxford.

an oath to preserve the Queen or King's peace. This connection with state power is still represented symbolically by the design of the police officer's badge which most uniformed officers have on their helmet: it contains a reference (EIIR) to the officer's role as a direct servant of the monarch.

The historical origins of policing have affected present organization, and have helped shape the pressures for changes in that organization. The police services in the United Kingdom were histor-

ically one of the most decentralized parts of the public sector. The territorial organization of police forces – into forces largely based on county boundaries headed by a Chief Constable – has been the dominant 'building block' of organization. These forces have had their own separate governing systems, in the past closely tied to local government; their own budgets; and, below the most senior levels, police officers generally made their whole careers in a single force. The contrast with a

European neighbour such as France, where policing has historically been closely controlled by central government in Paris, is striking. Even now, a separate police authority governs each of the regular police forces. Outside London, the authorities comprize local councillors and magistrates; under the provisions of the Police and Magistrates' Courts Act 1994, the police authorities also include independent members. This system is under the overall supervision of the Home Office but, as this formulation shows, there is plenty of room for manoeuvre in settling the balance of influence between centre and locality. London, as the largest and most complex police jurisdiction, has special arrangements. The government of policing in the capital was reformed as part of the changes of the government of London introduced in 1999 (see Chapter 12). The Greater London Authority Act of that year also created a Metropolitan Police Authority.

Although the historical imprint of decentralization is deep, in recent decades the balance of influence has swung in favour of the Home Office. The reasons for this take us back to the twin themes that we saw were important in the organization of the judicial system: the search for efficiency and the pressure to demonstrate impartiality.

## The efficiency of policing

The efficiency of public services has been a dominant theme of political debates for many decades. As Documenting Politics 22.1 shows, many of the key features of the New Public Management – notably concern with developing performance measurements – have reached into the police service, particularly through Home Office initiatives. In addition, there have been changes in the style of some traditional Home Office means of inspection, designed to squeeze more efficiency out of individual forces. Thus for over a century there has existed the Home Office-based HM Inspector of Constabulary, but only in the last couple of decades have inspectors' reports focused systematically and critically on the performance of individual forces measured by such indicators as clear-up rates of crimes.

The drive to organize policing more efficiently has had a number of important results. It has helped

accelerate a trend that we noted above: growing central control over what used to be a highly decentralized police service. One reason for this connection with centralization is that gauging and increasing efficiency involves developing common standards and targets: if we are to compare the efficiency of police forces in Manchester and London, we plainly need some standardized measures to make the comparison. The search for greater efficiency has also made the police a much more consciously *managed* service. Police operations are now organized around achieving a whole series of performance targets: for instance, detection and 'clear-up' rates for offences such as burglary. Promotion within the police depends much more than in the past on acquiring management skills. As a result, far more resources are today invested in the training of individual officers, not only in policing skills but also in general management skills, including control of budgets. The search for efficiency has also made policing a much more overtly political matter than in the past. This may seem an odd consequence, for we might expect the pursuit of efficiency to make policing more technical and organized around neutral 'management' issues; but much of the drive for more efficiency comes from the rising political sensitivity of policing. As a result, national politicians now openly compete for votes by promising to organize police services more efficiently than their party rivals.

The search for efficiency has been intensified by two other connected developments that transcend the influence of the New Public Management. Social and economic changes in the last generation have greatly increased the social sensitivity of policing, and therefore made more complex the task of the police in doing their job. The example of traffic offences shows the implications of change. Before the rise of mass car ownership, for most middle-class citizens the police officer was mainly a distant and fairly benign figure. The increasing regulation of the conditions under which we can drive vehicles – covering such sensitive issues as the narcotics and stimulants we may not consume before driving, and the speed at which we drive – has drawn into the law enforcement net millions of these citizens. The change highlights the delicate balance between

## DOCUMENTING POLITICS 22.1

## THE NEW PUBLIC MANAGEMENT COMES TO POLICING

### The Policing Performance Assessment Framework (PPAF)

*'Background*
The Policing Performance Assessment Framework is a joint initiative of the Home Office, the Association of Chief Police Officers and the Association of Police Authorities.

Improved police performance is central to the Government's vision of better public services. Until the Policing Performance Assessment Framework, the police service had lagged behind many other public services in terms of the extent, robustness and transparency of the framework for assessing its performance.

*Features*
The Policing Performance Assessment Framework is about 'policing' as a whole and is designed to reflect the breadth of modern policing. It is about the contribution of local communities and other organizations as well as the police service itself.

In addition to focusing on operational effectiveness, the Policing Performance Assessment Framework will provide measures of public satisfaction and overall trust and confidence in the police, as well as measures that put performance into context in terms of efficiency and organizational capability. In line with the Government's desire to enhance policing accountability at a local level, performance against both national and local priorities will be fully reflected in the assessment framework.

More specifically, the Policing Performance Assessment Framework will also demonstrate success in achieving the five key priorities of the National Policing Plan for 2004–7: providing a citizen focused service to the public, tackling anti-social behaviour and disorder, continuing to reduce crime in line with the Government's Public Service Agreements targets, combating serious and organized crime, and narrowing the justice gap.'

⮕ A major theme of this chapter is that the delivery of public order is a service in many ways like the wider range of services delivered by government. The New Public Management in recent years has increasingly tried to measure the effectiveness of service delivery, and to provide quantitative indicators against which service deliverers can be measured. The boxed material illustrates how this is increasingly being applied to the delivery of policing.

*Source*: Extracted from homeoffice.gov.uk/police reform

surveillance and voluntary obedience to the law. Technological developments – ranging from the breathalyser to 'speed cameras' – are designed to ensure more efficient surveillance. For the most part, however, police officers have no alternative but to rely on voluntary compliance. No matter how large a police force, and no matter how impressive its resources of surveillance, it could never hope to monitor the behaviour of millions of inhabitants of big cities. Police officers already have difficulties 'clearing up' house burglaries; if most of us practised theft as a way of life they would be overwhelmed. We often see the limits of policing when large groups in the community lose confidence in the police, or simply decide that they will not obey a law.

The second influence making more complex the search for efficient policing is the growing realization that effective policing is bound up with the effective management of multi-level government. Briefing 22.4, p. 486 illustrates this, from the vital state function of protecting against terrorism. It shows how police operations have to be fitted into a complicated institutional jig stretching right across the institutions of government. But this is only a single example. Briefing 22.2 shows the growth, presently small, of another important dimension of multi-level governance: the Europeanization of the policing function, as a result of our membership of the European Union.

## The impartiality of policing

It is fundamental to the theory of good policing in a democracy such as Britain that the police should be, above all, even-handed in the way they carry out their tasks. The perception of impartiality is also vital for effective policing: in the end the enforcement of the law depends on popular willingness to obey voluntarily, and that willingness will not appear if the police are seen as hostile or biased. As we saw in our discussion of Northern Ireland in Chapter 11, impartiality has been – and remains – a particularly difficult issue in that province. But it has also become increasingly clear that it is an issue in the rest of Britain. A number of scandalous cases have established that there have been spectacular instances of the police not acting in an even-handed manner: in Chapter 23, the Stephen Lawrence case provides one of our three boxes documenting scandalous breakdowns in the way public bodies have treated private citizens. (See Briefing 23.5, p. 504). Much more difficult than establishing these scandalous instances is working out how to organize policing so that they do not recur, and so that impartiality is assured. Discretion is engrained in policing. In enforcing the law police officers necessarily have to make thousands of decisions daily, often instantaneously and often under great stress and danger. The mechanisms for redress of complaints and grievances that are discussed in the next chapter are not themselves sufficient: indeed, they exist on the assumption that there will be lapses, and exist to remedy the results of those lapses. Many standard means to ensure impartial treatment are just not practical in the case of

---

# Briefing                                    22.2

## EUROPEANIZING POLICING: THE CASE OF EUROPOL

The extent to which the European Union should have jurisdiction over policing has proved a fraught issue, principally because policing is at the heart of the traditional functions of the nation state. The main EU agency at present is EUROPOL. Though its establishment was part of the Maastricht Treaty on European Union of 1992, the Europol Convention did not come into effect until 1998, following ratification by all member states. EUROPOL commenced full operations in July 1999. The Agency is located in The Hague (Netherlands). EUROPOL's mandate is wide: it covers drug trafficking, illicit immigration, terrorism, trafficking in humans, forgery and money laundering. However, its executive authority is slight, and it mainly acts as an information exchange, and as a source of expertize and advice to national forces.

*Source*: Information from www.europol.eu.int

➲ Even the 'core' domestic functions of the state, such as policing, are not immune from Europeanization, albeit at a slow and irregular rate, as this example shows.

---

policing. For instance anonymity is now widely used to guard against (often unconscious) bias in areas such as examination grading, but 'anonymized policing' does not make sense.

Faced with scandalous cases police forces have tried to restore the reputation for impartiality in three broad ways:

- By trying to recruit more officers from groups in the community who have particularly suffered in the past from partial policing, such as various ethnic minorities and other groups (gay people).
- By appointing senior officers with the special role of monitoring police behaviour, such as officers with responsibility for relations with ethnic minorities.
- By changing police education and training to make officers more aware of the problems of partial policing.

In the next chapter we will be setting these developments into the wider context of the relations between the state and the citizen in Britain. But, as we shall now see, many of these problems recur in other agencies charged with the maintenance of public order.

## Prisons and public order

The prison service has a unique importance in the government of public order in Britain. We turn to prisons for the maintenance of order more readily than almost any other country in Europe. The total prison population exceeds 70,000 and has grown steadily in recent years. Historically the prison system was also a centrally controlled organization, in the case of England and Wales from within the Home Office, much more than the police service. This historical centralization partly explains why the prison service is a uniquely politically sensitive area of the system for the maintenance of public order. There is no such thing as a 'non-political' area of prison management or administration. Even the most everyday matters of daily life – such as the kind of accommodation or food provided for prisoners – are grist for political struggle: good food and better accommodation are often cited as signs that prison is failing because it is insufficiently punishing; bad food and accommodation are as equally cited as failure because they are seen as part of a system which fails to deal with prisoners humanely. Thus the prison service is politically sensitive from the biggest issues of policy (such as the rights of prisoners) to the most routine (such as the kind of food served). The twin issues that have so far guided us in examining the institutions for the maintenance of public order – efficiency and impartiality – are more contested here than perhaps in any other public service.

We have indeed already encountered – in both Chapters 5 and 8 – just how difficult and politically sensitive the management of prisons can be. The Prison Service was part of the very first wave of Next Steps agencies, a testimony in part to the need for any Home Secretary to provide some distance between the office and the daily management of the system. (See Documenting Politics 8.3 for the formal position.) The attempt created one of the great constitutional crises of the 1990s, with accusations that, whatever the formal relationship between the Prison Service as an executive agency and the Home Office, the Home Secretary, faced with politically embarrassing escapes by prisoners, had exceeded his formal powers in securing the dismissal of a prison governor. (See Documenting Politics 5.2, p. 79 for some consequences.) The affair shows just how difficult the issues of efficiency and impartiality can be.

### Efficiency and the Prison Service

The Prison Service historically was a part of the public sector very far removed from the kind of pressures for efficiency associated with New Public Management. The system was highly centralized in a command structure controlled from the Home Office. Individual prisons were often 'total institutions', segregated from the wider society. Indeed, many virtually had their own independent domestic economy, with their own farms and workshops. The workforce of the prison service – prison officers – were well organized into a powerful, militant trade union with a high level of control over daily operational life in prisons.

In short, this was a very 'traditional' part of the public sector, and it is therefore not surprising that the rise of the culture of the New Public Management has forced some particularly radical changes in the way the service operates. Three are particularly important:

- *'Hiving off'*. As we have seen, the service was one of earliest candidates for 'hiving off' into a separate executive agency, with the aim of developing a relationship focused on the achievement of performance targets.
- *New styles of inspection*. A characteristic feature of the New Public Management – the more aggressive and adversarial inspection of the institutions of service delivery – has also developed in the Prison Service. This is a quite novel development in the case of prisons. The HM Inspectorate of Prisons was only established in 1980. It inspects prisons, reporting to the Secretary of State on the

treatment of prisoners and conditions in institutions. The style of successive inspectors has been consistently adversarial and critical. Inspectors have commonly used their power to arrive unannounced, and to offer highly critical verdicts on conditions in individual prisons. As a result they have had tense relations not only with those who work in the service, but with successive Home Secretaries who have found the reports politically embarrassing. Nevertheless, the institution of critical inspection is now built into the system.

- *Privatization to cut union power.* Determined attempts have been made to change working practices. As we have noted, the organization of this part of the public sector was very 'command' oriented, and was marked by a high level of militant trade union organization in the form of the Prison Officers' Association. Under the impact of the New Public Management this has produced successive efforts to change working practices in the search for efficiency. The most radical of these efforts have involved attempts to depart entirely from the old command system through the privatization of parts of the service. Briefing 22.3 shows the presently limited creation of private prisons contracted to deliver services. It exemplifies the attempt to shift to a performance-focused service based on contracted commitments from providers. But this is only part of the story, because there has also developed an increasing reliance on private delivery in the 'public' part of the service: for instance, through the use of private security firms to manage the transfer of prisoners between different parts of the justice system.

## Impartiality and the Prison Service

We have noted in the case of other institutions designed to ensure public order, such as the police and the courts, that impartiality in the way clients are treated is a core value about which there is widespread agreement; the arguments are about whether impartiality is actually practised. The agreement reflects the fact that Britain claims to be governed by a system where the rule of law is a paramount value. It is a foundation of the claim to rational-legal

## Briefing 22.3

### THE PRISON SERVICE AND THE NEW PUBLIC MANAGEMENT: THE CASE OF PRISON PRIVATIZATION

The Victorian era was a great period of both prison reform and prison construction. The state systematically organized for the first time the incarceration of offenders in a nationally organized public service. But, as with most other state services, in the closing decades of the twentieth century the traditional organization of the Prison Service was challenged by the model of privatization. Presently there are 11 private prisons, falling into two categories:

- 'Management only' prisons, where the prisons are managed by contracted private sector firms but were built by traditional procurement methods. Although just two prisons are 'management only', this is an obvious model of privatization for the large stock of prisons inherited from the Victorian era.
- 'Design, Construct, Manage and Finance' (DCMF) prisons, where the prisons are built and managed under the Private Finance Initiative, represent an increasingly popular method of organizing public services in which the capital for service provision is privately raised, and a long-term contract for service delivery is awarded to the service provider.

Both kinds of contract contain performance measures which, if not met, lead to reduced payments to the private contractor.

➲ The most radical manifestation of the New Public Management is privatization: the transfer of ownership or functions from public organizations to private firms. Here we see that it has even arrived in the Prison Service.

authority made by a state such as the British state. The 'clients' of the courts and the police are, however, citizens with all the full rights of citizenship, until found guilty of some offence. It is obvious that the main 'clients' of the prison service are different: they are both coerced clients, and are subject to varying degrees of control designed to modify their behaviour. The only remotely comparable group are those among the mentally ill who have been subjected to compulsory detention orders. Indeed, in the case of one particularly difficult category of prisoner – the criminally insane – there is necessarily a link with those parts of the public service concerned with management of extreme mental illness. Prisoners therefore manifestly do not have exactly the same presumed rights as other citizens. At the same time, prisoners are even more vulnerable than the free population. Prisons contain disproportionate numbers of the mentally ill and of those without basic life skills such as literacy. The fact that the suicide rate for prisoners greatly exceeds that for the general population is a summary indicator of this vulnerability.

The recent history of the Prison Service has exposed some scandalous examples of partiality, ranging from straightforward bullying and brutality to systematic racism among some prison officers. These examples have undermined the credibility of the traditional safeguard offered by the service to ensure even-handedness and impartiality. This traditional safeguard might best be summed up as self-regulation: relying on the internal control systems of prisons. In their place have developed externally organized systems of inspection and investigation. The issues reported on by the Prisons Inspectorate, though focused on issues of efficiency in service delivery, have also often been central to issues of impartiality. Thus evidence of bullying – one theme of some of the reports – plainly bears on this issue. But the efficient daily organization of the system, which is a main concern of the Inspectorate, also bears on impartiality. For instance, evidence that prisons are so badly run that basic hygiene, cleanliness and freedom from infestation by vermin cannot be guaranteed plainly bears on issues of how prisoners are treated. A second external mechanism has now been created in the form of the Prisons and Probation Ombudsman. All prisoners, whether sentenced or on remand, can complain about virtually any aspect of their treatment by the Prison or the National Probation Service. Complaints are only considered after the exhaustion of the relevant service's own internal complaints procedures; the

Ombudsman, if the complaint is considered and found to have substance, can issue a full report recommending to the Service remedial action.

The issue of how far such changes in formal organization effectively solve problems of partiality is examined at the conclusion of this chapter, and in Chapter 23.

## The armed services and public order

The conventional phrase 'the armed services' refers to the army, navy and air force. It conveys also an important conventional implication which the passage of time has made less true: that we can draw a clear line between services which are armed, for the purpose of defending the country against external threats; and forces (such as the police) which historically were unarmed, and concerned to maintain order domestically. The conventional division has partly been undermined by the increasingly common practice of arming the police, albeit only in explicitly prescribed circumstances; and also by the increasing extent to which the armed services have been drawn into public order roles within Britain. The use of the armed services in these domestic roles still only takes place in crises, but these crises are becoming more common. They mainly reflect a development mentioned at the start of this chapter: the fact that the conventional divide between internal and external threats to order is breaking down, principally under the threat of terrorism.

There are three sets of circumstances where branches of the armed services have been involved in maintaining order internally:

- *Where the civilian forces cannot keep the peace.* The single most important recent instance of this concerns the history of public order in Northern Ireland. For nearly 30 years after 1969 the army was the key agency in policing the province.
- *Where the provision of emergency services by normal service providers is disrupted.* The most important examples in recent years have occurred in industrial disputes: in both 1977 and 2003, when the

# Briefing

## COMBATING TERRORISM: AN EXERCISE IN MULTI-LEVEL AND MULTI-DIMENSIONAL GOVERNANCE

The threat of terrorism, a threat that obeys no departmental or geographical boundaries, compels coordination between agencies at the same, and at many different, levels of government.

- The Home Office is the 'lead' domestic department. The Home Secretary chairs the Cabinet committees on terrorism and related issues. The Home Secretary is also responsible for counter-terrorist policy and legislation, the police and the security and intelligence operations of the Security Service (MI5).
- The Foreign and Commonwealth Office is the 'lead' department in liaising with foreign governments and with international organizations to combat terrorism.
- The separate area-based police forces, under their Chief Constables, are responsible for operational decisions, such as investigating terrorism as a criminal offence. The Commander of the (London) Metropolitan Anti-Terrorist Branch is appointed by the Association of Chief Police Officers (ACPO) as national coordinator for investigating acts of terrorism.
- The armed forces have specialist equipment and expertize (for instance, in bomb detection and disposal). They are involved at the request of a police force, a request channelled through the Home Office to the Ministry of Defence.
- Immigration and Customs Officers have important anti-terrorist functions in their roles in the area of border control.
- The Security Service (MI5) is the main gatherer of intelligence within the UK about terrorist and potential terrorist groups, gathering intelligence by a wide range of methods, including covert surveillance. It reports to the Home Office.
- The Secret Intelligence Service (MI6) collects intelligence overseas for the British government, and reports to the Foreign and Commonwealth Office.
- The Cabinet Office is the location of the Security and Intelligence Co-ordinator, a civil servant of Permanent Secretary rank (the highest) charged with overall coordination of the government's anti-terrorist machinery. The Co-ordinator also oversees the work of the Civil Contingencies Secretariat in the Cabinet Office, which plans for a wide range of disasters, both natural and terrorist-produced.
- Local authorities have a key role in planning for emergencies, including terrorist emergencies, and in dealing with the consequences for the emergency services.
- The emergency services (police, fire, ambulance) have a lead role in responding to any terrorist attack.

⮕ This formal summary of the way responding to terrorism draws in agencies at all levels of government gives a sense of how multi-level governance is central to the management of any terrorist threat. But behind the formal demarcations lies an even more difficult reality: of competition for jurisdiction ('turf') between competing agencies, and of the sheer difficulty of deciding how to divide up the complex job of combating terrorism. It also shows that the problems of coordination are far more complicated even than getting a hierarchy of institutions in the right working order: there is a problem of coordinating different dimensions of institutional life.

fire services took industrial action, sections of the army were drafted in to provide emergency cover.

- *In planning against the threat of international terrorism.* While the army has now substantially withdrawn from an active policing role in Northern Ireland, this function is becoming increasingly

important, notably since the terrorist attacks in New York in September 2001. As we see from Briefing 22.4, the characteristic feature of modern planning against terrorist attacks is that it is a multi-level and multi-agency operation, involving the armed services.

There is no doubt that the threat of terrorist attacks is drawing the armed services into new roles in the maintenance of public order. Here, once again, the performance of these roles raises issues linked with efficiency and impartiality. In the case of the armed forces the efficiency and impartiality issues are so closely linked that they should be discussed together. They are connected because at root they concern the suitability of armed services trained to combat an external threat to the task of securing order in a domestic civil arena. The arguments have crystallized in a number of highly contentious cases, notably during the army's long service in policing Northern Ireland. Briefing 22.5 summarizes the most serious and the most long-drawn-out of these: the claim that on 'Bloody Sunday' in January 1972 in Derry armed paratroopers illegitimately opened fire on unarmed civilian demonstrators. In addition, the history of policing in Northern Ireland by the army was bedevilled by claims that there were problematic connections between the army and branches of the security services operating covertly. There are thus important overlaps between the role of the armed services and the security services. Indeed, one important component of the security services is the Defence Intelligence Staff, an integral part of the Ministry of Defence. It is to the security services that we now turn.

## The security services and public order

Britain has a long history of security services: Queen Elizabeth I (1558–1603) had, for example, a 'spymaster' who ran a large network of informers. But the present history of the security services largely dates from the twentieth century, a century dominated first by two global wars (1914–18 and 1939–45) and then a 'Cold War' between two super-powers, the United States and the Soviet Union, with the United Kingdom an ally of the former. The arms of the security services (see Figure 22.3) are all twentieth-century creations. The Secret Intelligence Service (MI6) and the Security Service (MI5) both originated in 1909 in a period when there were fears of a German invasion.

---

# Briefing 22.5

### THE SAVILLE INQUIRY AND THE PROBLEMS OF USING THE ARMED FORCES TO SUPPRESS CIVIL DISTURBANCE

The Bloody Sunday Inquiry (often called the Saville Inquiry, after its chairman, Lord Saville) was established in 1998 to inquire into 'the events of Sunday 30th of January 1972 which led to loss of life in connection with the procession on that day, taking account of any new information relevant to the events of that day'. This was the day members of the Paratroop Regiment, charged with maintaining order, shot and killed 13 members of the public in Derry, Northern Ireland. The Inquiry was established to discover the truth of claims and counter-claims; that there was a plot to shoot civilians in the security services, or alternatively that the paratroopers shot in response to fire from IRA paramilitaries. At the time of writing the Inquiry has taken over 1700 witness statements, and has cost over £113 million; it estimates that the final cost will exceed £150 million, and after a gap of more than 30 years it is unlikely to be able to establish any definitive truth.

*Source*: Information from www.bloody-sunday-inquiry.org

➲ Use of the armed forces to keep the peace is not unknown in Britain, but has usually been confined to individual, critical instances. But maintaining public order in Northern Ireland meant using troops for a whole generation and often, as in the case here, with catastrophic and highly acrimonious consequences.

---

Their later separation is the origin of the conventional distinction between the roles of the two agencies: MI6 is concerned with gathering intelligence abroad relevant to British national security; MI5 with gathering domestic intelligence. MI5 therefore has an explicit, historically established role in the maintenance of public order domestically.

Even at the height of the Cold War this distinction between the functions of the two agencies could not always be maintained, since governments and security services often took the view that domestic 'subversion' and foreign threats were

**Figure 22.3**   Structure of the security services: ministerial responsibilities

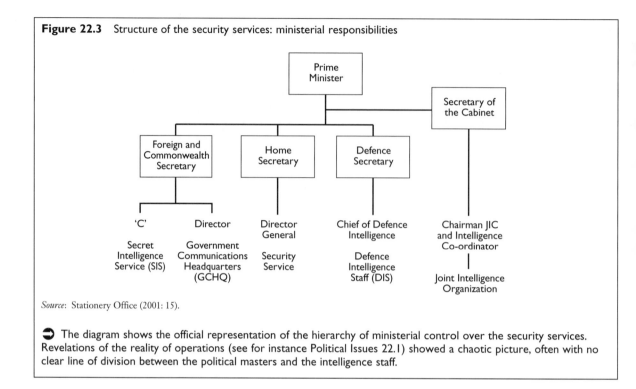

*Source*: Stationery Office (2001: 15).

➲ The diagram shows the official representation of the hierarchy of ministerial control over the security services. Revelations of the reality of operations (see for instance Political Issues 22.1) showed a chaotic picture, often with no clear line of division between the political masters and the intelligence staff.

connected. The end of the Cold War in the 1980s, followed by the collapse of the Soviet Union in 1991, led to the development of a new security doctrine: that the threat from a single foreign superpower had been superseded by the more diffuse threat from networks of terrorism. In this new doctrine the distinction between foreign and domestic security intelligence became even narrower than was the case in the Cold War. The potential link between the two is now recognized in the existence within the Cabinet Office of the Joint Intelligence Organization. The head of the Organization chairs a Joint Intelligence Committee, and acts as a coordinator of all state intelligence, both national and foreign.

The two most important secret intelligence services – MI5 and MI6 – were created in response to threats to national security in the early years of the twentieth century. It is not surprising, therefore, that for much of their history their operations were conducted with a degree of secrecy and lack of open democratic accountability unmatched by any other public service. Whatever the historical justifications for this secrecy, it created serious long-term

problems in assessing, and defending, the impartiality and efficiency of the security services. It was commonly alleged, for instance, that MI5 persistently identified those on the left of politics as potential threats to public order, and subjected them to surveillance. It has also been suggested in some of the great industrial disputes of recent decades (notably the great miners' dispute of 1984–5), that MI5 spied on some of the strikers and officials of the union. In the absence of an open account and defence of the agency's operations, it was hard either to estimate the extent of this partiality, or to hear a reasoned defence of the operations.

Secrecy also inhibited any systematic estimation of the efficiency of intelligence-gathering operations. It is hard to apply the performance measurement techniques of the New Public Management to intelligence gathering, since so much is concerned with long-term collation of information, much is covert, and success often consists in averting threats which are never made public. Nevertheless, the secrecy with which the system operated meant that even the most rudimentary scrutiny (for instance, of

**POLITICAL ISSUES**

## 22.1   THE BUTLER REPORT AND THE POLITICAL USES OF SECRET INTELLIGENCE

In Political Issues 16.1, p. 359, in connection with the Hutton Report, some of the implications of the reporting of intelligence in the approach to the Iraq War of 2003 for relations between government and broadcasters were outlined. But the prime minister also commissioned an inquiry into the quality of intelligence briefings from a Committee chaired by Lord Butler, a retired Cabinet Secretary (the most senior of senior civil servants). The Butler Report appeared in July 2004. Unlike the Hutton Report, which had completely exonerated officials and ministers of any blame, it was heavily critical of both the quality of intelligence and the processes by which it was assessed and communicated to the public. Butler looked closely at intelligence gathering and revealed a world of 'sub-sources' of intelligence: in simple English, reliance on second- or even third-hand information. It also showed that the sceptical evaluation of these sources was often lost in official intelligence briefings, and still more in the communication of intelligence to the public, as ministers, notably the Prime Minister, sought to find intelligence to justify going to war against Iraq. The single most contentious and influential claim in the whole period leading to war – that Iraq could launch weapons of mass destruction within 45 minutes – was dismissed as based on discredited intelligence and faulty analysis. On process, the Report criticized the style of decision making within 10 Downing Street, notably the Prime Minister's preference for often informal meetings with small groups of individuals instead of doing business in officially minuted committees, such as Cabinet and sub-committees of Cabinet.

The Butler Report is an invaluable document for any student of decision making in the core executive. Of the many issues it raises, three are particularly important here:

- *The 'style' of Prime Ministerial decision making.* In fact the criticisms of informality and by-passing official machinery are the latest in a long tradition: Mr Wilson as prime minister in the 1960s was similarly criticized, as was Mrs Thatcher in the latter days of her prime ministership.
- *The accountability of the security services.* The very nature of secret intelligence means that politicians and the public must take on trust much of what they are told about confidential intelligence. But Butler's picture of poor quality evidence and reliance on 'sub-sources' will make that trust harder to create in the future, especially when secret intelligence is being used to support a policy to which government is already committed.
- *The function and utility of official inquiries* such as that conducted by Butler. The Report concluded that there had been collective failures, but that no individuals were blameworthy. This is a striking contrast to the 'name and shame' strategy now commonly used to try to raise standards across the public sector. Journalistic reporting of the history of the Butler Committee suggest that this outcome was the result of lobbying against 'naming and shaming' powerful people, especially by supporters of the Prime Minister.

Source: Information from Butler (2004).

the disposal of public funds) was impossible: the budget for the security services is bundled into a single request for total resources. A number of scandals suggested that the services were poor at recruiting competent and reliable people. For instance, during the Cold War there were a number of spectacular instances of the Secret Intelligence Service being penetrated by foreign agents, in some cases to a very high level. In part these difficulties lay in recruitment practices. In place of the conventional, meritocratic methods employed throughout the rest of the civil service, as described in Chapter 18, the security services preferred to recruit by personal recommendation, often from a small number of universities. The result was a service with a strikingly narrow social range. All the services now profess a desire to recruit more diversely, though MI6 still practises a modified version of the 'talent spotting' method.

These difficulties in assessing efficiency and impartiality are part of the reason for a series of institutional changes dating from the late 1980s and 1990s. The Security Services Acts of 1989 and 1996 gave an openly acknowledged statutory foundation to the Security Service, under the political supervision of the Home Secretary. The Intelligence Services Act of 1994 performed a similar function for the Secret Intelligence Service under the political supervision of the Foreign Secretary. Attempts were also made to subject the operations of the services to more formal scrutiny. In 1994 the Intelligence and Security Committee of the House of Commons was established. The Committee is a cross-party mixture of senior backbenchers appointed by the Prime Minister in consultation with the Leader of the Opposition. It scrutinizes the services, delivers private ad hoc reports to the Prime Minister, and lays suitably censored reports before the House of Commons. It is an advance on what existed previously by way of Parliamentary scrutiny, but plainly does not operate remotely like other Select Committees of Parliament. The Investigatory Powers Act 2000 created three new public officers. The Intelligence Services Commissioner reviews all warrants issued by the different Secretaries of State authorizing surveillance by the Services; the Interception

Commissioner does likewise in respect of warrants to intercept messages or mail; while the Investigatory Powers Tribunal hears complaints about the activities of the security services, notably in respect of warrants and intercepts.

Recent developments in the government of the security services show two features, and both reflect general themes of this chapter. The first is the increasing extent to which the maintenance of public order involves the attempt to coordinate the activities of a wide range of public agencies at multiple levels. The effect in the case of the security services has been to diminish the traditional, conventional distinction between conducting surveillance operations abroad and at home. The second development is the rise of more formal ways of subjecting the services to public accountability. This parallels the development of more formally organized systems of inspection and complaint in other domains, such as the Prison Service. In Chapter 23 we shall look more closely at the wider significance of this shift to formality.

## Public order, efficiency and accountability

The agencies and institutions described in this chapter lie at the heart of state power in Britain, because they are concerned with what might be called the core functions of the state: exercising its claimed monopoly of the legitimate means of coercion in order to maintain public order. But special as these institutions are, we can still ask of them questions that we now routinely raise about other providers of public services. In particular, we can ask how efficiently they do their allotted jobs. As we have seen, the pressures and demands of the New Public Management have begun to penetrate even the most secretive security agencies of the state. Some other institutions of public order, such as the Prison Service, have been at the forefront of the changes associated with the New Public Management (hiving off, privatization and the development of performance targets).

As we shall see in Chapter 23, many of the issues raised by the workings of the agencies examined in

## DEBATING POLITICS

### 22.1 SECRECY AND NATIONAL SECURITY: NECESSARY DEFENCE OR DANGER TO DEMOCRATIC POLITICS?

| Special levels of secrecy are needed in any matter of national security | Excessive secrecy surrounds security operations |
| --- | --- |
| ■ We live in a threatening world where foreign powers and terrorist networks operate secretly.<br>■ Confidential reporting to groups such as ministers and senior backbenchers can adequately ensure accountability.<br>■ Public reporting can endanger the operations, and even the lives, of members of the security services.<br>■ Effective recruitment and promotion policies in the security services can ensure that they are staffed by those who respect democratic and constitutional government. | ■ The secrecy culture is an outdated legacy of the cloak and dagger atmosphere of the early twentieth century.<br>■ Ministers, and even civil servants, are too much at the mercy of what the security services decide to divulge.<br>■ The security services of other states operate as effectively with much higher levels of accountability and publicity.<br>■ The recruitment and promotion policies of the security services have too often promoted incompetents, and even traitors in the service of foreign powers. |

this chapter are only particular examples of those created by the exercise of authority by all public bodies over citizens and clients. The police, judges, prisons, security services: all have power to shape our lives, and all have discretion in the way they exercise that power. But so do many other public bodies, notably institutions of the welfare state. In this chapter, therefore, we have been examining just one special set of cases concerning the relationship between the state and the citizen in Britain, which nevertheless *is* a special set. The institutions examined in this chapter are special because they are able to employ the coercive resources of the state, often to inflict physical sanctions on us, and to deprive us of our liberty. Some are also special because – like the security services – they have been able to make special claims to secrecy in their operations on grounds of national security in a threatening world. Attempting to ensure that the great power physically to coerce, and to operate secretively, is compatible with the impartial treatment of citizens, is a difficult business (see Debating Politics 22.1). There is a pattern to developments in the different

services described in this chapter: there has been a growth of formal mechanisms of inspection and rendering accounts. The same pattern, we shall see in Chapter 23, is observable in the wider relations between the state and the citizen. The adequacy of that response is also examined in Chapter 23.

### REVIEW

Four themes have marked this chapter:

1 Agencies (the police and security services) and institutions (the courts) are both central to the exercize of state power in Britain;
2 Issues of efficiency and impartiality are often enmeshed in examining the operations of these institutions;
3 The most recent threats to public order, notably from terrorism, are demanding a much more conscious organization of multi-level and multi-dimensional governance;
4 There has been a growth of more formal means of accountability and inspection.

## Further reading

Reiner (1992) is authoritative on the development of politics and policing. Griffith (1991) began a prolonged debate about the impartiality of the judi-ciary, one which has deeply affected many of the changes described in this chapter. Le Seuer (2004) examines the most recent changes. Hood *et al.* (1999), Chapter 6, is a rare 'political' analysis of the prison service.

**CHAPTER 23**

# The state and the citizen

## CONTENTS

## AIMS

This chapter has the following aims:

❖ To sketch the main issues arising in relations between state agencies and private citizens

❖ To examine some of the most important institutions concerned with control of state power over individuals

❖ To examine the wider social and cultural constraints on these powers, and to evaluate how effectively they operate.

## Citizens, the state and British democracy

In the last chapter we concentrated on the organization of a fundamental function of any state: maintaining internal public order and external security. We also concentrated chiefly on how the various arms of the state are organized, and on the operational issues – such as efficiency – that are raised by the way they work. This chapter looks more closely at issues touched on only briefly in Chapter 22: at issues of accountability and liberty. As we saw in Chapter 22, the special powers conferred on the arms of the state concerned with preserving order – especially powers to engage in surveillance, to exercise physical force in the last resort, and to imprison – all raise sensitive questions about public accountability and the rights of us all against the state. But these are only the most extreme instances. Making all the operations of the state accountable, and not just those parts that have coercive power, is at the heart of the theory of democracy in Britain.

All states have great power over the lives of those who live in their territory. But over the course of the twentieth century Britain, like many other states, added to these traditional powers of compulsion huge powers in other social domains. As we saw in Chapter 21, the state allocates enormous resources to different social groups. Through devices including taxation and the distribution of social welfare it takes money from some in the community and gives it to others. It compels us literally from the cradle to the grave: when we are born our parents are obliged to register us with a public official; and when we die there is a similar obligation for our death to be registered. Between the cradle and the grave the state constantly intervenes in our lives: it obliges us to spend our childhood being educated; and when we go to work it takes a large proportion of the income of most of us through compulsory taxation. Throughout our lives it constantly collects information about us, and uses it to make policies. It has a huge say over what can and cannot be done to our physical environment: planning law stretches from the most minor matters (for instance, whether we can build an extension to our house) to the most important (such as whether

a nuclear power station can be built on our doorstep). The state has also become increasingly important in deciding who can live in Britain, and on what terms: asylum and immigration law has become one of the most difficult and contentious areas of public policy in recent decades.

The state in Britain has to provide a moral justification for the exercise of these great powers. We saw in Chapter 1 that the heart of this moral justification can be summed up in the claim that Britain is a *liberal democracy*. If Britain is a properly functioning liberal democracy, then the exercise of state power over individual citizens should be guided by certain principles.

*Liberties* should be protected. The 'liberal' in liberal democracy means that citizens are entitled to a range of freedoms (for instance, freedom of expression, organization, conscience), and that the exercise of state power should be governed by openly understood rules. These rules should set out clearly the boundaries of state power over all of us as individuals, and they should be applied impartially to everyone. As we shall see later in the chapter, some of these expectations have now also been embodied in a key law, the Human Rights Act.

*Democratic control* should be practised. Democracy refers to many features, which we have examined in earlier chapters: for instance, how adequate is the electoral system in allowing the people at large a voice in deciding who shall govern? But in relation to the state and the citizen it means that the exercise of state power over the individual citizen should be open and accountable. This means that when the state exercises power over us (whether it be in the form of a police officer questioning us about an offence or in the form of a tax inspector assessing our income tax obligations) that power should be subject to democratic checks. Institutions like the police and the Inland Revenue should be effectively under the control of elected representatives.

However, being answerable to elected representatives is not sufficient. What guarantee could we have that the elected in turn will respect liberty and legal restraints? That is why the exercize of great public power over individual citizens has to be surrounded by a range of rights of individual appeal and redress. If we feel that individual decisions that affect us are improper, or are not sanctioned by the law, we should find it easy to appeal against them; the appeal system should work impartially between us and the state; and if the appeal is upheld there should be swift and effective redress.

One of the most important ways these notions have been expressed in practice in Britain lies in the provision of safeguards against *maladministration*. Maladministration may summarily be defined as the excessive or incompetent use of administrative powers, 'administrative' being used here in the widest possible sense to encompass the powers of all public agents, including such powers as those of the police. But when the notion is unpacked it turns out to be highly complex, and this complexity means that the processes by which safeguards operate are also necessarily complex. *Maladministration* combines a number of disparate notions encompassing moral expectations about the exercise of public power coupled with expectations about its technical quality. The following definition, the standard in the work of public law, shows this. Encompassed are:

> corruption, bias, unfair discrimination, harshness, misleading a member of the public as to his [sic] rights, failing to notify him properly of his rights or to explain the reasons for a decision, general high-handedness, using powers for a wrong purpose, failing to consider relevant materials, taking irrelevant material into account, losing or failing to reply to correspondence, delaying unreasonably before making a tax refund or presenting a tax demand or dealing with an application for a grant or a licence. (de Smith and Brazier 1998: 641).

The statements of the democratic and liberal safeguards against maladministration are ideals. It would be amazing – a counsel of perfection – if in every case they were observed to the full in Britain. But they provide the standard against which to judge the state, and against which the state should judge itself, in the way it deals with citizens. But there is another extension to these principles that

## Briefing                                    23.1

### THE ABUSE OF STATE POWER, SCANDAL I: THE CASE OF MUNCHAUSEN'S SYNDROME BY PROXY

In 2002 and 2003 the courts overturned a series of convictions against mothers who had been sentenced to long terms of imprisonment for murdering their babies. The cases involved a series of miscarriages of justice. The convictions were based on a scientific theory associated with one particularly prestigious medical expert, who claimed to be able to detect a syndrome labelled Munchausen's syndrome by proxy, which disposed a mother to infanticide. It became clear from the judgments overturning the convictions that this theory was seriously flawed science. But the scandal turned out to be much greater even than these headline cases suggested. It transpired that many thousands of babies had been removed from mothers, often just after birth, and put into care and permanent adoption, in the name of this theory. Moreover, these decisions had been taken after secret discussions and decisions by a mix of social workers, medical professionals and children's courts, from which the parents had been excluded, and the proceedings of which the press were forbidden to report on pain of incurring contempt of court proceedings. At the time of writing investigation is just beginning into how public agencies and medical professionals could have used their power to destroy the lives of thousands of innocent parents and children so arbitrarily.

➲ In the last three decades numerous institutions have been created to protect the rights of citizens against powerful institutions. The crucial question, however, is how far these formal protections work. Three scandalous cases are summarized in this chapter (see also Briefings 23.5 and 23.7 below.) They are chosen to illustrate very different domains of government. As the 'scandal' cases show, there exist numerous instances of arbitrary and cruel treatment of private individuals by powerful public bodies. At the heart of the scandal summarized here lies a key feature of the modern welfare state: its necessarily heavy reliance on the discretionary judgement of professionals.

## Images 23.1–2
## The law, majestic and mundane

Image 23.1
The High
Court

Image 23.2
Employment
Tribunals
Offices

Photos: Michael Moran

⊙ Image 23.1 shows one of the most familiar and imposing images of the majesty of the law in Britain: the
entrance to the High Court on The Strand in London.
Most readers will have seen this on the television news,
usually in the aftermath of a highly publicized case. Behind
these grandiose buildings lies a set of leafy squares, the
'Inns', where leading lawyers have their chambers. All this
is calculated to impress normal people, but it is just the
showy pinnacle of a huge structure. Far more representative is Image 23.2, which shows the offices of the
Employment Tribunals in Manchester. As we shall see later
in the chapter, the tribunal system runs a little examined,
but hugely important, system of law which is quantitatively
far more important than the 'majestic' face of the law.

we should also bear in mind. The use of 'citizen'
here is fairly novel in discussing these matters in
Britain. Traditionally we have been 'subjects' of the
Crown, and a subtle but important shift in understanding lies behind the change in vocabulary. The
language of the 'subject' dated from a pre-democratic era when such rights as we had were privileges
granted us by the monarch. The increasingly
common use of 'citizens' reflects the fact that in a
system of government that claims to be democratic,
where the monarch occupies mostly a symbolic role,
we are much more than subjects. However, the
language of the 'subject' has buried in it an assumption that the state, through the Crown, has special
entitlements in its dealing with us all, and these
assumptions often shape arguments about how far
the powers of the state should be restrained. The
assumptions are particularly important when the
boundaries of citizenship start to run out. Who
exactly is a 'citizen' is often unclear. The problem is
particularly acute in dealings between the British
state and those who are not legally British, or whose
British status is uncertain. The most troubling
problems concern the treatment of those who wish
to come to live and work in Britain, either as permanent immigrants or as more temporary refugees.
How the state treats these vulnerable groups who
have few of the formal rights of the settled population is one of the greatest tests of liberal democracy
in Britain. We will see later in the chapter how
these difficult issues work in practice.

This chapter focuses in the main on the important issue of the direct protection that exists for
individuals against the power of the state. I spend
some time on institutions and procedures that
attract relatively little 'headline' attention because
they nevertheless lie at the heart of attempts to safeguard the citizen against state power. Tribunals are
a striking instance of this (see Images 23.1 and 23.2).
They are easy to picture as inhabiting a backwater
of dry legal technicalities; certainly anyone who
spent a day observing tribunal proceedings would
not have an exciting experience, and yet the
adequacy of the tribunal system critically affects the
defence of citizen rights against the state. It is to
tribunals that citizens – and non-citizens who wish
to live in Britain – look for defence against excessive

use of the great administrative powers of the modern state, and it is in the tribunals that the state in turn tries to defend the extent of its powers.

Formal institutions and procedures are therefore important, but they are not the whole story. Many of the wider mechanisms and institutions of accountability which we discussed in earlier chapters also, if they operate effectively, work to create a climate where individual rights are respected. They thus provide protection of a more indirect kind. If Parliament, the media, and the wider institutions of society (say, pressure groups) scrutinize and control the state effectively, it is more likely that individual citizens will be respected when they encounter the power of the state. The discussion of the role of the House of Commons in Chapter 10 can be taken as a twin of this chapter, for much that goes on in the Chamber and in Committees is designed to make executive power in Britain more accountable. And later in the chapter we directly address the contribution of wider social institutions like the media and pressure groups to the defence of citizens against the abuse of public power. The detailed examination in the chapter begins, however, with two critical sets of institutions: Administrative Tribunals and the Ombudsman system.

## The tribunal system

To examine the tribunal system (for an overview, see Briefing 23.2) is to appreciate immediately the complexity of the exercize of state power in Britain. Tribunals are essentially adjudicatory bodies: that is, they resolve, or attempt to resolve, disputes concerning the application of the law. These disputes can involve two separate categories of parties: they can concern disputes between two private parties; or they can concern disputes between a private party and a public body, normally in the latter case involving an appeal by a private individual or group against an administrative decision by a public agency. Among the most important of the former is, for instance, the system of tribunals concerned with adjudication of employment law, covering issues as various as appointment, promotion and dismissal. As Briefing 23.3 (p. 501) shows,

some of the busiest tribunals are concerned with this latter form of adjudication, but for present purposes our interest lies in the part of the tribunal system concerned with adjudicating on decisions made by public agencies.

Tribunals of this latter kind developed in response to the growth of the interventionist state in the twentieth century, to regulate the great power which the decisions of the servants of that state could have over the lives of individuals. These shaping decisions, as Briefings 23.2 and 23.3 show, are potentially very great indeed: they range from decisions over entitlement to a wide range of monetary benefits, to entitlement to the very right to settle in the country. In his classic study of the administrative system in Britain, Robson (1928/1947) showed that the tribunal system developed as an alternative to challenges through the court system for a variety of reasons:

- Because the size of the interventionist state, and the volume of adjudications to which its decisions gave rise, would have overwhelmed the traditional courts had appeals against administrative decisions been channelled only through these courts
- Because the tribunals were supposed to be more approachable to private citizens than were the courts: they conducted their affairs in a language closer to the everyday than the specialized jargon of the law; they conducted their proceedings without the 'dignified' features of the courts, such as the special uniforms of barristers and judges; and they conducted their hearings not in court settings but in ordinary offices
- Because tribunals were supposed to offer a less expensive form of adjudication (for instance, by making it more realistic than in the courts for individuals to present their own cases, and by offering speedier forms of adjudication).

These are the aspirations that lay behind the creation of the tribunal system. Realizing them has, unsurprisingly, proved more difficult than expressing them. In their beginnings, tribunals displayed many of the traditional features of the wider administrative system, notably an inclination towards

# Briefing                                                                    23.2

## THE SYSTEM OF TRIBUNALS

*Council on Tribunals*
The Council on Tribunals supervises the constitution and working of Tribunals and Inquiries in England, Scotland and Wales as listed in the Tribunals and Inquiries Act 1992. Thus, it is the 'tribunal for tribunals'.

*The Appeals Service*
Established in 2000; hears appeals against decisions on: Social Security; Child Support; Housing Benefit; Council Tax Benefit; Vaccine Damage; Tax Credit; and Compensation Recovery.

*Copyright Tribunal*
Decides, where the parties cannot agree between themselves, the terms and conditions of licences offered by, or licensing schemes operated by, collective licensing bodies in the copyright and related rights area.

*Employment Tribunals*
Resolve disputes between employers and employees over employment rights.

*General Commissioners of Income Tax*
Hear appeals against decisions made by the Inland Revenue on a variety of different tax related matters.

*Immigration Services Tribunal*
The Immigration Services Tribunal was created in October 2000 to hear appeals against decisions made by the Office of the Immigration Services Commissioner and to consider disciplinary charges brought against immigration advisers by the Commissioner.

*Rent Assessment Panels*
Deal with disputes arising from legislation regulating the private rented sector.

*Valuation Tribunal Service*
There are 56 Valuation Tribunals (VTs) in England. Each one is an independent organization that deals with appeals about Non-Domestic Rates and Council Tax.

*Source*: Information compiled from Department for Constitutional Affairs website.

➲ The listing of tribunals provided by the Department for Constitutional Affairs, on which Briefing 23.2 draws, documents 24 different categories of tribunal, and each single category in turn often contains numerous tribunals. The tribunal system thus administers what is in effect an elaborate system of administrative law, governing the powers of administrative bodies. The selected listing above is intended only to give a sense of their range: from the most detailed and technical, such as the Copyright Tribunal, to the most explosive (for instance, those hearing appeals against decisions of the Immigration Service).

secrecy in dealing with clients. The report of the Committee on Administrative Tribunals (Franks 1957) made a series of what now seem very modest proposals: that tribunal hearings be in public; that the parties should know in advance the cases they had to meet; that hearings should no longer be held on government premises; that reasons should be given for tribunal decisions; and that there should be rights of appeal against those decisions. These features are now a commonplace of most of the tribunal system (though we shall see that in the highly contested area of appeals by refugees and asylum seekers the state is making efforts to limit the range of appeal). Tribunals are normally chaired by an expert in the policy area involved in the appeal, commonly an individual with legal training; but in a further attempt to distance their proceedings from the formalities of court procedure, two lay members normally sit alongside the Chair.

The effective working of the tribunal system is vital to the exercize of state authority in Britain, and Figure 23.1 illustrates why. It picks up a trail that was originally laid down in Chapter 1 (see Briefing 1.1, p. 9 and Image 1.2, p. 11). There we saw that the most important foundation of authority in Britain is what Max Weber called 'rational-legal authority': obedience resting on the claim that decisions have been made under the authority of laws legitimately passed and correctly observed. Image 1.2 showed an illustration of this in action: a tax demand. Figure 23.1 shows what a tax payer who wants to challenge the demand can do, illustrating the quite complex trail of the appeal process to a panel of Tax Commissioners. The diagram is only illustrative of the wider adjudicatory character of the tribunal system, but it shows why tribunals are so central to the effective exercize of rational-legal authority, for on their efficient and impartial workings rests any guarantee that state authority in Britain does indeed have credible rational legal legitimacy.

In accomplishing the hard task of helping create legitimate rational-legal authority, tribunals face three main issues: efficiency, impartiality and informality. Each is now dealt with in turn.

## Efficiency

Tribunals only work as institutions for safeguarding the rights of individuals if they operate both efficiently and speedily. This is because many of the decisions appealed involve substantial deprivation of claimed entitlements. These claimed entitlements could be financial, most obviously to the wide range of benefits allocated by the welfare state. They can be literally matters of life and death, such as the claimed entitlements by asylum seekers to refuge in Britain from what they argue are murderous home regimes, a staple of the immigration appeals system. Getting the decision right, and getting it right quickly, are essential. It was concerns about the effi-

ciency of the tribunal system that led to the Leggatt Review of the tribunal system, whose Report has in turn produced the greatest reforms of the system since the aftermath of the Franks Report of 1957 (Leggatt 2001). The reforms in effect try to bring the world of New Public Management to tribunals. They establish a unified Tribunals Service, responsible to the Department for Constitutional Affairs. The service covers the 'big ten' tribunals (see Briefing 23.3) and other lesser tribunals as appropriate. The strategic aims of the service are couched in the efficiency language of the New Public Management: for instance, raising customer service and standards.

## Impartiality

The detailed work of tribunals can be highly technical, but the issues that they deal with are often politically fraught. It is hard to disengage them from partisan political debate. This constantly creates problems in operating the tribunal system in an even-handed manner. There are particular problems in deciding whether all classes of complainants about administrative decisions should be treated equally. An especially problematic area is created by the distinction between those who are full subjects of the state, and those who are not. Embedded in our thinking about the way the state should behave is the assumption that it is relations between the state and British subjects that should be closely controlled, rather than relations between the British state and those who cannot presently claim British nationality. This is why the part of the tribunal system that deals with appeals against decisions in respect of immigration is particularly troublesome.

As we saw above, the issue of immigration – notably in recent years applications to enter by refugees – has become politically highly contentious, and the individuals concerned are usually neither British nationals nor British residents. Yet as Briefing 23.3 shows, this is one of the busiest areas of the tribunal system. A particularly controversial change was proposed in the Asylum and Immigration Bill of 2004 (at the time of writing this was close to enactment). The Bill proposed to abolish an existing two-tier system of appeals against

**Figure 23.1**   Calling rational-legal authority to account: appealing against the Income Tax Commissioners

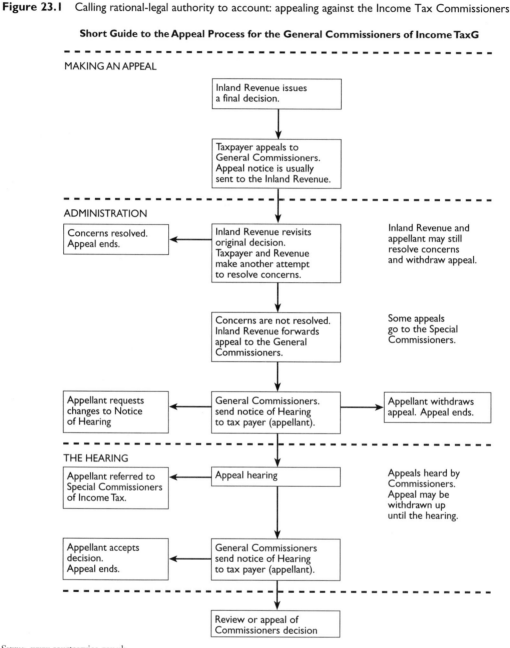

**Short Guide to the Appeal Process for the General Commissioners of Income TaxG**

- - - - - - - - - - - - - - - - - - - - - - - - - - - - - - - - - - - - - - - - - - - -

MAKING AN APPEAL

> Inland Revenue issues a final decision.

> Taxpayer appeals to General Commissioners. Appeal notice is usually sent to the Inland Revenue.

- - - - - - - - - - - - - - - - - - - - - - - - - - - - - - - - - - - - - - - - - - - -

ADMINISTRATION

> Concerns resolved. Appeal ends. ← Inland Revenue revisits original decision. Taxpayer and Revenue make another attempt to resolve concerns.   Inland Revenue and appellant may still resolve concerns and withdraw appeal.

> Concerns are not resolved. Inland Revenue forwards appeal to the General Commissioners.   Some appeals go to the Special Commissioners.

> Appellant requests changes to Notice of Hearing ← General Commissioners. send notice of Hearing to tax payer (appellant). → Appellant withdraws appeal. Appeal ends.

- - - - - - - - - - - - - - - - - - - - - - - - - - - - - - - - - - - - - - - - - - - -

THE HEARING

> Appellant referred to Special Commissioners of Income Tax. ← Appeal hearing   Appeals heard by Commissioners. Appeal may be withdrawn up until the hearing.

> Appellant accepts decision. Appeal ends. ← General Commissioners send notice of Hearing to tax payer (appellant).

- - - - - - - - - - - - - - - - - - - - - - - - - - - - - - - - - - - - - - - - - - - -

> Review or appeal of Commissioners decision

*Source*: www.courtservice.gov.uk

⮕ In Image 1.2 (p. 11) we used the demand to pay a tax bill from the Inland Revenue as an example of Weber's 'rational-legal authority', the commonest claimed foundation for the exercize of authority in Britain. Here we document the formal machinery which must be set in motion if the recipient of the demand wishes to challenge that attempted exercise of authority. It shows that initially an attempt is made to conciliate the differences between the Inland Revenue and the complainant; if that fails, a hearing is convened. If the Commissioners who hear the Appeal reject it, the complainant may carry the appeal forward, ultimately to the Courts. But this is a formidably expensive course of action, and success depends on the argument that the decision has not been based on rational-legal authority: in essence, that the Revenue exceeded its powers in law.

decisions of immigration officers in applications for asylum and, most controversially, to remove the safeguard of judicial review of the most important asylum decisions. In other words, it proposed to subject the tribunal system covering issues of immigration and asylum to a lower level of safeguards than applies to tribunals that deal with residents of the United Kingdom. From one point of view this is a serious departure from a key principle that should inform the operation of the tribunal system: impartiality and even-handedness in the treatment of all who resort to it. From another point of view, it not only recognizes the peculiar difficulties of making immigration policy work, but recognizes also that different standards of safeguards necessarily apply to British subjects and to foreigners.

## Informality

One of the important historical justifications for the tribunal system was that it created a more informally organized alternative to the procedures and styles of argument characteristic of the courts. This was supposed to make hearings more accessible to normal people, and therefore more open to effective participation by those without legal training. In some degree this aim has been achieved, in the sense that the style and setting of the typical tribunal is less surrounded by formality and a specialized legal language than we expect to find in a court. However, the very endurance and success of the tribunal system has made it difficult, whatever efforts are made to simplify language and relax the style of proceedings, to depart from the specialized world of the law. The tribunals are at the heart of a system of administrative law. Their style of reasoning is therefore inevitably coloured by the legal cast of mind, and success in hearings can depend on understanding a dauntingly complex body both of existing regulations and preceding adjudications. Although individuals can indeed present their own cases, the prudent citizen knows that effective presentation of a case is most likely if there is access to professional help (which more often than not means hiring a lawyer).

One special kind of tribunal has emphatically not conformed to a model of speed or informality. These

---

# Briefing                                23.3

●●●●●●●●●●●●●●●●●●●●●●●●●●●●●

## THE 'TOP TEN' TRIBUNALS

The Appeals Service
Immigration Appellate Authority
Employment Tribunals Service
Criminal Injuries Compensation Appeals Panel
Mental Health Review Tribunal
Office for Social Security and Child Support Commissioners
Tax tribunals
Special Education Needs and Disability Tribunal
Pensions Appeal Tribunal
Lands Tribunal

*Source*: Department for Constitutional Affairs.

●●●●●●●●●●●●●●●●●●●●●●●●●●●●●

➲  There are literally thousands of tribunals, but their workload is heavily concentrated on a 'top ten' now run by the unified Tribunals Service discussed in the text. The list shows how much the work of Tribunals is a reflection of twin forces: of the redistributive importance of the welfare state; and of immigration in a world of globalization.

---

are special Tribunals of Inquiry established under a variety of pieces of legislation stretching back to the Tribunals of Inquiry (Evidence) Act of 1921. These are 'one-off' tribunals established to examine particular issues. They have ranged diversely across cases of corruption, large disasters, and failures of regulation. Some have produced notoriously lengthy proceedings, with huge costs incurred in hiring lawyers. Among the most famous, or notorious, are the inquiry into the building of a nuclear reactor (Sizewell B) in 1985, which lasted 340 days; and the Bloody Sunday Inquiry (see Briefing 22.5, p. 487) which has been sitting since 1998 and has so far cost over £113 million, mostly in lawyers' fees.

## Ombudsmen: organized means of redress

We have already encountered the Ombudsman in Chapter 10 on the role of Parliament in the

Westminster system, when we described the Parliamentary Commissioner for Administration. It was appropriate that the Parliamentary Ombudsman was allotted an especially prominent role because there he is a pioneering figure. (Many Ombudsmen are women, but one of the quirks of the institution is that the original title has stuck.) The Parliamentary Commissioner for Administration has turned out to be an institutional innovation that has spread widely through British government and British society. As Briefing 23.4 shows, the very title itself is now used in many different settings, and the basic device is common even when some alternative title is used.

The world of British government now is very different from the world of 1967. It is therefore not surprising that as the original innovation has spread it has partly replicated, and partly altered, the terms of the original Ombudsman reform. Four important features of the original Ombudsman reform have been widely copied.

- *Reactive style.* All Ombudsmen are essentially reactive. They do not expect to intervene in the operation of institutions to improve their workings from the point of view of how citizens are treated, and neither do they expect actively to monitor the performance of institutions in the way they treat citizens. Of course, their decisions can and do have a wider impact than the substantive case in question, since decisions upholding complaints can both create precedents and highlight wider features of administrative systems that need to be reformed. Fundamentally, however, the Ombudsman system depends on waiting for a complaint, and then trying to put it right.
- *Conciliatory style.* All Ombudsmen practise a conciliatory adjudicatory style: that is, a critical judgement is a very last resort. In some cases the complaint only reaches the Ombudsman after earlier attempts to conciliate between the complainant and the offending public office have been exhausted. The Parliamentary Ombudsman described in Chapter 10 exemplifies this, for a complaint will only be referred after an MP has exhausted other means of seeking redress. But

even beyond this, when Ombudsmen are involved they will first attempt to agree a voluntary conciliation between complainant and the offending institution before moving to the point of issuing a critical judgement.
- *Recommendation over prescription.* One of the features of the original Parliamentary Ombudsman scheme was that the Ombudsman could only recommend, but not enforce, remedies to redress grievances if a complainant had been the victim of maladministration. The capacity to cause public embarrassment to ministers and civil servants; the sense of obligation among ministers and civil servants; these are the resources upon which the Parliamentary Ombudsman must in the end rely. This reliance on voluntary compliance has persisted in the numerous Ombudsmen schemes subsequently created. Curiously, private sector Ombudsmen sometimes have more teeth in this respect, if only because when a firm signs up to membership of an Ombudsman scheme it also often signs up to a willingness to abide by the decisions of the Ombudsman. In the public sector the only case of an Ombudsman with significant power to enforce decisions is the Police Ombudsman for Northern Ireland (a very special case given the turbulent policing history of the province, and frequent allegations that police forces have abused their power).
- *Informality over law.* Although the original Ombudsman has often been hard to reach, since access is via an MP, once access is gained the Ombudsman's services are available without the need for the formality or the expense of the law or lawyers. Successive Ombudsmen have followed this style. Indeed, in the private sector Ombudsman schemes have commonly been developed to support systems of self-regulation that are designed to avert regulation via the law, and access to the Ombudsman is available directly to any member of the public with a complaint.

There has therefore been continuity in the Ombudsman system in the nearly 40 years since the original innovation of 1967. But since the shape and

# Briefing

## THE ONWARD MARCH OF THE OMBUDSMEN

*Estate Agents Ombudsman* covers all the large chains of agents, and deals with complaints from private individuals as sellers or buyers. Disputes over surveys and lettings are excluded.

*Financial Services Ombudsman* covers most areas of personal finance, and also covers most financial firms.

*Financial Services Ombudsman for the Isle of Man* is a disputes resolution service for all customers of financial services firms operating in the island. (The Isle of Man operates preferential tax laws and is a major financial centre.)

*Gibraltar Ombudsman* is empowered by the government of Gibraltar to investigate all complaints by members of the public about alleged maladministration.

*Legal Services Ombudsman* investigates all complaints against legal professionals in England and Wales, providing the relevant professional body has first considered the complaint.

*Local Government Ombudsmen*: three cover England, Wales and Scotland, investigating complaints against most councils. Some key areas, such as internal running of schools, are excluded.

*Northern Ireland Ombudsman* has a very wide-ranging remit to investigate complaints in virtually any part of the public sector in the province.

*Health Services Ombudsman* considers complaints from members of the public from virtually any part of the Health Service in England and Wales – hospitals and all medical professionals.

*Independent Housing Ombudsman* considers complaints against a wide range of landlords in both the public and private sector in England.

*Independent Police Complaints Commission* investigates complaints about the conduct of police officers in England and Wales, and prescribes the disciplinary outcomes when complaints are upheld. Succeeded the Police Complaints Authority in April 2004, in part as a result of the reforms in the wake of the Stephen Lawrence scandal (see Briefing 23.5).

*Scottish Legal Services Ombudsman* covers for Scotland broadly the area covered for England and Wales by the Legal Services Ombudsman, see above.

*Scottish Public Services Ombudsman* considers complaints covering virtually the whole of the public sector in Scotland, analogous to the wide remit of the Northern Ireland Ombudsman, above.

*Prisons and Probations Ombudsman* investigates complaints about virtually any aspect of the Prison Service and the National Probation Service in England and Wales from all prisoners, sentenced and on remand.

*Northern Ireland Police Ombudsman* investigates complaints against police officers, a uniquely sensitive role given the policing history of the province.

*Parliamentary Ombudsman* investigates complaints passed on by Members of the Westminster Parliament. The Office was described in more detail in Chapter 10.

*Welsh Administration Ombudsman* investigates complaints of maladministration against the National Assembly and a wide range of Welsh public bodies.

*Pensions Ombudsman* considers complaints by individuals against most parts of the private and public pensions industry.

*Telecommunications Ombudsman* has been established by the private telecommunications industry to consider complaints against member companies.

*Source*: Information from www.bioa.org.uk

Until 1967 the 'Ombudsman' was a strange and little known Scandinavian institution. In that year the Parliamentary Ombudsman was established; now, Ombudsmen (many of whom are women) exist across both the public and private sector, for the purpose of investigating the complaints of individual citizens or consumers. There are so many that there exists a British and Irish Association of Ombudsmen, from whom the information in Briefing 23.4 is drawn. Not all industries have been welcoming: the Association's website notes that a Funeral Ombudsman scheme closed due to lack of support from the industry.

the social context of British government is very different from 1967, it is not surprising to see changes also in the way the Ombudsman system has evolved. Three developments are particularly noteworthy.

- *Devolution has reshaped institutions.* Devolution is one important reason for the proliferation of the Ombudsman as an institution. A glance back at Briefing 23.4 will show how many of the new Ombudsmen are the product of devolved government in Scotland, Wales and Northern Ireland. It is also striking that the 'devolved' Ombudsmen are often more formidable institutional creations than the original Parliamentary Commissioner for Administration, having a much wider jurisdiction across the public sector than had the original Parliamentary Commissioner.
- *Multi-level governance has reshaped Ombudsman institutions.* The public sector of the 1960s, when the original Commissioner appeared, was structurally a fairly simple affair, dominated by the Executive in Whitehall. The spread of Ombudsmen across public bodies – into local government, the health service, the agents of law enforcement – is in part a recognition of the importance of a wide network of agencies to the making and implementation of policy, and of the need to create some means to redress grievances when things go wrong with policy delivery in these networks (see Briefing 23.5).
- *The shifting public/private divide has reshaped Ombudsman institutions.* A glance at Briefing 23.4 shows a remarkable feature of the development of the Ombudsman system in recent years. Ombudsmen are no longer specialized figures designed to deal with redress of grievances against public sector bodies; they exist right across British society. Indeed, the list in Briefing 23.4 is selective, since it largely concerns those figures that have 'badged' themselves with the Ombudsman label; as we saw in the last chapter, there are many 'redress of grievance' institutions that are not formally labelled 'Ombudsman'. One reason for the rise of the Ombudsman institution is a change in the notion of what can be considered 'private' as distinct from 'public'. In Briefing

## Briefing                                    23.5

### THE ABUSE OF STATE POWER, SCANDAL II: THE STEPHEN LAWRENCE CASE

In July 1997 the then Home Secretary appointed an inquiry into the conduct of the investigation by the Metropolitan Police of the murder of a black teenager, Stephen Lawrence, following extensive public disquiet about the case. The inquiry, chaired by Sir William MacPherson, reported in February 1999. The report found that there had been numerous errors by the police in the conduct of the investigation. But its most important finding was that many of these errors were not the result of simple human error or administrative incompetence, but because of an institutional culture in the Metropolitan Police that systematically discriminated against members of the public on grounds of race. It made 70 recommendations, covering both the organization of the Metropolitan Police and policing in general. The aim was to combat *institutional racism* which, the Report argued, was embedded in the force. It defined institutional racism thus: 'The collective failure of an organization to provide an appropriate and professional service to people because of their colour, culture, or ethnic origin. It can be seen or detected in processes, attitudes and behaviour which amount to discrimination through unwitting prejudice, ignorance, and racist stereotyping which disadvantage minority ethnic people' MacPherson (1999: para. 6.34).

➲ The importance of the scandal of the conduct of the investigation into Stephen Lawrence's murder was twofold: it was part of a long history of difficulties in relations between the police and ethnic minorities; and the MacPherson Report argued that the problems were engrained in the police as an institution: hence the scandal of institutional racism. (See also Briefing 15.2.)

23.4, the final entry, for example, summarizes the Telecommunications Ombudsman, established by the privately owned telecommunications industries. But these industries are themselves the product of privatization measures dating from the 1980s when industries that had long been publicly owned were transferred to private ownership. As we saw in Chapter 8, these privatized industries are typically subjected to public regulation; in other words, they are presumed to have various kinds of public obligations because they exercise great potential power over consumers.

The example of the Telecommunications Ombudsman highlights a more general feature of the development of the Ombudsman as an institution designed to secure redress of grievances. The state in Britain has in recent years retreated on many fronts, notably in the range of direct public ownership of enterprizes. But, as we saw in Chapter 8, the range of regulatory duties undertaken by the state has actually widened greatly. That expansion of regulation partly reflects the blurring of the divide between the public and private, and in particular the growing concern with regulating private, as much as public, institutions. (Look back at Briefing 8.3, p. 150 for illustrations of this.) Many private sector Ombudsmen schemes are designed to protect private institutions against the threat of direct public regulation. Ombudsmen are created either to meet criticism in the wake of scandals that reveal the abuse of private power over consumers, or more generally are intended to strengthen the institutions of self-regulation: a good example of the former is the creation of the Pensions Ombudsman for an industry with a long history of marketing scandals; good examples of the latter are the Legal Services Ombudsman and the Estate Agents Ombudsman.

Arguments about the worth and effectiveness of 'private' Ombudsman schemes are very similar to those invoked about the effectiveness or otherwise of public sector Ombudsmen ever since the first appearance of the original Parliamentary Commissioner for Administration in 1967. The symbolism of the Ombudsman is very powerful. It borrows an institution from the Swedish system of government, a system with an open administrative culture and an egalitarian culture in the wider society, where public servants expect to have to give a very full account of their actions. In some cases, as we can see from the first entry in Briefing 23.4, the very title Ombudsman is borrowed to give added symbolic weight to quite limited schemes for

handling complaints. Debates about the effectiveness of this symbolically significant figure turn on how far the characteristic styles of British Ombudsmen are up to the job of redressing grievances: styles that are reactive, conciliatory, permissive and informal (see Documenting Politics 23.1 for an account of a day in the life of the Parliamentary Ombudsman in her own words). However, the Ombudsman institution is now embedded across British society, in private and public institutions. In multi-level governance it is taking increasingly diverse forms, departing in many ways from the single, simple template of the original Parliamentary Commissioner for Administration.

## Creating rights

In the tribunal system and in the spreading institutions of the Ombudsmen we see attempts to create organized means of regulating relations between the state and the citizen, and to provide organized means of defending the citizen against the abuse of public power. In recent years a new and, for the United Kingdom, constitutionally novel solution has been attempted to the problem of safeguarding citizens' rights: the creation of rights embodied in law.

As we have noted on several occasions in these pages, the dominant constitutional tradition pictured a monarchy with 'subjects', where claims against public power were privileges granted by monarchical government. These claims were not trivial. Historically they included, for example, such longstanding legal claims as those contained in the Habeas Corpus Act of 1679. The title literally translates from the Latin for 'you have the body'. In substance, it meant that in England (though not elsewhere in the Kingdom) those detained by Crown Servants – such as police officers – could apply to the courts to test the right of the Crown to detain them. In practice, the law limited the time span when institutions (say, the police) could detain individuals without bringing a charge to be tested in court.

Though often providing substantial protection

**DOCUMENTING POLITICS 23.1**

## SO WHAT DO YOU DO ALL DAY? THE WORKING LIFE OF THE PARLIAMENTARY OMBUDSMAN – IN HER OWN WORDS

**Example 1**
*Case study*
The Ombudsman found that the Benefits Agency and the Independent Tribunal Service had made serious mistakes which caused a long delay to a woman's appeal against a refusal of attendance allowance. An ex-gratia payment was made by the Independent Tribunal Service and the Benefits Agency agreed to consider further compensatory payments if it were shown that the woman's health had been affected.

**Example 2**
*Case study*
The Ombudsman found that Customs and Excise had made mistakes when measuring and recording the length of a fishing boat, with the result that the boat needed more safety equipment than the owner had been led to suppose. Customs paid £12,000 to the owner of the boat in recompense.

**Example 3**
*Case study*
Delay by the Ministry of Agriculture, Fisheries and Food in informing a farmer of the result of his application for sheep annual premium quota, led the farmer to incur additional costs due to his leasing, rather than purchasing, quota. After the Ombudsman's investigation the Ministry agreed to pay 191 farmers compensation totalling nearly £70,000.

**Example 4**
*Case study*
A man complained that the Inland Revenue had mishandled the tax affairs of a business in which he had been a partner. Following the Ombudsman's intervention, the Revenue took action to offset nearly £19,000 against the PAYE debt of the former partnership.

➲ The most recent annual report for the Parliamentary Ombudsman – formerly the Parliamentary Commissioner for Administration – shows a caseload for the year 2002–3 of 2,567. These examples, provided by the Ombudsman, show a slice of the working year, in the Ombudsman's own words. The present Parliamentary Ombudsman is a woman, and combines her post with the job of Health Service Ombudsman.

*Source*: www.ombudsman.org.uk

against the abuse of power by public institutions, the protections traditionally afforded had a number of important limitations:

- Their jurisdiction was often limited: habeas corpus, for example, was a protection extended only by the English courts.

- They were an incomplete net of protections, built up piecemeal historically, from a mix of individual statutes and the judgments and conventions of the common law. (See Chapter 22 for the significance of the common law.)
- The doctrine of the supremacy of the Westminster Parliament meant that any particu-

# Briefing

## THE HUMAN RIGHTS ACT

The Human Rights Act 1998 did the following:

- It made enforceable in domestic law the rights contained in the European Convention on Human Rights, an international agreement to which the British government was a signatory, but whose provisions could hitherto only be enforced by the expensive and time-consuming procedure of taking a case to the European Court of Human Rights.
- The Act (fully effective from 2000) makes it unlawful for a public body to violate Convention rights; if possible all UK law should be consistent with Convention rights; and it provides for the enforcement of those rights through a domestic court or a tribunal.
- The Convention guarantees 16 basic human rights. Some of these are uncontentious in a British setting, such as the prohibition of slavery. Some are uncontentious in general terms, but their application is highly contested: some anti-abortion groups contend that abortion violates the right to life. Some are uncontentious, but British governments have engaged in the prohibited practices in the recent past: for instance, torture was practised on some detainees in Northern Ireland.
- Documenting Politics 23.2 (below) shows that the Act is not simply a symbolic exercise: serious efforts are being made to shape British administrative culture around it.

➲ The Human Rights Act is a great innovation in a system of government where historically we were 'subjects' of the Crown rather than citizens with rights. It has not overturned the old practices totally, however. The Scottish Parliament and the Welsh Assembly must both be bound in all their decisions by the Act, but the Westminster Parliament still retains the sovereign power to claim exemptions from the Act and to pass laws in violation of its provisions. Following the terrorist attacks in New York in September 2001 the government passed anti-terrorist laws which involved an explicit departure from some of the Act's safeguards, such as right to liberty and fair trial.

lar protection could be suspended by a counter-manding item of legislation – as happened, for example, to habeas corpus in time of war, and as happened to a wide range of protections during nearly 30 years of the struggles with paramilitary forces in Northern Ireland from the early 1970s.

Two broad areas of change illustrate the developments that have been taking place. The first concerns the collection, holding and transmission of information, especially electronically collected and stored information; and the second concerns the broader regime of human rights.

Two pieces of legislation, and one important institutional innovation, mark the attempt to subject the use of information to closer legal control: the Data Protection Act, passed 1998 and in force from 2000, and the Freedom of Information Act 2000. The Data Protection Act principally gives rights to access data held both by private and public institutions about individuals, and to have mistakes in that data corrected. The information can range from the data about individuals' financial affairs, commonly held by private institutions such as credit rating agencies, to information such as character references, held by institutions as varied as universities about students, and both private and public employers. But the Act also for the first time subjects the rapidly spreading technology of surveillance by closed circuit television (CCTV) to legal control. In enforcing both the sections of the Act concerning the holding of data about individuals, and in respect of the regulation of CCTV, the Information Commissioner, an official established under the Act, is a key figure. For instance, the Commissioner is responsible for the creation and maintenance of a code of conduct governing the use of CCTV by those who establish

## DOCUMENTING POLITICS 23.2

### ATTEMPTING TO CREATE A HUMAN RIGHTS CULTURE WITHIN GOVERNMENT

Extract from a letter from the acting Permanent Secretary John Warne (Lord Chancellor's Department) to Sir Richard Wilson, and all permanent Secretaries, dated 9 April 2001

'Sir Richard Wilson KCB
Secretary of the Cabinet and Head of the Home Civil Service
Cabinet Office
70 Whitehall
LONDON
SW1A 2AS

HUMAN RIGHTS ACT:
BUILDING THE CULTURE OF RIGHTS AND RESPONSIBILITIES

1.  The Task Force set up by the Government to help implement the Human Rights Act has held its last meeting. I am writing to pass on some final recommendations which are relevant to mainstreaming the Act and to building the culture of rights and responsibilities. We shall be pursuing all these at Board level in the Home Office and I hope that colleagues will consider a similar approach.

2.  There are five main areas:

    • general aims and commitment
    • awareness raising in front-line services, subsidiary public authorities *etc*
    • formal training
    • monitoring
    • role of Inspectorates.

and operate these surveillance systems in public places. The Commissioner is also responsible for the implementation of some important EU regulations governing access to telecommunications traffic. For instance, the Telecommunications Regulation of the European Commission of 1999 gives effect to a Directive dating from 1997 guaranteeing a 'right to privacy' in respect of the telecommunications traffic of individuals.

The Data Protection Act is in essence intended to provide entitlements to individuals in respect of personal data held about them by institutions. The Freedom of Information Act 2000 is best conceived of as providing access not to data about individuals, but to a wide range of documentation held by public authorities (for instance, about the processes by which policy has been made). Thus it is not directly addressed to the question of redress of instances of grievances created by maladministration, but can be conceived of as one more attempt to create a more open and accountable culture of policy making, thus reducing the likelihood of the abuse of official

**DOCUMENTING POLITICS 23.2**    (continued)

*General aims and commitment*

3.    Task Force members have commented that, inevitably, initial thinking about the Human Rights Act
has tended to concentrate on legal questions about compliance. From that narrow perspective,
implementing the Act may be seen as complete once the relevant legislation and guidance have been
audited centrally, or not impugned by a court. Though it is clearly right that all public authorities
should not act incompatibly with the Convention rights, the Act was intended to do more than
merely avoid direct violations of human rights. As the senior judiciary have commented in their
early judgments on the Act, this is a constitutional measure, legislating for basic values which can be
shared by all people throughout the United Kingdom. It offers a framework for policy-making, for
the resolution of problems across all branches of government and for improving the quality of
public services. From this point of view it is not right to present the Human Rights Act as a matter
for legal specialists. The culture of rights and responsibilities needs to be mainstreamed. This
requires at least:

- developed awareness at all levels of the Convention rights *and the associated balances and
limitations*, as an integral part of public administration and policy-making
- frequent practical expression of the positive difference the Convention can and does make, by
voluntary good practice as well as by court decision
- clear and public demonstration of commitment to the Convention values and principles at the
highest levels of government and public authorities
- public recognition of the Convention values and principles in delivering quality public services.

4.    The Task Force recognizes that a good start has been made on this agenda, but that there is a lot to
be done. A sustained and focused effort over a long time scale is required.'

➲ The value of this edited document is that it shows how administrators attempt to convert the public rhetoric about
human rights into administrative reality, and it shows also how far the effective implementation of human rights law
depends on detailed changes in culture and working practices within departments. The original is about three times as
long as the extract and includes detailed prescriptions both about formal training of staff and the creation of a culture of
sensitivity towards the Human Rights Act.

*Source*: *Source*: www.dca.gov.uk

power. The rights under the Act in principle,
entitle anyone to request access to documents and
records held by public authorities. Requests must be
clear and specific enough to make it clear what is
being sought. In other words, it is not possible to
simply to carry out 'fishing expeditions' for information. Refusal to supply information can in the
last resort be appealed to the Information
Commissioner who has power to investigate and
adjudicate.

We shall see that there are different views of the
significance of these measures, but at the very least
they amount to important symbolic statements
about the rights of citizens to have access to information. The significance of the Human Rights Act
1998 is greater still (see Briefing 23.6). Formally the
Act might be thought to advance little in the way of
creating rights, for it only made enforceable in
domestic law the rights contained in the European
Convention on Human Rights. The United
Kingdom had been a signatory since the original
Convention of 1950 and thus bound itself to

observe the judgments of the European Court of Human Rights, sitting in Strasbourg. (The Court should not be confused with the European Court of Justice, the judicial body concerned with the interpretation of the law of the European Union, an institution described in Chapters 5 and 6.) Indeed, in the near half-century between the signing of the Convention and the passage of the Human Rights Act, the Court made a number of judgments that compelled important changes in law and policy. These included changing the law on contempt of court in 1979, when *The Sunday Times* successfully challenged its use to try to prevent the paper publishing details of a scandal concerning birth defects caused by a drug prescribed to expectant mothers; the abolition of corporal punishment in British state schools following a successful challenge that the practice infringed parents' rights concerning their children's education; and a judgement in 1995 which ruled that British soldiers used unreasonable force in shooting to death three suspected IRA terrorists in Gibraltar. (See Pyper 1998 and Pyper 2002 from where these examples are drawn.)

Before the passage of the Human Rights Act, however, the enforcement of rights under the Convention was both a protracted and expensive process. The Court of Human Rights could only be invoked at the end of domestic judicial process, and domestic law was not made by reference to the provisions of the Convention. As Briefing 23.6 summarizes, the Act attempts precisely to remedy this. Courts can make a declaration of incompatibility between a law and the Convention. The Act makes it unlawful for a public body to violate Convention rights; makes the Convention in effect enforceable in any domestic judicial arena, meaning that enforcement need not depend on the time consuming and expensive route of appeal to Strasbourg; and is designed to ensure that both legislative proposals and administrative practice are shaped around the provisions of the Act. This last is illustrated by the document reproduced in Documenting Politics 23.2.

The Data Protection Act, the Freedom of Information Act and the Human Rights Act are all comparatively recent creations. Since their avowed purpose is to alter the culture of the state, we should not expect their impact to be immediate. It is therefore difficult to arrive at any firm view of their wider importance in regulating the relations between the state and the citizen in Britain. Two contrasting interpretations might be considered. An optimistic interpretation – optimistic from the point of view of those who wish to entrench constitutional safeguards against state power – would note the timing of this legislation. It was passed as part of a wider raft of constitutional change, examined earlier in this book: the most notable examples are the devolution reforms, and the reform of the Second Chamber. In other words, whatever particular limitations exist on the range of rights practically enforceable under these laws, they can be viewed as part of a systematic modernization of the constitution in the United Kingdom. The package of modernization has both reduced the powers of the traditionally dominant Whitehall executive and opened the operations of public bodies to greater scrutiny and explicit control. Devolution has also widened the range and variety of controls: the devolved Scottish system, for example, has its own freedom of information regime.

A pessimistic interpretation of what rights reform amounts to stresses two points. First, these rights are anything but entrenched constitutional safeguards. They are surrounded by numerous exemptions. More important, the Whitehall Executive still has the power to suspend them on the basis of wider considerations, such as public security: measures passed to counter terrorism in the wake of the terrorist attack on the World Trade Center in September 2001 do precisely this in respect of some of the safeguards in the Human Rights Act. But a second ground for pessimism is even more fundamental, because it concerns the wider setting in which these formal rights have been enacted. Pessimism here begins with the incontrovertible observation that formal rights enshrined in statute mean very little without the existence of wider social and cultural safeguards for the citizen in dealing with public power. From this point of view, all measures such as the Data Protection Act can do is marginally rein in new forms of surveillance created by new technologies, including technologies of visual surveillance and technologies that allow centralized storage and onward passage of personal information. The Human Rights Act also, on this pessimistic view, is marginal in a world where the threats of terrorism and the desire to control the movement of immigrants across borders are pressing the state in the direction of increasing controls over personal freedoms and personal privacy.

Thus, whether we take a pessimistic or an optimistic view of the recent spate of rights creation depends on much more than an inspection of the content of those rights. It depends also on how we view the wider social and cultural context regulating the relations between the state and the citizen. It is exactly this setting that we next examine.

## Social and cultural institutions of control

We have seen that an important trend in the regulation of the relations between the state and the citizen is the growing shift to formality in the creation of safeguards. This formality encompasses the institutions of the tribunal system, the growth in the number of Ombudsmen, and the creation of a legally enforceable human rights regime. The effectiveness of these formal safeguards, however, depends on the existence of wider social and cultural forces that constrain government (see Briefing 23.7). Three are particularly important: self-regulation; media scrutiny; and pressure groups in the wider civil society.

# Briefing                                                                 23.7

## THE ABUSE OF STATE POWER, SCANDAL III: THE CASE OF MATRIX CHURCHILL AND ARMS TO IRAQ

In 2003 the British government went to war against Iraq on the grounds that its weapons capacity was a threat to both regional and world security. But in 1989 a different government had decided secretly to relax restrictions on arms exports to Iraq. The decision was taken by three junior ministers from the Foreign Office, the Ministry of Defence and the Department for Trade and Industry. Sir Richard Scott's subsequent investigation concluded that deliberately uninformative answers were given in Parliament to conceal the change of policy. So secret was the decision that the investigation branch of Customs and Excise did not learn of the change, and prosecuted the directors of a defence equipment firm, Matrix Churchill, for breaching export rules. In order to conceal the secret policy change, some senior Cabinet ministers were persuaded to sign 'public interest immunity certificates' on grounds of national security, allowing the prosecution to withhold documents from the court that would have cleared the Matrix Churchill defendants. The Deputy Prime Minister, Mr Heseltine, only signed a certificate on condition that his worries that innocent men were being prosecuted were conveyed to the judge; they were not. The case collapsed when one of the original junior ministers concerned (Alan Clark) admitted under oath, in a famously flippant phrase, that government had been 'economical with the *actualité*'. Sir Richard Scott's subsequent official report (1996) into the affair severely criticized ministers for persistently misleading Parliament, and for speciously claiming that public interest immunity certificates were needed in the public interest. But there were no resignations in the wake of these criticisms, and it was only in November 2001 that the directors of Matrix Churchill received financial compensation for a prosecution which had both damaged them personally and damaged their firm. In keeping with the culture of secrecy revealed throughout the whole affair, the details of the compensation remain confidential.

*Source*: Information from Scott (1996).

➲ Our first two scandals regarding the abuse of public power concerned relations between welfare state professionals, courts and families, and between the police and ethnic minorities. The Matrix Churchill affair concerned the abuse of power by institutions right at the heart of the core executive in Britain.

## Self-regulation

Relying on public servants and public institutions to observe self-imposed restraints on the exercize of their powers was traditionally the most important means of regulating relations between the state and the citizen. In their landmark study of systems of internal control in the public sector, Hood and his colleagues identified this method as 'collegial': it depended on the capacity of equals within the administrative system both to check themselves, and to check each other (Hood *et al.* 1999). In an important sense, self-regulation has to remain a key mechanism of control because discretion is inevitable in the administrative process. That discretion applies whether it is exercized by the police officer reacting to a problem on the beat, or by the official in the benefit agency deciding whether a client's circumstances amount to grounds for entitlement. A large amount of the training of public servants consists not just of acquiring techniques or formal knowledge of rules, but in absorbing the more informal codes of the organization – whether the organization be a police force or an executive agency (see Documenting Politics 23.3). Documenting Politics 23.2 shows that in the wake of the Human Rights Act attempts are being made to shape codes around the presumptions of the Act, so that self-regulation works to support the formal prescriptions of the law. Yet numerous developments summarized in this and the preceding chapter show decreasing confidence in the effectiveness of self-regulation. The spread of inspectorates, varieties of Ombudsmen, and the creation of formal entitlements in law all show that, however important self-regulation is, it is decreasingly relied on to provide safeguards.

## Media scrutiny

The mass media are important in regulating the relations between the state and the citizen for both particular and general reasons. Some of the most important individual scandals of abuse of public power have either been revealed, or pursued in detail, by the media. We saw in the last section, for instance, that the campaign to uncover the failings in drug safety revealed by the Thalidomide scandal by *The Sunday Times* led to the important judgments by the European Court of Human Rights in 1979, but this was only one episode in a long campaign by the paper to reveal the chain of incompetence and failures in safety regulation which inflicted birth defects on new born children. Another important European Court of Human Rights judgment referred to above – the judgment that unreasonable force had been used to kill suspected IRA terrorists in Gibraltar – was also greatly assisted by investigative journalism, notably by television journalists. These particular instances are important in their own right, since they concern scandals where public power inflicted suffering on individuals; but they also connect to the second, general, reason why media scrutiny is important. The presence of a scrutinizing mass media creates a wider climate where public institutions know that their actions may well be the subject of investigative reporting. The demonstration effect of particular investigations – the way they show to public servants the possibilities of media scrutiny and exposure – can plainly be important in fostering a culture of restraint in the exercize of power.

Just as we can be pessimistic or optimistic about the worth of creating a formal regime of human rights, so we can be pessimistic or optimistic about the effectiveness of media scrutiny in supporting that regime. Whether we are optimistic or pessimistic depends quite heavily on the time frame we use to examine the media. If we looked back to the mid-1950s it would be hard to argue against the view that media scrutiny has grown in volume and effectiveness since that time. Then, for example, there was only one licensed broadcaster – the BBC – and its coverage of politics was highly deferential to those in power. Investigative journalism in both the print and electronic media is now much more widespread than in the 1950s. On the other hand, much of this investigative culture was created in the 1960s, when small magazines (including *Private Eye*) pioneered investigative practices. Since then both the economics and institutions of journalism have become weighted against scrutiny. Investigation is both expensive and often demands willingness to pursue a story for a long period of time. Increasing competition for an audience – in the case of newspapers, for an audience in long-term decline – has

**DOCUMENTING POLITICS 23.3**

## THE SEVEN PRINCIPLES OF PUBLIC LIFE, ACCORDING TO THE COMMITTEE ON STANDARDS IN PUBLIC LIFE

'The Seven Principles of Public Life

*Selflessness*
Holders of public office should act solely in terms of the public interest. They should not do so in order to gain financial or other material benefits for themselves, their family or their friends.

*Integrity*
Holders of public office should not place themselves under any financial or other obligation to outside individuals or organisations that might seek to influence them in the performance of their official duties.

*Objectivity*
In carrying out public business, including making public appointments, awarding contracts, or recommending individuals for rewards and benefits, holders of public office should make choices on merit.

*Accountability*
Holders of public office are accountable for their decisions and actions to the public and must submit themselves to whatever scrutiny is appropriate to their office.

*Openness*
Holders of public office should be as open as possible about all the decisions and actions that they take. They should give reasons for their decisions and restrict information only when the wider public interest clearly demands.

*Honesty*
Holders of public office have a duty to declare any private interests relating to their public duties and to take steps to resolve any conflicts arising in a way that protects the public interest.

*Leadership*
Holders of public office should promote and support these principles by leadership and example.'

➲ We encountered the Committee on Standards in Public Life in Chapter 5, noting the way it was shifting constitutional understandings from informal understandings to explicit codes. One of the Committee's first actions, however, was to try to strengthen self-regulation as a mechanism of restraint, by enunciating these Seven Principles of Public Life. The seven principles are on its website and are always reprinted on the inside cover of the Committee's separate reports. Optimists will see the spelling out of the principles as an advance in the self-restraint with which all those in public life exercise authority and influence; pessimists might wonder why such self-evident principles of good conduct ever needed spelling out in the first place.

*Source*: www.public-standards.gov.uk

# Briefing

## THE REFUGEE COUNCIL AND THE DEFENCE OF THE RIGHTS OF REFUGEES

The treatment of refugees and asylum seekers is a particularly sensitive indicator of how public power is exercized over individuals. Many protections against public power in Britain are tied to nationality; thus refugees and asylum seekers occupy a particularly vulnerable status. The status of asylum seekers and refugees became a key issue in British politics from the end of the 1990s, but refugees have come to Britain for centuries. At the end of the seventeenth century Huguenots, a French Protestant sect, settled in London following Catholic persecution. At the end of the nineteenth century, East European Jewish refugees fled persecution, many settling in Britain. Between 1935 and 1950, over 250,000 East European refugees settled in Britain. In 1956, some 15,000 Hungarian refugees came here after the failed uprising against Communism. Since the 1990s, wars in the Balkans, in the Middle East and in central Asia have created millions of new refugees.

The Refugee Council thus deals with issues of long standing. It is an independent charity created in 1981 by the amalgamation of two organizations that had themselves originated out of the great refugee wave of 1935–50. It is a member organization: that is, composed not of individuals but of over 180 separate organizations, many of which are community-based refugee support groups. It provides both practical support services for individuals, and is also an advocacy organization for the voice of refugees in policy debates. It has a complex relationship with government. As one of the largest refugee support groups (alongside the British Red Cross) it is often used by government to establish support schemes for refugee groups; for instance, for the Kosovan refugees who fled war and terror in the 1990s. But as government policy increasingly turned to restrictions over the entitlements of refugees (for example, by trying to eliminate any entitlement to welfare benefits) the Council increasingly turned to criticism of policy and defence of refugee claims against public agencies.

*Source*: Compiled from information on www.refugeecouncil.org

➡ There are now numerous organizations concerned with the liberties of citizens in the face of public power. The Refugee Council occupies a particularly sensitive area because of the vulnerable status of refugees and asylum seekers.

produced pressure to cut expensive activities, and to produce 'news' (literally, a constant stream of fresh stories). At the popular end of the market, in both print and broadcast journalism, reporting is increasingly dominated by non-political material: sport, celebrity gossip, horoscopes, sexual peccadilloes.

## Pressure groups in civil society

Chapter 9 showed that pressure group formation has been particularly rapid in recent years, and Briefing 5.1, p. 75 provided examples of groups – Charter 88 and Liberty – that are concerned with issues central to this chapter. Briefing 23.8, a case study of the Refugee Council, shows the importance of organization in defending weak groups. Indeed, the organized defence of the interests of the citizen

against state power is, when considered in the light of group organization, not at all confined to what might conventionally be called 'civil liberties' groups. The examination of the tribunal system, for example, showed that one of the most vexatious areas of state–citizen relations is created by decisions about entitlements to the money and services allocated by the welfare state. Thus the wide range of advocacy groups that seek to represent potential benefit claimants – encompassing, for instance, the low paid, the disabled, the unemployed – are inevitably drawn into the domain of the regulation of state–citizen relations. Nevertheless, the example of the Refugee Council is particularly instructive because it is a sign of the increasing tendency to try to defend the rights of individuals by organized advocacy, standing alongside the groups already profiled in Chapter 5, such as Liberty. The Refugee Council, as a member organization, is the tip of the organizational iceberg, consisting as it does of over 180 constituent bodies. We can also see organizations at work that exemplify the workings of multi-level governance in this area: Amnesty, the organization founded in 1961 to campaign for prisoners of conscience across the globe, periodically issues critical reports on British domestic policy.

An equally striking area of institutional growth involves organizations that campaign to protect another marginalized and stigmatized group, prisoners. While prison reform movements are among the longest established groups in the British pressure group universe, with a continuous history going back to the nineteenth century, there has been a steady multiplication of groups in recent years, often dedicated to the defence of particular categories, such as women prisoners. The Penal Affairs Consortium, a member organization that tries to create a unified voice for those concerned with penal policy, presently has over 40 organizations in membership.

What sense can we make of the increasing tendency for the defence of individuals against public power to take this organized form? Just as we could arrive at competing pessimistic or optimistic interpretations in the case of the media, the same is true here. It is possible to see these developments as a response to a threatening change in the character of the state in the last 30 years: a shift to more authoritarian treatment of marginalized social groups. (This theory of a new authoritarianism is examined more closely in Chapter 24.) Two of the groups identified here could be invoked to support this argument. British penal policy has turned in a markedly punitive direction, with an increasing resort to incarceration in prison, and there is a growing tendency for politicians to use the language of retribution. In the case of refugees, a long history of hostility and suspicion culminated in the 1990s in increasingly active public policies designed to control entry, to limit entitlements to public services, and to hunt down illegal entrants. The turn to organization in this setting can be seen as an attempt to protect vulnerable groups against increasingly hostile public power.

However, the growth of these organizations has not taken place in isolation. As we noted in Chapter 9, there has been a wider growth in pressure group organization. Chapters 13 and 16 described some of the institutional, technological and cultural changes that underpin this growth. New forms of political mobilization have occurred because of a variety of developments: the success of some groups has encouraged others to learn the lesson that well organized groups can have a clear effect on public policy; new technologies of communication, such as mobile telephony and the web, have cut the costs of organization and communication in creating networks of activists; and cultural trends, such as rising levels of formal education, have increased the size of the pool of those with the skills to organize politically and to advocate causes. On this account, the rise of formal organizations designed to defend individuals against public power, including the most vulnerable and marginalized individuals such as prisoners and refugees, is a sign that we have in Britain a healthy wider culture and society that is increasingly able to scrutinize the power wielded by public servants. Thus public servants in Britain, on this account, actually operate in a wider civil society that creates organizations well able to scrutinize and check.

## The state: modernized or authoritarian?

The preceding two chapters paint a picture of a consistent pattern of change. This pattern takes three forms:

● Institutions have become more formally organized and entitlements have been increasingly codified. We can see this, for example, in the growth of more formally organized systems to ensure accountability and review of institutions as varied as the police and prison services, and the intelligence services. We can see it in the spread of the institution of the Ombudsman. We can see it in the increasingly explicit codification of entitlements and obligations, culminating in large-scale codifications such as the Human Rights Act.

## DEBATING POLITICS

### 23.1    SCANDALS IN THE EXERCISE OF PUBLIC POWER: OPTIMISM OR PESSIMISM?

| Scandals such as those documented in the boxes of this chapter make us pessimistic about the rights of citizens | Scandals such as those documented in the boxes of this chapter give grounds for optimism about the rights of citizens |
|---|---|
| ■ They cover a wide range of institutions and thus suggest that abuse of power is engrained in British government.<br>■ They involve abuse at the expense of a wide range of social groups: business people, young members of ethnic minorities, parents in families.<br>■ Their revelation and correction has typically come not through the formal mechanisms of redress, but as the result of public campaigns prompted by extreme scandal.<br>■ Redress and public apology have typically been delayed and grudging. | ■ They show that open scrutiny and reform are possible, albeit after a hard struggle.<br>■ Many arise from attitudes and practices that are being eliminated within government; they predate the new culture of the Human Rights Act.<br>■ They are revealed as scandals precisely because citizens are no longer prepared to put up with arbitrary and discriminating behaviour by public servants.<br>■ Cases such as the Stephen Lawrence case have prompted large scale reform of both practices and the means of redress. |

- The institutional architecture has become more diverse and complex, principally through the reshaping influence of the world of multi-level governance. This is partly visible in the immediate impact of the institutions of the European Union and the institutions of devolution, but it is also visible in the increasing recognition by policy makers that shaping policy in the areas of order and security is a matter of effectively securing multi-level, multi-agency coordination: the key example here is provided in Briefing 22.4 (p. 486), on multi-agency efforts to cope with terrorism.
- The domains examined in these two chapters have become more contentious and volatile. Part of the function of the three Briefings in this chapter that summarize recent scandals in the abuse of public power is to show that formal safeguards can coexist with great abuse; but the Briefings also show how scandal and intense controversy have become central features of the regulation of relations between the state and the citizen. The frequent references to decisions about asylum and immigration in this chapter

show how sensitive this area in particular has become, dramatizing the issue of what constitutes proper rights and safeguards, and highlighting the problem of which socially or legally defined groups should be entitled to which safeguards.

We have seen at several points in these two chapters that developments can be interpreted in contrasting ways. One way to see the growth of institutional safeguards, the increasing codification of entitlements, and the growing contestation of the use of power by public bodies is to view these as part of a highly desirable modernization of key parts of the constitution. They all amount to the creation of more robust institutional safeguards for citizens, and the emergence of a more assertive wider culture replacing the deference of the past. They are, in short, part of a passage from the status of 'subject' to the status of 'citizen'. Different views of the changes can still be held by 'modernizers', some viewing them as extensive, some as still modest; but the changes are in the right direction, and the differences are about how much further we need to go.

**REVIEW**

Four themes dominate this chapter:

1  The growth of institutional and procedural safeguards against some forms of maladministration

2  The recurrence of scandalous examples of the abuse of public power;

3  The problem of deciding how far safeguards should extend impartially, and in particular the problem of safeguarding the rights not only of nationals and residents, but of those who wish to enter Britain as immigrants, especially as refugees;

4  The problematic nature of our understanding of institutional and procedural change, notably how far to read it as democratic modernization or as a strengthening of authoritarian controls.

However, we have also encountered an altogether more pessimistic view of what has been happening: one that stresses the great surveillance resources of the state, and the way it treats the most vulnerable, such as would-be immigrants who do not have the resources of the native population. On this view, the recurrence of the scandals illustrated in some of this chapter's Briefings is not an unfortunate blemish in an otherwise improving picture. It is consistent with the growth of public power, and with an increasingly authoritarian exercize of public power, especially over the most vulnerable and stigmatized: ethnic minorities, prisoners, asylum seekers, the poorest benefit claimants. The spread of institutions such as the Ombudsmen, and the codification of rights in laws such as the Human Rights Act, are on this view symbolic measures designed to manage expectations: in the language of Bagehot, they are part of the 'dignified' rather than the 'efficient' machinery of the Constitution.

As will be obvious from this summary of contrasting views, how we view the present relations between the state and the citizen depends on more than how we evaluate specialized institutional safeguards and procedures; it depends also on our wider view of how democracy in Britain works. That wider view is the subject of our next, concluding, chapter.

## Further reading

For many years 'Democratic Audit', operating from the University of Essex, has been publishing audits of democracy and rights in Britain (and elsewhere). Its continuing work is always worth tracking down: see in particular Beetham *et al.* (2002). Moran (2003), Chapter 3, is a handy summary of the robustness, or otherwise, of the system of self-regulation. Senvirante (2002) is comprehensive and up-to-date on Ombudsmen, and has the added strength of some comparative material. Jowell and Cooper (2003) describe the latest important human rights developments.

CHAPTER 24

# Understanding the British state

## AIMS

This chapter:

❖ Looks back at the previous chapters, extracting the main lines of change in British government and politics

❖ Discusses competing views about what these changes imply for the wider system of government

❖ Discusses competing theories of how best to make sense of change.

❖ Looks to the future.

## Transformation and continuity in British government

Imagine studying British government a generation ago: say, at the moment in 1964 when the election of a new Labour administration under Harold Wilson as Prime Minister had produced the first change in partisan control of the Westminster government for 13 years. With the benefit of hindsight we can see that this moment also marked a turning point: it was the beginning of a long period of change in both the system of government and in the wider political system (see Timeline 24.1). The new era of change had comparatively little to do with the government that was elected in 1964; rather, the change in the partisan colour of government in that year was itself a symptom of deeper changes in the wider society and in the links between society and politics.

We can identify six important changes, and four lines of continuity, if we glance back over the last four decades. First of all, let us consider the changes.

### The rise of multi-level and multi-agency governance

In part this change is institutional, and in part it is a change in the mindset of those involved in making policy. The institutional changes that have cropped up in many of the chapters of this book are part of the story. The two most dramatic are the increasing intersection between all levels of government in Britain and the governing institutions of the European Union, notably the European Commission in Brussels; and the formalization of domestic multi-level governance which has taken place as a result of the devolution measures introduced from 1999. But just as important as the objective institutional change is the rising consciousness that government is a multi-agency matter: a matter of coordinating the activities of a wide range of agencies distributed both horizontally and vertically across society. 'Joined-up government', a slogan used by Labour administrations since 1997, is sometimes derided as a gimmick, but it expresses well this change in mindset. An institutional expression of the change in mindset is the growing amount of resources put into the coordination of policy initiatives, notably from the heart of the core executive. It is one of the most important reasons for a development we identified in Chapter 7: the increasing resources allocated to the institutions immediately surrounding the office of prime minister. This stress on coordination highlights an important point: we should not necessarily equate the rise of multi-level and multi-agency governance with greater decentralization. The change in mindset often only makes actors in the core executive more sensitive than in the past towards the need for central control over agencies, in the name of policy coordination.

### The Europeanization of British politics

Suppose someone had emigrated from Britain in 1964 to a country where British politics was rarely reported, and that she returned a generation later. She would probably find Europeanization the most remarkably changed feature of British politics. In 1964 we were not even members of the (then) EEC. Part of the change, as we saw above, lies in the intersection with multi-level governance. But Europeanization, as we have seen in numerous chapters, has deeply inserted itself into the wider workings of society and politics: into electoral competition, both because of the advent of direct elections to the European Parliament and because divisions over strategic choices in Europe have become critical lines of cleavage in and between the leading political parties; into strategies pursued by the institutions of devolved, local and regional government, because the European Union is a major funder of public investment schemes; into key areas of economic policy, such as competition policy, because the European Commission has a major say in domestic mergers and competition regulation; and into the strategies pursued by interest groups large and small, since virtually all treat the European Union as a level at which they can seek to shape policy outcomes.

### The reshaped public sector

The reshaping of the public sector has taken two important forms. The most visible is quite simply the shrinkage, in some cases to the point of disap-

## TIMELINE 24.1    A CHRONICLE OF POLITICAL EVENTS IN BRITAIN, 1964–2004

**1964**
Labour party returned to office for the first time in 13 years with tiny Commons majority.

**1965**
Labour government publishes *National Plan,* in an attempt to emulate French style of planning and French record of economic success.

**1966**
Labour wins general election with landslide Commons majority of almost 100 over other parties.

**1967**
Pound sterling devalued following currency crisis; *National Plan* effectively abandoned in ensuing economic crisis.

**1968**
Civil Rights marches in Northern Ireland show first sign of a generation of civil unrest in the province.

**1969**
*In Place of Strife,* Labour Government White Paper proposals on trade union reform, abandoned in face of trade union opposition. Troops committed to policing streets in Northern Ireland following riots and attacks on Catholics.

**1970**
Edward Heath returned unexpectedly as Conservative Prime Minister in general election.

**1971**
Negotiations begin to prepare way for UK entry into European Economic Community.

**1972**
Direct rule from Westminster imposed in Northern Ireland, beginning a history of direct rule which has lasted, with brief interruptions, for more than 30 years. Conservative government abandons free market policies, introducing statutory pay and prices policies.

**1973**
United Kingdom formally becomes member of the European Economic Community. 'Six Day War' in the Middle East leads to huge rise in oil prices and beginning of severe recession in Britain and in other advanced industrial nations. Prolonged dispute with miners over challenge to statutory pay policy leads to widespread social and economic disruption and imposition of a 'three day working week' on industry and many public services, and severe restrictions on use of energy.

**1974**
Conservatives expelled from office in February general election; second general election in October fails to give Labour government a clear majority.

**1975**
Year of unprecedented pay and price inflation, approaching annual rates of 30%.

**1976**
Following sterling crisis Labour government forced to seek financial support from International Monetary Fund in return for cuts in public spending plans.

**1977**
Clashes between police and mass picketing in dispute at Grunwick printers.

**1978**
'Winter of discontent' sees widespread public sector strikes, disruption of essential services and violent clashes between strikers and police.

**1979**
Margaret Thatcher returned as Prime Minister of Conservative government in general election.

**1980**
British and world recession following sharp rise in oil prices in preceding year.

**1981**
Widespread riots in London (Brixton) and in other cities.

**1982**
Argentine invasion of British possession in South Atlantic, the Falkland Islands, followed by short victorious military campaign to regain possession.

**1983**
Conservatives win landslide victory in general election.

**1984**
IRA bomb in Grand Hotel during Conservative Party conference kills five, injures many more and narrowly misses killing the Prime Minister.

⇨

## TIMELINE 24.1 (CONTINUED)

**1985**
Miners concede defeat in year-long strike aimed at challenging government authority to make coal policy.

**1986**
Single European Act passed committing the UK to further progress towards European integration. Michael Heseltine resigns from Cabinet, beginning train of events that will bring down Mrs Thatcher.

**1987**
Rupert Murdoch moves printing of his national newspaper titles, such as *The Times* and *The Sun*, from Fleet Street to Wapping, breaking power of print unions after long conflict. In general election Margaret Thatcher returned for third term as Prime Minister.

**1988**
Section 28 of Local Government Act forbids local authorities from 'promoting' homosexuality in schools.

**1989**
Nigel Lawson resigns as Chancellor of the Exchequer, signalling first public sign of infighting in the Thatcher Cabinet.

**1990**
Mrs Thatcher resigns as Prime Minister and Leader of the Conservative Party following failure to win required majority in first ballot of leadership challenge by Michael Heseltine. John Major becomes Conservative Leader and Prime Minister.

**1991**
Introduction of 'council tax' to replace 'poll tax', failure of which had helped depose Mrs Thatcher.

**1992**
On 'Black Wednesday', 16 September, government forced to take sterling out of European Exchange Rate Mechanism, destroying public faith in Conservative economic competence for over a decade.

**1993**
British government admits to holding secret talks with Provisional IRA.

**1994**
IRA declares first ceasefire in Northern Ireland. Tony Blair elected as Leader of Labour Party.

**1995**
In British Rail privatization Conservatives introduce last and most controversial of the large privatization schemes.

**1996**
IRA bomb Canary Wharf in London, ending first ceasefire on British mainland.

**1997**
Labour government returned to power with landslide Commons majority under Tony Blair.

**1998**
Signing of Belfast Agreement on Good Friday begins attempted 'peace process' in Northern Ireland.

**1999**
New devolved administrations established in Scotland and Wales.

**2000**
Euro introduced for daily transactions in most member states of the EU, with Britain as the most significant 'opt-out'.

**2001**
Labour returned for second term of office under Tony Blair with another landslide majority.

**2002**
Labour government commits British troops to campaign in Afghanistan to remove Taliban government following attacks on New York and Washington by terrorist-guided aircraft in September 2001.

**2003**
Government fights war in Iraq alongside the United States.

**2005**
Labour party, convulsed by divisions over the Iraq war sees sharp fall in popular support and parliamentary majority in general election.

⮕ The text of this chapter stresses continuity and change over the last generation. This timeline only selects key events for each year of the last 40. Not all readers will agree with my selection of highlights. It is an illuminating exercise for students to create their own timeline.

pearance, of what were some of the most important parts of the public sector a generation ago. If we look back at Timeline 21.1 we can see this change summarized in the great privatization programmes; these transferred the biggest nationalized corporations, and most important public utilities, to private ownership. The second change has been subtler. It has reshaped the boundary separating the public and the private, so that the boundary itself is more complicated and unclear. The 'reshaping' here has altered our view of where the public sector ends and the 'private' begins. Chapter 8 provided some very striking examples of this reshaping, showing how nominally 'private' institutions and activities were increasingly subject to regulation by public agencies.

## The reshaped world of interest representation

If we looked back to 1964 we would see that many of the present institutional giants of interest representation did not even exist: the Confederation of British Industry was only founded a year later, in 1965. Some of the most important features of the modern world of interest representation also either did not exist, or were present only in embryonic form. While giant firms certainly operated a generation ago, and advocated their own special interests, the importance of the giant multinational firm, which we stressed in Chapter 9, has grown exponentially. Many of the firms that are now classic examples of the giant firms as interest lobbyists – including the larger supermarket chains, such as Tesco (see Image 9.4, p. 164) – either did not exist, or were small in scale, as recently as the 1960s. There has also been a significant growth in the membership and resources of large, permanently organized campaigning groups, encompassing causes as diverse as civil liberties at home, the rights of prisoners of conscience abroad, and the protection of the environment. In Chapters 5, 22 and 23 we saw how the first of these two sets of issues – broadly constitutional in nature – have increasingly been the subject of well organized group campaigning. And in Chapter 9 (see Table 9.1, p. 174) we saw the transformed membership resources of some important environmental campaigning groups.

In the 1960s Britain was just beginning to experience something that has now become common to interest group organization: the rapid growth of mass, single-issue campaigning groups. In the middle of the 1960s the first great example of these – the campaign for unilateral nuclear disarmament by Britain, or CND – was just starting to decline (see Parkin 1968). As we saw, notably in Chapter 13, organizing this kind of mass single-issue campaigning group has become much commoner, and much easier, in recent years. Alongside this growing popularization of interest representation has gone a very different trend, also explored in Chapter 13: growing professionalization, marked by the appearance in recent years of an increasingly well organized corps of professional lobbyists, hired guns who will speak for any interest with the money to pay them. Finally, as we saw especially in Chapter 9, the strategies of interest representation are being adapted to the demands of multi-level governance, notably by targeting policy makers in such European institutions as the Commission in Brussels and the newly devolved administrations in Edinburgh and Cardiff.

## Reshaped participation

Some accounts of changing patterns of participation paint a picture of decline over the last generation, but this is only part of the picture. What is undoubtedly correct is that the shape of participation has altered dramatically in the last generation. Many of the key forms of participation of the 1960s are of either little, or declining, importance. The most dramatic fall concerns membership of, and activism in, the political parties. In Chapter 14 we painted a picture of institutions whose membership was shrinking, and whose local political and social life was in widespread decay. There has been marginal compensation in the rise of some third parties, such as the nationalists and the Greens, but the two giants of the 1960s, Labour and the Conservatives, are strikingly weaker (with the Conservatives probably the weaker of the two). An even gloomier picture for the big parties emerges if we look at the participation of young people: the youth wings of the parties, and the student wings of the parties, have suffered a particularly serious decline. Students – a much larger group in the population now than in the 1960s – rarely participate in politics via membership of the Conservative or Labour parties.

A second fall in 'official' participation concerns voting. In recent years, as we documented in Chapters 13 and 17, voting, especially in general elections for the Westminster Parliament, has fallen sharply. 'Official' political participation is less widespread than knitting (see Table 13.1, p. 276). But from Chapters 9, 13, 17 and 18 we can draw a very different, less pessimistic, picture of what has happened to participation. The *opportunities* to participate have widened. There are more opportunities to vote, in referendums and in competitive elections, and there are more routes to political office than existed in the days when the Westminster Parliament was virtually the only route to significant high office. Most important of all, there has been an explosion of new kinds of participation, notably in permanently organized campaigning groups, and in single-issue groups that come and go with great speed. This is why we should speak of the reshaping, rather than the decline, of participation.

## The codified constitution

The constitution of a generation ago was still a thing of understandings and conventions: a mostly unwritten patchwork. The intervening generation has seen a growing *codification*: this means the increasing tendency systematically to write down constitutional understandings, often in the form of laws. In part this is an aspect of 'Europeanization', because the British system of government has been drawn into other European systems where written constitutional rules are the norm. One big sign of the change, which we have come across in several chapters (especially Chapter 6), is the importance of the European Court of Justice as a kind of 'supreme court' arbiter of the meaning of EU Treaties, Directives and Regulations. In Chapters 22 and 23 we also saw a long-term tendency to try to create formally organized institutional safeguards (such as Ombudsmen) and a tendency to write down safeguards in forms such as the Human

### Image 24.1
### The symbol of statehood: the passport

⮕ A British passport, the opening pages of which are reproduced here, has powerful symbolic and practical importance. Symbolically, it defines identity in a world where every piece of territory is claimed by some state. Look closely at the second page: you will see that the designation 'United Kingdom of Great Britain and Northern Ireland' is reproduced in all the languages of member states of the European Union. (The passport was issued before the enlargement of the Union in 2004.) Practically, the passport confers the right to enter a wealthy part of the world. Its value is reflected in the fact that it is stolen, forged and even killed for in impoverished parts of the globe.

Rights Act. And in Chapter 5 we saw many signs of the growth of codification, such as that arising out of the work of the Committee on Standards in Public Life.

❖ ❖ ❖

Great changes have therefore come over British politics in recent decades; but the story is not only about change. If we scan over a generation there are also striking continuities. Some political worlds have shown great persistence. Four are sketched here.

## The world of Westminster

Much has changed in the world of Westminster politics in the last generation, but there are also remarkable continuities. The House of Commons remains one of the most important centres of public political life: if anything, it was perhaps strengthened by the broadcasting of debates and their consequential use as clips in news broadcasts. For the most ambitious political aspirants a seat in the House of Commons still remains a highly desirable prize, both for its own sake and because it is a virtual precondition of winning more glittering prizes, such as a seat in the Westminster Cabinet. Commanding the House of Commons in debates, and in the jousts of Prime Minister's Question Time, remains a key to the exercize of Prime Ministerial authority. A generation ago a political fan who wanted to 'rubberneck' the leading figures in British political life only had to hang round the Palace of Westminster for a few days; the same holds true today. For the most important part of the political class in Britain, political life still means Westminster life.

## The world of the core executive

A major theme of Chapter 7 was the way the core executive is changing, but as in the world of Westminster the continuities are also striking. A generation ago, for the most ambitious politicians, the Cabinet was the pinnacle of a political career, and a small number of key offices of state (Prime Minister, Chancellor, Foreign Secretary and Home Secretary) the very summit of that pinnacle. That is still true: in these offices we still find the 'big hitters' in politics. The increased use of the concept of the 'core executive' in many ways only recognizes what was already a reality a generation ago: that at the heart of British government were a few hundred people working in central departments grouped around Whitehall in London, encompassing elected politicians, permanent civil servants, and more temporary advisers and aides. That is still substantially the case.

## The world of liberal democracy

The two worlds of continuity identified so far are elitist worlds populated by a small group of the political class. The world of liberal democracy is different. It refers to the wider popular foundations of the system of government. A generation ago Britain claimed to be a liberal democracy, in the senses identified earlier in this text, notably in Chapter 1: that is, it claimed to combine the protection of liberal freedoms (such as freedom of conscience, speech, assembly) with control over, and selection of, government by the people at large. This is still the version of British politics to which virtually anyone in Britain who argues and thinks about the system of government aspires. Those who defend our governing arrangements argue that, whatever particular blemishes may exist on the liberal democratic record, ours is fundamentally a liberal democracy. Critics of this account argue a variety of cases: for instance, that the 'blemishes' are so great as seriously to compromise liberal and democratic claims; or even that the claim to abide by these standards, even imperfectly, is unsustainable. But both critics and defenders agree on liberal democracy as the critical measure by which we should judge the system of government (an agreement that also united critics and defenders a generation ago). A small minority of authoritarians of a variety of persuasions dissent from this liberal democratic consensus, as did a small minority a generation ago.

## The world of the United Kingdom

One surprising continuity should be highlighted: at least, it is surprising if we look back at the pessimistic, often crisis-laden atmosphere of British politics that was common about 25 years ago: the United Kingdom continues. The 1970s were a decade of particularly severe economic failure and political turmoil. By the end of the decade 'the break-up of Britain' – the title of a highly influential book by Nairn (1981) – seemed a possibility. That 'break-up' might have come in a variety of forms: from the challenge of separate nationalisms; or, as seemed possible on occasions in the 1970s, from a wider crisis of governability produced by economic failure and the inability of government to manage the demands of powerfully organized competing interests (see, for instance, King 1976). It has been a major theme of this book that the nature of United Kingdom government has indeed been transformed in recent decades, notably by the impact of EU membership and by the institutional reforms introduced after the return to power of the Labour party in 1997. But there has been no break-down of the United Kingdom itself. The Westminster system remains the single most important concentration of resources and authority in British politics (see Image 24.1). Actors from that system – notably from the core executive – are the most important British players in the politics of policy in the institutions of the EU. Indeed, involvement with the Union has given new roles to key actors: to the Prime Minister, for example, as a leading figure in the high diplomacy of the Union. In the 1980s and 1990s the Westminster govern-ment proved highly effective at confronting institu-tions and interests (such as the trade unions) against whom it had seemed ineffective during the 1970s. Far from break-up and economic chaos, the United Kingdom begins the new millennium with one of the best economic records in Europe, measured by such indicators as economic growth, employment, and average income per head. At the conclusion of this chapter we examine the possible reasons for this unexpected outcome.

## Understanding change and continuity

The forms of development in British politics are many and varied, as even the simple sketches provided above show. How do we make sense of them? In other words, how do we step back from the bare institutional detail and provide a general interpretation of the forces shaping government? Many possibilities exist, but three are especially important, both because they have been prominent in academic debates and because they have influ-enced practical political perceptions.

### The network state

We began this book with Max Weber's account of the nature of authority, and notably with the differ-ent grounds on which it could be exercized: charisma, tradition, or the claim to legitimacy by

virtue of rational legality. The last, we saw, was the commonest basis on which the state could claim to exercize authority in Britain: by virtue of the fact that the decisions and commands of public servants were in accordance with powers conferred by laws legitimately passed. Charisma, the claim to some divine anointment; tradition, the claim to authority by virtue of linkage to a long line of historically established custom; both of these are now only residually present, reflected in various antiquated ceremonies associated with a monarchy which exer-cizes hardly any real power.

There is no doubt that rational legality is the commonest basis for claimed authority in Britain, though traces of charisma and tradition may be more deeply buried in our unconscious when we are faced with authority than we actually realize. But what each of these pictures of authority shares, in any case, is a fundamentally hierarchical vision of how government should work, and does work: the state, through its public servants, tells us what to do, and we obey, if we acknowledge authority. But these conceptions of authority were formulated now virtually a century ago, and they were shaped by experience of the nineteenth-century state. (Weber was born in 1864). Can they adequately reflect the complexity of modern government? We do not expect nineteenth-century technologies, such as the steam engine, to power a modern economy, so why should we expect nineteenth-century ideas to power government? We do not expect social institutions (such as firms or universities) to be organized on the same principles as governed their workings in the nineteenth century, so why should we expect government to be organized by nineteenth-century principles?

It is exactly these thoughts that lie behind the title of this book, notably the reference to 'gover-nance'. In the twenty-first century British govern-ment cannot be described with nineteenth-century language. 'Governance' in the title is a modest recognition of the way policies and politics take place in a world of multi-level institutions and agen-cies. But there is an account that goes well beyond this modest linguistic shift, and it can be summarily described as the theory of the network state (see Briefing 24.1).

# Briefing                    24.1

## CASTELLS ON THE NETWORK STATE

'The network state is a state characterised by the sharing of authority (that is, in the last resort, the capacity to impose legitimized violence) along a network. A network by definition, has nodes, not a centre. Nodes may be of different sizes, and may be linked by asymmetrical relationships in the network. Not only do national governments still concentrate much decision-making capacity, but there are important differences of power between nation-states, although the hierarchy of power varies in different dimensions: Germany is the hegemonic economic power, but Britain and France hold far greater military power, and at least equal technological capacity.

However, regardless of these asymmetries, the various nodes of the European network are interdependent on each other, so that no node, even the most powerful, can ignore the others, even the smallest in the decision-making process. If some political nodes do so, the whole political system is called into question. This is the difference between a political network and a centred political structure. Amongst the responses of political systems to the challenge of globalisation, the European Union may be the clearest manifestation to date of this emerging form of state, probably characteristic of the Information Age.'

*Source*: Castells (2001).

➲ Castells (see also Castells 2000) is the foremost theorist of the network state and the network society. As this extract shows, he does not deny the persistence of traditional state authority, but here he gives his ideas a distinctly 'European' cast, picturing the emergent EU system as a network without clear, stable hierarchies. Castells has offered the most influential and emphatic version of the limited idea that has shaped much of this book: that traditional government hierarchies are under challenge from networks. The question is: has he pushed the argument too far?

At the heart of the idea of the network state is the proposition that we no longer live in a world of stable hierarchies, and that government can no longer be conducted in a hierarchical fashion, even where those hierarchies claim the legitimacy of rational legal authority. We live instead in world of networks: links of institutions and people that are highly dispersed, not necessarily hierarchical, and that cross the conventional public/private boundary. For government to be effective it is no longer sufficient for it to invoke authority, rational-legal or otherwise; it must mobilize and coordinate the actors in numerous different networks to address issues and problems.

Part of the power of the 'network' theory of the state is that it offers us both description and prescription: it suggests that the world is changing in particular ways, and that as a result the practice of making and putting into effect policy has to change, if policy is to be at all effective. Many of the features that are central to this book fit the network theory, and three are especially important.

First, the major theme of the development of multi-level and multi-agency systems, notably in the policy world, obviously chimes with the 'network' vision. The 'stretching' of policy making to span both the European and the devolved worlds plainly also fits the vision of a networked state.

Second, a large number of the wider political changes that have figured in these pages make sense when viewed through the vision of the network state. In the preceding section we summarized, for instance, the transformation of participation that has taken place in the last generation. That transformation has created a less hierarchical, more difficult to control world. In place of the small number of political parties that 'funnelled' most participation through their mass memberships a generation ago, there is now a more dispersed and chaotic world: a huge diversity of groups organizing different people with specialized, different interests and preferences; spontaneously created groups with mass memberships, often created extremely rapidly around single issues. Behind these developments in turn lie cultural and technical developments that have undermined hierarchical control: a better educated and more self-confident citizenry which no longer takes its political cues from a London-based elite; technologies of communication that can no longer be monopolized by the institutions of the state.

Third, theories of the network state help explain failure in government, and offer the prospect of avoiding it in future. We have seen at a number of points in this text that fiascos and failures are a common experience of British government. One of the most distinguished exponents of the network account, Rhodes, has argued that fiasco and failure are the product of an inability to recognize the reality of networks: that government can no longer be carried on by the tools given us by a Weberian hierarchical theory of the nature of the state (Rhodes 1997). Trying to use these tools is like attempting to steer a modern car with the skills of a nineteenth-century train driver: disaster is inevitable unless some more subtle form of coordination and manoeuvre is adopted.

The network vision plainly alerts us to important features of multi-level governance in Britain. But should we subscribe to it fully? We might have reservations on three grounds.

The first lies in the claim to *novelty*. Recall that in the hands of writers such as Rhodes this is an important part of the argument: modern society, and modern government, create new levels of complexity that make old-fashioned hierarchies ineffective. The new governance has to be about managing dispersed institutional networks, and seeking coordination across the old-fashioned public/private divide. But if we look at the past of government in Britain we can see numerous examples of precisely this kind of arrangement. Some examples will help to illustrate the point.

- We know from Chapters 22 and 23 that traditionally the relations between the state and the citizen in Britain were heavily reliant on voluntary coordination. This part of the constitution was strikingly lacking in codification, depending on understandings by a wide range of parties that were rarely written down. If anything, the developments described in those two chapters seem to move us away from models of coordination to more exact specification of the relationships between citizens and public institutions.
- Many of the key 'multi-level' relationships in government in the past were highly voluntary in nature: for instance, until the 1980s local authorities in Britain had a high level of autonomy, and the central state had to rely on voluntary cooper-

ation for the delivery of services. In other words, the centre truly had to try to coordinate networks of dispersed institutions. If anything, this declined from the 1980s as the central state intervened directly to control the actions of local government (a development described in Chapter 12).

- In the recent past central government relied on informal and voluntary agreements with many institutions and agencies to deliver services or to ensure regulation. Two very good examples are provided by universities, which were substantially independent of the central Education Ministry until the 1980s; and the City of London, which ruled itself through a complex network of private firms, semi-public agencies (including the Bank of England) and the informal guidance of agencies from the core executive, such as the Treasury. Here again since the 1980s there has been a move to more directive, legally-based modes of control and regulation.

Second, as some of the examples given above show, it may be a little sweeping to adopt the language of networks because there seems to be life in the old 'state' yet. The shape of state power in Britain is certainly changing. The old highly centralized, London-focused model has been greatly altered in recent decades. Many services that were delivered by state institutions are now delivered otherwise, either by private firms or – as in the case of a large amount of what used to be 'council' housing – by the voluntary sector. But, as we saw in Chapter 21, the state is still a massively important institution in raising and allocating economic resources. It wields highly traditional forms of state power, including the power to compel citizens to pay a variety of taxes, on pain of prosecution, confiscation and, in the last resort, imprisonment. In some areas of national life – such as in controlling who may enter and work in the country – the state is strengthening both its powers and its surveillance resources.

Third, it may be premature to write off forms of legitimacy based on Weberian models of authority, and one reason why it may be premature is that a 'network' state itself raises serious problems of accountability. It deliberately tries to blur the divide between the public and private, and to work through complex networks of institutions where coordination is valued over clear specification of hierarchical relationships. But one merit of hierarchy is that it identifies lines of responsibility: an aggrieved citizen has some notion of where the buck stops. That helps explain developments described in Chapters 22 and 23 which are otherwise puzzling if we are indeed moving into a world of self-organizing networks: the increased tendency to try to lay out more exactly the terms of rational-legal authority, by codifying more explicitly the powers of public servants and the rights of citizens, and by putting on a more formal basis the means by which aggrieved citizens may seek redress. These developments show the tenacity of the rational-legal model of authority. They show that a reaction to failures of the model (for instance, when public servants use their discretion to abuse their powers) is to try to strengthen the rational-legal model by specifying it more exactly, and making stronger the institutions that can pursue cases where it is abused.

## The regulatory state

The theory of the regulatory state is a relative of the network state theory, but it emphasizes different forces. There are also strikingly varied accounts of what the regulatory state amounts to, and these variations catch some of the contradictory developments in British government over recent years.

The essential idea of the regulatory state is well conveyed in the name, notably in the idea of the state as a 'regulator'. A regulator in any system – it could be as simple as that providing domestic central heating, or as complex as the computer-based navigation for a large ship – essentially balances the system: it receives information from the environment, and adjusts system performance in the light of that information and in the light of the pre-set aims of the system. For a simple domestic central heating system that means turning a boiler on and off according to a pre-set temperature target and what sensors indicate about ambient temperature; for a complex navigation system it means

adjusting the direction of the vessel on the basis of information received and processed about a wide range of factors, from likely obstacles to ambient weather conditions. Transferred to government, this language pictures the regulatory state as a kind of pilot for society, not actually supplying the motive power but providing overall guidance about direction. A famous American image expresses this as a state that is not 'rowing' but 'steering' (Osborne and Gaebler 1992: 35).

This picture of the regulatory state is actually as old as political philosophy. In Plato's *Republic*, one of the first great texts of political philosophy written in Greece over 300 years before the birth of Christ, there is an explicit identification of leadership in government with the role of a pilot. This early identification tells us something potentially significant about the democratic character of the idea of the regulatory state, for the *Republic* is a consciously anti-democratic work. If we move from ancient Greece to our own times, we find that the idea of government as the act of piloting has often been associated with authoritarian, not democratic, politics: Mao Zedong, one of the most brutal dictators of the twentieth century (who ruled China from 1949 to 1976), was known periodically as 'the Great Helmsman'. And when we interrogate the idea as applied to Britain, we shall find that in some accounts it actually has anti-democratic undertones.

The vision of the regulatory state in Britain begins with two key recent British experiences: a great economic crisis in the 1970s and the policy response which that produced; and the by now long history of the country's membership of the European Union. The great economic crisis of the 1970s produced, at the end of the decade, the return of a Conservative administration led by Margaret Thatcher as Prime Minister. Throughout Mrs Thatcher's long tenure (1979–90) the state withdrew from many areas of economic control. In particular, it 'privatized' many important industries (such as telecommunications and steel) and many providers of utilities (water, electricity and gas). In many cases these had been in public ownership and control for over a century. The state also sought to guide the economy according to free market principles. It thus tried to adopt a key notion of the regulatory state: that government would set the overall direction of economic life, providing the key background conditions for markets to operate, but allowing the wider institutions of civil society to do the 'rowing': that is, actually to produce goods and services for offer in the marketplace. It also moved in the direction of more regulation in a more immediate institutional way. For many of the privatized industries it developed specialized regulatory bodies whose purpose was to steer the privatized sector in certain key directions, such as free and fair competition. We discussed the growth of these regulatory agencies, together with examples, in Chapter 8. Though the most revolutionary changes happened in the Thatcher decade of the 1980s, they were confirmed by her successors. Mrs Thatcher's immediate successor as prime minister, John Major, continued the privatization programme; and the Blair governments after 1997 established many new regulatory agencies, such as the Food Standards Agency and the Financial Services Authority.

This account of the growth of the regulatory state in Britain therefore traces it to the response to a long history of British economic decline, and in particular to the severe crisis of the 1970s. It identifies it as part of a new consensus in politics, uniting both the major Westminster governing parties. But the British experience, though special in the severity of the economic crisis that brought it about, is not unique. The British economic crisis of the 1970s was part of a wider change in international economic conditions that created economic difficulties across the advanced industrial world. Many countries responded by trying to withdraw the state from areas of economic control and by trying to adopt a more regulatory mode: more 'steering', and less 'rowing'. (Recall that this original image actually came from a study of American government.) This wider significance of the regulatory state is at the heart of the most important and academically influential version of the theory, that offered by the Italian social scientist, Majone (see Briefing 24.2). One great strength of Majone's account is that it ties British to European developments.

Majone (1996) argues that the developments that produced the British crisis of the 1970s were part of a wider crisis, one that threatened what he

## Briefing 24.2

### MAJONE ON THE REGULATORY STATE AS AN ALTERNATIVE MODEL OF DEMOCRACY

'Independent regulatory bodies, like independent central banks, courts of law, administrative tribunals or the European Commission, belong to the genus "non-majoritarian institutions", that is, public institutions which, by design, are not directly accountable either to voters or to elected officials. The growing importance of such institutions in all democratic countries shows that for many purposes reliance upon qualities such as expertize, professional discretion, policy consistency, fairness or independence of judgement is considered to be more important than reliance on direct political accountability ... non-majoritarian decision-making mechanisms are more suitable for complex, plural societies than are mechanisms that concentrate power in the hands of the political majority.'

*Source*: Majone (1996: 286).

➔ Majone offers two especially important perspectives on the regulatory state. His stress on the importance of the 'EU' connection we have already encountered; the second is his direct challenge to 'majoritarian' democracy on the grounds that it is too crude to work in 'complex, plural societies'. Britain is a complex plural society which has up to now relied heavily precisely on majoritarianism – most obviously in the convention that control of a majority in elected assemblies confers the legitimate right to make policy.

calls the Keynesian welfare state. The Keynesian welfare state was an ambitious form of state intervention that developed across numerous advanced industrial nations after the Second World War, especially in Western Europe. It combined a large welfare state with a commitment to close control of the economy, including large-scale public ownership. In the 1970s this kind of ambitious state found it increasingly hard to deliver aims such as low inflation and full employment. Britain's problems, though extreme, were thus only part of this wider crisis. The regulatory 'turn' involves, as in the British case, withdrawing from direct ownership and control, and relying much more on 'steering'. But this regulatory turn has been strengthened in western Europe by the rise of the European Union as an actor in economic life. The EU, Majone argues, is necessarily a regulatory state; it just does not have the resources to act as an interventionist state. It has a tiny independent budget of its own and a tiny bureaucracy (both not much more impressive than the resources of a large British local authority). It cannot directly control the vast economy of the Union. It must do the best it can by laying down broad rules and relying on others to implement these rules. It expresses this reliance in the doctrine of *subsidiarity*: the doctrine that power and control should be exercized at the lowest feasible level of a governing system. In practice this means that responsibility for implementing the rules lies with national and sub-national institutions, and often with private institutions, such as professional regulatory bodies. Since these lower-level bodies have to implement rules, it is also only sensible that they should have a large say in their formation. The regulatory state is therefore a state where private interests have a big say in what broad policies are decided, since they often have the responsibility for carrying them out.

The accounts of the regulatory state summarized here share some common features: they offer a fundamentally benign view of this state, picturing it as a way of standing back from, and empowering, civil society. Difficulties immediately arise, however, in picturing the regulatory state as a 'light touch' steering state. It is true that, in such programmes as privatization, there has been significant retreat from the dominant forms of twentieth century state intervention, but we saw in Chapter 8 that this is far from the whole story: the age of the regulatory state over the last couple of decades has seen greatly widened legal regulation, usually through agencies empowered by statute. The story cannot be just be about shifting from 'rowing' to 'steering'. These sections of Chapter 8 show the state acquiring new means of control over areas of civil society, such as sport and financial regulation, which hitherto largely operated independently.

One way of solving this paradox – that the age of 'steering' is also apparently an age of increasing control – looks to the authoritarian strand in regulation that spans, as we saw above, Plato's 'pilot' and Mao's 'Great Helmsman'. Moran's (2003) account of the regulatory state recognizes this strand and paints the British regulatory state in a threatening and interventionist light. Here the state is using regulation not just as a response to residual problems of control left behind by privatization, but as a way of fundamentally reshaping civil society. This reshaping is taking place in the name of a variety of projects of wholesale social transformation: making the economy competitive in an age of global markets; intervening in the lifestyles of the population to manage their health; promoting and controlling education and scientific research.

It is obvious that one of the strengths of the 'regulatory state' theory is that it offers a number of different perspectives on the meaning of change in British politics. It can draw together the impact of the Thatcher revolution in economic policy and the long-term consequences of our membership of the European Union. But that diversity is also a weakness. Whatever the difficulties of the theory of the network state, it offers a fairly clear set of propositions that we can test against the evidence. What, by contrast, are we to make of theories of the regulatory state that do not seem to agree on whether regulation means retreat or advance, more liberal freedoms or more authoritarian controls?

One intriguing feature of the 'authoritarian' account of the regulatory state is that it connects to the third and final theory examined here: a theory that we are witnessing the rise of an authoritarian state in Britain.

## An authoritarian state

The two theories we have so far examined are chiefly academic in origin and circulation. They are in the main too technical to have attracted much attention in the world of practical political argument. Our third theory is especially interesting because it has crossed these two worlds: originating in both academic and polemical accounts of what is happening to British politics, it is now widely invoked, especially by radical critics of what has happened to government in the last couple of decades.

The theory of the rise of a new authoritarianism sprang from attempts to make sense of the Thatcher revolution in policy and organization of the 1980s: the destruction of trade union power; the more active use of policing to combat industrial militancy; the onset of a new age of foreign wars, beginning with the victorious campaign to expel Argentinian invaders from the Falklands in 1982 (see Timeline 24.1); and the growth of central controls over formerly locally controlled services, be they policing or schooling.

Some of these changes could be assimilated to the theory of a 'free market and strong state' developed by Gamble (1994). This argued that free market forces in a society with strong institutions of collectivism (such as trade unions) demanded powerful central state controls. These controls were needed both to impose the reforms in the first place, and then continually to police an economy where actors had incentives to try to subvert competitive forces in order to gain advantages in markets. But while Gamble's theory opened up the possibility that the new 'free market strong state' order might be authoritarian, it did not necessarily entail authoritarianism. It is easy to imagine that a strong central state could be combined with the preservation of both democratic practices and liberal freedoms, which is something that seems to approximate to Gamble's own view. Faced with the Thatcher revolution in the 1980s, Hall and Jacques (1983) offered a much darker picture of a new authoritarianism: an authoritarianism that not only policed in the name of the free market but summoned up old forms of repression, such as imperialism and racism (see Briefing 24.3).

This account was published at the height of the Thatcher revolution in the 1980s. Since then, radical critics have been able to accumulate continuing signs of this authoritarian 'turn' in British political life. Three pieces of evidence supporting this authoritarian account are: the new cross-party consensus; the impact of international events; and the development of surveillance technology. We examine each in turn.

## Briefing    24.3

### HALL AND JACQUES ON THE AUTHORITARIAN STATE

'The historic mission of Thatcherism has not been to win this or that election – astute as it has been at mastering the ebb and flow of the opinion polls. It is much more ambitious than that ... a new public philosophy has been constructed in the open affirmation of "free market values" – the market as the measure of everything – and reactionary "Victorian" social values – patriarchalism, racism and imperialist nostalgia. The whole shift towards a more authoritarian type of regime has been grounded in the search for "Order" and the cry for "Law" which arises among many ordinary people in times of crisis and upheaval.'

*Source:* Hall and Jacques (1983: 10–11).

➔ Hall and Jacques originally set out to understand Thatcherism at the height of its success, but their theory of a new authoritarianism has been echoed in many later radical accounts, including critical radical accounts of New Labour.

● *The new cross-party consensus.* When Hall and his colleagues produced their original account, the Conservatives under Thatcher were pioneers of a new kind of politics. The Labour party in Opposition was then opposed to much of what the Conservatives were attempting, but in the 1990s 'New Labour' accepted most of the Conservative reforms, and indeed in some areas sought to 'outdo' the Conservatives. Apart from accepting most of the Conservatives' reforms designed to strengthen market forces, new Labour was particularly enthusiastic about three key areas of reform. First, it strenuously pursued the agenda of *more centralized and more thorough policing*. Second, it sought to introduce reforms that tried to *police more closely the behaviour of the unemployed*, linking entitlements to benefits to willingness to be subjected to periodic assessments and to take offers of employment. Third, despite introducing the Human Rights Act, it tried to *restrict the range of some traditional liberties*, such as rights to trial by jury and defences against imprisonment without trial. Thus what were in the 1980s highly contested measures associated with the Conservatives are now supported and promoted by the majority of the governing class. One reason for this change we now examine: the impact of international events.

- *The impact of international events.* We saw earlier in this text (see Chapter 4, pp. 66–7) that the collapse in 1991 of the main perceived threat to British security, the Soviet Union, actually produced in many ways a more threatening and unstable world. British government lives in an era of small – and sometimes not so small –wars: two wars against Iraq (1990 and 2003); in the Balkans (1999); and in Afghanistan (2002). In the twentieth century war, because of the way it was accompanied by external threats to home security, was often accompanied by the curtailment of civil liberties. A perceived new threatening force is provided by international terrorism, the defining moment being the successful attack by hijacked civil airliners on the World Trade Center in New York, and on the Pentagon in Washington, on 11 September 2001. Most democratic states introduced curtailed civil liberties in the wake of that attack, taking power, for example, to imprison suspected terrorists without trial. As Political Issues 1.1 and Table 5.1 show, the response of the British government was among the most drastic. At the time of writing it imprisons without trial a small number of people it suspects of terrorist intent or links, and is preparing legislation which will make easier conviction of citizens charged with a variety of offences (not just terrorism) without many of the normal safeguards, such as open trial by jury.

- *The development of surveillance technology.* States have often wanted closely to monitor the lives of their subjects, but primitive technologies of surveillance set a limit to monitoring, and thus to control. If the state does not know what we are doing it is harder for it to punish us for doing it. Some of the possibilities of the new surveillance technologies have cropped up in the pages of this book: notably, the way a combination of huge computing power and digital technologies of

observation means that our daily movements, transactions and communications can now be recorded, stored, easily retrieved and passed between private and public agencies ranging from the police to credit rating firms.

The theory of a new authoritarianism therefore begins with fairly limited historical observations of the revolution in British government introduced by the Conservatives in the 1980s, as they tried to cope with the aftermath of the British economic crisis. But the power of this theory is greatly strengthened by the way it seems to fit with so many wider developments: a state struggling with the perceived threat of terrorism; an era of small wars often connected to the fight against terrorism; a consensus about the need for closer social control of the poor that unites large sections of the political class; new technologies that make surveillance and control ambitions more realizable than in the past.

There are two rather different grounds for scepticism in the face of this theory of a new authoritarianism. One partly accepts the argument that there has been a diminution of liberty; the other argues that this account entirely misreads what has been happening to British government and politics in the last couple of decades. (See People in Politics 24.1 for the input of three intellectuals over a broader time span.)

Partially accepting the theory of the new authoritarianism means admitting that restrictions on liberties have indeed grown, and are likely to continue to grow. That can be coupled with the argument that this is a necessary evil to avert a greater one: destruction of life, and even of our free institutions, by supporters of political violence. But the restrictions, viewed in the round of British political life, are still marginal, if worrying. Most people, most of the time, retain wide liberties (of speech, conscience, assembly). Virtually every conceivable body of opinion is still able to organize and campaign. Ninety-nine per cent of the population still speak, think and organize without any restriction; and the 1 per cent that expresses views deeply repugnant to those of the majority still has quite ample freedoms to speak and organize. No system

## *People in politics*

### 24.1   PUBLIC INTELLECTUALS IN POLITICAL LIFE

Cartoons: Shaun Steele

**Michael Oakeshott** (1901–90). Though he wrote comparatively little and avoided public engagements, Oakeshott had a deep effect on public life in Britain. He professed a profoundly sceptical conservatism in elegant English prose, and thus exerted a great effect over the minds of many practising Conservatives. Curiously, his influence did not extend to the greatest modern Conservative leader: Mrs Thatcher was instinctively a reformer of the kind Oakeshott disavowed.

**Anthony Crosland** (1918–77) was a quintessential public intellectual. His *The Future of Socialism* (1956) was the key restatement of 'revisionist' democratic socialism (see Documenting Politics 15.3, p. 331). For over 20 years following its publication Crosland remained the most prominent Labour party intellectual, but he was also a leading figure in successive Labour governments, being a member of Cabinets in 1965–70 and 1974–7. He died suddenly while holding office as Foreign Secretary.

**Eric Hobsbawm** (1917–), a refugee from German Nazism in the 1930s, is best known as one of the most distinguished social historians of the last century. But Hobsbawm also made a long journey from classical Marxism to more revisionist views characteristic of many public intellectuals. His 1978 Marx Memorial lecture, 'The forward march of Labour halted', although delivered in the spirit of revising Marx, anticipated many of the key conclusions of New Labour in Britain.

➲ Possibly the greatest public intellectual of the last century was J.M. Keynes (see People in Politics 21.1). He defined the importance of the public intellectual in a famous passage: 'The ideas of economists and political philosophers, both when they are right and when they are wrong, are more powerful than is commonly understood ... Madmen in authority, who hear voices in the air, are distilling their frenzy from some academic scribbler of a few years back' (Keynes, 1936, ch. 4). These three profiles show that 'academic scribbling' can take many different forms.

of liberal democratic government is perfect, but this does not seem a bad record in a dangerous world of terrorist threats.

A more thoroughgoing rejection of the theory of authoritarianism would argue that, far from growing authoritarianism, the range of liberty has widened in recent decades, and the state's coercive power has been more tightly controlled. Three pieces of evidence can be produced in support of this view.

The first is the evidence that *state coercion is actually in retreat, not advancing*. Suppose we compare the coercive activities of the British state now with its activities thirty years ago, before the onset of the new age of authoritarianism. We can see three areas where state coercion has declined.

- *Coercion by the police and the armed forces in Northern Ireland* has greatly receded. Mass internment without trial; almost daily shootings on the streets; massive undercover surveillance of the population; all these commonplace 1970s signs of state coercion have been eliminated. Since the signing of the Good Friday Agreement in 1998, indeed, the greatest coercion in the province comes from sections of nationalist and paramilitary loyalists, often to support criminal enterprizes such as drug dealing. The coercive arms of the state – notably the police – have actually been very ineffective at preventing this private enterprize coercion.
- *State coercion of important minorities conventionally labelled 'deviant'* has greatly declined. The most striking example concerns gay men. Many British cities now have openly run 'gay villages'; as recently as the 1970s (and indeed part of the 1980s), significant police resources went into the surveillance and attempted prosecution of gay people for allegedly breaching rules that same sex relations could only be practised in private.
- *Coercion of ethnic minorities* was widespread in the 1970s and 1980s, notably in police harassment of young black people using 'stop and search' laws. As we saw in our sketch of some scandals of recent years there is still intense argument about the extent of institutional racism in police forces. Periodic journalistic exposés still uncover examples of crude police racism and brutality against black people. But the arguments about institutional racism, and concerted official police campaigns to extinguish both conscious and unconscious racism, have greatly changed the climate of policing. It would be very hard to argue, whatever level of harassment now exists, that it is not significantly lower than was the case 30 years ago.

The second ground for scepticism about the 'new age of authoritarianism' thesis is that there has been a *rise in legal and institutional safeguards* against the arbitrary exercize of state power.

Chapters 22 and 23 painted a picture of great institutional and legal change in recent years, including the building of institutions concerned with the redress of grievances. The original creation of the Parliamentary Ombudsman in 1967 was the start of a movement of widespread institutional reform that has spread across the public sector. This movement has also increasingly involved, as we saw in Chapter 23, the transformation of informal codes into statutes, and therefore the embedding of many safeguards for citizens in the law. The culmination of this movement was the passage of the Human Rights Act. The 'derogations' (exemptions) from some of the safeguards of that Act, successfully claimed by the government in respect of its anti-terrorism measures after the attacks of September 2001, amount to serious breaches of its safeguards. But the passage of the Act, and the fact that most its measures remain unbreached, amounts to a great advance in safeguarding liberties.

A final ground for scepticism about the authoritarianism thesis is that we have seen *the rise of citizen activism*. The Human Rights Act did not appear unexpectedly: it was the product of profound changes in the British political culture that have made many old forms of coercion untenable. In some instances these changes have taken the form of the development of groups that campaign against the coercive exercize of state power, advocating the case for stigmatized groups, such as asylum seekers (see, for instance, Briefing 23.8). These advocacy groups are often weak and poorly resourced, but their emergence represents an increase, not a decrease, in resistance to state authoritarianism. More generally, in a number of chapters (notably 9, 13 and 16) we have seen that the picture of the British as politically apathetic is inaccurate. The biggest falls have been in 'officially' approved forms of participation, including voting, and in membership of the characteristic organization of the political class that still dominates Westminster government: the big political party. But there has been an explosion of single-issue groups, and of more long-term campaigning movements, such as those concerned with the environment. When the state has authoritarian ambitions it faces a better-organized and less deferential civil society than was the case even 30 years ago.

## Looking back at the future

Much of this chapter has tried to gain a perspective on British government and politics by looking back over recent decades. If we look back 25 years or so at how observers then pictured the future of Britain, what is striking is their pessimism. The prevailing images were of Britain in decline; of the likely break-up of the United Kingdom; of a society and a politics divided against it in ferocious, destructive sectional struggles (see Beer 1982; Gamble 1994; Moran 1985; Nairn 1981).

Why did British politics and government turn out to be more robust than expected? There are three main reasons, and they all illuminate important aspects of what shapes the fate of a system of government.

### It's the economy stupid

This slogan became famous after it was posted in the campaign headquarters of Bill Clinton, the successful Democratic candidate for the American presidency in 1992: it asserted that the fate of politics and politicians turns, above all, on the performance of the economy. The British economy, having performed poorly for a century up to the 1970s, and spectacularly badly during that decade, has performed unusually well since the early 1990s. We have enjoyed the longest uninterrupted period of economic growth since at least 1870. The rates of economic growth – the commonest measure of national economic success – have not been as high as those recorded at the peak of economic growth in the 1950s, but there is a critical difference: in those days Britain was an international laggard, her economy pulled along by the superior performance of miracle economies including the German and the Japanese; now, Britain has at least matched, and often outpaced, the performance of the other leading industrial nations. Historians will argue long about the source of this change, and they will have the advantage over us of knowing to what extent the change is producing a long-lasting transformation. But the consequences of a long economic boom have been both psychological and material. Whatever the real origins of the boom, political leaders in the Westminster system now widely believe that the transformation is due to revolutionary changes in policy introduced in the 1980s and 1990s. Tony Blair and Michael Howard both share the view that the original Thatcherite reforms have made Britain a model economy that our European neighbours should emulate (see Political Issues 24.1). Materially, perhaps the most important consequence of the boom has been to remove what had returned in the 1980s, mass unemployment: from over 3 million in 1984 to not much more than 1 million some 20 years later.

### Political creativity

Political creativity refers to the ability of political leaders and political institutions to learn from, and respond to, crises (see Image 24.2). Political creativity reminds us that there is a role for human agency in shaping political outcomes. It is possible to see four remarkable examples of this kind of creativity over the last 25 years, which contributed to the unexpected robustness of British institutions.

- One example concerns the intervention of a single individual, *Mrs Thatcher*. In her long tenure as prime minister, Mrs Thatcher was simultaneously the most reviled, and the most admired, figure in British politics. In retirement she continues to divide. But her opponents and friends agree on one thing: British politics would have been fundamentally different without her decade long influence at the centre of government.

- A second example of creativity is more contestable, because we cannot yet be sure that it has really made a difference; it concerns *Northern Ireland*. The long-term future of the devolved institutions and their creator, the Good Friday Agreement of 1998, is uncertain. But the military ceasefire, which originated now over a decade ago, has helped transform daily life in the province, largely for the better. The ceasefire and

## POLITICAL ISSUES

### 24.1   EXPORTING THE BRITISH MODEL

Should the British model of government be exported? Historically the answer given was a resounding 'yes'. Empire was used to export not only the general idea of a British style of democracy but even the particular forms of Westminster, leading to the notion of the Westminster Parliament as 'the mother of Parliaments'. The elites who ruled Commonwealth nations following decolonization in the 1950s and 1960s were very often educated at elite British universities, such as Cambridge, Oxford and the London School of Economics, and initially ran Westminster-style governing systems. Disillusionment with 'export' set in with the collapse of most of these Westminster-style democracies into dictatorships, and with the collapse of confidence within Britain in the face of imperial dissolution and economic crisis. But the idea of 'export' has revived in the last two decades. Two kinds of exports have been especially important:

- British institutions have tried to encourage international emulation of the British privatization revolution. Firms from the City of London have been in the forefront selling British privatization expertize.
- Through its influence in institutions such as the World Bank, Britain has supported the doctrine that aid to poor countries should be contingent on adopting 'good governance': in practice this means a stress on eliminating corruption from the administration of government.

Three important issues are raised by this new export trade:

- Is there 'a' British model to be exported? For instance, the merits of the British privatization programme, and the associated drive for deregulated markets, are deeply contested within Britain.
- The older attempts at export – for example, of the model of 'Westminster democracy' – failed in part because they were not adapted to the cultural and social settings to which they were transplanted. Opponents of the new export models also argue that mass privatization and free markets are entirely inappropriate to societies where poverty has prevented the development of any sophisticated infrastructure of services.
- The export of models is not always a voluntary exercize: in a deeply unequal world, countries may be given no choice. In the case of good governance, receiving aid is contingent on adopting a foreign model; in the extreme case, such as Iraq in 2003, an attempt is made to impose a democratic model by force, backed by American military power in partnership with the British.

the Good Friday Agreement are the product of learning on all sides: learning by the paramilitaries, both nationalist and unionist, that straightforward military victory was impossible; by Sinn Féin, the political wing of armed nationalism, that electoral success was highly possible; and by British and Irish governments that conclusive military victory was impossible, but that incorporation of paramilitary groups into peaceful politics was possible.

- A third kind of creativity is shown by the great burst of constitutional reform since the *return of*

**Image 24.2**
**Leading Britain's providential mission: Mr Blair and the Commission for Africa**

➲ The 'Commission for Africa' was established to coincide with Britain's assumption of the. Presidency of the 'G-8', the group of leading industrial nations in 2005. The Prime Minister and his Chancellor committed themselves to the goal of tackling African poverty as the 'big idea' of the Presidency. Note the now obligatory presence of an ageing rock star in the front row. But beneath the immediate politics lies a theme that we have encountered many times in this book: the revival of the notion (originating in the age of the British Empire) that Britain has a special providential destiny, in this case to bring peace and prosperity to less fortunate peoples, and to export British practices around the globe.

Members of the Commission for Africa: (front row L–R) Governor of the Bank of Botswana Linah K. Mohohlo, Britain's Chancellor of the Exchequer Gordon Brown, Irish singer and campaigner Sir Bob Geldof, Britain's Prime Minister Tony Blair, Tanzania's President Benjamin Mkapa, Ethiopia's Prime Minister Metes Zenawi, Britain's International Development Secretary Hilary Benn, (back row L–R) Personal Advisor to France's President Jacques Chirac on Africa, Michel Camdessus, Executive Director of the United Nations' (UN) Centre for Human Settlements (Habitat), Anna Tibaijuka, Chairman of the Board of the Uganda Investment Authority, Dr William Kalema, former U.S. Senator, Nancy Landon Kassebaum Baker, Group Strategy and Development Director of Aviva Plc, Tidjane Thiam, UN Under-Secretary-General and Executive Secretary for the Economic Commission of Africa, KY Amoaka, founder and Chairman of the FATE foundation, Fola Adeola, Canada's Finance Minister Ralph Goodale and South Africa's Finance Minister Trevor Manuel.

*Labour to office* in 1997. Labour, and other left-wing groups, had plenty of time to reflect in the long years of opposition to the Conservatives after 1979. The reforms – devolution, in the House of Lords, in the system for the administration of justice – are the greatest for a century, comparable in scope to the radical Thatcher economic reforms of the 1980s. They are the product of a long period of debate and reflection in the 1980s and 1990s.

● A fourth example of creativity is illustrated by the capacity of the institutions of British society to *reflect on failures and scandals*, and to try to do something about them. This source of creativity has been helped by greater assertiveness, and reduced deference, in the wider civil society. The 1980s and 1990s were marked by many scandals: miscarriages of justice; revelations of race hatred and homophobia in key institutions such as the police; callousness and incompetence

in many of the key institutions of the welfare state. But it became increasingly common to debate these as scandals, to argue intensely about them, and to try to do something about their causes: Briefings 23.1, 23.5 and 23.7 show the creative role, albeit limited, of these scandalous instances.

### Events

The everyday reality of trying to govern Britain is that most of what government tries to cope with is the product of what Harold Macmillan (Prime minister, 1957–63) called 'events': in other words, occurrences that take place apparently outwith the control of those who have to cope with them. Often these events produce unpleasant outcomes and difficult problems. In the early 1970s the end of a long period of sustained growth in the world economy created problems with which British governments

# ═══ DEBATING POLITICS ═══

## 24.1   THE FUTURE OF BRITISH DEMOCRACY: PESSIMISM OR OPTIMISM?

| The future of British democracy is secure | The future of British democracy is under threat |
|---|---|
| ■ Democratic government has shown an impressive ability to solve problems and learn from mistakes.<br>■ The vast majority of Britons support democratic freedoms.<br>■ The legal safeguards for democratic liberties have been strengthened in recent years.<br>■ In the wider society people are smarter and more confident than in the past in exercizing their rights of democratic citizenship. | ■ A world of terrorist threats is producing great pressure to curb democratic liberties, in Britain and elsewhere.<br>■ The state is continually increasing its control and surveillance capacities.<br>■ Although only a minority, those who reject democratic politics are vociferous, active and well organized.<br>■ Most people across the globe do not live under stable democratic government. Why should Britain remain an exception? |

struggled for two decades. In the same era the increasing importance of globalization – the growth of trading and production organized on a global scale – created great problems for British governments in independently managing the economy. As these examples show, 'events' are not random, accidental occurrences; they usually have deep historical roots. But they give an accidental flavour to the experience of government, because often they are occurrences over which British politicians have little control. Three sets of recent events show how British political history can be radically diverted.

● *The revival of the drive for European integration.* Throughout the 1970s, despite the accession of new states to the EEC, integration in Europe was largely stalled. (Britain, Ireland and Denmark joined together in 1973.) But in the 1980s there was a fresh burst of integration and growth: Greece joined in 1981 and Spain and Portugal were added in 1986. In the same year the Single European Act accelerated and broadened the range of integration. From this renewal dates one of the main themes of this text: the growing Europeanization of British government and politics.

● *The collapse of Communism.* In the late 1980s the control exercized by the Soviet Union over a large number of states in Eastern and Central Europe collapsed, and in 1991 the Soviet Union itself collapsed. This brought the Cold War to an end, changing radically the external environment of British politics. Radical consequences also followed for the European Union. In 2004 the accession of ten new members from the former 'Soviet bloc' was a direct, delayed consequence of the collapse of the old Soviet Empire.

● *The unsettled post-Cold War world order.* Since 1990 the British government has fought several important wars, often as the ally of the United States: in the Gulf against Iraq in 1990 and 2003; in the Balkans in 1999; in Afghanistan in 2002. These are all the direct, or the indirect, result of the collapse of Soviet power and the creation of a new international order in the wake of the Cold War that existed between the United States and the Soviet Union for over 40 years after the end of the Second World War.

'Events' such as these remind us how hard it is to predict. Twenty-five years ago few would have foreseen either the rejuvenation of the movement for

**REVIEW**

Four themes have dominated this chapter:

1 There is an important story to be told about change in British politics over the last generation, but equally a story to be told about continuity;

2 Explaining the new British system involves more than description: it also involves evaluating contestable theories of the governing process;

3 The British system turned out to be remarkably robust in coping with crisis;

4 How problems in the future are faced depends on the creativity of individuals and the wider creativity of the institutions of British society.

European integration or the collapse of the Soviet Union. Even as recently as the beginning of the 1990s few would have predicted that the economy was set on the start of a boom that would last more than a decade. We cannot, obviously, predict 'events', and we cannot know how long the new age of economic growth will last (see Debating Politics 24.1). The relatively open and democratic cast of British society does mean that we have a decent chance of addressing any problems with the creativity shown in recent decades. Whether any future British crisis will produce a figure as decisive as Mrs Thatcher is more uncertain.

## Further reading

The best way to carry forward the themes of this chapter, and this book, is to look back, to look out and to look forward. Colley (1996) is a wonderful study of the 'forging of the nation'. Coates (2000a) is a partisan, scholarly and highly original study of the world system and Britain's place in it. Gamble (2003) directly addresses the future of the 'world island', his evocative phrase for Britain.

# Bibliography

Alford, B. (1996). *Britain in the World Economy since 1880*. London: Longman.

Almond, G. and Verba, S. (1963). *The Civic Culture*. Boston, MA: Little, Brown.

—— (eds) (1980). *The Civic Culture Revisited*. Boston MA: Little, Brown.

Atkinson, A.B. (2000). 'Distribution of income and wealth', in A.H. Halsey and J. Webb, (eds), *Twentieth-Century British Social Trends*. London: Macmillan, pp. 348–81.

Audit Commission (2003). *Building Better Libraries*. London: Audit Commission.

Bagehot, W. (1867/1963). *The English Constitution*. London: Watts.

Bartle, J. and Griffiths, D. (eds) (2001). *Political Communications Transformed: From Morrison to Mandelson*. Basingstoke: Macmillan/Palgrave.

Beer, S. (1969/82). *Modern British Politics: A Study of Parties and Pressure Groups*. London: Faber & Faber.

—— (1982). *Britain Against Itself*. London: Faber & Faber.

Beetham, D., Byrne, I., Noan, P. and Weir, S. (2002). *Democracy under Blair: A Democratic Audit of the United Kingdom*. London: Politico's.

Bogdanor, V. (1999). *Devolution in the United Kingdom*. Oxford: Oxford University Press.

Bradley, A. (2000). 'The sovereignty of Parliament', in J. Jowell and D. Oliver (eds), *The Changing Constitution*, 4th edn. Oxford: Oxford University Press, pp. 23–58.

Brandreth, G. (1999). *Breaking the Code: Westminster Diaries, 1992–97*. London: Phoenix.

Brazier, R. (1999). *Constitutional Practice: The Foundations of British Government*, 3rd. edn Oxford: Oxford University Press.

Bromley, C., Curtice, J. and Seyd, B. (2001). 'Political engagement, trust and constitutional reform', in A. Park, J. Curtice, K. Thomson, L. Jarvis and C. Bromley (eds), *British Social Attitudes: The 18th Report. Public Policy, Social Ties*. London: Sage, pp. 199–225.

Brymin, M. and Newton, K. (2003). 'The national press and voting turnout: British General Elections of 1992 and 1997', *Political Communication*, 20:1, pp. 59–77.

BSE Inquiry (2000). *The Inquiry into BSE and variant CJD in the United Kingdom, Volume 1, Findings and Conclusions*. www.bseinquiry.gov.uk

Bulmer, S. and Burch. M. (2000). 'The Europeanisation of British central government', in R. Rhodes, (ed.), *Transforming British Government, Volume 1, Changing Institutions*. London: Macmillan, pp. 46–62.

Bulmer, S., Burch, M., Carter, C., Hogwood, P. and Scott, A. (2002). *British Devolution and European Policy-Making: Transforming Britain into Multi-level Governance*. Basingstoke: Palgrave Macmillan.

Burch, M. and Holliday, I. (1996). *The British Cabinet System*. London: Prentice Hall.

—— (2004). 'The Blair Government and the Core Executive', *Government and Opposition*, 39:1, pp. 1–21.

Butler, D. and Butler, G. (2000). *Twentieth-Century British Political Facts*, 8th edn. London: Macmillan.

Butler, D. and Kavanagh, D. (2002). *The British General Election of 2001*. Basingstoke: Palgrave.

Butler, D. and Stokes, D. (1974). *Political Change in Britain*. London: Macmillan.

Butler, R. (2004). *Review of Intelligence on Weapons of Mass Destruction: Report of a Committee of Privy Counsellors. Chairman: The Rt Hon Lord Butler of Brockwell*. HC898, 2003–4. Also accessible at http://www.butlerreview. org.uk

Cain, B., Dalton, R. and Scarrow, S. (eds) (2003). *Democracy Transformed? Expanding Political Opportunities in Advanced Industrial Democracies*. Oxford: Oxford University Press.

Castells, M. (2000). *The Rise of the Network Society*. Malden, MA: Blackwell.

—— (2001). 'European unification in the age of the network state', www.opendemocracy.net/debates/article-3-51-347.asp

Clark, T. and Dilnot, A. (2002). *Long-Term Trends in British Taxation and Spending*. London: Institute of Fiscal Studies, briefing note 25: also at www.ifs. org.uk/public/bn25pdf

Clarke, H., Sanders, D., Stewart, M. and Whiteley, P. (2004). *Political Choice in Britain*. Oxford: Oxford University Press.

Coates, D. (2000a). *Models of Capitalism: Growth and Stagnation in the Modern Era*. Cambridge: Polity.

—— (2000b) 'The character of New Labour', in D. Coates, and P. Lawler, *New Labour in Power*. Manchester: Manchester University Press, pp. 1–15.

Cohen, N. (2003). *Pretty Straight Guys*. London: Faber & Faber.

Colley, L. (1996). *Britons: Forging the Nation 1707–1837*. London: Verso.

Conservative Party (2004). 'European Constitution: bad for Britain', at www.conservative.com.campaigns. display

Cook, C. and Stevenson, J. (1983). *The Longman Handbook of Modern British History, 1714–1980*. London: Longman.

—— (2000) *The Longman Companion to Britain since 1945*, 2nd edn. London: Longman.

Cowley, P. (2002). *Revolts and Rebellions: Parliamentary Voting under Blair*. London: Politico's.

Crick, B. (1998). *Advisory Group on Citizenship. Education for Citizenship and the Teaching of Democracy in Schools. Final Report*. London: Qualifications and Curriculum Authority.

—— (2000). *In Defence of Politics*, 5th edn. London: Continuum.

Criddle, B. (2002). 'MPs and candidates', in D. Butler and D. Kavanagh, *The British General Election of 2001*. Basingstoke: Palgrave, pp. 182–207.

Crosland, C.A.R. (1956/64). *The Future of Socialism*. Revised paperback edn. London: Jonathan Cape.

Customs and Excise (2004). *Annual Report 2002–3*, at www.hmce.gov.uk/reports/ann/2002-3-stats

Dahl, R. (1984). *Modern Political Analysis*, 4th edn. Englewood Cliffs, NJ: Prentice Hall.

Day, J. (2002) 'Blair doubles the cost of spin', *The Guardian*, 25 July.

de Smith, S. and Brazier, R. (1998). *Constitutional and Administrative Law*, 8th edn. Harmondsworth: Penguin.

Denver, D. (2002). *Elections and Voters in Britain*. Basingstoke: Palgrave Macmillan.

Department for Local Government, Transport and the Regions (2002). *Local Government Financial Statistics*. London: DLTR.

Doherty, B., Paterson, M., Plows, A. and Wall, D. (2003). 'Explaining the fuel protests', *British Journal of Politics and International Relations*, 5:1, pp. 1–23.

Downs, A. (1957). *An Economic Theory of Democracy*. London: HarperCollins.

Dunleavy, P. (1981). *The Politics of Mass Housing 1945–75*. Oxford: Clarendon Press.

—— (1991/2001). *Democracy, Bureaucracy and Public Choice*. London: Longman Direct Editions.

Easton, D. (1965). *A Systems Analysis of Political Life*. New York: Wiley.

Economic and Social Research Council (2004). *Delivering Public Policy after Devolution: Diverging from Westminster*. Devolution and Constitutional Change Research Programme. Birmingham: University of Birmingham.

Electoral Commission (2002a). *Modernising Elections*. London: Electoral Commission.

—— (2002b) 'The electoral commission's youth campaign', at electoralcommission.org.uk

—— (2002c) *Voter Engagement among Black and Ethnic Minority Communities*. London: Electoral Commission.

—— (2004) *Delivering Democracy: The Future of Postal Voting*. London: Electoral Commission.

Farrell, D. (2001). *Electoral Systems: A Comparative Introduction*. Basingstoke: Palgrave Macmillan.

Fisher, J. (2003). 'Party finance – new rules, same old story?', *Politics Review*, April, 30–3.

Franks, Sir O. (Chairman) (1957). *Report of the Committee on Administrative Tribunals and Enquiries*. London: HMSO, Cmnd 218.

Gallie, D. (2000). 'The labour force', in A.H. Halsey and J. Webb, (eds), *Twentieth Century British Social Trends*, London: Macmillan: pp. 281–323.

Gamble, A. (1974). *The Conservative Nation*. London: Routledge.

—— (1981/1994). *Britain in Decline: Economic Policy, Political Strategy and the British state*. London: Macmillan (4th edn, 1994).

—— (1994). *The free market and the strong state: the politics of Thatcherism*, 2nd edn. London: Macmillan.

—— (2003). *Between Europe and America: The Future of British Politics*. Basingstoke: Palgrave Macmillan.

Geldof, Sir B. (2003). 'The father love that dare not speak its name', *Sunday Times*, 7 September.

George, S. (1998). *An Awkward Partner: Britain in the European Community*. Oxford: Oxford University Press.

Goodin, R. and Le Grand, J. (1987). *Not Only the Poor: The Middle Classes and the Welfare State*. London: Allen & Unwin.

Gould, P. (1998). *The Unfinished Revolution: How the Modernisers Saved the Labour Party*. London: Abacus.

Grant, W. (2000). *Pressure Groups and British Politics*. Basingstoke: Palgrave/Macmillan.

—— (2002). *Economic Policy in Britain*. Basingstoke: Palgrave.

—— and Marsh, D. (1977). *The Confederation of British Industry*. London: Hodder & Stoughton.

Griffith, J. (1991). *The Politics of the Judiciary*, 4th edn. London: Fontana.

Guttsman, W.L. (1963). *The British Political Elite*. London: MacGibbon & Kee.

Hall, P. (1999). 'Social capital in Britain', *British Journal of Political Science*, 29:3, pp. 417–61.

Hall, S. and Jacques, M. (eds) (1983). *The Politics of Thatcherism*. London: Lawrence & Wishart.

Halsey, A.H. and Webb, J. (eds) (2000). *Twentieth-Century British Social Trends*. London: Macmillan.

Harris, K. (1982). *Attlee*. London: Weidenfeld & Nicolson.

Harrison, B. (1996). *The Transformation of British Politics, 1860–1995*. Oxford: Oxford University Press.

Haubrich, D. (2003). 'Anti-terror laws and civil liberties', *Government and Opposition*, 38:1, pp. 3–28.

Hazell, R. (2003). *The State of the Nations 2003: The Third Year of Devolution in the United Kingdom*. Exeter: Imprint Academic.

Heath, A., Jowell, R. and Curtice, J. (2001). *The Rise of New Labour: Party Policies and Voter Choices*. Oxford: Oxford University Press.

Heath, A. and Payne, C. (2000). 'Social mobility', in A.H. Halsey and J. Webb, eds, *Twentieth-Century British Social Trends*, London: Macmillan, pp. 254–80.

Hennessy, P. (2001). *The Prime Minister: The Office and its Holders since 1945*. Harmondsworth: Penguin.

Heseltine, M. (2000). *Life in the Jungle: My Autobiography*. London: Hodder & Stoughton.

Hirst, P. and Thompson, G. (1999). *Globalization in Question*, 2nd edn. Cambridge: Polity.

HM Treasury (2004). *Economic Data and Tools*, at www.hm-treasury.gov.uk

Hobsbawm, E. (1962/97). *The Age of Revolution*. London: Abacus.

Hood, C., Rothstein, H. and Baldwin, R. (2001). *Government of Risk: Understanding Risk Regulatory Regimes*. Oxford: Oxford University Press.

—— Scott, C., James, O., Jones, G. and Travers, T. (1999). *Regulation Inside Government: Waste-watchers, Quality Police, and Sleaze-busters*. Oxford: Oxford University Press.

Houghton, Lord D. (1976). *Report of the Committee on Financial Aid to Political Parties*. London: HMSO, Cmd 6601.

Howell, D. (1980). *British Social Democracy: A Study in Development and Decay*. 2nd edn. New York: St Martin's Press.

Hutton, B. (2004). *Report of the Inquiry into the Circumstances Surrounding the Death of Dr. David Kelly*. London: The Stationery Office, HC 247.

Inland Revenue (2004). *Tax Receipts and Taxpayers*, at www/inlandrevenue.gov.uk/stats/tax_receipts/g_t01_1.htm

Jenkins, K. Caines, K. and Jackson, A. (1988). *Improving Management in Government: The Next Steps*. London: Her Majesty's Stationery Office.

Jones, B. (2004). 'Is Tony a Tory?', *Politics Review*, September, pp. 20–3.

Jowell, J. and Cooper, J. (eds), (2003). *Delivering Rights: How the Human Rights Act is Working and For Whom*. Oxford: Hart.

—— and Oliver, D. (eds) (2000). *The Changing Constitution*, 4th edn. Oxford: Oxford University Press.

Judge, D. (1993). *The Parliamentary State*. London: Sage.

—— (1999). *Representation: Theory and Practice in Britain*. London: Routledge.

Katz, R. and Mair, P. (1995). 'Changing models of party organization and party democracy: the emergence of the cartel party', *Party Politics*, 1:1, pp. 5–28.

Kavanagh, D. and Seldon, A. (1999). *The Power behind the Prime Minister: The Hidden Influence of Number Ten*. London: HarperCollins.

Kelly, R. (1999). 'Power in the Conservative Party: the Hague effect', *Politics Review*, February, pp. 28–30.

—— (2001). 'Farewell conference, hello forum: Labour and Tory policy-making', *Politics Review*, September, pp. 30–3.

Kennedy, P. (1989). *The Rise and Fall of the Great Powers*. London: Fontana.

Keynes, J.M. (1936). *The General Theory of Employment, Interest and Money*. London: Macmillan.

King, A. (ed.) (1976). *Why is Britain becoming Harder to Govern?* London: British Broadcasting Corporation.

Klingemann, H.-D., Hofferbert, R. and Budge, I. (1994). *Parties, Policy and Democracy*. Boulder, CO: Westview.

Laswell, H.D. (1950). *Politics: Who Gets What, When, How?* New York: Smith.

Le Seuer, A. (ed.) (2004). *Building the UK's New Supreme Court*. Oxford: Oxford University Press.

Leach, S. and Wilson, D. (2000). *Local Political Leadership*. Bristol: Policy Press.

Leggatt, A. (2001). *Review of Tribunals: one service, one system*, at www.tribunals-review.org.uk

Lilleker, D., Negrine, R. and Stanyer, J. (2003). 'Britain's political communication problems', *Politics Review*, February, 29–31.

Lindblom, C. (1959). 'The science of muddling through', *Public Administration Review*, 19:1, 79–88.

Local Government Association (2003a). *Fact Sheet: Dates in English and Welsh Local Government History*. London: Local Government Association.

—— (2003b). *Local Government Structures*. London: Local Government Association.

—— (2003c). *Our Work*, at www.lga.gov.uk.

Lovenduski, J. and Norris, P. (2003). 'Westminster Women: the politics of presence', *Political Studies*, 51:1, 84–102.

Lukes, S. (2004). *Power: a radical view*. Basingstoke: Palgrave.

Macpherson, C.B. (1971). *The Real World of Democracy*. Oxford: Oxford University Press.

MacPherson, Sir W. (1999). *The Stephen Lawrence Inquiry: Report of an Inquiry by Sir William MacPherson of Cluny*. London: HMSO, Cmd 4262–1.

Magee, E. and Outhwaite, M. (2001). 'Referendums and initiatives', *Politics Review*, February, 26–8.

Majone, G. (1996). *Regulating Europe*. London: Routledge.

Major, J. (1999). *John Major: The Autobiography*. London: HarperCollins.

Maloney, W., Smith, G. and Stoker, G. (2000). 'Social capital and urban governance: adding a more contextualised "top down" perspective', *Political Studies*, 48:4, pp. 802–20.

March, J. and Olsen, J. (1984). 'The New Institutionalism: organizational factors in political life', *American Political Science Review*, 78: pp. 734–49.

Marsh, D., Richards, D. and Smith, M. (2001). *Changing Patterns of Governance: Reinventing Whitehall*. Basingstoke: Palgrave Macmillan.

McKenzie, R. (1963). *British Political Parties*, 2nd edn. London: Heinemann.

Middlemas, K. (1979). *Politics in Industrial Society: The Experience of the British System since 1911*. London: André Deutsch.

Milward, A. (1992). *The European Rescue of the Nation-state*. London: Routledge.

Moran, M. (1985). *Politics and Society in Britain*. London: Macmillan.

—— (2001). 'Not steering but drowning: policy catastrophes and the regulatory state', *Political Quarterly*, 72:4, pp. 414–27.

—— (2003). *The British Regulatory State: High Modernism and Hyper-innovation*. Oxford: Oxford University Press.

Mughan, A. (2000). *The Media and the Presidentialization of Parliamentary Elections*. Basingstoke: Macmillan/Palgrave.

Nairn, T. (1981, 2000). *The Break-Up of Britain: Crisis and Neo-nationalism*, 2nd (expanded) edn 2000. London: Verso.

Newton, K. and Brymin, M. (2001). 'The National Press and Party voting in the UK', *Political Studies*, 49:2, pp. 265–85.

Norris, P. (2001). 'Apathetic landslide: the 2001 General Election', *Parliamentary Affairs*, 54:4, pp. 565–89.

—— and Lovenduski, J. (1995). *Parliamentary Recruitment: Gender, Race and Class in the British Parliament*. Cambridge: Cambridge University Press.

North East Lincolnshire Council (2002). *Renaissance: A Local Cultural Strategy for North East Lincolnshire*. North East Lincolnshire Council.

Norton, P. (1981). *The Commons in Perspective*. Oxford: Martin Robertson.

Nugent, N. (2002). *The Government and Politics of the European Union*, 5th edn. Basingstoke: Palgrave.

—— (ed.) (2004). *European Union Enlargement*. Basingstoke: Palgrave Macmillan.

Office of Telecommunications (OFTEL) (2003). *Consumers' Use of Internet*. OFTEL.

O'Leary, B. and McGarry, J. (1996). *The Politics of Antagonism: Understanding Northern Ireland*, 2nd edn. London: Athlone Press.

Osborne, D. and Gaebler, T. (1992). *Reinventing Government: How the Entrepreneurial Spirit is Transforming the Public Sector*. Reading, MA: Addison-Wesley.

Parkin, F. (1986). *Middle-class Radicalism*. Manchester: Manchester University Press.

Parry, G., Moyser, G. and Day, N. (1992). *Political Participation and Democracy in Britain*. Cambridge: Cambridge University Press.

Parsons, D.W. (1995). *Public Policy: An Introduction*. Aldershot: Edward Elgar.

Pattie, C., Seyd, P. and Whiteley, P. (2003). 'Citizenship and civic engagement: attitudes and behaviour in Britain', *Political Studies*, 51:3, pp. 443–68.

Pilkington, C. (1998). *Issues in British Politics*. London: Macmillan.

Pimlott, B. and Rao, N. (2002). *Governing London*. Oxford: Oxford University Press.

Pinto-Duschinsky, M. (1981). *British Political Finance 1830–1980*. Washington, DC: American Enterprise Institute.

*Politics Review* (2003). 'Fact file: trust and satisfaction', 12:4 (April).

Prison Reform Trust (2000). *A Hard Act to follow? Prisons and the Human Rights Act*. London: Prison Reform Trust.

Pulzer, P. (1967). *Political Representation and Elections in Britain*. London: Allen & Unwin.

Putnam, R. (2000). *Bowling Alone: The Collapse and Revival of American Community*. New York: Simon & Schuster.

Pyper, R. (1998). 'Redress of grievances', *Politics Review*, February, pp. 28–33.

—— (2002). 'Making government accountable', *Politics Review*, pp. 14–18.

*Regional Trends 2001*. London: The Stationery Office.

Reid, M. (1992). 'Policy networks and issue networks: the politics of smoking', in D. Marsh and R. Rhodes, (eds), *Policy Networks in British Government*. Oxford: Clarendon Press.

Reiner, R. (1992). *The Politics of Policing*, 2nd edn. London: Harvester Wheatsheaf.

Rhodes, R. (1988). *Beyond Westminster and Whitehall: The Sub-central Governments of Britain*. London: Unwin Hyman.

—— (1997). *Understanding Governance: Policy Networks, Governance, Reflexivity and Accountability*. Buckingham: Open University Press.

—— (1999). *Control and Power in Central-Local Relations*, 2nd edn. Aldershot: Ashgate.

—— (2000). *Transforming British Government: Volume 1, Changing Institutions; Volume 2, Changing Roles and Relationships*. London: Macmillan.

Robins, L. and Jones, B. (eds) (2000). *Debates in British Politics Today*. Manchester: Manchester University Press.

Robson, W.A. (1928/1947). *Justice and Administrative Law*. London: Macmillan.

Russell, M. (2000). *Reforming the Lords: Lessons from Abroad*. Oxford: Oxford University Press.

*Saga* magazine (2003). 'Tony Blair at fifty: the Saga interview', May, pp. 44–50.

Sanders, D., Clarke, H., Stewart, M. and Whiteley, P. (2001). 'The economy and voting', in P. Norris (ed.), *Britain Votes 2001*, Oxford: Oxford University Press, pp. 225–38.

Schon, D. A. and Rein M. (1994). *Frame Reflection: Toward the Resolution of Intractable Policy Controversies*. New York: Basic.

Schumpeter, J. (1943/1976). *Capitalism, Socialism and Democracy*. London: Allen & Unwin.

Scott, R. (1996). *Report of the Inquiry into the Export of Defence Equipment and Dual-use Goods to Iraq and Related Prosecutions*. London: HMSO, HC 115.

Select Committee on Public Administration (2001). *Mapping the Quango State*, 5th report, at www.publications.parliament-UK/pa/cm2001/cmselect/cmpubadmin/HC367

—— (2003). *Government by Appointment: Opening Up the Patronage State*, 4th report, at www.publications.parliament-UK/pa/cm2003/cmselect/cmpubadmin/HC165

Senvirante, M. (2002). *Ombudsmen: Public Services and Administrative Justice*. London: Butterworths.

Seymoure-Ure, C. (1996). *The British Press and Broadcasting since 1945*. 2nd edn. Oxford: Basil Blackwell.

Sikka, P. (2002). 'Show us the money: an international clampdown on tax avoidance is long overdue', *The Guardian*, 12 April.

Skelcher, C. (1998). *The Appointed State: Quasi-governmental Organizations and Democracy*. Buckingham: Open University Press.

Smith, M. (1999). *The Core Executive in Britain*. Basingstoke: Palgrave Macmillan

—— (2000). 'Prime Ministers, ministers and civil servants in the core executive', in R. Rhodes (ed.), *Transforming British Government, Volume 1, Changing Institutions*. Basingstoke: Macmillan, pp. 25–45.

*Social Trends 2002*. London: Office of National Statistics.

Stationery Office (2001). *National Intelligence Machinery*. Norwich: The Stationery Office.

Steinmo, S. (1993). *Taxation and Democracy: Swedish, British and American Approaches to Financing the Modern State*. London: Yale University Press.

Stoker, G. (2004). *Transforming Local Governance: From Thatcherism to New Labour*. Basingstoke: Palgrave Macmillan.

Sunkin, M. (2001). 'Trends in Judicial Review and the Human Rights Act', *Public Policy and Management*, July–September, pp. 9–12.

Thain, C. and Wright, M. (1995). *Treasury and Whitehall: Planning and Control of Public Expenditure*. Oxford: Oxford University Press.

Theakston, K. (1999). *Leadership in Whitehall*. Basingstoke: Macmillan.

Timmins, N. (1995). *The Five Giants*. London: HarperCollins.

Wainwright, M. (2003). 'Cleethorpes bucks trend of decline', *The Guardian*, 10 May.

Ward, S. and Gibson, R. (1998). 'The first internet election? United Kingdom political parties and campaigning in cyberspace', in I. Crewe, B. Gosschalk and J. Bartle (eds), *Why Labour Won the General Election of 1997*. London: Frank Cass, pp. 93–112.

Webb, P. (2000). *The Modern British Party System*. London: Sage.

Weber, M. (1918/1948). 'Politics as a vocation', in *From Max Weber*, London: Routledge, 1948, edited and introduced by H. Gerth and C.W. Mills, pp. 77–128.

Weir, S. and Beetham, D. (1999). *Political Power and Democratic Control in Britain*. London: Routledge.

White, R.J. (ed.) (1950). *The Conservative Tradition*. London: Kaye.

Whiteley, P. and Seyd, P. (2002). *High Intensity Participation: The Dynamics of Party Activism in Britain*. Ann Arbor, MI: University of Michigan Press.

Wilson, D. and Game, C. (2002). *Local Government in the United Kingdom*, 3rd edn. Basingstoke: Palgrave Macmillan.

Wilson, R. (1999). 'The civil service in the new millennium', at www.cabinet-office.gov.uk/1999/senior/rw

Worcester, R. and Mortimore, R. (2001). *Explaining Labour's Second Landslide*. London: Politico's.

# Index